CAMBRIDGE
UNIVERSITY PRESS

IT
for Cambridge International AS & A Level

COURSEBOOK

Paul Long, Sarah Lawrey & Victoria Ellis

CAMBRIDGE
UNIVERSITY PRESS

Shaftesbury Road, Cambridge CB2 8EA, United Kingdom

One Liberty Plaza, 20th Floor, New York, NY 10006, USA

477 Williamstown Road, Port Melbourne, VIC 3207, Australia

314–321, 3rd Floor, Plot 3, Splendor Forum, Jasola District Centre, New Delhi – 110025, India

103 Penang Road, #05–06/07, Visioncrest Commercial, Singapore 238467

Cambridge University Press is part of the University of Cambridge.

It furthers the University's mission by disseminating knowledge in the pursuit of education, learning and research at the highest international levels of excellence.

www.cambridge.org
Information on this title: www.cambridge.org/9781108782470

First published 2016
Revised edition 2019
Second edition 2021

20 19 18 17 16 15 14 13 12 11 10 9 8 7 6

Printed in the Netherlands by Wilco BV

A catalogue record for this publication is available from the British Library

ISBN   978-1-108-78247-0   Print Coursebook with Digital Access (2 Years)
ISBN   978-1-108-74932-9   Digital Coursebook (2 Years)
ISBN   978-1-108-79951-5   Coursebook eBook

Additional resources for this publication at www.cambridge.org/9781108782470

DEDICATED TEACHER AWARDS

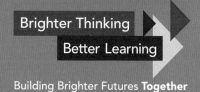

› Contents

> How to use this series

This suite of resources supports students and teachers following the Cambridge International AS & A Level Information Technology syllabus (9626). All of the books in the series work together to help students develop the necessary knowledge and critical skills required for this subject.

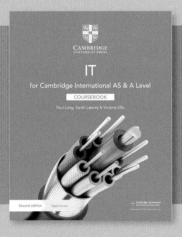

This coursebook provides 50% more practical activities than our previous edition and follows the same order structure as the Cambridge International AS & A Level Information Technology syllabus (9626). Each chapter includes questions to develop theoretical understanding or practical skills, and questions designed to encourage discussion. Exam-style questions for every topic help prepare students for their assessments.

The Teacher's Resource gives you everything you need to plan and deliver your lessons. It includes background knowledge at the start of each chapter, class activities with suggested timings, differentiation ideas, advice on common misconceptions, homework and assessment ideas.

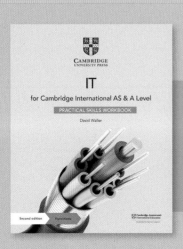

The Practical Skills Workbook contains worked examples and unique tasks to help learners practise core practical IT skills. With exercises increasing in challenge, it gives students further opportunities to undertake practice and refine their skills in the classroom or at home. It covers tasks for all of the practical chapters of the Coursebook that support many of the learning objectives required in the syllabus.

> How to use this book

Throughout this book, you will notice lots of different features that will help your learning. These are explained below.

LEARNING INTENTIONS

Learning intentions set the scene for each chapter, help with navigation through the coursebook and indicate the important concepts in each topic.

BEFORE YOU START

This contains questions and activities on subject knowledge you will need before starting this chapter.

REFLECTION

Reflection activities ask you to look back on the topics covered in the chapter and test how well you understand these topics and encourage you to reflect on your learning.

KEY WORDS

Key vocabulary is highlighted in the text when it is first introduced. Definitions are then given in the margin, which explain the meanings of these words and phrases. You will also find definitions of these words in the Glossary at the back of this book.

WORKED EXAMPLE

Wherever you need to know how to approach a skill, worked examples will show you how to do this.

Questions

Appearing throughout the text, questions give you a chance to check that you have understood the topic you have just read about. You can find the answers to these questions at the back of the book.

PRACTICAL ACTIVITY

Practical activities will help you to practise key skills. These may require you to use supplementary source files, which you can download from the digital edition of this book.

EXAM-STYLE QUESTIONS

Questions at the end of each chapter provide more demanding exam-style questions, some of which may require use of knowledge from previous chapters. Answers to these questions can be found at the back of the book.

TIP

Facts and tips are given in these boxes.

SUMMARY CHECKLIST

The summary checklists are followed by 'I can' statements which match the Learning Intentions at the beginning of the chapter. You might find it helpful to tick the statements you feel confident with when you are revising. You should revisit any topics that you don't feel confident with.

These boxes tell you where information in the book is extension content, and is not part of your syllabus.

> Introduction

Welcome to the second edition of our Cambridge International AS & A Level IT series.

This Coursebook has been written by experienced authors specifically for the Cambridge International AS & A Level Information Technology syllabus (9626) for examination from 2022.

The syllabus develops a broad range of IT skills. Throughout this Coursebook there are examples of IT in practice, practical activities which include extension activities for you to complete and reflection points to provoke further thought and discussion. There are questions that will test your knowledge and understanding. Whenever a task is presented, we would encourage you to carry it out before progressing further.

The key concepts for Cambridge International AS & A Level Information Technology (Impact of IT, Hardware and software, Networks and their role in the internet, mobile wireless applications and cloud computing, The internet, System life cycle, New technologies and how they may affect everyday life) recur throughout the syllabus. This Coursebook has been written to reflect these key concepts, in particular in the following chapters: Hardware and software (Chapter 2); IT in society (Chapter 12); New and emerging technologies (Chapter 13); Communications technology, including networks and the internet (Chapter 14); System life cycle (Chapter 16). It is not necessary to work through the book in order from start to finish.

The syllabus defines three assessment objectives: AO1 Recall, select and communicate knowledge and understanding of IT, AO2 Apply knowledge, understanding, skills and judgement to produce IT-based solutions and AO3 Analyse, evaluate and present reasoned conclusions.

The content of the syllabus focuses on current practice and practical applications of computers in everyday life. To reflect this, the practical elements of this Coursebook are not concerned with, for example, providing step-by-step advice on how to use particular software, but rather with helping you to discover what is available and have the confidence to apply your knowledge to different types of software. This will help you to prepare for the many different aspects of using computers that they will encounter in life, and not just in your exams.

This Coursebook makes reference to a variety of brand names. Note that marks will not be awarded for mentioning manufacturers' names in answers.

> Chapter 1

Data processing and information

By the end of this chapter, you will be able to:

- explain the difference between data and information
- explain the use of direct and indirect sources of data
- evaluate the advantages and disadvantages of direct and indirect sources of data
- describe factors that affect the quality of information
- understand the need for encryption
- describe different methods of encryption
- describe encryption protocols
- explain how encryption is used
- evaluate the advantages and disadvantages of different protocols and methods of encryption
- describe the use of validation methods
- explain the need for both validation and verification
- describe batch, online and real-time processing methods

CONTINUED

- give examples of when batch, online and real-time processing methods are used
- write an algorithm
- evaluate the advantages and disadvantages of different processing methods.

BEFORE YOU START

- Do you know the difference between input and output?
- Do you understand that when input data is processed it can be stored or sent to output?
- Do you understand the term encryption?
- Do you understand the term hacking?
- Do you know what a protocol is?
- Do you understand the structure of a table used in a database?
- Are you able to use a spell checker?

Introduction

We live in a world where we rely on data and information. It is important that data is accurate. Digital technology helps us to manage the input and transfer of data so that it is fit for purpose for its intended audience.

1.1 Data and information

Data

Data is raw numbers, letters, symbols, sounds or images with no meaning.

Some examples of data are:

P952BR
@bbcclick
359
23557.99

KEY WORD

data: raw numbers, letters, symbols, sounds or images without meaning

A picture without context is a further example of raw data.

Figure 1.1: Example of raw data.

The data P952BR could have several meanings. It could be:

- a product code
- a postal/ZIP code
- a car registration number.

Because we do not know what the data means, it is meaningless.

Data	Context	Meaning
P952BR	A product code	A product code for a can of noodles.
@bbcclick	A Twitter handle	The Twitter address for the BBC's weekly technology show, Click, which is worth watching on BBC World News and BBC2 to keep up to date with technology.
359	Price in Pakistani rupees	The price of a mobile phone cover.

Table 1.2: Examples of data being given context and meaning to become information.

Questions

A company creates websites using style sheets.

1 Identify one item of data that will be used by the company.

2 Describe how this item of data can become information.

Data sources

Direct data source

Data collected from a **direct data source** (primary source) must be used for the same purpose for which it was collected.

KEY WORDS

direct data source: data that is collected for the purpose for which it will be used

The data will often have been collected or requested by the person who intends to use the data. The data must not already exist for another purpose though. When collecting the data, the person collecting should know for what purpose they intend to use the data.

REFLECTION

When answering a question such as 'Give one item of data', do not try to explain what the data means because it then becomes information. Just give the raw numbers, letters, symbols or image.

KEY WORD

information: data with context and meaning

Information

When data items are given context and meaning, they become information. A person reading the information will then know what it means.

Data is given context by identifying what sort of data it is. This still does not make it information, but it is a step on the way to it becoming information.

Data	Context	Comment
P952BR	A product code	This is a product code, but it is still not known what it is a product code for, so it is still data.
@bbcclick	A Twitter handle	This is an address used for Twitter, but it is not information unless it is known to be a Twitter handle or used within Twitter software. It's also not known whose address it is.
359	Price in Pakistani Rupees	This is a currency value, but it is not known what the price is for, so it is still data.

Table 1.1: Examples of data being given context.

For the data to become information, it needs to be given meaning. Information is useful because it means something.

Figure 1.2: Direct data source.

For example, a sports shop wants to find out what other shops are charging for trainers. There are various direct sources from which this data can be collected. These could include:

- visiting the other shops and noting down the prices

- visiting the other shops' websites and noting down the prices

- carrying out a survey of other shop owners to ask their prices (although the shop owners are unlikely to want to give these).

Questionnaires can be used to gather specific data, such as opinions about an event that has taken place. Questionnaires are particularly useful when there are a large number of respondents and statistical analysis will be carried out on the results. Questions on a questionnaire need to be structured carefully to:

- elicit the information required

- enable analysis of the data effectively

- gather enough information without putting people off from completing the questionnaire.

Online questionnaires enable quicker analysis of data because the users fill in the data online and then the data is entered directly into a database. Online questionnaires save time because no further data entry by a third party is necessary.

Interviews are another direct source of information. Questions are asked directly to respondents and the interviewer can ask the respondent to elaborate on their answers.

Indirect data source

Figure 1.3: Indirect data source.

Data collected from an **indirect data source** (secondary source) already existed for another purpose. Although it may have been collected by the person who intends to use it, it was often collected by a different person or organisation.

> **KEY WORDS**
>
> **indirect data source:** data that was collected for a different purpose (secondary source)

For example, a sports shop could use various indirect sources to find out what other shops are charging for trainers, including:

- carrying out a survey of customers who have purchased trainers from the other shops (in this case, the price will be the one paid by the customer, which may have been a different price to that charged now, or it may have been discounted at the time)

- looking at till receipts from the shop (the price is printed on the till receipt for the purpose of providing proof of purchase, not for identifying prices).

Which of the following are direct data sources and which are indirect data sources?

Data	Reason collected	Reason used
Names and email addresses of members of a political party	To record their membership and to be able to contact them.	To contact members by email to see if they will donate some money.
Employee attendance dates and times	To identify when employees attended work and to calculate their wages.	To allow a police officer to check an employee's alibi if a crime has been committed.
Flight times and prices from airline websites	To compare the prices and times for a trip to Florida.	To decide the best flight to use for a trip to Florida.
Names, ages and addresses of people	For a national census.	To allow a marketing company to find out which areas have the highest population of children.
Weather measurements from a weather station	To record the current weather.	To show the current temperature and rainfall on a website.

Direct data is usually used by the person that collected it and for the purpose they collected it. However, it's also possible for a person to collect data from an indirect (secondary) source. For example, if a journalist is writing a news article and bases his story on existing news articles, then he has used indirect sources rather than interviewing the people involved in the original story.

One indirect source of information that is commonly used is an electoral register. Governments keep a register of people who are registered to vote in each household. This register includes names and addresses. Its main purpose is to enable those people to vote in elections. However, it can also be used by credit reference agencies to check whether a person lives at the address they say they do, or by marketing agencies to send direct marketing to the people listed on the register. There is an option for individual entries on an electoral register to be hidden from public view.

Businesses that want to send marketing letters will often purchase a list of email addresses or telephone numbers or addresses of people. Selling data is a big business, especially if the data enables a company to direct their marketing at their target market. For example, a company selling IT textbooks to schools would benefit greatly from a list of email addresses of IT teachers. Different countries have different laws about how personal data can be used in this way, but most developed nations have data protection laws that require companies to get consent from customers before the customers' data can be shared with a third party.

Advantages and disadvantages of gathering data from direct and indirect data sources

The general rule is that data collected directly for the purpose for which it is intended is more likely to be accurate and relevant than data that is obtained from existing data (indirect source).

Direct data source	Indirect data source
The data will be relevant because what is needed has been collected.	Additional data that is not required will exist that may take time to sort through and some data that is required may not exist.
The original source is known and so can be trusted.	The original source may not be known and so it can't be assumed that it is reliable.
It can take a long time to gather original data rather than use data that already exists.	The data is immediately available.
A large sample of statistical data can be difficult to collect for one-off purposes.	If statistical analysis is required, then there are more likely to be large samples available.

Direct data source	Indirect data source
The data is likely to be up to date because it has been collected recently.	Data may be out of date because it was collected at a different time.
Bias can be eliminated by asking specific questions.	Original data may be biased due to its source.
The data can be collected and presented in the format required.	The data is unlikely to be in the format required, which may make extracting the data difficult.

Table 1.3: Comparing direct and indirect sources.

Questions

This spreadsheet is used to calculate the area of a driveway.

	A	B	C
1	**Area calculator**		
2	Length =	3	m
3	Width =	5	m
4	Area =	15	m²

Figure 1.4: Part of a spreadsheet.

The builder using the spreadsheet needs to know the length and width of a driveway for a customer.

3 Identify one direct source the builder could use to find the length and width.

4 Identify one indirect source the builder could use to find the length and width.

5 Give one advantage of using the direct source instead of the indirect source to find the length and width.

Note: static and dynamic data is extension content, and is not part of the syllabus.

1.2 Quality of information

The quality of information is determined by a number of attributes.

Accuracy

Information that is inaccurate is clearly not good enough. Data must be accurate in order to be considered of good quality. Imagine being told that you need to check in at the airport 45 minutes before the flight leaves, so you turn up at 18:10 for a 19:05 flight, only to find that you were actually supposed to check in one hour before the flight leaves.

Examples of inaccurate information include:

- decimal point in the wrong place, for example $90.30 instead of $903.00 could suggest a product is much cheaper than it really is
- misspelling such as 'stair' instead of 'stare', where words have completely different meanings
- misplaced characters, such as a licence plate of BW9EP3T instead of BW93PET.

Relevance

Information must be relevant to its purpose. Having additional information that is not required means that the user must search through the data to find what is actually required.

Examples of irrelevant information include:

- being given a bus timetable when you want to catch a train
- being told the rental price of a car when you want to buy the car
- a user guide for a mobile phone that includes instructions on how to assemble a plug.

Age

Information must be up to date in order to be useful. Old information is likely to be out of date and therefore no longer useful. When using indirect data sources, always check when the information was produced.

Examples of out of date information include:

- the number of residents in a town based on a census from 2011, but 500 new homes have been built in the town since then
- a rugby score that has not been updated for 5 minutes, during which time a player scored.

Level of detail

There needs to be the right amount of information for it to be good quality. It's possible to have either too little or too much information provided. If there is too much information, then it can be difficult to find the exact information required. If there is not enough information, then it is not possible to use it correctly.

For example, a person orders a pizza. They ask for a large pepperoni to be delivered. They forgot to say what type of base they wanted and where it should be delivered to. The pizza company does not have enough information to fulfil the order.

Another example could be a traveller who needs to catch a train from Bhopal to Kacheguda. The traveller phones the rail company to find out the time of departure and arrival for trains, but they have to listen to all the times of the stations in between before they get the arrival time at Kacheguda.

Completeness

All information that is required must be provided in order for it to be of good quality. Not having all the information required means it cannot be used properly.

For example, a person has booked their car in for a service over the phone. The mechanic at the garage tells them the name of the street but doesn't give the building number.

PRACTICAL ACTIVITY 1.02

Look at this invitation.

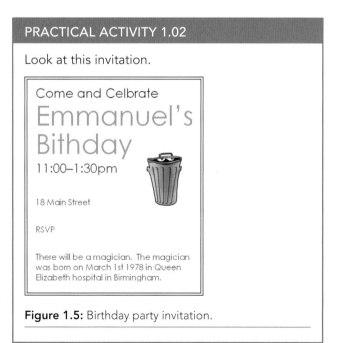

Come and Celbrate
Emmanuel's Bithday
11:00–1:30pm

18 Main Street

RSVP

There will be a magician. The magician was born on March 1st 1978 in Queen Elizabeth hospital in Birmingham.

Figure 1.5: Birthday party invitation.

CONTINUED

Describe how accuracy, relevance, level of detail and completeness affect the quality of information in the invitation.

Questions

6   Identify three factors that could affect the quality of information.

7   Describe how the age of information could affect the quality of information within a user guide for a mobile phone.

1.3 Encryption

One specific type of encoding is **encryption**. Encryption is when data is scrambled so that the data cannot be understood. Data can be encrypted when it is stored on disks or other storage media, or it can be encrypted when it is sent across a network, such as a local area network or the internet. Encryption is important when sending or storing sensitive data such as personal data or a company's sales figures. Data being sent across a network or the internet can be intercepted by hackers. Data stored on storage media could be stolen or lost. The purpose of encryption is to make the data difficult or impossible to read if it is accessed by an unauthorised user. Accessing encrypted data legitimately is known as decryption.

KEY WORD

encryption: scrambling data so it cannot be understood without a decryption key to make it unreadable if intercepted

---

Caesar cipher

A cipher is a secret way of writing. In other words it is a code. Ciphers are used to convert a message into an encrypted message. It is a special type of algorithm which defines the set of rules to follow to encrypt a message. Roman Emperor Julius Caesar created the Caesar cipher so that he could communicate in secret with his generals.

The Caesar cipher is sometimes known as a shift cipher because it selects replacement letters by shifting along the alphabet.

WORKED EXAMPLE 1.01

In this example the alphabet is to be shifted by three (+3) letters so that A = D, B = E and so on.

Original	A	B	C	D	E	F	G	H	I	J	K	L	M	N	O	P	Q	R	S	T	U	V	W	X	Y	Z
Encrypted	D	E	F	G	H	I	J	K	L	M	N	O	P	Q	R	S	T	U	V	W	X	Y	Z	A	B	C

So to encrypt the word 'Hello', you would use:

H = K, E = H, L = O, O = R

which gives KHOOR.

While the Caesar cipher is very easy to use, it's also very easy to crack.

PRACTICAL ACTIVITY 1.03

1   Using the Caesar cipher +3 example above, write an encrypted message to a friend. Ask your friend to decipher it.

2   Choose how many letters you are going to shift by and write another encrypted message to a friend. Don't tell your friend how many letters you shifted by. Your friend should try to decipher the code by working out which letters appear most commonly.

3   Look online for how to 'create a cipher wheel' and use it to encrypt and decrypt messages.

Symmetric encryption

Symmetic encryption is the oldest method of encryption. It requires both the sender and recipient to possess a secret encryption and decryption key known as a private key. With symmetric encryption, the secret key needs to be sent to the recipient. This could be done at a separate time, but it still has to be transmitted whether by post or over the internet and it could be intercepted.

Figure 1.6: Symmetric encryption.

Asymmetric encryption

Asymmetric encryption is also known as public-key cryptography. Asymmetric encryption overcomes the problem of symmetric encryption keys being intercepted by using a pair of keys. This will include a public key which is available to anybody wanting to send data, and a private key that is known only to the recipient. The key is the algorithm required to encrypt and decrypt the data.

The process works like this:

Figure 1.7: Asymmetric encryption.

Here is an example. Tomasz sends a message to Helene. Tomasz encrypts the message using Helene's public key. Helene receives the encrypted message and decrypts it using her private key.

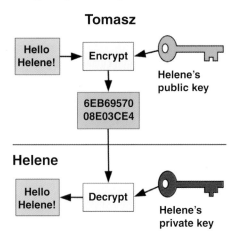

Figure 1.8: Example of asymmetric encryption.

Asymmetric encryption requires a lot more processing than symmetric encryption and so it takes longer to decrypt the data. However, as the decryption key does not have to be transmitted, it is more secure than symmetric encryption.

In order to find a public key, digital certificates are required which identify the user or server and provide the public key. A digital certificate is unique to each user or server. A digital certificate usually includes:

- organisation name
- organisation that issued the certificate
- user's email address
- user's country
- user's public key.

When encrypted data is required by a recipient, the computer will request the digital certificate from the sender. The public key can be found within the digital certificate.

Asymmetric encryption is used for Secure Sockets Layer (SSL) which is the security method used for secure websites. Transport Layer Security (TLS) has superseded SSL but they are both often referred to as SSL. Once SSL has established an authenticated session, the client and server will create symmetric keys for faster secure communication.

KEY WORDS
SSL: Secure Socket Layer
TLS: Transport Layer Security

PRACTICAL ACTIVITY 1.04
Find and watch a video about SSL.

Applications of encryption

Hard disk

Disk encryption will encrypt every single bit of data stored on a disk. This is different to encrypting single files. In order to access any file on the disk, the encryption key will be required. This type of encryption is not limited to disks and can be used on other storage media such as backup tapes and Universal Serial Bus (USB) flash memory. It is particularly important that USB flash memory and backup tapes are encrypted because these are portable storage media and so are susceptible to being lost or stolen. If the whole medium is encrypted, then anybody trying to access the data will not be able to understand it. The data is usually accessed by entering a password or using a fingerprint to unlock the encryption.

HTTPS

Normal web pages that are not encrypted are fetched and transmitted using Hypertext Transfer Protocol (HTTP). Anybody who intercepts web pages or data being sent over HTTP would be able to read the contents of the web page or the data. This is particularly a problem when sending sensitive data, such as credit card information or usernames and passwords.

Hypertext Transfer Protocol Secure (HTTPS) is the encryption standard used for secure web pages. It uses Secure Socket Layer (SSL) or Transport Layer Security (TLS) to encrypt and decrypt pages and information sent and received by web users. SSL was first used in 1996 and was replaced by TLS in 1999. SSL can still be used, but it has vulnerabilities so it's not recommended. TLS is the protocol that is used by banks when a user logs onto online banking. A secure web page can be spotted by its address beginning with https:// and in addition some browsers display a small padlock.

KEY WORD
HTTPS: Hypertext Transfer Protocol Secure

Figure 1.9: The 's' after 'http' and the padlock indicate that this is a secure website.

When a browser requests a secure page, it will check the digital certificate to ensure that it is trusted, valid and that the certificate is related to the site from which it is coming. The browser then uses the public key to encrypt a new symmetric key that is sent to the web server. The browser and web server can then communicate using a symmetric encryption key, which is much faster than asymmetric encryption.

WORKED EXAMPLE 1.02

The web browser requests the certificate from the web server.

Figure 1.10: Asymmetric cryptography.

The web browser then uses the web server's public key to encrypt a new symmetric key and sends that encrypted symmetric key to the web server. The web server uses its own private key to decrypt the new symmetric key.

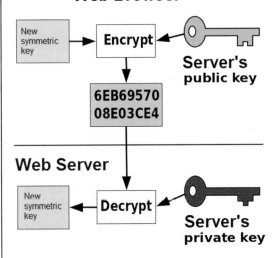

Figure 1.11: Secure website identification.

The browser and web server now communicate using the same symmetric key.

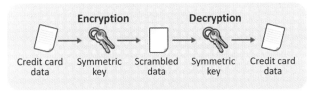

Figure 1.12: Symmetric encryption.

Email

Email encryption uses asymmetric encryption. This means that recipients of emails must have the private key that matches the public key used to encrypt the original email. In order for this to work, both the sender and recipient need to send each other a digitally-signed message that will add the person's digital certificate to the contact for that person. Encrypting an email will also encrypt any attachments.

How encryption protects data

Encryption only scrambles the data so that if it is found, it cannot be understood. It does not stop the data from being intercepted, stolen or lost. However, with strong 256-bit AES encryption, it is virtually impossible for somebody to decrypt the data and so it is effectively protected from prying eyes.

REFLECTION

Most Wi-Fi access points and Wi-Fi routers use encryption. This serves two purposes. The first is to only allow people who know the 'key' (usually a password) to access the network, so that any unauthorised users cannot gain access. The second is to encrypt the data, so that it cannot be understood by somebody 'snooping' on the Wi-Fi network.

Wi-Fi networks are particularly susceptible to 'snooping' because no wires are required to connect to the network. It is possible to sit in a car outside somebody's house and see the Wi-Fi network. The 'key' stops that person from accessing the network and also stops that person from understanding the data that is moving around the network.

Did you know that, if you access a public Wi-Fi hotspot that is 'open' and therefore not encrypted, anybody with the right software can see what you are sending over the network, including your emails? This applies to laptops, tablets and mobile phones or any other device using public Wi-Fi.

Question

8   Decipher this text that has been encrypted using the Caesar cipher with a shift of +4.

AIPP HSRI

1.4 Checking the accuracy of data

Validation

Validation takes place when data is input into a computer system. The purpose is to ensure the data is sensible and conforms to defined rules. A railway season ticket will have an expiry date. The season ticket is valid until it expires. Once it expires it is invalid. The rule here is that the date the season ticket is used must be before its expiry date.

When data is validated, if it conforms to the rules then it will be accepted. If it does not conform to the rules, then it will be rejected and an error message will be presented. Validation does not ensure that data is correct.

> **KEY WORD**
>
> **validation:** the process of checking data matches acceptable rules

> **PRACTICAL ACTIVITY 1.05**
>
> Create a flowchart to describe the process of validation. You should include the following:
>
> - Start
> - End
> - Input of data
> - Error message
> - Data accepted
> - Data rejected
> - Validation decision
>
> There are a variety of different validation checks that can be used to check whether data is acceptable. These different checks are the different types of rules that are used.

Presence check

A presence check is used to ensure that data is entered. If data is entered, then it is accepted. If data is not entered, then the user will be presented with an error message asking them to enter data.

Figure 1.13: Required data on a website.

> **WORKED EXAMPLE 1.03**
>
> When filling in a 'contact us' form on a website, it is essential that an email address is entered. These inputs would be valid if only a presence check is carried out:
>
> - a
> - a@bc.d
> - 372823
> - a@b
> - @
>
> Notice that none of these are correct but they pass the rule that data must be present.

Range check

A range check ensures that data is within a defined range. A limit check has a single boundary. This could be the highest possible value or the lowest possible value. A range check includes two boundaries, which would be the lower boundary and the upper boundary. These symbols are used when comparing with a boundary:

> greater than   > = greater than or equal to

< less than   < = less than or equal to

WORKED EXAMPLE 1.04

a   An opinion poll is taken and asks for the respondent's age. The respondents have to be at least 18 years old. The lower boundary is 18. There is no upper boundary, so this is a limit check. This could be written as:

Age > = 18

b   Letters representing grades for an exam are entered. Only the letters A–E are valid grades. The grade must be less than F. The upper boundary is E. There is no lower boundary, so this is a limit check. This could be written as:

Grade < F

c   The number of students in a class must be between 5 and 28. The lower boundary is 5 and the upper boundary is 28, so this is a range check. This could be written as:

Number of students > = 5 and < = 28

Data that is within the boundaries is valid. Data that is outside the boundaries is invalid. Data that is valid and within the boundaries is not necessarily correct. A grade of C could be entered when a grade A should have been entered. C is valid but incorrect.

Type check

A type check ensures that data must be of a defined data type.

Examples of a type check include:

- If an age is entered, it must be an integer.
- If a grade is entered, it must be text with no numbers.
- If a price is entered, it must be numerical.
- If a date of birth is entered, it must be a date.

Data that is of the correct data type is valid. Data that is valid and of the correct data type is not necessarily correct. A date of birth of 28/12/2087 could be entered. The date is valid because it is a date data type, but it is clearly incorrect.

Length check

A length check ensures data is of a defined length or within a range of lengths.

Examples of a length check include:

- A password must be at least six characters long.
- A grade must be exactly one character long.
- A product code must be at least four characters and no more than six characters.

Data that is of the allowed length is not necessarily correct. For example, a valid date might require six digits. A date of 2ndFeb would be a valid length because it contains six characters, but it would not be correct because it does not follow the required format.

Format check

A format check ensures data matches a defined format. It is sometimes known as a picture check and the data has to follow a pattern.

WORKED EXAMPLE 1.05

a   An email address must include an @ symbol preceded by at least one character and followed by other characters. These data would be valid:

- john@bldef.co
- a@b.dek
- fdc@jb

b   A student ID must be four numbers followed by two letters. These data would be valid:

- 3827BD
- 1111AA

Data that matches the pattern is valid. Data that is valid and of the defined format is not necessarily correct. An email address of fdc@jb meets the rules above but is clearly incorrect.

Lookup check

A lookup check tests to see if data exists in a list.

For example, when asking a user for their gender, they can respond with 'Male' or 'Female'. A lookup validation rule would check to see that the values are within this list. Students taking a qualification could be issued grades of pass, merit and distinction. When inputting the data, a validation rule could check that only 'X', 'P', 'M' or 'D' are entered ('X' would be for fail).

Consistency check

A consistency check compares data in one field with data in another field that already exists within a record, to see whether both are consistent with each other.

WORKED EXAMPLE 1.06

a When entering the gender of 'M' or 'F', a consistency check will prevent 'F' from being entered if the title is 'Mr' and will prevent 'M' from being entered if the title is 'Mrs' or 'Miss'.

b When entering data about dispatching products, it would not be possible to mark an item as being dispatched until after it has been packaged.

Check digit

A check digit is a number (or letter) that is added to the end of an identification number being input. It is a form of redundancy check because the check digit is redundant (not needed for the identification number, but just used for validation). When the identification number is first created, an algorithm (a series of calculations) is performed on it to generate a check digit. When the identification number is input, the same algorithm is performed on it. The result of the algorithm should match the check digit. The data is valid when the result of the algorithm matches the check digit. The data is not valid when the result of the algorithm does not match the check digit.

Original identification number = 20392
Algorithm is performed on 20392
Check digit = 4

Data including check digit = 203924

Valid Example
Identification number including check digit is entered into the computer: 203924
Algorithm is performed on 20392
Result of algorithm = 4

Result of algorithm (4) is compared with check digit that was entered (4).
They match.
Data is valid.

Invalid Example
Identification number including check digit is entered into the computer: 205924
Algorithm is performed on 20392
Result of algorithm = 7

Result of algorithm(7) is compared with check digit that was entered (4).
They do not match.
Data is invalid.

Figure 1.14: Valid and invalid check digit calculatons.

There are a variety of calculations that can be performed to determine what the check digit should be. The important thing is that the same calculation used to create the check digit in the first place should be used to confirm the check digit when the identification number is input.

WORKED EXAMPLE 1.07

Figure 1.15: Unique product code check digit.

The Unique Product Code (UPC) check digit is used with 13-digit barcodes. It is the last digit shown on a barcode. The algorithm for calculating the check digit is as follows.

1 Add all the digits in even numbered positions together.

2 Multiply the result (1) by 3.

3 Add all the digits in odd numbered positions together.

4 Add results (2) and (3) together.

5 Divide the result (4) by 10.

6 Calculate the remainder (modulo 10) of result (5).

7 Subtract (6) from 10.

Valid example

In this example, the International Standard Book Number (ISBN) is 978095734041-1 where the last 1 is the check digit. To calculate the check digit, this algorithm is performed on the ISBN (excluding check digit).

1 Add all the digits in even numbered positions together (978095734041): 7 + 0 + 5 + 3 + 0 + 1 = 16.

2 Multiply result (1) by 3: 16 × 3 = 48.

3   Add all the digits in odd numbered positions together (978095734041): 9 + 8 + 9 + 7 + 4 + 4 = 41.

4   Add results (2) and (3) together: 48 + 41 = 89.

5   Divide the result (4) by 10: 89 ÷ 10 = 8.9.

6   Calculate the remainder (modulo 10, when the number is divided by 10) of result (5): 89 MOD 10 = 9.

7   Subtract (6) from 10: 10 – 9 = 1.

The result of the algorithm is 1.

Invalid example

In this example, the ISBN has been entered incorrectly because two numbers have been transposed (7 and 3) accidentally: 978095374041-1.

1   Add all the digits in even numbered positions together (978095374041): 7 + 0 + 5 + 7 + 0 + 1 = 20.

2   Multiply result (1) by 3: 20 × 3 = 60.

3   Add all the digits in odd numbered positions together (978095374041): 9 + 8 + 9 + 3 + 4 + 4 = 37.

4   Add results (2) and (3) together: 60 + 37 = 97.

5   Divide the result (4) by 10: 97 ÷ 10 = 9.7.

6   Calculate the remainder (modulo 10) of result (5): 97 MOD 10 = 7.

7   Subtract (6) from 10: 10-7 = 3.

The result of the algorithm is 3. The result 3 is compared with the check digit of 1 that was entered. They do not match. The ISBN entered is invalid.

PRACTICAL ACTIVITY 1.06

Use a website to generate check digits for product codes.

REFLECTION

The usual algorithm for UPCs is to multiply the odd digits by 3 rather than the even digits. It is only for 13-character barcodes that the even digits are multiplied by 3.

Find out how to calculate a check digit for 10-digit barcodes.

Verification

Verification is the process of checking that the data entered into the computer system matches the original source.

KEY WORD

verification: ensuring data entered into the system matches the original source

Visual checking

A method of verification can be for the user to check visually that the data entered matches the original source. This can be done by reading the data displayed on screen and comparing it with the original data. If the data matches, then it has passed the verification process. If it does not match, then it has failed the verification process and needs to be re-entered. Visual checking does not ensure that the data entered is correct. If the original data is wrong, then the verification process may still pass.

For example, if the intended data is ABCD but ABC is on the source document, then ABC will be entered into the computer and verified, but it should have been ABCD in the first place.

Double data entry

Another method of verification is to input data into the computer system twice. The two items of data are compared by the computer system and, if they match, then they are verified. If there are any differences, then one of the inputs must have been incorrect.

For example, when changing a password, most systems will ask the user to enter the new password twice. This is because it is critical that the password is entered correctly in order that the user can gain access to the system in the future. If the new passwords match, then the password will be changed. If the new passwords don't match, then one of the passwords must have been entered incorrectly.

It is still possible to pass double entry verification and for the data to be incorrect. If the data is entered incorrectly twice, then the two values may match. For example, if the CAPS key is left on by mistake then both entries would match.

Hash total

Hash totals can be used when inputting a set of data. A hash total is calculated by adding together values from an input field for all the records that need to be input. Before input starts, the user will manually add up the values. Once input is completed, the computer will compare the hash total it calculates automatically with the hash total calculated manually before data entry. If the two totals are different, then a mistake has either been made during data input or in the manual calculation of the hash total.

WORKED EXAMPLE 1.08

A user is inputting these coursework marks for students.

Candidate number: 18292
Coursework mark: 74

Candidate number: 18264
Coursework mark: 38

Candidate number: 18279
Coursework mark: 82

The user adds up the total of all the coursework marks to give a hash total:

74 + 38 + 82 = 194

The user then inputs the coursework marks as follows:

Candidate number: 18292
Coursework mark: 74

Candidate number: 18264
Coursework mark: 83

Candidate number: 18279
Coursework mark: 82

CONTINUED

The computer calculates the hash total to be 239. As 239 does not match 194 there was either a data entry error or an error in the manual calculation of the hash total. In this case the error occurred with the input of candidate 18264 whose mark should have been 38 not 83.

A hash total is likely to find an error, but there are some occasions when an error wouldn't be found.

WORKED EXAMPLE 1.09

A user is inputting the following coursework marks for students:

Candidate number: 18292
Coursework mark: 74

Candidate number: 18264
Coursework mark: 38

Candidate number: 18279
Coursework mark: 82

The user adds up the total of all the coursework marks to give a hash total:

74 + 38 + 82 = 194

The user then inputs the coursework marks as follows:

Candidate number: 18292
Coursework mark: 73

Candidate number: 18264
Coursework mark: 39

Candidate number: 18279
Coursework mark: 82

The computer calculates the hash total to be 194. Because 194 matches 194 the data entry errors of 73 and 39 were not detected.

Control total

Control totals are very similar to hash totals. Hash totals can use any field and the sum of the data used may not have any meaning. Control totals have some useful meaning. For example, a control total could be the number of items in the batch that is to be input, or the total of prices for individual items on an order.

Parity check

A parity check is used to find errors during data transmission. Each byte (or word) of data is checked individually. For the purpose of explaining the parity check, we will assume that the parity check is on a single byte only. One of the bits in each byte is used as the parity bit and the other 7 bits are used to represent the data. There are two types of parity check: even parity and odd parity.

With even parity, the total number of on bits in a byte must be an even number. If the number of on bits within the 7 bits of data is odd, then the parity bit will be set to on to make the total on bits even. If the number of on bits within the 7 bits of data is even, then the parity bit will be set to off to keep the total on bits as even.

WORKED EXAMPLE 1.10

These seven bits of data are about to be transmitted:

1 0 0 1 1 0 0

Each on bit is represented by a 1 (one) and each off bit is represented by a 0 (zero). There are three on bits which is an odd number. The parity bit is therefore set to be on (1) so that the total number of on bits is an even number:

1 0 0 1 1 0 0 1

When this byte is received after transmission, the number of on bits are added up. If the total is even, then the data is accepted.

With odd parity, the total number of on bits in a byte must be an odd number. If the number of on bits within the seven bits of data is even, then the parity bit will be set to on to make the total on bits odd. If the number of on bits within the seven bits of data is odd, then the parity bit will be set to off to keep the total on bits as odd.

WORKED EXAMPLE 1.11

These seven bits of data are about to be transmitted:

1 0 0 1 1 0 0

There are three on bits which is an odd number. The parity bit is therefore set to be off (0) so that the total number of on bits is an odd number:

1 0 0 1 1 0 0 0

When this byte is received after transmission, the number of on bits are added up. If the total is odd, then the data is accepted. In this example, the data is received as:

1 1 0 1 1 0 0 0

The total on bits is in the received data is four. This is an even number so the computer system knows that an error occurred during data transmission.

Parity bits only check to see if an error occurred during data transmission. They do not correct the error. If an error occurs, then the data must be sent again. Parity checks can find an error when a single bit is transmitted incorrectly, but there are occasions when a parity check would not find an error if more than one bit is transmitted incorrectly.

WORKED EXAMPLE 1.12

These seven bits of data are transmitted using even parity with a parity bit of one:

1 0 0 1 1 0 0 1

The data is received as:

0 1 0 1 1 0 0 1

The data is accepted by the even parity check because there are four on bits. The parity check was not able to identify the error where the first two bits were transmitted incorrectly.

Checksum

Checksums are the result of a calculation on the contents of a file used to check whether a file has been transmitted or copied correctly. This can be especially useful if checking that a hacker hasn't disguised a malicious file as a genuine one. Any slight change in a file will mean that a different checksum is generated. The checksum is usually represented to the user as hexadecimal digits which are the numbers 0 to 9 and letters A to F with 2 hexadecimal digits representing a single byte.

Different algorithms can be used to generate the checksum. Popular algorithms include SHA-256, SHA-1 and MD5. Although it's very rare, MD5 and SHA-1 have been known to generate collisions. Collisions occur where the same checksum is generated for a different file. This can enable a hacker to disguise a malicious file as a genuine file, but is unlikely to happen by chance. Therefore, SH-1 and MD-5 are still suitable for checking for transmission errors. If the checksum at the start of transmission does not match the checksum at the end of transmission, then there will have been a transmission error. At the time of writing, there haven't been any reports of SHA-256 creating collisions and so it is currently the safest checksum method to use.

PRACTICAL ACTIVITY 1.07

1 Copy a file such as a word processed document to a different folder.

2 Compare the checksums of the original file and the copied file using an online checker. What do you notice about the checksums?

3 Now make a change to the copied file.

4 Compare the checksums of the original file and the changed copied file. What do you notice about the checksums?

You can also see other checksums that would be created using other methods.

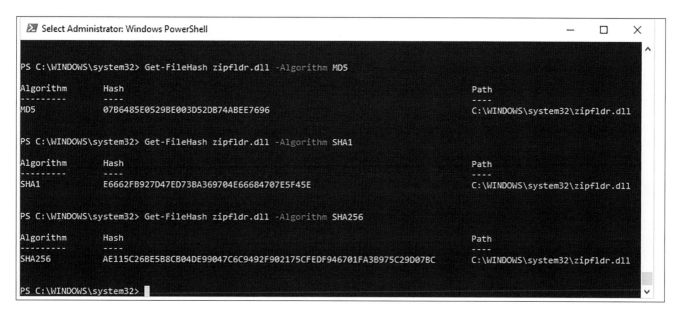

Figure 1.16: Checksums for a Microsoft® Windows® file.

The need for both validation and verification

It is possible to enter valid data that is still incorrect. It is also possible to verify incorrect data. By using both validation and verification, the chances of entering incorrect data are reduced. If data that is incorrect passes a validation check, then the verification check is likely to spot the error.

WORKED EXAMPLE 1.13

The validation rule is that a person's gender must be a single letter. N is entered. This passes the validation check but is clearly incorrect. When verified using double entry, the user enters N first followed by M the second time. The verification process has identified the error.

However, it is still possible that the user could enter N twice and both the validation and verification processes would fail.

PRACTICAL ACTIVITY 1.08

Perform a visual check on the following sentence.

I were walking along thc road yesterday wen I spotted a dog without a lead I called the dog but it did not respond. the dog ran away;

Questions

9   Describe the purpose of verification.
10 Identify three methods of validation.
11 Explain, using examples, why validation and verification do not ensure that data is correct.

1.5 Data processing

Data processing is any activity that manipulates or carries out operations on data.

Data processing includes actions such as:

*   collection and storage
*   editing and updating
*   sorting and searching
*   output and dissemination.

REFLECTION

The data to be processed is usually stored in files. Each file is a collection of records about a particular entity, for example, records of customers, employees or products.

Each record consists of items of information called fields, for example, customer surname, employee number or product price.

Organisations process data in different ways such as batch, online and real time processing.

Batch processing

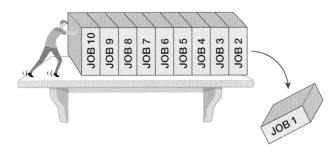

Figure 1.17: Batch processing.

In a **batch processing** system, the individual operations or transactions that need to be performed on the data are not done one by one by an operator in 'real time' but are collected together into a batch. At a later time, the system automatically carries out all of the transactions and updates the data file.

Examples where batch processing is used include automated backups, the processing of employees' wages, customer orders and stock control.

For data to be processed it is often stored first. This can be for long periods of time or momentarily. There are two main file types that are used to store data, **master files** and **transaction files**. A master file usually stores data about a thing such as a person, place or object. A transaction file usually stores data about an event, such as an order, electricity usage and travel expenses.

KEY WORDS

batch processing: sets of data are processed all at one time without user interaction

master file: a table in a database containing information about one set of things, for example, employees

transaction file: data that is used to update a master file

WORKED EXAMPLE 1.14

Businesses store customer details such as name, address and the total money they have spent in a file. There is a record for each customer.

Here is an example file.

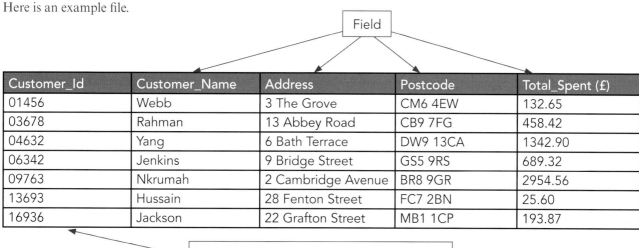

Field

Customer_Id	Customer_Name	Address	Postcode	Total_Spent (£)
01456	Webb	3 The Grove	CM6 4EW	132.65
03678	Rahman	13 Abbey Road	CB9 7FG	458.42
04632	Yang	6 Bath Terrace	DW9 13CA	1342.90
06342	Jenkins	9 Bridge Street	GS5 9RS	689.32
09763	Nkrumah	2 Cambridge Avenue	BR8 9GR	2954.56
13693	Hussain	28 Fenton Street	FC7 2BN	25.60
16936	Jackson	22 Grafton Street	MB1 1CP	193.87

Customer_Id is the primary key for each record. The data in the primary key field must be unique for each customer.

This file is called the master file. In a payroll system, used for processing employee wages, the master file would contain details of each employee, such as their ID number, name, address, hourly pay, total earned for the year and the amount of tax they have paid.

Whenever a customer orders a product, the transaction is recorded in another file called a transaction file.

Here is an example transaction file.

Customer_Id	Product_Ordered	Cost (£)
16936	Sweater	25.00
09763	Blouse	30.50
06342	Jeans	60.75
03678	Shirt	35.60
04632	Jacket	100.00

Table 1.4: Example transaction file.

After a regular interval, the complete batch of records in the transaction file are processed. In this example, invoices and delivery notes will be generated by merging the transaction and master files and the data in the master file is updated by recalculating the Total_Spent field.

At the start of the process, the transaction file is validated and any transactions that are invalid will be moved to an errors file.

The transaction file is sorted so that it is in the same order as the master file.

WORKED EXAMPLE 1.15

In this example the transaction and master files are sorted into ascending order according to the Customer_Id field.

Customer_Id	Product_Ordered	Cost (£)
16936	Sweater	25.00
09763	Blouse	30.50
06342	Jeans	60.75
03678	Shirt	35.60
04632	Jacket	100.00

Figure 1.18: Unsorted.

Customer_Id	Product_Ordered	Cost (£)
03678	Shirt	35.60
04632	Jacket	100.00
06342	Jeans	60.75
09763	Blouse	30.50
16936	Sweater	25.00

Figure 1.19: Sorted.

The batch process moves through the transaction file and finds the corresponding record in the master file with the same Customer_Id.

WORKED EXAMPLE 1.16

The first transaction in the previous worked example has a Customer_Id of 03678. This transaction is merged with the customer master file to produce an invoice and delivery note and to update the Total_Spent field in the master file.

Notice how the Total_Spent field of the second record has been updated.

Customer_Id	Customer_Name	Address	Postcode	Total_Spent (£)
01456	Webb	3 The Grove	CM6 4EW	132.65
03678	Rahman	13 Abbey Road	CB9 7FG	494.02

This continues until all the records in the master file have been copied to the new version.

The new master file will now hold this information.

Customer_Id	Customer_Name	Address	Postcode	Total_Spent (£)
01456	Webb	3 The Grove	CM6 4EW	132.65
03678	Rahman	13 Abbey Road	CB9 7FG	494.02
04632	Yang	6 Bath Terrace	DW9 13CA	1442.90
06342	Jenkins	9 Bridge Street	GS5 9RS	750.07
09763	Nkrumah	2 Cambridge Avenue	BR8 9GR	2985.06
13693	Hussain	28 Fenton Street	FC7 2BN	25.60
16936	Jackson	22 Grafton Street	MB1 1CP	218.87

One way of representing transaction processing as an algorithm could be as follows.

```
For each line in transaction file

   Repeat

      Read next record in master file

   Until transaction file ID matches master
file ID

   master file total for current record =
master file total + transaction file value

Next line in transaction file
```

Advantages and disadvantages of batch processing

Advantages	Disadvantages
It is a single, automated process requiring little human participation which can reduce costs.	There is a delay as data is not processed until the specific time period.
It can be scheduled to occur when there is little demand for computer resources, for example, at night.	Only data of the same type can be processed since an identical, automated process is being applied to all the data.
As it is an automated process there will be none of the transcription and update errors that human operators would produce.	Errors cannot be corrected until the batch process is complete.
There are fewer repetitive tasks for the human operators.	

Table 1.5: Advantages and disadvantages of batch processing.

Question

12 Describe how a telephone company might make use of both batch and interactive processing methods including the use of master and transaction files.

Online processing

There are differing definitions of online processing. For this syllabus, the focus is specifically on interactive processing.

> **KEY WORDS**
>
> **online processing:** also known as interactive processing, data is input by the user and feedback given in the form of outputs

Interactive processing is what you are most likely to be familiar with. Interactive means that the user and computer are communicating together. The user inputs data and the computer responds with an output. While processing takes place, data is stored in RAM and is not saved to non-volatile memory (for example, a disk) until the user saves the data. The computer will process the data as quickly as possible so that the user is able to see (or hear) the results of the processing. For everyday tasks such as word processing, analysing data in a spreadsheet, browsing the web and checking emails, the response times will be thousandths of a second.

One method of online processing is to deal with data as transactions. A certain amount of data is input as a transaction. This amount of data is usually small. Once the data for the transaction is collected it is processed and the next transaction can occur.

An online booking system, for example, an airline ticket booking system, will process data in transactions. All the data about the customer, flight and seat number will be collected in the transaction. This will then be processed and a ticket can be provided as an output. As each transaction is processed in turn, this avoids a seat on the aeroplane being double-booked. Once a seat has been allocated to a transaction, until that transaction is completed that seat cannot be booked by anyone else. This is because no transaction will be processed until the previous one is completed. The same would occur with a concert ticket booking system.

Electricity meter readings need to be recorded on a regular basis so that accurate bills can be calculated. The readings are taken interactively using methods such as:

- a PDA or smart phone is used by an employee of the electricity company
- the homeowner enters the meter reading using the world wide web

- the homeowner phones the electricity company and enters the reading using the phone.

Note that electricity meter readings can be taken automatically using a smart meter which does not require user interaction.

Electronic funds transfer

Electronic funds transfer (EFT) is the transfer of funds (money) electronically to or from a bank account. Some types of EFT payments include:

- Direct payments where money can be sent from one bank account to another. This can either happen immediately or within a given time frame or overnight. If it happens within a given time frame, then there is usually a batch process involved that processes a batch of direct payments at one time.

- Automated teller machines (ATMs) are used to withdraw cash from a bank account. The ATM will look up a customer's bank account in a database and, if there are enough funds, then it will allow a withdrawal to take place and deduct the amount withdrawn from the account balance.

- Debit cards can be used to give an instruction to your bank to take funds to pay for goods or a service. A debit card is linked to a bank account and, when used to make a payment, the transaction is sent to the bank. A customer has to confirm the card belongs to them by entering a PIN, although contactless payments are also possible without a PIN up to a limit for each transaction. Once the PIN is confirmed, the account number and amount requested will be sent to the bank. The bank's computer system will check that the balance available to the customer is sufficient for the transaction amount. If there are sufficient funds, then the bank will return a message to the retailer confirming that funds are available. The retailer will then confirm the purchase and the amount to transfer from the customer to the retailer is sent to the bank. The bank's computer system will then create a transaction for the amount of the purchase, subtract the funds from the customer's account and add the funds to the retailer's account.

- Direct debits are used where regular payments need to be made. The owner of a bank account can authorise an organisation to take payments automatically. This is often used for paying utility bills which may vary each month.

Online stores

Online stores enable a customer to purchase a product from anywhere in the world and have it delivered to their home address. An online store uses an interactive system where the customer can browse or search for products using a website. The customer can then add those products to a virtual shopping basket which can be paid for using electronic funds transfer. The online store will send a confirmation email to the customer and then email updates about the delivery of the product.

Automatic stock control

The purpose of a stock control system is to ensure that a shop always has enough stock (products) to sell and never has too many. It's also possible to have a stock control system that ensures there are always enough parts needed for a manufacturing process. The main feature of a stock control system will be a database which will store data about each product that the shop stocks. In addition to this, data will be stored about the suppliers.

The system will need to store the following data about stock in order to maintain healthy levels of stock within the shop:

- quantity in stock

- reorder level (the point at which more stock will be ordered)

- reorder amount (the quantity that should be ordered when the reorder level is reached).

Each time a product is purchased at the till, its barcode will be scanned. The barcode number will be found in the database and the quantity recorded as being in stock will be reduced by one. When the quantity in stock reaches the reorder level for that product, an automatic order will be placed for the reorder amount of that product. When the products that have been ordered arrive at the shop, the quantity in the database will be increased by the number of products that have arrived.

WORKED EXAMPLE 1.17

Table 1.6 shows an extract of data that could be stored about stock in a stock control system (many fields have been omitted such as Colour, Size, Category, Location etc):

Barcode	Description	Quantity in Stock	Reorder Level	Reorder Amount
012345678905	Male Polo Shirt	8	3	10
456789012343	Female Polo Shirt	4	3	10
567890123450	Boys Trainers	6	2	4
678901234567	Girls Trainers	1	2	4

Table 1.6

We can see from this that there are currently 4 female polo shirts in stock and the reorder level is 3. That means that next time a female polo shirt is purchased, the quantity in stock will reduce to 3 and so 10 female polo shirts will be reordered.

We can also see that there is only 1 girls trainer in stock and so it had already dipped below the reorder level so we would expect to see that 4 girls trainers are already on order. When these 4 girls trainers arrive in store, the quantity in stock will be increased by 4.

The system can be a little more complex than this in large supermarkets where they need to keep track of how much stock is on the shop floor and how much stock is in the on-site stock room. There will also be times when products go out of date and so have to be thrown away and the quantity in stock will need adjusting. Stock also goes missing, sometimes by accidental damage or by theft. There will therefore be regular stocktakes where the shop checks the amount of stock it has compared with what is stored in the database and then makes adjustments.

Electronic data exchange

Electronic data exchange, or electronic data interchange (EDI) is a standardised format for exchanging data between organisations. For example, your school will submit coursework marks and estimated grades to an awarding organisation, either online, or using software designed to facilitate the exchange of that data. Application program interfaces (APIs) are used to provide a standard interface for importing and exporting data between different software. Accounts software will often automatically send data to the government for tax purposes using an API.

Business-to-business buying and selling

When a business buys in bulk from a supplier, the process can be made easier by having a common interface for sending the order and receiving the order. Some large wholesalers may insist on clients using the wholesaler's own software, but most will provide an API for clients to link their own software to.

The traditional process of placing an order would involve the buyer creating a purchase order, printing it and posting it to the supplier. The supplier would then receive this paper copy, enter the order onto their order entry system, print a delivery note to send with the order and print an invoice to send to the buyer. The buyer would then receive the invoice and then arrange for payment to be made.

With business-to-business (B2B) electronic data interchange, the buyer can create a purchase order but, instead of printing it, the software will transmit the order using EDI directly to the supplier's ordering system. The supplier's system will be able to give immediate confirmation of receipt and updates relating to the order, such as when the products have been dispatched. Similarly, the supplier can create an electronic invoice which will be transmitted by their software to the buyer's software and matched with the original purchase order. Payment can then be made using electronic funds transfer once the buyer confirms the goods have been received.

Real-time processing

A **real-time processing** system processes data as soon as it has been input. Such systems are normally used when the immediacy of the data is vital.

> **KEY WORDS**
>
> **real-time processing:** data is processed as soon as it has been input and outputs are generated immediately

Air traffic control

Figure 1.20: Air traffic control.

In an air traffic control system, data such as the location of all the aeroplanes currently in the air, is processed immediately so that the location of the planes can be known by everybody using the system. This is vital because this data will need to be given back to each plane that is currently in flight to make sure no collisions occur. There cannot be any delay in the processing of this data because the result of a delay could be catastrophic.

Computer games

When playing computer games, the input from the user needs to be processed immediately so that it can take effect and the game can be controlled. Each time a user asks a game character to move forward by pressing a key or button, the character needs to do this immediately. In order to do this, the game needs to have a real-time processing system to process the data.

> **REFLECTION**
>
> Why would we not make every processing system a real-time system? What would be the impact if we did? List the advantages and disadvantages of real-time processing.

Some real-time systems use a feedback loop where the output directly affects the input.

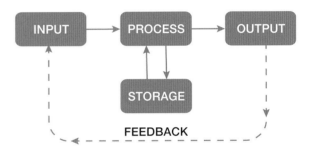

Figure 1.21: Feedback loop.

Central heating system

WORKED EXAMPLE 1.18

A central heating system is constantly monitoring the temperature of its surroundings. The desired temperature is stored, in this case 20 °C. When the temperature becomes too high, the boiler will be turned off. When the temperature becomes too low, the boiler will be turned on.

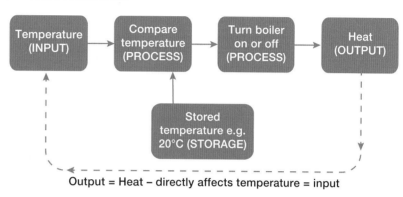

Output = Heat – directly affects temperature = input

Figure 1.22: Thermostat.   **Figure 1.23:** Temperature control.

When the boiler is turned on, it generates heat which will increase the temperature. This increase in temperature affects the input to the system and therefore feedback has occurred because the output (heat) has affected the input (temperature). The same happens if the boiler is turned off because the temperature in the room will be reduced and when it reaches a certain level the boiler will switch on again and generate heat.

Air conditioning system

PRACTICAL ACTIVITY 1.09

Draw a diagram similar to the one in worked example 1.18 to show how an air conditioning system would work.

Rocket guidance systems

When a rocket is launched, the launch happens in real-time. If the rocket veers off course, then any delay in receiving instructions could see the rocket continue in the wrong direction or, ultimately, crash. A rocket guidance system needs to provide stability for the rocket and to control its movement.

As a rocket moves, its position is constantly changing. If the position is off-course, then the rocket needs rotating back on course. As the rocket is rotated, this immediately affects its position, which is also the input to the control system.

REFLECTION

Find out how different rocket guidance systems operate and the inputs and outputs that are used to control the rocket's path.

Question

13 Explain why real-time processing is required for a video-conference.

EXAM-STYLE QUESTIONS

1 Using an example, define the term information. [2]

2 Users can pay for premium services on a website using their credit card.

   a Explain why the website uses https at the beginning of the website address instead of http. [4]

   b Explain symmetric encryption. [2]

   The journalists working for the website encrypt their emails.

   c Describe how asymmetric encryption is used with emails. [2]

   When the users subscribe to premium features, they have to choose a password.

   d Suggest how verification can be used when entering the password. [1]

   [Total 9]

3 There is a form on the website in question 2 that can be used to submit news stories.
   When data is entered onto the form, it is validated.

   a State what the purpose of validation is. [1]

   b Using an example related to submitting a news story, identify and describe one method of validation. [3]

   [Total 4]

4 Describe the difference between an online and a real-time processing system. [4]

5 Define the term 'master file'. [2]

6 Describe three characteristics of a stock control system. [6]

7 Describe how a stock control system maintains stock levels automatically. [4]

SUMMARY CHECKLIST

- [ ] I can explain the difference between data and information.
- [ ] I can explain the use of direct and indirect sources of data.
- [ ] I can evaluate the advantages and disadvantages of direct and indirect sources of data.
- [ ] I can describe factors that affect the quality of information.
- [ ] I can understand the need for encryption.
- [ ] I can describe different methods of encryption.
- [ ] I can describe encryption protocols.
- [ ] I can explain how encryption is used.
- [ ] I can evaluate the advantages and disadvantages of different protocols and methods of encryption.
- [ ] I can describe the use of validation methods.
- [ ] I can explain the need for both validation and verification.
- [ ] I can describe batch, online and real-time processing methods.
- [ ] I can give examples of when batch, online and real-time processing methods are used.
- [ ] I can write an algorithm.
- [ ] I can evaluate the advantages and disadvantages of different processing methods.

> Chapter 2

Hardware and software

LEARNING INTENTIONS

By the end of this chapter, you will be able to:

- describe the characteristics of mainframe computers and supercomputers
- give examples of the use of mainframe computers and supercomputers
- explain the advantages and disadvantages of mainframe computers and supercomputers
- describe types of system software and how they are used
- explain the advantages and disadvantages of system software
- understand the need for utility software
- describe types of utility software and how they are used
- explain the advantages and disadvantages of utility software
- describe the uses of customer written software and off-the-shelf software
- explain the advantages and disadvantages of custom written and off-the-shelf software
- describe different types of user interfaces and their uses
- explain the advantages and disadvantages of different types of user interfaces.

Introduction

Hardware **devices** are the physical components of a computer. Hardware includes the CPU, motherboard, RAM, ROM, graphics card, sound card, monitor, keyboard, mouse, printer and memory card, among others.

Software is also known as programs or apps (application software), such as word processing, spreadsheet, anti-malware or **operating system**. Each program consists of programming code which gives instructions to the computer in order to carry out a task. The code that is passed to the hardware is in binary format which consists of instructions in the form of lots of ones and zeros (for example, 101011101110).

KEY WORDS

device: a hardware component of a computer system consisting of electronic components

software: programs which give instructions to the computer

operating system: software that manages the hardware within a computer system

2.1 Mainframe computers and supercomputers

Uses of mainframe computers

Mainframe computers can serve many terminals, usually thousands, within an organisation. A terminal can be a computer that is connected to the mainframe, a dumb terminal that has very little processing power and memory of its own or even an ATM (automated teller machine). Mainframes are often used to host business databases that can be accessed by the business and also thousands of consumers simultaneously through a web interface. They are also used for large scale transaction processing and batch processing. Other uses include statistical analysis such as analysis of census data.

KEY WORDS

mainframe computer: powerful computer serving several terminals

Uses of supercomputers

While mainframes are designed to be used by thousands of users and carry out many different types of instructions, **supercomputers** are designed to carry out large numbers of complex calculations. A supercomputer will run very few computer programs and its focus is on executing instructions as quickly as possible for one purpose. They will be run at maximum capacity so that their full power is used to process data and solve a problem.

KEY WORD

supercomputer: large computer with parallel processing to complete highly complex tasks quickly

Supercomputers are required for research in quantum mechanics where billions of complex calculations need to be made to simulate the dynamics of millions of atoms. They are also used in weather forecasting and climate research where sophisticated numerical models of the atmosphere, ocean and space need to be created.

Figure 2.1: Sierra Supercomputer at Lawrence Livermore National Laboratory.

The supercomputers will process billions of observations from weather monitoring stations, satellites, weather balloons, buoys and radar among others.

Characteristics of mainframe and supercomputers

Figure 2.2: The IBM z13: mainframe computer.

Mainframe computers need to have reliability, availability and serviceability (RAS) characteristics.

This means that their design prioritises the system being available 100% of the time. To be reliable, the hardware components must be capable of extensively self-checking and recovering automatically in the case of failure. Software for use on the mainframe will have gone through extensive testing and should be able to be updated quickly if problems are detected.

To remain available, the mainframe must be able to continue to operate at all times. There will be redundant hardware components, such as storage and power supplies, that will take over automatically if an active component fails. This will also mean that a failed component can be swapped out with a replacement without affecting the operation of the mainframe which makes it serviceable. The term hot-swappable is used to refer to hardware components that can be replaced while the system is still running.

Mainframes can often operate without downtime for many years, but serviceability also requires that if the mainframe does need to be taken down for maintenance then it should be taken down for as short a period as possible. Longevity is important because mainframes and supercomputers are a large financial investment and so they need to be useful for several years. The ability to upgrade them by adding additional processors or memory is important to ensure they can cope with increasing demand.

Due to the power and quantity of processors, mainframe computers and supercomputers generate a lot of heat. This therefore requires cooling systems to be in place. One method is to use air cooling which cools the warm air in equipment racks and carries the heat to large chillers, but this uses up a lot of power. A more efficient method is to use liquid cooling which delivers cold liquid direct to the processor chip. Many data centres are now being built in colder parts of the world where natural cold air can be circulated.

As mainframes service many applications and thousands of simultaneous users, they require a multi-layer approach to security including identifying users, authentication and access control. Individuals and groups can be given permission to access different resources. Each resource will have different levels of access that can be granted to it. For example, web users would be allowed to see descriptions, images and prices of active products for sale but only product managers would be able to see non-active products or make changes to the descriptions and prices. Security software will also monitor the mainframe for potential security threats and alert administrators if a threat is suspected.

Historically, the performance of a mainframe computer has been measured by how many instructions its processors can perform every second. This is measured in MIPs (millions of instructions per second). However, this is not considered an accurate measure of performance of the mainframe as a whole for several reasons, including that a complex instruction can take longer to process than a simple one. CISC (complex instruction set computing) processors will have a single instruction doing many things at once whereas RISC (reduced instruction set computing) processors will have a single instruction that does very little but manages the instruction efficiently. Other factors that affect processing speed and mean that MIPs is not an accurate measurement include:

- workload mix
- memory and cache sizes
- amount of input and output activity
- operating systems and software
- changes made to hardware.

A batch workload that operates sequentially will make efficient use of resources, but online activity such as web access will have a much more random resource requirement. Larger memory and cache sizes can make a significant difference to the performance of a mainframe computer. Lots of input and output activity leads to less efficient use of processors with tasks being suspended while input/output interruptions are processed.

As the amount of input and output activity can have a detrimental effect on the performance of a mainframe, it's possible to include dedicated system assist processors (SAPs) which handle input/output requests. This frees up the main processors enabling them to operate without input/output interruptions.

Enhancements or bug fixes for operating systems and applications software can improve the efficiency of processing or can have an adverse effect on how efficiently processors are used.

In general, the cost of mainframes is evaluated by looking at how many MIPs can be delivered for the cost, despite the shortfalls of the measurement.

Another performance measurement is FLOPS (floating point operations per second), or MFLOPS (mega floating point operations per second). MFLOPS means mega FLOPS, which is one million floating-point operations per second. Floating point instructions are used in scientific computational research and so MFLOPS are more often used to compare the speed of supercomputers. MFLOPS give a more reliable measure of performance than MIPS but there are still discrepancies where some processors can carry out a single floating point operation but others would require several floating point operations for the same result. For example, the Cray-2 supercomputer has no divide instruction but the Motorola 68882 has divide, square root, sine and cosine functions. This means that the Cray 2 would require several floating point instructions to carry out a division but the Motorola 68882 would be able to do this as a single floating point instruction.

KEY WORDS

FLOPS: floating point operations per second – used to measure the performance of supercomputers

As with desktop computers, there are a variety of operating systems available for mainframe computers. Some operating systems such as z/OS are general purpose and offer a stable, secure and continuous environment for software that runs on the mainframe. Others such as z/VM specialise in offering virtual machines, each of which runs its own operating system. Some operating systems such as z/TPF specialise in transaction processing where there are a high volume of transactions taking place such as ticket sales. Most supercomputers run an operating system based on the Linux operating system which is Open Source and so freely available for development.

Questions

1 State **two** purposes of mainframe computers.

2 Give **two** examples of uses of a supercomputer.

3 State what is meant by RAS in relation to mainframe computers and supercomputers.

4 Explain why colder parts of the world are a favoured choice as a location for many data centres.

5 Explain why MFLOPS are used instead of MIPS as a performance measure for supercomputers.

Advantages	Disadvantages
They are designed to be reliable, available and serviceable (RAS) which makes them more reliable than regular computers.	The high cost of mainframes and supercomputers mean that they are only used by large organisations such as governments, banks and large corporations. They require specialist operating systems which are also very expensive.
They are scalable because processors and memory can be added as required.	A lot of space is required to install a mainframe or supercomputer and the temperature must be maintained so that it doesn't become too hot.
They are designed to last for at least 10 years.	Specialist support staff are required for maintenance.
They are able to store and process extremely large amounts of data.	The interface is command driven which can be difficult to understand.
More than one operating system can be used at once which can improve the overall performance of the system.	Supercomputers are processing big data and so need massive external storage drives that are capable of reading and writing data quickly enough for the processing.
Hardware failures are notified immediately so that replacements can be made very quickly.	
Terminals only require input and output devices and can take advantage of the processing power of the mainframe. Desktop computers connected to a mainframe can use their own processing power for smaller tasks and the mainframe can perform more complex tasks.	

Table 2.1: Advantages and disadvantages of mainframe computers

2.2 System software

Programs that are designed to maintain or operate the computer system are known as **system software**. The software that operates the computer hardware is known as the operating system.

> **KEY WORDS**
>
> **system software:** software needed to operate a computer system

Operating systems

An operating system manages the hardware within a computer system. When a computer is turned on and after the Basic Input/Output System (BIOS) has loaded, the operating system is the first piece of software that will load. It sits between hardware and applications software and manages any communication between the two.

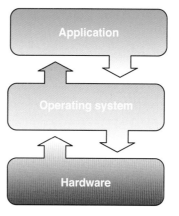

Figure 2.3: Operating system.

An operating system manages hardware by carrying out tasks such as:

- allocating memory to software
- sending data and instructions to output devices
- responding to input devices such as when a key is pressed
- opening and closing files on storage devices
- giving each running task a fair share of processor time
- sending error messages or status messages to applications or users
- dealing with user logons and security.

Device Drivers

While the operating system can manage the general instructions to deal with hardware such as displaying graphics on a screen, it requires the use of device drivers to deal with specific makes and models of hardware. A device driver is the software that comes with an external hardware component and sends customised instructions to that specific component. By using common device drivers, software applications are able to issue generic commands such as 'print' to the operating system without having to know the different instructions required for every different make and model of external hardware components.

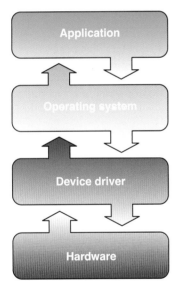

Figure 2.4: Device driver.

Translators

A translator translates a program written in a high-level programming language into machine code that a computer can understand.

Compilers

A **compiler** is a translator which creates a file containing the machine code known as an executable file because it can be executed by the processor. It can also be referred to as the object file. The original high-level programming language file is known as the source file.

KEY WORD

compiler: translates high-level programming language into an executable file in machine code

When a program is compiled, the whole source code is translated into the executable file at once and can then be distributed to resellers, customers and individual computers. As it is in an executable format, it can only run on operating systems for which the compiler has translated it. For example, programs that have been compiled for Windows© will not work on Linux© unless they are compiled again for Linux. The same situation exists with mobile phone and tablet operating systems.

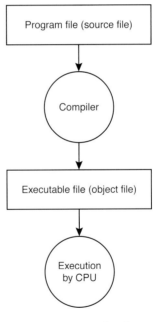

Figure 2.5: Compiler diagram.

The compilation process includes three stages:

- lexical analysis
- syntax analysis
- code generation.

During lexical analysis, any white space or comments will be removed and the code will be broken down into tokens. Each token will represent a keyword, constant, identifier, string, number, operator or punctuation symbol.

For example, in Python, the following code displays a value to the screen

    print("Hello" + forename);

The tokens would be:

- print   (keyword)
- ((symbol)
- "   (symbol)
- Hello   (string)
- "   (symbol)
- +   (operator)
- forename   (identifier)
-)   (symbol)
- ;   (symbol)

Some tokens will be replaced by shorter tokens, for example, ENDWHILE might be replaced by EW. Any errors detected during lexical analysis will be reported to the user.

During syntax analysis, the structure of the program will be analysed to check that it conforms to the syntax (grammar) of the programming language. Each set of tokens will be analysed separately to see if keywords, constants, identifiers, strings, numbers, operators and punctuation symbols have been used correctly. A dictionary will be created which is a list of variables used by the program, their data types and the memory location to be used.

The final phase is code generation when the source code is converted into machine code for the target machine type. Different machine types require different machine codes to carry out each instruction and so it's important that the source code is translated into the correct machine code.

Interpreters

Interpreters also translate a program written in a high-level programming language into machine code, but use a different method. Instead of translating the whole source code at once, it is translated one line at a time. This can be less efficient than a compiler because it takes time to do the translating as the program is being executed and also because statements within programming loops (e.g. FOR, REPEAT, WHILE) have to be analysed each time round.

KEY WORD

interpreter: translates and executes a high-level programming language one line at a time

---

An interpreter translates each line of the source code into an intermediate stage and then executes the line of code. It reports on errors as each line of source code is translated.

Interpreters are often used to translate macros or application-based script languages (for example, Visual Basic for Applications), which can be particularly useful when a document needs to be opened on a variety of operating systems. Interpreters are also used when testing programs so that parts of the program can be executed without having to compile the whole program.

Java uses both a compiler and an interpreter. The original Java source code (files with a .java extension) is compiled into Java bytecode (files with a .class extension) which is an intermediate code. In order that the Java program can work on any operating system, a Java Virtual Machine installed on the computer is used to interpret the bytecode at the time of execution.

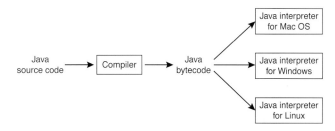

Figure 2.6: Java diagram.

Compiler and interpreter differences

Compiler	Interpreter
Translates source code into object code all at once in advance of execution.	Translates source code into object code one line at a time.
Compiled object code will only work on the operating system it has been compiled for.	Source code can be translated into object code for more than one operating system.
Object code is ready to be executed without delay.	Object code has to be generated, so additional time is added to the execution time.
Compiling can take a long time, which is not appropriate for on-the-fly testing.	Only the required code needs to be interpreted, so this is efficient for on-the-fly testing.
Errors are reported after compilation has completed.	Errors are reported as they are found during the interpretation.
The source code is optimised to run as efficiently as possible.	

Table 2.2: Compiler and interpreter differences.

Linkers

Computer programs often consist of several modules (parts) of programming code. Each module carries out a specified task within the program. Each module will have been compiled into a separate object file. The function of a linker (also known as a link editor) is to combine the object files together to form a single executable file. In addition to the modules used, the program may make reference to a common library. A common library contains code for common tasks that can be used in more than one program, such as mathematical functions, memory management, open and save dialogues, progress bars and input/output. The linker can link modules from a library file into the executable file, too.

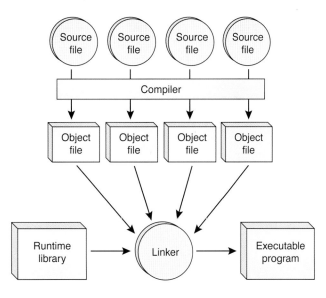

Figure 2.7: Linker diagram.

Not all modules are always needed and a linker is able to select which modules will form part of the executable file.

Questions

6 Identify two functions of an operating system.

7 Describe the function of a compiler.

8 Describe two advantages of an interpreter over a compiler.

2.3 Utility software

Utility software is system software that performs some sort of maintenance on the computer system. Utility software does not include the operating system, but an operating system may come pre-installed with some utility software.

> **KEY WORDS**
>
> **utility software:** software that performs some sort of maintenance on the computer system

Anti-virus

Anti-virus software is sometimes referred to as antimalware software, as it deals with other threats such as adware and spyware as well as viruses. It has two main functions. The first is an anti-virus monitor that is continually monitoring the system for viruses and malware. If the anti-virus monitor detects any unusual behaviour or tell-tale signs of viruses or malware then it will prevent them from being executed so they cannot cause damage to files or programs. The second function is to check for viruses or malware that may already be on a system. This is usually known as scanning the system. If anything is found then the user will usually be given the option to disinfect the affected area, put it into quarantine or ignore it. Ignoring it is very dangerous because it means the virus or malware will be executed and may have unexpected results. Disinfecting is the safest option as it completely removes the threat from the system, but it does mean that any data or program that had been affected would be deleted. The compromise is to put the affected area into quarantine. This is a safe area where the virus or malware cannot be executed, but the data or program remains isolated until it can be checked more thoroughly.

Backup

Backup utilities create a second copy of data and programs that are in storage. A backup utility can be executed by the user, in which case the backup takes place when the user asks it to, or it can be scheduled to execute at a predetermined time so that the backup takes place automatically. The user is usually able to select which folders and files will be backed up and can usually decide where the backup will be stored.

Data compression

Data compression utilities will reduce the original size of files so that they use up less storage space. This can be achieved on a file-by-file basis or for a set of files or even a set of folders. It will be slower to open the compressed file than the uncompressed file, but as it is smaller it will use up less storage and can be transferred from one location to another more quickly.

Disk defragmentation

Storing data on a hard disk

A hard disk drive (HDD) consists of two main parts: the device that is the electronics which store the data, and the disk that is the medium onto which the data is stored. The device (or drive) includes a read-write head which sits at the end of an access arm and magnetises sectors on the disk (platter).

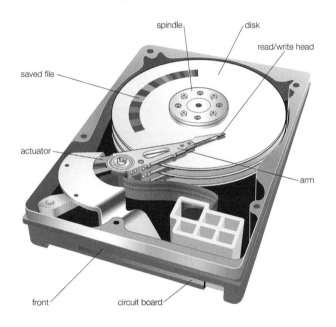

Figure 2.8: A hard disk.

There is usually more than one platter and therefore there will be several read-write heads for each side of each platter as shown in Figure 2.8. Each platter will have tracks and each track will be split into sectors. The tracks that are in the same position on each platter form a cylinder. Wherever possible, a computer will attempt to store data in clusters on a single cylinder because this requires the least access arm movement and the access arm is the slowest part of the hard disk.

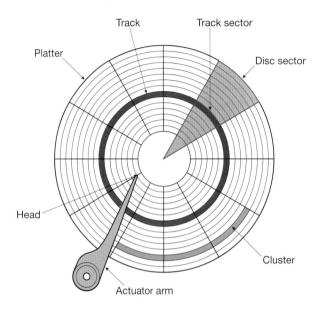

Figure 2.9: Structure of a hard disk.

REFLECTION

Do you know where the phrase 'my computer has crashed' comes from?

Fragmented files

As a hard disc gets used, files are kept together in storage on the same cylinder or adjacent cylinders. When files are deleted, gaps are left on the disc. As files grow in size, they use up more space on the disc and this may no longer be on the same or adjacent cylinder and will be spread across many clusters. When all the cylinders have been used, the only space to store files is within the gaps. If the gaps are not big enough, then files have to be split across gaps, meaning that they become fragmented. The problem with this is that when opening the file, the access arm of the hard disc drive has to keep moving to different locations which makes opening the file a slow process.

WORKED EXAMPLE 2.01

In Figure 2.10, files have been neatly stored on the disc with file A, followed by file B, then file C.

Figure 2.10: Non-fragmented files.

Figure 2.11 shows how each of the files has got bigger. First of all file A got bigger with an extra two sectors, then a new file D was added, then file B got bigger by a sector, then file A again by a sector and finally file C.

Figure 2.11: Fragmented files.

The files are fragmented and so they need to be defragmented as in Figure 2.12.

Figure 2.12: Defragmented files.

In Figure 2.13, files Q and S have been deleted.

Figure 2.13: Non-fragmented files.

A new file U needs to be stored but it requires four sectors. It could end up being stored as in Figure 2.14.

Figure 2.14: Fragmented files.

Defragmentation can solve this problem by temporarily moving U4, moving all of R next to P, moving all of T next to R and then moving all of U next to each other, as shown in Figure 2.15.

Figure 2.15: Defragmented files.

Defragmentation

A defragmentation utility will reorganise all the files so that each file is contiguous (kept together). It will do this by moving fragmented parts of files and small files to free space on the disc and creating space on whole cylinders or adjacent cylinders. It will then move the defragmented files to a place where the whole file is kept together. This can significantly improve the performance of a computer system, especially if program files have become fragmented and can be defragmented.

PRACTICAL ACTIVITY 2.02

Open **2.01 FragmentationDefragmentation.gif**.

In the grid, each colour represents a file, and each cell represents an item.

- The red file is originally stored as items 1 to 7.

- The blue file is then stored as items 1 to 4.

- Additional items 8 to 10 are added to the red file, which are fragmented from the red file items 1 to 7.

- The green file is then stored as items 1 to 3.

- The cyan file is then stored as items 1 to 5.

- Additional items 4 to 5 are added to the blue file, which are fragmented from the blue file items 1 to 3.

- Additional items 4 to 5 are added to the green file, which are fragmented from the green file items 1 to 3.

- The orange file is then stored as items 1 to 7.

- The blue file is then deleted.

Now watch what happens as the purple file is added as items 1 to 2 where the blue file used to be and the green file items 6 to 8 are added in a fragmented manner.

Finally, watch how the file is defragmented by moving files into blank spaces and then reorganising them so each file is kept together.

Formatting

When a disc is prepared for first time use, it needs to be formatted. Formatting is the process of organising the tracks on the disc into sectors. Each sector is where data will be stored. A used disc can also be formatted, in which case all data will be lost and the tracks prepared again as if the disc was being used for the first time.

File management

Files can be copied using features within an operating system's own interface. However, this can be slow and options are limited. File-copying utilities enable users to have more control over which files are copied and how they are copied. For example, a user may only want to copy word processing documents that are within a series of folders and they may want all the files to be copied to a single folder on the destination storage. It is also possible to synchronise files across multiple storage locations or even multiple computer systems, so that when a change is made to a file in one location, it will then be updated in all other locations.

Some files become locked by an operating system and it becomes almost impossible to delete them. Deleting utilities can overcome this problem by deleting locked files and folders. When files are deleted using normal deletion methods, the data is still on the disc although the user can't see it. Therefore another function of deleting utilities is being able to delete files permanently so that they cannot be restored or accessed. Some deletion utilities will remove temporary files that are no longer needed by the computer system, or files that are no longer used but haven't been deleted when a program has been uninstalled or a user profile removed.

Questions

9   List two utilities.

10   Describe the role of anti-virus software.

2.4 Custom-written software and off-the-shelf software

Custom-written software

When a client requires a software solution that will carry out a specific purpose that is unique to their organisation, they will ask for the software to be written for them. This is known as **custom-written software** because it is customised to the needs of the client and will meet the requirements of the client.

> **KEY WORDS**
>
> **custom-written software:** software that is written especially to meet the requirements of a client

Off-the-shelf software

When software already exists and is purchased online or from a shop, it is known as **off-the-shelf software**. The software will have been written for a general purpose that is likely to be useful to a large market. Anybody can purchase the software for a specified price.

> **KEY WORDS**
>
> **off-the-shelf software:** general purpose software available to a large market

Advantages and disadvantages

Custom-written software	Off-the-shelf software
The entire development cost of custom-written software is met by the client for whom it is written, which makes it very expensive.	The development cost of off-the-shelf software is spread between all the customers who purchase it at a specified price, which means the cost is much lower.
Custom-written software takes a long time to develop, so the client will have to wait before being able to use the software.	Off-the-shelf software is immediately available, so the customer can start using it straight away.
The requirements of the client can be met precisely with no additional features that are not necessary.	Some tasks that the customer needs to carry out may not be possible and there will be lots of features that the customer never uses.
The developers of the software will ensure that the software is compatible with the hardware, software and data used by the client.	The software may not be compatible with existing hardware, software and data used by the customer.

Custom-written software	Off-the-shelf software
As the software will not have been used before, apart from testing, it is likely that bugs will be found within the software as it gets used by the client.	The software will have been used by thousands of customers and bugs will have been identified and fixed, and patches will be released as more bugs are found so that the software runs as expected.
The client will have access to support from the company that developed the software.	Customers will be able to get support from a wide range of sources including telephone support, discussion forums and online training.

Table 2.3: Custom-written software versus off-the-shelf software.

Proprietary software

Proprietary software is owned by a single person or organisation who sells it for use under an agreed licence. Only the files needed to run the software are made available, with the source code used to create the software remaining with the owner. Different licences can be granted for the use of the software including freeware, shareware, single user, multi-user and site licence. For example, an office suite of software could be sold for use for business purposes on a single computer or it could be sold for use for personal purposes and allowed to be installed on up to five devices. Freeware can be used free of charge whereas Shareware can be used free of charge, but some features might be restricted or it might stop working after a trial period until payment is made.

REFLECTION

Explore examples of shareware software and discover what restrictions are in place if it's used without making a payment.

Open source software

Open source software has the source code freely available. This means that the source code used to create the software must be distributed with the executable version of the software. It can be freely accessed, used, changed or shared. There is often a community of developers that contribute to the development of open source software. Whilst open source software is often free of charge, it is not a requirement because the installation, distribution or customisation of open source software can be charged for.

REFLECTION

Visit the Open Source Initiative website and find out what defines open source software.

Questions

11 Describe off-the-shelf software.

12 Describe two disadvantages of custom-written software.

2.5 User interfaces

An interface is the boundary between two systems. A **user interface** is the boundary between the user and the computer system. A user interface represents the communication between a user and the computer system. This communication can take many forms.

KEY WORDS

user interface: communication between the user and the computer system

Command line interface

A command line interface (CLI) allows a user to enter text commands to which the computer system will respond. The computer system will respond by producing results in a text format.

For example, in Figure 2.16, the user has changed the directory (folder) to the logs directory ('cd logs').

Then the user has requested a listing of the directory ('dir'). Finally the user copies the file directx.log to the root directory of the f drive ('copy directx.log f:\'). The user gets a confirmation message that one file has been copied. The only prompt that the user gets is information about which directory is currently active ('C:\Windows\Logs>')

```
C:\Windows>cd logs

C:\Windows\Logs>dir
 Volume in drive C has no label.
 Volume Serial Number is C8FD-8C85

 Directory of C:\Windows\Logs

29/01/2015  12:07    <DIR>          .
29/01/2015  12:07    <DIR>          ..
18/05/2015  03:12    <DIR>          CBS
09/12/2014  13:53           254,487 DirectX.log
17/10/2013  17:00    <DIR>          DISM
17/10/2013  18:10    <DIR>          DPX
22/08/2013  16:36    <DIR>          HomeGroup
23/05/2014  00:09    <DIR>          Paragon
23/05/2014  00:10    <DIR>          Paragon Software
22/08/2013  16:36    <DIR>          SettingSync
19/10/2013  10:17    <DIR>          SetupCleanupTask
08/06/2015  03:40    <DIR>          SystemRestore
29/01/2015  12:07    <DIR>          WindowsBackup
               1 File(s)        254,487 bytes
              12 Dir(s)   5,402,001,408 bytes free

C:\Windows\Logs>copy directx.log f:\
        1 file(s) copied.

C:\Windows\Logs>
```

Figure 2.16: Command line interface.

CLIs use very little memory so they are useful in old systems or for maintenance of very small systems/devices (for example, engine management systems). They are also useful for technical users who need to carry out complex operations which cannot be performed using more user-friendly interfaces. However, CLIs can be difficult to learn and use because users have to learn and remember all the commands, and errors are easily made when entering those commands.

Graphical user interface

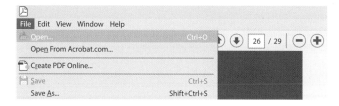

Figure 2.17: Graphical user interface.

The most common type of interface that we use is a graphical user interface (GUI). GUIs are found on desktop computers, tablet computers, mobile phones,

televisions, set-top boxes, photocopiers and some in-car entertainment systems.

GUIs can include some or all of the elements shown in Table 2.4.

The acronym WIMP is commonly used to remember these elements.

Complex GUIs require a lot of memory to operate, but simpler GUIs can be used where memory is limited. Although CLIs don't require much memory, simple GUIs can be used instead of a CLI in small systems such as embedded systems. It is commonplace to find simple web-based GUIs for the maintenance of devices such as routers, switches and printers.

GUIs are intuitive to use which means they are easy to learn because commands are represented by pictures and menus provide options that can be selected. However, they can be restrictive for some technical users who need to carry out unusual tasks.

Within a GUI, form controls can be used. These include labels, text boxes, tick boxes, option buttons, drop-down boxes and buttons.

Windows	An area of the screen devoted to a specific task, for example a software application, a file within a software application or a print dialog box.
Icons	An image that is used to represent a program, file or task. The icon can be selected to open the program, file or task.
Menus	Menus are words on the screen which represent a list of options that can be expanded into further sub-menus.
Pointers	This is the method of representing movement from a pointing device such as a mouse or the human finger on a touch screen. The pointer is also used to select and manipulate objects on the screen.

Table 2.4: Graphical user interface elements.

Control	Description	Example
Labels	Labels are used as prompts or instructions to enter data. They are text and cannot be edited by the user.	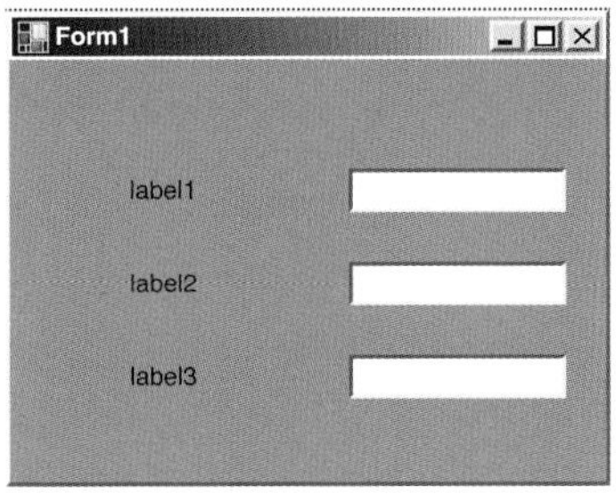 Figure 2.18: Label.
Text boxes	Text boxes are an area where the user can enter text such as their surname or credit card number. Errors can easily be made by the user when entering data into a text box, such as spelling things incorrectly.	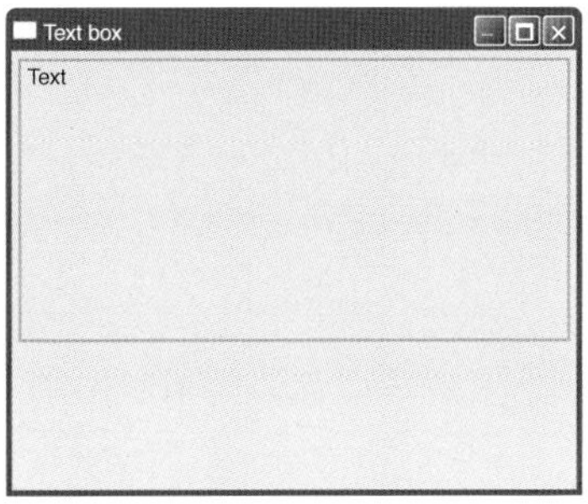 Figure 2.19: Text6 box.
Tick boxes	Tick boxes (also known as check boxes) allow the user to select from a set of options. The user can choose as many options that apply. For example, when printing, a user can choose to collate documents and to print on both sides.	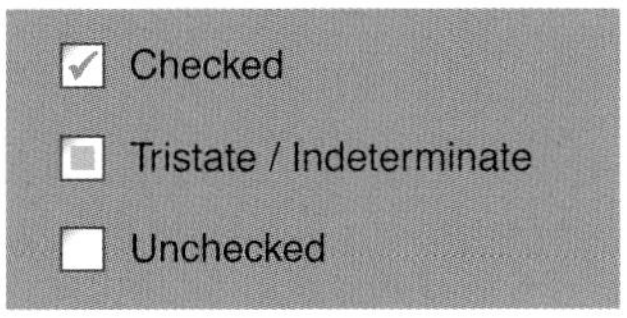 Figure 2.20: Tick box.
Option buttons	Option buttons (also known as radio buttons) differ from tick boxes in that only one option in a group can be selected at once.	 Figure 2.21: Option button.
Drop-down boxes	Drop-down boxes allow a user to select from a list that appears when the drop-down box appears on screen. Only one option can be chosen. The user can usually start typing the option so that it is found more quickly. Drop-down boxes are more appropriate than option buttons when there are a large number of options to choose from, as the drop-down box doesn't take up as much space on the screen.	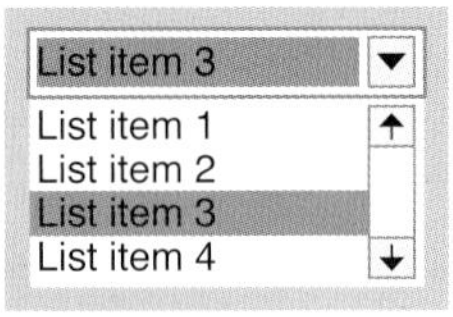 Figure 2.22: Drop-down box.
Buttons	Buttons can be used to navigate through an interface (forwards and backwards), to confirm that inputs have been completed, to clear inputs, to gain help and to access any other area of an interface.	 Figure 2.23: Confirm button.

Table 2.5: Form controls.

Dialogue interface

A dialogue interface refers to using the spoken word to communicate with a computer system. A user can give commands using their voice and the computer system can respond by carrying out an action or with further information using a synthesised voice.

Dialogue interfaces are very popular with mobile devices, including mobile phones and in-car entertainment systems. Some cars will accept commands such as 'Temperature 20' or 'Call John Smith at home'. Mobile phones will accept commands and questions such as 'What is the time in Islamabad?' or 'Give me directions to get home'. Some automated telephone systems will recognise voice, too, so that the user doesn't have to use the dial pad to input information.

A big advantage of dialogue interfaces is that no hands are required, which makes them suitable for use in cars or when holding a telephone. In many circumstances, words can be spoken by a user more quickly than a user can type them. There is no need for a physical interface with dialogue interfaces, so they are suitable for systems such as home automation where voice commands can be given from anywhere to control equipment such as lights, entertainment systems and curtains. With entertainment systems such as televisions, the user does not have to find a remote control to use and anybody in the room can give the command to increase the volume or change the channel.

The main problem with this type of interface is the computer system's ability to recognise the spoken word. Many things can make it difficult for the computer to understand, including accents, different voices, stammers and background noise (for example, a car's engine). Dialogue interfaces also require the user to know what commands are understood by the computer system as otherwise the system will not know how to respond. Some dialogue interfaces will give prompts telling the user from which options they can choose. Systems are not intelligent enough to simply understand requests in any format that the user chooses.

Gesture based interface

Gesture-based interfaces will recognise human motion. This could include tracking eyes and lips, identifying hand signals or monitoring whole body movement.

There are many applications of gesture-based interfaces, including gaming, which have led to the development of other gesture-based interfaces. The original Nintendo Wii® enabled gamers to move their hands while holding a remote controller and that movement would be mimicked in games such as ten pin bowling and boxing. Microsoft's Xbox® took this a stage further and was able to track whole body movement without any devices being held or worn by the user. This enabled gamers to fully engage with a game using their whole body, so boxing could now become kick-boxing and ten pin bowling could include a run-up.

Many computer systems, including mobile devices, are now starting to accept hand gestures as a way of controlling objects on screen. For example, a swipe of the hand across a screen may close a program, while pinching fingers together in front of a screen may zoom out on an image. This can avoid greasy screens and could help with infection control in hospitals, specifically in operating theatres.

Gestures can be an essential form of interaction for some disabled users who cannot use conventional input devices. A person who has no control from the neck downwards could control a computer system with their eyes because the computer can track the movement of each eye.

One of the biggest problems with gesture interfaces is accuracy. In order for a gesture interface to be effective, it needs to interpret the movements made by the human user accurately. Tracking individual fingers, arms, eyeballs and legs requires highly accurate cameras or sensors. This is why many virtual reality applications still use sensors attached to various parts of the body in order to improve accuracy. It can also be very difficult to control a pointer when a finger is in mid-air rather than when firmly fixed to a touch screen or holding a mouse.

Questions

13 Give **two** reasons why a CLI might be used instead of a GUI. [2]

14 Give **two** disadvantages of a CLI. [2]

15 Define the term WIMP. [1]

16 Explain two advantages of dialogue interfaces. [2]

EXAM-STYLE QUESTIONS

A local council uses a mainframe computer to host its databases and web-enabled applications.

1 a State one measurement of processor speed used for mainframe computers or supercomputers. [1]

  b Explain the importance of reliability, availability and serviceability for mainframe computers. [6]

[Total 7]

Geraldine in the accounts department has been issued with a new printer.

2 Explain why Nadia needs a device driver for her printer. [2]

Nadia has discovered that her laptop computer is running slower than usual. The IT Support team have run disk defragmentation software which has identified her hard disk is 70% fragmented.

3 a Explain how data is stored on a hard disk. [4]

  b Explain how the data on Nadia's hard disk may have become fragmented. [4]

[Total 8]

The council needs some new software for waste management that will link in with their website where residents can log problems such as missed collections.

4 Evaluate the use of a custom-written software solution for this purpose. [6]

The waste management software will use a Graphical User Interface (GUI).

5 a Identify and describe three different form controls that could be used in the GUI, giving examples of how they could be used. [6]

  b Identify two other types of user interface. [2]

[Total 8]

The development team will use an interpreter for testing during development of the software and a compiler to translate the final version of the software to machine code for the council.

6 Describe two differences between a compiler and an interpreter. [4]

SUMMARY CHECKLIST

- [ ] I can describe the characteristics of mainframe computers and supercomputers.
- [ ] I can give examples of the use of mainframe computers and supercomputers.
- [ ] I can explain the advantages and disadvantages of mainframe computers and supercomputers.
- [ ] I can describe types of system software and how they are used.
- [ ] I can explain the advantages and disadvantages of system software.
- [ ] I can understand the need for utility software.
- [ ] I can describe types of utility software and how they are used.
- [ ] I can explain the advantages and disadvantages of utility software.
- [ ] I can describe the uses of customer written software and off-the-shelf software.
- [ ] I can explain the advantages and disadvantages of custom written and off-the-shelf software.
- [ ] I can describe different types of user interfaces and their uses.
- [ ] I can explain the advantages and disadvantages of different types of user interfaces.

> Chapter 3
Monitoring and control

Introduction

You use **monitoring systems** and **control systems** every day. They are an important part of your life. These systems help with tasks such as keeping the temperature of your fridge at the correct level. They also help keep you safe in workplaces that may be dangerous. A monitoring system could collect data about the temperature in your local area so this can be reported. A control system could help keep a chemical factory worker safe as it will make sure that the production process is working correctly, so that the worker is not exposed to chemicals for a dangerous amount of time.

KEY WORDS

monitoring system: a system that observes and often records the activities in a process

control system: a system that manages or regulates a process by physically changing aspects of the system depending on collected data

It is important for you to learn how these important systems operate and how they help many aspects of daily life.

3.1 Sensors

A **sensor** is a type of input device. It is used to collect data about a physical environment automatically. This removes the need for a human to collect the data manually. The data collected from a sensor is input into a system and any necessary action required is taken.

KEY WORD

sensor: an input device that collects data from the surrounding physical environment

There are several advantages of using sensors to collect data.

1   Data can be repeatedly collected 24 hours a day. This means that a human does not need to be present all the time and can rest.

2   Data can be collected in harmful and dangerous environments, without the need for a human to be present. This means that the lives of humans are not endangered to collect the data.

3   A sensor may be more consistent in the data that it samples as it is a mechanical device. It is therefore likely to be accurate. A human may be inconsistent and this could lead to errors in data samples.

Figure 3.1: Collecting data.

If you look at the environment around you, you will see that it has many different elements to it.

Question

1 What kind of things can you see, hear and feel in your environment?

When answering Question 1, you may have noticed things such as:

- the temperature
- the level of sound
- the level of light
- movement.

There are also many more things that are changeable about the environment, such as:

- moisture
- electromagnetic fields
- pressure.

If you attempted to create a sensor to collect data about all these different aspects of the environment, it would probably need to be quite large. When you are trying to collect data, it is important that the sensor is quite small so that it can fit into convenient places. There are different sensors that collect data about different aspects of the environment. There are sensors for:

- light/UV
- temperature
- pressure
- humidity
- sound
- infrared
- touch
- electromagnetic field
- proximity.

Question

2 It may be obvious what some of the sensors collect data about, for example, light and sound. What sort of data do you think some of the less obvious sensors collect, for example:

- infrared
- electromagnetic field
- touch
- proximity?

You have learnt that there are advantages to using sensors, but there can also be disadvantages too. The biggest disadvantage is that a sensor can be subject to wear and tear and may become faulty. This might make it start to provide incorrect readings. This could be detrimental to the whole system.

Question

3 a Think of two situations where a sensor may start to provide incorrect readings.

b What detrimental effect could this have?

For this reason, sensors can be regularly put through a process of calibration, to make sure the readings they take are accurate.

3.2 Calibration

An inaccurate set of data is useless. It could also be very dangerous if the data is used in a control system that takes vital action based upon the data. To make sure that the data collected by a sensor is accurate it can be put through a process of calibration. No sensor will be absolutely perfect, but it is important to make sure that the readings that are taken are as accurate as possible.

> **KEY WORD**
>
> calibration: the process of testing and modifying a device to make sure that it is taking the correct readings

To calibrate a sensor, you need a calibration reference. This is a standard that you can calibrate against. A simple method of calibration is to test readings against another sensor that you know is calibrated, to see if the same readings are produced by both sensors. Another way to calibrate a sensor is by using another physical reference. For example, a ruler or measuring tape could be used to find out if an item that should trigger the proximity sensor does so from the correct distance set.

Each sensor has a characteristic curve. This curve maps the sensor's response in comparison to an ideal response. There are three main categories of result that can be given by a sensor. These are:

- Offset – this means that the readings are higher or lower than the ideal reference
- Sensitivity – this means that the readings change over a range at a different rate to the ideal reference
- Linearity – this means that the readings are directly proportional to the ideal reference.

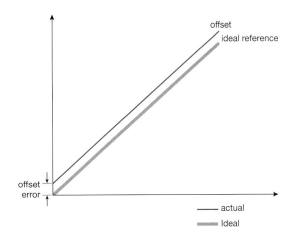

Figure 3.2: Offset.

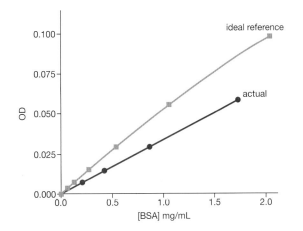

Figure 3.3: Sensitivity.

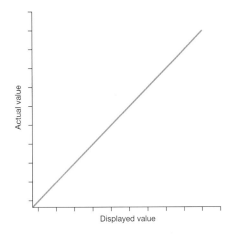

Figure 3.4: Linearity.

There are three different types of calibration that can be used for a sensor. These are:

- one point calibration
- two point calibration
- multipoint calibration.

One point calibration is the simplest form of calibration. It can be used to correct an offset calibration curve. This is because the sensor is reading partly correct, as it is changing at the same rate, but it is just consistently measuring too high or too low. The sensor can be calibrated based on a single reading to be brought closer to the ideal reference.

There are different methods for performing a one point calibration check depending on the sensor. One simple method could be:

1. Take a reading with the sensor.
2. Compare the reading with a device measuring at the ideal standard.
3. Subtract the reading from the reference to get the offset.
4. Add the offset to every reading to get the calibrated value.

For example, if a thermometer tells you the temperature of a room is 22 °C, but the reading from your sensor tells you that the room is 20.5 °C, the calculation would be:

$$22 - 20.5 = 1.5$$

This means the offset that needs to be added to each reading from the sensor is 1.5.

Figure 3.5: Calibration curve.

Two point calibration can be used to correct a data set suffering both offset and sensitivity. It rescales the output to do this. It can often be a more accurate method of calibration than one point calibration.

There are different methods, to perform a two point calibration check depending on the sensor. One method could be:

1   Take two different readings with your sensor. It works best if you take a reading at the lower end of the scale and a reading at the higher end of the scale.

2   Compare the readings to readings from a device measuring at the ideal standard.

3   Calculate the range value for the sensor readings by subtracting the low reading from the high reading.

4   Calculate the range value for the ideal standard by subtracting the low reading from the high reading.

5   Use a formula to calculate the correct value for each reading such as:

6   CorrectValue = (((SensorCurrentValue – SensorLowValue) * IdealRangeValue) / SensorRangeValue) + IdealLowValue.

For example, if a temperature sensor measures the temperature of an iced water bucket as 0.75 °C and a boiling kettle as 98 °C, you can use this two point calibration method to get a correct reading for the temperature sensor. You can use a current reading from the sensor of 37 °C. You can use a set of common ideal standard readings for iced water (0.01 °C) and boiling water (100 °C).

SensorRangeValue = 97.25

IdealRangeValue = 99.99

CorrectValue = (((37 – 0.75) * 99.99) / 97.25) + 0.01 = 37.28 (2dp)

This means that the correct value for the sensor reading of 37°C is 37.28 °C.

Multipoint calibration is similar to the other calibration methods but is performed using many different readings, at least three. This further increases the accuracy of the calibration and can help calibrate sensors that would produce readings that do not naturally form a linear line.

When a sensor has collected the data, this data will be sent to a computer system. What happens to the data at this stage will depend on whether the system is a monitoring system or a control system.

3.3 Monitoring systems

A monitoring system is designed to collect the data and then store it so that it can be used at a later stage. For example, data may be collected about the temperature in a garden over a period of 24 hours, for a week. The data could then be analysed at a later stage to see which day was the warmest and what time of the day the warmest temperature was recorded.

The main technologies used in a monitoring system are sensors. Other technologies that may be used are storage devices to store the data collected. Graphing software could also be used to create visual representation of the data to make it easier to interpret.

An example of this type of system could be a monitoring system for the level of chlorine in the water of a swimming pool:

•   a pH sensor is placed in the swimming pool

•   the pH sensor takes readings at regular intervals, such as every minute

•   the readings are sent to a storage device

•   the readings are put into a graph by the manager so that she can see the level of chlorine in the water throughout the day.

Figure 3.6: Thermometer.

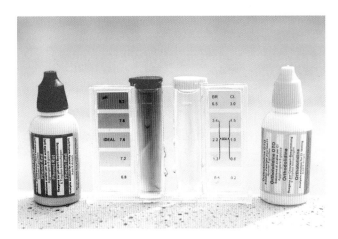

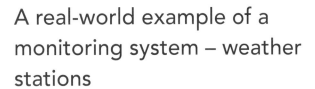

Figure 3.7: Monitoring chlorine levels.

Figure 3.8: Weather station.

A real-world example of a monitoring system – weather stations

Weather stations use many monitoring systems to provide everyone with daily information about the weather in their area, and all over the world. On an individual level, this daily information is important in knowing how to plan your day: how you should dress or how it will affect your activities. On a wider scale, industries such as the farming industry heavily depend on weather reports to make sure they task the right actions for their crops.

A weather station uses lots of temperature sensors that are spread across a region or country. These temperature sensors take data samples of the ambient temperature in that area. The data samples are sent back to the weather station. This data can then be used in many ways, for example, to report the current temperature. The weather station could also analyse lots of samples of data and predict what the weather may be in the future.

A weather station may also use pressure sensors, humidity sensors and light sensors.

Question

4   A textile factory is about to open. The factory is near a river. The local authority is worried that chemicals used to colour the textiles may leak into the nearby river. They decide to set up a monitoring system to check the pH level of the river at regular intervals. Explain what sensors could be used and how they could be used in this system.

3.4 Control systems

A control system is designed to collect data and then send this to a computer system so that it can be analysed (and any resulting action taken).

The main technologies used in a monitoring system are sensors, microprocessors and sometimes actuators. You have looked at the different kind of sensors that can be used and what the advantages and disadvantages are of using sensors. You also need to understand the use of microprocessors and actuators, and the advantages and disadvantages of each.

A **microprocessor** is an electronic component that can perform similar functions to a central processing unit (CPU). It can process instructions and perform mathematical comparisons and calculations. Microprocessors also have small areas to hold data called registers. Microprocessors are normally a single integrated circuit.

KEY WORD

microprocessor: an integrated circuit that is used in monitoring and control systems

Figure 3.9: Microprocessor.

There are both advantages and disadvantages to using a microprocessor in control systems.

Advantages	Disadvantages
They can be programmed to execute several different tasks.	There is a limit on the size of the data they are able to handle.
They are small in size so can be easily built into different technologies.	They are only small in size and can overheat if too much demand is placed on them.
They are relatively fast at moving data between different memory locations.	

Table 3.1: Advantages and disadvantages of microprocessors.

An **actuator** is used to move and operate other different mechanisms or devices. Actuators can be based on different methods of operation such as hydraulic, pneumatic or electric. Actuators could control operations such as opening and closing a valve, turning a switch on and off or driving a mechanism to open a door. They can also be used to drive each of the individual parts in a robot.

KEY WORD

actuator: a type of motor that is used to move and operate another mechanism or device

An actuator is vital in a control system because it is the element that drives the action to be performed to control the element of the environment that is at the focus.

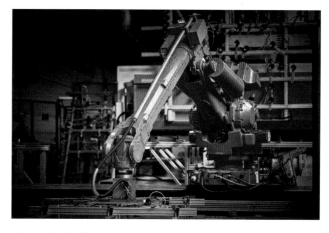

Figure 3.10: Robot arm.

There are both advantages and disadvantages to using actuators in control systems.

Advantages	Disadvantages
Hydraulic and electric actuators are fairly quiet.	Pneumatic actuators can be quite noisy.
The cost of pneumatic actuators is relatively low.	The cost of hydraulic and electric actuators is relatively high.
Most actuators have moderate to high speed abilities to perform an action.	Fluid leaks can be a problem in hydraulic actuators.

Table 3.2: Advantages and disadvantages of actuators.

Sensors, microprocessors and actuators are programmed to interact with each other to create a control system.

There are several stages in the process of a control system.

1 The sensor collects the data at set-time intervals, for example once every minute.

2 The data is sent to a microprocessor.

3 The microprocessor will analyse the data. This could involve comparing it to a pre-stored value, or range of values.

4 If the data does not match the pre-stored value, the microprocessor will send a signal to an actuator or device.

5 The actuator or device will trigger any action that needs to be taken.

An example of this type of system could be an air-conditioning system.

Figure 3.11: Air conditioning.

1 The user sets the temperature to 22 degrees Celsius.

2 This value is stored.

3 A temperature sensor collects data about the ambient temperature in the room.

4 The data collected by the sensor is sent to the microprocessor. The data is converted from analogue to digital.

5 The microprocessor analyses each data sample sent to see if it is equal to the stored value of 22 degrees Celsius.

6 If the data sample is greater than 22 degrees, the microprocessor sends a signal to an actuator, triggering the system to increase the cooling function.

7 If the data sample is less than 22 degrees, the microprocessor sends a signal to an actuator to trigger the system to increase the heating function.

8 If the data sample is equal to 22 degrees, no action is taken.

9 The whole process is then repeated at a set time interval, for example, once every minute.

This list represents an **algorithm**, which is a set of instructions or steps to be followed to achieve a certain outcome, for this example of a control system.

This system could also be represented as a flowchart:

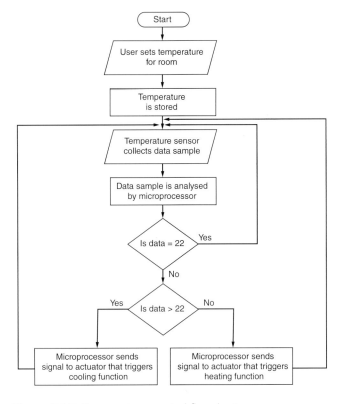

Figure 3.12: Temperature control flowchart.

A real-world example of a control system – growing crops

A farm that grows fruit and vegetables makes use of many different control systems. It relies on these systems to make sure that the produce it grows are kept in the correct conditions to make sure that they do grow. It would be a huge task for a farmer to constantly check his produce, so he relies on these systems to do this for him.

One control system that he could use is to control the conditions within his greenhouses. The correct level of light and temperature will need to be maintained. The control systems will incorporate light sensors, temperature sensors, microprocessors and actuators to maintain the correct conditions. The farmer wants to make sure the temperature is between 22 °C and 25 °C.

1   The control system uses a temperature sensor to read the temperature within the greenhouse on a regular basis.

2   The readings are sent to a microprocessor. They will need to be converted from analogue data to digital data to be processed by the microprocessor.

3   The microprocessor compares the reading to the set range.

4   If the reading is within the range, no further action is taken.

5   If the reading is greater than 25 °C, the microprocessor sends a signal to an actuator that could drive an action, such as open a window to the greenhouse.

6   If the reading is less than 22 °C, the microprocessor sends a signal to an actuator that could drive an action, such as turn on a heater in the greenhouse.

7   The whole process is repeated.

Question

5   a   Draw a flowchart to demonstrate how this environment control system will operate.

    b   The control is missing two vital processes, can you identify what they are?

Figure 3.13: Environment control.

PRACTICAL ACTIVITY 3.02

Discuss with a partner how the control system might work to control the correct level of light.

A real-world example of a control system – protecting against intruders

A jewellery store uses three main control systems to keep the jewellery they sell safe and secure. These systems are vital to the security of the jewellery and the store heavily relies on them.

Their first security control system detects if an intruder enters the store through a door or window. Infrared beams of light are run across each doorway and window. If one of these beams is broken, an alarm will sound and metal bars will close every door and window, trapping the intruder inside the room.

Question

6   Write an algorithm to demonstrate how this entry detection control system will operate.

Their second security control system detects if a window is broken by an intruder trying to enter. The sound of any breaking glass is measured. If the sound of breaking glass is detected, the alarm will sound again.

The jewellers' third security control system detects if any of the jewellery glass cabinets are opened by an intruder. The weight of the glass for each cabinet is 5 kg. If any of the glass is lifted up the alarm will sound and the bars will close every door and window.

Question

7   Draw a flowchart to demonstrate how this broken glass detection control system will operate.

REFLECTION

Look at your flowchart. Can you see any way that you can improve it? Is it easy to follow? Have you used the correct symbols?

Question

8   Either write and algorithm or draw a flowchart to demonstrate how this glass cabinet control system will operate.

REFLECTION

How did you work out which sensors would be used in each system?

EXAM-STYLE QUESTIONS

1   Define the role of a sensor.   [1]
2   Define the role of a microprocessor.   [1]
3   Define the role of an actuator.   [1]
4   Describe how a sensor is calibrated using two point calibration. [3]
5   State two advantages of using a microprocessor in a control system. [2]
6   Explain the difference between a monitoring system and a control system. [4]
7   Describe how a control system using touch sensors can be used to make sure the level of cooling liquid in a nuclear power plant is maintained at a certain level. [5]
8   Draw a flowchart to represent a control system with the following requirements:

  • A proximity sensor is used in a mobile phone.
  • The proximity sensor measures the immediate environment, using infrared (IR), to see if it is close to a human ear.
  • If an IR level of 12 micron is detected, the screen on the mobile turns off. The screen will immediately turn back on again when the IR level reduces. [6]

SUMMARY CHECKLIST

☐ I can identify a variety of different sensors and explain how they are used in monitoring systems.

☐ I can identify a variety of different sensors and actuators and explain how they are used in control systems.

☐ I can explain how sensors are calibrated, using different types of calibration.

☐ I can draw a flowchart to represent a control system.

☐ I can write an algorithm to represent a control system.

☐ I can explain at least two different advantages and disadvantages of control technologies.

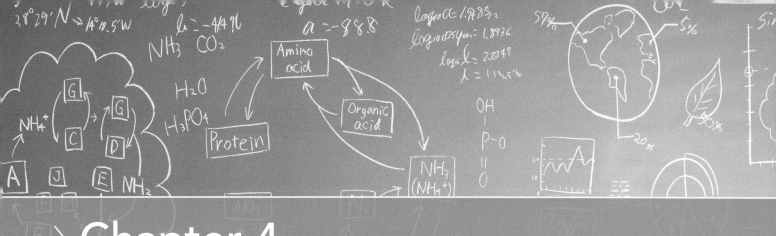

> Chapter 4
Algorithms
and flowcharts

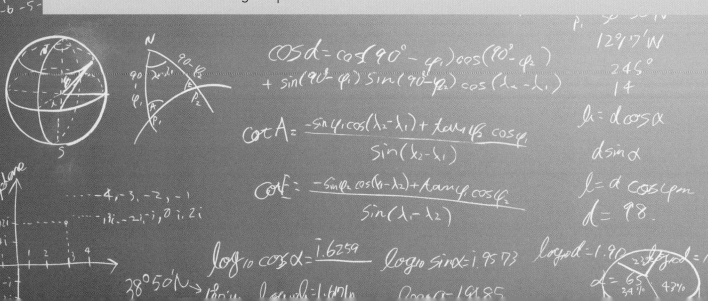

LEARNING INTENTIONS

By the end of this chapter, you will be able to:

- edit a given algorithm
- write an algorithm using pseudocode to solve a given problem
- edit a given flowchart
- draw a flowchart to solve a given problem.

Introduction

In this chapter you will learn how to develop algorithms to solve problems in a form that a computer could follow. All computer programs are simply a series of algorithms that are written in a specific way that the computer's processor can then follow one at a time.

4.1 Algorithms

An algorithm is a series of steps that are followed. You follow lots of algorithms without even realising it, for example, following a recipe or following a list of instructions. These are both examples of algorithms. Before you write algorithms on a computer, you can design them using a **flowchart** and/or using **pseudocode**. Pseudocode simply means there is no specific syntax that you have to use. It doesn't have to follow a set format, but it is more structured than English sentences.

KEY WORDS

flowchart: a set of symbols put together with commands that are followed to solve a problem

pseudocode: a language that is used to display an algorithm

A simple form of an algorithm is a series of steps to move someone (or something) through a maze. The instructions you can use are:

FD5 Move forward 5 spaces

BK2 Move backward 2 spaces

RT90 Turn right 90 degrees

LT90 Turn left 90 degrees

You start in the space labelled 'Start' in this maze, facing to the right.

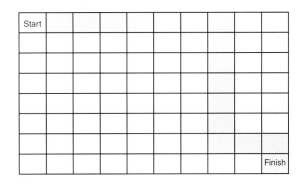

Figure 4.1: Maze 1, start.

To get to 'Finish' you would need to follow these steps:

Step 1:	FD7	**Step 5:**	FD2
Step 2:	RT90	**Step 6:**	RT90
Step 3:	FD6	**Step 7:**	FD1
Step 4:	LT90		

WORKED EXAMPLE 4.01

You are on Start, facing to the right.

Write an algorithm to move from Start to Finish.

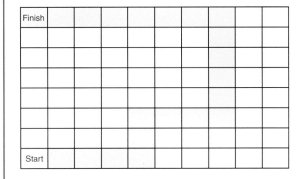

Figure 4.2: Maze 2, start.

You are facing to the right so need to count how many grey spaces there are until you need to turn. There are 4 spaces, so the command is:

FD4

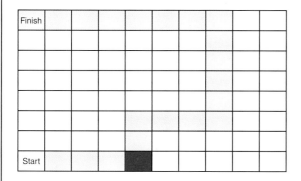

Figure 4.3: Maze 2, FD4.

You need to turn so you are facing up, this means turning to the left, 90 degrees. The command is

LT90

How many spaces forward? 2

FD2

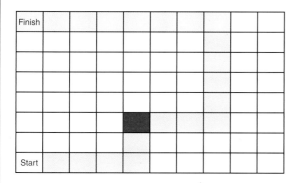

Figure 4.4: Maze 2, FD4, LT90, FD2.

You need to face to the right again, so:

RT90

To the next turn is 3 spaces:

FD3

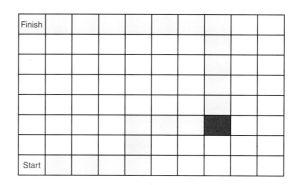

Figure 4.5: Maze 2, FD4, LT90, FD2, RT90, FD3.

You need to face up, so you are turning left again:

LT90

Now you need to move forward 5 spaces:

FD5

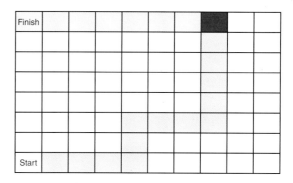

Figure 4.6: Maze 2, FD4, LT90, FD2, RT90, FD3, LT90, FD5.

CONTINUED

To get to the Finish you need to turn left:

LT90

Then move forward 7 spaces:

FD7

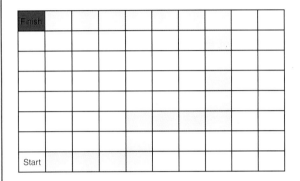

Figure 4.7: Maze 2, finish.

Together, the algorithm becomes:

FD4, LT90, FD2, RT90, FD3, LT90, FD5, LT90, FD7

Questions

1   What is meant by an algorithm?
2   How can an algorithm be represented?

PRACTICAL ACTIVITY 4.01

Write an algorithm to move from Start to Finish in this maze:

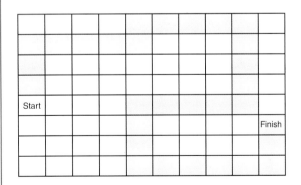

Figure 4.8: Maze 3, Start.

4.2 Flowcharts and pseudocode

A flowchart is a diagram that uses specific shapes and arrows to produce an algorithm that someone can then follow.

Pseudocode does not use symbols, but structured statements. There is no specific syntax (rules) that it must follow, but it should use key words (as in the flow diagrams) such as INPUT, OUTPUT, and so on.

Flowchart structure

There are set symbols throughout a flowchart. You will be introduced to these in each section. Every flowchart begins and ends with a terminator box (a Start box at the beginning and a Stop box at the end).

Figure 4.9: Start/Stop box.

The arrow is the flow line. When following a flowchart you follow the arrows. Algorithms don't go straight from start to stop. They also need **input**, **output**, **processes**, **decisions** and **loops**.

KEY WORDS

input: putting data into an algorithm

output: displaying data from an algorithm to the user

process: an action performed to some data to make a change

decision: a comparison is used to decide if code is run, or not

loop: code that is repeated

Input and output

Algorithms often need to output messages (such as text) to the screen, and therefore to the user. They may also need to take in data from the user, for example from the keyboard.

Flowcharts

If you want the algorithm to output something to the user, for example a word, a sentence or a number, then you will need an output box.

Figure 4.10: Output box.

After the word OUTPUT you put the text you want to display. If you want to output "Hello World", you use this,

Figure 4.11: Output box with text.

Notice how the words being output are in speech marks. This is because you want those actual words output, without them "Hello" could be a variable, or a command word.

If you want to input (or read) data from the user into the algorithm, you use an input box.

Figure 4.12: Input box.

When data is input into an algorithm it needs to be stored somewhere. This is done using a **variable**. A variable is a name (**identifier**) that is given to a space in a computer's memory that stores a value. Think of it like a box, with a name. You could call the box myNumber. You can then put data into myNumber. You can get data out of myNumber, and so on.

KEY WORDS

variable: a space in the memory of a computer, that has an identifier where you can store data; this data can be changed

identifier: the name given to a variable, subroutine or function

concatenate: to join two strings together

Here's the symbol for inputting a value into myNumber.

Figure 4.13: Input box with identifier.

Put these together with the Start and Stop to create a flowchart.

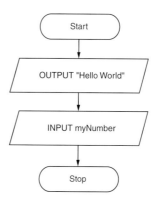

Figure 4.14: Flowchart "Hello World".

Once you have a variable, you can output this by using its name.

Figure 4.15: Output box with identifier.

You might want to output a variable and some text. You can combine them by using an ampersand (&). This is to **concatenate** (join) the values together. For example,

OUTPUT "My number is" & myNumber

Figure 4.16: Output box with concatenation.

Pseudocode

An output in pseudocode can use a command word such as OUTPUT, WRITE or PRINT, for example,

    OUTPUT "Hello World"

The words "Hello World" are a string as in the flowcharts, so are still in speech marks. There are many different words that you can use to output data, but they all perform the task, for example all of these have the same result.

    OUTPUT "Hello"
    WRITE "Hello"
    PRINT "Hello"

An input in pseudocode can use a command word such as INPUT. As with the flowcharts, this will need to be stored somewhere such as in a variable, for example,

    num = INPUT

or you could combine the input and output, for example,

    num = INPUT("Enter a number")

WORKED EXAMPLE 4.02

An algorithm needs to ask a user to enter their name. It should take their name as an input and then welcome them by name, for example, "Welcome Sasha".

Draw a flowchart for the algorithm.

Start by identifying the steps required.

Step 1: Ask them to enter their name.

Step 2: Take their name as input.

Step 3: Welcome them by their name.

Then identify what type of symbols these steps need.

Step 1: Ask them to enter their name.
Output

CONTINUED

Step 2: Take their name as input.
Input and store in variable

Step 3: Welcome them by their name.
Output including variable

Draw the flowchart following the steps identified.

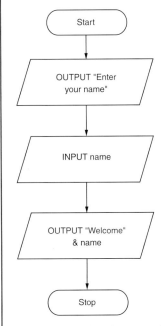

Figure 4.17: Flowchart-"Welcome".

WORKED EXAMPLE 4.03

Convert the flowchart into pseudocode.

Take each statement from within the flowchart and write it on its own line.

    OUTPUT "Enter your name"

    INPUT name

    OUTPUT "Welcome" & name

Questions

3   Identify the symbol for Start and Stop in a flowchart.

4   Describe the stages in this flowchart.

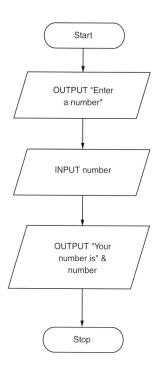

Figure 4.18: Flowchart-Enter a number.

There are different types of processes.

Table 4.1 shows the different mathematical processes that be performed.

Operator	Description	Example
+	Addition	`myNumber = 10 + 3`
−	Subtraction	`myNumber = 10 - 3`
*	Multiplication	`myNumber = 10 * 3`
/	Division	`myNumber = 10 / 3`
^	Power of	`myNumber = 10 ^ 3`
MOD	**Modulus division** (gives the remainder)	`10 MOD 3 = 1` `20 MOD 8 = 4`
DIV	**Integer division** (gives the whole number)	`10 DIV 3 = 3` `20 DIV 6 = 2`

Table 4.1: Mathematical (arithmetic) operators.

PRACTICAL ACTIVITY 4.02

1 Convert the flowchart in Question 4 into pseudocode.

2 An algorithm needs to take a word as an input, and then output the same word.

Draw a flowchart for this algorithm.

3 An algorithm needs to tell a joke. It should output the joke, and let the user give an answer, before outputting the actual answer.

Create a pseudocode algorithm for the problem.

KEY WORDS

modulus division: when the remainder is given from a division

integer division: where only the whole number is given from a division

---

Flowcharts

Processes are in rectangular boxes.

```
Process
```

Figure 4.19: Process box.

Processes

A process is an action that is performed. In a program it usually means that a change is being made to something. If you have a number stored in a variable, you could change this; you might add something to it, or subtract from it.

The mathematical calculations can make use of numbers, and/or variables. For example,

myNumber = 10 + 3	myNumber now stores 13
myNumber = myNumber + 3	myNumber now stores 16 (it already had 13 in and now has another 3)
myNumber = myNumber + myNumber	myNumber now stores 32 (it already had 16 in it, and it was added to itself, so 16 + 16 = 32)

Putting a value into a variable is called **assignment**.

KEY WORD

assignment: giving a variable a value

In this process box two numbers are multiplied together and stored in a variable.

newNumber = 3 * 8

Figure 4.20: Assignment in process box.

Follow this flowchart. What does it do?

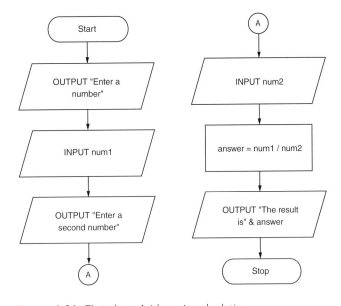

Figure 4.21: Flowchart-Arithmetic calculation.

Notice that a new symbol has been introduced here, a circle with a letter inside. This is a connector symbol. Sometimes, if a flowchart is long, then it is convenient to split it into smaller portions (perhaps to show it all on one page). The connector letter shows where the flowchart continues.

The algorithm takes in two numbers (num1 and num2), divides num1 by num2 and stores the result in answer. It then outputs the message "The result is" and the value in answer.

Pseudocode

Processes use the same structure as in a flowchart, but without the box. Therefore this:

newNumber = 3 * 8

Figure 4.22: Assignment in process box.

would become this:

```
newNumber = 3 * 8
```

WORKED EXAMPLE 4.04

A program needs to ask a person's age, then tell them how old they will be in 50 years.

Draw a flowchart for the algorithm.

Start by identifying the steps required.

Step 1: Ask them to enter their age.

Step 2: Take the age as input.

Step 3: Add 50 to their age.

Step 4: Output the new age.

Identify what type of symbols these steps need;

Step 1: Ask them to enter their age.
Output

Step 2: Take the age as input.
Input and store in a variable

Step 3: Add 50 to their age.
Add 50 to the variable and store the result

Step 4: Output their new age.
Output variable

CONTINUED

Draw the flowchart following the steps identified.

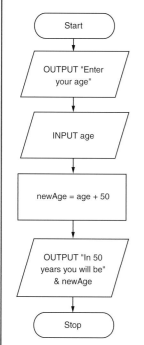

Figure 4.23: Flowchart-New age calculator.

WORKED EXAMPLE 4.05

Convert the flowchart into pseudocode.

Take each line and write it on a separate line.

```
OUTPUT "Enter you age"
INPUT age
newAge = age + 50
OUTPUT "In 50 years your will be" & newAge
```

Questions

5 What is a process?

6 What action does the operator ^ process?

7 Write a statement to multiply 3 by 7.

8 Describe the stages in this flowchart.

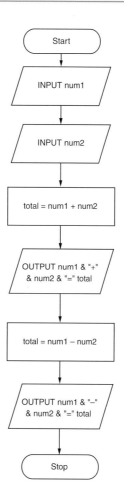

Figure 4.24: Flowchart-Arithmetic calculation.

PRACTICAL ACTIVITY 4.03

1 Convert the algorithm in Question 8 into pseudocode.

2 An algorithm needs to take 3 numbers as input. Add them together and output the result. Then divide the total by the quantity of numbers and output the average.

   Draw a flowchart for this algorithm.

3 Convert your algorithm from part 2 into pseudocode.

Decisions

A decision is also known as **comparison** and **selection**. It is a statement that involves a comparison and is either true or false. If the result is true, then some code is run, if it is false then either different code is run or some code is skipped.

> **KEY WORDS**
>
> **comparison:** comparing two items of data resulting in true or false
>
> **selection:** use of a conditional statement to decide a course of action or which section of code to run

A comparison needs two sides of the argument, and a comparison symbol. Table 4.2 shows common comparison operators.

Operator	Description	Example
>	Greater than	10 > 5 is true 5 > 10 is false
<	Less than	10 < 5 is false 5 < 10 is true
>=	Greater than or equal to	10 >= 5 is true 10 >= 10 is true 5 >= 10 is false
<=	Less than or equal to	10 <= 5 is false 10 <= 10 is true 5 <= 10 is true
=	Equals to	10 = 5 is false 10 = 10 is true
!= or <>	Not equal to	10 != 10 is false 5 <> 10 is true

Table 4.2: Comparison operators.

Either side of the operator can be a number or a variable.

Flowcharts

Single selection

The selection must be in the form of a question, for example 'is 10 > 5?' This is because it has two results: true and false.

The selection flowchart symbol is a diamond.

Figure 4.25: Selection box.

There are two options from a selection box: True and False, or Yes and No. This means selection has two arrows (two flow lines), that need to be labelled, for example.

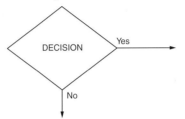

Figure 4.26: Selection box with options.

Follow this flowchart. What does it do?

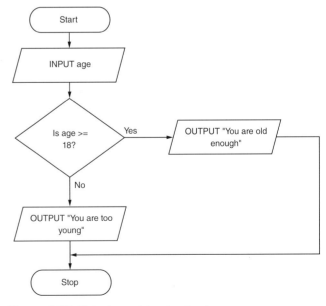

Figure 4.27: Flowchart with selection box.

This flowchart starts by the user inputting an age. The decision statement asks if age is greater than, or equal to, 18. If the result is Yes, then it outputs "You are old enough", if it is No it outputs "You are too young".

Multiple selection

If you have multiple options, then you will need multiple decisions. For example,

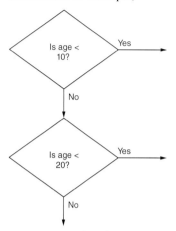

Figure 4.28: Flowchart with multiple selection boxes.

The first decision is 'If age is less than 10?' If it is not, then it goes straight to another decision, and asks whether age is less than 20.

Pseudocode

Selection uses the keyword IF and THEN. The question 'Is' in the flowchart is replaced with IF, and the '?' with THEN. All the code that runs when the condition is true goes beneath the IF and this is finished with an ENDIF to show where it ends.

For example, if the value in age is more than 18, then the output message will be displayed.

```
IF age > 18 THEN
   OUTPUT("You are old enough")
ENDIF
```

An IF statement can have an ELSE. This is what happens if the condition is true. For example, if the age is not more than 18, then "You are not old enough" will be displayed.

```
IF age > 18 THEN
   OUTPUT("You are old enough")
ELSE
   OUTPUT("You are not old enough")
ENDIF
```

Multiple conditions

These can be created using ELSEIF statements. Each condition has its own ELSEIF. You can even put an ELSE on the end in case none of the conditions are true. For example, each of the conditions are checked in the order they are written. If one of the conditions is found to be true, then the code within it runs, and then it jumps to the ENDIF; the other conditions after it are not checked.

```
IF cost >= 100 THEN
   OUTPUT "That is far too expensive"
ELSEIF cost >= 80 THEN
   OUTPUT "That's a bit too expensive"
ELSEIF cost >= 60 THEN
   OUTPUT "That is reasonable"
ELSEIF cost >= 40 THEN
   OUTPUT "That looks like a good deal"
ELSE
   OUTPUT "I think that is too cheap"
ENDIF
```

CASE...END CASE

This is a different selection statement. This is used when you are checking the value of one variable and you have many different values you want to check it against.

Pseudocode

CASE uses the keyword SELECT, followed by the identifier of the variable you are checking. Then it has the keyword CASE followed by the condition.

For example, if you are checking if a menu choice is 1, 2 or 3:

```
SELECT menuChoice
   CASE 1: OUTPUT "You chose 1"
   CASE 2: OUTPUT "You chose 2"
   CASE 3: OUTPUT "You chose 3"
```

A CASE statement can perform comparisons other than equals to, but this time you need to include the variable name to make it clear what the comparison is.

```
SELECT age
   CASE age < 12: OUTPUT "You can watch PG
   films"

   CASE (age >= 12 and age < 15): OUTPUT "You
   can watch PG and PG12 films"

   CASE (age >= 15 and age < 18): OUTPUT "You
   can watch PG, PG12 and 15 rated films"
```

```
CASE age >= 18: OUTPUT "You can watch all
films"
```

There is also a default keyword for CASE, the code in this will run if none of the conditions have been met.

```
SELECT symbol
    CASE "+":
        result = value1 + value2
```

```
CASE "-":
    result = value1 - value2
CASE "*":
    result = value1 * value2
CASE "/":
    result = value1 / value2
CASE DEFAULT:
    OUTPUT "Invalid symbol"
```

WORKED EXAMPLE 4.06

An algorithm needs to take two numbers as input, and output which is the largest.

Draw a flowchart for the algorithm.

Start by identifying the steps required.

Step 1: Ask the user to input two numbers.

Step 2: Input two numbers.

Step 3: Check if the first number is larger than the second.

Step 4: Output the first number if it is.

Step 5: Output the second number if it isn't.

Identify what type of symbols these steps need.

Step 1: Ask the user to input two numbers.
Output

Step 2: Input two numbers.
Input the store in a variable

Step 3: Check if the first number is larger than the second.
If first > second

Step 4: Output the first number if it is.
Output first number

Step 5: Output the second number if it isn't.
Output second number

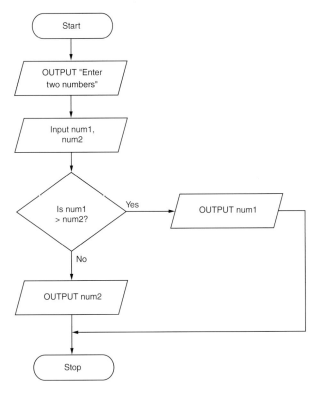

Figure 4.29: Flowchart-Compare two numbers.

WORKED EXAMPLE 4.07

Convert the flowchart into pseudocode.

Write each line separately. Only one value can be input at a time.

Replace Is with an `IF` statement.

```
OUTPUT "Enter two numbers"
INPUT num1
INPUT num2
IF num1 > num2 THEN
    OUTPUT num1
ELSE
    OUTPUT num2
ENDIF
```

Questions

9 How many arrows must come out of a selection symbol in a flowchart?

10 Define selection.

11 Is 956 >= 856?

12 Is 123 != 123?

13 Is 55 = 66?

PRACTICAL ACTIVITY 4.04

1 Describe the stages in the flowchart opposite.

2 Convert the flowchart in part 1 into pseudocode.

3 An algorithm needs to take three numbers as input, and output the smallest.

   Draw a flowchart for this algorithm.

4 Convert your flowchart from part 3 into pseudocode.

5 An algorithm needs to take two numbers as input, then subtract the smallest from the largest.

   Create a pseudocode algorithm for the problem using an IF statement.

6 Replace the IF statement in task 5 with a SELECT CASE statement.

CONTINUED

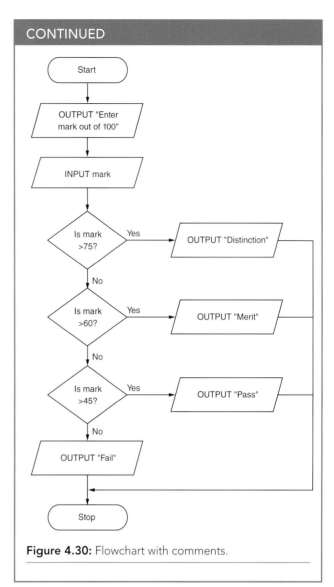

Figure 4.30: Flowchart with comments.

Loops

A loop means repetition; doing the same thing several times. Its technical term is **iteration**.

KEY WORD

iteration: a loop to repeat a section of code for a fixed number of times or until a required outcome is achieved

Loops are mainly used in two scenarios:

1   You know how many times you want to repeat the code. This might be 10 times, or `age` times (where `age` is a variable that stores a value). This is a **count-controlled** loop.

2   You don't know the number of times, but want to keep going until something happens. This is a **condition-controlled** loop.

> ### KEY WORDS
>
> **count-controlled loop:** a loop where you know the number of times it will run
>
> **condition-controlled loop:** a loop that runs based on a condition, not the number of times it will run

Count controlled

Flowcharts

This type of loop needs a counter to keep track of the number of repetitions you have done (the number of loops). The counter will be a variable. Before you start the loop, the counter needs to be set to the starting value (usually 0 or 1). Then inside the code that loops, you need to **increment** the counter (this means add 1 to it).

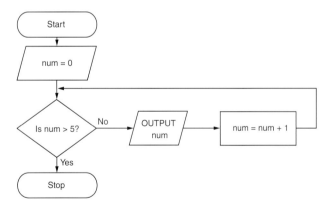

Figure 4.31: Flowchart with counter.

In this example, the counter variable is `num`. `num` is set to start at 0. Following the arrows, it keeps increasing by 1 until `num` is greater than 5, at which point the algorithm stops.

Pseudocode

A `FOR` **loop** is a count-controlled loop. You need to know what number to start with, and when you will end. The loop increments the number each time through.

> ### KEY WORDS
>
> **increment:** add 1 to something
>
> **FOR loop:** a count-controlled loop

In this example, the variable counter starts at 0 and continues until it is 9.

```
FOR counter = 0 to 9
    OUTPUT counter
NEXT counter
```

WORKED EXAMPLE 4.08

An algorithm needs to ask the user to input the 10 marks of its students, and then output the average.

Draw a flowchart for the algorithm.

Start by identifying the steps required.

Step 1:   Repeat 10 times.
Step 2:   Ask the user to input a mark.
Step 3:   Input the mark.
Step 4:   Add the mark to a total.
Step 5:   After all the marks are entered, calculate the average.
Step 6:   Output the average.

Identify what type of symbols these steps need.

Step 1:   Repeat 10 times.
Loop 10 times

Step 2:   Ask the user to input a mark.
Output

Step 3:   Input the mark.
Input and store in variable

Step 4:   Add the mark to a total.
Add input to total

Step 5:   After all marks are entered, calculate the average. *Total divided by 10*

Step 6:   Output the average.
Output

CONTINUED

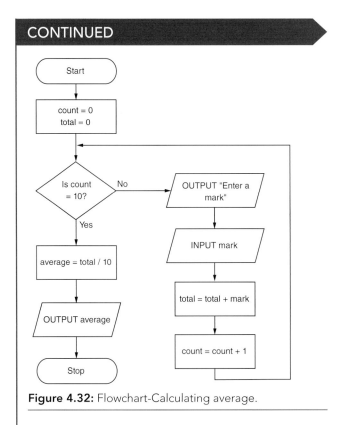

Figure 4.32: Flowchart-Calculating average.

WORKED EXAMPLE 4.09

Convert the flowchart into pseudocode.

Write each line separately. Replace the count and selection with a FOR loop.

```
total = 0
FOR count = 0 TO 10
    OUTPUT "Enter a mark"
    INPUT mark
    total = total + mark
NEXT count
average = total / 10
OUTPUT average
```

Questions

14 What is iteration?

15 What is a count-controlled loop?

16 When is it appropriate to use a count-controlled loop?

17 What three elements do you need in a count-controlled loop?

PRACTICAL ACTIVITY 4.05

1   Describe the stages in this flowchart.

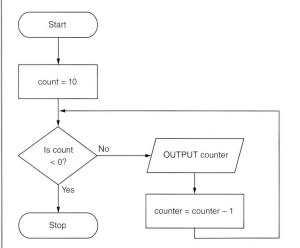

Figure 4.33: Flowchart with counter.

2   Convert the flowchart from part 1 into pseudocode.

3   An algorithm needs to output the 12-times table using iteration.

Create a flowchart for the algorithm.

4   An algorithm needs to ask the user how many numbers to output. The algorithm should then print out the numbers from 1 to that number input.

Create a pseudocode algorithm for the problem.

Condition controlled

A condition-controlled loop has the same structure as a count-controlled loop, but it doesn't need a counting variable, because something else is controlling it. This could be controlled by an input from the user (you could loop until it is a valid input), or until a specific number is greater than another.

Flowchart

The flowchart looks similar to a count controlled due to the condition, but it would be missing the variable counter and does not run a set number of times.

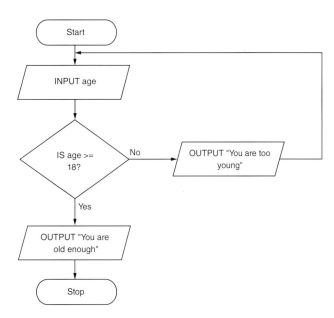

Figure 4.34: Flowchart with condition-controlled loop 1.

The following flowchart is an example of a **REPEAT UNTIL loop**. This is a type of condition controlled loop. The code inside the loop will always run once because the condition is at the end of the code. So the statement value = value * 2 repeats until the value is >= 100.

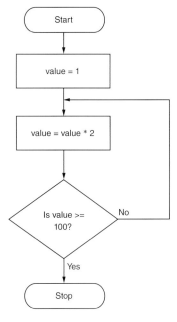

Figure 4.35: Flowchart with condition-controlled loop 2.

In this example, the loop keeps on going until the number in the variable `value` is greater than or equal to 100.

Pseudocode

A `WHILE` **loop** is a condition-controlled loop. It keeps looping while the condition is true.

In this example the loop will continue until the user enters an age greater than or equal to 18.

```
age = 0
WHILE age < 18
    INPUT age
ENDWHILE
```

In this example, the loop continues until loop is greater than 100.

```
value = 1
WHILE value <= 100
    value = value + value
ENDWHILE
```

WORKED EXAMPLE 4.10

An algorithm needs to continually ask the user to input numbers, and add them to a total, until the total is more than 100, then output the total.

Draw a flowchart for the algorithm.

Start by identifying the steps required.

Step 1:   Repeat until the total is more than 100.

Step 2:   Ask the user to input a number.

Step 3:   Input the number.

Step 4:   Add the number to the total.

Step 5:   When total is more than 100, output the total.

Identify what type of symbols these steps need.

Step 1:   Repeat until the total is more than 100.
          Loop until total > 100

CONTINUED

Step 2: Ask the user to input a number.

Output

Step 3: Input the number.

Input

Step 4: Add the number to the total.

Process – add number total

Step 5: When total is more than 100, output the total.

Output

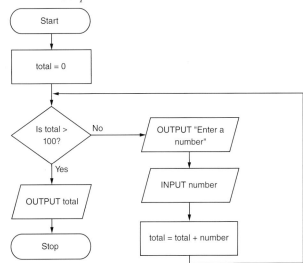

Figure 4.36: Flowchart-Totalling number with control loop.

WORKED EXAMPLE 4.11

Convert the flowchart into pseudocode.

Replace the selection condition with a WHILE loop.

```
total = 0
WHILE total < 100
   OUTPUT "Enter a number"
   INPUT number
   total = total + number
ENDWHILE
OUTPUT total
```

Question

18 When should a condition-controlled loop be used?

PRACTICAL ACTIVITY 4.06

1 Describe the stages this flowchart follows.

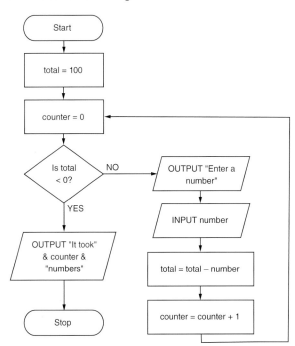

Figure 4.37: Flowchart with control loop.

2 Convert the flowchart into pseudocode.

3 An algorithm needs to ask the user to input a number between 100 and 200. Keep asking the user for the number until it is valid.

Draw a flowchart for the algorithm.

4 An algorithm stores a number. The user has to guess what this number is. They keep guessing until they get it correct. The algorithm then outputs the number of guesses the user took.

Write a pseudocode algorithm for this problem.

String manipulation

Strings are collections of letters, characters and numbers. They are represented by speech marks; this is because the variable `value` is different from the word "value".

You may need to manipulate strings, for example get one or more characters from it or find its length.

These are all processes, so would go inside a process box (apart from concatenation which can also be in an input or output box).

Table 4.3 shows some common string manipulators.

Command	Description	Example
length(string)	Returns the length of the string	length("Hello") would give 5
char(string, characterNum)	Returns the character at characterNum in the string.	char("Hello",0) would give "H"
mid(string, startingChar, numChars) or substring(string, startingChar, numChars)	Returns numChars number of characters from startingChar in the string	mid("Hello",1,2) would give "el"
upper(string)	Converts string to capitals	upper("Hello") would give "HELLO"
lower(string)	converts string to lowercase	lower("Hello") would give "hello"

Table 4.3: String manipulators.

In this example, the four digits of the year (1999) are extracted from the string and output.

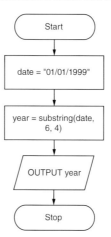

Figure 4.38: Flowchart to extract year from a date pseudocode.

The statements are the same in pseudocode, they are just written without the boxes.

WORKED EXAMPLE 4.12

A program is needed to input a word from the user, and then output alternate letters starting with the first letter.

Draw a flowchart for the algorithm.

Start by identifying the steps required.

Step 1: Ask the user to input a word.

Step 2: Input a word and store it in a variable.

Step 3: Count the number of letters in the word.

Step 4: Set a counter to start with the letter at position 0.

Step 5: Increase the counter by 2 each time through the loop.

Step 6: Output the letter of the counter in the loop.

Step 7: Loop until the counter is greater than or equal to the number of letters

CONTINUED

Identify what type of symbols these steps need.

Step 1: Ask the user to input a word.
Output

Step 2: Input a word and store it in a variable.
Input and store in a variable

Step 3: Count the number of letters in the word .
Find length of the word

Step 4: Set a counter to start with letter 0.
Process set counter to be 0

Step 5: Increase the counter by 2 each time through the loop.
Process, counter = counter + 2

Step 6: Output the letter of the counter in the loop.
Get mid at position counter

Step 7: Loop until the counter is greater than the number of letters.
Loop until counter > length

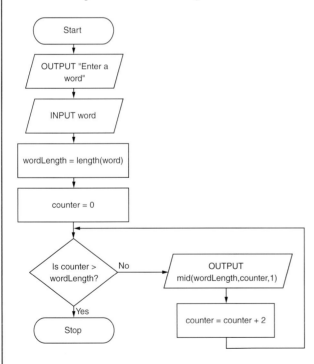

Figure 4.39: Flowchart with mid command.

WORKED EXAMPLE 4.13

Convert the flowchart into pseudocode. Replace the loop with a FOR loop (from 0 to wordlength) but it needs to add 2 each time.

```
OUTPUT "Enter a word"
INPUT word
wordLength = length(word)
FOR counter = 0 TO wordLength
    OUTPUT mid(wordLength, counter, 1)
    counter = counter + 1
NEXT counter
```

Question

19 What number is the first character in a string?

PRACTICAL ACTIVITY 4.07

1 Describe the stages in the flowchart in Figure 4.40.

2 An algorithm is needed to ask the user how many letters they want to enter. The program should then ask the user to enter that many letters, concatenate them and output the result.

Draw a flowchart for the algorithm.

3 An algorithm takes the date of a month a user was born, the name of the month, and the year. It creates a date of birth in the form DD/MM/YYYY and outputs this.

Create a pseudocode algorithm for the problem.

CONTINUED

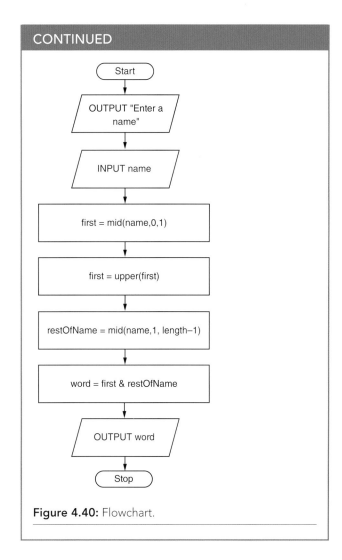

Figure 4.40: Flowchart.

Subroutines

A **subroutine** is a set of instructions that are independent. They have an identifier (a name) and can be called from other parts of the program. When it finishes running, control passes back to where it was called from.

KEY WORD

subroutine: a set of instructions that have an identifier and that are independent from the code; it is called from another part of the program and returns control when it was finished

There are two types of subroutine, a **procedure** and a **function**. A procedure performs a task and returns

control back to the program that called it. A function can return a value to the program that called it. You do not need to know about functions, or use them in this chapter, but it is useful to understand that a procedure is not the only form of a subroutine.

KEY WORDS

procedure: a type of subroutine that does not return a value to the main program

function: a separate piece of code that has an identifier and performs a task; it can be called from elsewhere in the code and returns a value

Flowcharts

Each subroutine is a separate flowchart, and instead of having a Start box, it has the name of the subroutine, for example,

Figure 4.41: Subroutine identifier.

In this example, the subroutine is called OutputText. Note that the symbol for a subroutine is similar to a process box but has a pair of parallel vertical lines at each side. The algorithm starts at Start, the process box tells the flowchart to go to Output. The output "Hello" runs, and Stop tells the algorithm to go back to the first flowchart, where it runs Stop.

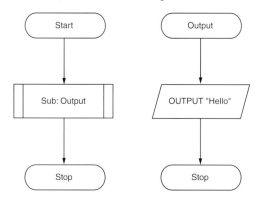

Figure 4.42: Flowchart calling subroutine.

Pseudocode

In pseudocode, a subroutine still has an identifier. It starts with the command PROCEDURE and ends with ENDPROCEDURE.

In this example, the procedure is called outputMessage(). The brackets identify it as a subroutine. The procedure outputs the words "Hello World" and then returns control.

```
PROCEDURE outputMessage()

    OUTPUT "Hello World"

ENDPROCEDURE
```

A procedure is called by using the name of the procedure, for example,

```
INPUT x

outputMessage()

OUTPUT "Finished"
```

Procedures are declared at the top of the program, and the main program beneath all the function calls.

Parameters

You can send data to a subroutine; this data is called a **parameter**.

Flowchart

In this example, the main flowchart (in Figure 4.44) calls the subroutine (in Figure 4.43), calculate and sends it the value in number. The function calculate renames this as value. It adds this to total and outputs it before returning control to the main program.

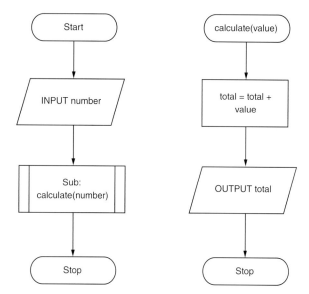

Figure 4.43: Flowchart calling calculate subroutine.

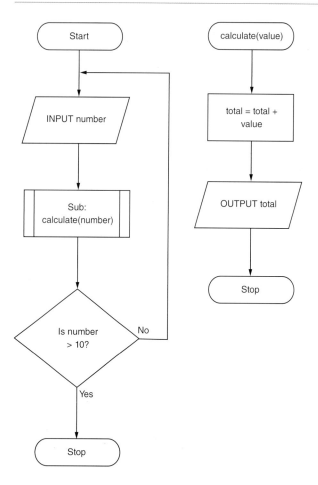

Figure 4.44: Flowchart with condition loop calling calculate subroutine.

Pseudocode

Parameters are identified within the brackets.

In this example, the main program (beneath the procedure), inputs a value into the variable `number` and then sends this to the procedure `calculate`. This is then named `value` and added to `total` before being output.

```
PROCEDURE calculate(value)
    total = total + value
    OUTPUT total
ENDPROCEDURE
INPUT number

calculate(number)
```

WORKED EXAMPLE 4.14

A program asks the user to input a number. It loops that a number of times. Each time through the loop, if the number is even it calls a subroutine to output the number multiplied by itself. If the number is odd it calls a subroutine to output the number to the power of itself.

Draw a flowchart for this algorithm.

Start by identifying the steps required.

Step 1: User inputs a number.

Step 2: Set the counter to 1.

Step 3: Loop until the counter is the number entered.

Step 4: If the number is even, call subroutine.

Step 5: Else if the number is odd, call subroutine.

Create a subroutine taking `number` as parameter.

a   Multiply the parameter by itself.

b   Output the result.

Create a subroutine taking `number` as parameter.

a   Calculate the parameter to the power of itself.

b   Output the result.

Identify what type of symbols these steps need.

Step 1: User inputs a number

Input number store in variable

Step 2: Set counter to 1.

Process counter = 1

Step 3: Loop until counter is the number entered.

Loop until counter = number

Step 4: If the number is even call subroutine

If counter is even call multiply( )

Step 5: Else if the number is odd call subroutine

else call powerof( )

Create a subroutine taking number as parameter.

multiply(number)

a   Multiply the parameter by itself.

*Process number * number*

b   Output the result.

Output result

Create a subroutine taking number as parameter.

powerOf(number)

a   Calculate the parameter to the power of itself

Process number ^ number

b   Output the result.

Output result

Draw the flowchart for the subroutines.

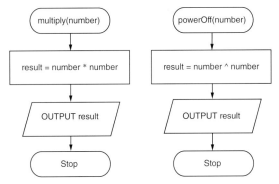

Figure 4.45: Subroutine flowcharts.

Draw the flowchart for the main program.

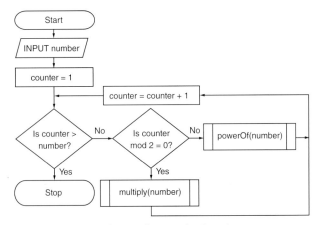

Figure 4.46: Flowchart calling multiple subroutines.

Convert the subroutines and main program to pseudocode.

Write each subroutine first, then the main program.

```
PROCEDURE multiply(number)
    result = number * number
    OUTPUT result
ENDPROCEDURE
PROCEDURE powerOf(number)
    result = number ^ number
    OUTPUT result
ENDPROCEDURE
INPUT number
Counter = 1
WHILE counter < number
    IF counter MOD 2 = 0 THEN
        multiply(number)
    ELSE
        powerOf(number)
    ENDIF
ENDWHILE
```

Questions

20 What is a subroutine?

21 Why are subroutines used in programs?

22 What is a parameter?

1 Describe what the flowcharts a to d show.

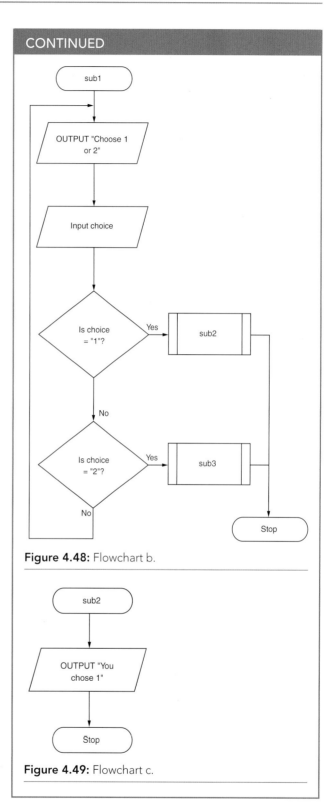

Figure 4.47: Flowchart a.

Figure 4.48: Flowchart b.

Figure 4.49: Flowchart c.

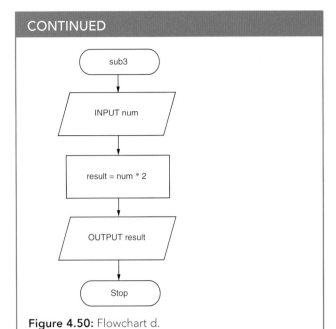

Figure 4.50: Flowchart d.

2   Convert the flowcharts in part 1 into pseudocode.

3   Create a program that asks the user whether they want to make word uppercase or lowercase. Create a procedure to turn a word uppercase and output it, and a second procedure to turn a word into lowercase and output it. Call the appropriate procedure for which choice the user inputs.

    Draw a flowchart for the algorithm.

4   Convert the flowchart from part 3 into pseudocode.

Nested construct

A nested construct is one **construct** (selection or iteration) inside of another construct (selection or iteration). For example, this could be a loop inside another loop, or a selection statement inside a loop, or a selection statement inside another selection statement. You can even have multiple **nested loops**, with several selection statements inside one loop. There is no end to the possibilities.

construct: a control structure, such as a loop or a conditional statement

nested loops: one construct that is inside another construct

In this example (see the flowchart and the pseudocode) there is a nested loop; a WHILE loop inside a WHILE loop.

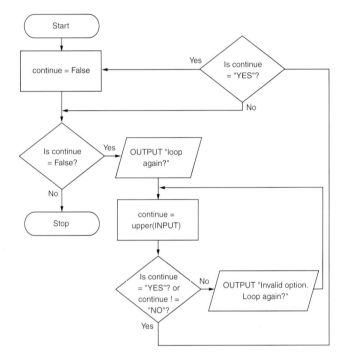

Figure 4.51: Nested loop.

```
continue = False
WHILE continue = False
   OUTPUT "Loop again?"
   continue = upper(INPUT)
   WHILE continue != "YES" or continue !=
   "No"
      OUTPUT "Invalid option. Loop again?"
      continue = upper(INPUT)
   ENDWHILE
ENDWHILE
```

WORKED EXAMPLE 4.16

A program needs to input the results for 100 students. Each student has 10 different results and the total needs to be output for each student.

Create a flowchart for the algorithm.

Start by identifying the steps required.

Step 1: Loop through all 100 students.

Step 2: Loop through all 10 results for each student.

Step 3: Ask for the student's result.

Step 4: Input the student's result.

Step 5: Add the result to their total.

Step 6: Output the total at the end of each student's results.

Identify what type of symbols these steps need.

Step 1: Loop through all 100 students.

Count-controlled loop

Step 2: Loop through all 10 results for each student.

Count-controlled loop

Step 3: Ask for the student's result.

Output

Step 4: Input the student's result.

Input and store the result

Step 5: Add the result to their total.

Process total = total + result

Step 6: Output the total at the end of each student's results.

Output

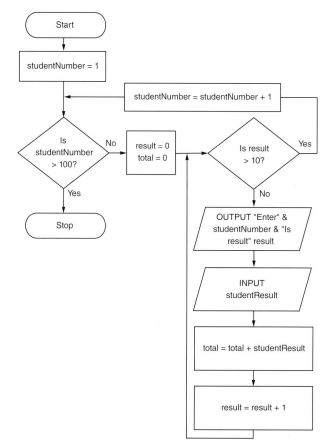

Figure 4.52: Flowchart-Totalling results.

WORKED EXAMPLE 4.17

Convert the flowchart into pseudocode.

Each loop is count controlled so replace with FOR loops.

```
FOR studentNumber = 1 to 101
   total = 0
   FOR result = 1 to 11
      OUTPUT "Enter " & studentNumber & "'s result " & result
      INPUT studentResult
      total = total + studentResult
   NEXT result
   OUTPUT "Total is" & total
ENDWHILE
```

Question

23 What is a nested statement?

PRACTICAL ACTIVITY 4.09

1   An algorithm should ask the user if they want to perform a calculation, and should continue asking this until they say Yes. Then the program should ask them how many numbers they want to add together. The program should input that quantity of numbers, add them together and output the result.

Draw a flowchart for the algorithm.

2   An algorithm should take a word as input from the user. Then take each letter in turn, and output it the number of times of its position in the alphabet. For example, 'a' would be output once, 'b' would be output twice, and so on.

Create a pseudocode algorithm for the problem.

Editing an algorithm/flowchart

You need to be able to read an algorithm, or flowchart, and be able to identify how to make changes to it.

To do this, you need to work out what the algorithm does first. Do this by using test data to run the algorithm, follow each step and write down what happens. Then look at the difference between what the algorithm did, and what you need to make it do.

WORKED EXAMPLE 4.18

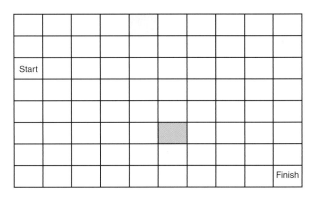

Figure 4.53: Maze 4.

The following algorithm visits the yellow box, then the green before moving to finish. Start facing up.

    FD2
    RT90
    FD4
    RT90
    FD5
    LT90
    FD1
    RT90
    FD2
    LT90
    FD4

Edit the algorithm so it visits the yellow box and then the Finish without visiting the green box.

The algorithm can stay the same up to the yellow box, so repeat this:

    FD2
    RT90
    FD4

Continue the algorithm from this point. There are many different ways you could go, for example:

    RT90
    FD7
    LT90
    FD5

WORKED EXAMPLE 4.19

This flowchart takes in a user's first name and favourite colour. It takes the first three letters of the first name, and the first three letters of the colour to create and output a username.

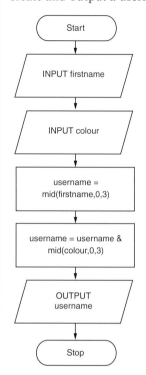

Figure 4.54: Flowchart-Create a username.

Change the algorithm so that is gets the last three letters of the colour instead of the first three.

The algorithm can stay the same up to where the letters are taken from the colour. This box was originally: username = username & mid(colour,0,3)

Instead it needs to get the last three, so it needs changing to:

username = username & mid(colour, length(colour)–4,3)

Questions

24 This flowchart takes 10 numbers as input, adds them together and outputs the total.

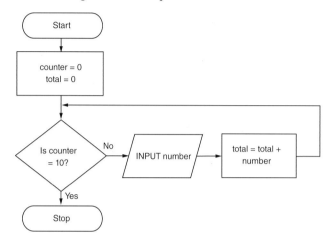

Figure 4.55: Flowchart-Total 10 numbers.

Change the flowchart so it inputs 20 numbers and adds them together.

25 This algorithm asks the user to input 50 numbers. It finds the smallest number and multiplies it by itself before outputting it.

```
smallest = 9999
FOR counter = 0 to 50
    INPUT number
    If number < smallest THEN
        smallest = number
    ENDIF
NEXT counter
answer = smallest * smallest
OUTPUT answer
```

Change the algorithm so it finds the largest number and multiplies this by itself before outputting it.

Correcting an algorithm/flowchart

You may need to find an error in an algorithm such as a flowchart. To do this, you need to follow each step of the algorithm, performing the actions it instructs to find where it goes wrong.

WORKED EXAMPLE 4.20

An algorithm should take three numbers as input, it should add together the two largest, and output the result.

Find the error in the algorithm.

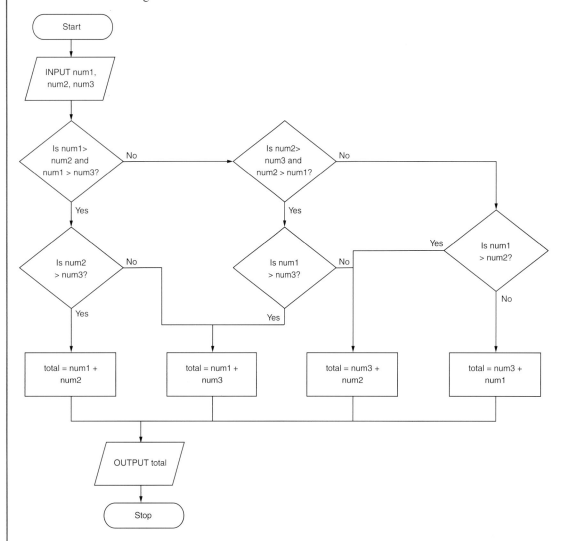

Figure 4.56: Flowchart with error.

Run the algorithm with all possible different types example data, for example,

Test 1: num1 = 10, num2 = 5, num3 = 3 (num1 and num2 are the largest), Output should be 15

Test 2: num1 = 5, num2 = 3, num3 = 10 (num1 and num3 are the largest), Output should be 15

Test 3: num1 = 3, num2 = 10, num3 = 5 (num2 and num3 are the largest), Output should be 15

Test 1

Is num1 > num2 and num1 > num3? Yes

Is num2 > num3 Yes this is true, total = num1 + num2 = 10 + 5

OUTPUT 15 – correct

Test 2

Is num1 > num2 and num1 > num3? No

Is num2 > num3 and num2 > num1? No

Is num1 > num2? Yes, total = num3 + num2 = 10 + 3

OUTPUT 13 – This is incorrect. It should have carried out total = num3 + num1.

The yes and no from the Is num1 > num2? Box are in the wrong order, they need swapping.

Test 3

Is num1 > num2 and num1 > num3? No

Is num2 > num3 and num2 > num1? Yes

Is num1 > num3? No total = num3 + num2 = 5 + 10

OUTPUT 15 – correct

PRACTICAL ACTIVITY 4.10

1   The algorithm should ask the user how many letters they want to enter, then let them enter that many letters. All the letters should be concatenated and output.

Find the error(s) in this algorithm.

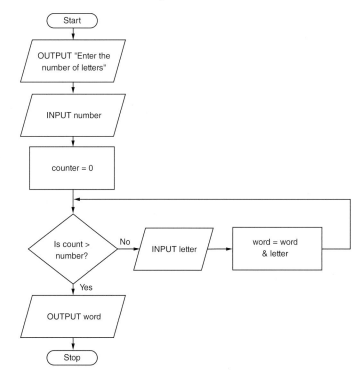

Figure 4.57: Flowchart with errors.

CONTINUED

2 The algorithm should repeatedly ask the user to input a number. The difference between that number and the previous number should be added to the total. This should continue until the total is more than 1000.

Find the error(s) in the algorithm.

```
total = 1
previousNumber = 0
WHILE total < 1000
    INPUT number
    total = total + (number - previousNumber)
    previousNumber = number
ENDWHILE
```

REFLECTION

1 What steps did you follow to plan an algorithm?

2 How did you find errors in an algorithm?

3 How did you work out how to edit an algorithm?

EXAM-STYLE QUESTIONS

1 Identify two ways that an algorithm can be expressed.   [2]

2 Name the actions for these flowchart shapes.

Figure 4.58: Flowchart symbols.

[3]

3 State what the output will be when this algorithm is run when the data input is 10. [1]

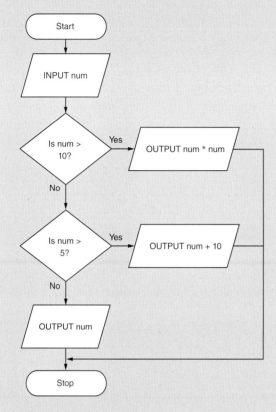

Figure 4.59: Flowchart.

4 Change this algorithm so it outputs the 9-times table.

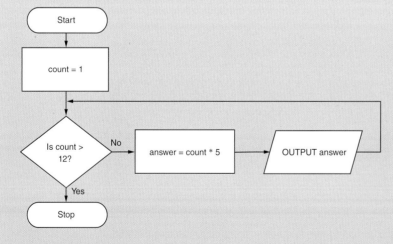

Figure 4.60: Flowchart.

[3]

5 This algorithm should loop until the user enters something other than 'Yes' or 'yes'. Each time through the loop, it adds the two numbers the user inputs to the total.

Find and correct the error(s) in the algorithm. [1]

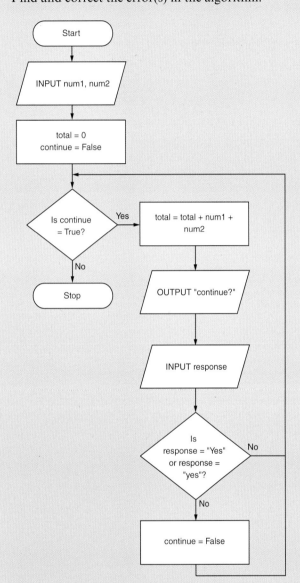

Figure 4.61: Flowchart.

CONTINUED

6 Follow this algorithm.

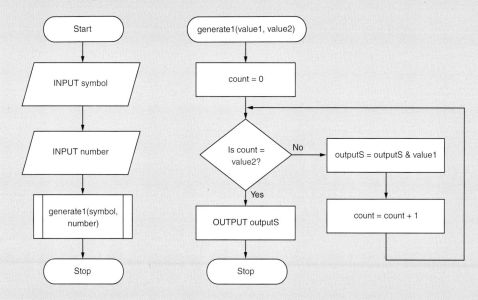

Figure 4.62: Flowchart.

a State the name of the procedure in this algorithm. [1]
b State the number of parameters that are passed to the subroutine. [1]
c State the name of two variables in the algorithm. [2]
d State what will be output from the program if the inputs are: "*" and then 5. [1]

[Total 5]

7 An algorithm is needed to output the odd numbers from 0 to 100.
Draw a flowchart for this algorithm. [6]

8 Write an algorithm for a calculator. The user should be able to input two numbers and a symbol (+ or −, or * or /). The algorithm should use subroutines for each of the calculations and output the result. [9]

SUMMARY CHECKLIST

- ☐ I can edit a given algorithm.
- ☐ I can write an algorithm to solve a given problem.
- ☐ I can edit a given flowchart.
- ☐ I can draw a flowchart to solve a given problem.
- ☐ I can identify errors in an algorithm/flowchart for a given scenario.
- ☐ I can use conditional branching.
- ☐ I can use looping.
- ☐ I can use nested loops.
- ☐ I can use procedures/subroutines.
- ☐ I can use input/output in a flowchart.
- ☐ I can use decisions in a flowchart.
- ☐ I can use start, stop and process boxes in a flowchart.
- ☐ I can use connecting symbols/flow arrows in a flowchart.

eSecurity

LEARNING INTENTIONS

By the end of this chapter, you will be able to:

- know and understand what is meant by personal data, how to keep it secure and prevent its misuse

- recognise types and uses of malware, their consequences for organisations and individuals and methods of prevention.

Introduction

The world of Information Technology can be a fun and exciting experience. It also comes with its dangers and it is important that you are aware of these, so that you can safeguard against them.

Sadly, there are people with malicious intentions online, and the more you are aware of the actions that they could take, the more protection you can put in place. This increased awareness and preventative measures can make sure that your time spent online, and further afield with technology, does not endanger you, your data or your identity.

5.1 Personal data

Personal data is any data that relates to you and your identity. This includes data such as:

- Name
- Address
- Telephone number
- Email address
- Bank details
- Medical records
- Salary
- Political opinions

You should be very careful about revealing any of your personal data! By revealing personal data to another, especially online, you are exposing yourself to dangers such as identity theft, fraud, bullying and blackmail. These types of dangers can be issues that arise as a result of revealing more personal thoughts and feelings to those that can use them against you. It is a more sinister viewpoint to take, but the moment you reveal any personal data to another, you are providing them with the potential to harm you or your identity. This isn't to say you should never speak to another, especially those unknown online, just understand how to recognise a danger and how to keep your identity secure.

To keep yourself safe in your daily life, you are likely to have been taught to take measures such as locking doors, not talking to strangers and not venturing into unsafe areas. However, when many people go online, they relax their safety measures, perhaps because they are in the comfort of their own home, so do not think anything negative will happen. Many people that use the internet are genuine, but knowing how to detect the few that aren't is important.

There are several guidelines for you to be aware of to keep your personal data confidential:

- Have strong passwords set on any account that holds personal data. Stronger passwords include characters, numbers and symbols and are not a recognisable word.

- Encrypt (scramble text so that it cannot be read without a decryption key) any personal data that you store on your computer.

- Have a **firewall** present, scanning incoming and outgoing data from your computer system.

- Regularly scan your computer with preventative software, such as an **anti-virus** package, that is used to identify a virus on a computer and remove it.

- Make use of any **biometric** devices (devices that measures a person's biological data, such as thumbprints), that are built into technology.

KEY WORDS

firewall: a security measure that can be implemented to monitor traffic into and out of a computer and prevent external users gaining unauthorised access to a computer system

anti-virus: software that is used to identify a virus on a computer and remove it

biometric: unique physical characteristic of a person that can be used by a computer for identification purposes

- Only visit and provide data to websites that are a trusted source.

- Do not open any email attachments from a sender you do not recognise.

- Check the URL attached to any link requesting data to see if it is genuine.

- Be cautious about any pictures or opinions that you post or send to people.

- Remove data about your location that is normally attached to your photos and videos that you may post, such as geotags.

- Do not become friends on social networking sites with people you do not know.

- Set all the privacy controls to the most secure setting that are available on social media accounts.

- Report and block any suspicious user.

- Use a nickname or pseudonym when using the internet for entertainment, for example, playing games.

- If it is possible, use a virtual private network (VPN), an encrypted connection that can be used to send data more securely across a network.

KEY WORDS

geotag: an electronic tag that assigns a geographical location

virtual private network: an encrypted connection that can be used to send data more securely across a network

The ways in which some of these guidelines can be used in more detail will be explored throughout this chapter.

REFLECTION

How many of the guidelines do you follow at the moment to keep your personal data confidential?

PRACTICAL ACTIVITY 5.01

Create a plan to implement any of the guidelines that you do not currently have in place to keep your data confidential.

How is personal data collected?

There are several ways that an unauthorised person can try and collect your data. These include:

- phishing
- smishing
- vishing
- pharming.

Phishing

Phishing is when a person sends a legitimate looking email to a user. The email contains a link to a website that also looks legitimate. The user is encouraged to click the link and to input personal data into a form on the website. The email could also simply ask the user to reply to the email with their personal data. The user is tricked into giving their personal data to a source that they believe is legitimate. However, both the email and the linked website are from a fake unauthorised source.

The personal data that is input is then collected by an unauthorised person. This person can then use this data for criminal acts, for example, to commit fraud or steal the person's identity.

Intimidation has become a common feature of phishing emails, threatening the user that they must click the link and rectify a situation immediately, or there will be a further issue.

The aim of a phishing attack is to steal the user's personal data.

Figure 5.1: Phishing.

A real-life example of phishing

PayPal have been the subject of several different phishing emails. Users receive an email that looks as though it has been sent from PayPal, as it has the PayPal branding. The email normally warns of an issue such as unexpected activity on their account, or that some kind of verification of their account is required. The user is then asked to click a link to log into their account and resolve the issue.

The link takes them to a webpage that looks like the PayPal login page. If the user inputs their login details into this page, they will not be taken to their account. It is often at this stage that the user may realise that the email and webpage are fake. However, they have already given the unauthorised person their PayPal login details.

PayPal

Problem with your account, rectify now to prevent deactivation!

Dear PayPal User,

Your PayPal account has generated some critical errors on our system. If this problem is not corrected, we will be forced to shut down your account. You are required to correct this problem immediately to prevent your account from being deactivated.

During our verification procedures we encountered a technical problem caused by the fact that we could not verify the information that you provided during registration. Most of your data in our database were encrypted to an unreadable format and could not be recovered due to system errors. Because of this, your account will not be able to function properly and will lead to account de-activation. We urgently ask you to re-submit your information so that we could fully verify your identify, otherwise your PayPal account will be shut down until you pass verification process.

Click here to rectify your account problem immediately

Verification of your Identity will further protect your account against possible breach of security. We urgently ask you to follow the link above to correct this problem as soon as you have read this message. Your PayPal account security is our concern. We are very sorry for the inconveniences this might have caused you.

Thank you for using PayPal!
The PayPal Team

Figure 5.2: An example of a phishing email claiming to be from PayPal.

How to recognise phishing

There are several guidelines to be aware of regarding emails to avoid being subjected to phishing. These include:

- Don't even open an email that is not from a sender that you recognise or a trusted source.

- Legitimate companies will never ask you for your personal data using email. Be immediately suspicious of any email that requests your personal data.

- Legitimate companies will normally address you by your name. Be suspicious of any email that addresses you as 'Dear Member' or 'Dear Customer'.

- Legitimate companies will send an email that uses their domain name. If you hover your mouse over the sender's name, it will show the email address that the email is sent from. If this does not look legitimate, for example, does not contain the correct domain name, then it is probably fake. For example, if the sender's email is user@paypall.com rather than user@paypal.com, this is from an incorrect domain name.

- Legitimate companies are protective of their professional reputation and thoroughly check any communications. They will make sure that all information given is grammatically and correctly spelt. Be suspicious of any email that contains bad grammar or spelling mistakes.

- A link in an email from a legitimate company will also normally contain the domain name of the company. You can sometimes hover over the link, or right click and inspect the link, to see the address of the URL that is attached. If the URL does not contain the domain name, or also contains typical errors such as spelling mistakes, then be suspicious of this.

PRACTICAL ACTIVITY 5.02

Ask a friend or a member of your family if they have ever received an email that they believed was a phishing email.

Ask them how they identified it was phishing. Ask them if they know all of the given guidelines for identifying phishing emails.

Smishing

Smishing (or SMS phishing) is a variant of phishing that uses SMS text messages to lure the user into providing their personal details. The user is sent an SMS text message that either contains a link to a website, in the same way that phishing does, or it will ask the user to call a telephone number to resolve an urgent issue.

The same advice can be followed for smishing as given for phishing. The user must question at all times any links that are sent from an unknown or suspicious user. It is advisable that if a user believes the message may be legitimate, to type in the domain name for the legitimate company website into their web browser, rather than following the link in the message.

Users should block any numbers that they believe are suspicious to prevent any further risk of smishing from that number.

Figure 5.3: Smishing.

Vishing

Vishing (or voice phishing) has the same aim as phishing, to obtain a user's personal details. The user receives a telephone call that could either be an automated system or could be a real person.

An automated voice could speak to the user and advise them that an issue has occurred, such as there has been suspicious activity regarding their bank account. The user may then be asked to call another number, or just to simply press a digit and be directed to another automated system. This system will ask them to provide their bank account details to resolve the issue. The bank account details have then been obtained by the unauthorised user and can be used to commit a crime against the user.

The automated system could be replaced by a real person who will try to do the same thing. They will try to convince the user that there has been an issue with an account they have and to provide the log-in details or PIN for the account to verify who they are so the issue can be resolved.

The precaution to take for vishing is that no company will ever call you and ask you to provide any log-in details or PIN details over the telephone. They may ask you to provide other personal information, and if you are in doubt that the person on the other end of the phone is legitimate, it is always advisable to put the phone down and call the company back on a legitimate number that you may already know or can obtain.

Figure 5.4: Vishing.

Pharming

Pharming is when an unauthorised user installs malicious code on a person's hard drive or server. The malicious code is designed to redirect a user to a fake website when they type in the address of a legitimate one. The fake website is designed to look like the legitimate one, to trick the user and make sure they are not aware that their request has been redirected. The user will then enter their personal details into the fake website, believing it is the legitimate one, and the unauthorised person will now have their personal data.

A common technique used in pharming is called domain name server (DNS) cache poisoning. This technique exploits vulnerabilities in the DNS and diverts the internet traffic intended for a legitimate server toward a fake one instead.

The unauthorised user needs to find a way to install the malicious code on the computer. They often hide the malicious code in an email attachment or link. When the user opens the email attachment or clicks the link, the malicious code is downloaded also.

Figure 5.5: Pharming.

The aim of a pharming attack is also to steal a user's personal data.

A real-life example of pharming

In 2007 50 different companies all over the world were subject to a pharming attack, these included PayPal, eBay, Barclays bank and American Express. Over a three-day period, hackers managed to infect over 1000 PCs a day with a malicious pharming code.

When users who had been infected visited the websites of the different companies, they were redirected to a legitimate-looking version of the site that was designed to steal their personal data.

The original email, containing the malicious code, was set up to look like a shocking news story. Users were encouraged to click a link in the email to find out more information. The code was downloaded when the user clicked the link.

This was quite a sophisticated attack that required legitimate looking websites to be set up for a large number of companies. It is not known how much money the hackers were able to retrieve as a result.

How to prevent pharming

All of the guidelines to avoid being subjected to phishing are also relevant for recognising pharming. There are also several other precautions that can be taken to check for pharming attacks. These include:

- Have a firewall installed and operational. A firewall monitors incoming and outgoing traffic from your computer. It checks this traffic against set criteria and will flag and stop any traffic that does not meet the criteria. A firewall could detect and block suspicious traffic, such as a malicious code trying to enter your system.

- Have an anti-virus program installed that is designed to detect malicious pharming code. You need to scan your computer on a regular basis to check for any malicious code. It is advisable to set up an automatic scan on a daily basis at a time when your computer will normally be switched on.

- Be aware when using public Wi-Fi connections. A hacker could look to directly access your computer and install the malicious code if you are connected to a public Wi-Fi connection. It is often advisable to use a VPN when using public Wi-Fi. This will help shield your internet activity and personal details from a hacker, making it more difficult for them to access your computer.

Smishing can also be used as a form of pharming. A user is sent a link, that when they click is designed to download malware onto their mobile device. Therefore, it is advisable to have security software installed on your mobile and also scan it regularly to detect any presence of malware.

Question

1   Investigate the use of a VPN. Find out what security benefits it may have.

5.2 Malware

Malware (or malicious software) refers to any software that is designed to disrupt or damage a computer system or sometimes a user.

KEY WORD
malware: software that is malicious

There are various types of malware. These include:

- virus
- trojan
- worm
- spyware
- adware
- rootkit
- malicious bots
- ransomware.

It is important that you understand how each of the given malware operates and what you can do to minimise the risk from each.

The consequences to the individual or to a business will depend on the type of malware. Some malware may just cause a minor irritation, such as slowing down a computer, but it could be much more serious, leading to identity theft, corruption of data or blackmail (either to do with personally collected data or to restore blocked data).

Virus

A virus is the most commonly known type of malware.

A virus is the only type of malware that infects new files in the computer system. It attaches itself to a clean file, replicates itself, then attaches itself to another clean file. It is designed to spread, much like a human virus.

Once a virus has infected a file, it may begin to replicate immediately, or it can lay dormant until actions performed by the computer cause the code to be executed. If an infected computer is part of a network, it can then begin to infect other computers on the network. A virus can be especially dangerous if it infects files on a server that are accessed by many different computers.

There are several signs that your computer has been infected with a virus. These include:

*   slower system performance

*   files multiplying or duplicating on their own

*   files being deleted without your knowledge.

The aim of a virus is to corrupt and disrupt data in a computer system. It is mainly a method of sabotage for this reason.

Figure 5.6: Virus.

Minimising the risk of a virus

If a virus manages to infect a computer system, it can be very difficult to eradicate. A robust anti-virus software is needed to minimise the risk of a virus. You should install an anti-virus program and regularly scan your computer. It is best to set up a daily automatic scan of your computer at a time when you know that your computer is likely to be switched on.

Anti-virus software scans a computer system and finds any files that it thinks contain a virus. It will quarantine these files and alert the user of their presence. The user can then select to delete these files. It is possible to remove this stage and set the software to automatically delete all quarantined files.

The anti-virus software can detect the presence of a virus in a file by comparing the code to a database of known virus codes. If it finds a code that matches it will quarantine the file.

One weakness of anti-virus software is that it is dependent on the database it holds. Therefore, if a perpetrator manages to hack a system with a virus that is not in the database, it will not be recognised and removed. This could leave it to do a great deal of damage. For this reason, it is also important to update your anti-virus software to make sure that it includes the latest known viruses.

Some anti-virus software can be set for real-time checking. This means that all programs that are requested for download are immediately checked for viruses. If the anti-virus detects the presence of a virus, it will alert the user and tell them not to download the file as it contains a virus.

A firewall can be used to minimise the risk of a virus. A firewall acts as a filter, monitoring incoming and outgoing traffic from a computer system. Therefore, if it detects malicious software trying to enter the system, it can stop it before it is able to enter. A firewall again relies on the necessary criteria to be set in order to detect the malicious traffic in the first place.

You should also be very careful when sharing any resources using portable storage devices such as a USB memory stick. You should immediately scan any USB memory stick that is inserted into your computer, even if it is your own storage device. It is very common for viruses to be spread through the use of portable storage devices.

Figure 5.7: Trojan.

Trojan

A Trojan is a type of malware that disguises itself as legitimate software, or is included in legitimate software that may have been infiltrated. They are mostly downloaded from an infected email or website.

The term Trojan comes from Greek mythology. The Greeks gave a wooden horse as a peace offering to the people of the city of Troy. The 'Trojan' horse was in fact a container that held several Greek soldiers who, when night fell, climbed out of the horse and opened the city to the rest of the soldiers, who were then able to conquer the city of Troy.

A malware Trojan works in a similar way. It looks harmless, but it hides a malicious program. When the Trojan file is opened, it will normally release another type of malware, such as a virus. A Trojan needs the user to run the program for it to release other malicious software. Therefore, it will usually encourage the user to run the program, for example, it will tell the user another program needs to be updated, and to click to run a program to update it. This then runs the Trojan and allows it to release further damage.

Minimising the risk of a Trojan

It is difficult to minimise the risk of Trojans because they mask themselves as legitimate software. They also require the user to make them run, so rely on the error of a user to operate, rather than detection by anti-virus or a firewall. It is more likely that a user would make an error and be tricked into running the software than malware going undetected by a firewall and anti-virus.

The main way to minimise the risk of a Trojan is to only open files and click to run software that you know is from a trusted source, for example, trusted software companies and trusted websites. If you are in any doubt about the program, do not run it!

Question

2   Find out what is meant by a backdoor Trojan.

Worm

A worm is a type of malware that acts in a similar way to a virus, but with a fundamental difference. A worm is a program that replicates itself, like a virus but, unlike a virus it does not need to attach itself to another program or file to cause damage. Worms exploit security holes and issues in a computer. These normally exist in the operating system.

A worm replicates itself and aims to fill up all the free space on a computer to slow it down and bring it to a halt. Therefore, the first signs for a user that their computer has been infected with a worm is that it starts to run slowly and the space on their hard drive begins to rapidly decrease.

A worm also tries to spread to different computers on a network. For this reason, worms are often used to infect a large number of computers on a network. If a worm is able to spread throughout a network, it can clog up bandwidth and slow the whole network down.

Worms are normally downloaded and spread through email attachments, peer-to-peer file sharing networks or using a link to a website or resource. Once downloaded, they do not need any other human interaction to replicate themselves.

A well-known example of a computer worm is Stuxnet. Stuxnet was a computer worm that was used as a cyber weapon in 2010. It was discovered by two security researchers who recognised that the worm was a great deal more complex than any they had seen at the time. The worm was being used to attack a power plant and security experts believed the aim was to sabotage nuclear weapon production.

Figure 5.8: Worm.

Minimising the risk of a worm

Worms often aim to exploit software vulnerabilities in a computer. These will normally be located in the operating system or applications. Therefore, you should regularly check for, and install, updates for your operating system and your applications. If this process can be set to automatically occur, then this can remove the need for you to remember to do it.

The same guidelines about minimising phishing should also be taken. This can help to reduce the risk of downloading a worm that is attached to an email attachment or a link.

Anti-virus software can normally check for a worm too. Therefore, regularly scanning your computer with anti-virus software can help identify a worm that has infected your computer.

Worms can be spread by network connections. Therefore, disconnecting your computer from a network, when the network resources are not required, can keep it safe during this time.

Question

3   Find out about another well-known example of a worm called Confiker.

 • What issues did Confiker cause?

 • Who did Confiker affect?

 • How was Confiker dealt with?

Spyware

Spyware is a global term that is used to describe malware that is designed to gather information about your interactions with your computer. As the name suggests, the aim of spyware is to spy on the user. Spyware is normally used to gather personal and sensitive data that can be used in fraudulent and criminal activity.

A common example of spyware is a key logger. A key logger is installed on a user's computer, normally without their consent. The key logger will then record any key presses that are carried out by the user. All this data is sent to a third party, normally the person who created the spyware, to be analysed. The data is analysed, normally by another computer, but can be done manually, to establish any patterns in the data. The patterns are then analysed to see if any of them look as though they could be personal or sensitive data, for example, a password.

Spyware can perform actions beyond just key logging. A user can sometimes unknowingly allow a commercial company to use spyware for several purposes, including:

- targeted marketing from tracking browsing habits
- sending unwanted and often irritating pop-up adverts
- installing add-ons and redirecting to advertising websites

You can often unknowingly download spyware whilst using the internet. It can be embedded into enticing opportunities, such as a pop-up advert offering a prize or a free product. It can also be embedded into the download of a video, music or application file, often those that are free of cost. Sometimes, this may involve you consenting to the download of the spyware as the consent is buried in the small print and can go unread and unnoticed.

Figure 5.9: Spyware.

Minimising the risk of spyware

Spyware is always roaming around the internet, so it is important to understand how you can minimise the risk of allowing it to be used to monitor your actions.

As always, be very careful about what you download, especially when downloading software that is free of cost, and downloading from video and music sharing sites. Make sure that this is only done from very trustworthy and reputable sources.

Do not click on any links or offers in pop-up adverts, no matter how enticing they may seem. If you find that there is no obvious way to close a pop-up window, you can press ALT and F4 and this will close your internet session.

Always read the small print when consenting to any user agreement. Commercial companies can sometimes list

in the small print that you are consenting to allowing spyware to be downloaded to track information such as your browsing habits. Look for clauses about sharing your data with third parties.

Cookies are a type of spyware that you may consent to be used to track your internet surfing habits. Even with cookies, you should always check what you are allowing the company to do with the cookies that you consent to being used to track your actions.

Anti-malware software can be used to scan your computer to see if any key logging software is present. This type of software will normally remove any key logger if it is found. If it does find a key logger it is advisable to change all your passwords immediately, in case your data has been gathered an analysed. Do not wait to see if any issue occurs in the future, be proactive!

Questions

4   How has the General Data Protection Regulation (GDPR) in the European Union (EU) affected the use of spyware?

5   Find out about mobile spyware.

   a   How are mobile phones infected?

   b   How is spyware used in mobile devices?

Adware

Adware is a type of software that is designed to display targeted advertising on your computer. It does this by collecting data about your internet browsing habits. Adware can be legitimate, but it can also be illegitimate. Some program developers will justify the inclusion of adware in their product by claiming that it will generate revenue for them, keeping the cost of the product lower.

Adware can be bundled in with legitimate software downloads. This means that you may end up with adware on your computer without actually asking to download it. This can happen when you are given the chance to customise what is downloaded. For example, there may be a hidden addition to the download of a task or search bar that is added into your current internet browser. You can customise the download and uncheck the box so that you do not get the adware, but if you do not know to do this you may download it unknowingly. Once downloaded, the adware can prove difficult to delete as they do not normally have any uninstall feature. It may not act maliciously, but will often serve as a method of advertising for the company, or try to get you to use their search function.

Adware as malware will present adverts when a user is browsing the web that are often shown constantly. They are normally in the form of pop-ups or windows that cannot be closed. They can often be very irritating.

Figure 5.10: Adware.

Minimising the risk of adware

You may be happy to allow some adware to track your browsing habits online. This will allow you to see adverts for products that you might be interested in. You may not be happy to allow adware to make your browsing experience become very irritating by having too many adverts popping up on a constant basis. Therefore, you may want to be careful about what adware you allow to be installed on your computer.

The most proactive measure you can take with adware is to make sure that you check exactly what is being downloaded onto your computer. Look at the list of component parts that will be downloaded and make sure that any that look like they could be adware (for example, a search bar or task bar addition to your browser) are not ticked. If they are present, untick them immediately before allowing the download to go ahead.

Once downloaded, unwanted adware can be very difficult to remove. It may take several scans with an anti-malware software to detect and remove the adware.

Rootkit

A rootkit is a computer program that enables a person to gain administrator access to a victim's computer. They are designed to stay hidden on a user's computer and allow the computer to be controlled from a remote location. A rootkit allows the unauthorised user to do several criminal acts with the computer, such as hide illegal files on the computer, use the computer as part of a larger cyber attack or to steal personal data and information.

Rootkits can get installed because a victim's password is cracked or a vulnerability in the security of a computer system is exploited. The person installing it can then use the access to stop the computer recognising that the rootkit is there, so the victim will not know that someone else has complete access to their computer system. The rootkit will normally be buried deep within the operating system. This is so that it can try to avoid any detection by anti-malware software. Other malware can be incorporated into a rootkit that can then be concealed on the computer to cause harm.

One very sneaky way that an unauthorised person can use to install a rootkit on a computer is by leaving USB memory sticks, infected with a rootkit, in places that they believe they will be found. They are relying on the curiosity of another user to insert the USB memory stick that they have found into their computer and therefore download the rootkit.

An early rootkit example is NTRootkit. This was a rootkit that appeared in 1999 and was designed to infiltrate Windows operating systems. A rootkit that was designed to do the same with Mac operating systems didn't appear until 10 years later.

Figure 5.11: Rootkit.

Minimising the risk of a rootkit

Rootkits are often installed through your computer password being cracked, or by another means such as embedded in a software download or installed on a USB memory stick.

It is advisable to have a strong password set for your computer to minimise the risk of it being cracked. A strong password should contain a random mixture of characters, numbers and symbols. It should not contain any data that could be connected to you or your likes and dislikes. It is also advisable to change your password on a regular basis in case it has been discovered.

Previous advice should also be followed about making sure that software is only downloaded from trusted and reputable sources. You should also, under no circumstances, insert a USB memory stick that you find into your computer system. It may be tempting to see what it contains, but the risks that could be attached to inserting it into your computer are not worth the temptation.

Removing a rootkit from a computer once it has been installed can be extremely difficult. It is software that is designed to be hidden and heavily relies on this feature. A rootkit may be detected by anti-malware, but this is highly unlikely. Often, one of the only ways to rid a computer of a rootkit is to completely uninstall the operating system.

Question

6 Rootkits can also be used a positive way. Find out how rootkits are used in connection with Digital Rights Management (DRM).

Malicious bots

A bot, short for robot, is an application that is automated and used to carry out simple and repetitive tasks. These are normally tasks that a human would find mundane and time-consuming. Bots can be used for very productive reasons, such as indexing a search engine, but they can also be used as a form of malware.

Malicious bots are used by cybercriminals in a variety of ways:

- SPAM bots are used to bombard people's email inbox with SPAM emails.

- Zombie bots are used to create a bot network. The bot will lay dormant on a computer until an attack

is launched. The computer will then be connected with lots of other computers that have been compromised by zombie bots to launch a large-scale attack on an organisation. Bots connected in this way can be known as a botnet.

- Chatter bots will pretend to be humans on sites such as social networking and dating sites. They try to emulate human interaction with the goal of obtaining personal data.

- File-sharing bots will provide a search result for a user's search request and offer a link for a file download.

Bots often have worm-like capabilities because they can replicate and spread themselves.

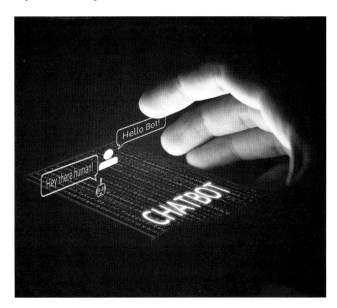

Figure 5.12: Bots.

Minimising the risk of bots

Bots are often embedded into links or software downloads and are often spread in the same way that phishing is carried out. Therefore, the same measures that can be taken to minimise phishing can be applied to bots. The best advice is not to click on any links without knowing who they are from and that they will link you to a trusted and reputable source.

As bots can often be used in a chat situation, you should never give out any personal data when chatting online. Even if you feel this is in a private environment, one on one with a person, you should still never provide any personal data. If you are chatting to friends, you should agree to never request any personal data from each other online. If you are chatting to what you believe is as friend, if you feel they ask you an odd question, or for personal data, then contact them by another means, such as calling them, and double check that you are speaking to your friend.

If you suspect that you have downloaded a bot, anti-malware software can be used to detect and remove it.

A firewall can also be used to detect the activity of a bot as it may recognise suspicious traffic created by the bot. However, if a bot is sophisticated and can disguise its communications as legitimate traffic, it will go unnoticed by a firewall.

Question

7   Bots can be used in both positive and negative ways.

a   How are bots used in a positive way as web crawlers?

b   How are bots used in a negative way in distributed denial of service (DDoS) attacks?

Ransomware

Ransomware is a type of malware that restricts a user's access to their computer system and files. The ransomware will normally demand that the user pays a ransom in order to regain access to their computer system. Some ransomware programs will completely lock a user's system, and some will encrypt all of the files on their system in a way that renders them useless. Ransomware will normally try to enter a system in a similar way to a Trojan. If the user doesn't pay the ransom in a set amount of time, they risk losing their data forever.

A well-known example of Ransomware is WannaCry. The unauthorised user demands that the infected user pays a $300 ransom. If the user does not pay within three days, the amount is doubled. If payment is not made within a week, the unauthorised user will delete the infected user's files forever.

The success rate of a person paying the ransom relies on the user's attachment to the data that is stored on their computer. Users that do pay the ransom can often be exploited further and asked for a further payment to release their data.

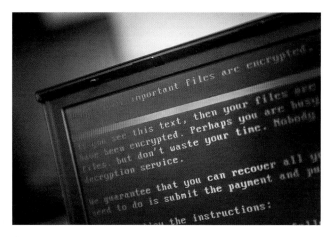

Figure 5.13: Ransomware.

Minimising the risk of ransomware

As ransomware is distributed in a similar way to Trojans, the same guidelines for minimising the risk of Trojans can also be followed.

In addition to this, you can counteract the risk of losing your data in this type of attack by making sure that you have a copy of your data. If you create a separate back-up of your data, and keep this up to date, then the risk of losing your data in a ransomware attack becomes greatly reduced. This means that you can reinstate your data, if it is deleted.

The risk of losing data can also be reduced by storing data in the cloud. Cloud systems often have a facility that can allow the user to roll back to a previous version of the data, so it can be reinstated if lost.

Question

8   A company can use a practice called principle of least privilege (POLP) to help keep data safe and secure.

Find out what POLP is and how it can help keep data safe and secure.

REFLECTION

What kind of resources did you use for the research questions?

If you used the internet, what kind of measures did you take to minimise the risk of malware?

EXAM-STYLE QUESTIONS

1 Identify three guidelines that can help keep personal data safe. [3]
2 Explain one difference between phishing and pharming. [1]
3 Explain two similarities between phishing and pharming. [2]
4 Identify four different types of malware. [4]
5 Describe how a firewall can be used to help prevent a virus infecting a computer system. [5]
6 Describe how spyware can be used to obtain a user's password for an online account. [5]
7 Rootkits can be used to allow an authorised person to hide illegal files on a user's computer.
   a State what is meant by a rootkit. [1]
   b Explain how the risk of rootkits can be minimised. [2]
   c Identify two other malicious ways that rootkits can be used. [2]

[Total 5]

8 Ransomware can be used to prevent a user gaining access to their data.
   a State how ransomware prevents the user gaining access to their data. [1]
   b Explain two measures that can be taken to minimise the risk of ransomware. [2]

[Total 3]

SUMMARY CHECKLIST

- [ ] I can identify what is meant by personal data.
- [ ] I can understand the importance of keeping personal data confidential.
- [ ] I can describe several guidelines that can help keep personal data confidential.
- [ ] I can explain how personal data is collected by unauthorised people, using practices such as phishing, smishing, vishing and pharming.
- [ ] I can describe how a range of malware operates.
- [ ] I can identify a range of consequences of malware to organisations and individuals.
- [ ] I can explain what measures can be taken to minimise the risk of each type of malware.

› Chapter 6
The digital divide

Introduction

You live in an ever-increasing digital world. The digital divide is therefore a complex and growing issue. The term refers to the technology divide between countries, **demographic** groups (particular sections of the population) and **economic** areas (areas defined by their production and use of goods and services). A lack of access to technology, such as mobile telephones, personal computers and the internet, is seen as an issue and a disadvantage because of the range of benefits that technology can provide. The digital divide that people experience can depend on several aspects, such as age, status and location.

KEY WORDS

demographic: a particular section of a population

economic: considering a country in terms of their production and consumption of goods and services

Groups affected by the digital divide:

- people living in cities versus people living in rural areas

- people educated in using technology versus people uneducated in using technology

- older people versus younger people

- areas that are more industrially developed versus areas that are less industrially developed

- different socio-economic groups.

All countries experience a digital divide at one level or another. At a national level, the digital divide describes the difference between those who have regular access to modern technology, and those who have the necessary skills to make good use of the technology. At an international level, the digital divide describes the difference between developed and developing countries.

REFLECTION

Do you think there is anything that can cause a digital divide in your country?

The digital divide matters because those without access, and those without developed skills, are missing out on the many advantages the digital world can offer.

Figure 6.1: The digitally-connected world.

6.1 City versus rural living

The geographical location of where a person lives can have an affect on their access to technology services. One aspect of this is whether they live in a city or a rural location.

One of the main services that can be affected by geographical location is access to the internet. The **infrastructure** for the availability of **broadband** (a method of data transmission that is capable of transmitting a high level of traffic) and high-speed internet connections is much more developed in city locations than it is in rural locations. Why has this happened?

KEY WORDS

infrastructure: the facilities that are needed for the operation of a society, such as roads, buildings and utilities

broadband: method of data transmission that is capable of transmitting a high level of traffic

Figure 6.2: Countryside and rural.

The most likely cause is linked to the higher concentration of people that live in a city, compared to a rural area. This means that the potential customer base for broadband providers is much greater in a city. This may mean that both the government and an internet provider are able to recuperate the costs of implementing more advanced infrastructure far quicker in urban areas than in rural areas.

One issue that could be caused by a lack of high-speed internet access is a reduced level of enjoyment of online entertainment. People in rural areas may not be able to use the services offered by some online television broadcasting companies. Therefore, they may find they have other friends and family that are able to watch television shows and films they do not have access to, due to their rural location. This could result in a person feeling isolated, as they cannot have a conversation with friends and family about the television shows and films they are currently watching.

Question

1   a   How could a lack of high-speed internet access affect a person's ability to use online learning platforms?

b   How could this affect the digital divide between those living in a city and those living in a rural location?

The issue of a lack of access to high-speed internet access can extend to mobile telephone internet services. In a rural location, a person may find that they have limited connection to 3G or 4G connections, or may not get any connection at all.

Question

2   a   How could a lack of mobile telephone internet services affect a person's ability to communicate with others?

b   What kind of services may they not be able to use?

c   How might this lack of ability to communicate in certain ways make them feel?

Real-life example

Sofia lives in a rural area of Spain. Access to high-speed internet in her rural village is very limited. She is a furniture designer who works from home.

Sofia currently creates her designs and sends them to clients using the internet. She would like to be able to video-conference with her clients because she feels this would provide her with a better platform to explain her vision. The internet speeds available to her, because of her rural location, will not allow her to use video conferencing technologies effectively. Sofia feels that this reduces her competitive advantage in comparison to other designers that live in the city, who have access to internet speeds that allow them to video-conference with their clients.

Figure 6.3: Video-conferencing.

Reducing the digital divide in rural areas

The quality of the infrastructure in rural areas could be improved. Many governments around the world are working with internet providers and offering incentives to improve the infrastructure in rural areas.

In certain rural locations, the practicality of building infrastructure capable of high-speed internet, or even any internet access at all, can be very challenging. This is normally because the task and cost of building the infrastructure needed is just so large. One solution to this is to use satellite technologies. This limits the amount of infrastructure that needs to be developed, whilst still providing access to the internet.

Real-life example

A report released at the India Mobile Congress 2017 highlighted that only 16% of people in rural areas of India have internet access. The India government are looking into ways to improve this figure.

BharatNet is an initiative of the government of India that focuses on developing infrastructure in rural India in order to provide affordable internet connectivity up to 20Mbps. They are planning to do this through increasing the infrastructure based on fibre optic cabling. They are also planning to deliver access through satellites in approximately 5300 locations.

Figure 6.4: Building digital infrastructure.

6.2 Technology educated versus technology uneducated

Using technology can be complex. Different types of technology have different interfaces and different methods for use. Without a certain level of education in how to use technology, it can often seem very daunting. This can begin to make those who are not educated in using technology very uncomfortable.

Many companies now have online systems that allow people to buy products, book tickets or book services. This may seem simple and convenient for people who are educated in using technology and are confident in navigating the systems. However, for those who are not educated in using these systems it can seem frustrating and people may miss out on opportunities.

There may be several different reasons why people are not technologically educated. It may be that they do not have much access to technology and therefore do not have much experience in using it. Some people simply do not have an interest in using technology, but they are sometimes forced to use it to be able to access certain products and services.

Question

3 Think of two advantages that people who are educated in using technology may have over those who are not educated in using technology.

Real-life example

Zhen wants to buy tickets to see her favourite band in concert. Tickets go on sale on a Friday morning and are only available online. Zhen has never used an online ticket booking system before and feels very nervous about doing so. She would much rather be able to ring the venue and purchase tickets over the telephone, but this option is not available.

Zhen doesn't have a computer, so she goes to use one in a local coffee shop, to purchase tickets online on the Friday morning. Zhen struggles to navigate the booking system and by the time she has managed to get to trying to pay, all the tickets have sold out and there are no more tickets available.

Zhen was unable to buy the tickets to see her favourite band because she did not have the education in technology and experience needed to navigate the ticket system.

Figure 6.5: Buying online.

Reducing the digital divide with the technologically uneducated

One effective way of reducing the digital divide with the technologically uneducated is to provide accessible technology courses in local communities. This is often offered as a service by colleges, schools and libraries. Courses can be offered for free, or at a low cost, that people can attend to improve their education in the use of technology. This will allow people to learn with others who are of a similar level to them, so they do not feel too uncomfortable. They can also have a teacher or leader who will help them with any problems they have. People can then use the skills they learn to use technology to their advantage in the future.

Real-life example

Pakistan are offering a 12-week course to its citizens for learning skills in everyday software. The course is provided as a collaboration with the Virtual University. The course will provide people with basic knowledge on everyday software and also a better understanding of using the internet for communication.

This education will provide Pakistani citizens with a basic education in the use of technology and allow them to feel more comfortable and confident in their skills. The country believes this will help its people be more competitive in an advancing digital world.

Figure 6.6: Virtual education.

6.3 Older people versus younger people

Technology has developed a huge amount over the last 50 years. This means that some people have grown up with technology as an integral part of their life, and others have witnessed the development of technology, along with experience of a world without it.

Some younger people have only ever known the use of smart phones and the internet. This means that social media has been their main understanding of communication with the outside world. Some older people have known other methods of communication and may have preferred those, but this group are now finding that older methods of communication are becoming increasingly dated. This can cause a divide in the ability of a younger and an older generation to communicate.

Younger people may feel much more confident using technology as they have far more experience with it. It is often just their 'go to' resource for many aspects of their life, including communication, entertainment and research. Older people may feel less confident about using technology because they have experienced a world before smart phones and the internet and have used alternative methods. These include a landline telephone for communications, written letters using the postal service and using libraries for research.

As older people have known other methods, this can cause resentment if they are presented with the need to use technology to complete a task. They may feel that the use of technology makes the task much more difficult and this can also affect their confidence in using technology for other tasks in the future.

PRACTICAL ACTIVITY 6.02

Make it your mission to help an older member of your family, or an older family friend, do something that they have never done using technology. This could be as simple as sending a message, watching a video online, or showing them how to research a topic they love, using the internet. Ask them why they have never used the technology before and ask them how they felt about using it to complete the task.

Question

4   To gain an understanding about how younger and older people may complete tasks, copy and complete the following table about pre-available technology and post-available technology for completing these tasks.

Task	Pre-technology	Post-technology
Sending a list of places you want to visit, to a friend.	Writing them a letter and sending it by post.	Sending them a text message.
Arranging to meet a friend for lunch.		
Buying a cinema ticket.		
Researching recipes for your favourite food.		
Finding out how much money is left in your bank account.		

PRACTICAL ACTIVITY 6.03

Think of three ways that you could pitch using technology to an older person. Think of how the technology would benefit them and how you would gain their confidence in its use.

Real-life example

Jack is an elderly gentleman who needs to attend several hospital appointments. The hospital has a brand-new technology that collates all the data about appointments at the hospital and sends out reminders to people who need to attend appointments. The previous system was to send a letter to people reminding them of their appointment.

Jack has a mobile telephone that his daughter bought for him. He doesn't know how to use it though, other than to make a telephone call to his daughter. Jack keeps receiving text messages from the hospital about his appointments. The messages ask him to reply if he will still be attending the appointment. Jack doesn't know how to reply to the messages and this makes him very worried that he will lose his hospital appointment. Jack doesn't know who to call at the hospital to say he will still be coming to his appointment, there is no telephone number to do this. Jack is already worried about needing to go to the hospital and now he is even more worried because of the messages. He wishes they would just go back to the old system and write to him.

Reducing the digital divide between younger and older people

One of the biggest barriers to older people using technology is likely to be their fear of it. They will have more familiar ways to do things with which they are comfortable. They may feel that they are too old to learn how to use technology and see it more of a young person thing.

What they may not see is that the use of technology can be hugely beneficial to older people. One of the things that can happen with older people is that as they become less mobile and are able to go outside their home less frequently they can start to become cut off and feel isolated. By being able to use platforms such as social media, they can improve their feelings of isolation and have regular contact with their friends and family.

Incentives to get older people to see the advantages of technology are developing in many countries.

Real-life example

Singapore is a country that are trying to encourage their older generation to see the advantages of technology. Retirement villages are built incorporating several different technologies so that older people who live there can experience how the technology can benefit their lives. Sensors can monitor a patient's health and doctors can take advantage of the high-speed broadband to make video-conference calls to check in and look over the elderly, who find travel to a clinic difficult.

Additionally, initiatives have seen many public buildings, such as libraries and community centres, offering free internet access to the elderly in the hope of encouraging them to get online. The country sees the internet as integral to economic and social success and is striving to reduce the gap for all its population.

Figure 6.7: All-age technology.

6.4 More industrially developed areas versus less industrially developed areas

The parts of the world that have greater access to modern technology are the USA, Europe and northern Asia. These areas mostly consist of developed countries. Areas where access is more restricted are in some parts of Africa, India and southern Asia. These are areas that have countries that are less industrially developed. Access to technology may be less in these areas because the countries are having to use their financial resources to provide more important services and do not have the funds available to concentrate on the development of their technology services.

The start-up costs for these countries to build the infrastructure would be very great. However, not having the same access to technology and the internet could put them at both a competitive and economic disadvantage. They may not have the ability to trade using modern technologies and therefore cannot access the same customer and supplier base as businesses in developed countries. It may also affect the level of education that can be provided as there may be a wealth of information unavailable to them that is accessed using the internet. This can have an impact on both the education and the skill level of people in those countries and prevent them from competing on an international level.

PRACTICAL ACTIVITY 6.04

Business and education are two areas that could be affected by a digital divide in respect of the industrial development of a country. With a partner, think of one other area that could be affected and discuss what impact this could have on the country.

PRACTICAL ACTIVITY 6.05

How aware are you of the infrastructure in your country? Make a list of the facilities that you think your country provides. Use the internet to see if you are correct and to see what other facilities it provides. Do further research using the internet to find out what future plans your country has to improve its infrastructure in terms of technology.

Real-life example

Elinah lives in a village in Kenya. She makes beautiful woven baskets that can be used for a range of purposes, including storage of items and as a plant holder. Elinah sells her products to local customers and tourists. The tourists often say to her that they wish they could buy her products online.

Elinah would like to be able to sell her products online. She knows how to set up a website and distribution channel, but the internet access to her village is very limited, meaning that she cannot be effective in running an online business. Even if Elinah moved to a different location, access to the internet in her country is limited in many places, although it is improving.

Reducing the digital divide in less industrially developed areas

The internet has become one of the most fundamental global infrastructures. Those with limited access to the internet often find it difficult to access the benefits of the internet.

Satellite technology may assist remote areas to access the internet. Large companies plan to implement satellite technologies that allow such areas better access to the internet.

Governments in many less industrially developed areas try to promote the business and products that they could offer if they had better infrastructure and access to the internet. They hope that other countries will invest and help the country to build the necessary infrastructure. These coordinated efforts can benefit the world on a global scale.

Real-life example

A developing method of accessing the internet is called TV white space. This technology uses unused channels in radio frequencies within the range that is normally used for broadcasting television.

Microsoft have an initiative called the Affordable Access Initiative that is making use of the TV white space technology to provide internet access to developing parts of the world. One example of this is to provide access to the internet in solar powered internet cafes in Kenya.

This technology is allowing more access to be developed in countries that lack the infrastructure, because it is removing the need for the traditional infrastructure to be put in place.

Figure 6.8: Access to technology.

6.5 Different socio-economic groups

The digital divide between different socio-economic groups often revolves around cost. Richer people can afford higher-speed internet connections and expensive advancements in technology. This can mean they have a better standard of living, due to an increased level of experience, as they have access to higher quality entertainment, a wealth of information and the level of convenience that technology can bring.

The lack of access to information can greatly impact the poor. It is often people in poorer circumstances that would benefit from the education that access to services such as free online learning platforms would provide. The lack of access to this kind of service can create a greater digital divide between the rich and the poor. Education in poorer communities can often be an important way of improving the socio-economic circumstances. Therefore, greater access to online learning platforms could help rectify this.

Questions

5 How could the ability to access free online learning platforms improve circumstances for those in poorer communities?

6 How could access to high-speed internet connections for entertainment purposes improve the lifestyle of a person?

Real-life example

Taliya is a film studies student. She has high quality recording equipment, a 4K monitor and a high spec computer system at home. She really enjoys recording scenes for her movie projects and editing them on her computer system at home.

Jane is also a film studies student. She is becoming increasingly frustrated by her course as she has to film and edit all her movie projects on her low spec mobile

Figure 6.9: Video recording.

telephone. She feels that she could produce much better work, and enjoy her studies much more, if she had access to a better computer system to edit her work.

Reducing the digital divide in different socio-economic groups

Many countries are developing initiatives that provide technology at a subsidised rate or even for free to those in poorer communities. This is helping close the digital divide by giving those who would not normally be able to afford those technologies access to the advantages that the technologies can provide.

Many organisations are starting to work together to provide the internet in developing countries. Large organisations, such as Facebook and Google, are working with internet service providers to implement facilities, such as Wi-Fi hotspots, that can be used to bring internet access to these countries at a lower cost. The larger organisations will collaborate in this way as it can help bring them a wider customer base and therefore generate more profits.

Real-life example

One Laptop Per Child is an initiative that helps provide technology to poorer and developing communities. Its primary goal is to improve the education for children by enabling those in low-income communities to have access to a laptop and the benefits that brings.

The initiative has been running since 2005 and continues to provide laptops to low-income communities around the world, including the USA, Rwanda, Paraguay, India, Nepal, Kenya and Peru. Some of the original organisations that funded the initiative are AMD, Google and Quanta.

> **REFLECTION**
>
> How does the existence of a digital divide make you feel? What do you think you can do about the digital divide?

EXAM-STYLE QUESTIONS

1   Define the term 'digital divide'.   [1]
2   Identify two aspects that can create a digital divide.   [2]
3   Explain the impact of the digital divide on a person's geographical location.   [4]
4   Explain how a person's education can be affected by the digital divide.   [4]
5   Explain two strategies that can be implemented to reduce the digital divide.   [4]

SUMMARY CHECKLIST

☐   I can explain what is meant by the digital divide.

☐   I can explain what kind of aspects can affect the digital divide, such as age, socio-economic status and geographical location.

☐   I can discuss what measures can be taken to reduce the digital divide.

Chapter 7
Expert systems

LEARNING INTENTIONS

By the end of this chapter, you will be able to:

*   recognise and understand how expert systems are used to produce possible solutions for different scenarios.

Introduction

You spend your life developing your knowledge, thinking and making decisions. Decisions are fundamental parts of life. It is also possible to develop systems to aid this process and they are called expert systems.

An expert system is a computerised system that attempts to reproduce the decision-making process of an expert human being. The person who designs and develops an expert system is called an expert system engineer. They are designed to try and replicate the judgement of a human that has expert knowledge in a certain field. By doing this they can be used to replace or assist a human expert.

Figure 7.1: Thinking about decisions.

An expert system consists of several components. These components include:

- a user interface

- a knowledge base

- an inference engine

- a knowledge base editor

- an explanation system

- method of output, e.g. screen.

An expert system operates by prompting the user to enter certain data using the user interface, referring to the knowledge base and using the inference engine to aid the decision-making process it is designed to simulate.

Expert systems are versatile and can be used in a range of different applications. Expert systems can be used as a diagnostic tool, in financial planning and risk analysis. Expert systems can even be used for a more fun purpose, such as a challenging chess opponent. They are also a form of **artificial intelligence** which is a computer system designed to simulate human intelligence.

KEY WORDS

artificial intelligence: a computer system designed to simulate human intelligence

7.1 Components of an expert system

User interface

The user interface is the way that a user interacts with the expert system. This could include using a keyboard to enter criteria into text query boxes, or choosing options by pressing offered choices on a touch screen.

The user interface will guide the user about what data they need to input into the expert system and will then display any output from the expert system.

Without the presence of a user interface, a user would need to know how to program each of the interactions they want to make with the expert system. The quality of the design of a user interface is very important.

Question

1   What could happen if the user interface design for the expert system is poor?

Figure 7.2: Touch screen interface.

Knowledge base

The **knowledge base** is a database of related information about a particular subject. It allows the storage and retrieval of the knowledge required for an expert system to operate.

When an expert system is developed, several experts will be interviewed and asked to contribute the knowledge they have of a given field. This knowledge is then used to build a database that is the knowledge base for the expert system. The developers will want two types of knowledge from the experts, factual knowledge and heuristic knowledge. Factual knowledge is knowledge that is definitive and widely shared amongst experts in the field. Heuristic knowledge is knowledge that is acquired through personal experiences and built on reasoning.

Part of the knowledge base is the **rules base**. The rules base is a set of rules that will be used to produce an output or decision by the expert system. These rules are used by the inference engine as a base for reasoning, to obtain a solution to a problem or a decision. Each rule will contain two parts, the IF and the THEN. A rule can also have multiple IF parts that will be joined together by Boolean operators including AND and OR.

KEY WORDS

knowledge base: a component of an expert system that stores the knowledge provided by experts

rules base: a part of the knowledge base that contains all the rules to be analysed by the expert system

A simple example of a rule could be:

IF a > b AND a > c THEN highest = a

Figure 7.3: Experts pooling knowledge.

The knowledge base should be a dynamic resource, therefore the expert system needs to have a **knowledge base editor**. The knowledge base editor allows the knowledge base to be edited and updated when necessary.

KEY WORDS

knowledge base editor: a component of an expert system that is used to amend or update the knowledge base

Question

2   What could happen if the expert system did not have a knowledge base editor?

Inference engine

The inference engine is the part of the expert system that makes judgements and reasoning using the knowledge base and user responses. It is designed to produce reasoning based on the rules and the knowledge base.

It will ask the user questions and, based on their answer, it will follow a line of logic. This may then lead to further questions and, eventually, to a final result.

The inference engine is mostly a problem-solving tool. It organises and controls the steps to providing the desired output. There are two main methods that an inference engine can use to simulate reasoning, these are **backward chaining** and **forward chaining**.

Backward chaining is based on goal driven reasoning, i.e. is dependent on a finding a desired goal. This type of chaining is used when the possible outcomes are limited and definitive in nature. In backward chaining, the system tries to take a goal and repeatedly split it into sub-goals that are simpler to achieve. The nature of this type of system is that it moves backward from the goal to be achieved, using the sub-goals to inform the next piece of data that is needed by the system, to reach a goal.

A simple diagram that represents the process of backward chaining would be:

Sub-goals ◄——————— Rules ◄——————— Goal

Figure 7.4: Backward chaining.

Forward chaining is based on data driven reasoning and is dependent on the data that it is provided with. This type of system is used when a problem is more open ended, and the outcome is not necessarily definitive in nature. The system will take data input by the user and move forward from rule to rule to suggest a possible outcome. It will take the data input by a user, then move from rule to rule to find one where the clause for the data input is true. It will then ask the user for more data and repeat this process until it can suggest an outcome.

KEY WORDS

backward chaining: breaking a goal down into sub-goals that allow the system to work backward from the goal

forward chaining: a system that moves forward from rule to rule until it reaches a possible outcome

goal driven: a system that is dependent on a finding a desired goal

data driven: a system dependent on the data that it is provided with

A simple diagram that represents the process of forward chaining would be:

Data ——————► Rules ——————► Outcome

Figure 7.5: Forward chaining.

Explanation system

The conclusion or decision the expert system provides may not always be an obvious choice to a user. The user may want to gain an understanding of how the conclusion or decision was determined. In order to allow this facility, some expert systems have an explanation system built into them. This will provide an explanation of the reasoning process and show how the output given by the system was achieved.

KEY WORD

explanation system: a component of an expert system that provides an explanation of how an outcome was achieved

Method of output

The output method is the method the user will use to view any results produced by the expert system. This will often be in the form of a display screen that will allow them to see the results on screen, or may include an output, such as a printer, that allows the results to be printed and viewed.

7.2 Are expert systems useful?

There are several advantages that can be gained from using an expert system.

Expert systems:

- can provide answers to questions that are outside the knowledge that you currently have
- can aid professional people by prompting them and guiding them to look at areas of knowledge they may not have considered or remembered
- are consistent in the responses they produce as they are arrived at in a logical way
- can be used at any time, so you do not need to contact another person who may have the knowledge at an unsuitable time
- can sometimes arrive at a solution to a problem quicker than a human would.

There are clear advantages to using an expert system, however there are also disadvantages to using them as well.

Expert systems:

- do not have the intuition that humans have. This means that their response can only be a logical one and may not be useful.
- are only as good as the rules and data they are provided with. If there are errors in the data or rules, then this will produce incorrect results.
- are expensive to create. Many experts need to be consulted and a high level of skill is required to build the component parts.
- cannot adapt a great deal to their environment and may require the knowledge base to be edited in order to do this.

Questions

3   Think of a scenario in which an expert system would be an advantage.

4   Think of a scenario where an expert system would not be very suitable.

REFLECTION

Do you think you have ever used an expert system?

7.3 How are expert systems used?

Expert systems are used by many individuals and organisations for a variety of different reasons. These include:

- medical diagnosis
- car engine fault diagnosis
- a digital opponent in games such as chess
- providing financial planning and investment advice
- providing insurance planning advice
- plant and animal identification
- planning and scheduling routes for delivery vehicles
- mineral prospecting.

Medical symptoms

The organisation WebMD have a website that offers a medical expert system called 'symptom checker'. It asks the user a series of questions about the user's symptoms

and then provides possible conditions that match the symptoms. It lists the possible conditions in order, starting with the one it finds to be the closest match.

Figure 7.6: Medical diagnosis interface.

PRACTICAL ACTIVITY 7.01

Do you think a medical expert system will be a data driven or goal driven expert system? Discuss with a partner your thoughts about which it could be and why.

Question

5   What could be the benefits and the disadvantages of people using online self-diagnosis systems?

Car engine fault diagnosis

Most modern cars have an abundance of technology built into them. Car mechanics will often be very knowledgeable about the mechanical parts of the car, but they may not have as much knowledge about the modern technology.

The cars often have a system of symbols on their dashboard that light up when an issue is detected in the car, such as a problem with the engine. The driver of the car sees the engine symbol light up and this shows that the car may need to be taken to a garage.

When the driver takes the car to a garage, the mechanic plugs the expert system into the car engine. The expert system then interrogates the engine management system to discover all the information available about the fault, so that it can provide a diagnosis. The expert system provides a list of possible diagnoses to the mechanic, who can then use their knowledge to fix the car.

Figure 7.7: Car fault warnings.

Chess player

One of the most famous examples of an expert system used as a chess player is a computer called Deep Blue. Deep Blue was developed by the organisation IBM. On 11 May 1997, Deep Blue beat the world champion chess player Garry Kasparov. The victory received press coverage around the world, as people were amazed at the abilities of the computer. The success of Deep Blue inspired computer scientists around the world to develop the abilities of expert systems much further.

People were quite sceptical about the victory of Deep Blue. They could not believe that a computer could play with the capabilities that it showed. It was one of the first realisations that computers had great capabilities when it came to simulating thinking. This scared some people.

Deep Blue is now stored in the Smithsonian Museum in Washington DC.

Figure 7.8: Computer chess master.

PRACTICAL ACTIVITY 7.02

Find out what Deep Blue was developed to do after its chess victory.

PRACTICAL ACTIVITY 7.03

Find out about another chess playing system called AlphaZero.

Financial planning

Expert systems can be a very useful tool in financial planning. They can help individuals on a small scale or companies on a large scale. They can create a financial plan or assess what financial actions need to be taken to achieve a desired outcome.

They can help people to:

- manage their debt
- organise their investments
- reduce their taxes
- plan for retirement.

A user enters information about their financial situation and personal circumstances. The expert system will then produce a financial plan, or a list of possible outcomes, based on this information.

Figure 7.9: Financial planning.

Insurance planning

Many insurance company websites use an online expert system so that users can quickly see if the company has a policy that would be suitable for them. The system will ask a user for their circumstances and it will then provide a result to say whether the insurance company would be willing to give the user an insurance policy. If the expert system is able to match their data to a possible policy, it will inform the user with details about the policy, such as how much it will cost and what benefits it will provide.

Question

6   An insurance company offers life insurance policies. What kind of questions do you think the expert system will ask in order to establish whether an insurance policy would be issued to a user?

Plant identification

A website called Botanical keys allows users to enter a range of characteristics about a plant. It mostly covers plants in the UK and Ireland area.

The website takes the data input about the plant and analyses it against its rules and knowledge base. It then tells the user what kind of plant it could be.

A user could find out what kind of plant is growing in their garden, or try to discover the type of plant they have seen when on a walk.

Figure 7.10: Identifying plants.

Question

7   What kind of questions would an expert system ask in order to identify a type of animal?

Planning a route for a delivery company

Delivery companies can use expert systems to find out the best route for a delivery driver for all the deliveries the driver needs to make on a given day.

Each of the deliveries the driver needs to make is put into the system. The system then outputs a route that will be the most efficient route for the driver to follow, in terms of time or fuel used, etc. to make each delivery. It may request further information, such as the type of delivery vehicle and how long each delivery will take. The system may make further recommendations about how many drivers are needed to deliver all the parcels that day and what kind of vehicle each driver will need to take for the parcels they need to deliver.

It is likely that an expert system could work out this type of outcome quicker than a human, due to the amount of data it is likely to handle, especially in large delivery companies.

called **PROSPECTOR** was one of the first expert systems developed to aid geologists in exploring for minerals. Digging for minerals can be very expensive, so companies want to be sure that minerals will be present when they break ground. **PROSPECTOR** can be used to calculate the probability of minerals being present in a certain location.

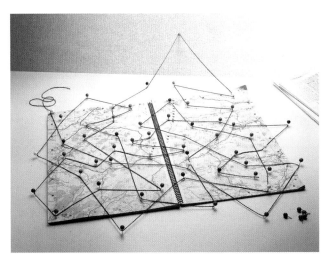

Figure 7.11: Route planning.

Figure 7.12: Prospecting.

Mineral prospecting

Minerals can be very precious, and geologists can spend a long time trying to source them. An expert system

EXAM-STYLE QUESTIONS

1	Identify the name of the component in an expert system that stores the data required for the system to use in decision making.	[1]
2	Identify the name of the component in an expert system responsible for reasoning and judgement.	[1]
3	Explain the role of an expert system.	[2]
4	Describe the concept of forward chaining.	[3]
5	Identify the type of problem for which backward chaining would be more suitable.	[1]
6	Explain two scenarios where an expert systems can be used.	[4]

SUMMARY CHECKLIST

- [ ] I can identify the different components in an expert system including the user interface, the inference engine, the knowledge base, the knowledge base editor and the explanation system.
- [ ] I can explain the role of each component in an expert system.
- [ ] I can describe the concept of backward chaining and understand it is goal driven reasoning.
- [ ] I can describe the concept of forward chaining and understand it is data driven reasoning.
- [ ] I can understand how expert systems are used in a range of different scenarios.

> Chapter 8
Spreadsheets

LEARNING INTENTIONS

By the end of this chapter, you will be able to:

- create structure
  - create page/screen structures to meet the requirements of an audience and/or task specification/house style
  - create/edit spreadsheet structures
  - protect cells and their content
  - freeze-panes and windows

- create formulas and use functions
  - use formulas
  - use absolute reference, relative reference, named cells, named ranges
  - know and understand why absolute and relative referencing are used
  - use functions

- use validation rules

- create formatting
  - format cells
  - format cell emphasis

- test a spreadsheet structure

CONTINUED

- extract data
  - sort data
  - summarise and display data using pivot tables and pivot charts
  - import and export data
- create macros
- create a graph or chart appropriate to a specific purpose
- apply chart formatting.

BEFORE YOU START

- Do you know that spreadsheets can be used to manipulate numbers, perform calculations, present summary data and make predictions?
- Are you able to create a basic spreadsheet structure using cells, rows and columns?
- Do you understand the purpose of cells, rows, columns and ranges within worksheets?

Introduction

A **spreadsheet** is a software package that organises data in rows and columns. There are many actions that a spreadsheet can perform on the data, these include carrying out calculations and creating charts and graphs.

KEY WORD

spreadsheet: software that can organise, analyse and manipulate data that is organised in a grid of rows and columns

8.1 Create a spreadsheet structure

Page and screen structures

Pages within a spreadsheet can be formatted in a variety of ways as shown in Table 8.1.

You need to consider the needs of the audience when formatting pages or screens. If the person reading the document doesn't need to view all the data, then consider hiding columns or rows. If fitting all the data onto one page will make it too small to read, then consider fitting the data to spread across more pages. Reducing margins can enable more data to fit on one page, but consider whether a space is needed for hole punches, making notes or binding in a book. If a spreadsheet is to be printed across several pages, then including the title of the document and the page number in a header or footer will help the audience to follow the document in the correct order.

PRACTICAL ACTIVITY 8.01

Open **8.01 Page Formatting.xls** which currently requires 20 pages to print.

1   Add a header of 'Chapter 8 figure list'.

2   Remove gridlines from printing and also on the sheet view.

3   Remove row and column headings from printing.

4   Add a footer of 'Page # of n' where # is the current page number and n is the total number of pages.

5   Change the settings described so that the document fits onto just three pages.

Page setup	The size of paper to print on (e.g. A4, Letter) can be set as well as the orientation (portrait or landscape). It's also possible to decide whether to print gridlines for all the cells (rectangles within a spreadsheet where data can be positioned), whether to include row and column headings and whether certain rows will be repeated at the top of each page.
Fit to page	Sometimes large spreadsheets cover several pieces of paper. In order to make it easier to follow the data and save paper, it is possible to set the spreadsheet to fit a specific number of pages. Options include, fit all columns on one sheet, fit all rows on one sheet, fit the sheet to one page or fit the sheet to a specified number of pages across and down.
Margins	The top, bottom, left and right margins can be adjusted to provide space at the edges (e.g. for hole punches) or to reduce the space at the edge and provide more space on the paper for printing.
Header and footer	Information can be included at the top and bottom of each printed spreadsheet. This could include the title and author of the document, page number, file name and date.

Table 8.1: Formatting pages.

KEY WORD

cell: a single unit/rectangle of a spreadsheet formed at the intersection of a column and a row where data can be positioned; its reference (name/address) is based on its column and row

Create and edit spreadsheet structures

It is possible to add rows and columns by inserting them. Rows are inserted above existing rows and columns are inserted to the left of existing columns. Rows and columns can also be deleted.

WORKED EXAMPLE 8.01

In this example, you can see the option to insert a row which will be inserted above row 3.

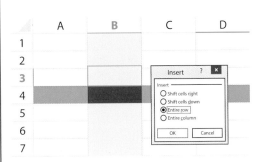

Figure 8.1: Inserting a row.

Now you can see the effect of having added the new row.

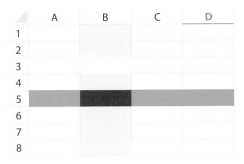

Figure 8.2: An inserted row.

Rows and columns can be resized. Rows can be made taller or shorter and columns can be made wider or narrower. Rows are resized to enable different sizes of text to fit or to allow multiple lines of text within one cell or row. Columns are resized to allow more data to fit in the column or to save space by narrowing the column.

WORKED EXAMPLE 8.02

The rows and columns in this spreadsheet have been resized.

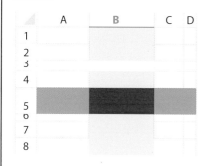

Figure 8.3: Height and width resized.

It is possible to hide a row or column. Rows or columns are hidden because they may contain information that does not need to be seen by the user or they may contain private or confidential data that should not be seen by the user.

WORKED EXAMPLE 8.03

Here you can see the process of hiding column C.

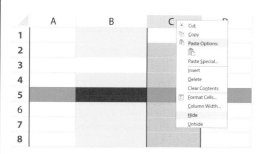

Figure 8.4: Hiding a column.

Now you can see that column C has been hidden.

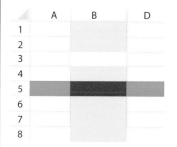

Figure 8.5: Hidden column.

Sometimes it can be useful to merge two cells together. Merging multiple cells will create a single cell with the cell reference being the original upper-left cell of the merged cells.

WORKED EXAMPLE 8.04

8.02 Merging.xlxs cells has a title of 'Staff Hourly Rates' in cell A1.

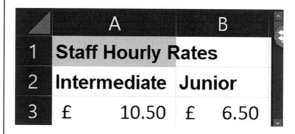

Figure 8.6: Hourly rates.

The data is in cell A1 but overflows into cell B1. Cell A1 has been shaded. Cells A1 and B1 can be merged so that it is one single cell as shown in Figure 8.7.

Figure 8.7: Hourly rates merged.

Cell B1 no longer exists as the space is used for the larger cell A1.

PRACTICAL ACTIVITY 8.02

Open 8.03 Rows and Columns.xls.

1   Insert a row above row 5.

2   Delete column C.

3   Increase the height of row 1.

4   Decrease the width of column B.

5   Hide rows 2 and 3.

6   Merge cells A4:C4 to become a single cell.

Protect cells and their content

Depending on the software being used, different parts of spreadsheets can be secured in a variety of ways. The simplest form of security is to protect a whole workbook from having any new worksheets added or existing worksheets removed.

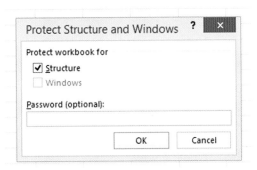

Figure 8.8: Workbook protection.

Following on from this, it is possible to protect a worksheet from having any changes made to it.

WORKED EXAMPLE 8.05

In this example, the worksheet is protected to the extent that no changes can be made to any data and no data can be selected. No columns can be added and no rows can be added. Cells and rows cannot be formatted. This is useful if the whole worksheet contains just output data or a data table.

Figure 8.9: Worksheet protection.

It is also possible to protect a worksheet but allow the user to change certain cells within that worksheet. This enables a developer to protect all the formatting, titles and structure but allow the user to enter and change input data. To do this, cells that may be edited must be unlocked prior to protecting the worksheet. It is then necessary to protect the sheet but allow unlocked cells to be selected.

WORKED EXAMPLE 8.06

In this example, the commission and prices can be changed by the user so those cells have been set to be unlocked.

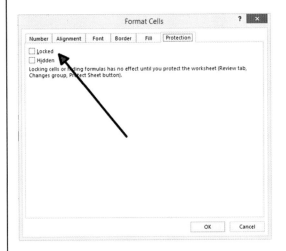

Figure 8.10: Unlocked cell.

Now that those cells have been unlocked, the sheet can be protected and only the unlocked cells can be selected.

Figure 8.11: Worksheet protection with unlocked cells.

Cells can also be protected so that the **formula** cannot be seen by a user. This may be used to prevent users from seeing how certain confidential calculations are made but still letting them see the results of the calculation based on changing input data.

WORKED EXAMPLE 8.07

In this example, there is a formula in cell C2. It is currently visible.

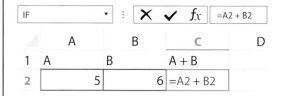

Figure 8.12: Formula visible.

After the cell has been set to hidden, the formula is now hidden from the user.

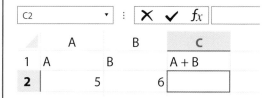

Figure 8.13: Formula hidden.

There will be occasions when some users will be allowed to change some data but not all data. In this case, it is possible to protect a worksheet but allow a specific set or **range** of cells to be edited by users who have knowledge of the correct password, or by selected users within the computer network.

WORKED EXAMPLE 8.08

In this example, the prices cells are left unlocked but the commission cell (B2) has been locked. In order to allow some users to edit the commission, a password has been set on that cell so that anybody with the password can edit the cell.

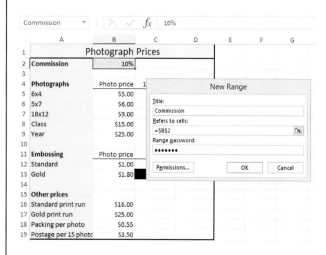

Figure 8.14: Range protection.

Freezing panes and windows

Spreadsheets can sometimes become so large that they cannot fit visibly onto a single screen. It's possible to freeze panes so that the top row remains on the screen as the user scrolls down the spreadsheet. Similarly, the first column can be frozen so that it remains on screen as the user scrolls across the spreadsheet.

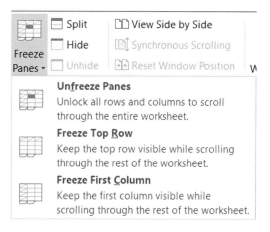

Figure 8.15: Freeze pane options in Microsoft Excel.

To freeze more rows or more columns, the user can select the first cell that should not be frozen and then freeze the panes. This will freeze all rows above and all columns to the left of the selected cell.

WORKED EXAMPLE 8.09

This example from **8.04 Freezing panes.xls** shows which cells will be frozen when cell B4 is selected and freeze panes is applied.

	A	B	C	D	E
1	Physics				
2	Student	Test 1	Test 2	Test 3	Test 4
3	*Max Marks*	*40*	*30*	*50*	*20*
4	Matthew	3	27	5	12
5	Elijah	6	21	10	2
6	Caleb	36	8	34	18
7	Joshua	32	7	29	12
8	Sheila	30	29	17	20
9	Junayna	4	28	41	4
10	Jordan	21	11	38	11
11	Sharon	39	29	26	17
12	James	12	15	7	7
13	Naomi	38	27	49	20

Figure 8.16: Cell selected for freezing panes.

As the user scrolls down and across the screen, rows 1 to 3 and column A remain visible as shown in Figure 8.17.

	A	D	E	F	G
1	Physics				
2	Student	Test 3	Test 4		
3	*Max Marks*	*50*	*20*		
4	Matthew	5	12		
5	Elijah	10	2		
6	Caleb	34	18		
7	Joshua	29	12		
8	Sheila	17	20		
9	Junayna	41	4		
10	Jordan	38	11		
11	Sharon	26	17		
12	James	7	7		
13	Naomi	49	20		

Figure 8.17: Panes frozen as user scrolls down and across.

PRACTICAL ACTIVITY 8.03

1   Open **8.05 Worksheets.xls**.

   a   Try to add or delete a worksheet. The workbook has been protected to prevent this from happening.

   b   Unprotect the workbook using the password 'openme'. Now try to add a new worksheet.

2   Select the **Invoice** worksheet.

   a   Try to select any cell. This worksheet has been protected completely to prevent this from happening.

   b   Unprotect the worksheet using the password 'payment'. Now try to select cells and make changes to data.

3   Protect the **Breakdown** worksheet so that no changes can be made at all.

4   Open the **Prices** worksheet.

   a   Try to change one of the titles in column A. These cells are locked so that you cannot edit them.

   b   Now try to change the prices of the photos. These cells have been unlocked so the prices can be changed.

   c   Now try to change the commission rate in cell B2 (10%). Notice how an additional password is required to do this. This is because this cell has been set to allow users with that password to change it.

   d   Enter the password 'special' and then change the rate of commission.

5   Open the **Purchases** worksheet.

   a   Lock the cells in columns A, B and C. Unlock the cells in columns D and E. Then protect the worksheet and see what you can and cannot change.

   b   Scroll down the purchases worksheet and across to the right and notice how the top row and first 2 columns remain in place.

CONTINUED

c   Unfreeze the panes and then try scrolling again. Notice how all of the data moves, including the top row and left hand columns.

d   Freeze the top row. Scroll down and across. Which cells remain on the screen?

e   Freeze the first column. Scroll down and across. Which cells remain on the screen?

f   Freeze the panes so that columns A, B and C and row 1 remain on the screen. Which cell did you click on to achieve this?

8.2 Create formatting

Format cell contents

Format data type

Cells within a spreadsheet can be formatted for an appropriate data type. Dates can be formatted to be dd/mm/yyyy where dd is the day, mm is the month and yyyy is the year. In countries like the USA, the date would be formatted mm/dd/yyyy. It is also possible to display the whole month, use leading zeros for days and months and use four digits or two digits for the year. Times can be formatted to include hours, minutes and seconds or just hours and minutes. Some times may have a.m. or p.m. whereas others will use a 24-hour clock.

Cells can be set to contain text. This is particularly useful if a set of numbers need to be entered that start with zero. Numeric cells can be set to include a specific number of decimal places including no decimal places. Currency can also be set to include a specific number of decimal places, and the currency symbol can also be chosen.

A number can be set as a percentage, in which case the number is divided by 100. For example, 58% is used in calculations as 0.58. Decimals can be entered into a cell and turned into fractions. For example, entering 0.25 would give a fraction of ¼.

WORKED EXAMPLE 8.10

These examples from **8.06 Data Types.xls** show different ways in which data can be formatted according to the data type. Notice how C4 contains text. This is because, although it looks like a number, it starts with zero and numbers do not include leading zeros.

	A	B	C
1	**Data Type**	**Example 1**	**Example 2**
2	Date	02/05/2015	02 May 2015
3	Time	3:44 PM	15:44
4	Text	abcdefg	09876
5	Numeric	25	25.33
6	Currency	$15.45	₱15.45
7	Percentage	25%	0.30%
8	Fractions	1/4	4/5

Figure 8.18: Data types.

PRACTICAL ACTIVITY 8.04

Open **8.07 Data Types Task.xls**.

1   Change cell B2 to be a date with no leading zeros for the day and month and two digits for the year.

2   Change cell C2 to be a date with leading zeros for the day, the full name of the month and four digits for the year.

3   Change cell B3 to be a time with a.m./p.m.

4   Change cell C3 to be a time with hours, minutes and seconds.

5   Enter the value 0382 in cell B4. What happens?

CONTINUED

6 Change cell C4 to be text and then enter the value 0382. What is different from B4?

7 Change cell B5 to have two decimal places. What happens?

8 Change cell C5 to have one decimal place. What happens?

9 Change cell B6 to be currency in euros with two decimal places. What happens?

10 Change cell C6 to be currency in Japanese yen with two decimal places. What happens?

11 Change cell B7 to be a percentage. What happens?

12 Change cell C7 to be a percentage. What happens?

13 Change cells B8 and C8 to be fractions up to one digit. Are they both correct? What do you think needs to be done to fix this?

Text orientation

Often it is difficult to fit all the necessary text into a column title without the column becoming too wide. In these circumstances, the text **orientation** can change so it is diagonal or vertical.

KEY WORD

orientation: the direction of text, for example horizontal or vertical

WORKED EXAMPLE 8.11

This spreadsheet shows the scores between international football teams. The number of goals scored by the team is shown in each row and the number of goals scored against a team is shown in each column. You will notice that in the first version the columns are too narrow to fit in the full team name and in the second version the columns are too wide.

	A	B	C	D	E	F
1		Japan	Mace	Unite	Pakis	Ukrai
2	Japan		3	2	4	1
3	Macedonia	2		3	0	0
4	United States of America	1	0		0	2
5	Pakistan	2	3	2		0
6	Ukraine	0	1	2	5	

Figure 8.19: Columns too narrow.

	A	B	C	D	E	F
1		Japan	Macedonia	United States of America	Pakistan	Ukraine
2	Japan		3		2	4	1
3	Macedonia	2		3	0	0
4	United States of America	1	0		0	2
5	Pakistan	2	3		2		0
6		0	1		2	5	

Figure 8.20: Columns too wide.

To overcome this problem, the text can be orientated vertically.

	A	B	C	D	E	F
1		Japan	Macedonia	United States of America	Pakistan	Ukraine
2	Japan		3	2	4	1
3	Macedonia	2		3	0	0
4	United States of America	1	0		0	2
5	Pakistan	2	3	2		0
6	Ukraine	0	1	2	5	

Figure 8.21: Columns rotated vertically.

Alignment

By default, the **alignment** of text is to the left and numbers are aligned to the right. However, it is possible to change the way that data is aligned within columns. Data can be aligned to the left, right or centre.

KEY WORD

alignment: positioning text so that it is in line, for example on the left, right or centre

WORKED EXAMPLE 8.12

One problem that often occurs is when different numbers of decimal places are used in the same column. The numbers are aligned to the right of the cell rather than by the decimal point.

	D
3	87.23
4	18.5
5	23.56
6	34.23472

Figure 8.22: Decimal point alignment problem.

Unlike a word processor, it is not possible to change the alignment to be by the decimal point. Therefore, the number of decimal places needs to be made equal.

	D
3	87.230
4	18.500
5	23.560
6	34.235

Figure 8.23: Decimal point alignment solved.

PRACTICAL ACTIVITY 8.05

Open **8.08 Alignment.xls**. This shows the election results for three areas of the UK in 2015.

1. Change the names of the parties in C2 to P2 to be vertical orientation.
2. Increase the height of row 2 if necessary.
3. Change the names of the parties to be centred.
4. Change the number of votes in C3 to I5 to be right aligned.
5. Change the number of decimal places for the percentages in K3 to P5 to be one decimal place.
6. Change the titles in B2 to B5 to be right aligned.

Format cell emphasis

Cell emphasis is about changing a cell so that it stands out from the others. There are lots of ways this can be done, including changing data to be bold, italic, underlined, in a different font and in a different font size.

WORKED EXAMPLE 8.13

The cells in figure 8.24 have been emphasised as indicated.

	A	B
1	colour of text	font size
2		
3	shading of cell	**font style**
4		
5	cell borders	

Figure 8.24: Cell emphasis.

Comments

Spreadsheets can contain a lot of data and some of it may need additional information to explain what it is. However, there may not be space for that information or it may be too confusing to include the information with the data. In this case, comments can be added to cells that can be seen when selected.

WORKED EXAMPLE 8.14

Comments have been added to cells B5 and E2 for the Japan versus Pakistan game. Cell B5 has been selected and so the comment is showing. A comment is indicated in cell E2 by the red triangle.

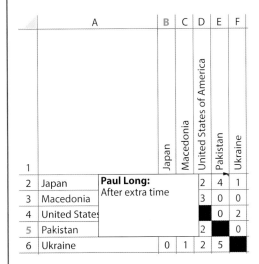

Figure 8.25: Comments.

PRACTICAL ACTIVITY 8.06

Open **8.09 Emphasis.xls**.

1   Change cells A2, A4, A11 and A15 to be bold and font size 14.

2   Add borders to the bottom of cells B4, C4, B11, C11 and D11.

3   Add a thick blue border around cells A1 to D19.

4   Shade A1:D1 and A1:A19 in yellow.

5   Shade C13 and D13 in black.

6   Add a comment to cell B2 to read 'This is the commission a school will earn'.

Conditional formatting

Cells can be formatted based upon certain conditions being met. This is known as conditional formatting. Conditions can include:

- values in a cell that are equal to a set criterion (e.g. = 'Good')
- values in a cell that are greater or less than a set criterion (e.g. >5)
- values in a cell that are between set criteria (e.g. between 2 and 10)
- values in a cell that are duplicated elsewhere in the worksheet
- values that are above or below average
- a scale of values from lowest to highest.

WORKED EXAMPLE 8.15

In **8.10 Conditional Formatting.xls**, a questionnaire has been sent out and respondents have had to give a priority to each question from 1 to 5 or x if they disagree completely.

The average response, total x responses and total blank responses has been calculated. The following conditional formatting rules have been used:

- Respondent reply = 1: white text with green shading
- Respondent reply >= 4: white text with red shading
- Respondent reply = x: white text with red shading
- Respondent reply between 2 and 3: yellow shading
- Average response < 2: white text with green shading
- Average response >= 4: white text with red shading
- Average response between 2.0 and 2.9: yellow shading
- Total x >= 4: red text with light red shading.

Open **8.11 Member List.xls** and conditionally format cells according to the following rules:

1   Female members: pink shading
2   Male members: white text, blue shading
3   Full, junior or patron members: green text
4   Lapsed members: red text
5   Do not email = TRUE: yellow shading with red border
6   Number of years >=10: green text
7   Number of years between 5 and 9: purple text.

8.3 Create formulas and use functions

Use formulas

A formula uses basic arithmetic calculations. These are plus, minus, divide and multiply, for example, =B5+B6. There is no limit to the number of arithmetic calculations that can be used, for example, =(B5+B6)*3/100-(D1-D2).

WORKED EXAMPLE 8.16

This spreadsheet is used to calculate the cost of broadband, TV and phone packages. The formula in cell B9 adds up the monthly costs of line rental (B6), TV (B7) and broadband (B8) then multiples the result by 6. Finally it adds any setup costs from B3.

	A	B	C
1		**Broadband 1**	**Broadband 1**
2		Original	Family
3	Initial cost	$ 15.00	
4			
5	1st 6 month		
6	Line rental	$ 15.40	$ 15.40
7	TV	$ 10.75	$ 16.50
8	Broadband	$ 20.00	$ 20.00
9	Total 6 months	=6*(B8ıB7ıB6)ıB3	

Figure 8.26: A formula.

Indices can be used within formulas to raise a number to a power. For example =4^3 would raise 4 to the power of 3 which is $4^3 = 64$.

Referencing cells and ranges

Relative cell references

Relative cell referencing is used when you want the content of a cell to change based on its relation to its row and column position. Often the formulas being used are performing the same calculation for a whole row or column. When this happens, it is possible to replicate the formula rather than typing it in each time.

KEY WORDS

relative cell reference: a cell reference that changes when it is copied into other cells

WORKED EXAMPLE 8.17

This spreadsheet lists the number of hours it takes to produce a promotional leaflet, the cost to be charged for the leaflet and the quantity to be produced. The total to be charged is then calculated by multiplying the cost (C4) by the quantity (D4).

	A	B	C	D	E
3	Job	Hours	Cost	Quantity	Total
4	A5 Leaflet	1	$ 12.50	3	=C4*D4
5	A4 Leaflet	1.5	$ 18.75	1	
6	A3 Leaflet	2.5	$ 25.00	2	

Figure 8.27: Replication 1.

One way of entering the formula in E5 for the total cost of A4 leaflets is to type it in again but changing row 4 to row 5 so the formula would be =C5*D5. However, it is much quicker and more accurate to replicate the formula by copying it from E4 and pasting it into E5 and E6.

	A	B	C	D	E
3	Job	Hours	Cost	Quantity	Total
4	A5 Leaflet	1	12.50	3	=C4*D4
5	A4 Leaflet	1.5	18.75	1	=C5*D5
6	A3 Leaflet	2.5	25.00	2	=C6*D6

Figure 8.28: Replication 2.

The cell references used in the formula in the previous example were relative cell references. This is because they point to another cell in a position relative to the current position. When referring to C4, it is pointing to a cell that is two columns to the left of column E. When referring to D4 it is pointing to a cell that is one column to the left of column E. Therefore, when the formula is replicated down to rows 5 and 6, the references continue to point to the same columns but the row reference is incremented.

WORKED EXAMPLE 8.18

The same process happens when copying formulas across a spreadsheet. The formula in B3 calculates the number of kilometres travelled. When it has been replicated to columns C and D, instead of the row numbers changing, the column letters change. B2 is referring relatively to one row above and B1 is referring relatively to two rows above.

	A	B	C	D
1	Start distance	38029	38098	39273
2	End distance	38087	39137	39410
3	Distance travelled	=B2-B1	=C2-C1	=D2-D1

Figure 8.29: Replication across.

Formulas can be used to retrieve a value from another worksheet. To do this you should include the name of the worksheet before the cell reference.

WORKED EXAMPLE 8.19

To use the value in cell B4 in a worksheet called 'Data source', use the following formula:

='Data source'!B4

The inverted commas are only required if the name of the worksheet includes a space, but the exclamation mark must always be used.

The following formula will multiply the value in B4 on the 'Data source' worksheet by C15 on the current worksheet:

='Data source'!B4 * C15

Absolute cell references

PRACTICAL ACTIVITY 8.08

Open **8.12 Absolute References.xls** and use the worksheet Absolute 1, which is similar to the example used for relative cell references. The cost is calculated by multiplying the hourly rate in B1 by the number of hours in B4.

1   Replicate (copy) the formula from C4 to C5 and C6.

2   What has gone wrong?

3   Why has it gone wrong?

Absolute cell referencing is used when you do not want a cell reference to change when other cells are filled in, or when replicating formulas. Either a row, a column, or both can be set to be relative or absolute referencing.

KEY WORDS

absolute cell reference: a cell reference that does not change when it is copied into other cells, usually by placing a $ sign before the cell reference

To stop a row from being changed, a $ symbol must be put before the row number. So C5 would become C$5. This makes the row an absolute reference but leaves the column as a relative reference.

PRACTICAL ACTIVITY 8.09

Continuing with **8.12 Absolute References.xls** and the worksheet Absolute 1:

4   Change the formula in C4 to be =B$1*B4.

5   Replicate (copy) the formula from C4 to C5 and C6.

6   Examine the formulas in C5 and C6.

7   Which cell references have changed and which have not?

To stop a column from being changed, a $ symbol must be put before the column letter. So C5 would become $C5. This makes the column an absolute reference but leaves the row as a relative reference.

To stop both the row and column from being changed, a $ symbol must be put before both the column letter and row number. So C5 would become $C$5. This makes the whole cell reference an absolute reference.

PRACTICAL ACTIVITY 8.10

Continuing with **8.12 Absolute References.xls**, open worksheet Absolute 2. This worksheet is used to calculate the wage bill each month.

8 Look at the formula in C4 which calculates the cost of workers in week 1 month 1.

9 Make any changes necessary to the formula in C4 before replicating it for months 2 to 4.

10 Try copying the formula from C4 to E4 for week 2 workers.

11 What has gone wrong?

12 Why has it gone wrong?

13 Change the formula in C4 so that when replicated both across and down it will still work.

14 Now replicate the formula down column C and across to columns E, G and I.

15 Complete the spreadsheet with formulas in column J.

Named cells and ranges

Ranges were introduced earlier in this chapter. A named cell is when a name is used instead of the cell reference and a named range is when a name is used instead of cell references.

Named cells can be used as absolute cell references. When referring to a named cell, whenever it is replicated it will still point to the same named cell.

WORKED EXAMPLE 8.20

8.13 Tax Rate.xls contains a named cell of 'TaxRate' which is cell B1. The formula in C4 is =B4*TaxRate

	A	B	C
1	**Tax rate**	0.15	
2			
3	**Product**	**Cost**	**Tax**
4	6 × 4 frame	12	=B4*TaxRate
5	5 × 7 frame	15	=B5*TaxRate
6	10 × 8 frame	18	=B6*TaxRate
7	12 × 8 frame	21	=B7*TaxRate

Figure 8.30: Tax rate named cell.

When this formula is replicated down column C, the reference to TaxRate remains the same because it is an absolute reference.

Named ranges can also be used within formulas. It is easier to understand formulas with named cells and ranges than to understand formulas with cell references.

WORKED EXAMPLE 8.21

In **8.13 Tax Rate.xls**, cells C4:C7 have been named as 'TaxCharged'. Instead of using a function of =SUM(C4:C8) for the total tax charged, the named range can be used instead.

	A	B	C	D
1	**Tax rate**	15%		
2				
3	**Product**	**Cost**	**Tax**	**Cost inc tax**
4	6 × 4 frame	$12.00	$ 1.80	
5	5 × 7 frame	$15.00	$ 2.25	
6	10 × 8 frame	$18.00	$ 2.70	
7	12 × 8 frame	$21.00	$ 3.15	
8	Total tax charged:		=SUM(Tax Charged)	

Figure 8.31: Total tax charged name range.

When a range of vertical cells has been named, it is possible to make reference to any individual cell in that range by using the name of the range, as long as the reference is being made in the same row.

WORKED EXAMPLE 8.22

	A	B	C	D
1	Tax rate	0.15		
2				
3	Product	Cost	Tax	Cost inc tax
4	6 x 4 frame	12	=B4*TaxRate	=Cost+TaxCharged
5	5 x 7 frame	15	=B5*TaxRate	=Cost+TaxCharged
6	10 x 8 frame	18	=B6*TaxRate	=Cost+TaxCharged
7	12 x 8 frame	21	=B7*TaxRate	=Cost+TaxCharged

Figure 8.32: Referencing a named column.

In 8.13 Tax Rate.xls, cells C4 to C7 have been named 'TaxCharged' and cells B4 to B7 have been named 'Cost'. The formula in D4 calculates the cost including tax by adding the Cost to the Tax. To do this, it makes reference to the whole named range for Cost and the whole named range for TaxRate. The spreadsheet software can see that the range is in the same row so it uses the values in the same row from the Cost and TaxRate ranges. This can be replicated down and the reference is relative rather than absolute because it is relative to the same row.

PRACTICAL ACTIVITY 8.11

Open 8.13 Tax Rate.xls.

1 Change the formula in C4 so that it uses a named range for the cost.

2 Replicate this formula to C5:C7.

3 Use a named range to calculate the total cost in B8.

4 Name the range for cost including tax.

5 Use a named range to calculate the total cost including tax in D8.

PRACTICAL ACTIVITY 8.12

Open 8.14 Times Table.xls which will be used to show the times table.

1 Create a formula in B2 that will calculate the value in B1 multiplied by the value in A2. Do not use numbers, only use cell references.

2 Change the formula so that it has absolute references where needed so that you can replicate the formula across and down. You should only need one formula.

Named ranges can be used across multiple worksheets within the same spreadsheet. When referencing a named range in a different worksheet it is not necessary to reference the name of the worksheet. Examples of this being used can be found in the Lookup functions section.

Functions

A **function** is a ready-made formula representing a complex calculation, for example =SUM(A5:B10) or =AVERAGE(cost). It is a reserved word within the spreadsheet software that processes a series of predefined formulas.

KEY WORD

function: a ready-made formula representing a complex calculation

Summary functions

Table 8.2 shows some of the summary functions.

Function	Purpose	Example
SUM	Calculates the total of values within a range.	=SUM(B3:E3)
AVERAGE	Calculates the average of values within a range.	=AVERAGE(B3:E3)
MINIMUM	Calculates the smallest value within a range.	=MIN(B3:E3)
MAXIMUM	Calculates the largest value within a range.	=MAX(B3:E3)

Table 8.2: Summary functions.

WORKED EXAMPLE 8.23

8.15 Student Marks.xls calculates the total, average, minimum and maximum mark that each student scores in a set of four tests. In row 2, the total has been calculated by adding up each cell individually using a formula. In row 3, this has been done using a function that requires much less effort. In row 2, the average has been calculated using a formula, but it is necessary to know how many marks there are to complete this calculation. In row 3, this has been done using a function which does not require knowledge of the number of values to be averaged and will allow extra values to be added in the future by inserting columns.

	A	B	C	D	E	F	G	H	I
1	Student	Mark 1	Mark 2	Mark 3	Mark 4	Total	Average	Minimum	Maximum
2	Name 1	98	40	36	84	=(B2+C2+D2+E2)	=F2/4		
3	Name 2	31	67	61	77	=SUM(B3:E3)	=AVERAGE(B3:E3)	=MIN(B3:E3)	=MAX(B3:E3)
4	Name 3	62	58	29	38	=SUM(B4:E4)	=AVERAGE(B4:E4)	=MIN(B4:E4)	=MAX(B4:E4)
5	Name 4	64	83	85	27	=SUM(B5:E5)	=AVERAGE(B5:E5)	=MIN(B5:E5)	=MAX(B5:E5)
6	Name 5	87	45	64	42	=SUM(B6:E6)	=AVERAGE(B6:E6)	=MIN(B6:E6)	=MAX(B6:E6)
7	Name 6	93	58	43	73	=SUM(B7:E7)	=AVERAGE(B7:E7)	=MIN(B7:E7)	=MAX(B7:E7)
8	Name 7	99	29	55	92	=SUM(B8:E8)	=AVERAGE(B8:E8)	=MIN(B8:E8)	=MAX(B8:E8)
9	Name 8	57	58	44	93	=SUM(B9:E9)	=AVERAGE(B9:E9)	=MIN(B9:E9)	=MAX(B9:E9)
10	Name 9	45	43	98	55	=SUM(B10:E10)	=AVERAGE(B10:E10)	=MIN(B10:E10)	=MAX(B10:E10)

Figure 8.33: Summary functions.

PRACTICAL ACTIVITY 8.13

Open **8.15 Student Marks.xls**. Use functions to calculate the average, minimum and maximum mark for each of the four tests.

Rounding functions

Numbers can be rounded to whole numbers or decimal places. Table 8.3 shows the functions that can be used.

Function	Purpose	Example
INT	Returns the whole number value of a decimal number (the value before the decimal point). The INT function effectively rounds the number down to the nearest whole number.	=INT(A2)
ROUND	Rounds a number to the nearest decimal place specified. This example rounds the value in A2 to three decimal places.	=ROUND(A2,3)
ROUNDUP	Rounds a number up to the nearest decimal place specified. This example rounds up the value in A2 to two decimal places.	=ROUNDUP(A2,2)
ROUNDDOWN	Rounds a number down to the nearest decimal place specified. This example rounds down the value in A2 to four decimal places.	=ROUNDDOWN(A2,4)

Table 8.3: Rounding functions.

WORKED EXAMPLE 8.24

In **8.16 Rounding.xls** you can see how the functions in table 8.3 have been used:

	A	B	C	D	E
1	Original number	Integer	Round	Round up	Round down
2	25817.32817	=INT(A2)	=ROUND(A2,3)	=ROUNDUP(A2,2)	=ROUNDDOWN(A2,4)
3	3852.876985	=INT(A3)	=ROUND(A3,3)	=ROUNDUP(A3,2)	=ROUNDDOWN(A3,4)
4	928.2341	=INT(A4)	=ROUND(A4,3)	=ROUNDUP(A4,2)	=ROUNDDOWN(A4,4)
5	0.03256	=INT(A5)	=ROUND(A5,3)	=ROUNDUP(A5,2)	=ROUNDDOWN(A5,4)

Figure 8.34: Rounding functions.

You can also see the results of the calculations made by the functions:

	A	B	C	D	E
1	Original number	Integer	Round	Round up	Round down
2	25817.32817	25817	25817.328	25817.33	25817.3281
3	3852.876985	3852	3852.877	3852.88	3852.8769
4	928.2341	928	928.234	928.24	928.2341
5	0.03256	0	0.033	0.04	0.0325

Figure 8.35: Rounding values.

PRACTICAL ACTIVITY 8.14

Create a new spreadsheet and experiment with the four rounding functions using different values for decimal places.

REFLECTION

What happens if you change the number of decimal places to a negative number? How does this relate to rounding to significant figures? Notice how −1 rounds to tens, −2 rounds to hundreds and −3 rounds to thousands. The minus number relates to rounding to the power of 10 rather than rounding to a set number of significant figures.

Indices

If you need to calculate indices (powers), then the POWER function can be used. It uses the syntax =POWER(number,power). For example, =POWER(6,3) would raise 6 to the power of 3. It is also possible to use the ^ symbol and so =6^3 would also raise 6 to the power of 3.

WORKED EXAMPLE 8.25

8.17 Powers.xls raises the numbers in column A to the power given in row 1.

	A	B	C	D
1	Original number	Power 2	Power 3	Power 4
2	4	=POWER(A2,2)	=A2^3	=POWER(A2,4)
3	3	=POWER(A3,2)	=A3^3	=POWER(A3,4)
4	7	=POWER(A4,2)	=A4^3	=POWER(A4,4)

Figure 8.36: Powers.

PRACTICAL ACTIVITY 8.15

Open **8.17 Powers.xls**, which contains random values for the number to be raised and random values for the power.

1 Create a function in B8 that raises the value in A4 to the power given in B7. Do not use any numbers, only use cell references.

2 Using absolute cell referencing where needed, copy the function from B8 across the row and down the column. You should not need to change any cell references if you have used absolute references properly.

Date and time functions

Calculations can be performed on dates and times.

Function	Purpose	Example
DAY	Calculates the day part of a date.	=DAY(B1)
MONTH	Calculates the month part of a date.	=MONTH(B1)
YEAR	Calculates the year part of a date.	=YEAR(B1)
DATE	Calculates the date from a given year, month and day.	=DATE(B4,B3,B2)
HOUR	Calculates the hours part of a time.	=HOUR(B8)
MINUTE	Calculates the minutes part of a time.	=MINUTE(B8)
SECOND	Calculates the seconds part of a time.	=SECOND(B8)
TIME	Calculates the time from given hours, minutes and seconds.	=TIME(B9,B10,B11)
NOW	Gives the current date and time (can be formatted for just date or just time).	=NOW()
WEEKDAY	Gives the number of the day in the week.	=WEEKDAY(B1,2)

Table 8.4: Date and time functions.

PRACTICAL ACTIVITY 8.16

Explore **8.18 Date and Time.xls**.

Text functions

Calculations can be performed on text to extract parts of text, join text together, calculate the length of text or change the case of text.

Function	Purpose	Example
CONCATENATE	Joins together text values.	=CONCATENATE (A1,B1,C1) =A1&B1&C1 =A1 & '.' & B1 & '@' & C1 & '.it.com'
LEFT	Extracts the furthest left characters.	=LEFT(A1,4)
RIGHT	Extracts the furthest right characters.	=RIGHT(A1,2)
MID	Extracts characters from a starting point.	=MID(A2,4,6)
LEN	Calculates the length of a string.	=LEN(A1)
UPPER	Converts text into upper case.	=UPPER(A1)
LOWER	Converts text into lower case.	=LOWER(A1)
FIND	Searches for a substring within a string and returns its position.	=FIND('@', A2)

Table 8.5: Text functions.

WORKED EXAMPLE 8.26

In **8.19 Text functions.xlsx**, text functions have been used to extract data. Before looking in detail at how each function works, can you predict which function has been used in each of the cells D1, D2, A5, B5, C5, D5, row 7 and row 8?

	A	B	C	D
1	Mr	Minjun	Park	Mr Minjun Park
2				Mr Minjun Park
3				
4	Apples	Bananas	Strawberries	Pears
5	App	as	awb	5
6				
7	APPLES	BANANAS	STRAWBERRIES	PEARS
8	apples	bananas	strawberries	pears

Figure 8.37: Extracted data.

We can now look at each of the functions that have been used. Experiment by changing values and looking at what difference it makes.

	A	B	C	D
1	Mr	Minjun	Park	=(A1 & " " & B1 & " " & C1)
2				=CONCATENATE(A1," ", B1, " ", C1)
3				
4	Apples	Bananas	Strawberries	Pears
5	=LEFT(A4,3)	=RIGHT(B4,2)	=MID(C4,4,3)	=LEN(D4)
6				
7	=UPPER(A4)	=UPPER(B4)	=UPPER(C4)	=UPPER(D4)
8	=LOWER(A4)	=LOWER(B4)	=LOWER(C4)	=LOWER(D4)

Figure 8.38: Extracted data functions.

Notice how D1 and D2 return the same values. These are two different methods of concatenating data.

For apples, the first three characters from the left are extracted which are 'App'. For bananas, the last two characters from the right are extracted which are 'as'. For strawberries, the three characters starting at character 4 ('a') are extracted which are 'awb'.

For pears, the length is shown which is the number of characters in 'Pears' which is '5'.

Row 7 converts the data from row 4 into upper case and row 8 converts the data from row 4 into lower case.

PRACTICAL ACTIVITY 8.17

Look at the spreadsheet in Figure 8.39 and the function used to calculate the username of students in a school.

	A	B	C	D
1	Forename	Surname	Year	Username
2	Harjinder	Singh	2013	=UPPER(RIGHT(C2,2)&LEFT(A2,3)&LEFT(B2,3))
3	Abigail	Drew	2009	=UPPER(RIGHT(C3,2)&LEFT(A3,3)&LEFT(B3,3))
4	Poonam	Patel	2011	=UPPER(RIGHT(C4,2)&LEFT(A4,3)&LEFT(B4,3))

Figure 8.39: Text functions.

1. Describe what the function does and how the username is formed.

2. Calculate the usernames for each of the three students.

3. Write a function that will work out their email addresses. Their email addresses are surname.i.yy@ textfunctionschool.edu where surname is their surname, i is the first initial of their forename and yy is the last two digits of the year they joined the school. The email address should be in lower case.

4. Write a function to calculate the length of the email address.

The FIND function can be used to find the position of a substring within a string. For example, FIND('@', 'username@domain.com') will return the number 9 because the @ symbol is in position 9.

WORKED EXAMPLE 8.27

In **8.20 Find.xlsx**, the FIND function has been used to calculate the position of a specific character in A1, A2 and A3. Can you predict which character the FIND function is looking for?

	A	B
1	Train	5
2	Aeroplane	8
3	Lorry	#VALUE!

Figure 8.40: Finding a character.

CONTINUED

In this example, the FIND function was being used to find the value 'n'. As 'n' does not exist in 'Lorry', it returned an error. Later in this chapter you will find out how to manage errors in spreadsheets.

	A	B
1	Train	=FIND("n",A1)
2	Aeroplane	=FIND("n",A2)
3	Lorry	=FIND("n",A3)

Figure 8.41: Finding a character function.

The next part of the spreadsheet uses the FIND function to find the @ symbol in an email address and then returns the characters after the @ symbol. These characters form the domain name of the email address.

	A	B
5	mpark@dmail.com	
6	Domain:	dmail.com
7		dmail.com

Figure 8.42: Extracting a domain name.

In cell B6, the RIGHT function is used to extract data from the right-hand side of the email address. However, to do this the number of characters to extract needs to be calculated. This can be done by subtracting the position of the @ symbol from the length of the email address.

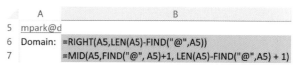

	A	B
5	mpark@d	
6	Domain:	=RIGHT(A5,LEN(A5)-FIND("@",A5))
7		=MID(A5,FIND("@", A5)+1, LEN(A5)-FIND("@",A5) + 1)

Figure 8.43: Extracting a domain name functions.

Notice how cell B7 uses the MID function instead of RIGHT to return the same result. Can you explain how this function is working?

PRACTICAL ACTIVITY 8.18

1   Create a function to find the position of the phonetic sound 'igh' in a word.

2   Create a function to extract the part of a word that comes before the phonetic sound 'igh'. For example, for 'bright', the function should extract 'bri'.

Data type functions

Questions can be asked about data to determine if it is of a particular type or even if a cell contains an error.

Function	Purpose	Example
ISTEXT	Returns TRUE if a value is text.	=ISTEXT(A1)
ISNUMBER	Returns TRUE if a value is a number.	=ISNUMBER(A1)
ISNONTEXT	Returns TRUE if a value is not text.	=ISNONTEXT(A1)
ISERROR	Returns TRUE if a cell contains an error.	=ISERROR(A1)

Table 8.6: Data type functions.

WORKED EXAMPLE 8.28

The file **8.21 Data type functions.xlsx** uses the ISTEXT, ISNUMBER, ISNONTEXT and ISERROR functions:

	A	B	C	D	E
		ISTEXT	ISNUMBER	ISNONTEXT	ISERROR
1					
2	Hello	TRUE	FALSE	FALSE	FALSE
3	012 555 555	TRUE	FALSE	FALSE	FALSE
4	BD54QRT	TRUE	FALSE	FALSE	FALSE
5	258	FALSE	TRUE	TRUE	FALSE
6	19.32	FALSE	TRUE	TRUE	FALSE
7		FALSE	FALSE	TRUE	FALSE
8	#DIV/0!	FALSE	FALSE	TRUE	TRUE
9	#VALUE!	FALSE	FALSE	TRUE	TRUE

Figure 8.44: Data type results.

CONTINUED

These are the functions that were used in the example above:

	A	B	C	D	E
1		ISTEXT	ISNUMBER	ISNONTEXT	ISERROR
2	Hello	=ISTEXT(A2)	=ISNUMBER(A2)	=ISNONTEXT(A2)	=ISERROR(A2)
3	012 555 555	=ISTEXT(A3)	=ISNUMBER(A3)	=ISNONTEXT(A3)	=ISERROR(A3)
4	BD54QRT	=ISTEXT(A4)	=ISNUMBER(A4)	=ISNONTEXT(A4)	=ISERROR(A4)
5	258	=ISTEXT(A5)	=ISNUMBER(A5)	=ISNONTEXT(A5)	=ISERROR(A5)
6	19.32	=ISTEXT(A6)	=ISNUMBER(A6)	=ISNONTEXT(A6)	=ISERROR(A6)
7		=ISTEXT(A7)	=ISNUMBER(A7)	=ISNONTEXT(A7)	=ISERROR(A7)
8	=A6/0	=ISTEXT(A8)	=ISNUMBER(A8)	=ISNONTEXT(A8)	=ISERROR(A8)
9	=FIND("b",A2)	=ISTEXT(A9)	=ISNUMBER(A9)	=ISNONTEXT(A9)	=ISERROR(A9)

Figure 8.45: Data type functions.

The file **8.22 Using data type functions.xlsx** contains some examples of using some of these functions in practice. Earlier in this chapter, you saw how using the find function to search for a value would return an error if the value is not found:

	A	B
1	Train	5
2	Aeroplane	8
3	Lorry	#VALUE!

Figure 8.46: Find function causing error.

We can fix this by using the iserror function to check if an error has been found. If an error is found, then the value 0 could be returned, or something else like 'Not found':

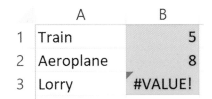

	A	B
1	Train	=IF(ISERROR(FIND("n",A1)),0,FIND("n",A1))
2	Aeroplane	=IF(ISERROR(FIND("n",A2)),0,FIND("n",A2))
3	Lorry	=IF(ISERROR(FIND("n",A3)),0,FIND("n",A3))

Figure 8.47: Removing an error.

CONTINUED

The ISNUMBER function could be used to check a value is a number before performing a calculation on it. This could avoid errors. In the example below, ISNUMBER is used to check a value is a number before trying to divide it by two:

	A	B
5	one	=IF(ISNUMBER(A5),A5/2,"")
6	1	=IF(ISNUMBER(A6),A6/2,"")
7	1.5	=IF(ISNUMBER(A7),A7/2,"")

Figure 8.48: Avoiding errors.

If the value in column A is a number, then it is divided by 2, otherwise a blank value is displayed.

PRACTICAL ACTIVITY 8.19

1   Modify the function below from the file **8.20 Find.xlsx** so that it returns the value 'Invalid email address' if the @ symbol is not found:

mpark@dmail.com
Domain: =RIGHT(A5,LEN(A5)-FIND("@",A5))

2   Test the function works by inputting an invalid email address without the @ symbol.

Lookup functions

Lookup functions will look up a value in a table and return another value in the same row or column. VLOOKUP is used to look for a value in a column and return a value from the same row. HLOOKUP is used to look for a value in a row and return a value from the same column.

The VLOOKUP function uses the syntax:

=VLOOKUP(Search Value, Lookup Table, Column, Match)

Search Value is the value being looked up in the table. Lookup Table is the range of cells that define the location of the table. Column is the number of the column that should be returned as the result in the matching row of the value that was found. Match defines whether an exact match should be found – TRUE for approximate match or FALSE for exact match.

WORKED EXAMPLE 8.29

8.23 Months.xls contains a table in the worksheet **Months** that lists the numbers that represent months, the three-letter shortened version of each month's name, the full name of each month and the French name of each month.

	A	B	C	D
1	Number	3 Letter	Month	Francais
2	1	Jan	January	Janvier
3	2	Feb	Febuary	Février
4	3	Mar	March	Mars
5	4	Apr	April	Avril
6	5	May	May	Mai
7	6	Jun	June	Juin
8	7	Jul	July	Julliet
9	8	Aug	August	Août
10	9	Sep	September	Septembre
11	10	Oct	October	Octobre
12	11	Nov	November	Novembre
13	12	Dec	December	Décembre

Figure 8.49: Lookup table.

The worksheet **Number** asks the user to enter a number that represents a month and it will then look up that number in the table and return the three-letter code, full month name and French month name.

	A	B
1	Enter the number of the month:	
2	2	
3		
4	3 Letter code:	Feb
5	Month:	Febuary
6	Francais:	Février

Figure 8.50: Number worksheet.

These are the VLOOKUP functions that were used:

	A	B
1	Enter the number of the month:	
2	2	
3		
4	3 Letter code:	=VLOOKUP(A2, Months!A2:D13,2,FALSE)
5	Month:	=VLOOKUP(A2, Months!A2:D13,3,FALSE)
6	Francais:	=VLOOKUP(A2, Months!A2:D13,4,FALSE)

Figure 8.51: Lookup functions.

VLOOKUP functions can also be replicated in the same way as any other function. The main problem with this though is that the lookup table cell references will change as they are copied down the rows.

PRACTICAL ACTIVITY 8.20

Open **8.24 VLookup Price Categories.xls** which calculates the prices of tickets purchased for a show.

1. Look at the lookup table on the **Ticket Categories** worksheet. It shows the prices for each category.
2. Look at the function in C2 on the **Ticket Sales** worksheet. Describe what this function is doing.
3. Replicate the function from C2 down the column.
4. What has gone wrong?
5. Why has it gone wrong?

One way of overcoming this is to change all the cell references in the lookup table (but not the lookup value) to be absolute cell references. An easier way of overcoming this is to name the lookup table as a named range.

PRACTICAL ACTIVITY 8.21

Continue using **8.24 VLookup Price Categories.xls**.

6. Name the range containing the lookup table on the **Ticket Categories** worksheet (do not include the titles in the range).
7. Change the VLOOKUP function in C2 to include the named range instead of the range 'Ticket Categories'!A1:B5
8. Replicate the function from C2 down the column and it should find the correct prices for each category of ticket.

So far you have seen VLOOKUP functions that find an exact match within a table. However, there are occasions when an exact match is not required, but the closest value below or equal to the search value should be found.

WORKED EXAMPLE 8.30

8.25 Exam Results.xls includes a lookup table of the minimum mark required to achieve each grade. This table has been called 'GradeBoundaries' as the named range.

GradeBoundaries

	A	B
12	Mark	Grade
13	0	U
14	24	E
15	30	D
16	36	C
17	42	B
18	48	A

Figure 8.52: Non-matching VLOOKUP table.

Each student's marks are entered in cells B2 to B10 which has been named 'Mark'. The VLOOKUP function is then used to look up the Mark in the GradeBoundaries table and return the second column, which is the grade. Not many of the marks are an exact match and so the TRUE element at the end of the function means that the closest mark below or equal to the student's mark will be found and the grade returned as the answer.

	A	B	C	D
1	Student	Mark	Grade	Function
2	1	5	U	=VLOOKUP(Mark,GradeBoundaries,2,TRUE)
3	2	30	D	=VLOOKUP(Mark,GradeBoundaries,2,TRUE)
4	3	35	D	=VLOOKUP(Mark,GradeBoundaries,2,TRUE)
5	4	22	U	=VLOOKUP(Mark,GradeBoundaries,2,TRUE)
6	5	49	A	=VLOOKUP(Mark,GradeBoundaries,2,TRUE)
7	6	47	B	=VLOOKUP(Mark,GradeBoundaries,2,TRUE)
8	7	48	A	=VLOOKUP(Mark,GradeBoundaries,2,TRUE)
9	8	39	C	=VLOOKUP(Mark,GradeBoundaries,2,TRUE)
10	9	25	E	=VLOOKUP(Mark,GradeBoundaries,2,TRUE)

Figure 8.53: Non-matching VLOOKUP function.

It is essential that the lookup table's first column is in order from lowest to highest for this to work.

The HLOOKUP function works in a very similar way to the VLOOKUP function, but instead of searching for values down the table, it searches for values across the table.

The HLOOKUP function uses the syntax:

=HLOOKUP(Search Value, Lookup Table, Row, Match)

Search Value, Lookup Table and Match are the same as in the VLOOKUP function. Row is the number of the row that should be returned as the result in the matching column of the value that was found.

WORKED EXAMPLE 8.31

8.26 HLookup.xls lists products and their prices and the discounts that are currently being applied to each of those products. The function used in D2 for the Discount Rate is:

=HLOOKUP(C2,DiscountRates,2,FALSE)

The discount rate code (C2) is looked up in the named range DiscountRates (B13:F14) and the corresponding rate in the second row of the table is returned as the discount rate.

	A	B	C	D	E	F
1	Product	Price	Discount rate	Discount	Discounted value	Discounted price
2	Product 1	$ 101.96	B	30%	$ 30.59	$ 71.37
3	Product 2	$ 99.51	A	40%	$ 39.80	$ 59.71
4	Product 3	$ 142.15	C	20%	$ 28.43	$ 113.72
5	Product 4	$ 186.94	B	30%	$ 56.08	$ 130.86
6	Product 5	$ 171.80	D	10%	$ 17.18	$ 154.62
7	Product 6	$ 215.88	B	30%	$ 64.76	$ 151.12
8	Product 7	$ 213.39	E	5%	$ 10.67	$ 202.72
9	Product 8	$ 222.17	A	40%	$ 88.87	$ 133.30
10	Product 9	$ 199.98	C	20%	$ 40.00	$ 159.98
11	Product 10	$ 86.40	E	5%	$ 4.32	$ 82.08
12						
13	Code	A	B	C	D	E
14	Rate	40%	30%	20%	10%	5%

Figure 8.54: Hlookup.

The INDEX function will find a value based on its position within a table. The INDEX function uses the syntax:

=INDEX(Lookup Table, Row, Column)

Lookup Table is the table where the value will be found. Row is the number of the row to use within the table (different to the worksheet row number) and column is the number of the column to use within the table.

WORKED EXAMPLE 8.32

8.27 Months index.xls includes a table of months in short form, full word and the French translation. The table has been called 'Months' as the named range.

	A	B	C	D
1	3 Letter	Month	francais	
2	Jan	January	janvier	
3	Feb	February	février	
4	Mar	March	mars	
5	Apr	April	avril	
6	May	May	mai	
7	Jun	June	juin	
8	Jul	July	juillet	
9	Aug	August	août	
10	Sep	September	septembre	
11	Oct	October	octobre	
12	Nov	November	novembre	
13	Dec	December	décembre	

Figure 8.55: Table of months.

To find the French word for July, this INDEX function would be used:

=INDEX(Months,7,3)

Months is the name of the table used to lookup the value. The number 7 is the row where the month of July is to be found. The number 3 is the column where the French translations are to be found.

PRACTICAL ACTIVITY 8.22

Open 8.28 Days index.xls

1 Create an INDEX function in C10 to find the full name of the 5th day of the week.

2 Create an INDEX function in C12 to find the 3 letter version of the 2nd day of the week.

3 Create INDEX functions in B16, B17 and B18 to find the 3 letter version, full name and German names for the day number input by the user in cell F14. The INDEX function should work for any value between 1 and 7 that is input in F14.

The MATCH function will find the position of a value in a list. Its MATCH function uses the syntax:

=MATCH(Search Value, Lookup Table, Type)

Search Value is the value to be found in the list. Lookup Table is the table to find the value. Lookup Table must be a one-dimensional list (e.g. values in one row or one column only). Type is a type of search which can be one of 3 values:

Type	Description
0	Finds the position of the value that is EQUAL to the Search Value. The Lookup Table can be in any order.
1	Finds the position of the largest value that is less than or equal to the Search Value. The Lookup Table must be in ascending order.
−1	Finds the position of the smallest value that is greater than or equal to the Search Value. The Lookup Table must be in descending order.

Table 8.7: Type values.

WORKED EXAMPLE 8.33

8.29 Match.xls includes a list of products and their prices in Turkish Lira. Figure 8.56 shows the list of products and their prices.

	A	B
1	**Product**	**Price**
2	Clock	₺30.80
3	Water bottle	₺6.50
4	Crisps	₺3.70
5	Calculator	₺59.50
6	Ring binder	₺13.20
7	Telephone	₺95.00

Figure 8.56: List of products and prices.

To find the position of Crisps in the list of products, the following function can be used:

=MATCH('Crisps', A2:A7,0)

This will search for Crisps in the Lookup table A2:A7 and find the position for an exact match.

Amir has ₺10 available to spend. To find the most expensive product that he can buy with his ₺10 he needs to find the position of the largest value that is less than or equal to ₺10. First, the table needs to be sorted into ascending order of price:

	D	E
1	**Product**	**Price**
2	Crisps	₺3.70
3	Water bottle	₺6.50
4	Ring binder	₺13.20
5	Clock	₺30.80
6	Calculator	₺59.50
7	Telephone	₺95.00

Figure 8.57: Product list in ascending price order.

Now a MATCH function can be used:

=MATCH(10,E2:E7,1)

The number 1 indicates that the largest value that is less than or equal to the search value should be found. This will return the value 2 which is the position of the largest value that is less than or equal to 10 (6.50).

To find the cheapest product that Amir could not afford, the list needs to be sorted into descending order.

	G	H
1	**Product**	**Price**
2	Telephone	₺95.00
3	Calculator	₺59.50
4	Clock	₺30.80
5	Ring binder	₺13.20
6	Water bottle	₺6.50
7	Crisps	₺3.70

Figure 8.58: Product list in descending order of price.

The MATCH function can then be used to find the position of the smallest value that is greater than or equal to ₺10:

=MATCH(10,H2:H7,−1)

The number −1 indicates that the smallest value that is greater than or equal to the search value should be found. This will return the value 4 which is the position of the smallest value that is greater than or equal to 10 (6.50).

PRACTICAL ACTIVITY 8.23

Open **8.30 Match marks.xls**

1   Create a MATCH function in E11 to find the position of Balraj in the list of names.

2   Create a MATCH function in E12 to find the position of the highest mark that is below 90. (Remember to sort the list)

3   Create a MATCH function in E13 to find the position of the lowest mark that is above 50. (Remember to sort the list)

4   Use an INDEX function and the result in E13 to find the value of the lowest mark that is above 50.

Nested formulas and functions

A nested formula or function is one which can include more than one function or formula. Each nested formula or function is surrounded by brackets and will be calculated before the formula or function surrounding it is completed.

WORKED EXAMPLE 8.34

8.31 Nested Formula.xls calculates the average mark using separate total and average functions in columns F and G.

	A	B	C	D	E	F	G	H	I	J	K	L	M
1	Student	Mark 1	Mark 2	Mark 3	Mark 4	Total	Average						
2	Name 1	98	40	36	84	258	65	=IF(G2>(SUM(G$2:G$10)/COUNT(G$2:G$10)),"Above","Below")					
3	Name 2	31	67	61	77	236	59	Below					

Figure 8.59: Nested IF.

In column H, a nested formula has been used to calculate whether each student is above or below the average mark. It examines the average mark for the student in column G, then divides the total of all the average marks by the number of average marks to see if column G is higher. If column G is higher then 'Above' is displayed otherwise 'Below' is displayed.

PRACTICAL ACTIVITY 8.24

Open **8.32 Profit calculator.xls**.

1   Create a single nested formula for E2 that will calculate the total profit made for product 1.

2   Replicate this formula for products 2 and 3.

3   Without using the AVERAGE function, create a nested formula to calculate the average total profit in E5.

Conditional functions

The functions you have seen so far will always perform their calculation. However, a conditional function will only perform the calculation if certain criteria are met.

WORKED EXAMPLE 8.35

8.33 IF functions.xls contains a simple quiz that asks users what the capital city of a country is. If the user gives the correct answer then they are told 'Well done' otherwise they are told 'Oops'.

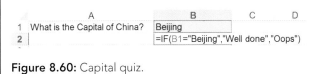

	A	B	C	D
1	What is the Capital of China?	Beijing		
2		=IF(B1="Beijing","Well done","Oops")		

Figure 8.60: Capital quiz.

An IF function has three elements as shown in Table 8.8.

Element	Purpose	Example
Condition	Specifies the rules to be checked.	B1 = 'Beijing'
True Value	Specifies what to display if the condition is met.	'Well Done'
False Value	Specifies what to display if the condition is not met.	'Oops'

Table 8.8: IF function elements.

PRACTICAL ACTIVITY 8.25

Open **8.33 IF functions.xls** and use the **Capitals Quiz** worksheet.

1 Why does the spreadsheet say 'Oops' when the answer for the capital of France is correct?

2 Fix the IF function for the capital of France so it works properly.

3 Test your function by entering an incorrect answer.

4 Add another question in row 7 and write an IF function to give feedback to the user.

CONTINUED

This is quite a slow way of creating a quiz. Try this more efficient method:

1 Put the answers to each question in column C next to where the user will put their answer in column B.

2 Change the IF function in B2 to be =IF(B1=C1,'Well done','Oops')

3 Now replicate this to the other two questions and write another two so you have five in total.

Notice how much quicker it is now to add the new questions because you don't have to keep editing the IF function. However, the user can see the answers. Use security measures such as hiding columns and worksheet protection to hide the answers from the user.

Open the worksheet **Mark Book**.

1 Students need to get 75 marks or more to pass maths, otherwise they fail. Write a function in D4 to display Pass or Fail.

2 Replicate this function for the other maths results.

3 Students need to get 60 marks or more to pass English, otherwise they fail. Write a function in D12 to display Pass or Fail.

4 Replicate this function for the other English results.

If needed, more than one criterion can be used by using AND or OR within the condition element of the IF function.

Nested IF

It is possible to have an IF function nested within another IF function. This can be useful if there are two or more alternative outputs. Sometimes the same result can be achieved with a lookup function.

WORKED EXAMPLE 8.36

8.34 Nested IFs.xls contains a mark book on the **Mark Book** worksheet. Students who get a mark of 80 or above get a distinction. Those who get a mark below 40 get a fail. All other students get awarded a pass. Notice how a nested IF has been used to show the grades.

	A	B	C	D	E	F	G
1	**Maths**						
2	**Student**	**Mark**	**Grade**				
3	Matthew	94	=IF(B3>=80,"Distinction",IF(B3<40,"Fail","Pass"))				
4	Elijah	75	Pass				
5	Caleb	39	Fail				

Figure 8.61: Nested IF example.

PRACTICAL ACTIVITY 8.26

Open **8.34 Nested IFs.xls** and use the worksheet **Mark Book**.

1   Create a lookup table for the grades.

2   Change the nested IF functions to lookup functions.

Using the same file, switch to the **Ticket Sales** worksheet which shows ticket sales for three different price categories.

1   Change the lookup function for the price to a nested IF function.

2   Replicate the function down the column.

Where the option for a lookup function exists, it is better to use this than a nested IF, especially if there are lots of options to choose from. However, sometimes decisions are made based on more than one item of data, in which case a nested IF function is the only possible option.

WORKED EXAMPLE 8.37

Open **8.35 Photo frames.xls**, which shows the charges made for a photo frame with a standard embossing or a gold embossing. The user can select Standard or Gold embossing and the quantity to purchase. The price can be determined by this algorithm:

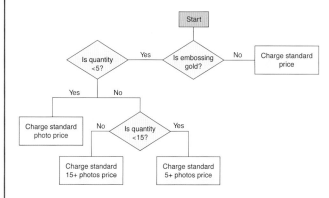

Figure 8.62: Flowchart algorithm.

A nested IF function is used to determine the price by following the same algorithm:

	A	B	C	D	E	F	G
1	Embossing	Photo price	5+ photos	15+ photos			
2	Standard	$ 1.00	$ 0.80	$ 0.70			
3	Gold	$ 1.80					
4							
5	Embossing:	Standard					
6	Quantity:	5					
7	Unit price:	=IF(Embossing="Gold",B3,IF(Quantity<5,B2,IF(Quantity<15,C2,D2)))					
8	Total price:	$ 4.00					

Figure 8.63: Nested IF for unit price.

A nested IF can become quite complex and difficult to follow. To overcome this, IFS can be used instead. This works by using pairs of conditions and outputs:

=IFS(condition1, output1, condition2, output2, condition3, output3 .....)

The only downside of IFS is that it does not have an ELSE option.

WORKED EXAMPLE 8.38

8.36 IFS instead of nested IF.xlsx contains the same mark book used in example 8.36 . The nested IF has been replaced with the IFS function. Notice how the condition and output pairs are used and also how an extra condition has had to be included for 'Pass' because there is no ELSE option.

	A	B	C	D	E	F	G
1	**Maths**						
2	**Student**	**Mark**					
3	Matthew	29	=IFS(B3>=80,"Distinction",B3>=40,"Pass",B3<40,"Fail")				
4	Elijah	22	Fail				
5	Caleb	32	Fail				
6	Joshua	61	Pass				

Figure 8.64: IFS instead of nested IF.

PRACTICAL ACTIVITY 8.27

Open 8.37 Photo Frames.xlsx.

1   Replace the nested IF function in B7 with an IFS function.

WORKED EXAMPLE 8.39

8.38 Maths results.xls results shows the marks and grades awarded to students taking a maths test. In cell C3, a COUNTIF function is used to count only those students who achieved a Pass.

	A	B	C	D	E
1	**Maths**				
2	**Student**	**Mark**	**Grade**		
3	Matthew	91	Distinction		
4	Elijah	89	Distinction		
5	Caleb	51	Pass		
6	Joshua	38	Fail		
7	Huan	92	Distinction		
8	Junayna	42	Pass		
9	Yuki	32	Fail		
10	Menekse	54	Pass		
11					
12	Total students				
13	Passes		=COUNTIF(C3:C10,"Pass")		
14	Fails				
15	Distinctions				

Figure 8.65: Maths results COUNTIF.

Conditional statistical functions

You have already been introduced to the SUM function and the AVERAGE function. Both of these have similar functions that will only perform that function if a certain condition is met. There is also a count function that will only count items that meet certain criteria (see Table 8.9).

Function	Purpose	Example
COUNTA	Counts all values in a range.	=COUNTA(H3:H200)
COUNTIF	Counts all values that meet a criterion within a range.	=COUNTIF(H3:H200,'Yes') Only counts cells that contain 'Yes'.
SUMIF	Adds up all values that meet a criterion within a range.	=SUMIF(J3:J200,'<0') Only adds up negative numbers.
AVERAGEIF	Calculates the average of all values that meet a criterion within a range.	=AVERAGEIF(J3:J200,'>0') Only finds the average of positive numbers.
MAXIFS	Calculates the largest numeric value that meets one or more criteria in a range of values.	=MAXIFS(value_range, range1, criteria1, range2, criteria2, …)

Table 8.9: Conditional statistical functions.

PRACTICAL ACTIVITY 8.28

Open **8.38 Maths results.xls** used in worked example 8.39.

1   Use a function to count all the students in cell C12.

2   Use a function to count all the students who failed the test in C14.

3   Use a function to count all the students who achieved a distinction in cell C15.

4   Use functions to calculate the average distinction mark, pass mark and fail mark in cells C17 to C19.

Open **8.39 Member ratings.xls** which shows how many meetings each member of a club has attended. Members who have attended 50 meetings or more are awarded 'Gold member' status.

1   Use a function in B13 to calculate how many members have Gold member status.

2   Use a function in B14 to calculate the total number of meetings that have been attended by Gold members.

The MAXIFS function works slightly differently to the other functions above. It can use a single range to check that a condition is met or it can use multiple ranges to check if multiple conditions have been met. It will then calculate the maximum value within a different range that relates to the ranges used for conditions.

WORKED EXAMPLE 8.40

8.40 Maxifs.xlsx contains a set of class marks, together with the names, gender and class of each student who achieved those marks. It also calculates the maximum female mark, maximum male mark and can also use two conditions to calculate the maximum female mark from class A and the maximum male mark from class A.

CONTINUED

	A	B	C	D
1	Name	Gender	Class	Mark
2	Alfie	M	A	16
3	Ramesh	M	A	15
4	Gertrude	F	A	14
5	Samir	F	A	19
6	Tavleen	F	B	17
7	Roy	M	B	16
8	Sky	F	B	14
9	Donald	M	B	18
10				
11	Max female mark:			19
12	Max male mark:			18
13	Max female mark class A:			19
14	Max male mark class A:			16

Figure 8.66: IFS instead of Nested IF.

To calculate the maximum female mark and maximum male mark, only one criterion is needed for each. In cell D11, the range D2:D9 refers to the rang that will be used to calculate the maximum mark. The range B2 to B8 is the range that will be used for the criteria which in this case will be that the gender must be female.

	A	B	C	D
1	Name	Gender	Class	Mark
2	Alfie	M	A	16
3	Ramesh	M	A	15
4	Gertrude	F	A	14
5	Samir	F	A	19
6	Tavleen	F	B	17
7	Roy	M	B	16
8	Sky	F	B	14
9	Donald	M	B	18
10				
11	Max female mark:			=MAXIFS(D2:D9,B2:B9,"F")
12	Max male mark:			=MAXIFS(D2:D9,B2:B9,"M")
13	Max female mark class A:			=MAXIFS(D2:D9,B2:B9,"F",C2:C9,"A")
14	Max male mark class A:			=MAXIFS(D2:D9,B2:B9,"M",C2:C9,"A")

Figure 8.67: IFS functions instead of Nested IF.

To calculate the maximum male mark in class A, two criteria are needed. This is where MAXIFS enables more criteria to be used. In cell D14, the same range of D2:D9 is used to find the maximum mark. Similarly, the same range of B2:B9 is used to check that the value is 'M' for male. However, another range and criterion pair has been added which is that within C2:C9, the class must be 'A'.

PRACTICAL ACTIVITY 8.29

Open **8.40 Maxifs.xlsx** which you saw in worked example 8.40.

1 Create two new functions to calculate the maximum female mark for class B and the maximum male mark for class B.

Open **8.38 Maths results.xls** which you saw in worked example 8.39.

2 Create a new function to calculate the highest distinction mark achieved, highest pass mark achieved and highest fail mark achieved by students in this class.

Questions

1 Describe the purpose of a named range of cells.
2 Describe the difference between a formula and a function.
3 Compare absolute cell referencing with relative cell referencing.
4 Using an example, describe how absolute cell referencing could be used in a spreadsheet.

8.4 Validation rules

The principle of validation was introduced in Chapter 1. Spreadsheet software can apply validation rules to data that is input. If data passes the validation rule, then it will be accepted. If data fails the validation rule, then it will be rejected and an error message may be shown.

WORKED EXAMPLE 8.41

In this spreadsheet, the user is asked to enter a person's gender. They have two valid options – 'Male' or 'Female'. The user has accidentally entered 'Mal' which is not a valid option. An error message has appeared telling the user what to do to fix the problem.

CONTINUED

Figure 8.68: Male/female validation fail.

This is the rule that had been set up:

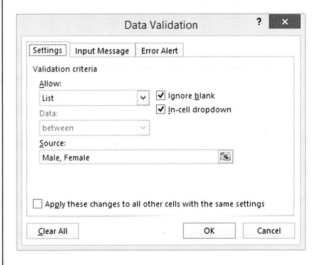

Figure 8.69: Male/female validation setup.

The rule ensures that the only data that can be entered must exist in the list that contains 'Male' and 'Female'. It is a lookup in list method of validation.

PRACTICAL ACTIVITY 8.30

Create a new spreadsheet.

1 Create a validation rule that will only allow the entry of 'Junior', 'Intermediate' or 'Senior'.

2 Set up an appropriate error message.

Error messages must clearly tell the user what they have done wrong and what they should do to put it right. An error message that simply says 'Error' or 'Invalid Data' is not helpful to the user.

The validation rules that can be used in spreadsheet software include lookup in list, range, type (integer and real) and length. A range check can be set up with the following properties:

- between two values
- equal to a value
- not equal to a value
- greater than a value
- greater than or equal to a value
- less than a value
- less than or equal to a value.

WORKED EXAMPLE 8.42

This validation rule is a range check that checks input data is a whole number between 1 and 99.

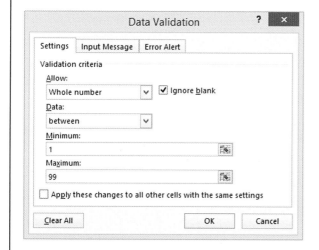

Figure 8.70: Range validation.

Question

5   The data below is an extract from a spreadsheet.

Customer	Product Code	Price	Quantity
K&N Motors	QRV58N	$28.50	2
Cosmic Flavours	PWC48H	$19.23	1
Boldmere Carpets	GEV28X	$218.29	1

a   Using the example shown, describe **three** types of validation rule that could be applied to the Product Code.

b   Using the example shown, describe **two** different types of validation rule that could be applied to the Quantity.

8.5 Test a spreadsheet structure

Test validation

When testing validation rules work, it is important to enter four different types of test data as part of a test plan.

Type of test data	Purpose
Normal (valid / acceptable data)	Data that should pass the validation rule.
Abnormal (erroneous / invalid data)	Data that should generate an error message.
Extreme	Data that will only just pass the validation rule because it is on the boundary of acceptable data.

Table 8.10: Types of test data.

WORKED EXAMPLE 8.43

Here is some test data that could be used to test the validation rule whole number BETWEEN 5 and 20:

Test data input value	Type of test data	Expected result
10	Normal	Accepted
5	Extreme	Accepted
20	Extreme	Accepted
3	Abnormal	Error message
−10	Abnormal	Error message
abc	Abnormal	Error message
10.5	Abnormal	Error message

PRACTICAL ACTIVITY 8.32

Generate test data that will test the following rules. You should use a table with three columns: test data value, type of test data and expected result. Ensure you cover all four types of test data.

- input value is a whole number <1000
- input value is a decimal >25
- input value is between 100 and 200
- input value = PASS or FAIL (there are no extreme tests for this)
- input value exists in list Junior, Intermediate, Senior (there are no extreme tests for this)

Test formulas and functions

Testing of validation rules is just one aspect of testing. All formulas and functions also need testing. To test a formula or function, you need to identify input data that will be used for the calculation and the expected output data (result of calculation). The expected output data should be calculated using traditional methods and then compared with the result from the spreadsheet. It is also essential to identify which worksheet the input data and output data are on as they may be on different worksheets and the tester will need to find the data. Other aspects such as cell and worksheet protection and conditional formatting can also be tested. It is not possible to test every possible input value, but a good range should be used, especially extreme values which are small and large. Abnormal input values should only be used if validation rules have been set up.

WORKED EXAMPLE 8.44

This test plan tests the formula in C6 of = A6 + B6

Test data input value	Type of test data	Expected result
A6 = 5, B6 = 8 on Addition worksheet	Normal	C6 = 13 on Addition worksheet
A6 = 30 000 000, B6 = 80 000 000 on Addition worksheet	Extreme	C6 = 110 000 000 on Addition worksheet and is fully visible
A6 = 0, B6 = 0 on Addition worksheet	Extreme	C6 = 0 on Addition worksheet

When a tester runs a test plan, there will be an additional column called 'Actual result' where the results of the test will be entered.

PRACTICAL ACTIVITY 8.33

Open **8.42 Testing task.xls** and run the tests from Worked Example 8.44.

1 Record the results in **8.43 Test results.doc**.
2 If a test fails, record what happened.

PRACTICAL ACTIVITY 8.34

Open **8.44 Invoices.xls** and **8.45 Test plan.doc** and complete the test plan with at least six other tests. Calculate the expected result using traditional methods and then enter the input data and compare with the actual result.

Test data input value	Type of test data	Expected result	Actual result
Quantity for Product 3 on Invoice worksheet = 36 Cost for Product 3 on Invoice worksheet = $1,345.00 VAT rate on Data worksheet = 20%	Normal	VAT for Product 3 on Invoice worksheet = $9,684.00	

Test plans are often written during the design stage of a system life cycle. At this point, cell references are unlikely to be known. Therefore, cell references can be replaced with a description of the input. It must be clear to the tester where to input the test data.

Question

6   The data below is an extract from a spreadsheet.

Customer	Product Code	Price	Quantity
K&N Motors	QRV58N	$28.50	2
Cosmic Flavours	PWC48H	$19.23	1
Boldmere Carpets	GEV28X	$218.29	1

A customer name should always be present, a product code should be exactly 6 characters long and the quantity must be an integer above zero.

Using the example shown, complete the test table below.

Test data input value	Type of test data	Expected result	Reason for choosing data
Customer = Null			
Customer = _____	Normal		
Product Code = XYZ12AB			
Product Code = _____		Error: 'You must input a product code with 6 characters'.	
Quantity = 'a'			
Quantity = _____	Extreme	Value accepted	It's the smallest allowable quantity.
Quantity = _____		Value accepted	

8.6 Use a spreadsheet

Extract data using filters

Figure 8.71: Coffee filter paper in use.

When there is a lot of data listed in a spreadsheet, users may want to view just some of that data. This can be achieved by filtering the data that is required. The term filter is used to relate to the user's mental model. When coffee is filtered, the granules are left in the filter while the flavoured drink flows through the filter.

WORKED EXAMPLE 8.45

In this example, people with a title of 'Dr' have been filtered.

	A	B	C	D	E
1	Title	First Name	Surname	Membership status	Gender
67	Dr	Forename 141	Surname 141	Full	Patron
111	Dr	Forename 57	Surname 57	Full	Male

Figure 8.72: Dr filter.

PRACTICAL ACTIVITY 8.35

Open **8.11 Member List.xls** and apply the following filters:

1 People with a membership status of Full.

2 People who do not want to be emailed.

3 People who have been a member for one year.

4 People who are either Full or Patron members.

In practical activity 8.35, the last filter that you applied was to find members who were either Full or Patron members. This uses a Boolean operator known as OR. It means that either condition can be true. Other Boolean operators include AND and NOT.

WORKED EXAMPLE 8.46

This filter shows members who have NOT lapsed their membership:

Figure 8.73: NOT.

This filter will show members who have five or more years of membership AND less than seven years of membership:

Figure 8.74: AND.

CONTINUED

This is the result of the filter:

	A	B	C	D	E	F	G
1	Title	First Name	Surname	Membership status	Gender	Do not email	Number of years
13	Mrs	Forename 3	Surname 3	Full	Female	FALSE	5
23	Mr	Forename 50	Surname 50	Full	Male	FALSE	5
24	Mrs	Forename 7	Surname 7	Full	Female	FALSE	5
37	Mr	Forename 90	Surname 90	Lapsed	Male	FALSE	6
38	Miss	Forename 10	Surname 10	Full	Female	TRUE	6
39	Mr	Forename 110	Surname 110	Full	Female	FALSE	6
50	Ms	Forename 24	Surname 24	Patron	Female	FALSE	5
52	Mr	Forename 69	Surname 69	Full	Male	FALSE	6
53	Mr	Forename 15	Surname 15	Junior	Female	TRUE	5
58	Mr	Forename 129	Surname 129	Lapsed	Female	FALSE	5
61	Mr	Forename 133	Surname 133	Patron	Female	FALSE	6
74	Mr	Forename 122	Surname 122	Lapsed	Female	FALSE	5
78	Mrs	Forename 14	Surname 14	Lapsed	Female	FALSE	6
83	Mr	Forename 108	Surname 108	Patron	Male	FALSE	5
88	Mr	Forename 37	Surname 37	Full	Male	FALSE	5
114	Mr	Forename 48	Surname 48	Full	Male	FALSE	5
128	Mr	Forename 89	Surname 89	Lapsed	Male	FALSE	5
132	Mr	Forename 78	Surname 78	Full	Male	FALSE	6
146	Mr	Forename 70	Surname 70	Full	Male	FALSE	6

Figure 8.75: AND result.

Special text filters can be applied as shown in Table 8.11.

Filter	Purpose	Example
Contains	Selects data in a column that includes the text specified.	Contains 'CH' will select all data in a column where CH exists anywhere within each data item. Chicken, Reach, Church and Ache would all be included, but not Card.
Starts with	Selects data in a column that starts with the text specified.	Starts with 'CH' will select all data in a column where the data starts with CH. Chicken and Church would all be included, but not Reach, Ache or Card.
Ends with	Selects data in a column that ends with the text specified.	Ends with 'CH' will select all data in a column where the data ends with CH. Church and Reach would be included but not Chicken, Ache or Card.

Table 8.11: Text filters.

Filters that find a range of data can be used with numbers, dates and times as shown in Table 8.12.

Filter	Purpose	Example
Greater than	Selects data in a column that is greater than the value specified.	>10 Lists 11 but not 9 or 10.
Less than	Selects data in a column that is less than the value specified.	<10 Lists 9, but not 10 or 11.
Greater than or equal to	Selects data in a column that is greater than or equal to the value specified.	>=10
Less than or equal to	Selects data in a column that is less than or equal to the value specified.	<=10

Table 8.12: Filtering for a range.

PRACTICAL ACTIVITY 8.36

Open **8.46 USA addresses.xls** and apply the following filters:

1   State is Arizona 'Az' OR California 'CA'.

2   City starts with 'San'.

3   Company ends with 'Inc'.

4   Company includes '&'.

5   Position is <=10.

6   Position is >10 AND <=50.

7   State is NOT = 'FL' AND NOT = 'OH'.

Sort data

It is possible to sort data into ascending or descending order. If only a selection of columns are sorted, then only the data within those columns will be sorted. To keep all data in each row together, do not highlight the data. To sort on more than one column, it is necessary to specify the sort order for each column and which column should be sorted first. If you wanted to sort by surname and then sort any matching surnames by forename, then you would sort by surname first.

PRACTICAL ACTIVITY 8.37

Open **8.46 USA addresses.xls** and sort data into the following order:

- Position from 1 to 500.

- Position from 500 to 1.

- State in alphabetical order from A to Z.

- City in reverse alphabetical order.

- Surname in alphabetical order from A to Z with Forename as the secondary sort.

It's not just text and numbers that can be sorted into order. Dates and times can also be sorted.

Summarise and display data

Pivot tables

A pivot table will provide summary data such as totals and averages for a data set. It's a very powerful feature because it replaces the need for several functions. Summary data can also be grouped by chosen items.

WORKED EXAMPLE 8.47

The file **8.11 Member list.xls** contains a list of members of a club including their membership status, gender, whether they want to be contacted by email and how many years they have been a member. There are 148 members in total. Figure 8.76 shows an extract of the data.

	A	B	C	D	E	F	G
1	Title	First Name	Surname	Membership Status	Gender	Do Not Email	Number of Years
2	Mrs	Forename 6	Surname 6	Full	Female	FALSE	13
3	Mr	Forename 32	Surname 32	Full	Male	FALSE	11
4	Ms	Forename 22	Surname 22	Patron	Female	FALSE	1
5	Mr	Forename 144	Surname 144	Junior	Female	TRUE	14
6	Mr	Forename 101	Surname 101	Patron	Male	FALSE	15
7	Mr	Forename 85	Surname 85	Lapsed	Male	FALSE	4

Membership List | Pie Chart | Pivot Tables

Figure 8.76: Extract of members list.

The Pivot Tables worksheet of the file includes some more pivot tables. One of the pivot tables shows the average number of years of membership for each type of member and gender of member. This can be seen in Figure 8.77

	A	B	C	D
30	Average of Number of Years	Gender		
31	Membership Status	Female	Male	Grand Total
32	Full	7.9	9.2	8.9
33	Junior	9.6	8.8	9.4
34	Lapsed	7.1	5.5	6.6
35	Patron	6.5	9.6	7.8
36	Grand Total	7.6	8.8	8.3

Membership List | Pie Chart | Pivot Tables

Figure 8.77: Pivot table.

CONTINUED

Figure 8.78 shows how the membership status has been selected as the row, the gender as the column, and the average number of years as the value to display.

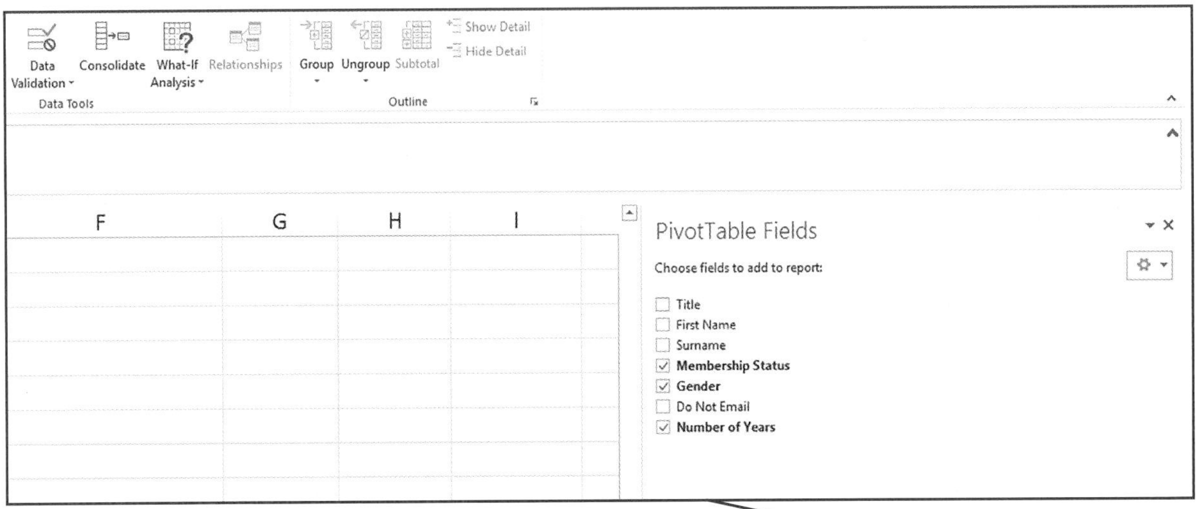

Sum of Number of Years	Gender		
Membership Status	Female	Male	Grand Total
Full	12.26%	44.64%	56.90%
Junior	8.60%	4.30%	12.91%
Lapsed	10.88%	3.57%	14.45%
Patron	7.95%	7.79%	15.75%
Grand Total	39.69%	60.31%	100.00%

Figure 8.78: Pivot table configuration.

A pivot table can sumarise data based on any row or column in the data source. Summary data can include the sum, count, average, maximum, minimum and standard deviation. The data can also be shown as a percentage of the total set of values.

WORKED EXAMPLE 8.48

Figure 8.79 shows the number of years for each type of member grouped by gender as a percentage of the total number of years of membership. For example, 4.3% of all members are junior male members.

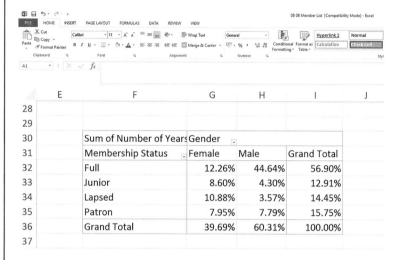

Figure 8.79: Pivot table showing percentage of total.

Pivot charts

A pivot chart works in a similar way to a pivot table but shows the data graphically. It takes just a few seconds to set up a pivot chart showing summary data.

WORKED EXAMPLE 8.49

This pivot chart shows the number of members in each membership category and how many are male and female.

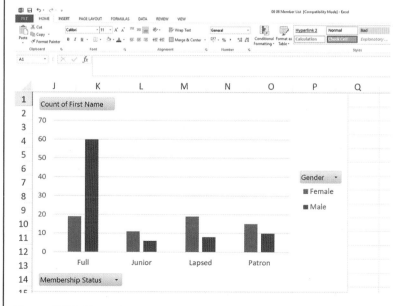

Figure 8.80: Pivot chart.

CONTINUED

To set up this pivot chart, the membership status was selected for the axis, the gender for the series and the number of first names for the values.

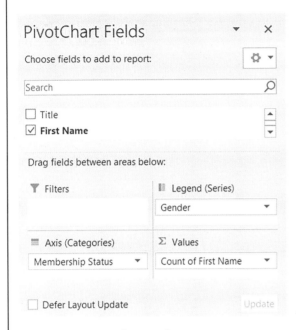

Figure 8.81: Pivot chart configuration.

PRACTICAL ACTIVITY 8.38

Open **8.47 IQ.xls** which shows the IQ of 500 people. Create pivot tables to show:

1   The number of people in each state.
2   The number of people in each age group in each state.
3   The number of people in each county of the state of Arizona (AZ). [Hint: use a filter for the state.]
4   The average IQ for each state.
5   The average IQ for each age group in each state.
6   The number of people and the average IQ for each age group in each state.
7   Create pivot charts to show the data in tasks 1, 3, 4 and 5.
8   Create a pivot chart to show the number of people in each age group in the state of New York (NY).

Import and export data

Data can be **imported** from other formats such as a comma separated values (CSV) file, text (TXT) file or from a database. When importing, you should already have the spreadsheet software open and open the file to be imported from within the spreadsheet software. You will often have to ensure that when opening you have selected the option to show all files.

PRACTICAL ACTIVITY 8.39

Within your spreadsheet software, open **8.48 Instructor.txt** and select options which will cover the following:

1   This is a delimited file that is separated by commas.

2   The file has data headers in the first row.

3   The Date of Birth should be in date format with no time.

4   The charge should be in currency.

5   Use the find and replace option in the Weekends column only to replace 1 with 'Yes' and 0 with 'No'.

Within your spreadsheet software, open **8.49 Driving school.accdb** and import the Learner table.

Try to open **8.50 Lessons.doc** from your spreadsheet software. It is unlikely that your spreadsheet software will recognise how to import this data. It is essential to ensure that the data being imported is structured in a way in which the spreadsheet software can understand it by using rows of data and separating columns with a special symbol such as a comma.

Data can also be **exported** so that it can be used in other software. If it is exported in a common format such as CSV or TXT, then other software will be able to recognise the rows and columns. Formats such as portable document format (PDF) will enable the data to be viewed by a wide variety of users but not manipulated, so PDF is good for showing output data.

PRACTICAL ACTIVITY 8.40

Open **8.46 USA addresses.xls** and export it to the following formats:

- CSV
- TXT
- PDF
- Open Document Spreadsheet (ODS) – works with Open Office
- Web page (HTML).

View the files that you have exported the data to and note how the data has been stored.

8.7 Automate operations within a spreadsheet

Create macros

Macros are a set of instructions that run all at once. They are usually created by recording a set of actions. This is done by defining a starting point (e.g. clicking on a record button), then performing the actions, and then defining a stopping point (e.g. clicking on a stop button). The actions that have been recorded can then be repeated at any time by running the macro. A macro is usually run by clicking on a button, selecting a menu option or by using a shortcut key combination. Once a macro has been recorded, it can also be edited to make fine adjustments to it.

Examples of macros could include:

- moving to a different worksheet
- changing the style of a cell
- sorting data into a set order
- finding specific items of data
- resetting input cells so they are blank.

WORKED EXAMPLE 8.50

8.51 Macro Cuboid.xlsm calculates the volume of a cuboid. Dimensions can be input in the yellow cells and the volume is shown in the blue cell.

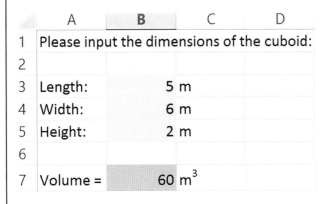

	A	B	C	D
1	Please input the dimensions of the cuboid:			
2				
3	Length:	5 m		
4	Width:	6 m		
5	Height:	2 m		
6				
7	Volume =	60 m^3		

Figure 8.82: Cuboid calculation.

A macro has been recorded to clear the contents of the input values for length, width and height.

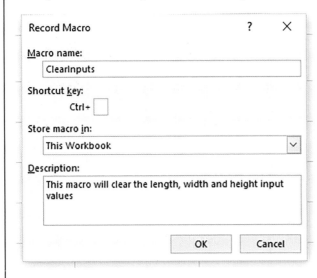

Figure 8.83: Recording the macro.

The following steps were taken to record the macro:

- The Start Recording option was chosen
- Macro was given a name 'ClearInputs'
- Cells B3:B5 were selected
- The delete key was pressed
- Cell B3 was selected
- The Stop Recording option was chosen.

Each time the macro is run, the length, width and height inputs are cleared:

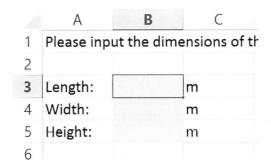

	A	B	C
1	Please input the dimensions of th		
2			
3	Length:		m
4	Width:		m
5	Height:		m
6			

Figure 8.84: After macro has been run.

When recording a macro, the spreadsheet software will usually generate some code for the macro which will allow the developer to fine tune how the macro works.

The code generated for the macro that was recorded to clear the cuboid input values is:

```
Sub ClearInputs()
' ClearInputs Macro
' This macro will clear the length, width and height input values
    Range("B3:B5").Select
    Selection.ClearContents
    Range("B3").Select
End Sub
```

Figure 8.85: Code for macro.

PRACTICAL ACTIVITY 8.41

Open **8.52 Macros.xlsm**

1   Click on the buttons on the **Macros Examples** worksheet and see what the macros do.

2   Create the macros suggested in the workbook.

Table 8.13 shows advantages and disadvantages of macros.

Advantages of macros	Disadvantages of macros
Repetitive tasks can be performed quickly rather than having to perform them manually over and over again.	The macros need to be created before they can be used.
Complex tasks can be completed quickly by simply clicking a button or a shortcut key.	Macros can easily go wrong and perform the wrong actions if they have not been created properly or are not started from the intended starting point.
Enables software to be tailored to meet the needs of users.	If only shortcut keys are used then it can be difficult for users to remember the shortcuts.

Table 8.13: Advantages and disadvantages of macros.

Customise the user interface

Macros can be run from a menu but this can often require quite a few actions. For example, in Microsoft Excel this would require the following actions:

• Click on Developer ribbon

• Click on Macros button

• Select the macro to run

• Click on Run.

Instead, a button can be added to the spreadsheet screen that will run the macro with a single click.

WORKED EXAMPLE 8.52

8.51 Macro Cuboid.xlsm includes a button that runs the macro to clear the input values.

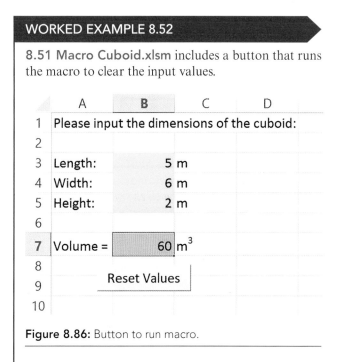

Figure 8.86: Button to run macro.

Other form controls include those shown in Table 2.5 in Chapter 2.

WORKED EXAMPLE 8.53

8.53 Form Controls.xlsx has a data entry screen for applying for a lease for a holiday home using a spreadsheet.

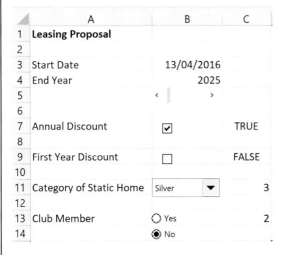

Figure 8.87: Form controls.

Below the End Year is a scroll bar, sometimes called a spinner, which changes the value of the contents of cell B4. Although it looks like the scroll bar is in B5, it is actually an object that is 'floating' above the spreadsheet.

Next to Annual Discount is a tick box, often called a check box, which changes the value of cell C7. If it is ticked, C7 will be TRUE but if it is not ticked then C7 will be FALSE. Similarly, the tick box next to First Year Discount is linked to cell C9.

The drop down box, often called a combo box, can have three values of Platinum, Gold or Silver. When a value is selected, the value in C11 changes to match the position in the list of the value in the drop down box. For example, Silver is the 3rd item in the list, so the value of C11 is 3.

The option buttons for Yes or No are linked to cell C13. If Yes is selected then the value of C13 will be 1 and if No is selected then the value of C13 will be 2.

PRACTICAL ACTIVITY 8.42

You are going to create a worksheet that will be used as an input form for data relating to feed in tariffs for renewable energy. Feed in tariffs are payments made to a customer for supplying electricity back to the national grid. You do not need to create any calculations. Figure 8.88 shows an example of what the input form might look like.

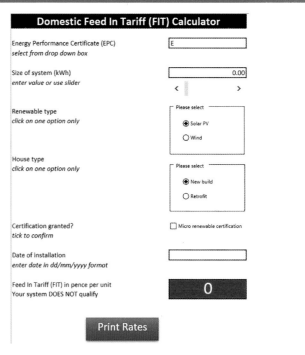

Figure 8.88: Feed in tariff input form.

CONTINUED

1   Create a drop-down box (combo box) for the Energy Performance Certificate (CPC) which can be A, B, C, D, E, F or G.

2   Create a scroll bar or slider or spinner to change the size of the system. The size of the system can range from 0.01 kWh to 9.99 kWh. Hint: use values 1 to 999 and divide the result by 100.

3   Create a grouped set of option buttons for the renewable type which can either be 'Solar PV' or 'Wind'.

4   Create a grouped set of options for the house type which can either be 'New build' or 'Retrofit'.

5   Create a tick box for the micro renewable certification.

8.8 Graphs and charts

Analyse and select a chart

Graphs or charts are used to show information in a way that makes it easy to compare values. This could be as simple as showing the monthly sales in a column or bar chart or it could be more complex and show how hospital waiting times vary during a month compared with their targets. Charts that show more than one set of data are known as comparative charts because data for one set can be compared against data for another set.

WORKED EXAMPLE 8.54

8.54 Graphs and Charts.xls includes some examples of graphs and charts. The worksheet **Monthly Sales** contains a bar chart showing the Monthly sales over a period of 12 months. Notice how a chart title and x-axis title have been included:

Figure 8.89: Monthly sales bar chart.

The comparative bar chart on the worksheet **Worldwide Sales** compares the sales of different continents for each of the months in 2015. Notice how a legend is used to show which continent is represented by which colour:

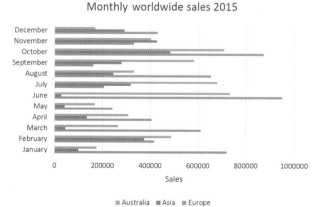

Figure 8.90: Worldwide sales comparative bar chart.

CONTINUED

The chart currently shows sales for Australia, Asia and Europe but it may be that only the sales for Europe and Australia need to be shown. Australia and Europe are in non-contiguous (non-adjacent) columns. One way of creating the graph would be to select only the columns that are required. Depending on the software being used, this can often be achieved using the Ctrl key to highlight non-contiguous columns:

	A	B	C	D
1	Monthly Sales	Europe	Asia	Australia
2	January	767784	153710	444583
3	February	845619	483590	495572
4	March	547861	10578	537289
5	April	487561	122980	513220
6	May	876780	470416	454170
7	June	719862	46656	534387
8	July	258994	156400	648415
9	August	527236	340102	542103
10	September	790027	175028	782983
11	October	683973	370258	244798
12	November	843379	438223	656699
13	December	395084	288689	667735

Figure 8.91: Selecting non-contiguous columns.

Note that this method can be used to select any specified range of data. Another way to achieve this would be to remove the Asia data series from the chart:

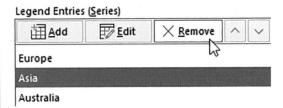

Figure 8.92: Removing Asia data series.

The chart is also only showing the sales values at intervals of 200,000. This can be changed to a different data interval by setting the major units. In the example below, the data interval (major units) have been set to 100,000 and to enable more space on the graph, the display units have been set to Thousands:

Figure 8.93: Changing data interval.

The graph now looks like this:

Figure 8.94: Monthly worldwide sales bar chart.

CONTINUED

If we wanted to add the Asia series of data back again, then we could add a new series and specify the range of data to use (C2:C13) and the name of the series (C1 = 'Asia'):

	A	B	C
1	**Monthly Sales**	**Europe**	**Asia**
2	January	767784	153710
3			483590
4			10578
5			122980
6			470416
7	June	719862	46656
8	July	258994	156400
9	August	527236	340102
10	September	790027	175028
11	October	683973	370258
12	November	843379	438223
13	December	395084	288689

Edit Series dialog box overlay:
Series name: ='Worldwide Sales'!$C$1 = Asia
Series values: ='Worldwide Sales'!$C$2:$C$13 = 153710, 483590...
OK   Cancel

Figure 8.95: Adding Asia data series.

Line graphs are similar to bar charts in that they show the size of data, but they are mainly used to show how data changes over a period of time.

WORKED EXAMPLE 8.55

The first line graph on the worksheet **Waiting List** in **8.54 Graphs and charts.xls** shows how waiting times at the Kerslake Hospital have fallen over a four-year period. Notice how the minimum value on the y-axis scale is 2.0 hours and the maximum value is 3.6 hours. The y-axis scale has intervals of 0.2 hours. Both y and x-axes have been given axis titles.

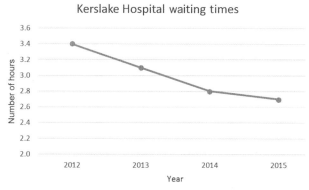

Figure 8.96: Kerslake Hospital line graph.

The comparative line graph on the worksheet Waiting List compares the waiting times of three hospitals over a four-year period with the target waiting time of 2.5 hours. Notice how the y-axis scale has intervals of 0.5 hours, the maximum value for the y-axis scale is 5.0 and the minimum value for the y-axis scale is 1.5.

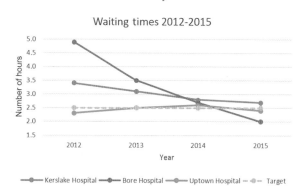

Figure 8.97: Hospital waiting times comparative line graph.

While pie charts can also sometimes be used to show actual values, they are usually used to show proportional data. Pie charts showing proportional data show the proportion or percentage of each data item.

WORKED EXAMPLE 8.56

The worksheet Head Boy in **8.54 Graphs and charts. xls** contains a pie chart showing the proportion of votes received for each student standing in an election for head boy of a school. Notice how a legend is not necessary because each segment has been labelled with the name of the data item. Each segment has also been labelled with the percentage of the total vote that each data item represents, and the sector for the boy with the most votes has been extracted (exploded).

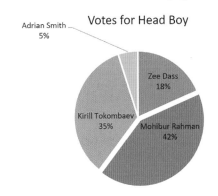

Figure 8.98: Head Boy pie chart.

Finally, look at the Financial Performance tab on the worksheet. It contains a combination chart. Think about what information is being conveyed here.

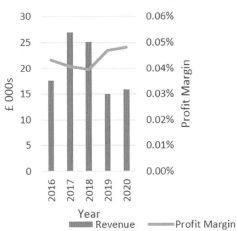

Figure 8.99: Combination chart.

Sometimes, two different data series relating to different data sets need to be plotted on the same chart but they have a different set of values. In this case, a combination (combo) chart can be used which would include a column chart for one set of data and a line graph for the other set of data.

WORKED EXAMPLE 8.57

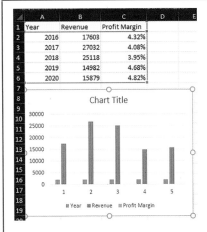

Figure 8.100: Column chart.

In this example, the contiguous (adjacent) columns for Year, Revenue and Profit Margin have been selected to create a column chart. However, the Year has not been automatically selected as the value for the x-axis. The horizontal axis labels are currently shown as:

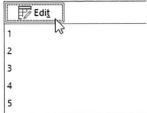

Figure 8.101: Horizontal axis labels.

CONTINUED

This can be changed by editing the horizontal axis labels to use the specified range A2:A6 where the years are found in the table:

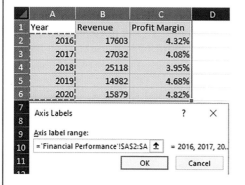

Figure 8.102: Editing horizontal axis labels.

The Year can also be removed from the legend and series data:

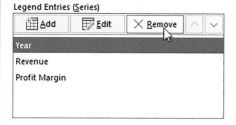

Figure 8.103: Removing the Year.

The graph now includes the revenue and profit margin but the profit margin is so small compared with the revenue that it can't be seen:

Figure 8.104: Chart with revenue and profit margin.

A secondary axis is required for the profit margin data series. The chart type can be changed to a combination (combo) chart with the Profit Margin as a Line Chart and having its own secondary axis:

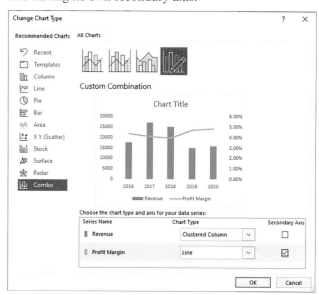

Figure 8.105: Combination chart.

Finally, the chart title, axis labels and units can be added:

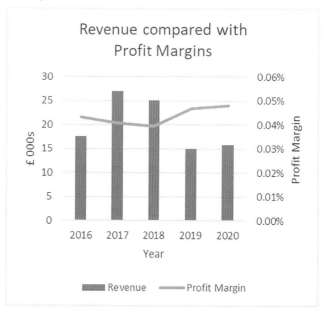

Figure 8.106: Final chart.

When selecting which type of graph or chart to produce, you should consider the general rules shown in Table 8.14.

Type of graph / chart	Purpose
Bar / column chart	Used to show a single series of data in columns or rows.
Comparative bar / column chart	Used to compare more than one series of data in columns or rows.
Line graph	Used to show how a single series of data changes over a period of time.
Comparative line graph	Used to compare how more than one series of data changes over a period of time.
Pie chart	Used to show the proportion that is used by each item of data.
Combination (combo) chart	Used to show more than one series of data using a combination of a column and line chart where there is a secondary axis.

Table 8.14: Rules for selecting type of graph or chart.

Formatting a graph or chart

When creating a graph or chart, you should ensure that it is formatted appropriately.

Label	Purpose
Title	A brief overview of what the graph or chart is showing.
Legend	A key to show what the colours used represent.
Series label	The name given to a series which can be used on a legend.
Value axis label	Each of the axes (usually x and y) should include the values including any units.
Category axis label	Each of the axes should include a title to state what the data represents.

Label	Purpose
Secondary axis	A second axis used to show data for a different set of values to the primary axis but using the same direction of axis.
Percentages	When using a pie chart, the percentages may need to be displayed for each segment.
Segment label	Instead of a legend, each segment in a pie chart could be labelled with its description.
Segment value	As well as, or instead of the percentage, each segment in a pie chart could be labelled with its quantity.
Extract / explode pie chart sector	Extract one sector of a pie chart from the rest of the pie chart by moving its position.
Scale	The scale of the y-axis can be set to a normal or logarithmic scale.
Data interval / major units	The interval between values on an axis.
Axis scale maximum	The maximum value to be used on an axis.
Axis scale minimum	The minimum value to be used on an axis.

Table 8.15: Labelling graphs and charts.

PRACTICAL ACTIVITY 8.43

Open **8.38 Maths results.xls**.

1   Create a bar chart to show the marks for each student.
2   Include a title and axis titles.

Open **8.41 Physics results.xls**.

1   Enter some marks for each student for each test.
2   Create a comparative bar chart to show the marks for each student in each of the tests 1, 2 and 3.

CONTINUED

3 Include a title and axis titles.

4 Include a legend for the tests.

5 Change the y-axis maximum scale value to be 50.

6 Change the y-axis scale to have intervals of 5.

Open **8.55 School attendance.xls**.

1 Create a comparative line graph to show the attendance of each of year 1 and year 2 over the period of the year compared with the target.

2 Label the chart appropriately.

3 Adjust the y-axis scale and maximum scale values appropriately.

4 Include a legend.

5 Change the line type of the target series to be dashed.

Open **8.11 Member List.xls**.

1 Open the worksheet **Pie Chart**. Change 'Count of Membership Status' to 'Count of membership status', 'Membership Status' to 'Membership status' and 'Grand Total' to 'Grand total'.

2 Create a pie chart to show the proportion of members for each status.

3 Give the chart a sensible title.

4 Add the percentages and membership statuses to the pie chart segments.

Open **8.26 HLookup.xls**.

1 Create an appropriate chart to show the products, original price and discounted price.

2 Label the chart appropriately.

A chart can be created in a spreadsheet and then used within other software by copying the graph and pasting it into the other software, such as word processing for a report, or presentation software for a presentation. It is also possible to link the exported chart to the original spreadsheet data so that if the data changes within the spreadsheet then the chart will update in the software to which it has been exported.

PRACTICAL ACTIVITY 8.44

Open **8.54 Graphs and charts.xls**.

1 Copy the graph Monthly sales 2015.

2 Open a word processor or presentation software.

3 Select the option to paste as a link (you may find this under paste special).

4 Ensure that the link option is selected and the object type (graph) is identified.

5 Save this new document and close it.

6 Change some of the data in the Monthly sales worksheet.

7 Save the spreadsheet.

8 Reopen the new document you created and check that the graph has changed to reflect the updated data in the spreadsheet.

Questions

7 Identify and give reasons for the most appropriate type of chart or graph to show the number of missed refuse collections shown in Table 8.16.

Year	Vesey	New Hall	Trinity
2010	2502	4571	3271
2011	2786	5728	3102
2012	1987	5645	2905
2013	2057	4972	2647

Table 8.16: Missed refuse collections.

8   Identify and give reasons for the most appropriate type of chart or graph to show the data shown in Table 8.17.

Student	Mark 1	Mark 2	Mark 3	Mark 4	Average
Name 1	98	40	36	84	65
Name 2	31	67	61	77	59
Name 3	62	58	29	38	47
Name 4	64	83	85	27	65
Name 5	87	45	64	42	60
Name 6	93	58	43	73	67
Name 7	99	29	55	92	69
Name 8	57	58	44	93	63
Name 9	45	43	98	55	60

Table 8.17: Student marks.

REFLECTION

How would you have drawn a graph or chart without being able to use a spreadsheet? What would happen to that graph or chart if the original data changed?

Discuss situations where data could be valid but incorrect.

Think about projects you have completed at school where you could have used a spreadsheet. What features of a spreadsheet would have been useful for this project and how would you have used them?

REVIEW PRACTICAL ACTIVITY

Open **8.56 Review Task.xlsx** and look at the **VehicleRates** worksheet.

A vehicle hire company rents out vehicles to customers. The types of vehicle available are shown in A4:A11 which has a named range of 'VehicleTypes'.

The table in columns A to F shows the types of vehicles available, the minimum age of drivers for each vehicle, and the charge rates for each vehicle.

The table of points in cells G7:G9 refers to a set of ranges for the number of penalty points a driver may have on their driving licence. Cells G6:G9 have been named **Points**.

Cell B13 refers to the number of drivers that will be hiring a vehicle.

1   Merge cells C2:F2, give the merged cell a yellow shading and align the text centrally in the cell.

2   Resize columns A to F so that all the data is visible.

3   Name the range A4:E12 as **VehicleRates**.

4   Insert a new row between rows 5 and 6 for an 'Estate' vehicle which has a minimum age of 21 and charging rates of £34, £38 and £42.

The charge rate is determined by the number of driving conviction points that a driver has had in the last 5 years.

- 0 conviction points = Rate 1
- 1–3 conviction points = Rate 2
- 4–6 conviction points = Rate 3

CONTINUED

If there are any additional drivers, then whoever has the highest number of conviction points is used to determine the charge rate. The driver in the example above has 3 penalty points and so would be charged rate 2.

Switch to the **Quote** worksheet.

The Quote worksheet is an input form used to calculate the cost of hiring a vehicle.

5   Create a validation rule in C16 that will only accept vehicles that exist in the named range **VehicleRates**. Use an appropriate error message if invalid data is input.

6   Create a drop-down box for the number of Conviction Points. The input range of the drop-down box should only contain the values from the named range **Points** and must be a form control, not a validation rule. The charge rate should be stored in F12.

7   Create option buttons for the number of additional drivers which can be 0, 1 or 2. The option buttons should be linked to cell B2 on the VehicleRates worksheet.

The quote reference is calculated by taking the initials of the driver and adding the year of the current date, followed by a hyphen, followed by the month of the current date, followed by another hyphen, followed by the day of the current date. For example, the reference for Caleb Andrews on 20th May 2019 would be CA2019-5-20.

8   Create a formula in F6 to calculate the quote reference.

The expiry date is calculated as 7 days after the date of the quote. Assume the date of the quote is the current date.

9   Create a formula in F8 that calculates the expiry date of the quote.

The minimum driver age is calculated by looking up the type of vehicle in the **VehicleRates** table.

10   Create a function in F10 to find the minimum driver age.

11   Create a validation rule in C18 for the youngest driver age to be at least 16. Use an appropriate error message if invalid data is input.

12   The hire rate per day is calculated by looking up the type of vehicle in the VehicleRates table and finding the correct column for the charge rate. Create a function in F14 to find the hire rate per day.

13   The number of days is calculated to be inclusive of both the date of hire and the date of return. Create a formula in F16 to show the number of days the vehicle will be hired for.

14   The hire rate is calculated by multiplying the number of days by the hire rate per day. Create a formula in F18 to calculate the hire rate. You should only use named cells within your formula.

If there is one additional driver, then there is a 15% additional cost. If there are two additional drivers then there is a 22% additional cost.

15   Create a function in F20 to calculate the additional percentage based on the number of additional drivers selected. Format the cell to display this value as a percentage.

16   Create a formula in F22 to calculate the additional charge for additional drivers.

17   Create a formula in F24 to calculate the total cost of the quote including additional drivers.

18   Format any cells that contain currency to include a currency symbol and 2 decimal places.

CONTINUED

19 Test your spreadsheet works using the following test plan:

Test data input value	Type of test data	Expected result
Firstname: Merrick Surname: Woodward Date of Hire: 21/12/2020 Date of Return: 28/12/2020 Vehicle: Hatchback Youngest driver age: 23 Conviction Points: 5 Additional drivers: 1	Normal	Quote reference: MWyyyy-mm-dd (where yyyy is current year, mm is current month and dd is current year) Expiry date: (one week after current date) Minimum driver age: 18 Charge Rate: 3 Hire rate per day: £38.00 Number of days: 8 Hire rate: £304.00 Additional drivers %: 15% Additional drivers amount: £45.60 Total quote: £349.60

20 Print a copy of the Quote worksheet in both normal view and showing formulas ensuring that no formulas or functions are truncated.

21 Protect the worksheet so that only input cells can be edited with all other cells being read-only.

22 Create a macro that will clear any input data. The macro must not clear any formulas or functions.

23 Complete the test plan below for the input of Vehicle.

Test Number	Description	Type of Test	Input Data Value(s)	Expected Output Value(s)
1	Vehicle validation		Transit	
2	Vehicle		Sedan	'You must select a vehicle from the list'

24 Complete the test plan below for the input of Youngest driver age when booking a 9-seater vehicle.

Test Number	Description	Type of Test	Input Data Value(s)	Expected Output Value(s)
3	Youngest driver age validation	Normal		
4	Youngest driver age validation	Extreme		
5	Youngest driver age validation	Abnormal		

Figure 8.107 shows cars that are owned by a driving school. It calculates the fuel type of each car, the cost per litre of each fuel type and the cost per gallon.

	A	B	C	D	E	F
1	**Registration**	**Make**	**Model**	**Fuel type**	**Cost per litre**	**Cost per gallon**
2	BX56JWL	Ford	Mondeo	Diesel	$ 1.25	$ 5.69
3	BX56JWM	Saab	Saab 9-3	Petrol	$ 1.17	$ 5.32
4	BX56JWN	Land Rover	Discovery	Diesel	$ 1.25	$ 5.69
5	BX56JWP	Smart	Smart Car	LPG	$ 0.85	$ 3.87
6	BX56JWR	Ford	Mondeo	Petrol	$ 1.17	$ 5.32
7	BX56JWS	Saab	Saab 9-3	Diesel	$ 1.25	$ 5.69
8						
9					**Fuel type**	**Cost per gallon**
10					Diesel	$ 5.69
11					Petrol	$ 5.32
12					LPG	$ 3.87

Figure 8.107: Driving school spreadsheet.

Rows and columns are used in the spreadsheet.

1 a Use an example from this spreadsheet to describe a row. **[2]**

Formulas and functions have been used in the spreadsheet. There are 4.55 litres in a gallon.

b i Using an example, describe a formula. **[2]**

ii Write the formula used in F2. **[1]**

iii Describe a function. **[2]**

iv Identify the type of formula used in E2. **[1]**

[Total 8]

The driving school would like to see all their petrol cars but not the other cars.

2 a Explain how the driving school could see all their petrol cars but not the other cars without losing any data. **[2]**

b Explain how the fuel types could be identified quickly using a different colour for each without changing them all one by one. **[2]**

[Total 4]

Absolute and relative cell referencing have been used within the spreadsheet.

3 Using examples, explain how absolute and relative cell referencing have been used. **[4]**

The spreadsheet model is going to be used to calculate the costs of using each car.

4 a Explain three advantages of using a spreadsheet to model the costs of using each car. **[3]**

b Explain one disadvantage of using a spreadsheet to model the costs of using each car. **[1]**

[Total 4]

SUMMARY CHECKLIST

- [ ] I can create and edit a spreadsheet structure to meet the requirements of an audience.
- [ ] I can protect cells and their content.
- [ ] I can freeze panes and windows.
- [ ] I can create formulas and use functions within a spreadsheet.
- [ ] I can use absolute reference, relative reference, named cells and named ranges.
- [ ] I can know and understand why absolute and relative referencing are used.
- [ ] I can use validation rules within a spreadsheet.
- [ ] I can format the content of cells and the emphasis of cells.
- [ ] I can test a spreadsheet structure including formulas, functions and validation rules.
- [ ] I can extract data from a spreadsheet using search facilities.
- [ ] I can sort data in a spreadsheet.
- [ ] I can summarise and display data using pivot tables and pivot charts.
- [ ] I can import and export data to and from a spreadsheet.
- [ ] I can create a graph or chart in a spreadsheet for a specific purpose.
- [ ] I can apply formatting to a graph or chart.

> Chapter 9

Modelling

LEARNING INTENTIONS

By the end of this chapter, you will be able to:

- use what-if analysis

- test a spreadsheet model

- describe the characteristics of modelling software

- explain the need for computer models

- evaluate the effectiveness of spreadsheet models

- explain how a model can be used to create and run simulations.

Introduction

A computer **model** is a representation of a real-world process. A model is created through mathematical analysis of the real-world process. A **simulation** is the use of a computerised model to predict how a real-life system might behave. Details in a computer model can be easily changed to see what effects they would have. This is often cheaper and safer than trying out changes on the real-world process.

KEY WORDS

model: a representation of a process

simulation: using a model to predict real-life behaviour

9.1 Characteristics of modelling software

Modelling software is used to create a model. Spreadsheets can be used to create computerised models, but there are also custom-written solutions that are used to model specific processes.

For example, a network simulator such as Cloonix can be used to model a computer network. The software produces a diagrammatic view of the devices connected to the computer network. It will be possible to identify the Internet Protocol (IP) addresses used on the network and how they are assigned through a Dynamic Host Configuration Protocol (DHCP) server. Wireless networks can be added and security can be configured to see what the effects will be. Devices can be connected to specific switches and the throughput of data traffic can be analysed.

Computer Aided Design (CAD) enables designers to produce a model of a physical object. This could include a kitchen, a building, a motor vehicle or an aeroplane. CAD software can include features such as viewing an object in two dimensions (2D) or three dimensions (3D), manipulating objects within the model, adding or removing objects, viewing the model from different angles, applying different effects such as colour and lighting, and focusing on specific features such as the electrical cabling or heating system within a building.

Modelling software will include some essential features:

- the ability to change variables within the software

- asking what-if questions to see what the result of changing variables might be

- formulas and functions to carry out the mathematical calculations that form the basis of the model

- automatic recalculation of formulas and functions

- rules that define how the model behaves

- layers of abstraction so that different parts of the model can be viewed and analysed separately.

An example of the use of modelling is to create a model of a roller coaster. Variables can include the height of each drop, the radius of loops, the starting speed of the carriage, length of each section and the weight of each carriage. Calculations will be used to define rules such as the amount of friction and how that will slow carriages down, the effect of gravity on carriages as they move up and down and the g-force that will be experienced by passengers. What-if questions could be asked such as 'What would happen if we increased the starting speed by 2 km/h?' or 'What would happen if we increased the initial drop by 5 m?' The effect of these changes in variables can then be modelled.

Experiment with a digital single-lens reflex (DSLR) camera simulator by changing the variables and seeing how this affects the end results. You can find an example simulator on the Cameraism website.

9.2 The need for computer models

There are a variety of reasons why models might be used, including training, forecasting and construction. Whatever the reason, a model must be able to answer what-if questions.

Models can be used for the purpose of training people to use equipment. This could range from learning to drive a forklift truck to flying an aeroplane or operating a nuclear power plant. Models are used for training because there is less risk of injury to the trainees and instructors than learning in a real environment. When learning to drive a forklift truck, the trainee may make a mistake by lifting a load too high and toppling the truck. In real life this could cause serious injury as well as costing money in terms of repairs, but using a model removes both of these risks. Costs are saved because real equipment does not suffer wear and tear, fuel is not required to operate machinery and instructors do not need to be present all of the time. It is also possible to test the trainee in unpredictable situations such as turbulence for an aeroplane or driving a heavy goods vehicle on ice. Unpredictable situations that would happen in real life can also be removed for trainees when they first start learning so they can focus on basic controls.

Models can also be used for forecasting. One of the most common models for this purpose is weather forecasting. Patterns that have happened in the past can be analysed along with current data to predict what the weather might be in the future. Businesses and governments use financial modelling to predict what might happen to profits or the economy. It is too risky for a business to make sudden changes in the marketplace without testing them out with a model first. A variety of what-if questions can be asked using a model to determine how to make the most profit. Variables that could be changed include selling prices, adjusting the quantity of products to supply at any given time, times of year to sell products and the effect of weather on seasonal sales.

Constructing buildings, kitchens, gardens, motor vehicles and other objects can be a very costly process. It is important to get it right first time as any adjustments that have to be made in the real world will incur financial costs. Models help to experiment with different designs to see which look is most aesthetically pleasing and which ones react best to environmental conditions. When designing a kitchen using modelling software, variables such as lighting, worktops, cupboard doors, position of units, flooring and tiling can be changed to see which configuration looks the best. Cupboards, drawers, dishwashers and cookers can be opened to see if they use the space efficiently. The angle of view can be changed in a 3D environment to see what the kitchen might look like from a variety of angles.

Models can be used to predict population growth. It's important for governments to know what future populations will be so they can plan for housing, transport infrastructure and public services. Scientists model population growth within natural habitats. They can identify the existing population and reproduction rates and predict what future populations will be. There will come a point when the population will outgrow its carrying capacity (number of inhabitants that can survive on limited resources) and the growth rate will adjust. This is known as density-dependent growth. If there are no limiting resources, then the growth rate would be expected to increase exponentially. This is known as density-independent growth.

Experiment with the Wolfram population growth model, which you can find on the Wolfram Demonstrations Project website, by changing the initial population, growth rate and carrying capacity variables.

Climate change models consider the interactions between the atmosphere, oceans, land, ice and the sun to estimate climate trends. Climate change models are used for long-term predictions and it can be decades before it will be known if the model is accurate. Models will include several scientific rules such as the first law of thermodynamics, the Stefan-Boltzmann Law, the Clausius-Clapeyron equation and the Navier-Stokes equations, but they include so many uncertainties and are so complex that there is no known exact solution. These complex models require the use of supercomputers. Climate change models differ to weather forecasting in that they predict average weather conditions over a long period of time rather than specific weather conditions on a given day. Models from the past can be tested against what really happened to see if the model was accurate, enabling the models to be improved for the future.

PRACTICAL ACTIVITY 9.03

Search on Youtube for the video of the installation of the final phase of the Met Office Supercomputer to see the scale of just one of The Met Office Hadley Centre's three Cray SC40 supercomputers which are capable of 14,000 trillion calculations a second.

Models can be used to help with queue management. This can include queues at a supermarket, telephone helpline queues and amusement parks. Being able to predict the number of customers and having rules that define how long it takes to serve each customer can help to determine how many staff are needed to serve the customers. Queues can be quite simple as in a supermarket or they can be complex where different customers are given different priorities. These rules such as 'first in first out' or 'shortest job first' will form part of the model. The behaviour of customers can also form part of a model, including balking (deciding not to join a queue if it is too long), jockeying (switching between queues) and reneging (leaving a queue). Variables will include number of customers, number of servers, time to serve a customer and expected number of customers at different times of the day.

Models can also be used for traffic flow. This can help with planning new roads, improving existing roads or building new shopping centres or residential areas. Models will take into account existing traffic movement and projected changes in the number of vehicles expected along a route. The model can be used to experiment with different traffic control measures such as traffic lights, traffic islands or traffic calming measures. Transport planners can then see what effect making changes to the roads would have without committing to projects that might not be suitable. Variables within the model can include length of vehicles, vehicle speed, average acceleration of vehicles and congestion. Different modelling techniques are used, such as microscopic models that model the behaviour of single vehicles, and macroscopic models that model the behaviour of a stream of vehicles.

PRACTICAL ACTIVITY 9.04

Go to the Onramp traffic simulation website and try out their model of road traffic flow.

Identify the variables that can be changed and what the effects are of changing these.

What questions could you ask of the model?

9.3 What-if analysis

What-if analysis is the process of asking the question 'what would happen if … ?'.

KEY WORD

what-if-analysis: experimenting with changing variables to see what would happen to the output if those variables changed

---

Some examples of what-if questions in a financial spreadsheet model might include:

- What happens to the total income for the month if we increase the selling price by 20%?

- What happens to our costs if we use a different supplier for one of our parts?

- What happens to our total expenditure for the next five years if we move to new premises?

Part of what-if analysis includes the use of goal seek. It is possible to set a goal and find out what needs to be done to achieve that goal. Some examples of goal-seek questions might include:

- What price do we need to sell at in order to sell 5000 items per month?

- How many items do we need to sell to break even (zero profit and zero loss)?

KEY WORDS

goal seek: seeing what a variable needs to change to for a goal in terms of output to be achieved

---

PRACTICAL ACTIVITY 9.05

Open **9.01 bike hire.xlsx** which is a model to calculate the profit that would be made for different numbers of bikes being hired.

1   a   What would happen to the profit if the number of short male mountain bikes booked was changed to 70?

    b   What if there were no short male mountain bikes booked? Did any other data change when you changed the quantity booked?

2   What would happen to the profit if the junior hourly rate was increased to £12.50?

3   Experiment with changing other variables within the spreadsheet model and watch what happens to the outputs.

WORKED EXAMPLE 9.01

9.01 bike hire.xlsx calculates the profits for a bike hire company. In this example, the company wants to see how many bikes of a particular type they need to hire out to increase their profit to £2500:

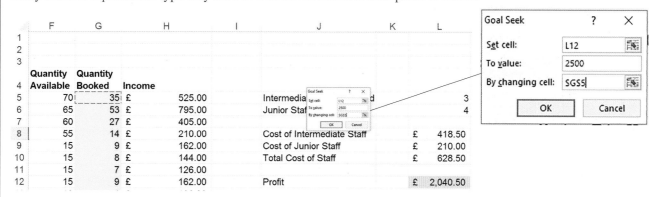

Figure 9.1: Goal seek configuration.

Figure 9.2 shows the result of the goal seek being 65.63333 bikes, which would of course need to be rounded up to 70 bikes:

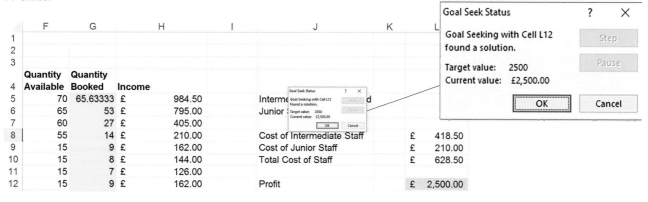

Figure 9.2: Goal seek result.

PRACTICAL ACTIVITY 9.06

Open **9.02 student marks.xlsx** which shows exam and coursework marks for students in a class.

Use goal seek to answer these questions.

1   What coursework mark would John need to increase his total mark to 390?

2   John resits exam 3. What mark does he need to increase his total to 425?

3   Sameena resits her coursework. What mark does she need to get a total of 380?

4   Fathima hasn't taken exam 3 yet. What mark does she need to get a total of 250?

5   Experiment with setting your own goals.

9.4 Test a spreadsheet model

In Chapter 8 you learned how to choose test data and to test formulas, functions and validation rules within a spreadsheet. When testing a spreadsheet model, it is important to test all aspects of the model. This could include:

- formulas and functions
- validation rules
- conditional formatting
- form controls
- graphs and charts
- cell and worksheet protection
- macros.

A test plan needs to be created to test all these aspects of the spreadsheet model. It needs to include clearly identified input values and the expected output values.

WORKED EXAMPLE 9.02

9.03 Block Paving.xlsm produces a quote for block paving a driveway. Here is an extract of a test plan for the model:

Number	Description	Type	Input Value	Expected Result
1	Area calculation	Valid	Input Screen: Length = 12, Width = 7	Area on Invoice = 84
2	Customer Name on Invoice	Valid	Input Screen: Customer Name = 'Mr. Marzi'	Invoice customer name = 'Mr. Marzi'
3	Length validation	Invalid	Input Screen: Length = 'twelve'	Error Message = 'Only use real numbers (e.g. 12.3)'
4	View Invoice Button	Button	Input Screen: Click on 'View Invoice Button'	Invoice displays in print preview mode with same data from input screen

---

PRACTICAL ACTIVITY 9.07

Open **9.03 Block Paving.xlsm**

1 Follow the test plan in Worked Example 9.02 and see if the actual results match the expected results.

2 Create another four entries for the test plan in Worked Example 9.02

3 Ask somebody else to follow your test plan entries exactly as they are written and see if there is anything you could have put more clearly.

Extension 1: add cell protection, additional form controls and conditional formatting to the spreadsheet. Extend your test plan to cover these new features of the model.

Extension 2: open **9.04 Theme Park Queue Model.xlsm** and create a test plan to test the theme park queue model. You will need to spend a bit of time understanding how the model works and how the graph and conditional formatting respond to input values.

9.5 Evaluating the effectiveness of spreadsheet models

There is a variety of tools within a spreadsheet that can be used to help with modelling:

- variables that can be changed to ask what-if questions

- formulas and functions which define the rules of the model

- graphs and charts which can show a graphical representation of the forecast

- instant, automatic recalculation of formulas, functions and graphs/charts to answer what-if questions immediately

- conditional formatting to highlight the effects

- goal-seek to find out what variables need to be changed to achieve a given outcome.

Other advantages of spreadsheet models include the ability to share the spreadsheet with colleagues easily so that many people can experiment with the model, and the fact that most organisations already own spreadsheet software which reduces the need for training and purchase costs.

Spreadsheets do have their limitations though. They are only as accurate as the formulas and functions that are the rules that represent the real world. Unless extremely complex rules are used, then a spreadsheet model will never be an accurate representation. These complex rules require mathematical and computer expertise in order to set them up and it can take a very long time to create models that are truly representative of the real world. Spreadsheets can only be used to simulate numbers, but cannot simulate the effect on objects.

Questions

1 Identify three characteristics of modelling software.

2 Describe, using examples, how a spreadsheet could be used to model the costs or savings to an organisation of moving premises.

9.6 Simulations

Advantages and disadvantages of using a model to create and run simulations

A simulation is the use of a computerised model to predict how a real-life system might behave. As with modelling, simulations can be used for training, forecasting and construction.

Advantages include:

- expensive prototypes or the real thing do not need to be created in order to experiment with different variations and answer what-if questions

- changes to the model can be made very quickly and the effect can be seen just as quickly

- alternative models and designs can be used to see how they react differently

- unusual events (for example, earthquakes) can be tested without the need to wait for them to happen in real life

- equipment does not suffer from wear and tear or damage when being tested or experimented with

- dangerous situations such as aeroplane equipment failure can be simulated without putting people in danger

- simulations can be 'sped up' so that effects can be analysed over a long period of time without having to wait for that period of time to elapse.

Disadvantages include:

- the way a simulation reacts is only as good as the model it is based upon

- simulation software and equipment can be very expensive to purchase

- people need to be trained to use simulation equipment and software

- complex models take many years to develop, especially if they are designed to react like the real process

- it is impossible for a simulation to be a perfect representation of the real-world process.

The use of simulation

Natural disaster planning

When planning for natural disasters, people need to know what the effects of a natural disaster might be.

It is impossible to do this in real life without the actual disaster happening and, as they are natural disasters, it is impossible to force them to happen. If the planners wait for the natural disaster to happen, then it is too late to plan.

Simulations based on models of natural disasters such as earthquakes, volcanic eruptions, hurricanes, bush fires and tsunamis can be used to see what the effects might be. Planners can experiment with different variables such as wind speed and direction to see how quickly a fire might spread, which will help them to plan evacuations and firefighting.

As with all simulations, these rely upon the accuracy of the model. There will be many things that the model can't predict completely, such as sudden changes in

wind direction or wind speed and emotional reactions to being evacuated. However, planners can experiment with lots of what-if questions in order to plan for a large variety of circumstances, which means that when a natural disaster does occur people can be better equipped to deal with it.

Pilot training

When it comes to large aircraft, it can cost thousands of pounds just to take off, fly and land. This cannot be repeated too often as it will become too costly to train pilots. Flight simulators can help by removing the fuel costs associated with flying. They can also remove the danger that a trainee pilot might pose if they make a mistake while in the air.

Flight simulators not only include software, but very specialised equipment which can cost hundreds of thousands of pounds. The equipment will be designed to react in a similar way to a real aircraft, so that the pilot can feel the physical effects of any movements that they make (including take off, landing, turbulence or even a crash landing) in a way that is as close to real life as possible. The software will include the rules of the model that define how the aircraft should react in a variety of circumstances.

Pilots can also practise landing and taking off at airports they have not visited before, including some of the most dangerous airports in the world such as Toncontin Airport in Honduras. Simulations give pilots the opportunity to respond to malfunctions such as an engine failure, cabin pressure failure or landing gear failure. These would be far too dangerous to attempt in real life.

Figure 9.3: Toncontin Airport.

Car driving

Simulators can be used to help to learn to drive a car. In most countries, learner drivers start immediately on the road having never used any of a car's controls before. They immediately have to deal with hazards such as other cars, pedestrians, cyclists, potholes and dangerous junctions. In addition to this, other drivers on the road are held up because of the learner driver being slow and hesitant.

Simulations can enable a learner driver to become familiar with the controls of a car and dealing with hazards before taking a car onto the road for the first time. A simulator is a safe environment and could reduce insurance premiums for driving instructors. The simulator could also be used when the learner driver needs to attempt manoeuvres such as turning in the road or reversing around a corner for the first time, rather than having to do this straight away on a real road. Even after a learner driver has passed their test, they could use simulators to learn how to drive on a motorway, drive in icy conditions and how to handle a car if it gets out of control, such as in a skid.

Simulations can also be used for racing drivers to experiment with different car setups to find the optimum configuration for a racing circuit, rather than risking crashing. Racing drivers would be able to take the car to the limit knowing that the virtual crash will not result in an injury. However, a simulation will never behave exactly the same as the real car as the rules of the model will never be perfect. Therefore it is still necessary to practise using a real racing car.

Nuclear science research

Nuclear science is very dangerous. Even a small accident could expose a person to radiation that could cause serious disfigurement or death. It is therefore not possible to experiment with nuclear reactions in the real world in the hope that something might work. Simulations can be used to try out different nuclear reactions by adjusting the coolant temperature, changing the way the control rods are used and the rate of reaction. What-if questions can be asked such as

'What happens if I increase the temperature?' and the outcomes can be seen. It's also possible to speed up the simulation so that rather than waiting hours, days or even years to see what the effects might be, results can be seen much more quickly.

Nuclear science requires a lot of computing power in order to simulate nuclear reactions. For example, reactors convert uranium and plutonium through nuclear fission which involves millions of collisions every microsecond. Even with supercomputers, nuclear scientists cannot represent all of these collisions in a simulation.

PRACTICAL ACTIVITY 9.08

Look online for a nuclear power plant simulator. An example can be found on the Dalton Nuclear website.

Questions

3   Describe two advantages of using a simulator for pilot training.

4   Describe one disadvantage of using a simulator for learning to drive.

REFLECTION

1   Consider the implications of not being able to model the effectiveness of changing the timing of traffic lights, but instead having to try it out over a period of time.

2   Think about situations that would be too dangerous for a pilot to learn how to react to in a real aircraft but would be better suited to a flight simulator.

3   Discuss what other models and simulations are used in real life.

EXAM-STYLE QUESTIONS

The spreadsheet shows cars that are owned by a driving school. It calculates the fuel type of each car, the cost per litre of each fuel type and the cost per gallon.

	A	B	C	D	E	F
1	**Registration**	**Make**	**Model**	**Fuel type**	**Cost per litre**	**Cost per gallon**
2	BX56JWL	Ford	Mondeo	Diesel	$ 1.25	$ 5.69
3	BX56JWM	Saab	Saab 9-3	Petrol	$ 1.17	$ 5.32
4	BX56JWN	Land Rover	Discovery	Diesel	$ 1.25	$ 5.69
5	BX56JWP	Smart	Smart Car	LPG	$ 0.85	$ 3.87
6	BX56JWR	Ford	Mondeo	Petrol	$ 1.17	$ 5.32
7	BX56JWS	Saab	Saab 9-3	Diesel	$ 1.25	$ 5.69
8						
9					**Fuel type**	**Cost per gallon**
10					Diesel	$ 5.69
11					Petrol	$ 5.32
12					LPG	$ 3.87

Figure 9.4: Driving school spreadsheet.

1 The spreadsheet model is going to be used to calculate the costs of using each car.

    a Explain three advantages of using a spreadsheet to model the costs of using each car. [3]

    b Explain one disadvantage of using a spreadsheet to model the costs of using each car. [1]

                                                                                                    [Total 4]

The driving school is considering purchasing a simulator to help students to learn to drive.

2 a Explain why a simulator would be used for this purpose. [4]

    b Explain the disadvantages of using a simulator for this purpose. [4]

                                                                                                 [Total 8]

3 Evaluate the use of simulators for nuclear science research. [8]

SUMMARY CHECKLIST

☐ I can use what-if analysis.

☐ I can test a spreadsheet model.

☐ I can describe the characteristics of modelling software.

☐ I can explain the need for computer models.

☐ I can evaluate the effectiveness of spreadsheet models.

☐ I can explain how a model can be used to create and run simulations.

> # Chapter 10
> # Database and file concepts

CONTINUED

- validate and verify data entry

- perform searches

- use arithmetic operations and logical functions to perform calculations within a database

- sort data

- design and create an appropriate data entry form

- design and create a switchboard menu within a database

- import and export data

- understand the characteristics of data in unnormalised form, first, second and third normal forms

- understand the advantages and disadvantages of normalisation

- normalise a database to first, second and third normal form

- understand the components of a data dictionary

- create a data dictionary and select appropriate data types for a given set of data and a given situation

- identify different data types

- use static and dynamic parameters in a query and understand their use

- understand when static and dynamic parameters should be used in queries

- understand when simple, complex and nested queries should be used

- understand when summary queries, including cross-tab queries, should be used

- understand different file types and their uses

- understand what is meant by proprietary and open-source file formats and why open-source file formats are needed

- understand why generic file formats are needed

- understand the use of indexed sequential access

- understand the use of direct file access

- understand the use of a hierarchical database management system

- understand the features of a management information system (MIS)

- understand how a MIS can be used by organisations.

- Do you understand the difference between data and information?

- Do you know what a database table is?

- Are you able to create a single database table with records and fields?

Introduction

A **database** is a structured method for storing data in sets of tables. Each **table** contains similar data about people, places, objects or events. Data can be sorted and filtered to respond to queries. Databases are used in applications such as inventory tracking and payroll management and can be used as source files for mail merge.

KEY WORDS

database: a structured method of storing data

table: a collection of related data, organised in rows and columns (for example, about people, places, objects or events)

10.1 Create a database

WORKED EXAMPLE 10.01

Figure 10.1, from **10.01 Sales processing.mdb**, contains data about customers (people):

Customer ID	Contact Forename	Contact Surname	Street Address
1	Reina	Wolchesky	305 W Washington St
2	Marc	Wenger	33 Harrison Ave
3	Damion	Matkin	5830 Downing St #-d
4	Lucius	Winchester	670 S Barrington Rd
5	Petra	Mcnichol	670 S Barrington Rd
6	Katina	Ramano	580 Fountain Ave

Figure 10.1: Customer table.

Data that is stored in a single table is called a **flat file**. Within a table are rows known as **records**. Each record is an **entity** which is a set of data about one single thing (person, place, object or event). An entity can also refer to a table within a database. In Worked Example 10.01, the data about Marc Wenger is a single record/entity.

Each entity has categories of information. These categories are known as **attributes** or **fields**. In Worked Example 10.01, Customer ID, Contact Forename, Contact Surname and Street Address are all field/attribute names.

One of the fields will be known as the **primary key**. The primary key contains a unique value for each record. This means that each value can only exist once in that table so it is possible to uniquely identify each record using the primary key. In Worked Example 10.01, Customer ID is the primary key.

The software that is used to manage the database is called a **database management system** (DBMS). Sometimes, this is referred to as a relational database management system (RDBMS) as it is managing a database that includes **relationships**.

KEY WORDS

flat file: a database stored in a single table

record: a common word for entity

entity: a set of data about one thing (person, place, object or event) or a table within a database

attribute: a category of information within an entity

field: a common word for attribute

primary key: a field that contains the unique identifier for a record

database management system: software used to manage a database

relationship: the way in which two entities in two different tables are connected

Open **10.01 Sales processing.mdb** and then open the table **Product**.

1   Identify four field names in the Product table.

2   Identify the primary key in the Product table.

3   How many records are in the Product table?

4   Identify two other tables within the database.

Data types and field sizes

Each field in a table will have a data type assigned to it. Data types include:

- text
- alphanumeric
- numeric (integer/decimal)
- date/time
- Boolean.

The Product table in **10.02 Sales processing 2.mdb** has the following data types:

Field Name	Data Type
Product ID	AutoNumber
Product Name	Short Text
Supplier ID	Number
Category ID	Number
Quantity Per Unit	Short Text
Unit Price	Currency
Units In Stock	Number
Reorder Amount	Number
Units On Order	Number
Reorder Level	Number
Discontinued	Yes/No

Figure 10.2: Product data types.

- Product Name and Quantity Per Unit are alphanumeric (Short Text is the term used by Microsoft Access) which means they can include letters, numbers and symbols.

- Units in Stock is a Number (numeric) which has been set as an integer because it only contains whole numbers.

- Unit Price is Currency (numeric) which has been set as a decimal (real) because it can contain decimal values.

- Discontinued is Yes/No (Boolean) because it can only contain Yes or No values.

The Order table has the following data types:

Field Name	Data Type
Order Number	AutoNumber
Customer ID	Number
Order Date	Date/Time
Notes	Long Text

Figure 10.3: Order data types.

- Order Number is numeric but it is also set as an AutoNumber which means a numeric value will be automatically assigned to it.

- Customer ID is numeric which has been set as an integer. It also matches the data type of the Customer ID in the Customer table which you can find within the database.

- Order Date is Date/Time and has been set as a date.

- Notes is alphanumeric but has been further defined as Long Text which means that any amount of text can be assigned to it.

Different database management systems use different names for data types. If you are using Microsoft Access, you will notice that text is used for alphanumeric data and number is used for numeric data. Sometimes the software will also use formatted data as a data type, such as currency. Currency is numeric (usually decimal) and is just formatted by displaying a currency symbol with the number.

Fields within a table will have field sizes applied to them. This is because most fields are a fixed length. This means that only a specified amount of data can be stored in each field.

Text and alphanumeric fields will have a length to specify the maximum number of characters that can be stored. For example, the Product Name in the Product table is limited to 40 characters. This avoids having lots of wasted storage space where field space is not used if the length is too long.

Numbers can also have a field size. This could be defined as the number of digits or it could be defined as the maximum numeric value.

Dates will always be the same field size as they will always store the date is the same way, but they can be formatted to be displayed differently.

Some text fields can be formatted to be a variable length which means they can store as little or as much data as possible. These are sometimes referred to as memo or long text data types. These are useful for fields that will contain notes or comments.

It is important to ensure that the field length is not too long because this will waste storage space, but it is also important to ensure that the field length is long enough to store the longest required data item.

The three relationships

Relationships within a database can be used to connect entities together. A **foreign key** is an attribute (field) in one entity that connects to a primary key in another entity. This allows related data to be looked up and found.

a

Order Number	Customer ID	Order Date
1	2	28/05/2015
2	1	22/05/2015
3	5	06/05/2015
4	3	05/04/2015
5	7	06/05/2015

b

Customer ID	Contact Forename	Contact Surname
1	Reina	Wolchesky
2	Marc	Wanger
3	Damion	Matkin
4	Lucius	Winchester
5	Petra	Mcnichol
6	Katina	Ramano

Figure 10.4: Foreign key. **a** Order table; **b** Customer table.

In the Order table, the foreign key is Customer ID which connects to the primary key Customer ID in the customer table. For Order Number 4, the Customer ID 3 is looked up in the Customer table to find Damion Matkin.

One-to-one

A one-to-one relationship is when each record in one table only connects to one record in another table. Each foreign key value will link to one primary key value and each primary key value will only be linked to by one foreign key value. The foreign key can exist on either side of the relationship.

WORKED EXAMPLE 10.04

a

Sales Rep ID	Last Name	First Name	Job Title	Title	Employee ID
1	Davolio	Nancy	Sales Representative	Ms	5
2	Fuller	Andrew	Vice President, Sales	Dr	6
3	Leverling	Janet	Sales Representative	Ms	1
4	Peacock	Margaret	Sales Representative	Mrs	2

b

Employee ID	Birth Date	Hire Date	Address
1	08-Dec-48	01-May-92	507 - 20th Ave. E.
2	19-Feb-52	14-Aug-92	908 W. Capital Way
3	30-Aug-63	01-Apr-92	722 Moss Bay Blvd.
4	19-Sep-37	03-May-93	4110 Old Redmond Rd.
5	04-Mar-55	17-Oct-93	14 Garrett Hill
6	02-Jul-63	17-Oct-93	Coventry House

Figure 10.5: One-to-one relationship. **a** Sales Rep table; **b** Employee table.

The Sales Rep table stores details of the sales representatives within a business. This only contains basic information about their name but their full employee details are stored in a separate table called Employee. Each sales representative only has one employee record and each employee record can only refer to one sales rep record.

One-to-many

A one-to-many relationship is when each record in one table can connect to many (zero or more) records in another table. A foreign key will exist within the table on the *many* side of the relationship and will connect to a primary key in the *one* side of the relationship. This is the most common type of relationship within relational databases.

WORKED EXAMPLE 10.05

The Category table stores data about the different categories of products being sold. Its primary key is Category ID. The Product table stores data about the products. The Product table has a foreign key of Category ID. Each product can only have one category. Each category can have many products. There is *one* Category to *many* Products.

a

Product ID	Product Name	Category ID
1	Chai	1
2	Chang	1
3	Aniseed Syrup	2
4	Chef Anton's Cajun Seasoning	2
5	Chef Anton's Gumbo Mix	2
6	Grandma's Boysenberry Spread	2
7	Uncle Bob's Organic Dried Pears	7
8	Northwoods Cranberry Sauce	2
9	Mishi Kobe Niku	6
10	Ikura	8
11	Queso Cabrales	4
12	Queso Manchego La Pastora	4

b

Category ID	Category Name	Description
1	Beverages	Soft drinks, coffees, teas, beers, and ales
2	Condiments	Sweet and savory sauces, relishes, spreads, and seasoning
3	Confections	Desserts, candies, and sweet breads
4	Dairy Products	Cheeses
5	Grains/Cereals	Breads, crackers, pasta, and cereal
6	Meat/Poultry	Prepared meats
7	Produce	Dried fruit and bean curd
8	Seafood	Seaweed and fish

Figure 10.6: One-to-many. **a** Product table; **b** Category table.

Many-to-many

Many-to-many relationships are only conceptual. They are not used in relational databases because they are converted into two sets of one-to-many relationships. In a many-to-many relationship, each record in one table can connect to many records in another table but each record in the other table can also connect to many records in the original table.

The Order table stores data about the orders that are placed including which products are being sold. It has a field called Product IDs which lists the products being sold on each order. Each order can have many products. Each product can exist on many orders. There are *many* Orders to *many* Products.

a

Order Number	Customer ID	Order Date	Product IDs
1	2	28/05/2015	1, 8, 4, 3
2	1	22/05/2015	1, 7
3	5	06/05/2015	2, 5, 6
4	3	05/04/2015	4
5	7	06/05/2015	3, 8

b

Product ID	Product Name	Category ID
1	Chai	1
2	Chang	1
3	Aniseed Syrup	2
4	Chef Anton's Cajun Seasoning	2
5	Chef Anton's Gumbo Mix	2
6	Grandma's Boysenberry Spread	2
7	Uncle Bob's Organic Dried Pears	7
8	Northwoods Cranberry sauce	2
9	Mishi Kobe Niku	6
10	Ikura	8
11	Queso Cabrales	4
12	Queso Manchego La Pastora	4

Figure 10.7: Many-to-many. **a** Order table; **b** Product table.

The problem with the many-to-many relationship is that it is not possible to store single data items within the foreign key. In the Order and Product example, the Product ID field contains more than one Product ID per Order and this causes a problem of non-atomic data, breaking the rules of first **normal form** which you will learn about later in this chapter.

- the table on the *many* side will have a foreign key
- the data type and field size of the foreign key must match the primary key on the *one* side
- only data items that exist in the primary key on the *one* side can be used in the foreign key.

KEY WORDS

normal form: the extent to which a database has been normalised

PRACTICAL ACTIVITY 10.04

Open **10.01 Sales processing.mdb** and open the relationships.

1   Create a one-to-many relationship between Supplier and Product.

2   Create a one-to-many relationship between Order and the Sales Rep that dealt with the order. You will need a new foreign key in the Order table.

PRACTICAL ACTIVITY 10.03

Open **10.01 Sales processing.mdb** and examine the relationships. Identify the relationships that currently exist. For example, the relationship between Sales Rep and Employee is One Sales Rep to One Employee.

Create and use relationships

One-to-many

When creating a one-to-many relationship, there are some rules to follow:

- the table on the *one* side must have a primary key

One-to-one

When creating a one-to-one relationship, there are also some rules to follow:

- at least one of the tables (table A) must have a primary key
- the other table (table B) must either have a primary key that is also a foreign key and will link to the primary key in table A or a foreign key field with a unique **index** that will link to the primary key in table A

- the data type and field size of the foreign key in table B and primary key in table A must match
- only data items that exist in the primary key in table A can be used in the foreign key in table B.

KEY WORD

index: a list of keys or keywords which identify a unique record and can be used to search and sort records more quickly

PRACTICAL ACTIVITY 10.05

Open 10.01 Sales processing.mdb and open the relationships.

Create a one-to-one relationship between Sales Rep and Employee. Employee ID should be used as the foreign key in the Sales Rep table and it will need a unique index.

If you don't have a unique index or a primary key as the foreign key, then the database software is likely to assume you want to create a one-to-many relationship instead of a one-to-one relationship.

Create and interpret an entity relationship diagram

An **entity relationship diagram** (ERD) shows the relationships (connections) between each entity.

KEY WORDS

entity relationship diagram: a diagram that represents the relationships between entities

There are three types of entity relationship diagram:

Type of ERD	Purpose
Physical	The structure of data that is or will be used within a relational database that meets both business and data needs.

Type of ERD	Purpose
Conceptual	Used during the analysis stage of the system lifecycle, a conceptual ERD shows the relationship between existing entities within a business and the attributes for each entity.
Logical	This is an extension of the conceptual ERD that includes data types. These are for analysis purposes only and the data types used in the physical ERD may be different.

Table 10.1: Types of entity relationship diagram.

In an ERD, each entity is represented by a rectangle. Each relationship is represented by a line.

WORKED EXAMPLE 10.07

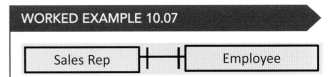

Figure 10.8: One-to-one relationship.

Figure 10.8 shows a one-to-one relationship between a Sales Rep and an Employee. Each sales rep is related to one employee and each employee can only be one sales rep.

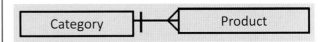

Figure 10.9: One-to-many relationship.

Figure 10.9 shows a one-to-many relationship between Category and Product. Each category can have many products, but each product has only one category.

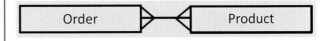

Figure 10.10: Many-to-many relationship.

Figure 10.10 shows a many-to-many relationship between Order and Product. Each order can be for many products and each product can exist on many orders. This is used in a conceptual or logical ERD only and should not be used for a physical ERD.

PRACTICAL ACTIVITY 10.06

Describe each of the relationships in Figure 10.11.

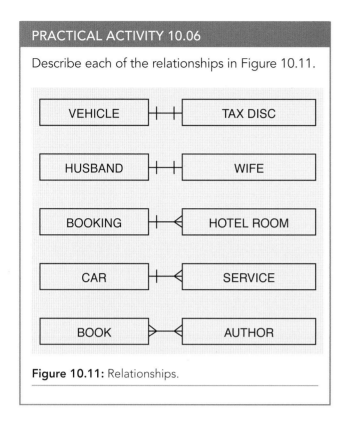

Figure 10.11: Relationships.

Different RDBMSs and analysts use different symbols. For example, Microsoft Access uses the infinity symbol for the many side of a relationship.

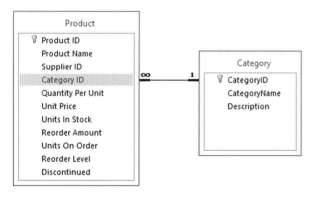

Figure 10.12: Infinity symbol.

Other RDBMSs may use two symbols at each end of the relationship. For example, 0:1 or 0| could be used to depict that there can be between zero and one related record on that side of the relationship, whereas 1:1 or || could be used to depict that there must be exactly one related record on that side of the relationship.

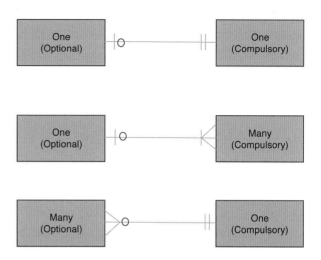

Figure 10.13: Alternative symbols.

0:M or 0< can be used to depict between zero and many related records and 1:M or |<can be used to depict that at least one record must be used on the *many* side of the relationship.

An ERD will usually have more than just two tables. The ERD in Figure 10.14 shows the relationships that exist within a bank.

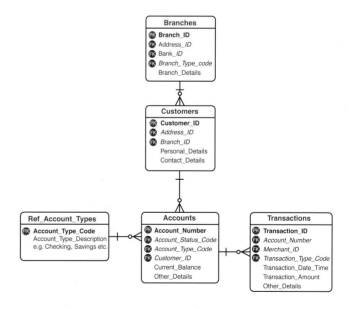

Figure 10.14: Bank relationships.

Each branch of the bank can have many customers. Each customer can have many accounts. Each account can have many transactions taking place. Each account can be of only one type but each type of account can exist as many accounts.

WORKED EXAMPLE 10.08

The Product table in **10.02 Sales processing 2.mdb** has the following relationships that have been implemented:

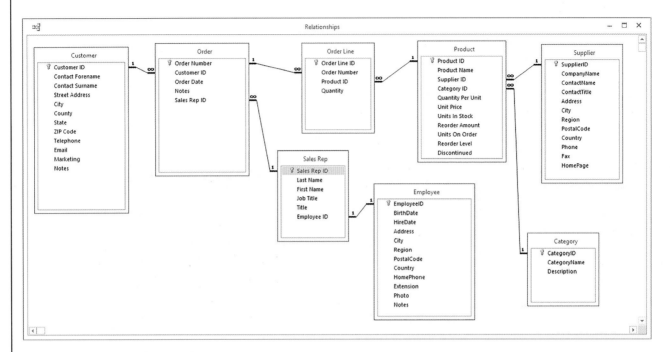

Figure 10.15: ERD Implemented.

PRACTICAL ACTIVITY 10.07

1   Draw ERDs to represent the following relationships:

   a   One Airline Seat to one Customer.

   b   One House to many Occupants.

   c   Many Coaches to many Drivers.

2   Draw an ERD to represent a library model. Within the library, there are several *books*. There may be many copies of the same *book* which are known as *book copies*. *Customers* can *loan* a *book copy*. A *customer* can have many *loans* but a *loan* will be for just one *customer*. Each *loan* will be for one *book copy* but over a period of time each *book copy* can be *loaned* out many times.

When a many-to-many relationship exists, it is necessary to break it down into two one-to-many relationships. The general rule for this is to put a LINK table between the two entities as shown in Figure 10.16.

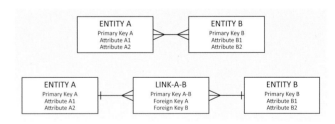

Figure 10.16: Many-to-many.

A new primary key (Primary Key A-B) is created in the LINK table. The primary keys for each of the original entities are then used as foreign keys in the LINK table.

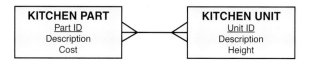

Figure 10.17: Kitchen.

In this example, each *kitchen unit* can include many *kitchen parts*. As each *kitchen part* can be used for many *kitchen units*, a LINK table is required.

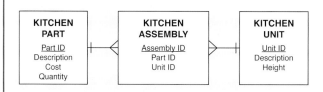

Figure 10.18: Kitchen resolved.

The LINK table *kitchen assembly* is for each combination of unit and part. It has its own primary key, but the primary keys from *kitchen unit* and *kitchen part* are also used as foreign keys. The quantity of each part needed for each unit is also stored. This is what some of the data might look like:

KITCHEN UNIT

Unit ID	Description	Height
DR3-700	3 drawer unit	700
BU-700	Base unit	700
LR-2000	Larder unit	2000

KITCHEN PART

Part ID	Description	Cost
HNG	Hinge	0.30
HND	Handle	1.45
SHL	Shelf	4.50

KITCHEN ASSEMBLY

Assembly ID	Unit ID	Part ID	Quantity
1	DR3-700	HND	3
2	BU-700	HND	1
2	BU-700	HNG	2
2	BU-700	SHL	2
3	LR-2000	HND	1
3	LR-2000	HNG	4

Resolve the following many-to-many relationships and suggest attribute names for all three tables:

- many Orders to many Products
- many Hire Cars to many Drivers
- many Authors to many Books
- many Students to many Classes
- many Employees to many Skills
- many Doctors to many Patients.

The difference between a flat file and a relational database

A flat file is a database that consists of a single table with no relationships. It is like looking at all the data in a single worksheet in a spreadsheet. It is called 'flat' because it only has two dimensions – fields and records.

WORKED EXAMPLE 10.10

This is an example of a simple flat file to store data about cars:

ID	Registration	Reg Year	Transmission
1	BX03HMW	2013	M
2	BR54URS	2011	M
3	BA55WEP	2012	M
4	BC53PRS	2013	M
5	BD05ABC	2012	A
6	BE04RTJ	2011	M

WORKED EXAMPLE 10.11

The flat file below stores data about driving lessons, the cars used and the learners taking the lessons.

LESSON

Lesson ID	Lesson Date	Time Slot Start	Registration	Reg Year	Transmission	Forename	Surname	Telephone
1	27/08/2013	08:00	BR54URS	2011	M	Nadia	Afzal	0555 555 556
2	28/08/2013	08:00	BD05ABC	2012	A	Roger	Drake	0555 555 557
3	31/08/2013	11:00	BD05ABC	2012	A	Roger	Drake	0555 555 557
4	31/05/2014	16:00	BC53PRS	2013	M	Nadia	Afzal	0555 555 556
5	01/06/2014	16:00	BR54URS	2011	M	Nadia	Afzal	0555 555 556
6	29/08/2013	19:00	BC53PRS	2013	M	Sally	Mastock	0555 555 555

The data about the car is repeated and the data about the learner driver taking lessons is also repeated. This example only contains a small amount of redundant data, but imagine if data about the distance each car had travelled, or the full address of the learner and their date of birth was stored.

In the flat file example about driving lessons, the data about cars was very similar to a table you would find in a relational database. However, with larger flat files there is a problem when all the data is in one table, because there will be redundant data (that is, data that is unnecessarily repeated).

Redundant data uses up additional memory. It can also cause problems with inconsistency and maintaining the flat file. If, for example, Aimee Fenson changes her telephone number, then it will need to be changed for every lesson that Aimee has taken. If some are missed, then there will be inconsistent data, meaning that a search will not produce accurate results because Aimee has more than one phone number listed. When a new lesson is entered, all the details of the car and the learner have to be entered rather than just their primary keys. This can lead to further inconsistent data and errors.

Flat files do have their uses though. They are often simple to set up as sometimes data can be entered into the file without needing to set up data types, field sizes or relationships. They can be shared easily through email and across the internet because the data is not dependent upon specific file types or software. It is also easy to add additional information to a flat file because it's a simple case of adding new columns. As all the data is in one single table, it is also very quick for the computer to process the data.

Relational databases are more useful when data needs to be managed properly. They resolve the problems of inaccurate data, inconsistencies and redundant data by using related tables.

Relational databases are used to reduce redundancy. Where data is likely to be repeated if stored in a single flat file then it is preferable to store this data in a set of related tables. For example, a relational database about a library would include separate tables for books, borrowers and loans. Flat files are used when processing speed is essential. Data is likely to have been stored in a relational database originally but exported to a flat file for processing. Flat files would be used in transactional processing systems such as when processing monthly salary payments by updating the master payment file from employee transactions such as hours worked and expenses claimed.

Links are created between the tables which means data can be looked up from one table to another. This takes time and expertise to plan in order to ensure that it is all set up correctly. It also means that processing time can be a bit slower, especially when there are large data sets. It is possible to share a relational database across a network or even the internet and apply security permissions to each table so that different types of users can access different tables. This is not possible with a flat file as it is all in one table. Queries can be created that enable data to be searched and sorted efficiently using a relational database and they can also join data together from related tables. It's also possible to produce detailed and customised reports of the data stored within a relational database. Relational databases are also flexible because additional fields and tables can be added without disturbing the rest of the data.

WORKED EXAMPLE 10.12

The flat file in Worked Example 10.11 could be stored in a relational database as a set of three tables:

LESSON

Lesson ID	Lesson Date	Time Slot Start	Registration	Learner ID
1	27/08/2013	08:00	BR54URS	10
2	28/08/2013	08:00	BD05ABC	11
3	31/08/2013	11:00	BD05ABC	11

CAR

ID	Registration	Make	Model	Reg Year	Transmission
2	BR54URS	Vauxhall	Astra	2011	M
4	BC53PRS	Mini	Cooper	2013	M
5	BD05ABC	Nissan	Almera	2012	A

LEARNER

Learner ID	Forename	Surname	Address 1	Address 2	Post Code	Gender	Telephone	Mobile	Licence Number
9	Sally	Mastock	15 Cloud Road	Kingston-Upon-Hull	KI8 6GU	F	0555 555 555	0777 777 777	MAST9999999SA9XX
10	Aimee	Fenson	23 Yandle Lane	Shrewsbury	KN3 7YY	F	0555 555 556	0777 777 778	FENS9999999AI9XX
11	Roger	Drake	19 Spion Kop	Liverpool	L15 9PL	M	0555 555 557	0777 777 779	DRAK9999999RA9XX

Table 10.2 further examines the types of searches and queries that can be applied to flat files and those that can be applied to relational databases.

CONTINUED

Flat file database	Relational database
A search or query has to load the entire database in order to find the data needed. For example, to find information about the car with registration BC53PRS, the database would need to search for every occurrence in the whole LESSON flat file.	A search or query only has to load the tables required. For example to find the same information, only the CAR table would need to be loaded.
A search or query will find all the data required in one file. For example, to find all lessons taken by Aimee Fenson, a filter could be applied to the Forename and Surname columns.	A search or query would have to assimilate data from more than one table. For example, to find all the lessons taken by Aimee Fenson, her Learner ID would need to be looked up in the LEARNER table and then the Learner ID would need to be found in the LESSON table.
Running a query to find the number of vehicles with manual transmission would mean searching the whole file and then identifying unique occurrences of each car and then counting only those that are manual transmission.	To run the same query would simply require filtering the CAR table to show only manual transmission and then a summary count of the number of records.

Table 10.2: Types of searches and queries that can be applied to flat file databases and relational databases.

Import data

Data can be imported from text files so that data that has been created in another system or for another purpose can be used within the database. The text files must be structured in such a way that fields can be recognised and records can be separated. Comma separated values (CSV) is a common format used for this purpose. Fields are separated by commas, records are separated by line breaks and speech marks are used to identify text. The use of a separation character means that the field lengths are delimited, which means each field can be any length.

WORKED EXAMPLE 10.13

This is a CSV file for books. The first row contains the field names.

"ID","Book title","Genre","Reading age","ISBN","Author"

1,"A Soldier's Tale","Thriller",12,"0-321-93561-1","B Rushmore"

2,"Hidden Gold","Mystery",10,"0-342-92763-X","J T King"

3,"Fearless","Action",14,"0-250-34751-9","K Lawrence"

CSV is only one common format. Text files (TXT) can also be used. Text files can be formatted in exactly the same way as a CSV file or they can use different characters to separate fields. They can also be structured to have fixed length fields, which means spaces are used to fill the gaps.

WORKED EXAMPLE 10.14

This is a fixed length field text file for students.

1	Smith	Larry	9F
2	Nyakatawa	Paul	9B
3	Kalsi	Waheed	10R
4	Woolfenden	Howard	11M
5	Patel	Poonam	9N

Create a new database and import the following files:

- 10.03 Book.xlsx (file includes row headings)
- 10.04 Student.xlsx.

Create a relational database

The first step in creating a database is to create the file that will be used. Other steps can then include creating:

- tables
- forms
- relationships
- reports.

Create a new database called **10.15 My library** that will be used to store information about books in a school library.

1 Create a new database file.
2 Import the files:
   a   **10.03 Book.xlsx**
   b   **10.05 Student.txt**
   c   **10.06 Copy.xlsx**
   d   **10.07 Loan.xlsx**.
3 Check the data types for each field in each table and change if necessary.
4 Check the field lengths for each field in each table and change if necessary (do not leave them as 256 characters in length).

Save this file for use later in this chapter.

10.2 Keys
Primary key

A primary key is a unique identifier for each record in a table. Therefore, the field used for the primary key must contain unique values and not have any repeating values.

Examples of primary keys could include:

- registration plate for a car
- student number for a student
- product code for a product.

It is important that data within primary keys never changes as it can be used within a relationship. Therefore, some fields that may appear on the surface to be suitable as a primary key may not be suitable in the long run. For example, a registration plate for a car can be changed in some countries. For this reason, it is always best to use separate ID fields as primary keys.

Table name	Primary key
Car	CarID
Student	StudentID
Product	ProductID

These ID fields should be used purely for the structure of the database. It is still possible to set another field to be unique, but the primary key should be used for relationships. If possible, the primary key should be set to increment automatically (e.g. AutoNumber).

Compound key

Sometimes, none of the fields have a unique identifier. In this case a **compound key** is used. A compound key is two or more fields combined to form a unique identity. These can be complex to use, especially within relationships. Examples of the concept of compound keys are shown in this section.

compound key: two or more fields that form the primary key. Each field that comprises the compound key are themselves keys from another table.

WORKED EXAMPLE 10.16

Table 10.3 shows the products and quantities ordered for each order. If each order only includes each Product on one Order Line, then the combination of Order Number and Product ID is unique.

Order Number	Product ID	Quantity
1	1	1
1	2	2
2	3	1
2	3	1
3	4	1
4	5	1
4	6	1
5	5	1
5	6	2

Table 10.3: Order Line.

WORKED EXAMPLE 10.17

Table 10.4 shows appointments for a doctor. If Doctor ID and Patient ID were selected as the compound key, then this would mean each patient could only see each doctor once and so this combination would not be suitable. If Doctor ID, Patient ID and Date were selected as the compound key then this would mean each patient could only see each doctor once each day. It may be acceptable to the doctor to see a patient only once per day, but if the doctor needs to see the same patient more than once on the same day, then a combination of all four fields including Time would be needed as the compound key.

Doctor ID	Patient ID	Date	Time
1	1	5/11/20	12:00
1	2	2/9/20	13:00
2	3	18/9/20	13:00
1	1	12/11/20	12:00
2	3	18/9/20	17:30

Table 10.4: Appointments for a doctor.

PRACTICAL ACTIVITY 10.11

1   Create a table of appointments as shown in Table 10.4.

2   Try to set the compound key to be a combination of Doctor ID and Patient ID. What went wrong and why did it happen?

3   a   Set the compound key to be a combination of Doctor ID, Patient ID and Date.

    b   Create a new appointment for Doctor ID 1 with Patient ID 2 on 12/2/20 at 14:00. Was the new appointment accepted?

    c   Create a new appointment for Doctor ID 1 with Patient ID 2 on 2/9/20 at 14:00. What went wrong and why did it happen?

Foreign key

A foreign key is a field in a table that refers to the primary key in another table. It is used to create the relationship between the two tables. The foreign key must always have the same data type and field size as the primary key to which it is linking. The foreign key must always be on the *many* side of the relationship. The foreign key will always link to a single primary key field.

WORKED EXAMPLE 10.18

Customer ID in the Order table is a foreign key which links to the Customer ID in the Customer table.

Order

Order Number	Customer ID	Order Date
1	2	28/05/2015
2	1	22/05/2015
3	5	06/05/2015
4	3	05/04/2015
5	7	06/05/2015

Customer

Customer ID	Contact Forename	Contact Surname
1	Reina	Wolchesky
2	Marc	Wanger
3	Damion	Matkin
4	Lucius	Winchester
5	Petra	Mcnichol
6	Katina	Ramano
7	Leslie	Cackowski
8	Cristopher	Wiget

Figure 10.19: Foreign key.

Open **10.15 My library.mdb** that you created earlier.

1 Assign primary keys to existing fields in each table.

Each book has several copies. Each copy of the book can be loaned out several times. Each loan is for only one student and only one copy of a book. Each student can take out several loans.

2 Create relationships between the tables.

Open **10.08 Driving school.mdb**.

1 Set the primary key for the **Instructor** table.

2 Create a new primary key for the **Car** table (do not use Registration).

3 Create a new primary key for the **Learner** table.

4 Create a compound primary key for the **Lesson** table. You will need at least three fields for this.

Each car can be used in several lessons. Each student can have several lessons. Each instructor can give several lessons. Each lesson will be for one student with one instructor in one car.

5 Create relationships between the tables.

Referential integrity

Referential integrity exists when data in the foreign key of the table on the *many* side of a relationship exists in the primary key of the table on the *one* side of a relationship.

KEY WORDS

referential integrity: data in the foreign key of the table on the *many* side of a relationship must exist in the primary key of the table on the *one* side of a relationship

WORKED EXAMPLE 10.19

In Figure 10.20, Customer ID 5 does not exist in the Customer table. This means that the Order table does not contain referential integrity because the related customer does not exist.

Order

Order Number	Customer ID	Order Date
1	2	28/05/2015
2	1	22/05/2015
3	5	06/05/2015

Customer

Customer ID	Contact Forename	Contact Surname
1	Reina	Wolchesky
2	Marc	Wanger

Figure 10.20: No referential integrity.

Without referential integrity a relationship cannot be properly set within a database. It is a type of lookup validation where the database will check to see if the related record exists before allowing it to be entered. If the related record does not exist, then the database will prevent the foreign key data from being entered.

This is important for maintaining the accuracy of the data within the database. If details of which classes you attend were entered into a database, but those classes did not exist, then the database would not be able to give you any information about the classes.

PRACTICAL ACTIVITY 10.13

Open **10.09 Sales processing 3.mdb**

1 Open the **order** table and add Sales Rep IDs 4, 5, 8, 11 and 15 to the records.

a Which ones worked?

b Which ones did not work?

c Why didn't they work?

CONTINUED

2   Try to create a relationship between Product and Category and enforce referential integrity.

  a   What happens?

  b   Why has this happened?

  c   Correct any data that is causing this problem and try to create the relationship again.

Validate and verify data

Validation rules

The principle of validation was introduced in Chapter 1. Database management systems can apply validation rules to data that is input. If data passes the validation rules, then they will be accepted. If data fail the validation rules, then they will be rejected and an error message may be shown.

WORKED EXAMPLE 10.20

In this database, the user is attempting to enter the title that a Sales Rep will be addressed by. They have four valid options – "Mr", "Mrs", "Miss" or "Dr". The user has accidentally entered "Msr" which is not a valid option. An error message has appeared telling the user what to do to fix the problem.

Figure 10.21: Error message.

This is the rule that had been set up:

| Validation rule | In('Mr', 'Mrs', 'Miss', 'Dr') |
| Validation text | Title must be Mr, Mrs, Miss or Dr |

Figure 10.22: Validation rule.

The rule ensures that the only data that can be entered must exist in the list that contains "Mr", "Mrs", "Miss" and "Dr". It is a lookup in list method of validation.

PRACTICAL ACTIVITY 10.14

Open **10.10 Sales processing validation.mdb** and open the table **Employee**.

1   Create a validation rule that will only allow the entry of "UK" or "USA" for the Country.

2   Create an appropriate error message.

There are a variety of validation rules that can be used within a database including:

- lookup in list (by looking up in a list entered within the rule)

- lookup in list (by using referential integrity)

- lookup in list (by using a lookup table)

- range

- data type

- format

- length

- presence.

Table 10.5 gives some examples of validation rules.

Type	Field	Rule
Lookup in list	Gender	"M" or "F"
Lookup in list	Title	IN ("Mr", "Mrs", "Miss", "Dr")
Range	Date of Birth	>DATE() (must be after today's date)
Range	Date Joined	> 28/02/1995
Range	Reorder Amount	Between 1 and 2000
Range	Reorder Level	>0
Data Type	State	Like "[A-Z][A-Z]" (must be two text characters)
Format	Email Address	Like "*@*.*" (* means any character)
Length	Colour	Like "??" (must be two characters)
Presence	Forename	IS NOT NULL

Table 10.5: Examples of validation rules.

PRACTICAL ACTIVITY 10.15

Open **10.10 Sales processing validation.mdb** and open the table **Customer**.

1   Create a validation rule to ensure the surname is present.

2   Create a validation rule to ensure that an email address includes the @ symbol and a full stop.

3   Create a validation rule to ensure the telephone number is 12 characters long.

Open the table **Product**.

4   Create a validation rule to ensure the Units in Stock is a positive number.

5   Create a validation rule to ensure the Reorder Amount is less than 1000.

6   Create a validation rule to ensure the Reorder Level is at least 0 and no more than 100.

Open the table **Employee**.

7   Create a validation rule to ensure the Hire Date is at least today.

8   Create a validation rule to ensure the region is two characters long and only contains letters.

9   Create a validation rule to ensure the extension is either three or four characters long and only contains numbers.

10 Create a validation rule to ensure the Hire Date is after the Birth Date.

Validation applied to a database

You should follow the same process that you learned in Chapter 8 by using valid, invalid and extreme.

PRACTICAL ACTIVITY 10.16

Open **10.10 Sales processing validation.mdb** and open the table **Customer**.

1   The State field has a validation rule applied to it.

   a   Try changing the state for Reina Wolchesky to NN. What happens? Why does this happen?

   b   Try changing the state for Reina Wolchesky to NM instead of MN. Why was this error allowed to happen?

   c   Identify five items of test data that could be used to test this validation rule.

2   The ZIP Code field has validation applied to it.

   a   Try different combinations of data to see if you can work out what the validation rule is.

   b   Identify eight items of test data that could be used to test this validation rule. You should use valid, invalid and extreme.

Verify data entry

In Chapter 1 you learned that data that has been validated is not necessarily correct. It is therefore necessary to verify data. When inputting data into a database, you should verify that the data input has been entered correctly by comparing what has been entered with the original source.

PRACTICAL ACTIVITY 10.17

Open **10.10 Sales processing validation.mdb** and open the table **Customer**.

1   Visually check that the data for Damion Matkin matches the original data below:

Contact Forename	Contact Surname	Street Address	City	County	State
Damion	Matkin	5830 Downing St	Denver	Denver	CO

ZIP Code	Telephone	Email	Marketing	Notes
80216	303-295-4797	damion@matkin. com	Yes	

2   Add the following data to the customer table and then visually check the data matches the source:

Contact Forename	Contact Surname	Street Address	City	County	State
Joel	Nardo	5150 Town Cir	Boca Raton	Palm Beach	FL

ZIP Code	Telephone	Email	Marketing	Notes
33486	561-395-2277	joel@nardo.com	Yes	

Searches

So far you have looked at whole tables. It is also possible to view only records which meet certain conditions known as criteria. This can be achieved by creating a **query** which asks questions about the data in order to retrieve the required records.

KEY WORD

query: a question used to retrieve data from a database

Simple queries

A simple query has only one criterion (singular for criteria). A criterion is the rule that will be applied to the data.

Table 10.6 shows examples of when you would use a simple query for a particular outcome.

When creating a simple query, it is also possible to specify which fields will be listed.

Field	Criterion	Outcome
State	="CA"	Lists all customers who live in CA (California)
Marketing	True	Lists all customers who have agreed to receive marketing
Mark	100	Lists all students who achieved 100 marks
Mark	<50	Lists all students who achieved less than 50 marks
Price	>3.99	Lists all products with a price more than 3.99 (i.e. 4.00 or above)
Distance covered by car	>=50000	Lists all cars with a distance travelled of at least 50 000 kilometres
Width	<=50	Lists all products with a width up to and including 50 mm
Date of Joining	< 01/01/2010	Lists all employees who joined the company before 1 January 2010
Appointment Time	>= 12:00pm	Lists all appointments in the afternoon
Surname	Like "A*"	Lists all customers with a surname starting with A
Product Code	Like "??B??"	Lists all product codes where the third character is B
Allergy	NOT "Nut"	Lists all students who do not have a nut allergy

Table 10.6: Query criterion and outcomes.

Wildcards can be used to replace one or more characters in a search to mean any value. Table 10.6 shows two examples of how wildcards can be used. The * symbol replaces any number of characters. The ? symbol replaces one single character. For example, Like "?'*" would find anybody with an apostrophe as the second letter of their surname or Like "*-*" would find anybody who has a hyphen in their surname.

WORKED EXAMPLE 10.21

In **10.02 Sales processing 2.mdb** a simple query has been created to show all Sales Reps who have a Job Title of Sales Representative:

The criterion of Job Title = "Sales Representative" means that only sales reps with that job title will be listed. The only fields that will be listed are Last Name and First Name. Job Title will not be listed because the option to show it has been deselected. This is what the result of the simple query looks like:

Figure 10.23: Sales Rep query.

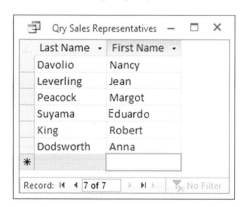

Figure 10.24: Sales Rep query result.

It is also possible to include data from a related table.

WORKED EXAMPLE 10.22

In **10.02 Sales processing 2.mdb** a query has been created to show all Products over $75 including their categories:

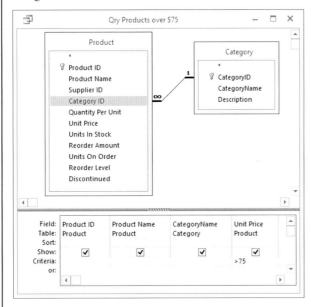

Figure 10.25: Product Category.

The CategoryName has been included from the Category Table which is related to the Product Table through the Category ID.

PRACTICAL ACTIVITY 10.18

Open **10.02 Sales processing 2.mdb**, identify which query is most suitable and then create queries for the following:

1 All UK employees.

2 All employees from Seattle.

3 All employees who were born on or after 1/1/1960.

4 All products that include the word "bottles" in the quantity per unit.

5 All products with no units in stock.

6 The product name and supplier company name of all products that have been discontinued.

7 The names and categories of all products with at least 100 units in stock.

8 The names and price of products that are in the category "Condiments".

9 A list of all orders that were not placed on 6/5/15.

10 A list of all Sales Reps who do not have a job title of "Sales Representative".

11 A list of all products where the Units in Stock is less than or equal to the Reorder Level.

Complex queries

Complex queries are queries that have more than one criterion. They use either the AND or OR Boolean operators. If all specified criteria need to be satisfied, then the AND operator is used. If any one of the specified criteria needs to be satisfied, then the OR operator is used.

Complex queries are not restricted to just two criteria. They can have as many criteria as necessary for the query.

WORKED EXAMPLE 10.23

The table below lists characteristics about some people.

Surname	Forename	Height	Shoe Size	Eyes	Nationality	Occupation	Sex
Greer	Wendy	1.85	7	Blue	British	Firefighter	F
Percy	Hugo	1.75	8	Blue	French	Welder	M
Pearce	Madison	1.85	8	Blue	American	Musician	F
Gardiner	Felicia	1.85	9	Blue	South African	Waitress	F
Ivanova	Sofia	1.65	8	Brown	Russian	Road sweeper	F
Joo	Haeun	1.35	9	Brown	South Korean	Firefighter	F
Goswami	Lamar	1.75	9	Brown	Indian	Shop Assistant	M
Kaya	Yusuf	1.95	10	Blue	Turkish	Teacher	M
Danshov	Aleksander	1.8	6	Hazel	Russian	Politician	M
Mallapati	Smriti	1.6	11	Hazel	Indian	Singer	F
Martinez	Maria	1.85	5	Green	Argentinian	Bus Driver	F

The complex query Eyes = Blue AND Shoe Size = 8 would return the following:

Surname	Forename	Height	Shoe Size	Eyes	Nationality	Occupation	Sex
Percy	Hugo	1.75	8	Blue	French	Welder	M
Pearce	Madison	1.85	8	Blue	American	Musician	F

As both parts of the query have to be satisfied, only people with both blue eyes and a shoe size of 8 will be listed.

The complex query Eyes = Hazel OR Eyes = Green would return the following:

Surname	Forename	Height	Shoe Size	Eyes	Nationality	Occupation	Sex
Danshov	Aleksander	1.8	6	Hazel	Russian	Politician	M
Mallapati	Smriti	1.6	11	Hazel	Indian	Singer	F
Martinez	Maria	1.85	5	Green	Argentinian	Bus Driver	F

As any one part of the query can be satisfied, all people with either hazel or green eyes are listed.

The complex query Eyes = Brown OR Nationality = Russia would return the following:

Surname	Forename	Height	Shoe Size	Eyes	Nationality	Occupation	Sex
Ivanova	Sofia	1.65	8	Brown	Russian	Road sweeper	F
Joo	Haeun	1.35	9	Brown	South Korean	Firefighter	F
Goswami	Lamar	1.75	9	Brown	Indian	Shop Assistant	M
Danshov	Aleksander	1.8	6	Hazel	Russian	Politician	M

Aleksander Danshov does not have brown eyes, but he is Russian and so is included in the list. Similarly, Haeun Joo and Lamar Goswami are not Russian but because they have brown eyes they are included in the list.

WORKED EXAMPLE 10.24

The following nested query uses a combination of AND and OR and includes more than two criteria:

Sex = F AND (Eyes = Blue OR Eyes = Brown) AND Height > 1.5

These are the results of the nested query:

Surname	Forename	Height	Shoe Size	Eyes	Nationality	Occupation	Sex
Greer	Wendy	1.85	7	Blue	British	Firefighter	F
Pearce	Madison	1.85	8	Blue	American	Musician	F
Gardiner	Felicia	1.85	9	Blue	South African	Waitress	F
Ivanova	Sofia	1.65	8	Brown	Russian	Road sweeper	F

PRACTICAL ACTIVITY 10.19

Open **10.02 Sales processing 2.mdb**, identify which query is most suitable and then create queries for the following:

1 All customers from Texas (TX) or Illinois (IL).

2 All customers who would like to receive marketing and live in Ohio (OH).

3 All products priced at least $50 with no units in stock, showing the Product Name and Supplier's Company Name.

4 All products over $30 supplied by companies in Germany.

5 All products under $30 supplied by companies in Denmark or Sweden.

6 A list of all products where the Units in Stock is less than or equal to the Reorder Level and the Units on Order is zero.

Nested queries

So far, each query that you have seen has been based upon existing tables within a database. It is also possible to create a query on an existing query. This means that the results of the original query will be narrowed down further by the new query. This is called a nested query.

WORKED EXAMPLE 10.25

In **10.02 Sales processing 2.mdb** a query has been created to show all customers who live in California (CA). A nested query is then created on top of the California Query to find customers in the California Query who placed an order on 6/5/15:

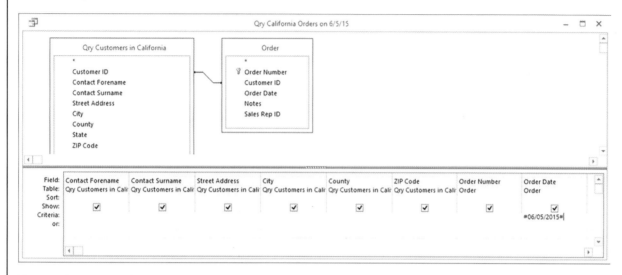

Figure 10.26: Nested query.

The new query is based upon the California query and the Order table.

A nested query is effectively a query that has multiple criteria and is equivalent to using AND. However, they can be used to make very complex queries easier to follow and set up by breaking down the individual steps required to create the query. There are also occasions when a nested query is necessary to achieve the desired results, such as creating a cross-tab query based on two or more tables.

PRACTICAL ACTIVITY 10.20

Open **10.02 Sales processing 2.mdb**, identify which query is most suitable and then create a query based on the existing query "Qry Products over $75" that will show those products in the Meat/Poultry category.

Queries to find duplicate records

There may be occasions when duplicate records are accidentally created within a table. It is possible to run a query to find those duplicate records. One method is to use Structured Query Language (SQL) or some software packages include a wizard to create a query to find the duplicate records.

WORKED EXAMPLE 10.26

Open **10.11 Duplicate Records.mdb** and open the table called **People**.

This table contains duplicate entries for Marlene Atack and Wendy Greer:

Surname ▾	Forename ▾	Sex ▾
Greer	Wendy	F
Barnard	Alan	M
Pearce	Katherine	F
Atack	Marlene	F
Briars	Sandra	F
Greer	Wendy	F
Briars	Simon	M
Pearce	Catherine	F
Atack	**Marlene**	F
*		

Figure 10.27: Duplicate records.

A find duplicate queries wizard can be used to create a query to find the duplicate records:

Surname Fie ▾	Forename F ▾	Sex Field ▾	NumberOfC ▾
Atack	Marlene	F	2
Greer	Wendy	F	2

Find duplicates for People

Figure 10.28: Finding duplicate records.

The query above has been called "Find duplicates for People".

Once the duplicate records are known, they can be found in the original table and deleted. It is also possible to use Structured Query Language (SQL) to create a query to find and remove duplicates automatically.

Summary queries

A cross-tab query is a type of summary query used to summarise data. It can be used to show the total number of records, the sum of values within a field, averages or other statistical data.

WORKED EXAMPLE 10.27

10.12 People.mdb contains a cross-tab query that shows the total number of people of each nationality. It also breaks this down into how many males and females there are in each nationality.

Qry People Summary Nationality and Gender

Nationality ▾	Total Of Surname ▾	F ▾	M ▾
America	9	7	2
Belgium	8	1	7
England	20	4	16
France	6	4	2
Greece	8	4	4
Ireland	11	2	9
Israel	1	1	
Italy	9	1	8
Russia	11	3	8
Scotland	16	10	6
Spain	1		1
Wales	6	1	5

Record: I◄ ◄ 1 of 12 ▶ ▶I ▶ 🏹 No Filter   Search

Figure 10.29: Cross-tab query.

In order to set this up, it is necessary to identify which fields will be used as row headings, which fields will be used as column headings and which field the summary of data will be used:

Nationality	Sex1	Sex2	Sex3
Nationality 1	Count (Surname)		
Nationality 2			
Nationality 3			
Nationality 4			

Figure 10.30: Cross-tab wizard.

CONTINUED

This can also be seen in the configuration settings where the data is grouped by nationality and sex as row and column headings and the surname is counted:

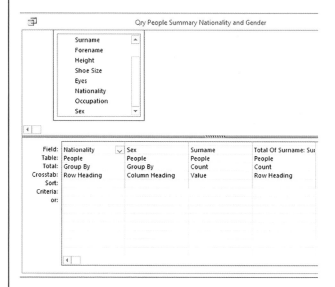

Figure 10.31: Cross-tab configuration.

You will notice that a new calculated field of "Total of Surname" has been added that counts the total number of people. This is not essential unless the overall totals are required.

To create a cross-tab query based on data from more than one table, you should use a nested query by first creating a query that joins the tables together and then creating the cross-tab query based on the original query.

PRACTICAL ACTIVITY 10.21

Open **10.12 People.mdb** and create cross-tab queries to show:

1 The number of people of each gender with eyes of each colour.

2 The number of people of each occupation (no need to have a column grouping).

3 The number of people of each gender with each shoe size.

Open **10.02 Sales processing 2.mdb** and create cross-tab queries to show:

1 The number of suppliers in each country.

2 The number of customers in each state.

3 The number of products in each category (the category names must be showing so you will need to join the Product and Category tables first).

4 The total price of each product in each category.

Using simple, complex, nested and summary queries

Simple queries should be used when only one criterion is required, such as Gender = Male.

Complex queries should be used when more than one criteria are required, such as Gender = Male AND Country = Israel, or Gender = Male OR Country = Israel.

A nested query can be used in the following situations:

• When an OR needs to be combined with an AND as this will avoid the problem of having to repeat the AND part of the query for each OR. It will also avoid the problem of not getting the criteria in the correct order.

• When there are lots of criteria and nesting the queries will make the criteria easier to understand.

• When a query can be reused and so creating a nested query saves the developer having to recreate some of the criteria.

A summary query can be used in the following situations:

- when multiple tables are required within a cross-tab query

- when a cross-tab query is summarising data from another cross-tab query.

Static parameters

So far all the queries you have used include static **parameters**. The parameters are the values used within the criteria. Each time the query is run, the values of the parameters will not change.

KEY WORD
parameter: data used within the criteria for a query

WORKED EXAMPLE 10.28

The query for all customers from Texas (TX) or Illinois (IL) had static parameters of TX and IL. These values do not change.

Dynamic parameters

Dynamic parameters allow the values within the criteria to be chosen at the time of running the query. This can be useful when the user needs to decide what those parameters might be.

WORKED EXAMPLE 10.29

In **10.02 Sales processing 2.mdb**, a query has been created to show all customers in the state that will be chosen by the user:

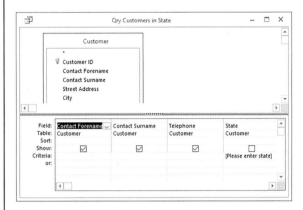

Figure 10.32: Dynamic query.

The criterion of [Please enter state] will be a prompt to the user to enter the state. This is what the prompt looks like when the query is run:

Figure 10.33: Parameter.

If the user enters AZ then all the customers in Arizona will be listed:

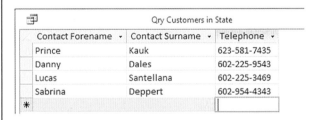

Figure 10.34: Arizona.

Dynamic parameters can be used with ranges (<, >, <=, >=) and Boolean operators (NOT, AND, OR). They can also be used alongside static parameters within a complex query.

Open **10.02 Sales processing 2.mdb** and create queries for the following (identifying whether to use static or dynamic parameters):

1   All sales reps with a Title of the user's choosing.

2   All products with a price below the user's choosing.

3   All products with a reorder amount above the user's choosing.

4   All products with more than 100 units in stock that have a unit price below the user's choosing.

5   All products with a category of the user's choosing that are also above a price of the user's choosing.

Analysing and evaluating when static and dynamic parameters should be used in queries

Static parameter values should be used when those parameter values will not change, no matter how many times the query is used. For example, if you wanted to search a table on a regular basis for all customers based in China, then you would use a static parameter query with the criterion of Country = "China". Dynamic parameters should be used when the user is likely to want to change the value each time the query is run. For example, if you wanted a query that would enable you to search for a specific product code, but that product code could be different each time, then you would use a dynamic query with the criterion of Product Code = [Please enter product code].

Perform calculations within a database

Within a database, calculations can be performed on fields. This can be done within forms, reports and queries. Within a form, a text box can be added to the form which includes the calculation. As with spreadsheets, the calculation must start with the equals (=) sign.

In the Order Form from **10.02 Sales processing 2.mdb**, the Total Price for each order line has been calculated by multiplying the Quantity by the Unit Price. The Order Total has been calculated by adding up all the Quantities multiplied by their corresponding Unit Prices.

The calculation for Total Price is
= [Quantity] * [Unit Price]

The calculation for Order Total is
= SUM ([Quantity] * [Unit Price])

Figure 10.35: Order Form.

In some database management systems, such as Microsoft Access, calculated fields such as Total Price cannot be used in a SUM function. Therefore, the SUM has to use the full calculation rather than simply referring to =SUM([Total Price]).

Calculations within reports are carried out in the same way as within forms. Within a query, the calculation needs to be defined by giving it a name and then identifying what the calculation will be.

WORKED EXAMPLE 10.31

In **10.02 Sales processing 2.mdb**, a query has been created to calculate how many products are left to sell before more need to be reordered:

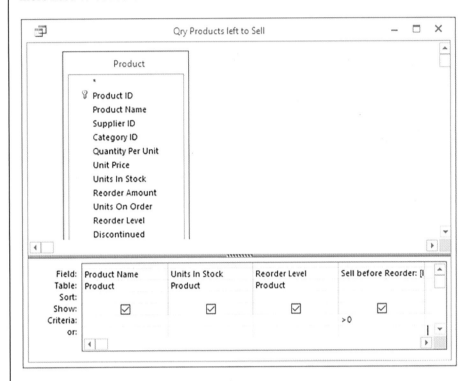

Figure 10.36: Query calculation.

The calculation subtracts the Units in Stock from the Reorder Level. In order to remove any products that are already below their Reorder Level, a criterion has been added that the total must be greater than zero. Here is an extract of the result of the query:

Product Name	Units In Stock	Reorder Level	Sell before Reorder
Chang	17	25	8
Aniseed Syrup	13	25	12
Queso Cabrales	22	30	8
Sir Rodney's Scones	3	5	2

PRACTICAL ACTIVITY 10.23

Open **10.02 Sales processing 2.mdb** and create a query to calculate the new Units In Stock when the Units On Order are added to the current Units In Stock.

Sort data

Ascending/descending

Data can be sorted in ascending or descending order. This can be done within a table, within a query or within a report. The order can be based on numbers, alphabetical characters, dates or times.

Grouped

More than one field can be used to create the sort. This is commonly used when sorting names into order. The surname would be set as the first sort order and then if there are any people with the same surname, the forename would be set as the second sort order.

WORKED EXAMPLE 10.32

The data below is sorted in order of colour of eyes and then within each colour, it is sorted by height:

Surname	Forename	Eyes	Height
Percy	Hugo	Blue	1.75
Hughes	Carl	Blue	1.8
Gardiner	Felicia	Blue	1.85
Greer	Wendy	Blue	1.85
Young	Rose	Blue	1.9
Cox	Arnold	Blue	1.9
Inan	Menekse	Blue	1.9
Hansen	Mathias	Blue	1.95
Xu	Huan	Brown	1.35
Li	Fen	Brown	1.64
Petrova	Alisa	Brown	1.7
Truong	Dinh	Brown	1.85
Saltings	Damien	Brown	1.85
Fontana	Giuseppe	Brown	1.95
Himura	Yuki	Green	1.75
Martinez	Maria	Green	1.85
Brown	Joseph	Green	1.9
Danshov	Aleksander	Hazel	1.8
Banton	Cedric	Hazel	1.85
Hammer	Daniel	Hazel	1.9

Data entry forms

As its name suggests, a data entry form is used for the entry of data. It can also be used to view existing data.

When designing a data entry form, you should consider who will be using it and how to make the form effective and user friendly by using some of the following techniques.

Appropriate font styles and sizes

Fonts should be plain and easy to read. A consistent font style should be used throughout so the user does not have to adjust to viewing different font styles. The colour of fonts should either be dark on a light background or light on a dark background so that the user can read the fonts clearly. The size should be big enough for the user to read but not so big that all the data does not fit on the screen. Titles and subtitles should be in larger fonts.

Spacing between fields

There should be enough space for the user to be able to distinguish between the data within each field. If you look at Figure 10.37, you will see that the fields on the left are separated by providing space between them and each field has a box around it to separate it from other fields. On the right you will see that there is sufficient horizontal space between each field to know which field belongs to which title.

WORKED EXAMPLE 10.33

The form from **10.13 Outlet monitoring.mdb** is used for monitoring inspections carried out at retail outlets within a shopping centre.

Outlet Inspection Data Entry Screen

Outlet Code	01029
Outlet Name	Pizza Parlour
Floor	1
Location	B9
Telephone	0121392038
Opening Date	05/01/2011
Annual Fee	£140,000.00
Penalty Percentage	1.65
Penalty Fee	£2,310.00
Total Fee	£142,310.00

Renewal is due shortly – write to outlet

☐ Renewal Letter

Inspections

Inspection Name	Agency	Inspection Date	Pass	Penalty Incurred
Health & Safety	H&S Executive	07/01/2011	☑	0
Health & Safety	H&S Executive	11/06/2011	☑	0
Food Hygiene	Trading Standards	28/02/2011	☐	35
Food Hygiene	Trading Standards	14/03/2011	☑	0
VAT	HM Revenue & Customs	19/08/2011	☐	20

Total Penalty Points: 55

Record: 1 of 5 · No Filter · Search

Print Record · Main Menu

Figure 10.37: Good data entry form.

Figure 10.38 shows an example of a badly designed input form with poor data flows.

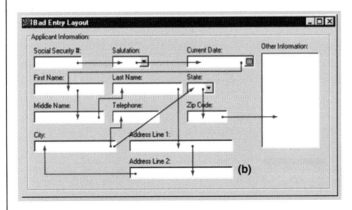

Figure 10.38: A badly designed input.

Character spacing of individual fields

There should be enough space between each character within the data for each field to enable the data to be viewed. If there is too much spacing then the user will struggle to read the data because it is spread out too much. If there is too little spacing then characters will overlap. If single words have been used for field names (e.g. Outlet Code), then when using field names on the form, the labels for the fields should include appropriate spacing (e.g. Outlet Code).

Use of white space

White space can be used to separate data and also to make sure a screen does not look too cluttered. In Figure 10.38, you will see that there is white space used between the left and right hand sides, between field names and the data and between buttons. Having white space between controls such as buttons means that the user is less likely to select the wrong button by having the pointer slightly in the wrong position.

Navigation buttons

Navigation buttons allow the user to browse through records by choosing the next record, previous record, first record in a file or last record in a file.

Radio buttons

Radio (option) buttons allow a user to select one mutually exclusive option.

Check boxes

Check (tick) boxes can be used to select an item. It can be true (ticked) or false (not ticked). Check boxes are used for Boolean data types. In Figure 10.37, a tick box has been used for whether or not a renewal was sent to the outlet and tick boxes have been used to identify whether each inspection was passed or not.

> ### WORKED EXAMPLE 10.34
>
> When printing a document, print options may be available regarding how much of the document to print, such as all of the document, a range of pages or selected records (or pages).
>
>
>
> **Figure 10.39:** Radio buttons.
>
> Only one of the radio (option) buttons can be chosen at a time.

Drop-down menus

Drop-down menus allow the user to select from a set of options. They are used instead of radio buttons when space is limited. In Figure 10.37 you can see that each inspection can be selected from a drop-down menu. This means that the user is only able to select from the list so will not make any spelling mistakes or enter an inspection that does not exist. This also helps to maintain referential integrity.

Highlighting key fields

If the key field is useful to the user, then it may be appropriate to highlight it. Figure 10.37 shows the Outlet Code in bold. However, if the key field is only used for the database structure, then it may not even be displayed. In Figure 10.37, there are no key fields displayed for the inspections or agencies.

Subforms

A subform shows data from related tables. The main data entry form will include data from the *one* side of a relationship and the subform can include data from the *many* side of a relationship.

> ### WORKED EXAMPLE 10.35
>
> The file **10.13 Outlet monitoring.mdb** includes a form called "OutletInspectionDataEntryScreen", shown in Figure 10.38. This form includes a subform showing the inspections that have taken place at each outlet. There are *many* inspections to *one* outlet.

PRACTICAL ACTIVITY 10.24

1   a   Evaluate the data entry form from **10.14 Library.mdb**.

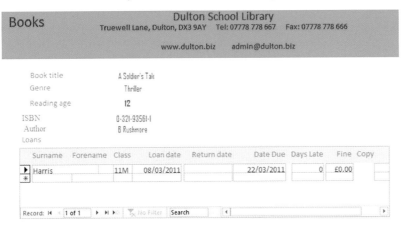

Figure 10.40: Bad data entry form.

b   Using the same database, create a data entry form for students.

c   Using the same database, create a data entry form for books without the sub-form.

2   Using **10.13 Outlet monitoring.mdb**, recreate the data entry form named
"OutletInspectionDataEntryScreen". You will need to use data from all three tables.

3   a   Using **10.08 Driving School.mdb**, create a data entry form for lessons which shows all the details of
each lesson. You should:
   - use an appropriate title
   - group information appropriately
   - use drop down menus to select the instructor, learner and car
   - create navigation buttons.

b   Create a data entry form for learners which includes a subform showing the date and time of any
lessons they have. You should:
   - use an appropriate title
   - create navigation buttons
   - use radio buttons to select a learner's gender.

c   Extend the subform to show the name of the instructor and the make and model of the vehicle that
will be used for each lesson.

4   Using **10.14 Library.mdb**, create a data entry form for students that includes a subform to show which
books they have on loan. Your subform will need to include the tables Loan, Copy and Book. The Copy
table shows each copy of each book as there are multiple copies of some of the books. You should:
   - use an appropriate title for the form and subtitle for the subform
   - use a drop-down menu to select the copy of the book that is on loan
   - create navigation buttons on the main form
   - ensure all the necessary data on the subform is showing and any unnecessary data is deleted.

Reports

Reports show data from a table or query in a structured format. Reports should always include a title and the data for each field will be displayed in columns.

Like a query, a report can be sorted into any order. A report can also include summary data, such as the total number of records, an average value and a total value. Unlike a query, a report can be grouped to show records in groups, such as grouping books by their genre. Summary data can be shown for each group as well as for the report as a whole.

WORKED EXAMPLE 10.36

10.08 Driving School.mdb includes a report showing all the instructors for a driving school.

Instructors

Job Title	Instructor						
Surname	**Forename**	**InstructorID**	**Date of Birth**	**Gender**	**Charge**	**Max Hours**	**Weekends**
Riaz	Serena	11	12/08/1980	F	£17.00	6	☑
Rogers	Sally	13	14/08/1982	F	£16.00	3	☑
Saxby	Wendy	10	11/08/1979	F	£16.00	1	☑
Smith	Jock	5	06/07/1974	M	£17.00	2	☑
Uxpern	Jean	2	03/04/1971	F	£16.00	4	☑
Walters	Peggy	8	09/08/1977	F	£15.00	3	☑

Total number of instructors in group: 6
Average charge for group: £16.17

Job Title	Senior Instructor						
Surname	**Forename**	**InstructorID**	**Date of Birth**	**Gender**	**Charge**	**Max Hours**	**Weekends**
Dean	Ben	17	02/07/1968	M	£19.00	3	☑
Kaur	Sameena	15	01/05/1969	F	£18.00	2	☑
Senior	Jon	16	18/05/1971	M	£17.00	8	☑

Total number of instructors in group: 3
Average charge for group: £18.00

Total number of instructors 9
Average charge £16.78

Figure 10.41: Report showing instructors at a driving school.

It has been grouped by Job Title so the Instructors are shown first followed by the Senior Instructors. It has also been filtered to only show instructors who are willing to work weekends. Within each group, the data is sorted by surname and the total number of instructors in each group are shown along with the average charge for the group. The total number of instructors willing to work weekends is also shown together with their average charge.

CONTINUED

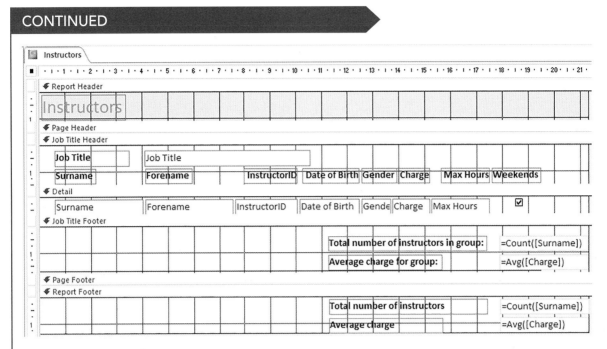

Figure 10.42: Report design.

Figure 10.42 shows how the report has been set up. The report header is the heading that appears at the top of the report. Page headers and footers can appear at the bottom of multi-page reports. The detail shows the data that will be listed. The Job Title header is the heading used for each group in this report. Data in the Job Title Footer appears at the bottom of each group in this report and shows the summary data. The report footer includes summary data for the whole report.

Reports are used to show the output of data either on screen or in a printed format. Therefore, they do not include form controls, such as drop-down menus, navigation buttons, radio buttons or check boxes.

PRACTICAL ACTIVITY 10.25

1 a Using **10.12 People.mdb**, create a report to show all people in alphabetical order of surname.

   b Create a query that shows all people from Italy. Create a report based on this query.

   c Create a report to show all the people grouped by their nationality. For each group, show the average height.

2 a Using **10.14 Library.mdb**, create a report to show all of the books grouped by Genre.

   b Create a report to show all the books that have been loaned grouped by each student. You will need to include the following fields from multiple tables:

   - Student.Surname
   - Student.Forename
   - Student.Class
   - Loan.Loan date
   - Loan.Return date
   - Copy.Copy
   - Book.Booktitle

Switchboards/menus

A menu can be used to help users navigate between elements of a database including forms, reports and action queries. A menu should include a title, clear instructions and buttons for each element. A switchboard is a Microsoft Access term used for creating a menu automatically. A switchboard manager is used to create the menu with links to forms, reports, macros and exiting the application. It creates a form which acts as the switchboard and a table which contains the switchboard data such as actions to take and objects to open. It is possible to have multiple switchboards so a menu could have sub-menus.

WORKED EXAMPLE 10.37

10.02 Sales Processing 2.mdb includes a switchboard.

The switchboard manager was used to add items to the menu. This example shows the "Open Order Form" button being added to the switchboard:

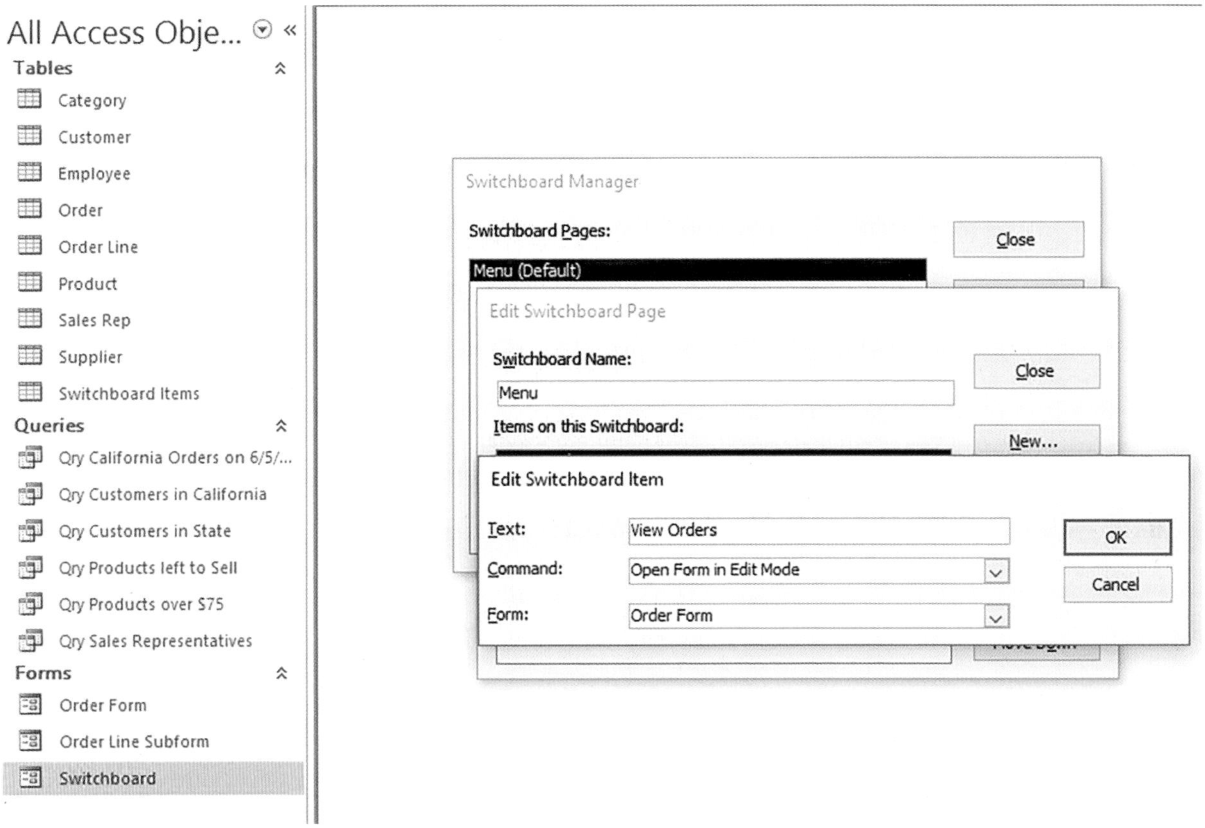

Figure 10.43: Switchboard Manager.

CONTINUED

The switchboard items were automatically stored in a table:

Figure 10.44: Switchboard Table.

The form was created automatically:

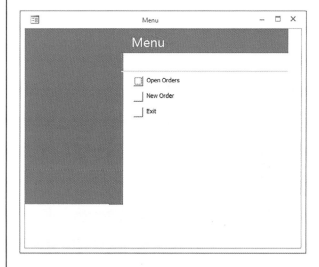

Figure 10.45: Switchboard Form.

Export data

In the same way that data can be imported from common formats, it can also be exported to common formats. This allows data to be used by other users who either do not have DBMS software or do not know how to use it. It can also be used to transfer data to other systems.

Table

Data in tables can be exported as a delimited file in CSV format, as fixed length fields in text format or as a table within a RTF file. It is sensible to save the field names when saving to CSV or text files.

Query

Data from queries can be exported in the same way as tables, but only the data that meets the criteria of the query will be exported.

Report

Reports include formatting, so the best method of export is to a RTF file which will include all the original formatting. Data that is exported from a report to a text file will lose its formatting.

Open **10.01 Sales processing.mdb** and export the following:

1   The Customer table in CSV format.
2   The UK Sales Reps query in fixed length fields text format.
3   The Categories of Products report in RTF format.

Questions

1   Define the term primary key.
2   Describe the difference between a simple query and a complex query.
3   Give an example of when a dynamic parameter query might be used.
4   Identify the decisions involved in exporting data from a table.
5   Explain the importance of referential integrity.

10.3 Normalisation to third normal form

Introduction to normalisation

Normalisation is the process of structuring data within a database. The process starts with a flat file and finishes with a set of related tables. It is a formal method of ensuring that each table is structured correctly and does not contain redundant data. There are stages throughout the process known as normal forms. Each normal form measures the extent to which the data has been normalised.

KEY WORD

normalisation: process of structuring data in a database

When describing tables, the following conventions will be used:

TABLENAME

Primary Key

Attribute 1

Attribute 2

TABLENAME (Primary Key, Attribute 1, Attribute 2)

Table names will be in capitals, primary keys will be underlined and all attributes will be listed below the table name or within brackets.

Normal forms

Unnormalised form

Data in unnormalised form (UNF) is a flat file. It will contain non-atomic data, repeating groups of data and possibly redundant data. Non-atomic data is where a field contains more than one item of data.

Repeating groups of data is when fields are repeated for each record or a record appears to have more than one set of data for a group of fields.

Redundant data exists when data is repeated unnecessarily. This can be spotted when data can be identified by knowing it is dependent upon another field.

WORKED EXAMPLE 10.38

This table contains non-atomic data:

Product ID	Description	Price
327BLF	Brown, Leather, Female	₹ 3510
327BPM	Brown, Plastic, Male	₹ 2540
327CLF	Cream, Leather, Female	₹ 3510

The colour, material and gender are three separate items of data within the description. This causes a problem when trying to sort data by a specific characteristic, such as colour, or when trying to search by a specific characteristic. (Note: ₹ is the symbol for rupees.)

First normal form

Data in first normal form (1NF) must satisfy the following criteria:

*   all fields must contain atomic data
*   there must be no repeating groups of data
*   there must be a unique key.

WORKED EXAMPLE 10.39

This table contains fields that are repeated for each record:

Surname	Forename	Subject 1	Subject 2	Subject 3	Subject 4
Jones	Ifor	Welsh	English	History	
Rushton	Ken	Politics	Literature	Philosophy	Physics
Smallwood	Steven	Maths	Physics	German	

The Subject field has been repeated. This can be a problem when trying to search for all students studying the same subject or when a student only studies one subject (leaving several blank) or when a student needs to study a fifth subject.

This table contains more than one set of data for a group of fields:

Surname	Forename	Book	Date Out	Date Due
Jones	Ifor	Everything in Colour Guardian	12/5/19 12/5/19	12/6/19 12/6/19
Rushton	Ken	Saving Grace	14/5/19	14/6/19
Smallwood	Steven	Delirious Stretch Out Always Faithful	26/11/19 5/1/20 5/1/20	3/1/20 5/2/20 5/2/20

Some students are borrowing more than one book and so the fields Book, Date Out and Date Due contain more than one set of data per record. This could also be classed as non-atomic data as there is more than one data item per field.

WORKED EXAMPLE 10.40

The table below contains redundant data:

Order ID	Order Date	Product	Quantity	Price
3857	12/9/19	Marzipan	1	$1.50
		Flour	2	$0.75
2320	15/10/19	Marzipan	3	$1.50
		Sugar	1	$0.83
		Eggs	6	$0.15

The price is dependent upon the product and therefore it is being repeated unnecessarily. If we know the product, we know the price.

PRACTICAL ACTIVITY 10.27

Describe the characteristics of data in 0NF using examples from the table of driving lessons:

Learner	Lesson Date	Instructor ID	Instructor	Price
Rob	30/5/16	4	Marcus Brown	$35
Pocock	6/6/16	4	Marcus Brown	$35
Graham	31/5/16	3	Mike Joyce	$30
Alkins	1/6/16	4	Marcus Brown	$35

WORKED EXAMPLE 10.41

The ORDER table below contains details of products ordered by customers:

ORDER
Order Date
Customer ID
Customer Name
Customer Address
    Product Code
    Description
    Quantity
    Price

Indented fields are a repeating group for each order.

To be in 1NF, this table needs:

- a unique key (Order Number)
- atomic data (Customer Name and Customer Address need breaking down)
- no repeating groups of data (products being ordered).

The ORDER table becomes:

ORDER (Order Number, Order Date, Customer ID, Customer Forename, Customer Surname, Customer Address 1, Customer Address 2, Customer Address 3, Customer ZIP Code)

A new table for the order of products needs to be added, but it needs to retain information about which order each order of products belongs to:

ORDERLINE (Order Number, Product Code, Description, Quantity, Price)

Order Number is retained in the ORDERLINE table as a foreign key. However, it is not unique and so cannot be used as the primary key. However, a combination of Order Number and Product Code are unique and so these become a compound key.

PRACTICAL ACTIVITY 10.28

Normalise the table of driving lessons below to 1NF: LESSON (Learner, Lesson Date, Instructor ID, Instructor, Price)

Learner	Lesson Date	Instructor ID	Instructor	Price
Rob	30/5/16	4	Marcus Brown	$35
Pocock	6/6/16	4	Marcus Brown	$35
Graham	31/5/16	3	Mike Joyce	$30
Alkins	1/6/16	4	Marcus Brown	$35

Second normal form

Data in second normal form (2NF) must have no partial key dependencies. This means that no non-key fields can be dependent upon part of a primary key. This therefore only applies to tables with compound keys because they are the only tables that can have partial keys. Dependencies exist when the data is known because of its direct relationship to another field.

When identifying partial key dependencies, there will be fields that are dependent on just one part of the compound key. These fields and that part of the compound key will form a new table.

WORKED EXAMPLE 10.42

The orders database from the previous example now contains two tables:

ORDER (Order Number, Order Date, Customer ID, Customer Forename, Customer Surname, Customer Address 1, Customer Address 2, Customer Address 3, Customer ZIP Code)

ORDERLINE (Order Number, Product Code, Description, Quantity, Price)

Only the ORDERLINE table contains partial keys. Description and Price are dependent on Product Code which is part of the compound primary key. Therefore, a new table needs to be created for products:

PRODUCT (Product Code, Description, Price)

The information stored in the ORDERLINE table that is not part of the PRODUCT table needs to be retained:

ORDERLINE (Order Number, Product Code, Quantity)

The Product Code field is retained in the ORDERLINE table as a foreign key because it is still necessary to know which products were ordered.

PRACTICAL ACTIVITY 10.29

Normalise the table of ingredients below to 2NF: RECIPE-INGREDIENT (Recipe ID, Ingredient ID, Ingredient Name, Measure, Quantity)

Recipe ID	Ingredient ID	Ingredient Name	Measure	Quantity
1	B	Flour	Grams	200
1	D	Eggs	Eggs	2
1	K	Water	Table-spoons	2
2	C	Milk	Millilitres	250
2	B	Flour	Grams	100

Third normal form

Data in third normal form 3NF must have no non-key dependencies. This means that there should be no fields that are dependent upon another field that is not a primary key. Therefore primary keys and compound primary keys can be ignored. All other fields should be examined to see if they are dependent on any other non-key field.

WORKED EXAMPLE 10.43

The orders database from the previous example now contains three tables:

ORDER (Order Number, Order Date, Customer ID, Customer Forename, Customer Surname, Customer Address 1, Customer Address 2, Customer Address 3, Customer ZIP Code)

PRODUCT (Product Code, Description, Price)

ORDERLINE (Order Number, Product Code, Quantity)

In the ORDER table, all the customer data is dependent on the Customer ID which is a non-key field. A new table needs to be created called CUSTOMER:

CUSTOMER (Customer ID, Forename, Surname, Address 1, Address 2, Address 3, ZIP Code)

The ORDER table now becomes:

ORDER (Order Number, Order Date, Customer ID)

Customer ID is retained in the ORDER table as a foreign key so it is still known which customer placed the order.

PRACTICAL ACTIVITY 10.30

Normalise the table of students below to 3NF: STUDENT (Student ID, Forename, Surname, Class, Teacher Title, Teacher Surname)

Student ID	Forename	Surname	Class	Teacher Title	Teacher Surname
1	Hayley	Barrow	3	Mrs	Stokes
2	Harriet	Chew	1	Miss	Spicer
3	Jessica	Lang	3	Mrs	Stokes

PRACTICAL ACTIVITY 10.31

This PROJECT table contains details of the employees working on projects for clients. It is currently in 0NF. Normalise the data to 3NF.

PROJECT   Company

Description   Contact Name

Start Date   Employee ID

End Date   Employee Name

Client ID   Employee Hours

Here is an example of the data:

Description	Start Date	End Date	Client ID	Company	Contact Name	Employee ID	Employee Name	Employee Hours
Barton	28/2/15	31/12/16	512	Barton	Jerry	PK32	Fred Havers	1052
Towers				Estates	Dean	JH45	Janice Spring	575
Haywoo	31/3/15	15/6/15	987	Haywood	Peter	JH45	Janice Spring	153
Manor				Estates	Gates	YR27	Mike Rawson	372

Advantages and disadvantages of normalisation

Normalisation removes duplicate data from a database. Not only does this reduce the size of the database, it also removes the potential for errors and inconsistencies. Data that is duplicated may be edited for one record but not another, meaning that it becomes inconsistent. This causes problems when searching for matching data.

The database will perform better if it is normalised because searches can be carried out on indexed fields and data can be looked up from related tables. However, each lookup does take time to perform and will use up processor time, which means that some queries that require access to more than one table may be slow.

As tables no longer contain redundant data, maintenance tasks such as rebuilding indexes can be completed more quickly. However, it can be difficult to understand the data stored in each table because foreign keys consisting of numbers or codes are used and they mean very little to the user. This means that the user will need to build queries to look up data from related tables. These queries can be quite complex and require expertise from the user.

The database becomes more flexible in that it is easy to add new fields to tables without affecting other columns

and it is easy to add new tables without affecting existing tables. Having smaller tables also means that data can fit onto one screen or one page more easily because there are fewer fields and security permissions can be applied to individual tables. However, it is also necessary to design the database properly and to understand the process of normalisation. This is a high-level skill that requires a database designer to understand the real world data structures and represent them in a relational database. An average user would not be able to do this.

Questions

6   Identify two characteristics of data in 1NF.

7   Describe one characteristic of data in 3NF.

8   Explain two advantages of normalisation.

10.4 Data dictionary

Metadata

A **data dictionary** is a document or file that describes the structure of the data held within the database. It is known as metadata which means 'data about data'. It is a tool that is used by database developers and administrators. It will include the following items:

data dictionary: metadata (information) about the database

- data about fields:
  - field names to identify each field
  - data types, such as text, integer, date/time
  - field size, such as the length of a text field or the maximum value of a numeric field
  - format of fields
  - default values which are values a field is set to be initially when a new record is created
  - primary keys, compound keys and foreign keys

  - indexed fields which improve search times
  - validation rules that restrict data entry for that field
- data about tables:
  - the primary key of the table
  - what sort order to use when displaying data
  - relationships to other tables
  - total number of records
  - validation rules that apply based on multiple fields within the table
  - permissions and security as to which users can access the table.

WORKED EXAMPLE 10.44

This is part of a data dictionary for fields in a product table:

Attribute	Data Type	Field Size	Format
Product Code	Alphanumeric	6	XX99XX
Description	Alphanumeric	20	
Category Code	Integer	4	9999
Price	Decimal	3.2	$999.99

Attribute	Validation Type	Rule	Error Message
Product Code	Format	Must be in the format of two letters, two numbers, two letters	Please enter a code that is two letters, two numbers, two letters
Description	Presence	Must be present	Please enter a description
Category Code	Look up in List	Must exist in Category Code in Category table	Please enter a category code that exists in the category list
Price	Range	Between 0.01 and 999.99	Please enter a price between 0.01 and 999.99

Complete this data dictionary for employees:

Attribute	Data Type	Field Size	Format
Employee ID			
Surname			
Forename			
Date of Birth			
Telephone			
Email			
Year Joined Company			
Pension Scheme?			

Data types

It is necessary to know the type of data in order to store it correctly and process it efficiently.

Field Name	Data Type
Product ID	Number
Description	Short Text
Retail Price	Currency
Date Started	Date/Time

Figure 10.46: Product data types.

Text

Text data types come in different formats. They can also sometimes be known as string or alphanumeric. A text data type can contain any letter, number or symbol.

Jane Atkins

M

Female W6749PR

O'Connor

info@alphabeta.rtq

00 44 208 555 5555

Numeric

Numbers can be stored in two main formats which are integer and real.

Integers are whole numbers. These can be negative or positive but must not contain decimals.

Real numbers can contain decimals. They can be positive or negative.

Numbers can also be formatted as percentages or as currency. Currency values are presented with a currency symbol. The currency symbol isn't actually stored with the data, but is presented when the data is displayed.

Percentage values are stored slightly differently to other number values. The number that is displayed is stored as a one hundredth (1/100) of the value. When using 25%, for example, the computer would store it as 0.25 (25/100). However, it would display 25%. So when the computer displays a percentage data type, it multiplies what is stored (e.g. 0.63) by 100 and adds the percentage symbol (e.g. 63%).

The table 10.7 shows examples of the different number format.

Integer	Real	Currency	Percentage
9	9.05	$9.05	0.09 (9%)
−6	−6.2	−$6.20	−0.06 (6%)
232 382 109	232 383 109.00	$232 383 109.00	2 323 821
−238	−238.00	−$238	2.38 (238%)

Table 10.7: Examples of number formats.

PRACTICAL ACTIVITY 10.33

Use a spreadsheet to enter the following numbers:

5	0.32
60	0.2

Now format the cells as percentages. What has happened to the data and why?

Some people get confused with telephone numbers because the word 'number' is used. However, a telephone number is actually a set of digits. The number data types cannot include the spaces or hyphens or brackets which are often used within telephone numbers. The number data types also cannot start with a zero because numbers cannot start with a zero. Arithmetic calculations can be performed on numbers but not on telephone numbers. Therefore telephone numbers are stored as text.

Try typing this telephone number into a spreadsheet (without using spaces) and see what happens: 00442085555555

If this was a number it would actually be 442 085 555 555 which is 442 billion, 85 million, 555 thousand, 5 hundred and fifty-five.

Date/time

This data type is used to store dates and times. The number data type cannot be used because it works in 10s, 100s, 1000s, but a date/time data type will be able to work with days, months, years, hours, minutes and seconds. It will also enable dates and times to be sorted into a logical order.

WORKED EXAMPLE 10.46

Dates can be formatted in a variety of ways such as:

18/7/1965

18-07-65

18th July 1965

July 18, 1965

However, they are always stored in the same way: day 18, month 7, year 1965. The symbols (such as th, / and -) are not stored. They are just displayed.

WORKED EXAMPLE 10.47

Times can also be formatted in a variety of ways:

12:55 p.m.

14:02.45 (hours, minutes, seconds)

0305 hrs (five past three in the morning)

Dates and times can also be combined to give a specific time on a specific date, for example:

12:55 18-07-65

Internationally, days, months and years can be stored in a different order. It is important to specify this order when setting up a data type. For example, in America, they use month, day, year (e.g. 7/18/1965), whereas in the UK they use day, month, year (e.g. 18/7/1965). This can become a problem when the day part is 12 or less. What date is 5/10/2019? Is it 5 October or 10 May?

Boolean/logical

Boolean or logical data types can have only one of two values. These two values are TRUE and FALSE, but are sometimes represented as YES and NO. If you use

Microsoft Access you will notice that this data type is referred to as the Yes/No data type.

Data is only a Boolean data type if the two possible answers are TRUE/FALSE or YES/NO. Boolean/logical data types do not include data like 'M' or 'F' for Male or Female. These are actually text data types. Just because there are two possible answers for the data does not mean that it is a Boolean.

Select appropriate data types

You will need to know how to choose an appropriate data type for a given situation. You will also need to be able to select appropriate data types when creating spreadsheets and databases. The following guidelines should help you:

Rule	Data type
The data contains whole numbers only	Integer
The data contains a decimal number	Real
The data starts with a zero (e.g. telephone number)	Text
The data includes letters, symbols or spaces	Text
The data is a date, a time or both	Date/Time
The only values for the data are TRUE/FALSE or YES/NO	Boolean/Logical

Table 10.8: Data type rules.

PRACTICAL ACTIVITY 10.34

Data is to be stored in a database about party bookings. Select the most appropriate data type for each of the following fields:
- Date of Party
- Time of Party
- Room being Booked
- Number of Guests
- Deposit
- Price Charged
- Paid?

Questions

9 Identify and describe three components of a data dictionary.

10 Select the most appropriate data type for the following information stored about flights:

Flight number (e.g. BA372)

Departure date

Departure time

Airport code (e.g. ACF)

Max number of passengers

Type (e.g. scheduled or charter)

Arrived?

11 Give reasons for the use of the text data type for storing a mobile phone number.

10.5 File and data management

File types

When data is saved it is stored in a file. Different software applications use data in different ways and so the way the data is stored differs between application types. For example, a database stores data in tables, whereas graphics software stores data about pixels.

Each file will typically include a header, which will be metadata (data about the file), then the main content will be stored followed by an end-of-file marker.

To a user, file types are usually identified by their extension. For example, Students.txt has an extension of txt which identifies it as a text file.

Examples of file types include:

Extension	File type	Purpose
.txt	Text	Stores plain text without any formatting. It is useful for transferring data between applications, but any formatting is lost.
.csv	Comma separated values	Stores structured data as plain text in rows with each column separated by commas. It is useful for transferring data between databases and spreadsheets or other applications which require data in a structured format.
.rtf	Rich text format	Stores text-based documents and includes the formatting (rich text). It is used to transfer data between different word processing or other text-based applications.
.docx	Microsoft Word XML	document Stores Microsoft's word processing documents in open XML format by saving all objects separately within a compressed file.
.pdf	Portable Document Format	Used to share read-only documents in a common format that can be accessed by any PDF reader software. It is commonly used for storing documents on the web as its contents can be indexed by search engines.
.odt	OpenDocument Text	An open-source file type for word processor documents that is used by open-source word processors and is not tied to one manufacturer.
.ods	OpenDocument Spreadsheet	An open-source file type for spreadsheets that is used by open-source spreadsheet software and is not tied to one manufacturer.
.odp	OpenDocument Presentation	An open-source file type for presentations that is used by open-source presentation software and is not tied to one manufacturer.
.html	Hypertext Markup Language	Stores web pages that can be opened by any web browser.
.xml	Extensible Markup Language	A data file that uses markup language to define objects and their attributes. They are used to transfer data between applications and can be read by a simple text editor.
.avi	Audio Video Interleave (video file)	Microsoft's method of storing video files with very little compression. File sizes are very big but no data is lost.
.mp4	Moving Pictures Experts Group (MPEG) Layer-4 (video file)	Audio and video are compressed and videos can be shared across the internet.
.wav	Waveform Audio File Format	Stores audio files as waveform data and enables different sampling rates and bit rates. This is the standard format for audio CDs but does not include compression so files are large.
.mp3	MPEG Layer-3 audio compression	Stores audio files in a compressed format approximately 10% the size of .wav files. Enables audio files to be shared across the internet.
.bmp	Bitmap image	Stores images as uncompressed raster images, storing each pixel individually. They are large files but can be accessed by any software.
.jpg	Joint Photographic Experts Group (compressed image)	Stores images as compressed raster images. It is used by most digital cameras and is a common format for web graphics but its use of lossy compression can mean some quality is lost.

Extension	File type	Purpose
.png	Portable Network Graphic	Stores images as compressed raster images and can include background transparency making it useful when images are required on different colour backgrounds.
.svg	Scalable Vector Graphics	Stores images as two-dimensional (2D) vector graphics. It is a standard format for using vector graphics on the web.
.exe	Executable program file	Stores program object code which enables the program to be executed by the computer.

Table 10.9: Examples of file types.

File formats

Proprietary file formats

Proprietary file formats are file types that have been developed by software manufacturers solely for use within their software. Using their own formats means that software manufacturers are free to develop software features that will store data in a way that is most suitable for the software and without waiting for a standard format to adapt to the software's needs. This enables software to improve and provide new features that otherwise would not be available.

Some examples of proprietary file formats include:

Extension	Software / file type	Manufacturer
.docx	Word processor	Microsoft Word
.wpd	Word processor	Corel Word Perfect
.msg	Email message	Microsoft Outlook
.ra	Audio / video streaming	Real Networks
.MOV	Movie	Apple
.psd	Graphics	Adobe Photoshop
.ai	Graphics	Adobe Illustrator
.accdb	Database	Microsoft Access

Table 10.10: Examples of proprietary file formats.

Open-source file formats

Open-source file formats are file types that have been developed for the purpose of being used by any proprietary software or open-source software. They are free from copyright, patents and trademarks, and their structure is known publicly. They are usually maintained by an international standards organisation or a public interest group. Their main advantage is that the files can be shared between users of different software. However, they can hold back development of open-source software because new features will require the file format standard to be updated.

Some examples of open-source file formats include:

File type	Type of data	Standards organisation
JPG	Compressed raster graphics	Developed by the Joint Photographic Experts Group (JPEG) and standardised by the International Organization for Standardization (ISO)
PNG	Compressed raster graphics with transparency support	ISO
ePub	E-book	International Digital Publishing Forum
XML	Extensible Markup Language	World Wide Web Consortium (W3C)
MPEG	Compressed video	Developed by the Moving Picture Experts Group (MPEG) and standardised by the ISO

Table 10.11: Examples of open source formats.

Generic file formats

Generic file formats enable data to be transferred between software. Data can be exported from software to a generic file format and generic file formats can be imported into software. They store the essential data but will not include any formatting.

The two main file formats used within databases are CSV and TXT. These were described earlier in this chapter in the section about importing data.

Types of file access

Indexed sequential access

Many years ago, data was often stored on tape, which required records to be written one after another onto the tape. This was known as storing the data serially. To access the data, all the records would need to be read from the first onwards until the required record was found or until the end of the file was reached. It could take a very long time to read through a whole table of data and so indexed sequential files were developed.

Indexed sequential files still store records one after each other but they are sorted into an order based upon a field. For example, data about customers might be sorted into surname order or customer ID order. Sequential files are particularly useful when data is being batch processed such as when gas bills are being generated and the master customer file will be processed in order of customer ID and any transaction files will also be processed in order of customer ID.

WORKED EXAMPLE 10.48

Here is an example of part of a master customer file showing the customers, the date the current meter reading was taken, the previous meter reading (amount of gas used) and the current meter reading:

Customer ID	Surname	Date of reading	Previous reading	Current reading
10	Black	12/1/20	32721	34872
11	Brown	15/12/19	02717	03281
12	White	8/1/20	47270	48572
13	Green	8/1/20	21827	23593

Here is an example of part of a transaction file that will be processed to update the master customer file with new gas meter readings:

Customer ID	Date of reading	Meter reading
11	12/3/20	03692
13	12/3/20	23997

This is what the master customer file will look like once the transaction file has been processed:

Customer ID	Surname	Date of reading	Previous reading	Current reading
10	Black	12/1/20	32721	34872
11	Brown	12/3/20	03281	03692
12	White	8/1/20	47270	48572
13	Green	12/3/20	23593	23997

When reading the data in sequential files, it was necessary to read the whole file serially from the beginning because there was no way of knowing where each record was stored. Indexed sequential files are stored in exactly the same way as sequential files but the file also has an index based on the field used to sort the file. A field with an index is known as a secondary key. The index file stores each secondary key value and the address in storage (e.g. tape or disk) where the first record containing that value is stored.

The index is small enough to store in main memory and so all that needs to be done to find a record is to search the index, find the location in storage and then read the records from that point until the record is found.

WORKED EXAMPLE 10.49

If Employee ID is the secondary key, then an index will exist with Employee ID as one column and the storage address as the other column. Rather than storing every single Employee ID, the index may store every tenth Employee ID for example.

Employee ID	Storage address
0001	A8FB2DC3
0011	9AEB08E3
0021	8C4DDDF5

Direct file access

The use of indexed sequential file access still requires some serial access of data and there are problems with trying to maintain a file in a sequential order as new records are added and old records deleted.

With direct file access, records are stored in a random order. There is no sequence. When storing a file, a hashing algorithm (calculation) is performed on the key field to determine the storage address where the record should be stored. Then, when the record is searched for, the same hashing algorithm will be performed on the key field to determine where the record can be found. The computer system can then directly access that record without having to read through other records.

Hierarchical database management systems

The hierarchical database model was created in the 1960s and is not commonly used today. The model relies upon a tree structure where each parent branch is the *one* side of a relationship and each child branch is the *many* side of a relationship. The tree structure can only deal with one-to-many relationships and can only work in one direction. Hierarchical databases are only suitable for models which have a strict hierarchy.

One such hierarchy is the file system used within computer systems. The file system may look something like this:

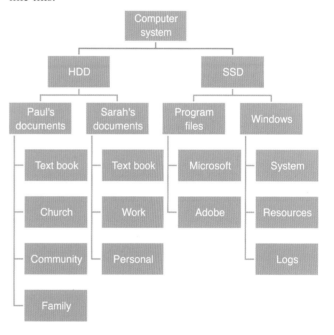

Figure 10.47: Folder structure.

Each disk contains folders and there may be further subfolders within each folder. Each subfolder has only one folder at the level above it. To find the data, the user browses through the system, selects the disk the data is stored on, then selects the folder, then selects the next subfolder until eventually the file is found.

This same process is used when searching for data within a hierarchical database. This means that data at the top of the tree is very quick to access.

WORKED EXAMPLE 10.50

A bank could store data about customers and the accounts they hold:

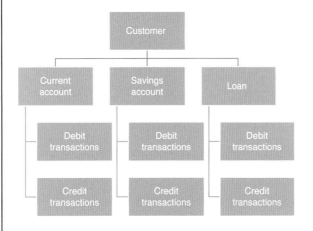

Figure 10.48: Hierarchical bank.

Management information systems

Introduction to management information systems

A management information system (MIS) provides summary information to managers to enable them to make decisions. The MIS will collate data from a database and present it in the form of reports and charts. These reports and charts can be produced within the database system itself or they may be part of an additional piece of software that is used to analyse the data.

The additional software is likely to collate data from more than one database and interconnect the data from those databases to produce reports that analyse all the data together. When additional software is used to collate data from more than one database, it is often referred to as an executive information system (EIS).

A MIS has the following essential features:

- data is collated from databases and other sources
- data is interconnected from different sources

- data is analysed to provide the data that is required by management
- summary reports and charts are produced for managers that will help with decision making.

The reports and charts are created by people, but once they are created they can be reused as the data changes within the data sources. It's important that the reports and charts provide information that managers need.

Using MISs

Information from a MIS is used by managers to make decisions. Managers can examine the summary information and then decide upon actions to take. Reports are provided at regular times and it's also possible for managers to request ad hoc reports if they need additional information.

WORKED EXAMPLE 10.51

Managers within a large second-hand car dealership need to be able to monitor sales. They need to be able to identify trends in sales for different makes and models of cars at different times of the year. This will enable them to identify which cars are selling the most and which are making the most profit. They can then decide which second-hand cars they want to acquire to sell.

Marketing managers can analyse how effective a marketing campaign was by comparing sales figures during an advertising campaign with sales figures outside the advertising campaign. This will help them to decide whether to run similar campaigns in the future.

Questions

12 Explain why generic file types are needed.

13 Describe the steps involved to find a file using indexed sequential access.

14 Explain why direct access is used for databases in preference to indexed sequential access.

15 Describe two features of management information systems (MISs).

Consider how long it would take to find a single record of data from 10,000 records on paper rather than using a database.

Discuss the problems that would occur with written data rather than a database if changes needed to be made to the data, if the data needed to be sorted, if queries needed to be performed on the data or if calculations needed to be performed on the data.

Discuss what problems might be experienced if a relational database didn't use referential integrity.

Consider times when you have used data in generic file formats, proprietary file formats and open source file formats. What was the purpose of using these formats and how did it help you complete a task?

REVIEW PRACTICAL ACTIVITY

A shopping centre would like to monitor the inspections that are carried out at their food outlets. These inspections include Health & Safety, Food Hygiene, VAT and Franchise Quality Control, amongst others. Figure 10.49 is an example of an Outlet Inspection Card that the organisation currently uses in a paper based format:

OutletCode	00929
OutletName	Wimpy
Floor	3
Location	C4
Telephone	0121392075
AnnualFee	£85,000.00

InspectionName ▾	Agency ▾	InspectionDate ▾	Pass ▾	Penalty Points ▾
Health & Safety	H&S Executive	08/01/2011	☑	50
VAT	HM Revenue & Customs	09/02/2011	☐	20
Food Hygiene	Trading Standards	23/02/2011	☐	35
Food Hygiene	Trading Standards	04/03/2011	☑	35
Franchise Quality Control	Franchise Partners	29/03/2011	☐	20
Health & Safety	H&S Executive	10/06/2011	☑	50

Figure 10.49: Outlet inspection card.

1   Create a database that can be used by the shopping centre to monitor these inspections. Import the three files **10.16 outlet.txt, 10.17 inspectionvisits.txt** and **10.18 inspectiontypes.txt**. Normalise the data to third normal form by removing redundant data and replacing it with appropriate foreign keys and adding any primary keys that might be needed.

2   Create relationships and enforce referential integrity for the database.

3   Penalty points are only applied if the inspection is failed. Using a query, create a calculated field that will show the 'Penalty Incurred' only if an inspection is failed.

4   a   Create a data entry screen that will look similar to Figure 10.49 and will allow the entry of data about outlets and their inspections. It should include a subform and only show the penalty if one was incurred.

   b   Create a drop down menu that can be used to select the inspection type on the subform.

CONTINUED

c   Add a calculation to the form to calculate the total penalty due. The penalty is calculated as £100 multiplied by the total penalty points.

d   Create a button that will print the Inspection Data Entry Screen for a single outlet.

5   Create validation rules that will prevent invalid data being entered for the following scenarios:

   a   There are 4 floors in the Sheep Square Shopping Centre from 0 (ground) to 4

   b   Inspection dates must always be after the opening date of an outlet

6   a   Produce a query to show the number of inspections passed between 1/2/2011 and 30/6/2011 for each type of inspection.

   b   Produce a query showing a list of the outlet codes for any outlets that have failed at least 2 inspections.

7   Create a graph that will show the Inspection Names on the *x*-axis and the Number of Passes on the *y*-axis using an appropriate title and clearly labelled axes.

8   Create a report which shows all failed inspections grouped by the type of inspection. The report should include the name of each outlet, the agency used for the inspection and the inspection date.

9   Create a menu that will open the following items and include an option to exit the application:

   •   Outlet Data Entry Screen

   •   Inspection Passes Graph

   •   Inspection Failure Report.

EXAM-STYLE QUESTIONS

1   A website accepts donations for charities. Each donor may make several donations to one or more charities. This information is stored in a relational database.

   a   Identify three tables that should be used within the database. [3]

   b   Describe two relationships that would be used within the database. [2]

   c   Explain how referential integrity is important to this database. [2]

   [Total 7]

2   An apartment complex stores data about its customers, their bookings and the rooms they are staying in. The entity relationship diagram (ERD) is shown in Figure 10.50:

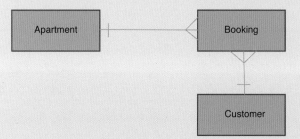

Figure 10.50: Entity relationship diagram.

CONTINUED

a   Identify two foreign key fields that should be used within the database.   [2]

b   Select the most appropriate data type for each of the fields below in the apartment table: [3]

   i   Telephone Number

   ii   Swimming Pool

   iii   Bedrooms

c   Describe how a dynamic parameter query could be used to produce a list of customers that have stayed in an apartment during a specified time period.   [4]

d   Explain why this query would be a complex query.   [2]

e   Identify and describe three items of a data dictionary that could be used in this database.   [6]

[Total 17]

3   Students in a college belong to tutor groups. Each tutor group has one tutor. The students are able to borrow books from the college library.

Normalise the unnormalised data below to 3NF. Show each table, its attributes and its primary keys.   [4]

STUDENT

Name

Address

Telephone

Tutor Group

Tutor Name

Book ID

Title

Due Date

4   Describe the difference between proprietary and open-source file formats.   [2]

SUMMARY CHECKLIST

☐   I can assign a data type and an appropriate field size to a field.

☐   I can understand the three relationships: one-to-one, one-to-many and many-to-many.

☐   I can create and use relationships.

☐   I can create and interpret an entity relationship diagram.

☐   I can understand the difference between a flat file and a relational database and when one might be preferred in certain situations.

☐   I can create a relational database.

☐   I can understand the function of key fields.

☐   I can set primary, compound and foreign keys.

☐   I can understand referential integrity and its importance.

☐   I can use referential integrity.

CONTINUED

- [ ] I can validate and verify data entry.
- [ ] I can perform searches.
- [ ] I can use arithmetic operations and logical functions to perform calculations within a database.
- [ ] I can sort data.
- [ ] I can design and create an appropriate data entry form.
- [ ] I can design and create a switchboard menu within a database.
- [ ] I can import and export data.
- [ ] I can understand the characteristics of data in unnormalised form, first, second and third normal forms.
- [ ] I can understand the advantages and disadvantages of normalisation.
- [ ] I can normalise a database to first, second and third normal form.
- [ ] I can understand the components of a data dictionary.
- [ ] I can create a data dictionary.
- [ ] I can select appropriate data types for a given set of data and a given situation.
- [ ] I can identify different data types.
- [ ] I can use static and dynamic parameters in a query and understand their use.
- [ ] I can understand when static and dynamic parameters should be used in queries.
- [ ] I can understand when simple, complex and nested queries should be used.
- [ ] I can understand when summary queries, including cross-tab queries should be used.
- [ ] I can understand different file types and their uses.
- [ ] I can understand what is meant by proprietary and open-source file formats.
- [ ] I can understand why open-source file formats are needed.
- [ ] I can understand why generic file formats are needed.
- [ ] I can understand the use of indexed sequential access.
- [ ] I can understand the use of direct file access.
- [ ] I can understand the use of a hierarchical database management system.
- [ ] I can understand the features of a management information system (MIS).
- [ ] I can understand how a MIS can be used by organisations.

Chapter 11

Sound and video editing

LEARNING INTENTIONS

By the end of this chapter, you will be able to:

- edit a video clip to meet the requirements of its intended application and audience
- know and understand how and why typical features found in video editing software are used
- know and understand the effects of different methods of compression on video
- edit a sound clip to meet the requirements of its intended application and audience
- know and understand how and why typical features found in sound editing software are used
- know and understand why file size depends on sampling rate and sampling resolution
- know and understand the effects of different methods of compression on sound.

Introduction

Sound and video editing skills are increasingly desirable for the individual and businesses.

Some people find that they can make money to supplement their income by creating high-quality videos about anything from video games to makeup tutorials. There are also internet stars who build a whole business around their video channels and rely on their video editing skills. There are also people who do the same using podcasts and rely on their sound editing skills.

Many businesses also use the media of video and sound to market their product or service. They hire whole teams of people to use their video and sound editing skills to ensure they produce high quality marketing media.

The ability to create high-quality videos and sound files is much dependent on creativity and accuracy. Creativity allows you to produce unique media that is attractive to the intended audience. Accuracy ensures that the media meets any given brief for the media, and that a refined product is produced.

Editing video and sound files can be a lot of fun. You will find that out as you progress through this chapter. You will begin by editing video clips to create a video, you will then edit sound clips to create a soundtrack that you will add to your video.

11.1 Video editing

Video editing is the manipulation and organisation of video **clips**. Video editing software is used to do this. Before the development of video editing software, the only way to edit videos was to physically cut and stick the analogue tape that the video had been recorded on.

KEY WORD

clip: a short piece of a video or audio file

Figure 11.1: Cutting and sticking film.

There are a wealth of skills that you can learn to edit videos. This chapter will cover many of them. You will read about the skill, why it is used and how to use it, then you will complete practical activities to practise using the skill.

You may be using different video editing software to that used in this chapter. However, you will find that most video editing software has similar features that can be used in similar ways. This may mean you need to search the menus of your software to find an equivalent feature.

Setting the aspect ratio and resolution

The **aspect ratio** of a video refers to the size proportions of a video. It is the ratio of the width of an image in comparison to the height. Choosing the right aspect ratio for your video is important. Deciding which is the right aspect ratio will depend on the platform on which the video will be played. The two most common aspect ratios are 4:3 and 16:9.

The aspect ratio 4:3 is an older, traditional ratio for videos. It comes from the shape of a **frame** on a traditional film strip.

Figure 11.2: Film strip frame.

It is the ratio used for most old film and television programmes. For many years, people were happy viewing videos in this ratio, until the development of wide screen. When videos using the 4:3 ratio were played on widescreen televisions, the image became distorted because the picture was stretched to fit the screen. This led to the creation of the 16:9 ratio.

The aspect ratio 16:9 is used for almost every digital media today. Film, television and online video platforms mostly use this ratio, so it is often the most suitable ratio to set when creating a video. Video developers in the 1980's decided that this would be the industry standard.

Here is a comparison of the different ratios:

Figure 11.3: Comparison of aspect ratios.

A **resolution** can also be set for a video. The resolution is the number of pixels in width compared to the number of pixels in height. A resolution of 1920 × 1080 would mean that each frame of the video has 2 073 600 pixels. Different platforms require different resolutions, depending how large the image will be when displayed and the quality required. 1920 × 1080 is the industry standard for high definition. The resolution for standard definition is 640 × 360.

Questions

1   Find out what the resolution is for 4K.
2   Find out why black bars are sometimes added to the top or sides of a video.

Setting the aspect ratio and resolution of a video can be done when setting up the video for editing. It can also be set or changed when rendering a video file when the editing process is completed.

The software this chapter uses for video editing is Davinci Resolve. This is a powerful video editing software that has a wealth of different features that you will learn to use.

The aspect ratio and resolution settings are combined in this software. You can select a pre-set aspect ratio, where you can then change the resolution is required.

To open the menu for aspect ratio you need to click the small settings icon (cog) in the bottom right corner.

You can select one of the settings from the drop-down menu at the top. This will also provide a resolution for the video in the boxes below. You can manually change the resolution in these boxes, if required.

PRACTICAL ACTIVITY 11.01

Open your video editing software. Save the file for the video that you will create with the filename **BeeProject**.

Locate the aspect ratio and resolution settings. View the settings available in the timeline resolution drop-down menu.

For the activities in this book, you can leave the setting at 1920 × 1080.

Adding a title slide

Title slides are a text-based slide that are used in videos. Text based slides can be used at various points in a video to provide written information for the viewer. This text-based information can be used for various reasons:

- to introduce the viewer to the video
- to clarify what the viewer will see, or has just seen, in a video
- to provide relevant facts and figures
- to provide information such as company contact details.

To create a title slide you need to click the 'Effects Library' icon in the top left corner. This will open menus in the bottom left corner. Select the 'Toolbox' option, then from this menu select the 'Titles' option. Locate the 'Text' option in the panel to the right. Click and hold this option and drag it right to the timeline.

You can then double click the title slide in the timeline to edit it. This will open an editing panel for the slide at the right of the screen. Within this panel you can scroll down and there are options to change the font style, size, colour and alignment.

To change the timing for the title slide, right click on the title slide in the timeline and a menu will appear. Select 'Change Clip Duration' from the menu and a window will open that you can enter the duration you require for the title slide.

PRACTICAL ACTIVITY 11.02

Add a title slide to your video. Edit the text to read:

Did you know that bees are very important to our world?

Edit the slide by:

- splitting the text across two lines
- changing the font style to Courier
- changing the font size to 80
- changing the alignment to centre
- changing the timing for the slide to three seconds.

Keep the background colour as black and keep the text white.

Importing a video

To insert a video clip into your video, you will need to import the file into the software. To import a video file, select the 'File' option from the menu bar across the top of the screen. This will open a menu. Select 'Import File' from the menu and this will open a sub-menu. Select 'Import Media' from the sub-menu and this will open up your files. Locate and select your video file and click 'Open'.

The video will appear in the file panel in the top left corner. To insert the clip into the video, click and drag the video clip to the timeline. You can then move the video to where it is required by clicking and dragging it up or down the timeline.

PRACTICAL ACTIVITY 11.03

Import the video file **11.01 BeeFly.mov** into the software. Insert the video into the timeline, next to the title slide.

Trimming a video clip

Trimming a video clip is an essential skill. Most video clips are not likely to contain exactly what you require. The clip may have unnecessary content at the start or finish, and this means that it will need to be trimmed to remove this content.

To trim a video clip, select the clip in the timeline and select the 'Trim' option in the menu bar at the top of the screen. Select the option 'Trim Mode' and this will enable you to trim the video clip. You can also select trim mode by clicking the second icon in the tool bar directly above the timeline.

Move the cursor to the start or end of the video clip and it will change to become square brackets. Click and drag the video clip left or right to trim the content that you do not require in the video clip.

You may need to play the clip first to note the timings for the content that you want to trim out of the video.

If you want to trim content off the end of the clip, you can also right click on the clip and use the 'Change Clip Duration option' from earlier. This will trim the content off the end of the clip to the timing that you enter.

The software will remain in trim mode until you change the mode again. If you want to revert to normal mode, select the option 'Normal Edit Mode' from the 'Trim' menu, or click the first icon in the tool bar above the timeline.

PRACTICAL ACTIVITY 11.04

Trim the end of the BeeFly video clip to make it five seconds long.

Adding captions and subtitles

Captions and subtitles are text-based content that appear over the top of the video content. Captions can be used to provide further information about what is being shown in the video clip. Subtitles can be used to provide a text-based version of any dialogue that is being spoken in the video. This is useful for any viewers who may be deaf, allowing them to read any speech that occurs in the video. Subtitles can also be used to display the spoken content in a different language, allowing viewers of different languages to understand the speech in the video. Subtitles usually appear at the bottom of the video.

Captions and subtitles are created by adding a text layer over the video. To add text to a video clip you need to use the same option that you used to add a title slide. This time, you need to drag the 'Text' option to be placed above the video clip that you want the text to appear on. This will create a second track in your video. You can then edit the text in the same way that you did for the title slide.

You can place the text in the exact place that you want it on the video clip. To do this, forward the video to the clip with the text, so that you can see it in the video preview pane. A quick way to do this is to use the small, red arrow that appears at the top of the timeline. If you drag this left or right, it will allow you to move forward or backward through the video. To move the text, click on the text and a white box will appear around it. Click and hold in the centre of the box and you can drag the text to the place that you want it to appear.

You can also add subtitles with a separate subtitle option. You will find this in the effects library under the titles section, right at the bottom. This will add a new track to your video that will display subtitles as text at the bottom of your video.

Figure 11.4: Adding a caption.

PRACTICAL ACTIVITY 11.05

Add a caption to the BeeFly video that displays the text:

Bees are very important pollinators for fruits and vegetables. They help them grow!

Edit the text so that is appears on three lines, with a font style courier, font size 60 and the colour is black.

Move the caption so that it appears in the top left corner of the video.

Adding animations

Animations can be used to create an attractive **transition** from one video clip to the next. This can help keep the attention of your audience and raise the quality of your video. However, used incorrectly, animations can be very distracting. Imagine watching a video and there is a long animation from one clip into the next, or different effects and animations have been added to so many different parts, they stop you being able to watch some of the content. Would that make you feel frustrated?

KEY WORD
transition: the method with which one video clip merges into a second clip

The simplest animation that can be added between video clips is a fading effect. This is where the first clip will fade out at the end and the next clip will fade in at the beginning. This can help create a higher quality video as it looks more attractive than one video clip stopping and the next abruptly starting. It helps blend the video clips together for a smoother viewing experience.

It is simple to add a fade effect between videos. If you hover over the top corner of a video clip, with your cursor, you will see a small white box appear. If you click on this white box you can drag it left or right, into the video clip. You will see a timing box appear and the corner of the video will become shaded. The timing box shows how long the fade will be and the shaded area shows when the fade will start and finish in the video. If you apply this to the top right corner of the video clip, this will create a fade in effect. If you apply it to the top left corner of the video clip, this will create a fade out effect.

Figure 11.5: Adding a fade effect.

You can add different animations between videos using the effects library. Select the 'Effects Library' and select the option for 'Video Transitions'. Several different transitions will appear in the panel. To add an animation, click the animation and drag it to the video clip that you want to apply it to.

PRACTICAL ACTIVITY 11.06
Import the video clip BeeFlower **11.02 BeeFlower.mov** and insert it into your timeline, after the BeeFly video clip. Fade out the BeeFly video clip for one second. Fade in the BeeFlower video clip for one second. Add the animation 'Additive Dissolve' to the beginning of the BeeFly video clip. Add text to the BeeFlower video that displays: Honey bees must gather nectar from approximately 4 million flowers Format the text to match the BeeFly video clip. Display the text for three seconds. Add a second text box to the BeeFlower video that displays: just to make one kilogram of honey. Format the text to match the previous text, but with a size of 80. Place this text in the centre of the video clip. Display the text for three seconds. Create a 0.2 second fade out of the first text and a 0.2 second fade in of the second text Trim the video clip to be six seconds.

Zooming and panning

Zooming and panning are used often in video editing.

Zooming is moving the camera closer to or further away from the whole or part of a video clip. You can zoom in or out of a video clip to highlight a certain part of it.

Panning a video clip is when the camera moves across the video clip from one side to the other, or sometimes top to bottom, or vice-versa.

To zoom a video clip, you can use the zoom settings in the panel to the right side of the video viewing panel. Scroll this panel and you will find the zoom settings in the 'Transform' section. If you want to zoom in or out on the whole of a video clip, you can just increase or decrease the zoom values. The simplest way to do this, is to click and hold in the 'x' value box, drag your mouse right to zoom in and left to zoom out.

If you want to create a zoom on part of a video clip, you will need to use the key frame feature. You will need to set a key frame at the point you want the zoom to start, and at the point you want it to stop.

- To create a key frame, you will need to use the small diamond box to the right of the zoom values.

- Move the red arrow above the timeline, to the point in the video that you want the zoom to begin and click the small diamond. It will turn red.

- Move the red arrow to the point that to want the zoom to stop and click the small diamond to make it red again. This will add two key frames to the video clip.

- At the second key frame, zoom the video clip in or out to the point required.

If you play the video, you will see that the zoom will begin at the first key frame and end with the required zoom amount at the second key frame.

Figure 11.6: Zooming and panning.

To pan a video clip, you follow very similar instructions to zooming. Instead of using the zooming values, you use the position values. You also need to change the position values if you want to change the position at which the zoom in placed.

PRACTICAL ACTIVITY 11.07

Import the video clip **11.03 BeeHoneycomb.mov** and insert it into your timeline, after the BeeFlower video clip.

Trim the clip to eight seconds.

Create a zoom in effect on the honeycomb in the video, starting five seconds into the video clip and finishing at the end of the clip.

Add text to the clip to display:

Honey bees live in hives

Format the text to match the previous text.

Place it in the top right corner of the video clip.

Display the text for three seconds.

Add further text to the clip to display:

They create honeycomb by making wax, to store their honey

Format the text to match the previous text.

Place it in the bottom right corner of the video clip.

Display the text for five seconds.

Create a 0.2 second fade out and fade in between the two text elements.

Altering speed

When creating a video, you may find that you want to alter the speed of a video clip. You may have a video clip that you want to slow down. This could be because you want to make it clearer and easier to see what is happening in the video clip. It may also be because creating a slow-motion effect in a video can often make it more entertaining. You may find that you want to speed up a video clip. This could be because you have quite a long clip, that you do not want to trim, as all of the content is important, but you just want to speed it up so that it can be all shown in a quicker time. It may also be that creating a sped up effect in a video can also make it more entertaining.

To alter the speed of a video clip, right click on the video clip in the timeline and select the option 'Change Clip Speed' from the menu. This opens a window that allows you to alter the speed of the clip. The clip is set at 100% speed. Increasing this percentage will speed up the clip, decreasing this percentage will slow down the clip. You will notice that the 'Frames per Second' setting will automatically change when you alter the percentage. It is the number of frames per second that are used that sets the speed of the clip. The more frames per second there are, the faster the clip will play. You can also change this value, rather than the percentage, to speed up or slow down the clip.

Figure 11.7: Changing clip speed.

PRACTICAL ACTIVITY 11.08

Import the video clip **11.04 BeeFlySlow.mov** and insert it into your timeline after the BeeHoneycomb video clip.

Trim the clip so that it is five seconds long.

Alter the speed of the clip to 200%.

Joining video clips

When you are editing video clips, you may want to join them together. This is useful as it means that if you apply any kind of effect or animation, it will be applied to the whole clip. If two clips are joined together, they will be treated as a whole clip. It also means that you can create a smooth transition between the clips to make it look like they appear as one.

To join two video clips together you need to select both of the clips. Select the first clip and press and hold shift, then select the next clip. This will allow you to select both clips. When you have both clips selected, select the 'Timeline' option from the menu bar at the top of the screen. From the timeline menu, select the option 'Join Clips'. This will join the clips together. If you try and move the clips now you will see that they both move together.

PRACTICAL ACTIVITY 11.09

Insert another copy of the BeeFlySlow clip into your timeline, after the previous copy.

Trim the clip so that it is also five seconds long.

Join the first and second BeeFlySlow video clips together.

Add the video transition 'Smooth Cut' to the beginning of the second BeeFlySlow video clip.

Add a one second fade out and fade in effect between the BeeHoneycomb and BeeFlySlow video clips.

If you play the video now, you will see that a smooth transition is created between the two BeeFlySlow clips, the first playing at double speed, then smoothly transitioning into the normal speed.

PRACTICAL ACTIVITY 11.10

Add text to the BeeFlySlow video clip to display:

We need to take care of our bees.

Set a suitable format for the text.

Set the timing for three seconds.

Add further text to the BeeFlySlow video clip to display:

Without them we'll lose products such as honey, coffee and many fruits and vegetables.

Set a suitable format for the text.

Set the timing for seven seconds.

Create a smooth transition effect between the two text elements.

Add a text-based slide to the end of the video to display:

To find out more about bees visit the website [Insert a suitable website here]

Find a suitable website about the importance of bees to use in your video.

Format the text to be yellow this time.

Set the timing for five seconds.

Extracting a still image

A video may have a certain small part of it that you think would be a really good still image to have. A still image is just like a normal image. It is extracting one frame from the video that is a single image.

You may want to use this image in the video to highlight this particular part and allow it to be displayed on screen for a few seconds. You may want to use the image as a background for certain text in your video.

To extract a still image from a video, you will need to use a different section in the software, the 'Colour' section. At the bottom of the screen you will see various sections of the software. You have been working in the 'Edit' section. You need to click on the 'Colour' section, this will open a new panel, where you will see the video clips that you have used.

Click the video that you want to extract the still from. Wind the video to the place that you want to extract the still image, using the scroll bar at the bottom of the preview pane. Right click on the video in the preview pane and select the option 'Grab Still'. This will extract a still image of the video at this point. You will see this image appear in the panel on the left. Right click the still image and export it. You can choose various file options to export the file. You can return to the 'Edit' section of the software and import the still image to use in your video.

Figure 11.8: Extracting a still image.

Once you have inserted the image still into your video, you can crop it in the same way that you crop a video clip, by adjusting the cropping values in the window on the right of the screen.

You can also resize the image if required. To resize the image, click the settings cog in the bottom right corner of the screen. This will open the window that you used initially to set the resolution of the video. Click the option in the window labelled 'Image scaling'. This will show some options for changing the size of the image. The image size will be automatically set to match the timeline settings. You can see this box ticked in the bottom half of the window. If you untick this box, you can use the boxes below this to type in the size that you want the image to be changed to.

Using filters

Filters can be used on both videos and images to change the look and feel of them. They may be used to correct the colour of an image or to change the feel and look of a video or an image.

To add a filter, locate the filters section. This can be found in the effects library under the option 'Open FX' and 'Filters'. Select the filter and drag it to the video or image on the timeline that you want to filter.

Removing sound

You may have sound on a video clip that you do not want. This may be because you intend to put a different sound file with that video clip, or just that you don't want any sound on that part of the video.

To remove sound from a video you need to first unlink the soundtrack from the video track. To unlink the soundtrack, click the video clip and you will see a red box appear around both the video clip and the soundtrack. The soundtrack appears underneath the video clip. Right click on the video clip and select the option 'Link Clips'. This will untick this option and unlink the soundtrack from the video clip. Click off the video clip and then click just the soundtrack. Make sure the red highlight box is only around the sound track this time. Right click on the soundtrack and select the option 'Delete Selected'. This will remove the soundtrack from the video clip.

Figure 11.9: Deleting a sound track.

Adding credits

Credits normally appear at the end of a video and are used to display information about the creation of the video. They are used to show information such as who created the video, who produced it, who directed, who wrote the script, and they are also used to give credit to authors of any material that may have been used in the video, for copyright reasons. The text for credits is normally set to scroll up the screen from bottom to top.

The option to add credits to a video is in the effects library, under the option 'Titles'. Before, you have selected the 'Text' option in this section, but to create credits, you need to select the 'Scroll' option. Drag the 'Scroll' option to the timeline to the place that you want to add the credits. This will create a text box, as before, and you can edit the text in the same way.

You are starting to have the makings of an excellent video editing project!

Exporting a video clip

You need to export your video clip to a suitable file format for the platform on which it will mostly be played. Most people will choose a universal file format to allow the video to be played on many devices, using different software. At present, the only people that would be able to play your video file is those that have the software used to create it. This is because it is saved in a particular file format for that software.

When you export a video, it combines all the elements in the video together and changes them into the format that you have selected.

You will need to select different formats depending on whether the video will be used on platforms such as websites, or a large screen television. Except for a RAW file format, that will save the 'raw' data in the file, each file format will compress the file using either a lossy or lossless **compression** method.

KEY WORD

compression: reducing the size of a file, for example, an image

Lossy compression will remove unnecessary data from the video file to make the file size smaller. Lossy will slightly affect the quality of the video file, but most of this will go unseen or unheard by the average human eyes and ears.

Lossless compression will not remove any data in the compression process and will allow the original data file to be reinstated. This means the original quality of the video will be retained. Lossless compression can work in various ways. One method is for the compression software to identify repeating patterns in the file and group them, often using an index.

The type of file format you choose for a video file will depend on how important the quality of the video is, how big the file size can realistically be for the platform and the type of platform it will be played on.

If you wanted to export the video in a lossless format, as you want to play it on a larger screen at full quality, you may choose a file format such as MOV or AVI. If you want to export the file in a lossy format as the quality of it isn't essential, but you need the file size to be smaller, you may choose a file format such as MP4.

If you wanted your video to be displayed on a website, you need to choose a file format that is suitable for the web.

Questions

3   Find out which video file formats are suitable for the web.

4   Find out whether the file formats for the web use lossy or lossless compression.

To export your video, you will first need to render it. Rendering a video is where your computer processes all the data that you have included in your video and changes it to the format you require, to create your video file. Rendering a video can be one of the most demanding jobs for a computer and often takes a lot of processing power.

To render your video, you need to use a different section of the software again, the 'Deliver' section. Click the 'Deliver' section at the bottom of the screen and a new panel will open.

You will see a panel at the top left of the screen that you will use to select the options for rendering. Make sure that the 'Custom' option and 'Video' section are selected. You need to enter a suitable file name and choose a suitable location to save the file.

You will need to scroll down to find the 'Format' drop down box. Click this drop down and you will see several different formats that you can select for your video. Once you have selected a suitable file format, click 'Add to Render Queue'. This adds the file to your render queue which appears at the right side of the screen. When you are ready to render your video, you need to click 'Start Render'. You will see the software start to work through the video and render it.

You can now go to the location that you chose to render your video and play the video file.

PRACTICAL ACTIVITY 11.15

Export your video in a file format that is lossless.

Export your video in a file format that is suitable for the web.

TIP

You should practice always saving a copy of the file in a generic file format as well as in the proprietary software format.

11.2 Sound editing

Sound editing is the manipulation and organisation of sound clips. Sound editing software is used to do this. Before the development of sound editing software, the only way to edit sound was also to physically cut and stick the analogue tape that the sound had been recorded on.

Figure 11.10: Analogue audio tape.

There are a wealth of skills that you can learn to edit sound files. This chapter will cover many of them. You will read about the skill, why it is used, how to use it, then you will complete practical activities to practise using the skill.

You may find that you are using different sound editing software to that used in this chapter. However, you will find that most sound editing software has similar features that can be used in similar ways. This may mean you need to search the menus of your software to find an equivalent feature.

The software this chapter uses for sound editing is Audacity. This is a widely used sound editing software that has a wealth of different features that you will learn to use.

Importing a sound file

To have sound to edit, you need to import a sound file. You will probably need to import multiple sound files into the software throughout a sound editing project. Each time you import a sound file it will be imported in a new **track**. A track in the software is a layer of sound. When multiple tracks are layered together this means that different sound files can be played at the same time.

KEY WORD

track: a specific recording, for example, of one instrument or voice – the tracks can then be edited separately and combined to play concurrently

To import a sound file, select the 'File' option in the menu bar at the top of the screen. It is the first option in the top left corner. This will open another menu, select 'Import' and 'Audio'. Find the audio file that you want to import and select 'Open'. You will now see the sound file imported into a track in the software.

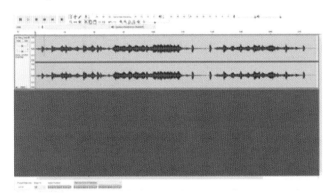

Figure 11.11: Imported sound tracks.

PRACTICAL ACTIVITY 11.16

Import the sound file **11.05 Piano_track.mp3**.

Trimming a sound clip

Trimming a sound clip is an essential skill. Most sound clips are not likely to contain exactly what you require. The clip may have unnecessary content at the start or finish, and this means it will need to be trimmed to remove this content. You may also need to trim a sound clip to make it match the timing of a video that you intend to add the sound to.

To trim a sound clip, you need to select the part of the clip that you want to remove. To begin to select the sound clip you will need to make sure that you have the selection tool selected. This is the tool that is automatically selected when you open the software, but to make sure it is the tool that you have selected, you can find it on the tool bar located at the top of the screen in the centre. The selection tool looks like an uppercase I. Once the selection tool is selected, move your cursor to the point in the sound clip that you want to remove. Click and hold the left mouse bottom and drag the cursor along the sound clip to highlight the part of the clip that you want to remove. You will see that it has been highlighted in a blue-grey colour. Click the cut tool, that looks like a pair of scissors in the tool bar, and the highlighted section of the sound clip will be removed.

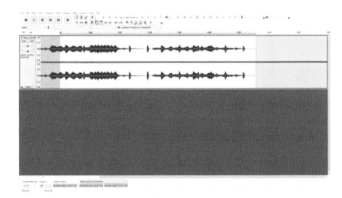

Figure 11.12: Selecting part of a track.

PRACTICAL ACTIVITY 11.17

Check the timing of your BeeProject video. You should find that it is approximately 41 seconds long.

Trim the sound clip to match the length of your video.

Splicing and joining sound clips

Splicing a sound clip is cutting it up into different parts so that you can use what you require of the different parts. You can then join the parts that you require, to edit the sound clip that you are working on. This helps cut out parts of the clip in the middle that you may not want, and to join the parts that you do want. You may find that you like the start of the sound clip and a certain part in the middle. You can use editing tools to help you first select the middle section you require and copy that, trim the clip to the part that you liked at the start, then paste the middle section into the track that was copied, to join the parts of the clip you require.

To splice a clip, highlight the part of the clip that you require and select the copy tool from the toolbar. This looks like two pieces of paper layered. You can also use the keyboard shortcut, Ctrl + C.

To paste the copy that you have made of the clip, move the cursor to the place in the track that you want to add the copied clip and click the paste tool in the tool bar. This looks like a clipboard. The copied clip section will then be pasted.

PRACTICAL ACTIVITY 11.18

Import a copy of **11.5 Piano_Track.mp3**. You will see this has imported as a second track under the one you already have. At approximately 39 seconds into the sound clip, you should see the sound wave section that looks like this:

CONTINUED

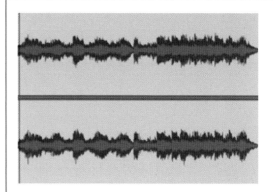

Figure 11.13: Piano_Track at approximately 39 seconds.

Highlight this section of the clip and copy it. Paste this section of the clip into your first soundtrack at the 16 second point.

Delete the second soundtrack that you imported. You no longer need it.

You should now have a sound clip that is approximately 50 seconds long. Trim the end of the clip again to the correct length for your video.

Fading in and fading out a sound clip

If a sound clip suddenly starts or suddenly stops, it can seem quite a harsh entrance or exit for the sound. This may be the effect that you require if you are trying to make a loud and exciting impact for your sound file. However, you may want to create a softer, more gentle entrance and exit for your sound file, this can be done by fading in and fading out the sound clip.

To add a fade effect to the sound clip, highlight the part of the clip that you want to fade in or out. Select the 'Effect' option in the tool bar at the top of the screen. This will open a large menu. To fade the sound in, select the 'Fade In' option, or to fade the sound out, select the 'Fade Out' option.

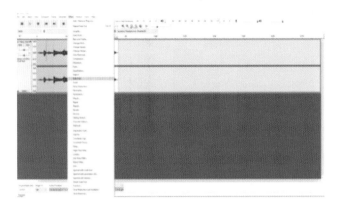

Figure 11.14: Fade out effect.

PRACTICAL ACTIVITY 11.19

Add a fade out effect to the last five seconds of your sound clip.

Changing the pitch of a sound clip

All sound is made by vibrations of particles. The faster they vibrate, the higher the pitch of the sound. The pitch of a sound is a measure of the sound frequency. The higher the frequency, the higher the pitch of the sound.

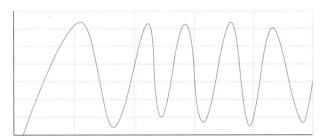

Figure 11.15: Example of high pitch sound wave.

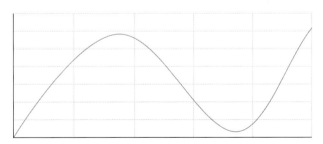

Figure 11.16: Example of low pitch sound wave.

You may find that a certain sound or sound clip is too high or too low. You can change the pitch of a sound clip to make it the pitch that you require.

To change the pitch of a sound clip, select the 'Effects' option in the menu bar at the top of the screen. Select the option 'Change Pitch' from the menu. You can change the pitch in two ways, by changing the key of the sound clip, or changing the frequency of the sound. You can use the key if you know that the music is played in a certain key and you need it in a different key. For example, the music is recorded in the key of A Major, but you want to change it to the key of C Major. If you are not a musical person, the key of music may not be familiar to you, therefore, a better option to use is changing the frequency values. The simplest way to do this is to use the blue arrow on the sliding bar underneath the frequency values. You can slide this right or left to make the pitch higher or lower, respectively.

PRACTICAL ACTIVITY 11.20

Import the sound clip **11.06 Bee_Voiceover.mp3** and move it to be played at the end, so that it finishes at the same time as the piano music.

[Hint: You can use the 'Time Shift Tool' in the tool bar to move a section of sound.]

Lower the pitch of the voiceover by 5%.

Adding or adjusting reverberation

Reverberation is a very old and traditional effect that is used with sound. It is an effect on the sound that is used to make it sound like it is being played in a larger room. If you play sound in a larger room, the acoustics of the room often change the sound, creating a slight echo effect. It can be used to create a fuller and softer feel to sound.

KEY WORD

reverberation: the number of echoes of the sound and the way that they decay – reverberation can be natural (caused by the room in which the sound is played) or introduced by editing software

---

To add reverberation to a sound clip, highlight the sound clip and select the 'Effects' option from the menu bar at the top of the screen. Select the option 'Reverb'. There are several values that can be used to change the reverberation, but the simplest value to change is the 'Reverberance' value. Increase it to add reverberance and decrease it to remove reverberance.

PRACTICAL ACTIVITY 11.21

Increase the reverberance by 10% for the Bee_Voiceover.

Overdubbing a sound clip

Overdubbing is when sound is layered so that each layer can be individually edited. When songs are recorded by professional music artists, overdubbing is used. Each musical instrument will be recorded on its own, so that it can be imported into its own track. The vocals will also be recorded on their own and imported into their own track. All the tracks are then layered to create the song. The benefit is that each layer can be edited independently of each other, to get the exact sound required for the song.

The addition of the Bee_Voiceover clip to your sound file in the previous activities is an example of overdubbing.

PRACTICAL ACTIVITY 11.22

Write a five second intro to your bee video.

Record your intro and import it into the software, overdubbing the piano music at the start.

Adding echo and delay to a sound clip

An echo is a reflection of the original sound, with a slight delay. This can often result in the original sound heard, then the echo heard slightly afterwards. It is caused by sound waves being reflected back off obstructions, such as walls. Adding an echo to sound can make it sound more distinctive. This is useful if you want a particular sound to be heard.

To add an echo to your sound clip, highlight the sound clip and select the 'Effects' option from the menu bar

at the top of the screen. Select the option 'Echo'. There are two values that you need to consider for your echo. The first is the delay value and the second is the decay value. The delay represents how long it will take to echo the sound and the decay value represents how much the echo will fade.

An echo effect can also be created using a different option in the 'Effects' menu. This is the 'Delay' option. This option can be used to create multiple echoes of the sound and change how the sound is echoed. There are three types of delay options you can choose. These are: regular, bouncing ball and reverse bouncing ball. These three options can be found in the drop down menu at the top of the window that opens when you select the 'Delay' option from the 'Effects' menu.

A regular delay will set a fixed time between each delay, a bouncing ball delay will make the echoes increasingly closer together and the reverse bouncing ball will make the echoes increasingly further apart. You can also set the number of times that you want the sound to echo.

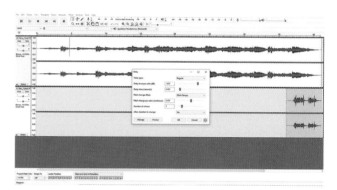

Figure 11.17: Adding a delay.

PRACTICAL ACTIVITY 11.23

Add an echo to your voiceover intro. Set the delay to 0.5 seconds and the decay to 0.5.

Applying noise reduction to a sound clip

Sometimes when audio is recorded there can be unwanted background noise that gets recorded too. This could simply be a low hum of any other equipment being used, or a soft hissing noise that can sometimes occur on recordings. It is possible to remove this kind of background noise using a setting called noise reduction.

To apply noise reduction, select a part of the track that contains just the background noise only that you want to reduce. This will allow the software to gain an understanding of what you want to reduce. Select the 'Effects' option from the menu bar at the top of the screen. Select the option 'Noise reduction'. Click the option to 'Get noise profile'. This will allow the software to analyse the noise in that part of the track. You can then select the whole track and use the Noise reduction setting again, but this time by clicking 'OK' rather than 'Get noise profile'. This will apply the profile created of the background noise to the whole track and reduce it throughout.

If you have any unwanted background noise in your recording of your intro for the video, you could try and remove it with noise reduction.

Applying Equalisation

Equalisation is the boosting or reducing of different frequencies in sound. The most common application of equalisation in everyday sound equipment is the ability to control the level of bass or treble on a sound system.

When used in sound editing, equalisation can also be used for this purpose and it can also be used to make certain sounds less prominent or eliminate unwanted sounds.

To apply equalisation to your soundtrack, select the section of sound that you want to alter. Then click the 'Effect' option on the top tool bar and select the option 'Equalization'. You will see a window open that looks like a graph.

Select the drop-down menu labelled 'Select Curve'. In this drop-down menu, you will see several different options. Each of these options will change the curve on the graph, altering the frequency of the sound, by adding or removing certain aspects to or from it. For example, the bass boost option will add more bass to the sound by increasing the lower frequencies. Another example is the treble cut. Treble refers to the higher frequencies in the sound, so this will cut all the higher frequencies out of the sound. Other options such as Telephone and Walkie-Talkie will change the frequencies of the sound to make it sound like it is being played through that equipment.

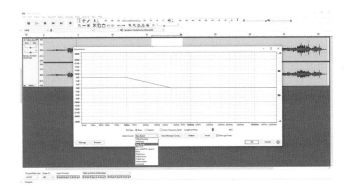

Figure 11.18: Applying a pre-set effect.

These options are pre-set options, but you can manually adjust the frequencies yourself to alter the sound. Click the radio button next to 'EQ Type' to select the option 'Graphic'. This will change the window to include a range of sliders that can be used to alter the different frequencies. Remember, if you alter the lower frequencies, this will alter the lower more bass tones in the sound, If you alter the higher frequencies, this will alter the high, more treble tones in the sound. The frequency on the graph is measured in Hertz (Hz) and it starts at approximately 20Hz at the lower frequencies and goes up to approximately 20000 Hz at the higher frequencies.

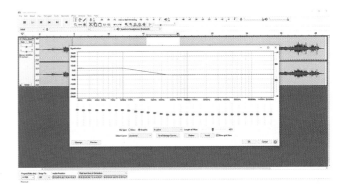

Figure 11.19: Manually adjusting the sound.

If you want to hear what the sound is like when you have moved some of these sliders, you can click the 'Preview' button in the bottom left corner of the window to hear the changes. One of the most useful applications of equalisation is to the sound of a voice. You can use it to make the voice sound clearer and of the tone that you want for your spoken aspects.

There are two other types of equalisation that you can apply, these are called high pass and low pass filters. A High-Pass filter is a type of equalisation effect that allows higher frequencies through, whilst cutting out lower frequencies. The cut-off for lower frequencies can be set and applied to any sound selected for the filter. A Low-Pass filter works in a similar way, except it cuts the higher frequencies rather that the lower ones. The High-Pass filter and Low-Pass filter options can also be found in the 'Effects' menu. Once you have selected either the High-Pass or Low-Pass filter, you can type in the frequency value that you want to be the cut-off value.

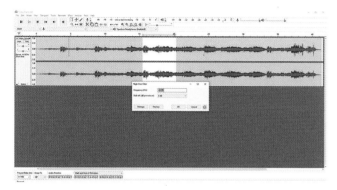

Figure 11.20: High-pass filter.

Changing the speed of a sound clip

It's possible to slow down or speed up a sound clip and there can be several advantages to this. Speeding up a sound clip can often have a very entertaining effect, especially if it is done with voices, as it can make them sound very squeaky. You may also need to speed up a sound clip to create a different effect with the music, for example, making it seem more upbeat. Slowing down a sound clip can also affect the feeling the sound creates, it could make it more relaxing. Musicians can often slow down a sound file when using it to practise a song. It can

allow them to get used to playing the song at a slower speed, before speeding up to play it at the correct speed.

To change the speed of your sound clip, highlight the sound clip and select the 'Effects' option from the menu bar at the top of the screen. Select the option 'Change Speed'. The simplest way to change the speed is to use the blue arrow on the sliding bar underneath the speed values. You can slide this right or left to make the speed faster or slower, respectively.

Normalising a sound clip

Sometimes when you take an audio recording, you play it back and find it is quieter than you had hoped for. There is a way to increase the volume of the recording, beyond just requiring the listener to turn the volume up. The setting that can be used to increase the volume is called normalisation.

Normalisation analyses the audio recording. When it has finished analysing it, it measures the difference between the highest peak in the audio and the maximum decibel limit (often automatically set to 0 decibels). It then calculates the difference. So, if the highest peak is −20 decibels, the difference will be 20 decibels. When the sound file is normalised, all the audio in the file will be increased by 20 decibels, which will result in it being made louder. One problem to be aware of when using normalisation is called clipping. This is when sounds get so loud that they sound distorted.

A setting that is often combined with normalisation is DC offset. When sound is recorded, it is desirable when it is played for it to centre vertically on 0.0. However, displacement can sometimes occur that can cause the recording to sit above or below 0.0. This too can cause distortion in the sound. This offset can simply occur when sound is converted from analogue to digital. Selecting the setting to remove DC offset will bring the recording back to vertical 0.0 and limit any distortion of the sound.

To normalise a sound clip, select the sound clip and choose the 'Effects' option from the menu bar at the top of the screen. Select the option 'Normalize '. This will open a window that will allow you to set the maximum amplitude (this shouldn't be set higher than 0) and choose whether to remove the DC offset.

PRACTICAL ACTIVITY 11.26

This is just a fun activity and not an effect that you are going to keep in your final sound file.

Try normalising all or part of your sound clip. Try setting the maximum amplitude to 2 to experiment with what happens to the sound when you do. Try setting the maximum amplitude to −1 and see what effect this has on the sound. Try doing each of those with and without DC offset.

Remove any normalisation effects that you have added.

Change a stereo sound clip to a mono sound clip

You may notice that the piano sound clip in your sound file has two different tracks. This is because it is **stereo**. When a sound file is set to stereo, it has multiple tracks. These two tracks can be just a duplicate of each other, as they are in the piano sound clip. They can also have different content. If they do have different content, the different tracks can be set to play through different speakers in a sound system. This is very useful when trying to create a 3D effect in films, as different sound effects can be heard from different speakers, making it seem like the sound is coming from different places. A technical term for this type of sound system is surround sound.

A sound clip can also be **mono**. This is when it has a single track, and when played through multiple speakers, they will all play the same track.

KEY WORDS

stereo: a sound clip that has multiple tracks

mono: a sound clip that has a single track

To change a sound clip from stereo to mono, highlight the sound clip and select 'Tracks' from the menu bar at the top of the screen. Select the 'Mix' option, then 'Mix Stereo Down to Mono'.

Figure 11.21: Stereo.

Figure 11.22: The same sound clip in mono.

PRACTICAL ACTIVITY 11.27

Change the piano sound clip from stereo to mono.

Sampling rate and resolution

It is important to understand the concept of **sample rate** and **sample resolution** when recording sound files. They both affect the size of the sound file and the quality of the sound recording.

KEY WORDS

sample rate: the number of times sound is sampled in a second

sample resolution: the number of bits that are used to represent each sound sample

---

When recording sound, samples of the analogue sound are taken at set intervals. This is called sampling. The number of samples taken in a period of time is called the sample rate. Sample rate is measured in hertz (Hz). If one sample is taken per second, this would be a sample rate of 1 Hz. Most music recordings are taken at a sample rate of 44.1 kHz. This means the sound is sampled 44 100 times in a second.

The effect of the sample rate can be seen by looking at a simple example of a sound wave representing analogue sound:

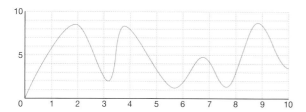

Figure 11.23: Analogue sound wave.

The sample of sound that is recorded at each time interval can be represented in a table:

Sample value	6	8.5	2.5	8	3.5	2	4.5	3	8.5	3.5
Time sample	1	2	3	4	5	6	7	8	9	10

If these sample values are then plotted on the same graph, this shows the difference in the initial sound, to the sound sampled.

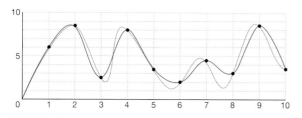

Figure 11.24: Analogue sound wave with sampled sound wave.

You can see that the sound wave differs significantly in places. This is because a sound sample wasn't taken at that certain point, so the detail in that part of the analogue sound is missed.

If the sample rate was doubled in the given example, the resulting sound wave after sampling would be a closer representation of the initial analogue sound wave. This means that the quality of the recorded sound would be a truer representation of the analogue sound that is recorded.

It also means that the file would need to store twice as many samples, so this will increase the size of the file.

The sample resolution of a sound file is the number of bits there are per sample. Sample resolution is important when recording the different volumes of sound. A low sample resolution, for example, 4-bits, would limit the level of volume that could be recorded. A high sample resolution, for example, 32-bits, would allow for a very accurate recording, but the size of the file created would be very large, so streaming could be affected by buffering, downloading could take a long time and it may affect your data allowance. The usual sampling resolution used for music files is 16-bit.

The size of a sound file is dependent on the sample rate and sample resolution. The approximate size of a sound file can be calculated using:

Sample rate × sample resolution × length of sound file

Question

5 a   Calculate the size of a file in megabytes (MB) that is two minutes in length, has a sample rate of 44.1 kHz and a sample resolution of 16-bit.

   b   Compare the file size if the sample resolution is increased to 32-bits.

      As size is an important factor when streaming or downloading music, sound files are often compressed.

Exporting a sound clip

You need to export your sound clip to a suitable file format for the media on which it will be mostly played. Most people will choose a universal file format to allow the sound file to be played on many devices, using different software platforms.

You will need to select different file formats depending on the type of media used to play the sound file, and the limitations of the file size required. Each file format will compress the file using either a lossy or lossless compression method.

Lossy compression will remove unnecessary data from the sound file to make the file size smaller, for example, sound that may not be audible by the human ear. Lossy will slightly affect the quality of the sound file, but most of this will not be heard by the human ear.

Lossless compression will not remove any data in the compression process and will allow the original sound file to be reinstated. This means the original quality and accuracy of the sound will be retained. Lossless compression can work in various ways. One method is for repeated patterns in the sound file to be identified and grouped together to be stored.

If you wanted to export the sound file in a lossless format, you may choose a file format such as FLAC. Lossless compression is often used for recording of live music, especially with orchestras. This allows the listener to have the most accurate experience of the sound created.

If you want to export the file in a lossy format as the accuracy and quality of it isn't essential, but you need the file size to be smaller, you may choose a file format such as MP3. This type of compression is often used when streaming music, so that less bandwidth is required to stream the sound file. This makes the ability to stream the music accessible to more people, especially those that only have access to low bandwidth connections. It would also mean that those users streaming via a mobile connection would not use as much of their data allowance.

When compression file formats such as MP4 are used, the compressed sound and video files are stored in a structure called a container. All the information needed for the sound or video is stored within the container. Other file formats that can operate as contains are AVI, MOV and WAV. The container manages the packing of the compressed files, as well as the transportation and the presentation of them when the file is opened.

To export your sound file, select 'File' from the menu bar at the top of the screen and select the option 'Export'. You will see several file formats that you can use for your sound file. Select a suitable format and give the sound file a suitable filename and location.

PRACTICAL ACTIVITY 11.29

Export your sound file in a file format that is lossy.

Export your video in a file format that is lossless.

TIP

You should practice always saving a copy of the file in a generic file format as well as in the proprietary software format.

The last task left to do is import your sound file into the video editing software and add it to your video file. Import the file in the same way that you imported the video clips. You can simply drag the file from the media section, to the timeline, when imported, to add it to your video.

PRACTICAL ACTIVITY 11.30

Export your BeeProject video with the sound and be proud of your sound and video editing skills!

REFLECTION

1 Who do you think the audience is for the video that you have created?

2 What do you think the intended purpose is of the video that you have created?

EXAM-STYLE QUESTIONS

1 Define what is meant by the aspect ratio of a video. [1]
2 State why a trimming tool would be used on a video clip. [1]
3 Explain two advantages of using captions on a video clip. [2]
4 Explain two advantages of using a lossy compression method on a video file. [2]
5 Explain one disadvantage of using a lossless compression method on a sound file. [1]
6 Explain what is meant by the sample rate of a sound file and how it affects the file size. [2]

SUMMARY CHECKLIST

- [ ] I can edit a video clip to meet the requirements of its intended audience and purpose.
- [ ] I can edit a sound clip to meet the requirements of its intended audience and purpose.
- [ ] I can know and understand the different compression methods and file formats that can be used for sound and video.
- [ ] I can know how to use typical editing features in sound and video editing software and know why they are used.
- [ ] I can know how the size of a sound file is affected by the sample rate and sample resolution.

> Chapter 12
IT in society

LEARNING INTENTIONS

By the end of this chapter, you will be able to:

- know and understand what is meant by an electronic currency, including:
    - different types
    - characteristics
    - advantages and disadvantages
    - uses
    - impact and risks
- know and understand what is meant by data mining, including:
    - processes of data mining
    - uses
    - advantages and disadvantages
- know and understand what is meant by social networking, including:
    - types
    - uses
    - impact
    - advantages and disadvantages of different types
- know and understand the impact of IT on a range of areas in society, including monitoring and surveillance

- know and understand technology enhanced learning, including:
    - methods of delivery
    - impact
    - advantages and disadvantages of different methods of delivery.

BEFORE YOU START

- Do you understand what is meant by information technology?
- Do you understand that technology is used extensively in many parts of our society?
- Do you understand that our data is valuable to companies and is used extensively to aid decision making in companies?
- Do you understand what is meant by social networking?

Introduction

IT has become an integral part of our society and some would argue that it is very difficult to imagine a society without it. It affects many aspects of our lives, including how we spend our money, how our data is stored and mined, how we communicate and how we learn, amongst many other aspects.

Figure 12.1: Electronic payment.

12.1 Electronic currency

An **electronic currency** is a payment method that occurs in digital form. It does not involve the exchange of physical currency, such as coins and bank notes. There are several types of electronic currency. These include: digital currency, virtual currency, cryptocurrency, central bank digital base money and stored value cards. These terms can sometimes be used interchangeably, but some information, for clarity, is given for each. The terms electronic currency and digital currency are often used interchangeably.

KEY WORDS

electronic currency: a payment method that occurs in a digital form

Digital currency

A digital currency is a method of payment that is similar to paying with coins and bank notes. However, rather than exchanging physical bank notes and coins to make the payment, the currency is exchanged digitally using computers. There are several different forms of digital currency. The most popular are payments using credit cards, mobile phones and smart watches. A common reference for this kind of payment is that it is like having an electronic wallet.

Credit cards can be used with card payment machines that will either allow the magnetic stripe to be swiped, the card to be inserted into the machine and the chip to be read, or touching the card to the computer using a method called contactless payment. In all cases, data that is stored on the card is read by the computer. This data will contain the information required to locate the user's bank account. The business can then request that the correct sum of money is deducted from the user's bank account and sent to the business's account.

Another form of digital currency that is similar to a credit card is a stored value card. This is a type of card that has a set amount of currency stored on it, for example, $100. The card can be used to pay for items and the value stored on the card will decrease until it reaches 0. Banks often provide the cards to people who are not able to have a credit card due to issues such as credit rating. There are two kinds of stored value card. The first is the closed-loop card. This is where a monetary value can only be loaded onto it once, and it is discarded when all the money is spent. The second is the open-loop card. This is where a monetary value can be repeatedly loaded onto the card.

Mobile phones and smart watches can be used in a similar way to the contactless payment that can be made with credit cards. A user can install an app onto their mobile device that acts as a digital credit card. Examples of this would be Apple Pay and Google Pay®. The user can touch

their mobile device to the card payment machine and the app will provide the data to access the user's bank account, in a similar way to the credit card method.

Virtual currency

Virtual currency is also a type of digital currency. However, unlike the digital currencies discussed, which are centralised systems, virtual currency is a decentralised system. In simple terms, a centralised system is one that has a central body that is managing and regulating the use of the currency. In most cases this is the government and banks. A decentralised system is therefore one that does not have a central

Advantages	Disadvantages
A person doesn't need to carry physical money around, which could be easily lost.	There is often a monetary limit on contactless payments.
If a card or mobile device is lost, the user can contact their bank to stop any monetary transactions from the card or device.	As data is sent electronically, there is always the risk that the transactions could be hacked.
All transactions are completed using encrypted methods, so data is sent securely.	Some people are anxious about the thought of contactless payments, believing that they could walk near a payment machine and money could be deducted from their account.
The use of contactless payments can speed up payment for products and services.	Some may think that people can lose track of their spending as they are not handing over physical money for the transaction.
If a user is in a different country, they don't need to have the physical currency of that country available in their wallet. They can use a digital method and the banks involved will electronically change the transaction from one currency to the other.	If a card or device is lost, it is possible for another person to use it for contactless payments, before the user has chance to cancel it.
The user doesn't necessarily need to remember their PIN number each time, if they are using contactless payments methods.	
The use of payment methods, such as stored value cards, can prevent a person from getting into debt, as they can only spend the set amount that is stored on the card.	

Table 12.1: Advantages and disadvantages of digital currency.

body managing the process. The most common way to manage transactions with a decentralised system is through the use of a ledger, for example, blockchain.

> **PRACTICAL ACTIVITY 12.01**
>
> Use the internet to research what blockchain is and how it is used to monitor payments transactions.

Virtual currency also differs from the digital currencies already discussed, in that it only exists within a virtual environment, and does not have a physical representation as bank notes and coins. An example of a virtual currency would be tokens that can be collected or bought, for example, within a computer game, that allow players to buy different items within the game, such as new clothing or armour. The player can buy a certain number of tokens and use this as virtual currency in the game. For this reason, a virtual currency is normally specific to the particular game or application for which it was created, and cannot normally be traded anywhere else.

Advantages	Disadvantages
It can personalise a game or application by making it fun to collect and spend the specific virtual currency.	Is a decentralised system, so has little regulation.
	Normally specific to the context for which it was created and cannot be spent elsewhere.

Table 12.2: Advantages and disadvantages of virtual currency.

Cryptocurrency

The most well-known examples of cryptocurrencies are Bitcoin and LiteCoin. Some cryptocurrencies, like these, are tracked using systems such as blockchain.

These cryptocurrencies are also a type of peer-to-peer electronic monetary system. This type of payment system is designed to allow peers to send electronic payment to each other without the need for it going via a central body, such as a financial institution.

The value of a cryptocurrency can often fluctuate a great deal. In 2011, 1 bitcoin was worth 1 US dollar. At the end of 2017, 1 bitcoin was worth close to 20 000 US dollars. In 2018, it fell again and was worth approximately 6000 US dollars.

> **PRACTICAL ACTIVITY 12.02**
>
> Use the internet to find out what 1 bitcoin is worth today in your country's currency.

Figure 12.2: Bitcoin.

Many people use bitcoin to buy and sell products over the internet. Some support the use of a decentralised currency, as it allows people, especially businesses, to make payments that do not involve the usual charges that are applied by banks in a centralised system. Others have a more controversial stance on the use of a decentralised currency, as they believe it can allow a level of anonymity in payments, that means criminal activity is difficult to trace.

Advantages	Disadvantages
The usual charges that can apply to bank transactions are not present for cryptocurrency.	The decentralised systems allows a level of anonymity that some believe encourages criminal activity and allows it to go untraced.
People are able to invest in bitcoin and possibly make money if they can sell it for a higher rate.	There have been a number of instances where businesses have been hacked and bitcoin has been stolen. As the system is decentralised, there is no bank to help resolve this kind of theft.
It is very difficult to create counterfeit currency for a cryptocurrency, because of all the security it involves.	

Table 12.3: Advantages and disadvantages of cryptocurrency.

The growth of cryptocurrency has proved troubling to banks around the world. Businesses have begun using it more, preferring the free nature of which they can exchange the currency. This is a threat to traditional banks offering traditional methods, because they rely on the fees generated and the cash input from businesses to survive. This has led to some banks considering creating their own cryptocurrency.

REFLECTION

What do you think about banks creating their own cryptocurrency? What advantages and disadvantages to you think this would create?

Central bank digital base money

Central bank digital base money (also known as central bank digital currency (CBDC)) is the digital form of what is known as fiat money. Fiat money is the currency that is the physical currency used in a country, that is issued by governments and banks. It is the bank notes

and coins that you can use in payments every day. Creating digital fiat money in this way would mean that banks effectively create a digital currency. Each unit of currency in CBDC will act as an equivalent of a paper bank note. It will be similar to bank notes, in that it will have a serial number. There will also be distinguishable characteristics on the unit that will prevent fake units being created.

Banks intend to use it as part of the controlled supply of currency by the central bank, and it will work alongside existing currency such as physical bank notes and coins. There are several banks around the world that are currently looking into the development and use of CBDC. These include The Bank of England, People's Bank of China and the Bank of Canada.

Advantages	Disadvantages
As no physical currency will need to be exchanged between banks, the cost of transactions will be reduced.	Some people like the privacy of the anonymity that they can have with using physical currency. If a person pays with cash, there is no record of their details attached to that payment, by the bank.
The banks' ability to speed up the exchange of money will be greatly improved.	
Some believe that if physical currency became obsolete, in favour of CBDC, criminal acts such as money laundering and tax evasion would decrease, as these often rely on the use of physical currency.	
It costs money to produce physical currency, therefore if it ceased to exist, then these costs would be saved and could be invested into the security of a CBDC.	

Table 12.4: Advantages and disadvantages of CBDC currency.

12.2 Data mining

Data mining is a form of data analysis. It is also a form of artificial intelligence. The process of data mining involves searching through and analysing large sets of data to establish patterns and trends. This information can be used to help identify future trends that could be very valuable to a company. The large sets of data used are stored in data warehouses.

> **KEY WORDS**
>
> **data mining:** the process of collecting large sets of data and analysing them to identify patterns and trends

> **REFLECTION**
>
> Why could the ability to identify future trends be so valuable to a company?

Computers are used for data mining because of the sheer volume of data that is searched and analysed.

Figure 12.3: Data mining.

The process of data mining

The process of data mining is complex and involves several different stages.

Stage 1: Business understanding

There are three main elements to the business understanding stage: setting the objectives, developing the project plan and establishing the criteria for success.

In order to establish the kind of data that needs to be mined and analysed, the objectives of the business need to be understood. The business understanding stage is where the needs of the business are discovered, and an in-depth analysis takes place to ascertain these.

Once the business needs have been established, other important factors, such as the resources available, the constraints on the process and a data mining plan and goals must be considered. The data mining plan will involve developing queries to interrogate the data.

Stage 2: Data understanding

The data understanding stage involves an initial collection of data. This is normally collected from various sources that are available. Once the data is collected, the integrity, accuracy and the properties of the data are considered, to make sure that it is viable.

Once the data is established as viable, it can be interrogated using queries that were developed in the business understanding stage. This interrogation will help the business understand whether the data is complete and will provide them with the desired outcome.

Stage 3: Data preparation

This is the largest stage in the project and the most time consuming. During this stage the data is taken through a whole process of selection, cleansing, construction and formatting, to make sure that it is in the form required for the business. This can then allow for patterns and trends to be established in the data, relating to the business needs.

Stage 4: Data modelling

During this stage, various test scenarios are generated to model the data. This will allow the business to understand whether the models are suitable for the business needs, and that the models fall in line with the business initiatives.

Stage 5: Evaluation

In the evaluation stage, the results generated by the models are evaluated. The outcome of this evaluation may produce new business needs, depending on the patterns and trends that have been identified in the process.

Stage 6: Deployment

The deployment stage normally involves creating a report and other visual material to present the findings of the data mining process to the stakeholders of a business. This information can then be used by the stakeholders to decide what actions the business will take next.

If the stakeholders feel the business hasn't achieved an informative enough result, they may choose to repeat the data mining process to further refine the information gathered from the process.

Figure 12.4: Refining the data mining process.

Use of data mining

The use of data mining is increasing. Many different organisations make use of data mining to aid their planning and the actions they choose to take. Sometimes, the use of data mining can be critical to highly sensitive situations.

National security and surveillance

Governments make continued use of data mining to aid nation security. It is used to analyse intelligence that is gathered to highlight the current activity in a country and predict possible future activity. This can help reduce the risk of attack or dangerous activity in the country.

The use of data mining in surveillance is an ongoing controversial matter. In surveillance, data mining is used in a similar way to how it is used in national security.

Surveillance data, such as CCTV footage and recorded telephone calls, are analysed to predict issues such as criminal activity. Some people agree with the use of data mining in this way because they believe it keeps people safer. Others completely disagree with the use of data mining in this way because they believe it is a violation of privacy.

> ### REFLECTION
>
> How do you feel about the use of data mining in surveillance?

One type of surveillance that data mining is used for is corporate surveillance. This is when corporations mine people's data that can be used for marketing purposes or sold to other companies. A business can use this information to tailor their products or advertising to individuals. This is also known as data profiling.

Figure 12.5: Surveillance.

Business

Businesses use data mining for a variety of different reasons, from predicting customer spending habits, predicting product trends and even in hiring staff. Data mining is valuable to a business because, if they are able to predict what products customers will buy, they can beat their competitor to market and gain a competitive advantage. This can ultimately result in increased sales revenue, and possibly profits, for the business.

One business application of data mining is customer relationship management (CRM). The aim of CRM is to improve customer loyalty and to implement business strategies that are customer focussed. In order to build customer loyalty, a business needs to predict the needs of the customer, this is where data mining can be used.

Question

1   How do you think a business could make use of data mining when hiring staff?

Research

Research is a fundamental and imperative part of so many areas in society. It helps revolutionise industries such as medicine, space exploration, engineering and technology. Data mining is often the underpinning tool in research. Research companies can also make use of other research company's data, through the use of data mining. This can speed up core developments in these key industries.

One research and healthcare application of data mining is bio-informatics. This is the practice of mining biological data to extract medical patterns and trends. This can be used in practices such as gene finding and disease research and diagnosis.

Health care

Data mining is increasingly used to improve health care. It can be used to identify success practices in health care and to also help reduce costs. It can also be used to predict the volume of patients that will visit medical institutions, so that appropriate levels of staffing can be put in place.

Figure 12.6: Data mining for improved health care.

Predicting social and economic trends

Data mining has a large role in predicting future social and economic trends. Many institutions are concerned with the stabilisation and growth of the global economic market. Any data and intelligence that can predict what might happen in future with the economy can help important institutions, such as governments, to prepare for any possible crisis that may occur. Companies can also use the ability to predict what may lay ahead with the economy to make important business decisions, such as where they should plan to expand their business.

Ethical and privacy implications

Individuals and organisations have concerns about the ethical and privacy implications of data mining. This often revolves around the use of data mined about individuals that is then used to target them with products and advertising. There can be certain issues with this. If a person searches for a certain product or service, they may be bombarded with similar products for a long time afterwards. This might not be too bad if this was for something they like, but if the search was for a product that can then create upsetting feelings at a later date, the constant reminder of the targeted advertising may be harmful. For example, if a person searches for their favourite chocolate, but then decides to start a healthy eating diet, they may keep being tempted by targeted adverts about chocolate. Another example could be a person who searches for symptoms of a medical ailment that they have. This data is then available and mined by lots of companies, and the individual may never want people to be aware of their medical issues.

The ethical issues also prompt privacy issues that many individuals have. Many people feel it is a violation of their privacy, and also unethical, for companies who have collected their data to share this with other companies.

> **REFLECTION**
>
> How would you feel about a company sharing data they have collected about you with another company? Do you feel this affects your privacy? Do you think this is an ethical practice?

Advantages and disadvantages of data mining

You may have realised there can be both advantages and disadvantages of data mining. These may be for the individual or the organisation:

Advantages	Disadvantages
Allows organisations to make strategic decisions that can help maintain or increase their revenue.	The process of data mining, the software tools and the skilled staff required are all very expensive.
Allows organisations to understand their customers and create the products they need.	Many people see the practice of data mining as both unethical and an invasion of their privacy.
Allows individuals to see targeted product advertising based on the things they already like. This means adverts could be more meaningful to them. It could also help them see products they would like but do not currently know about.	Storage costs for data are very expensive, therefore this can also increase the cost of the process of data mining.
Allows important institutions to predict future crisis that they can then plan strategies and solutions to help handle or avoid them.	The masses of data stored prove a great security issue, as hackers will want to gain access to the data because it has a high value.
Allows businesses to save costs either by understanding how to streamline what they already do, or by not investing in a future product that they can now be aware may not be desired.	The outcomes produced by data mining are only predictions based on patterns and trends in past data. They are not an accurate science and it is very possible for them to be incorrect.

Table 12.5: Advantages and disadvantages of data mining.

Example case study of data mining

A very high-profile case involving data mining was the Facebook-Cambridge Analytica scandal. The whole case involved the way companies collect, use and share people's data. The case occurred not because the companies involved necessarily broke the law, but because ethical issues were raised about their activities in collecting data. This occurred as there were no strict laws in place within the countries concerned that necessarily governed this practice. The companies involved were accused though of exploiting loopholes in the law to unethically mine data.

The scandal revealed that Cambridge Analytica, a political consultancy firm that mined data, had collected the personal data available from millions of people's Facebook profiles. They did this without the consent of the Facebook users. This data was then analysed and used for political advertising purposes. The data was used to influence public opinion.

As a result, on 25th May 2018, a new law was implemented to help govern the practice of data mining for EU residents. This has meant that any companies wanting to gather the data of EU citizens must seek their permission to do so. It details clear guidelines and definitions about how data can be collected and used. It also forces companies to consider questions such as 'Why am I collecting this data?', 'What do I intend to do with this data?' and 'Do I have the users consent to use this data?'.

12.3 Social networking

It can often seem that the world is obsessed with **social networking**, but it has grown to be an inherent part of many people's lives. They rely on it for entertainment, communication and often as a source of news. People use social networking methods to share information about their daily lives, including how they feel, what makes them happy, what irritates them, what they are eating, where they are on holiday and what their beliefs are. The world likes to share!

KEY WORDS

social networking: the use of websites and apps that allows users to communicate and interact

Figure 12.7: Sharing data on social networks.

There are several different types of social networking. These include chat rooms, instant messaging, forums, email, blogs and microblogs. These are all forms of communication technologies that are also known as social media. Users normally use these technologies on a personal computer or a mobile device and they are often accessed using a website or an app.

Chat rooms

A chat room is an online service that allows multiple users to type messages to each other, allowing them to chat. They are meant to be similar to people gathering in a room and chatting about what interests them.

Chat rooms are often created to allow users to discuss a particular topic or issue. Users are given a username and password to enter the chat room. When they log in, they can normally see which other users are online and type messages into a text input box. These messages are then displayed as a dialogue onscreen. The process is interactive and designed to allow multiple users to communicate and discuss the chosen topic.

Figure 12.8: A 'chat' room.

Chat rooms are mainly used by individuals, but they could be used by businesses and organisation as a type of marketing tool. A business who wanted to expand a current product or service, or launch a new one, could use it as a method of gaining feedback. A chat room could be set up to discuss the product and a selection of users could be sent the log-in details. When the users enter the chat room, the business could ask questions or make comments about the product to prompt discussion.

Instant messaging

Instant messaging is one of the earlier forms of social networking. It is designed to allow two users to send messages to each other in real-time. Although this often happens between two users, it is possible for more to be included if a group instant message thread is created. Several social media platforms have an instant messaging service built into them. These include Facebook, Instagram and Skype. Some other media, such as online gaming, also have instant messaging facilities built into them.

Many individuals and organisations use instant messaging facilities. Individuals use them to converse using text with friends and family. They can also use them to contact a business, who have a social media presence, to ask them a question, or make a complaint. Many instant messaging facilities have a reporting function that allows a user to see when the other person has read their message, and when they are currently replying. A user can also see when another user is currently online. Instant messaging can also be used to send other media, such as sound files, images, video files and emojis.

Figure 12.9: Instant messaging.

Businesses and organisations have begun to develop internal instant messaging facilities. This allows departments to message other workers in the department to ask a quick question or make a quick observation or comment about a current issue or idea. This facility is also known as a LAN messenger.

Forums

Forums are an online place that users can post thoughts, ideas and questions. Other users can then reply to the post with their thoughts, feedback and answers to any questions. Forums are different to chat facilities because they do not have the same level of live interaction. A user who posts a question on a forum is not likely to be needing an immediate reply from other users. They can post their question, then return to the forum at a later time to see what answers and advice other users have given. Other users can also search a forum to see if someone has already asked for an answer to their question and they can read the previous responses given if it has already been asked.

Some forum platforms will have a user who is called a moderator. The forum will have rules that users must abide by to post on the forum. The role of the moderator is to check the forum on a regular basis to make sure that users are abiding by the rules. The moderator will remove any posts and can block any users from posting if they break the rules. Some forums may be very strict and will only allow posts to be visible on the forum when they have been approved by the moderator. Most forum platforms will require users to register to be able to post or reply to comments. If users do not want to post or reply to posts, then they can normally read the forum posts without the need to register.

In a forum, posts are structured as threads. A user posts a question, which starts a thread. Other users post their reply to the question, which are all added to the same thread. This allows the original user who posted to be able to see all the replies to their post. A forum will normally have a particular topic as a theme, for example, technical support, healthcare issues, computer games and makeup tips.

Forums are mainly used by individuals, but businesses and organisations do also use them. A business can use a forum as a support facility. It can have a forum

platform that allows users to post questions or ask for support about their product. A moderator or other can then reply to users' requests and provide any support needed. This type of support facility can be useful to a business as a method of customer service.

Forums can also be used to seek advice and support on issues such as health, education and finances. Users may post about a particular health issue, such as their symptoms, and other users can provide information about what health issue they think the person has. Users can also share information about what advice they have been given regarding a particular health issue, and ask other users to post whether they have received similar or different advice. A user could also post seeking financial advice about a certain scenario they find themselves in, or for advice about investments, and other users could post offering their advice.

Forums sometimes have dedicated professionals that will post experienced advice to the initial user, but there can also be posts from other users who may be offering personal advice, but are not professionals. Therefore, users should always be cautious about any advice given by other users as this may not be correct or accurate.

Email

An email (short for electronic mail) is a message that can be sent by a user to one or more users. Email is similar to sending an electronic version of a letter. The user writes the letter then addresses it to send it to another user using their email address. This is an address that is linked to their email account. A user registers for an email account with an email provider, and as part of their registration they choose a unique email address. They can then give this address to any other user so they can be sent emails.

It is easy to identify if an address is an email address as they normally have an '@' symbol within them, and a domain name (for example.com).

Businesses and organisations use email extensively. For many, it is one of their main methods of communication. It can be used to easily send information to everyone within a company. Businesses can also use email to send information to customers and potential customers to provide them with information, such as a recent offer they have or a new product. This is a more direct method than requiring their customers to look at their other social media platforms.

Individuals also use email communication to contact family, friends and organisations. Email is used to send messages to family and friends that the writer may feel is more extensive than what they would put in an instant message. People can also use email to contact an organisation, for example, to make a complaint.

PRACTICAL ACTIVITY 12.05

Use the internet to research the first emails that were sent. Find out who sent them and what they contained.

Blogs and microblogs

A blog (which is short for weblog) is an online version of a journal. Blogs are set up by individuals, or groups of individuals, normally to report on their lives or a particular topic. Blogs are structured in reverse chronological order, which means that the most recent post to the blog will appear first.

Blogs are read by people all over the world. They have become a very popular way of people finding out about lots of information in which they are interested. The blogger will usually use some online software to create their blog. Popular online blogging software includes WordPress and Squarespace.

Microblogs are similar to blogs, but posts are created with a much smaller level of content. A blog may have posts that are a thousand words or more. However, a microblog will have posts that are just a couple of sentences or just an image. Popular microblogs include Twitter and Instagram.

Businesss and organisations can make use of blogs as a method of providing information, to customers and potential customers about developments within the company. Education facilities, such as schools, can use blogs to allow parents and students to see what has been happening in different departments within the school, including any recent school events.

Organisations such as police and law enforcement can use microblogs to provide regular updates to communities about problems and issues on a local or national scale. Schools could also use microblogs to provide a stream of information for parents about recent updates in the school. Microblogs have become a popular source of news for people around the world. News platforms will post a headline on their microblog that can provide a link to a full article for the user to view.

Some individuals make a living as a full-time blogger. They have so many users that read their blog that it attracts companies who want to place adverts on their blog. They are paid for the adverts that are displayed on their blog, which provides them with an income. Video has become a very popular media in blogging, and people who use videos to blog are known as vloggers.

Figure 12.10: Video blogging.

Impact of social networking

Social networking has had a huge impact on both individuals and businesses.

Some feel that it has had a positive impact on the lives of individuals. It has allowed us to communicate with people on a global scale. This means that family and friends that live in different countries can share more about their lives which can help people feel more connected and so happier and less alone. Some also feel that it has allowed us to connect with strangers and make more friends with people who share similar thoughts and beliefs to us. The result of this is that people feel happier and more passionate about their thoughts and ideas because they are able to share and develop them with those that think alike.

Some feel that social networking has had a negative impact on the lives of individuals. They believe it has a detrimental effect on our mental health. Social media has created a culture of constant sharing which has led to constant comparison of our lives to others. This can result in people feeling very unhappy with their lives, because they look at how others portray their lives on social media and feel that their own life does not compare. Others also think that social networking can be used to influence minds, often of the younger generation, to think in certain political or stereotypical ways.

Some feel that social networking allows people to hide behind an anonymous online profile, which allows them to post controversial and often harmful comments that can result in cyberbullying. There have been detrimental results of cyberbullying that have even led to some people taking their own life.

One growing concern about the use of social networking is that it has created a generation that needs a sense of immediacy to everything they do. This is creating cognitive issues that may result in people having very little concentration to be able to complete daily tasks because they are taking in a constant stream of information, without focussing on a one particular task.

REFLECTION

Some people believe that social networking has improved our ability to communicate, others believe it has caused it to deteriorate. What impact do you think social networking has had on our ability to communicate?

Social networking has had a large impact on businesses. It is used by businesses on a regular basis as an effective marketing tool. It can be vital to the success of a business to have an active online social networking presence. Some argue that the impact a business can have by using social networking is starting to deteriorate. Individuals now see so many different online adverts that they are likely to just bypass the advert, meaning it has little effect at all. However, social networking has allowed businesses to reach audiences on a global scale which can help increase their sales revenue.

REFLECTION

What's the most effective way that you have seen a business use social networking?

Social networking has had a positive impact on organisations because it allows them to distribute important information on a large scale. For example, if there is a natural disaster within a country, the police and government can use social networking to distribute vital information about how people can keep themselves safe, or get to safety. They can also use it to give people prior warning of an issue, such as an approaching tornado or other bad weather. This can help people have precious time to prepare safety measures that could save their lives. One cause for concern about organisations using social media is their ability to censor the information that is released. A government may choose to censor information about a current issue occurring within the country so that people have a false impression of what is occurring, distorting their opinion. For example, they could underplay or sensationalise a political protest, influencing the opinions of others in the country.

Here is a summary of the advantages and disadvantages of social networking:

Advantages	Disadvantages
Allows communication to occur on a global scale between individuals, businesses and organisations.	People can feel overwhelmed by all the information and communication they encounter.
Allows people to feel included as they can share thoughts and ideas with those who share similar opinions.	Some people can feel excluded and feel that everyone seems to have a better life than they do.
Allows organisation to distribute important information to people that could be lifesaving in critical situations.	Some organisations could falsely represent certain situations and influence opinions of people that are built on censored information.
Allows some individuals to make a living writing an online blog that others enjoy reading.	Social networking influencers can sometimes lead people to think or do things that are harmful, such as over exercise or spend too much on expensive clothing.

Advantages	Disadvantages
Allows people to seek advice or support on various issues, including technical support and healthcare. This can result in an improved level of customer service and care.	Contributions to platforms, such as forums, can often be made by people who may not be qualified to give advice or support. This could lead to a person acting on incorrect advice and possibly causing harm.
Provides a stream of entertainment for people.	It may be causing people's attention span to decrease as they no longer are able to focus on a single activity for any length of time.
Can expose people to news stories that they otherwise may not be aware of.	News stories can se sensationalised and falsely reported.
	It allows a level of anonymity that can encourage users to participate in bad or sometimes illegal behaviour that they would not otherwise do, if they thought people would know who they are.

Table 12.6: Advantages and disadvantages of social networking.

12.4 Technology enhanced learning

Teaching and learning has been improved by technology. A large part of technology's growing influence on society is the introduction of online learning and online courses.

There are many tutorials available on websites such as YouTube, and more educationally oriented sites like Lynda.com and edx.org. This means that people can now gain access to teaching, often without a fee, other than the cost of their internet connection. This also means they can learn at their own pace and in their own time.

The quality of the resources available through these sites can often differ greatly. On sites like YouTube there may be no governing body looking at the level of teaching that is taking place, in the way that there often is with schools. This means it may be difficult and time-consuming for a person to pick through all the tutorials they can find to get one that is of a high quality. It could also mean that a person could use a tutorial that teaches them incorrectly.

There are several different types of platform for technology enhanced learning. These include computer-based training, online tutorials, networked learning, massive open online courses (MOOC) and video conferencing.

Computer-based training

Businesses and organisations can create extensive training programs for their staff that can be accessed using computers. Often just the training resources created are available and this normally doesn't involve the presence of a tutor. The resources can be a mixture of text, sound, video and images to present the training information in the most effective way. Computer-based training is normally designed to deliver small chunks of training to people, as a step-by step process. It normally allows the user to learn at their own pace.

Many companies develop and make available this kind of training to their staff to allow them to develop their work skills. This can mean that the worker can improve their knowledge and skillset to a point that may allow them to be awarded a pay rise or a promotion. There can be tests incorporated into the training, that are automatically marked, that can show how much the user has learnt.

Advantages	Disadvantages
Users can learn at their own pace.	Learners may not have a tutor to answer any questions that they have.
Different media can be used to create an interesting set of resources.	Staff may not be motivated to follow the computer-based training as they aren't being watched and driven to do so.
Staff can improve their own skills set and knowledge resulting in promotion or additional pay.	

Table 12.7: Advantages and disadvantages of computer-based training.

Online tutorials

One of the biggest online platforms used for tutorials is YouTube. There is an extensive set of tutorials and a huge variety of different topics, from baking a cake, to fixing a car, to putting on makeup. An online tutorial is normally delivered using different media and aims to teach the viewer how to achieve a specific goal or outcome. Online tutorials also allow a user to learn at their own pace and in their own time. They are also able to view the tutorial repeatedly until they think they have the understanding that they need for the desired outcome.

Advantages	Disadvantages
There are online tutorials available on almost any skill or issue that a person may want information about.	The quality of online tutorials may differ greatly, and some may be poor quality, meaning it is time consuming to find one that is good.
Users can learn in their own time and at their own pace.	An online tutorial could teach a person in an incorrect manner. This will depend on the ability of the person who is acting as the educator.
Different media can be used to create an informative tutorial.	

Table 12.8: Advantages and disadvantages of online tutorials.

Networked learning

Networked learning is a form of online collaborative learning that helps learners to connect with other learners as well as their tutors. It is designed to help learners develop relationships with each other as well as their tutor. This can help the learning process because there are a number of different people from whom learners can gain feedback and partake in discussions.

The aim of networked learning is that learners are encouraged to support the learning of other learners. The whole process is normally facilitated by a tutor, who actively encourages participation from all learners. Learners are often asked to share thoughts, opinions and resources from their work or educational practices. Other learners are then asked to comment on each

other's contributions, offering advice about how to improve their skills and knowledge.

The time scales are more limited for networked learning as the current task will be dependent on everyone participating in a similar time frame.

Advantages	Disadvantages
Learners get to work with other learners and build relationships that they could take forward beyond the course.	Some learners may find it difficult to contribute to the process, as they aren't sure what to give as feedback.
Learners are exposed to both the ability to gain and provide feedback. This means that they build new skills and knowledge and offer the skills and knowledge they have to others also.	Some learners may be overbearing and dominate all the discussions that take place, not allowing enough contribution to encourage learning from others. Some tutors may find these people difficult to manage.
Learners may be more motivated to complete the tasks as the learning of others is also dependent on them.	Learners may be inclined to just provide positive feedback as they do not feel comfortable criticising the work of others.
	If some learners do not complete tasks or provide the necessary feedback, this may limit the learning ability of other users, as the timescales for learning are more limited.

Table 12.9: Advantages and disadvantages of networked learning.

MOOC (Massive Open Online Courses)

One of the biggest online learning methods is MOOCs. These are courses that are not limited in the number of people that can access them and have open access using the web. MOOCs are free and will be used by a large number of learners at any one time. They will often include filmed lectures and other resources, and have forums that can be used to interact with other learners and the educators. MOOCs allow people in similar industries to learn more about their industry from other people within that industry. They allow this to happen at the convenience of the learner. People can use MOOCs to develop additional career skills or explore new interests. Progress through courses available on a MOOC could be assessed using peer review, written assignments or online tests that are automatically marked. They may not provide a person with a formal professional qualification, but they can demonstrate that a person will expand their own learning, in their own time, which could be appealing to an employer.

Advantages	Disadvantages
Large selection of courses available.	Some people may get overwhelmed by the number of courses available, and may not know which one would be best to take.
Can provide an employee with a competitive advantage as it demonstrates the motivation to learn and improve in their own time.	There are often large numbers of people on the courses, so the educators may not have a lot of time to dedicate to helping each learner.
They are free of cost.	It may be difficult for educators to keep track of the progress of all learners, so they may not recognise that some are struggling.
The number of people on a course is often a large amount or unlimited, so people do not have to wait for a place to become available.	Some learners may struggle with the motivation to complete the tasks, and may only choose to complete those properly that they know will be assessed.
Users can learn at their own pace in their own time, often only limited by the submission deadline for assignments.	

Table 12.10: Advantages and disadvantages of MOOC.

Video conferencing

Video conferencing is when people communicate using computers, displaying a video stream, using an internet connection. The video will often show the user and any other resources that they want to provide. Video conferencing software often has a facility that will allow a user to share the content on their screen with other users that are part of the conference.

Teaching and learning can be carried out using video conferencing. An educator can carry out a lesson that allows them to speak to the other learners and also show them any resources that can aid the learning process. This can feel like a more personal learning experience as learners are able to see and speak to the educator. The quality of the lesson will depend on the communication abilities of the educator, and could also be dependent on the quality of the video conferencing software and the internet connection. Video conferencing can often require a relatively high broadband speed to be able to deliver smooth viewing of the video for the user. Video conferencing can allow learners to ask questions in real-time and clarify any points of learning that they may be unsure about.

Advantages	Disadvantage
As learners can ask questions in real-time, this may improve their level of learning and understanding.	Video conferencing software can require high broadband speeds that may not be available in some areas.
As learners can see and hear their educator, this may feel like a more personal learning experience and may create an increased level of motivation for the learner as they may find it more engaging.	Only a small number of learners will be able to be part of the video-conference, and this will be limited by the capabilities of the software and the internet connection. This may leave some people waiting a long time for a place on a course.
The educator can often share what is displayed on their screen with other learners, which could be useful if a demonstration needs to be given.	

Table 12.11: Advantages and disadvantages of video-conferencing.

Technology enhanced learning can vary a lot in terms of quality, cost and the subjects offered. Whether it is for self-interest or accreditation, it is often much easier to learn at your own pace and in your own time. It can sometimes be difficult to find the exact course you want as there are so many available. Another issue with online learning is finding effective teachers that are able to break down problems and help students in the process. This is partly because of the difficulty in finding someone who is capable, but also it can be because of the way in which the customers want to learn. Do they prefer to be lectured or do they want a small bit of information and then to be set a task and learn as they go?

12.5 The impact of IT

The use of IT has revolutionised many of our industries and areas of society.

IT in sport

In sport, IT has been introduced to aid referees in making important decisions that could change the outcomes of a game. In rugby union, the referee regularly uses IT to see if the ball was put over the goal line for a try to be scored. This was sometimes difficult to judge without the use of IT, as the referee often had to see around a pile of players trying to aid or stop the try occurring.

IT was used in the women's football world cup in 2019. Many important decisions, in the process of play, were aided by the video assistant referee (VAR). This meant that goals were allowed or disallowed based on the ability to re-watch important footage, to allow an improved refereeing decision to be made. Some people welcomed the use of VAR in this way, as they believed that it made the play fairer, allowing correct decisions to be made in games. Others believed that it stilted play and made the viewing experience less enjoyable.

IT, such as hawk eye, is used in sports such as tennis, to allow players to challenge the decisions of the officials judging the match. Some feel this is a welcome addition to the game as it can help the decision-making process become more accurate. Some feel that the system used is not very accurate and will often provide incorrect outcomes as a result.

> **PRACTICAL ACTIVITY 12.06**
>
> Find out how IT, such as AR and VR, can be used to improve the performance of sports players and teams.

IT in manufacturing

Manufacturing uses robotics to create assembly lines for products such as cars, where heavy elements like the chassis are moved to an area where humans can then fit items to them to build a car. This has meant that humans can be removed from working on the more dangerous elements of manufacturing. By using robotics in manufacturing, it is possible to create a more consistent and accurate product. This is because the robot can be programmed to produce a product and will do this to the same standard repeatedly. A human may differ in their standard of production depending on the mood they are in or how tired they feel that day. Also, if a manufacturing system is completely robotic, it can run for much longer periods of time and will not require the same level of rest as a human. With the correct level of maintenance, robotic manufacturing could be set to run for 24 hours a day.

Some feel that the introduction of robotics into manufacturing has resulted in a loss of jobs for people. This has often created animosity toward the use of robotics in manufacturing, despite their advantages. Also, if a company cannot afford the robotic equipment, this can sometimes put them at a competitive disadvantage against those companies in their industry that can.

Figure 12.11: IT in manufacturing.

Find out how computer aided design (CAD) and 3D printing are used in manufacturing.

IT in medicine

In medicine, IT has given us the ability to monitor patients and make sure they are healthy. We're able to measure their heart rate, analyse DNA samples to see if an infection is present, and even use technology to train doctors and nurses in how to perform certain procedures through simulations.

IT has enabled many advancements to occur in medicine. It is now possible to provide people with artificial limbs that can be controlled through the use of technology. This means that people who previously had debilitating disabilities can be provided with a new life by using these artificial limbs. They could be given the ability to walk again or regain the use of their arms and hands, allowing them to live a fuller life. This type of treatment has been very beneficial to soldiers who have been wounded by providing them with the ability to use their wounded limbs again, or have them replaced altogether.

The use of nanotechnology in medicine has provided great advancements, especially in the use of drugs to treat disease. This is when technology is used to manipulate individual atoms and molecules. In medicine, it can be used to target the delivery of drugs in a very precise way. Particles can be engineered to locate particular cells in the body, for example, cancer cells, and deliver the drug directly to them. This can help to reduce any damage or unnecessary treatment being delivered to healthy cells.

The use of IT in medicine is constantly developing because of the vast benefits it can bring. One development in progress is the use of smart devices that are designed to be implanted into different parts of the body, such as the brain or heart. By monitoring the body, these devices can detect health issues, for example, Parkinson's disease, a long time before they fully develop. This can enable treatment to start much sooner and this may prove more effective, or avoid the disease developing altogether.

IT in education

The use of IT in education is a growing trend. Technology, such as interactive whiteboards, can be used in the classroom to make lessons more visual and appealing. This may enhance the learning process for students.

It is also being used to aid learning online with the practice of technology-based learning that was discussed previously in the chapter.

Discuss with your teacher whether your school has any plans to introduce any new IT into your school in the future. If this isn't possible, discuss what IT you think would benefit your learning.

IT in banking and finance

You have already studied how IT is used in the development and management of a range of electronic currencies. Banks rely heavily on the use of IT to keep very large databases of records about all the transactions that are made on a daily basis. If this had to all be recorded on paper, the physical storage space required in buildings to do this would be immense!

IT is used to enable people to access physical currency through the use of ATMs. The introduction of IT for this purpose meant that people no longer needed to queue in the bank to withdraw their money. It also introduced the ability for people to access their money 24 hours a day, and not only when the bank was open.

Many banks now also provide access to an online bank account using a mobile app. Customers download the app onto their mobile device, set up access to their account by entering their personal details, and use their login details (or set up new ones) to access their online account using the app.

Online banking services now allow people to check their bank account quickly using IT. They can carry out most banking services online, such as:

- checking their bank balance
- viewing bank statements
- setting up direct debits
- applying for loans and overdrafts
- paying bills
- transferring money between accounts.

To be able to use services such as these, people would previously have needed to go into a bank. Often, they would only have one or two local bank branches, so their choice of bank may have been limited if they wanted their bank to be close to home. Also, those people that live in remote locations may have had to travel a great distance in order to get to a bank. The introduction and developments in online banking have allowed people to have more choice over which bank to choose and it saves people a lot of time in using banking services.

There are many advantages brought about by online banking. These include:

- Needing to visit a branch less as many services can be used online.

- Avoiding queues in bank branches.

- The ability to use banking services 24 hours a day, 7 days a week.

- Using banking services without leaving home.

- Viewing transactions online without needing to wait for paper statements to be delivered.

Some banks have chosen to encourage online banking by offering better deals on interest rates and loans online. They have done this because online banking can help cut their costs, from printing statements to the number of branches they need to have.

People can access many different financial services using IT. People can set up online investment portfolios and use IT to monitor them on a daily basis. They can also use IT to apply for financial services such as loans, mortgages and insurance. The use of IT can allow them to compare and contrast the deals on offer by different finance companies from the comfort of their own home. They can also use aggregate websites that will find all the deals available to them on the internet and show them which deals would be best for their needs.

E-business

Business has changed hugely through the introduction of IT. Online business is now commonplace and is often seen as an easier way of buying goods and services than in a physical store. Goods and services are often cheaper online because of cost savings from businesses not needing a shop space and from reduced utility bills.

IT has caused the rise of online shopping by providing a more convenient platform on which to sell items to a customer or purchase items as a customer. One of the main advantages of this is how quickly the customer receives products.

Online shopping has become even more popular with the rise of smart devices, because of applications that allow you to order anything online by using your phone, regardless of where you are. This is even more convenient for the customer as they could be out shopping, not able to find their product in store, but able to order it from the online store straight away from their phone.

Online shopping can be better for the environment, because fewer vehicles may be used as people are not driving to shops. This will depend on whether the amount of people travelling to the shops is reduced by people shopping online. Some people argue that the number of vehicles on the road that are delivering the online shopping does not make it much better for the environment. It is also very difficult for people to see the quality of products online or check the size of them. This can mean that many products end up being returned. This may also increase the number of vehicles used.

News and media

In the social networking section of the chapter, you studied how it is now being used on a regular basis and how it is a source of news and media for people. This has allowed people to have quick access to news stories around the world and has made people more aware of world events. The use of IT has also allowed people to be amateur journalists themselves, by recording events as they happen and using social media platforms to broadcast this to a wider audience. This has had both a positive and a negative effect. It has allowed people to see what has happened in certain events, when the media may have chosen to censor the content of those events. This gives people a truer impression of what is actually happening. Others believe that this could also be harmful and will argue that the media sometimes chose to censor what happens at events, because they believe it could be harmful for people to be fully aware.

People are able to use IT to set up news feeds that are able to draw news stories from all different kinds of media sources. This means that they save time as they do not need to go to the site of each individual source and find the news stories that they want to read. They can set their news interests for the feed and then the software will search for stories that it thinks will interest the user.

Figure 12.12: The news online.

Family and home

The introduction of IT into the home has developed in many ways. People now have devices, for example Amazon's Alexa and Google's Home systems, and use them for many different services in the home. They can be used to control many aspects in the home, such as lighting and heating. A user is even able to use the IT to control these systems from a remote location. This facility can help people save money and can also be better for the environment. This is because, rather than having the heating on all day, or having it on a timer system to start at a certain time, the user can choose to remotely start the heating system at a precise time that they are about to travel back to their home.

These devices can also prove to be a source of entertainment to families at home. Families can gather and play lots of games and quizzes using the devices. They can also use the device to stream music. This can help families interact and spend quality time together.

IT can also be present in many everyday devices in the home, such as washing machines and refrigerators. IT can be used to provide information to the user, for example, how long a washing machine has left to finish washing clothes. This can allow people to plan their time and know when they will need to remove their washing.

Figure 12.13: Home IT control devices.

Government and politics

The use of IT, especially social media, has become more prominent in government and politics. Social media is often used to raise awareness of different political causes and issues. Many online petitions are set up daily that try and encourage people to sign for the resolution of issues that they support. The use of IT in politics in this way can allow government to see what issues the people have, and this may help them prioritise what they discuss in government. It can also help the people have a voice and force government to discuss issues that they believe need resolving.

IT has allowed governments to make services they provide accessible online. For example, people may be able to pay their taxes online, and apply for documents such as a passport or a driving licence. This can make access to these services much more convenient for people and could also save costs for government, because they need fewer staff available than if people needed to meet face to face for these services.

Monitoring and surveillance

The use of IT in monitoring and surveillance has become very prominent. Many police authorities around the world use it to monitor possible criminal activity and to locate criminals when crimes have been committed.

One example of its use in this way is to combine facial recognition software with CCTV footage. Often a criminal will try and flee an area or a country if they believe they will be caught. This could involve them making a journey using a train or an aeroplane. Train stations and airports often have a lot of CCTV footage available. This footage could be scanned using facial recognition software to see whether the criminal has passed through the train station or the airport. This type of analysis can save a lot of time, as previously, a person would need to have watched hours of footage to see if they could spot the criminal in the footage. This type of technology could also be useful in finding a missing person. The police could analyse the CCTV footage in certain areas with facial recognition technology to see if the last known location for the missing person can be detected.

More people are adding CCTV technology to their home. Special systems can be set up that will monitor the area around a house. If any motion is detected in this area, a user can get an alert to their mobile phone and can instantly view footage of their home to see what or who has created the motion. Some systems also incorporate a speaker that will then allow the user to speak to whoever is moving outside of their house. This may scare off any person who may be planning to burgle the house, as they know they have been seen already.

People are also starting to use surveillance methods in their vehicles. Some drivers are adding dashcams (dashboard cameras) into their vehicles. These are cameras that will start recording the journey of the driver when the car is switched on. The intention of this footage is if another driver crashes into the car, the driver of the car will have video footage of the accident for their insurance company. This can help prove that they are not at fault for an accident (if, of course, it isn't their fault!). This footage has also started to serve a secondary purpose for some police authorities. Some police have requested if any drivers have dashcam footage of a certain area at a certain time. They are hoping to be able to analyse this footage to see if they can get evidence of a crime that may have been committed on the street at that time.

It is argued by some that use of IT in these ways, as methods of monitoring and surveillance, is relatively

unpoliced at present. It can take a long time to pass laws and regulations to police this type of technology, and the development of the technology can often move quicker that the ability to police it. Some people highly disagree with the ability of the average person to record them walking down the street or past their home, which is what can be done at present with home CCTV systems and dashcams. They believe that this is an invasion of their privacy and that there needs to be a greater level of laws and regulation governing there use in this way.

REFLECTION

How do you feel about a person's ability to record you walking down the street, without your knowledge or consent?

Do you feel this is an invasion of your privacy?

Do you think that the improved level of security that it may create is more important?

EXAM-STYLE QUESTIONS

1	Explain what is meant by a cryptocurrency.	[3]
2	Explain two advantages and two disadvantages of the use of digital currency.	[4]
3	Explain the difference between a chat room and a forum.	[4]
4	Describe the process of data mining.	[8]
5	Explain two ways that data mining can be used.	[4]
6	Explain two advantages and one disadvantage of learners using a MOOC to improve their work-based skill set.	[6]
7	Discuss the impact of the central bank moving to a digital based currency only.	[6]
8	Discuss the impact of the use of IT in banking and finance.	[6]

SUMMARY CHECKLIST

- [ ] I can recognise a range of different electronic currencies, how they are used and the advantages and disadvantages of each.
- [ ] I can describe the processes involved in data mining, how it is used and the advantages and disadvantages.
- [ ] I can recognise a range of different types of social networking, how they are used and the impact they have.
- [ ] I can recognise the different methods that can be used to deliver technology enhanced learning, including the advantages and disadvantages of each method.
- [ ] I can understand the impact IT has on a range of different areas of society.

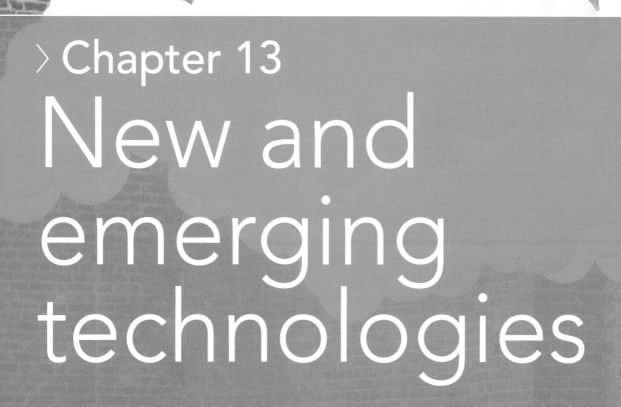

Chapter 13

New and emerging technologies

LEARNING INTENTIONS

By the end of this chapter, you will be able to:

* know and understand a range of new and emerging technologies

* know and understand the impact of new and emerging technologies on a range of areas of society.

Introduction

The world of technology is ever evolving. This results in the development of new and **emerging technologies**. Many of these technologies have a positive impact on our society. They aid both individuals and organisations, medicine and healthcare, scientific research and the environment.

KEY WORDS

emerging technologies: technologies that are still in development to allow them to reach their full potential

An emerging technology may be a new technology, but it may also be an existing technology that is still being developed. An emerging technology is still being developed to reach its full potential because this hasn't yet been realised.

You are going to learn about a range of emerging technologies and their application. You will develop your understanding of the impact of these technologies through the use of examples.

Figure 13.1: Emerging technology.

13.1 Near field communication (NFC)

NFC is a wireless technology that is similar to Bluetooth. It is a communication **protocol** that enables two devices to connect and share data. Unlike Bluetooth, which has an average range of 10 m, devices using NFC must be within 4 cm of each other.

KEY WORD

protocol: a set of rules or standards that ensure data is transferred between devices correctly

NFC is a technology that is present in most modern mobile telephones and smart watches. Users can bring their devices close together and use NFC to share data securely within seconds, without the need for an internet connection.

Some users are apprehensive about NFC. Unlike Bluetooth, it does not require a pairing code or password. Therefore, users are worried that someone could easily steal the data stored on their device. The very close proximity required for NFC means that this would be quite difficult. Many organisations that make use of NFC plan to add in other security methods to prevent this issue. As NFC doesn't require a pairing code, one advantage is that a connection between two devices can be established much quicker than with other wireless technologies.

Advantages	Disadvantages
Wireless communication so no cabled connection is required.	Can be seen as less secure as user does not need to authenticate the pairing of devices.
Fast method of data transfer.	Users are concerned that the technology could be used to steal their data.

Advantages	Disadvantages
Present in many modern mobile devices so is becoming more universal.	
Does not require an internet connection.	
Does not require a paring code.	

Table 13.1: Advantages and disadvantages of NFC.

Figure 13.2: Data sharing with NFC.

Passive NFC chips

There is a growing use of NFC by organisations to distribute data. Passive NFC chips can be built into information points in buildings and used to provide visitors with necessary information. Their use in this way is similar to QR codes, but without the need for a QR code reader, and with a more efficient process. Instead of having to open a QR reader application and wait a few seconds for the code to scan, a user with an NFC enabled device can touch their device to the information point and receive the data almost instantly.

Question

1   How could NFC be used in a hospital?

Electronic wallet

One of the fastest developing ways of using NFC is the electronic wallet. NFC chips are built into many credit cards. This is the technology that enables individuals to make contactless payments. The NFC technology in mobile phones and smart watches is also beginning to be used by companies like Apple, for services such as Apple Pay. This enables the user to use NFC technology in their mobile device to make a contactless payment.

> **REFLECTION**
>
> How do you feel about your mobile device and NFC becoming your electronic wallet in the future?

> **PRACTICAL ACTIVITY13.01**
>
> Use the internet to research how computer games, such as Skylanders and Disney Infinity, make use of NFC technology.

13.2 Ultra-high definition television systems

The quality of the image produced by a television system often depends on the resolution of the screen. The resolution of a screen is measured in pixels. It refers to the number of pixels wide and the number of pixels high that a screen can produce.

Standard high definition (HD) was once thought to be the highest quality that a picture could be displayed. This has a resolution of 1920 × 1080. However, 4K and, more recently, 8K screens have been developed and produce ultra-high definition (UHD). The resolution of 4K screens is 3840 × 2160. This is double the number of pixels than HD. This allows a sharper, clearer image to be created as the level of detail that can be replicated is greatly increased. 8K is double the resolution again!

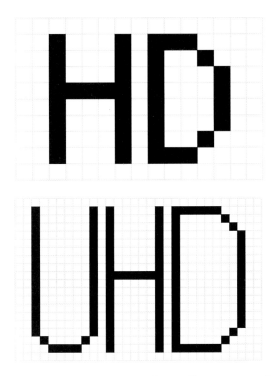

Figure 13.3: An example of the difference in pixels used between HD and UHD.

The average user will see a difference in an image or video produced by a UHD screen, compared to an HD screen. One way to enhance this difference is by viewing the image up close on each. The grid-like structure of an image will be more visible up close on an HD screen than a UHD screen, because the pixels are so much smaller on the UHD screen.

4K television systems are commercially available and are beginning to become more commonplace in our homes. 8K systems are mostly used on a commercial basis in applications such as cinema screens. It is possible to purchase an 8K television for the home, but there are very few entertainment services that can be used that will allow this kind of definition to be used. This is because to broadcast data to fulfil this level of resolution would require a very high-speed internet connection. Most television services are still working on managing to broadcast at a 4K resolution. This requires them to develop a method to broadcast four times as much data than it does for HD, if the file is considered in its raw form.

Question

2   How could a television broadcaster reduce the amount of data it needs to transmit, but still achieve a 4K resolution?

Advantages	Disadvantages
Quality of the image is sharper and clearer.	The technology required for UHD screens is more expensive to manufacture.
Can produce a higher level of detail in an image.	It requires a large amount of data to be transmitted by television broadcasters to achieve a UHD image.
Can improve the viewing experience for the user.	An internet connection of at least 25mbps is normally required to stream content at a UHD level.

Table 13.2: Advantages and disadvantages of UHD.

UHD in surgery

CyberMed NB24k and the Davinci is a medical grade computer that has a 4K screen. It is a computer that is used in surgical situations to allow surgeons to view the surgery in progress. The 4K resolution of the screen allows the surgeon to have a higher level of visibility of the surgery. This allows the surgeon to have a greater level of precision when carrying out tasks such as surgical incisions.

4K televisions systems are increasingly used this way in surgery to allow a greater level of precision, and to allow the possibility for surgery to be carried out remotely, using a very high-quality image.

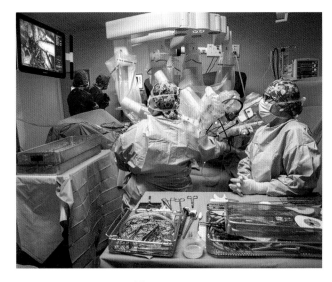

Figure 13.4: UHD used for imaging in surgery.

Question

3   What advantages could there be for using UHD to allow remote surgeries to take place? What disadvantages could there be to such surgery?

UHD in cinemas

Cinema saw the first mainstream Hollywood movie to be filmed in 8K in 2017, *Guardians of the Galaxy Vol. 2*. Most cinemas were not able to display the film at this resolution, but cinemas are gradually updating their technology to allow future movies to be displayed in 8K.

The difference in clarity for the 8K resolution is more likely be seen on large screens. It will create the most visually entertaining experience for the viewer and will allow a greater level of immersion.

The 8K resolution may be the highest resolution that is seen for a long time for cinema screens. Visual specialists have advised that it is probably the maximum level of pixels that our eyes can take, and anything above it would go completely unnoticed.

Question

4   What impact will UHD have on the technology required to create movies, including the computers often used to edit them?

13.3 Artificial intelligence

Artificial intelligence (AI) is one of the fastest developing areas of technology. AI is the creation of computers that are designed to have human-like capabilities. AI can react to stimuli and make decisions much like a human does. On a simple level, it is giving computers the ability to simulate the act of thinking.

AI is capable of actions such as learning, planning, recognising speech and problem solving. One of the earliest pioneers of AI was Alan Turing. During World War II he cracked the Enigma code, the code generated from the Enigma machine used by the German army to communicate, and decrypted German messages about the war strategies. He became intrigued by the possible intelligence of machines. This came from the notion of providing machines with **heuristic** knowledge to enable them to make decisions in a more human-like way.

AI systems are based around the creation of rules. The AI system uses these rules to make decisions based on input. It will then begin to adapt the decisions it makes as these rules allow it to learn and make decisions based on its own learning.

Knowledge engineering is important to the abilities of AI. To learn, AI machines need access to a knowledge base and need to be able to establish the relations between the knowledge available. Machine learning is also a core part of AI. This allows AI machines to establish patterns in the received input that can inform its ability to analyse and learn.

Advantages	Disadvantages
Increased level of precision and accuracy as will likely have a lower error rate than a human.	Requires a high level of skills to program so can be very expensive to create.
Can replace the need for humans in tedious, repetitive or dangerous tasks.	The storage requirements for the program and knowledge base can be very extensive, creating greater expense.
Machines do not require rest, so can be used 24/7.	People have ethical and moral issues with computers being used to recreate intelligence.
Can make logical decisions, void of emotion, so can provide a rational outcome.	They do not consider emotion when making decisions, so this is not considered. This also means they are not fully capable of human emotions such as sympathy and empathy.
Can analyse large sets of data in a much more efficient fashion than a human.	As they are fundamentally based on rules, this can affect their ability to be creative.

Table 13.3: Advantages and disadvantages of AI.

Figure 13.5: Artificial intelligence.

Self-driving cars

Several organisations, for example, Google and Tesla, are developing self-driving cars. Many people find driving a car, especially on a long journey, a tedious task. Therefore, these companies are trying to create a self-driving car that will remove the need for humans to drive. They believe it will greatly increase the quality of life for humans, especially those that commute by car on a regular basis.

Some people view the development of self-driving cars as an advantage. It will remove the possibility that people will drive when tired, and remove the emotional reactions that drivers can have in certain situations encountered on the road. Both of these aspects can often cause accidents. Therefore, if they are removed, then fewer accidents should occur.

Some people view the notion of self-driving cars as a disadvantage. They believe there are several moral and ethical aspects that will occur as a result. One aspect is that the quality of the algorithm that the car is based upon will be affected by the abilities of the programmers that created it. The standard of the programmers involved will differ, therefore the quality of the algorithm as a result could affect the AI's ability to make an effective decision in critical situations. Another aspect is the concept of responsibility if two self-driving cars have an accident. Who is at fault and should pay for the damage?

Scientific analysis

The level of data produced daily in relation to science is phenomenal! Many scientific research organisations record terabytes of data each day. This has caused many

of these organisations to use AI to analyse the extensive amount of data they collect.

AI is used to identify patterns and trends in the data that can then be used to form future scientific discoveries or hypotheses. The learning ability of AI can also be used to ask the machine itself to provide its own hypothesis that can be considered.

The level of data analysis that can be carried out by AI far outweighs the capabilities of a human in this application. Therefore, this could mean that scientific discoveries can be made quicker and with a greater level of accuracy.

13.4 Augmented reality

Augmented reality (AR) is where technology overlays computer-generated images onto a user's view of the real world. It creates an interactive experience by enhancing the user's view of the real world with multimedia elements such as text, sound, animations and video.

AR is a relative old technology. It has been in existence since the 1960's, but it is an example of an emerging technology that is only just starting to realise its potential. The technology commonly makes use of a digital camera and sensors to read data from the surrounding environment. It then uses a method of output to display the augmented reality.

AR can be created with mobile devices such as smart phones. It can also be created with pioneering technology such as smart glasses. If you have watched a science fiction movie, you have probably seen an example of augmented reality in action, for example, as a head up display in an aircraft or a vehicle. This type of technology is used in the real world, by organisations such as the military, to train professionals such as pilots.

Advantages	Disadvantages
Can make a learning experience both entertaining and more immersive.	It is based on the collection and analysis of data. This has caused some people to be concerned about the privacy and security of the data.
Can be used to simulate and communicate immediate information, creating a better experience when used in a learning and training capacity.	Some people believe that it can modify a person's perception of reality and can cause a blurred distinction between the two.
Can allow a user to simulate everyday experiences in an efficient manner. It can allow a shopper to simulate trying out different clothing and hairstyles, without actually changing their clothing or hairstyles.	The technology required to process the data needed for a smooth AR experience needs to be fairly powerful. This type of technology is expensive to manufacture.
Can be used to allow a user to navigate a new place, helping them to easily find the services and attractions they require.	

Table 13.4: Advantages and disadvantages of AR.

Figure 13.6: Augmented reality.

Gaming

One example of AR that continues to develop is its use in gaming. *Pokémon Go,* released in 2016, became a global sensation in the gaming world. It allowed players to augment their surround reality to find and collect different Pokémon. A second AR based game, released in 2019, *Wizards Unite,* augments the world of Harry Potter onto a player's surrounding reality, allowing them to immerse themselves in the Harry Potter world. In both cases, players use their mobile device to create the augmented reality.

Medicine

The use of AR in medicine is growing. Technology that allows surgeons access to immediate and vital information whilst performing surgery is in development. Surgeons can wear technology such as smart glasses. This technology would allow them to request access to any of the patient's records immediately during surgery and they could then see this data without having to look away from the surgery they are performing. This could also allow data such as scans of the patient to be superimposed onto the patient to allow a surgeon to clearly visualise the issue they are addressing in surgery.

> **PRACTICAL ACTIVITY 13.04**
>
> Research which companies are developing smart glasses and what they intend their uses to be.

> **PRACTICAL ACTIVITY 13.05**
>
> Find out how IKEA are allowing users to make use of AR.

13.5 Virtual reality

Virtual reality (VR) allows a user to experience a computer-generated reality that doesn't immediately exist in their real-world reality. A computer is used to generate a 3D space of a digital reality. The user is then immersed into this computer-generated reality, often through the use of a headset. The headset will normally incorporate a visual display and headphones to allow a fully immersive experience for the user.

Whilst wearing the headset, a user can then walk around the computer-generated reality and interact with it. The headset uses two camera feeds, one for the left eye and one for the right, in an attempt to mimic the human field of vision.

VR is becoming a more prominent technology in the gaming world, with the release of technology, such as PlayStation VR, allowing users to enjoy an even greater immersive experience.

Advantages	Disadvantages
Can be used to simulate critical situations for organisations such as hospitals and the military, to provide a training tool to develop the necessary skills required for dealing with the crisis.	Achieving perfect calibration between the cameras and the user can be very difficult. If it is not accurate enough, it can cause the user to get a feeling of motion sickness.
Can be used to provide a very immersive experience into a different reality than the immediate real world. This can enhance the gaming experience. It can also provide a relaxing or calming environment, to help people with stress or mental health issues.	The technology required to create the VR experience is often expensive to manufacture.
Can help build a person's confidence if they can replicate a situation that allows them to practise for a certain scenario.	Some people think that there is a danger that people can be seduced by an alternate reality and neglect their real world reality as a result.

Table 13.5: Advantages and disadvantages of VR.

Figure 13.7: Virtual reality headset.

Scientific research

Scientific organisations are beginning to use VR in their research. In the past, scientists have relied on using 2D visualisations of elements, such as atoms and molecules, to explore their structure and appearance. VR can now allow scientists to create a VR representation of this kind of aspect of our world that they can interact with and see an immersive visual representation of their research. They could use this kind of technology to combine molecular structures to see what affect it will have. This may help in the development of new medicinal drugs to treat new and existing medical conditions.

Tourism

Organisations around the world are using VR to allow users, particularly those who have disabilities and are unable to travel, to experience a computer-generated reality of tourist attractions. It could allow the users to experience a walk around the ancient ruins of Rome, or to admire all the art at the Louvre.

This type of technology can allow people to experience many tourist attractions around the world that they would otherwise be unable to experience. This can help create a better quality of life and can also be used for educational purposes in a similar way.

PRACTICAL ACTIVITY 13.06

Discuss with a partner what your perfect VR world would look like. Discuss whether you think it would help your quality of life if you could immerse yourself in this world on a regular basis.

13.6 Robotics

Robotics involves the study of designing, building and the application of robots. A robot is any machine that can perform tasks that would otherwise be performed by a human. Robots can be programmed to do this automatically or through the direct instruction of a human. The word Robot has Slavic origins and comes from the word robota, which means 'forced work or labour'.

Robots seem like a modern-day technology, but their origins are quite old. The **automation** aspect of robotics can be traced back to ancient Greece and Rome, where there is evidence of automation in toys. This kind of automation can be seen throughout history.

> **KEY WORD**
>
> **automation:** the ability to operate automatically

In the 1960's robots were introduced on a more industrial scale by General Motors. They introduced them into their automotive factories and used them to move car parts around to make it easier to assemble the cars. They are still used in automotive factories around the world today and have become a large part of the process of constructing cars.

Robots are normally automated using microprocessors and sensors. Sensors sample data from the surrounding environment and send this to the microprocessor. The microprocessor analyses the data and sends signals to instruct the robot on what action to take as a result.

Advantages	Disadvantages
Can perform tasks that might be tedious or dangerous for a human.	Can be used to replace humans in certain jobs and may take much needed jobs from some humans.
Do not require a break, so can work 24/7 if necessary.	Can be paired with artificial intelligence and can therefore learn, but are not capable of an emotional response.
Can improve a person's quality of life.	Require a constant supply of power. This can be expensive and can have a lasting impact on the environment.
Not prone to error like a human can be.	Designing and building robots requires a high level of skill and high-quality materials, to make sure they are reliable. This can be very expensive.

Advantages	Disadvantages
Can help reduce time and costs in manufacturing as can often complete tasks quicker and more consistently than a human is able to.	Some humans fear the use of robots and do not agree with our current dependence on them.
Robotic pets can be used to increase the quality of life for those who are not able to have real life pets, due to issues such as allergies. Robotics pets have also been used to help people with depression.	

Table 13.6: Advantages and disadvantages of robotics.

Prosthetic limbs

The use of prosthetic limbs in humans, to replace those lost, has been a medical practice for a long time. The use of prosthetics is now in further development due to the use of robotics. Robotic prosthesis is a rapidly developing area in medicine. A robotic prosthetic can be connected to a human mind. This can allow a human to train their brain to be able to move the robotics in the prosthetic, creating a working limb again. This advancement in medical technology will vastly improve the quality of life for those who have lost limbs.

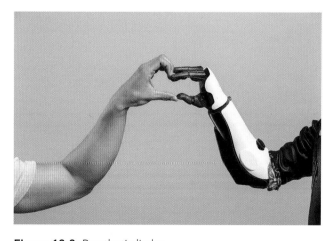

Figure 13.8: Prosthetic limbs.

Nano-robots

Nano-robots are robots that have been scaled down to a microscopic size. The ability to do this to robots could prove to be extremely useful in medical procedures. It could be possible to put nano-robots into a human's blood stream to track down and eliminate certain medical conditions. They could also be used to perform internal surgery in places that are normally very challenging to reach for surgeons.

Nano-robots could revolutionise cancer treatment, by tracking down and destroying cancer cells in the body. This could save the lives of many people in the future.

PRACTICAL ACTIVITY 13.07

Discuss with a partner about how you feel about having nano-robots released into your blood stream. Would you feel this is an invasion of your body, or would you feel that it is a very beneficial medical advancement?

PRACTICAL ACTIVITY 13.08

Use the internet to research how robots are helping in the fight against environmental issues such as climate change.

REFLECTION

Some people are concerned that advancements in robotics will one day cause them to take over the world. How do you feel about this?

13.7 Computer-assisted translation

The ability to translate from one language to another has allowed a greater level of communication in the world. It is an essential process on a global scale for the practice of business and politics.

Computer-assisted translation tools have been developed to help support this essential practice. They can be used to increase the productivity and accuracy of human translators, especially when vital information needs to be translated immediately.

The tool normally works by providing the software with a document for translation. The software will identify the text elements in a document and translate them into the required language. An important point to note about computer-assisted translation is that is a not like a human translator. It is a database-driven software that matches words to those in its database and is capable of using the grammatical rules of a language to piece together a translation.

There are some well known computer-assisted translation tools available, such as Google Translate, WordBee and memoQ.

Advantages	Disadvantages
People can get access to an instant translation of a document from one language to another. This can save time and improve communication.	Some people are sceptical about the accuracy of the translation that computer-assisted translators are capable of.
It can help reduce errors that may be present in manual translation methods.	Some people find that certain terms in a language are used in a context, for example, slang or colloquial language. Translation tools can often struggle to interpret these terms if used within a certain context.
Translation tools are quite widely available and are therefore a relatively inexpensive tool. Some companies offer them for free, for example, Google Translate.	

Table 13.7: Advantages and disadvantages of computer-assisted translation.

Figure 13.9: Language translation.

Foreign-language websites

Computer-assisted translation can be very useful when accessing websites from around the world. If you want to use a website from a different country, it is likely to be written in the language of that country. This can mean that you are not able to read the language it is written in. Computer-assisted translation tools can be used to translate the website content into the language that you require. This can help improve communication and make a lot more information accessible to people around the world.

PRACTICAL ACTIVITY 13.09

Use the internet to find a website that is written in a different language to your own. If you do this using a search engine, such as Google Chrome, this has a built-in computer-assisted translator. Ask the translator to translate the website into your language. Look at the translation and consider how accurate it is. Can you see any errors that the translator may have produced?

Spell checking

Another way that computer-assisted translation can be used is as a spell-checker tool. The database stored of all the words for a language can be used to compare text that is typed. This will allow the tool to identify any words that may be incorrect and offer a corrected spelling for them.

13.8 Holographic imaging

Holographic imaging is also known as a **hologram**. A hologram is a 3D image that is created using laser beams and mirrors. The laser beam is split up by reflecting it off mirrors and when they recombine, they create the holographic image.

KEY WORD

hologram: a 3D image that is created using laser beams and mirrors

Holograms were originally invented in the 1950's by a Hungarian born physicist called Dennis Gabor. He was awarded a Nobel prize in Physics in 1971 for his invention and development of the holographic method.

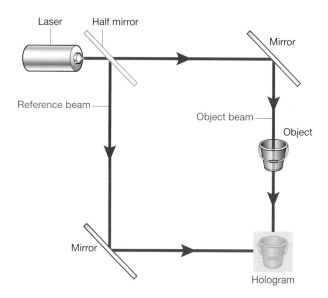

Figure 13.10: Creating a hologram.

Holograms can be a 2D image that appears to look 3D, as it is moved. Holograms can also be an image that is actually 3D and free standing. This kind of hologram also uses photographic projection. You may have seen this kind of hologram appear in movies such as *Star Wars* and *Iron Man*.

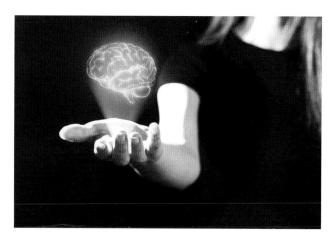

Figure 13.11: Holographic image.

Advantages	Disadvantages
They do not require special glasses to view the 3D effect.	3D projected holograms require expensive equipment to create.
They are very difficult to replicate so can be useful as a security measure.	A lot of data needs to be stored in order to create holograms and the cost of data storage can often be expensive.
If is much easier to see depth perception on a 3D projected hologram, than in ordinary 3D images.	

Table 13.8: Advantages and disadvantages of holograms.

Security

Holographic images are used on many items around the world. They appear on credit cards, currency and other secure documents such as driving licenses and passports. They are used as a method of security, to stop fraud, as they are difficult to replicate.

Holograms add an extra layer of security to sensitive items and information. This is an important benefit as these documents can be the target of many acts of fraud.

Figure 13.12: Hologram used on currency.

Architecture

The use of holograms has become more prominent in architecture and the construction industry. Holographic images can be used to see a true 3D visualisation of what a building will look like when constructed. They can offer additional benefits over the use of on-screen simulated 3D models, which is the older alternative. This can help architects of buildings provide further understanding to construction companies, by allowing them to see an actual representation of what the they intend the building to look like. This means that construction companies do not need to spend as much time deciphering the plans and ideas of an architect.

Figure 13.13: Hologram of a building structure.

PRACTICAL ACTIVITY 13.10

Use the internet to research one other application of holographic imaging. Create a short presentation that could be used to inform the members of your class about how holographic imaging is used in this application.

REFLECTION

It may become possible to transmit holographic images into individual homes. This means that we could actually see a true 3D representation of the person we are talking to. How do you think this will affect our communication with each other and our daily lives?

13.9 Holographic data storage

The use of light to store data is common. Optical data storage uses light to burn data onto a reflective surface, and also uses the reflective properties of light to read the data from the reflective surface. The concept of optical storage is also the underlying principal behind holographic data storage.

One possible way of holographic data storage will use a laser beam. The laser beam is fired, and it is then split. The splitting process is important, as this is what helps create the hologram. The split beams will be bounced off mirrors and they will both travel to a crystal. When the two beams meet again, they will create a hologram that is stored in the crystal.

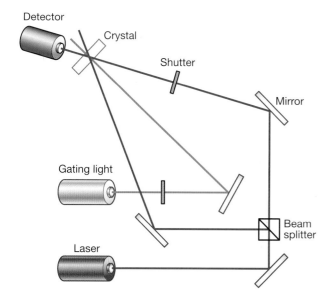

Figure 13.14: Beam splitter.

A single storage crystal is about the size of a grain of sugar. Each storage crystal could be capable of storing a single terabyte of data. Imagine how much data could be stored on a single disk as a result!

Advantages	Disadvantages
Large amounts of data can be stored on a very small medium.	It is not compatible with current methods of data storage. This would make reading the data very difficult.
It will make the storage of large amounts of data much more portable.	The technology required to use holographic data storage is currently very complex and expensive.
It is capable of storage millions of bits of data at a time, making transfer rates much faster than current methods.	

Table 13.9: Advantages and disadvantages of holographic data storage.

Taking data into space

Holographic data storage could be extremely useful when transporting large amounts of data, for example, taking data into space. It can be difficult to send large amounts of data into space to a space station that may require it. It has to travel a long way and that limits the amount of data that can sent at any given time.

The amount of space available to send items to space in a rocket is also very limited. Therefore, if holographic data storage could be used to store data that can be transported into space, this would enable very large amounts of data to be sent with each mission to space.

Archiving data

Large corporations often archive large amounts of data. This can often be to refer to in future, or sometimes for legal reasons. Data storage currently can take up a lot of space in a storage unit and to buy or rent the building space necessary to hold the large data storage units can be very expensive.

If the size of the data storage units could be greatly reduced, through using holographic data storage, this could potentially save large organisations a lot of money. The CERN data centre, a large particle physics laboratory in Switzerland, generates 30 petabytes of data a year to be archived. They could definitely benefit from smaller data storage units!

Figure 13.15: Data storage facility.

PRACTICAL ACTIVITY 13.11

Use the internet to research information about the longevity of holographic data storage.

13.10 3D printing

The concept of 3D printing is now a relatively developed technology. It has been in development since the 1980's. It is the application of 3D printing that continues to develop. There are increasingly more ways that 3D printing is used and many past methods are being revolutionised.

Figure 13.16: 3D printing.

3D printing is a form of additive manufacturing. A 3D software-based model is created using computer aided design (CAD) software. The data to create this model is transmitted to a 3D printer. The 3D printer creates the physical model by layering very thin materials, such as plastic, to build the model.

Advantages	Disadvantages
The speed at which certain objects can be created is greatly increased through the use of 3D printing.	It has become much easier to build dangerous and counterfeit items, which causes greater security and fraud issues.
A 3D printer will consistently create the exact same product from a model. The level of consistency would be much greater than when created by a human.	At present, 3D printers are only capable of creating relatively small items. Developments are progressing to increase the size of the objects that a 3D printer is capable of creating.
Much more flexible when creating complex models, especially those that have hollow cavities within solid parts.	3D printing reduces the number of manufacturing jobs, as it is able to replace the need for humans to create the products.
Although the initial setup costs will be high, the cost of creating each product with a 3D printer will often be much cheaper than alternative manufacturing methods.	3D printing requires a relatively high level of power consumption. This can be harmful to the environment as it increases emissions.
	At present, ABS filament is the most common type of material used in 3D printing. The by-product of this plastic is increasingly dumped in landfill and negatively affects the environment.

Table 13.10: Advantages and disadvantages of 3D printing.

Bespoke prosthetics

The application of 3D printing has revolutionised many areas of the medical industry. It is possible to print bespoke prosthetics, making limb replacement much more accessible to many.

3D-like printing is also being used as a method of bio-printing. This is allowing practices such as tissue engineering to be developed. The layer-by-layer method used in 3D printing is used in tissue engineering, layering biomaterials to create tissue-like structures. This technique can also be used to print organs and artificial blood vessels that can be used to aid drug and other medical research. This reduces the need to harvest organs for medical research. The hope is that these biomedical printing techniques will lead to the ability to create artificial organs that can be used in humans in the future. This will replace the need to have long waiting lists for organ transplantations, due to the need for a human donor.

Printing in space

3D printing has become an increasingly valuable practice in space. As storage space in a rocket is limited, a limited number of items can be taken into space with each visit. If a part breaks on a space station, the crew may be waiting for a quite a while for the next mission to be sent to get a replacement part. It has now become possible to take a 3D printer into space. This means that if any parts break on the space station, it is possible to print a copy and repair the space station much quicker.

REFLECTION

How would you feel about having a 3D printed artificial organ inserted into your body?

13.11 Vision enhancement

Vision enhancement is a field of technology which can restore vision, one of our five senses, to those who have lost it. Vision enhancement is normally provided in the form of a type of glasses or lenses. These alter the stimulus that enters through the eyes and filters it in a way that can enhance a person's vision. The glasses or lenses can be tailored to the person and their current level of vision for greatest effectiveness.

The ultimate goal of vision enhancement is to be able to provide blind people with images of their surroundings so that they can work and enjoy themselves just as others do. However, this field is not solely focused on those who are blind. A recent development in the field has allowed those who are colour-blind to see the world in the same way that everyone else sees it. This means that they are better able to distinguish between colours and in some cases see new colours that were muted before.

Vision enhancement can also be used to enhance the vision of all in situations where visibility is limited, for example, in the dark. Two types of vision enhancement that can be used for these situations are night vision and thermal vision. Night vision devices, such as night vision goggles, operate by collecting all available light, including infrared light and ultra-violet light, and amplifying it to create a more visible image. Thermal vision devices, such as thermal vision goggles, operate by using thermal imaging technology to capture the infrared light emitted as heat by objects such as humans.

Advantages	Disadvantages
It can improve the vision of those with limited or poor vision, which can provide them with a better quality of life.	The technology involved is expensive to manufacture.
It can improve the vision of those who are colour blind, allowing them to see a greater scope of colours, and colour correct the issue they may have.	The use of night and thermal vision devices is limited or illegal in some countries.
It can help improve visibility in scenarios where visibility is limited.	

Table 13.11: Advantages and disadvantages of vision enhancement.

Improving vision

People with poor vision can wear a headset that allows images of a person's surroundings to be projected inside the headset in front of their eyes. This allows them greater awareness and vision of their surroundings, allowing them improved navigation.

Seeing in the dark

Night vision and thermal vision devices are often used by military, to allow soldiers to have enhanced visibility at night. This can aid strategy necessary in combat, making it possible for soldiers to move around or assess a dangerous situation, at a time when they will be less visible also.

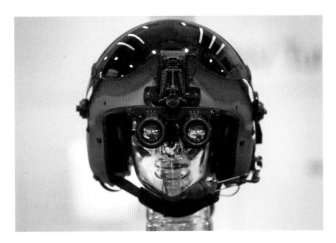

Figure 13.17: Night vision goggles.

13.12 Wearable computing

Wearable computing can take many different forms. One of the most common items of wearable computing is a fitness tracker. These are used by many people to see how many steps they have taken during a day, and often provide other health information, such as how many calories they have burned.

Wearable computing refers to clothing or accessories that have some form of computer-based components embedded into them. This could include glasses, headsets, watches, t-shirts and any other item that can be worn. Some of these serve a functional purpose that will provide information to the user, some are merely to look stylish and fashionable.

Figure 13.18: Wearable technology.

Advantages	Disadvantages
It allows greater access to important statistics regarding our daily health. This can improve our ability to monitor our health.	Users can become obsessed with their health statistics, which can lead to damaging thoughts.
Users can sync their fitness devices together and can encourage each other and set each other challenges, improving people's motivation to exercise.	There can be compatibility issues between devices, such as fitness trackers and mobile phones, that may mean data cannot be shared between them.
It can aid communication by allowing a user to see alerts for any text messages or emails that they have received, on their wearable device. Some can even be used to make telephone calls. This removes the need for the user to take their mobile out of the pocket or bag.	The accuracy of some health trackers can be dubious, as they are designed to monitor the 'average' person and not the bespoke health of each person.
	Some people are concerned about the security of their data that is gathered by their wearable device. It is also possible for companies to use the data that is collected for marketing purposes, which users may not be aware of.

Table 13.12: Advantages and disadvantages of wearable computing.

Exercise brings rewards

Companies are now providing employees with health trackers and rewarding them for the amount of exercise they record. They are provided with points for the steps that they record each day and these points can be spent on rewards for the employee. Rewards can often be in the form of gift vouchers for the employee, or a choice of products they are able to purchase.

Monitoring health issues

Heath trackers can also be used to monitor those with serious health issues. A user could have their heart rate constantly monitored, and if they have a heart issues, the device could be set to alert a medical professional or family member the instant that medical assistance is required.

13.13 Environmental issues

Whilst emerging technologies can be used to create many positive impacts on our lives, there is always the issue they can cause for our environment. The more we use and rely on technology, then more power consumption we will create. This will increase the level of emissions created in order to continue to power all our technology.

Despite the environmental issues that the power consumption of technology can create, some of these emerging technologies can be used to aid our environment. AI can be used to monitor current trends and patterns in our environment, and predict future trends. This can help identify information that could be useful to governments, so they can prepare for natural disasters and adverse weather possibilities. It could also be used by industries, such as farming, so that they can create the best conditions for their crop growth.

There will always be the added issue of e-waste from people throwing away technology in favour of new technology. This discarded technology often ends up being disposed of in landfill, where harmful metals from the technology can leach into the soil and infiltrate water supplies. Governments around the world are trying to encourage the recycling of technology to limit the issue created with this kind of disposal.

EXAM-STYLE QUESTIONS

1 Identify one advantage and one disadvantage to the user of wearable technology such as a health tracker. [2]
2 Explain three ways that 3D printing can be used in medical circumstances. [3]
3 Explain two advantages to a surgeon of using ultra-HD technology when performing surgery. [4]
4 Explain two disadvantages that emerging technologies have on the environment. [4]
5 Describe how near field communication (NFC) can be used in electronic payments. [3]
6 Discuss the impact on employees of the use of AI in manufacturing. [8]
7 Evaluate the potential impact on an organisation of using holographic data storage to archive data. [6]

SUMMARY CHECKLIST

- [ ] I can understand what is meant by an emerging technology.
- [ ] I can recognise a range of emerging technologies and understand how they are used.
- [ ] I can understand the impact of a range of emerging technologies and the impact they have on areas of society such as individuals, organisations, medicine and the environment.

> # Chapter 14
Communications technology

LEARNING INTENTIONS

By the end of this chapter, you will be able to:

- know and understand the different types of network, their characteristics and uses, and their advantages and disadvantages

- know and understand the role and operation of different components in a network

- know and understand the different types of network server, their role and operations in a network

- know and understand the characteristics, uses and advantages and disadvantages of cloud computing for a given scenario

- know and understand about data transmission across networks; speed of transmission; bandwidth and bit rate; and data streaming

- know and understand different methods of routing data over a network, including packet switching, circuit switching and message switching, and the purpose and use of network addressing systems

- know and understand the definition of a network protocol and the purpose and use of protocols in the preparation, addressing, sending and receiving of data across a network, including the internet

- know and understand about the management of network traffic; static and dynamic routing; the function of routing protocols; and the use of layers in protocols

- know and understand about data transmission methods; the properties, features and characteristic of different transmission methods; typical applications of each transmission method; and the advantage and disadvantages of each method

- know and understand the methods, uses and operation, and advantages and disadvantages of different methods of wireless data transmission technology

- know and understand about mobile communication systems, including cellular networks and how satellite communication systems are used for transferring data

- know and understand a range of network security threats to stored data and files, the impact of network security threats on individuals and organisations, and a range of prevention methods of network security issues, including the advantages and disadvantages of each method

- know and understand how threats and risks are identified in disaster recovery management, how to control threats and about the strategies to minimise risks.

BEFORE YOU START

- Do you have a basic understanding of a LAN, a WAN and a range of network topologies?

- Do you have a basic understanding of a range of network components including hubs, switches, routers and bridges?

- Do you have a basic understanding of security methods that can be used in a network?

Introduction

Until the 1990's, most computers found in the home and even in a workplace were stand-alone computers. This means that they were not connected to other computers. When computers are connected together, a **network** is created. This can be as simple as connecting two computers together.

KEY WORD

network: two or more computers or devices connected together so they can communicate and share data and resources

The primary reason why we create networks is to share data and resources, and to communicate with each other. There are three fundamental aspects to a network. These are the network components, the structure of the network and the protocols used. Protocols are vital in the effective transfer of data across a network and there is a wealth of them that have been created to make sure this is done efficiently and securely.

PRACTICAL ACTIVITY 14.01

Use the internet to research information about ARPANET, one of the first networks created.

14.1 Fundamental network models

There are two fundamental network models that many networks are built upon. These are the transmission control protocol/internet protocol (TCP/IP) suite and the open systems interconnection (OSI) model. Both outline rules and standards about how communications should take place over a network. Each is split into several layers. This is so that each layer can operate independently of another, which allows the functions that take place at each layer to be easily adapted, if necessary.

The OSI model has seven different layers:

Layer	Function
Application	This is the top layer of the model that directly interacts with data from the user. Software applications, such as web applications and email clients, rely on the applications layer to communicate. However, user applications, such as word processing packages, are not included in this function. The applications layer is responsible for managing the protocols that allow meaningful data to be presented to the user. It manages protocols such as hypertext transfer protocol (HTTP) and simple mail transfer protocol (SMTP) (you will learn about the function of these later in the chapter).
Presentation	The primary function of the presentation layer is to prepare data ready for use in the applications layer. This could involve the translation, encryption and compression of data. It makes sure that the data is translated into a form that will be understood by the receiving device. If the devices are communicating over a secure connection, the data will be encrypted. It will also decrypt any data that is received. It will also compress any data that is required to increase the speed of transmission.
Session	This layer is responsible for opening and closing communication links between devices. The time that passes between a communication link being opened and closed again is called a session. This layer makes sure that the session is open for long enough to allow all the data to be transmitted and then closes it immediately, as soon as transmission is completed.
Transport	This layer is responsible for breaking down the data from the session layer into segments. These segments are then given to the network layer. It is also responsible for reassembling the segments at the receiving device. This layer is also responsible for flow control (the best speed for transmission) and error checking. It checks that all the data has been received and will request a retransmission if it is not complete.
Network	The network layer breaks down the segments from the transport layer into smaller units, known as packets. It is also responsible for reassembling the packets after transmission. This layer is also responsible for routing, which is the process of finding the best path across the network. The network layer performs these tasks when data is transmitted from network to network. A router is one of the key network components in this layer. You will learn more about the role of a router later in the chapter.
Data link	This layer performs a very similar role to the network layer, but rather than transmitting data from network to network, it is responsible for transmitting data from node to node within a network. It takes the packets created at the network layer and converts them into frames. A switch is one of the key components in this layer. You will learn more about a switch later in the chapter.
Physical	This layer involves the physical equipment that is used to transmit the data, such as the cables. In this layer, data is broken down into bits to be transmitted as binary. This layer is also responsible for reassembling the bits into frames, after transmission.

Table 14.1: Layers in OSI model.

KEY WORDS

packet: a unit of data in data transmission

router: a network component that uses a computer's IP address to send data packets to a destination outside the current network

switch: a network component that uses a computer's MAC address to send data packets to a destination within a network

The OSI model is a logical model that can be applied when creating a network. An alternative setup is the TCP/IP model. In its basic form the TCP/IP model is a condensed version of the OSI model. It has four layers, rather than the seven outlined in the OSI model. The TCP/IP model was developed by the US department of defence and is intended to be a more advanced version of the OSI model.

The four layers of the TCP/IP protocol are:

Layer	Function
Application layer	This layer condenses the role of the application, presentation and session layers from the OSI model. It uses several protocols to provide a standardised exchange of data. The protocols it uses include HTTP, SMTP, post office protocol (POP) and file transfer protocol (FTP). You will learn more about the function of these protocols later in the chapter.
Transport layer	This layer is comparable to the transport layer in the OSI model. It is responsible for maintaining end-to-end communications between devices. There are two main protocols that are used at this level. The first is the transmission control protocol (TCP) and the second is the user datagram protocol (UDP). You will learn more about the function of these protocols later in the chapter.
Network layer	This layer can also be known as the internet layer and it is comparable to the network layer in the OSI model. It breaks data down into packets and transmits it network to network. There are two main protocols that are used at the level. The first is the internet protocol (IP) and the second is the internet control message protocol (ICMP).
Link layer	This layer can also be known as the physical layer and it condenses the role of the data link layer and physical layer from the OSI model. A protocol used at this level is the address resolution protocol (ARP).

Table 14.2: Layers in TCP/IP model.

14.2 Structure of a data packet

The prime function of a network is to transmit data from one device to another. In order to begin to understand how this occurs and how networks are structured, it is important to understand how the data is packaged to be transmitted across the network.

A data packet is normally the smallest unit of data that is sent across a network and it contains several elements. These elements can depend on the network used to send the packet. For example, if a packet is sent using the internet, it will contain more elements to allow to it to be directed to the right place. All the normal elements of a packet of data are the header, the payload and the trailer.

The header could include:

- the IP address of the sender. This is called the source IP address.
- the IP address of the receiving device. This is called the destination IP address.
- the sequence number of the packet. This is so the receiving device can reorder the packets to obtain the original data.
- the MAC address of the sender and the receiver. If the packet passes through a router, these will be removed, as they are no longer necessary, as they are only used by a switch. You will learn the roles of a router and a switch later in the chapter.
- any protocols used.

The payload will include:

- the actual data from the file that is being transmitted.

KEY WORDS

IP address: (Internet Protocol address): a unique address given to a device, normally by a router

MAC address: (Media Access Control address): a unique address given to a device by the manufacturer

The trailer could include:

- a flag that tells a device it has reached the end of the packet.

- any error checking methods that are used.

The data sent in the header and trailer are all designed to make sure that payload data arrives at its intended destination without any errors.

14.3 Transmitting data packets

The term used for transmitting data packets across a network is switching. There are three main types of switching, circuit switching, packet switching and message switching.

Circuit switching

In circuit switching, a direct path is created between the sending and the receiving device. These are dedicated pathways to transmit the data packets from one device to another across the network. The data is transmitted each time using this dedicated path.

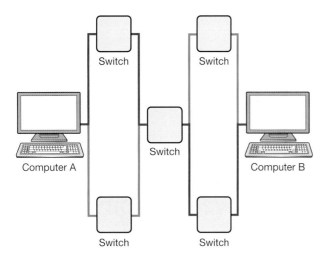

Figure 14.1: Circuit switching.

Whilst data is being transmitted from computer A to computer B, no other computers in the network can use the same pathway. When the data transmission is completed, the path is then released for use by other data transmission across the network.

Packet switching

In packet switching, the data packets sent across the network can take any available path. There is no set pathway and each data packet could be sent along a different pathway. In the diagram in Figure 14.1, data packets sent from Computer A and could be sent via any of the five switch components in the network. The packets will be collated and reordered when they reach Computer B. Packet switching is normally used when packets are sent across the internet. In this case, they will be sent via routers. You will learn later in the chapter how routers are used in this way.

There are two main methods of transmission in packet switching. These are connection-oriented (also known as virtual circuit switching) and connectionless (also known as datagram switching). Frame relay and transmission control protocol (TCP) are two types of connection-oriented packet switching. Ethernet, internet protocol (IP) and user datagram protocol (UDP) are types of connectionless packet switching. In connection-oriented packet switching, a session is created before any data is transferred. This becomes a fixed channel for the data to travel. In connectionless packet switching, there does not need to be any prior arrangement set up between devices to transmit the data.

Connection-oriented

Method	Function
Frame relay	In frame relay, data is separated into units called frames. Any methods of error correction that are used are carried out by the devices at the end points of transmission, which is one advantage of frame relay, as it helps speed up transmission.
	If an error is detected in a frame, that frame is dropped. The devices at the endpoints will then detect the dropped frames and retransmit them. This makes frame rate most suitable for sending data where the error rate is likely to be low.
	There are two main methods of connection in frame relay. The first is permanent virtual circuits (PVC), which are connections intended to exist for long periods of time, even if data is not currently being exchanged. The second is switched virtual circuits (SVC), which are temporary connections designed to exist for a single session.

Method	Function
TCP	In this protocol, a connection is created and maintained until the application software at each endpoint have finished exchanging data. It determines how the data is broken down into packets, which it gives to and receives from the network layer in the TCP/IP model. It is responsible for providing error free data transmission and managing the flow of the data.

Table 14.3: Connection-orientated packet switching methods.

Connectionless

Method	Function
Ethernet	This is a traditional protocol used to connected devices, using a wired connection, to form a network. It makes sure that network devices format and transmit data in a way that other devices on the network will understand. Most networks that are set up within a home or school are likely to use ethernet.
IP	This is the protocol that is used when data is sent across the internet. It is the protocol that is responsible for delivering the packets of data to the receiving device.
UDP	This is an alternative protocol to the TCP. There are two main differences between this protocol and the TCP. The first is that this protocol sends the data in units called datagrams. The second difference is that this protocol does not control the flow of data or carry out error checking. For this reason, the exchange of data using UDP is often faster than using TCP.

Table 14.4: Connectionless packet switching methods.

Message switching

Message switching is a little like an intermediate method between circuit switching and packet switching. It is like circuit switching in that all the data packets are sent along the same path, and it is like packet switching in that any path from Computer A to Computer B can be taken. The data packets are sent from Computer A to the first switch device. The device holds the data packets until all of them have arrived. This switch then sends the data packets onto the next switch, which holds onto the data packets until all of them have arrived. The data packets are sent from switch to switch in this way, until they reach Computer B. This is known as the store and forward method.

> **PRACTICAL ACTIVITY 14.02**
>
> Draw a diagram to represent the method of message switching.

14.4 Network structures

There are several different structures that can be used to create a network. You are going to learn about six different structures.

Peer-to-peer

A peer-to-peer network is one that contains computers known as **peers**. A peer-to-peer network can be as simple as two computers connected in a home. It can also be as extensive as hundreds of peer computers connected using the internet. The main reason that peer-to-peer networks are created is to share data. A peer-to-peer network has a decentralised structure, which means that is doesn't have any central point of control. Therefore, each peer in the network has the same level of responsibility and capability.

> **KEY WORD**
>
> **peer:** a computer of equal importance in a peer-to-peer network

Each user in the peer-to-peer structure stores data on their computer. They can choose to keep this data private, which means other peers in the network are not able to view it. They can also choose to make the data public, which means that other peers in the network are able to view the data too. If a peer computer in the network has a peripheral, such as a printer attached to it, the user can make the printer public so that other peer computers can print to it also.

Peer-to-peer networks have evolved into being used as a file sharing system for digital media, such as sound and video. Sound and video files are accessed by users using a dedicated peer-to-peer software. The software links people who have the files with people who want the files, so that the data can be exchanged. This method of file sharing has proved controversial because of its use in the piracy of music and movies.

There are several advantages and disadvantages of a peer-to-peer network:

Advantages	Disadvantages
Relatively cheap to setup as no need to buy expensive servers.	If a peer computer is being accessed by another peer computer, it can affect the performance of the computer and cause it to run slower.
Requires little technical knowledge to set up.	The data stored on each peer computer is not centrally backed up by the network. Therefore, if a peer loses the data, it is lost for everyone, unless they have a copy saved locally on their computer.
Users are able to share data and resources.	The public files shared by a peer computer may be disorganised and difficult to navigate, because there is no central organisation system in place.
Often has less traffic than the alternative client-server structure.	Each user in the network is responsible for the security of their peer computer. If users are not vigilant, and their computer gets a virus, this could be passed to other peer computers in the network.
Users have full control over the data stored on their computer.	
If a peer computer fails, this will only have a minor effect on the rest of the peers in the network. It will just mean that any data that the user had made public will be temporarily unavailable.	

Table 14.5: Peer-to-peer network advantages and disadvantages.

PRACTICAL ACTIVITY 14.03

Draw a diagram to represent a peer-to-peer network. The network must contain four computers and a printer and a scanner.

Client-server

A client-server network is one that contains two types of computers, a **client** and a **server**. The server or servers in a client-server network are a central point of control and provide a dedicated function for the network. All other computers in the network are called clients. The client computers in the network are all connected to the server to allow it to perform its dedicated function.

Most client server networks operate using a request-response method. A typical operation in this method is a client sends a request to a server to ask the server to perform a task and the server responds by performing the task.

KEY WORDS

client: a computer in a network that is not a central point of control

server: a computer in a network that is a point of control

There are several types of server that could be included in a client-server network that perform a dedicated function. These include:

Server type	Function
File server	Stores and manages data files. This saves the need for extensive storage space on client computers. They allow a user to use any client computer in the network and still be able to access their files and also any publicly shared files available. They also allow a central backup of all data to be made.
Web server	Stores, processes and transmits web pages.
Mail server	Sends and receives emails. It stores incoming emails for the user that can be downloaded when requested. It forwards outgoing messages to the correct destination. Most mail servers have security checking software that will scan emails for issues such as known viruses and malware. They can also be set to check for inappropriate content and spam.
Application server	Installs and runs software applications. They provide a platform to run both desktop and web applications.
Print server	Receives print jobs from client computers and sends them to the correct printer. This allows many client computers in a network to use the range of printers available. They can be set to print to a specific printer. They can also be set to find the next available printer, or the closest printer to the client. If many jobs are sent to the print server at a time, it will queue the jobs until it can deliver them to a printer.
FTP server	Manages the transfer of data that uses the file transfer protocol (FTP). It keeps a log of all activity involving FTP. Uses a lot in the transfer of files over the internet.
Proxy server	Acts as an intermediary between clients and other servers by receiving client requests and forwarding them on to the relevant server. It provides an added level of security in a network, protecting clients directly accessing resources on another server. For this reason, it can also be set to act as a firewall.
Virtual server	Shares the hardware of another server. Created using virtualisation software on another server. Multiple virtual servers could be created on one physical server. A virtual server can be given the capabilities of any of the above physical servers. Businesses sometimes use third party virtual servers that will act as a web server, for the business to host its website. This allows the hosting company the ability to host several businesses websites on the hardware of a single physical server.

Table 14.6: Server types.

Spreading the functionality of the network across several servers can help a network run more efficiently. However, servers are very expensive computers, because of the performance power and sometimes high levels of storage space they are required to have. For this reason, some businesses are planning to have fewer physical servers and to divide them up into enough virtual servers for the functionality they require.

There are several advantages and disadvantages of a client-server network:

Advantage	Disadvantage
Files can all be located in a single place and backed up on a regular basis. This means each user does not need to be responsible for this.	Can be very expensive to set up due to the need to buy expensive equipment, such as servers.
Security for the network can be controlled from a central point, meaning each user does not need to be responsible for this.	Expensive to maintain as specialist knowledge is required to setup and maintain the servers.
Levels of access can be applied to resources and data on the servers, so only those that should have access will do so. This is very beneficial when some data and resources have to be kept confidential.	Failure of a server will mean that functionality is unavailable for all users. For example, no user can access their files if a file server fails.
Updates for any software or network peripherals can be rolled out from a central location. Therefore, the business is not reliant on each user installing updates.	

Table 14.7: Client-server network advantages and disadvantages.

Servers can be grouped together to provide functionality that would be beyond a single computer. As a collective, the servers have a huge amount of processing power and require a large amount of power to keep cool, so that they can all run. Servers that are grouped in this way are called a server farm and they can be used to execute very large tasks, as all servers can be used to execute one or more parts of the task simultaneously. There are often thousands of servers present in a server farm. One of the largest server farms to exist is owned and maintained by Google. It has over 10,000 servers.

> **PRACTICAL ACTIVITY 14.04**
>
> Draw a diagram to represent a client-server network. The network must contain eight computers, two printers, a print server and a file server.

LAN and WAN

A **local area network (LAN)** is a network of computers and other devices that are connected within a small geographic area, such as a home, school or small business. A LAN could be as simple as two computers connected within a home. It could also be as extensive as one hundred computers, several peripheral devices and other network components, such as switches and servers, connected in a small business. Individuals and organisations create LAN networks to allow them to efficiently share data and resources, such as peripherals.

A **wide area network (WAN)** is a network of computers and other devices that are connected over a large geographical area. The largest example of a WAN is the internet. Businesses and organisations, such as banks and the police force, use WAN networks because they have multiple branches over a large geographical area that need to be connected to share data and resources. A WAN in these examples is normally a LAN network in each branch location that are all connected to create a WAN.

> **KEY WORDS**
>
> **local area network (LAN):** a relatively small network that is located within a single building or site
>
> **wide area network (WAN):** a relatively large network that is normally two or more LANs that are linked

LAN and WAN networks are set up with a purpose to share data, storage and peripheral devices. There are several factors that can be considered about their structure.

Factors	LAN	WAN
Data transfer rate	Capable of higher transfer speeds up to 1Gb per second.	Often restricted to lower transfer speeds, normally less than 200Mb.
Data transmission errors	Fewer errors are likely to occur because data is transferred over a shorter distance.	Greater chance of errors occurring as data is transferred over longer distance.
Method of connection	Normally connected using copper wire, fibre optic cables or radio waves. It could be a mixture of all three.	Connections could include copper wire, fibre optic cables, radio waves, microwaves, public telephone systems, leased lines, transmission towers and satellites.
Security	Can normally be kept more secure as a smaller number of devices need securing. Most of the security required is the responsibility of the network owners.	More susceptible to security issues as a larger number of devices need securing. The organisation will normally need to rely on the security measures of others for part of the network, so they will not be able to control security in these areas.
Ownership	Most of the network components and devices are owned by the individual or organisation, so they can control and maintain them.	Elements of the network are often owned by a third party, so they have to rely on the control and maintenance of others.

Table 14.8: LAN and WAN factors.

Virtual private network

Individuals or organisations may want to access sensitive data from a remote location to where it is stored. It is possible that a request to access this data could be intercepted by a hacker. This security issue can be overcome by using a virtual private network (VPN).

To us a VPN, a user needs to open their VPN client. This is the software that they have used to create the VPN. The VPN software will encrypt any data that the user wants to transmit before it gets sent across the internet. The data will first be sent to the VPN server. From here, it will be sent to its required destination. The data sent is encrypted and the when the data arrives at the destination, it only shows that it was sent from the VPN server, and not the details of the original sender.

When data is sent without the use of a VPN, it could be intercepted by another user and the contents of the packets examined. This would show who sent the data and where it is going to. This may mean that a hacker could then use this data to hack the accounts of the user. The security of data is increased in several ways by using a VPN:

- The data is encrypted, so even if it is intercepted, it will be meaningless.

- If the data is intercepted between the user's computer and the VPN server, a hacker would not know the final destination of the data.

- If the data is intercepted between the VPN and the final destination, the hacker would not know who the original sender of the data is.

Because the VPN server connects to the rest of the internet on your behalf, this adds a level of security and privacy to data that is beneficial to both an individual and an organisation.

Advantages	Disadvantages
Data is encrypted before it is sent across the network.	In some countries the use of a VPN is illegal or controversial, as some people can use them to create anonymity in certain criminal activity.
The identity of the sender is kept private from the destination and any hacker who intercepts a data package.	The security of the data is reliant upon a third party and their ability to create effective software and maintenance of the VPN server.

Advantages	Disadvantages
The maintenance of the VPN server is not the responsibility of the user, so they do not need to think about this.	There is often a cost involved in purchasing a VPN. This could be a monthly subscription fee.

Table 14.9: VPN advantages and disadvantages.

Mobile network

A mobile network (also called a cellular network) is a wireless WAN that uses radio to transmit and receive communications from portable devices, such as smartphones. Mobile networks now cover a considerable amount of the inhabited areas of world.

Mobile networks are broken down into small areas called cells. At the heart of each cell is a radio base station that transmits and receives messages. The base stations connect to public telecommunications services allowing access to the internet.

Cells vary in size:

- picocells cover an area of less than 200 metres
- microcells cover an area up to 2 kilometres
- macrocells cover larger regions.

There have been several generations of mobile networks, each providing faster access speeds and greater reliability:

- 1G networks – This is the first generation of mobile networks. They use analogue signals. 1G networks are largely limited to voice and text message communications.
- 2G networks – This is the second generation of mobile networks. They switched from analogue to digital transmission, improving signal quality. 2G networks were able to connect with each other, allowing a phone to use other networks.
- 3G networks – This is the third generation of mobile networks. 3G networks increased data transmission speeds up to 2 Mbps, allowing internet access, video transmission and online gaming.
- 4G networks – This is the fourth generation of mobile networks, and is a relatively recent generation of mobile network technology. In theory, 4G networks allow data transmission speeds of up to 1 Gbps, allowing greater use of video streaming facilities.
- 5G networks – This is the fifth and most recent generation of mobile networks. 5G networks offer

the fastest and most reliable connections available. When they are fully established the average download speed should be approximately 1 Gbps. They have tested speeds up to 1.5 Gbps at present, but could prove to be capable of even faster speeds.

Mobile networks have their advantages and disadvantages:

Advantages	Disadvantages
Mobile networks have enabled users to communicate with others and access the internet while on the move, often through the use of smartphones.	Quality of reception can vary and can be poor towards the edge of a cell, leading to interrupted or delayed transmissions.
Breaking the network down into cells allows for lower power radio transmitters to be used, bringing energy and cost savings.	The use of frequency must be carefully planned to avoid interference between cells.
There are only so many radio frequencies that can be used for mobile communications. These frequencies can be split among neighbouring cells, and reused in more distant cells, thereby increasing the number of communications that can take place at the same time.	The technology for 5G technology is limited at present and it could take a while and be costly to make the technology full useable.
Larger geographical areas can be covered than by using a single transmitter. Even high-power transmitters are limited in range. By using several low power transmitters, a wider area can be covered.	
The use of multiple transmitters means the network is more robust. Failure of one base station only affects one cell, leaving other areas of the network unaffected.	

Table 14.10: Mobile networks advantages and disadvantages.

14.5 Network protocols

Some of the main network protocols have already been discussed. However, there are several other protocols that you need to understand.

These protocols are mainly designed to increase the privacy and security of data. They include:

Protocol	Description
Tunnelling	This is a communications protocol that allows for the secure transmission of data from one network to another. It allows private data packets to be sent across a public network through a method called encapsulation. This is when private data packets are made to look like public data packets, so that they can be sent across a public network. Tunnelling is an important protocol used in VPNs.
Secure sockets layer (SSL)	This is a network protocol that is designed to ensure connections made between web clients, such as user devices, and web/mail servers are secure. It uses both public and private keys to encrypt data that is transmitted over the secure connection. It is still used in some applications, but it has now mostly been replaced by the use of TLS.
Transport layer security (TLS)	This is a network protocol that is the updated version of SSL. It uses updated and more secure encryption algorithms.
Internet protocol security (IPsec)	This is a network protocol that is designed to encrypt and authenticate data packets that are sent across the internet. IPSec is also part of the tunnelling process for a VPN.

Table 14.11: Network protocols.

Another protocol that is used in the transmission of data over a network is BitTorrent. This is a communications protocol that is often used in peer-to-peer file sharing. It allows the transfer of large files such as videos. It does this through distributing the load of downloading the file across several sources on the network. Several sources (known as hosts) are collated

to create a swarm. Each host will be given pieces of the file. The BitTorrent protocol allows the user to join the swarm and download the file from the available hosts. The protocol will download the file in pieces, simultaneously, from various hosts in the swarm. The protocol can then rearrange the pieces to create the completed file.

Each piece of the file is protected to stop it being modified by any users. Each user trying to download the file is called a peer and each user that is providing an upload of the file, as part of the swarm, is called a seed.

Further network protocols include:

Protocol	Function
Internet control message protocol (ICMP)	This is an error reporting protocol that is used to generate error messages, to transmit to the sender, when network problems cause delivery problems with data packets.
Address resolution protocol (ARP)	This protocol is responsible for translation of an IP address into a MAC address for a device. It is necessary for use between the network layer and the data link layer of the OSI model.
Inverse address resolution protocol (InARP)	This protocol performs the opposite role to the ARP. It translates a MAC address into an IP address.
Dynamic host configuration protocol (DHCP)	This is a network management protocol that is used to assign IP addresses to devices on a network. It manages the assignment of the addresses so that a network administrator does not need to manually carry out this task.
Hypertext transfer protocols (HTTP and HTTPS)	HTTP is the protocol that is used for transferring the content of web pages across the internet, from a web server to a browser. HTTPS is the secure version of this that incorporates the use of the SSL protocol.
File transfer protocol (FTP)	This protocol is responsible for the transfer of files between a client and a server in a network.

Protocol	Function
Simple mail transfer protocol (SMTP)	This protocol is used to send email from a computer to a mail server, and between different mail servers.
Post office protocol (POP)	This protocol is used to retrieve emails from a mail server. When the user checks their mailbox, the email is sent from the server to their device. The protocol then deletes the email from the server.
Internet message access protocol (IMAP)	This protocol is also used to retrieve email from a mail server. It has one main difference from POP and that is that the email is not deleted from the server by the protocol. The only time it is deleted is when the user chooses to delete it.
Telnet	This protocol allows a user to connect remotely to another computer, using the internet.
Secure shell (SSH)	This protocol provides a secure way to access a computer over an unsecure network. It does this using strong authentication and encryption methods for communication.

Table 14.12: Network protocols.

14.6 Components in a network

A network can often include several different components, that each have a role within the network.

Network interface cards and wireless network interface cards

The first component a device needs to connect to a network is a **network interface card (NIC)**. These can allow a wired connection to a network, but also exist in wireless form as wireless network interface

cards (WNIC). A NIC is an electronic circuit board that is inserted into a device's motherboard. More modern devices can have the NIC already built into the motherboard, which removes the need to have a separate component. When a manufacturer provides a device with a network interface card, it also provides the card with a media access control (MAC) address. This address is unique to the NIC and is made up of the manufacturer's ID and the serial number. The MAC address is used to uniquely identify the device when it is connected to a network. A cable, called an ethernet cable, is connected into a port on the NIC. The cable can then simply be connected to another computer, or to another network component, such as a router or a switch. This is the basis of creating a simple network of computers. If a WNIC is used, rather than a wired NIC, there is no requirement for an ethernet cable, as the devices can be connected using the wireless capabilities of the cards.

> **KEY WORDS**
>
> **network interface card:** a network component required to attach a computer to a network

Figure 14.2: Wireless network interface card.

Hubs and switches

If only a couple of computers are connected in a network, a simple ethernet connection between the two can be made. If several computers need to be connected, a component needs to be used to connect the devices and manage the traffic. There are two devices that can be used for this purpose. They are a **hub** and a switch.

A hub is a component in a network to which each device is connected using a wired connection. If one device wants to send data to another device in the network, it will go via the hub. The hub receives the data from the sender and then forwards the data on to every other device connected to the hub. The other devices connected to the hub will ignore the data sent to them if they are not the intended destination. The computer that is the intended destination will receive the data. A hub can be described as an active or passive hub. A passive hub will just send the data to the other devices as described. An active hub will amplify and regenerate the signal used to send the data to make it stronger. Because the hub forwards the data to all connected devices the process is inefficient. There is lots of unnecessary traffic present in the network and this can often cause an issue called data collisions. The data sent only needs to be received by the intended destination device. This inefficiency was recognised and, as a result, another network component was developed, the switch.

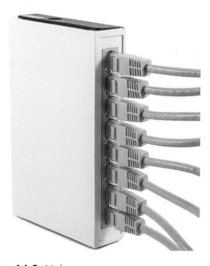

Figure 14.3: Hub.

A switch is a component in a network that is used in the same way as a hub, to connect devices together. The difference between a hub and a switch is the way it forwards the data received on to its destination. A switch has the capability to examine each data packet it receives and forward the data packet onto the

intended destination only. It knows which device to send the data to because, when the devices are connected to the switch, it creates a MAC address source table. When it receives a data packet, it looks which MAC address is the intended destination of the packet and then forwards it to that device. This greatly reduces the amount of traffic on the network, because data is only sent to the destination device, and not to every device it is connected to on the network. This also greatly reduces the possibility of data collisions occurring.

Figure 14.4: Switch.

Repeaters

As signals sent by devices travel around a network, they can be prone to deterioration. This can often occur because of interference that can occur in the transmission media (the cables that are used to transmit data around a network). To try and retain the original quality of the signal as it travels around a network, a component called a **repeater** can be used. A repeater can be used at various points in a network to boost the signal as it passes through the repeater. A repeater can be used to boost a wired signal, or a wireless signal, and they are capable of retransmitting both analogue and digital signals.

Wireless access points

There may be requirement in a network for devices to connect to the network using a wireless connection. The network component required for this is a **wireless access point (WAP)**. A WAP allows a wireless device to connect to a wired network. It receives wireless data signals and then uses the wired network to transmit them to their destination, often via a switch. It supports the connection of multiple wireless devices to the same WAP, therefore it connects the devices to the network by effectively creating a wireless LAN. Although a WAP will support the connection of multiple devices, they often have a limit, for example, 15 to 20 devices. For this reason, larger organisations will have multiple WAPs. They will distribute these throughout the building as the signal strength for connection to a WAP also deteriorates with distance.

> **KEY WORDS**
>
> **wireless access point:** a network component that receives and transmits radio signals to allow wireless (Wi-Fi) connection to a network

Figure 14.5: Wireless access points.

Bridges

Some organisations may have a site for their business that has several different buildings. This may mean that they have a LAN network that is split up and segregated between the different buildings. This can result in the parts of the LAN being too far apart to operate effectively, the signal can deteriorate too much, travelling from one device to another. The parts of the LANs can be connected more effectively using a network component called a bridge. A bridge also uses MAC addresses to forward data to the correct destination, like a switch. It works slightly differently to a switch in one way though. It examines the data packets it receives, checking them against the MAC address source table. If it finds that the data packet's destination is in another segmented part of the network, for example, another building on the site, it will forward

the packet 'across the bridge' to that part of the LAN. If the bridge finds that the packet's destination is within the same part of the network, for example, within the same building, it will just ignore the packet and allow it to continue to its destination.

> **KEY WORD**
>
> **bridge:** a network component that connects segregated parts of a LAN

Gateways and routers

Some organisations may find that they have different branches, sometimes within the same city, for example, a bank. Each branch will have its own LAN network. The branches may want to share data about their customers, so they need to connect their LANs together. They do this using a component called a gateway. A common gateway component that is used to connect LANs is called a router.

> **KEY WORD**
>
> **gateway:** a network component that joins different LANs together

One of the primary roles of a router is to assign each device that is connected to it with an IP address. This is an address that is unique to the device and can be used to identify its location in the network. There are two current versions of IP address, IPv4 and IPv6. IPv4 was the original version, that is a 32-bit numerical address. As more devices connected to the internet, we started to run out of possible combinations for IP addresses, so IPv6 was developed. IPv6 is a 128-bit address that allows for many more possible combinations of IP address. An IP address can also be static or dynamic. A static IP address means that the device will always have the same IP address. A dynamic IP address means that the IP address could change for each internet session. Most devices operate with a dynamic IP address setup. A user will normally need to request a static IP address from the internet provider if they want one.

> **PRACTICAL ACTIVITY 14.05**
>
> See if you can find out the current IP address of your computer.

A router is used to connect LANs and also to connect LANs to WANs. A router acts in a similar way to a switch, but with two main differences. The first is that a switch will only forward on data packets to their destination within a single network. However, a router is used to forward data packets outside the current LAN to other networks. The second is that a switch examines data packets and looks for the MAC address to establish the packet's destination, but a router looks for the IP address of the destination device and uses this to send it there. Routers use routing tables to do this, which allow them to establish the most efficient route the data packet should take to reach its destination. A routing table is stored on the router and lists all the available routers to particular network destinations. Routers need to use routing protocols to specify how they communicate with each other. Routing protocols help select the route that data travels from one device in a network to another. There are three main types of routing protocol – interior gateway protocols, exterior gateway protocols and border gateway protocols. Interior gateway protocols are used to specify how routers communicate with each other within a network, such as a local area network. Exterior gateway protocols are used to specify how routers communicate with each other between different networks. Border gateway protocols are a specific kind of exterior gateway protocol that manage the process of exchanging packets of data across the largest network, the internet.

Many of us have routers in our home that we use to connect our devices to the internet. The router devices we have within our home can be quite neat little devices. They are often a router and a WAP all in one.

14.7 Network connections (physical)

To connect devices together in a network, either some kind of wired or wireless connection will be necessary.

There are three main types of cable that can be used to create a wired connection between devices, these are coaxial, twisted pair and fibre optic.

Coaxial

Coaxial is a type of copper cable that has a central wire surrounded by an insulating layer. Coaxial cables also have an outer layer that acts like a jacket. Coaxial cables are used to carry radio frequency signals. They are used in applications such as TV and Cable TV connections as well as some internet connections.

Advantages	Disadvantages
Low cost to manufacture and purchase.	Has the lowest level of bandwidth of the three cable types.
Lower error rate because the central wire is within a faraday shield (a special shield used to block electromagnetic interference).	The way in which a coaxial cable is insulated can make it difficult to install and maintain.

Table 14.13: Advantages and disadvantages of coaxial cable.

Twisted pair

Twisted pair is a type of copper cable that has two separate insulated wires that are twisted around each other. These cables are then covered by an outer layer that acts like a jacket. Twisted pair cables transmit electric current. They are used for telephone communications and normally as part of an ethernet network.

Figure 14.6: Twisted pair cables.

Advantages	Disadvantages
Crosstalk (a signal transmitted from one channel to another) is minimised.	Can be susceptible to electromagnetic interference.
Is the lowest cost to manufacture and purchase.	Has the shortest distance that a signal can be carried before it will begin to deteriorate.
Has a higher level of bandwidth than coaxial.	

Table 14.14: Advantages and disadvantages of twisted pair cable.

Fibre optic

Fibre optic is a type of cable that is made up of lots of very fine threads of glass. These are covered with an outer layer. The use of fibre optic cables is becoming more prominent in networks, because they can transmit data much faster. Fibre optics cables use the properties of light to transmit data. They are used in modern internet connections and in high performance networks where large amounts of data are transmitted.

Advantages	Disadvantages
Has the highest level of bandwidth available of the three cables.	Has the highest cost for manufacture and purchase.
Can carry signals for a much longer distance without deterioration.	Can be difficult to install due to how fragile the glass tubes can be.

Table 14.15: Advantages and disadvantages of fibre optic cable.

14.8 Network connections (wireless)

There are several types of wireless methods that can be used to connect devices in a network. These include Wi-Fi, Bluetooth, infrared, microwaves and radio.

Wi-Fi

Wi-Fi uses radio signals and is the most commonly used wireless communication method. Each device that wants to make a wireless connection will broadcast a radio signal. A router or a WAP will receive these wireless signals and process them. The router or WAP will also broadcast radio signals that will be received and processed by each device when it is receiving data that has been transmitted. Wi-Fi currently transmits data at frequencies of 2.4 GHz and 5 GHz. These frequencies are much higher than those used by mobile networks. These are considered high frequencies, which are required to send larger amounts of data. The current limit for Wi-Fi data transmission is approximately 450 Mbps.

Figure 14.7: Wireless communication.

Advantages	Disadvantages
Several wireless capable devices can connect to a single router or WAP.	The speed at which data can be transferred decreases as more devices connect to a wireless network.
The high level of frequency used means that large amounts of data can be transmitted at a time.	Less secure than a wired connection.
More recent Wi-Fi standards are backward compatible with previous ones.	Radio signals can be subject to interference.
Has quite a large range of approximately 100 m.	
It doesn't require a line of sight, so it can work through obstacles.	

Table 14.16: Advantages and disadvantages of Wi-Fi.

Bluetooth

Bluetooth also uses radio signals to create a wireless connection between two devices. It uses the radio frequency 2.45 Ghz. To establish a connection, devices need to be within 10 m of each other and there is currently a limit of eight devices that can be connected at any given time using Bluetooth. The two devices requesting a wireless connection using Bluetooth must have matching profiles. For example, if a mobile device wants to connect to a headset to allow sound to be transmitted, they must both have the profile that allows this. This is to stop pointless Bluetooth connections being made. For example, connecting a wireless mouse to a digital camera – the mouse cannot be used to control the camera as it is not designed for this function.

To create a connection, the Bluetooth transmitter is turned on in a device. This device will then begin to transmit the radio signals. Any device that has a matching profile, within range, will pick up the radio signals and will then identify with the sender as a possible device to connect to. The required device for connection can then be chosen. The devices will then be paired together. This can sometimes require entering a pin code for added security.

Figure 14.8: Establishing Bluetooth pairing.

Advantages	Disadvantages
It requires a low level of power consumption.	Has a limit of 10 m for a connection.
It doesn't require a line of sight, so it can work through obstacles.	A limit of eight devices can be connected at a time.
Can be made more secure by requiring a pin code for connection.	Has a lower level of bandwidth available than Wi-Fi.
There will be less interference as other wireless connections transmit on different frequencies.	

Table 14.17: Advantages and disadvantages of Bluetooth.

Infrared

Infrared connections use infrared radiation as their method of connection. Two different types of infrared connection can be made. These are line-of-sight mode and scatter mode. In line-of-sight mode, there must be a direct line of sight between the sending device and the receiving device. This means that there can be no obstacles in the way. In scatter mode, a device broadcasts infrared into a certain area and any device may receive it directly or through reflection of an obstacle. The sending device will need the ability to produce an infrared signal and the receiving device needs an infrared sensor to capture the infrared signal.

Infrared lasers can also be used to transmit data from one device to another in a network. The infrared laser beam needs to have a direct line of sight in order to be able to connect the devices. Laser data transmission works in a similar way to fibre optic, in that it uses the properties of light to transmit the data. Rather than travelling through physical transmission media, like fibre optic transmission, laser transmission relies on data travelling through free space.

Advantages	Disadvantages
It is the most secure form of connection.	Cannot be transmitted through obstacles.
Low cost to manufacture and purchase.	If it uses line-of-sight mode, there must be a direct line of sight between the two devices.
It requires a low level of power consumption.	It can only be used to connect two devices.
It doesn't get any interference from radio frequencies.	It has a short range with a limit of approximately 1 m.
	May be subject to interference from bright sources.

Table 14.18: Advantages and disadvantages of infrared.

Question

1   Identify two examples where an infrared wireless connection could be used.

There can be security issues associated with the use of wireless data transmission. This is because wireless connections do not have the same level of protection as a wired connection. Wired networks are normally limited to the confines of a building or single site, and there are often locks and other security methods in place to stop an unauthorised person entering that area and gaining access to that network.

As a result, there are two main protocols that are designed to improve the level of security of a wireless network. These are wired equivalent privacy (WEP) and wi-fi protected access (WPA):

Protocol	Function
WEP	This protocol is designed to provide a wireless network with a compatible level of security to a wired LAN. It does this by encrypting data transmissions sent using a wireless connection.
WPA	This is a standard required of devices equipped with a wireless internet connection. It is designed to provide a more sophisticated encryption method than WEP.

Table 14.19: Wireless security protocols.

Microwaves and radio waves

In data transmission, the terms 'microwaves' and 'radio waves' are often used interchangeably. This is because microwaves and radio waves are both types of electromagnetic radiation that can be used to transmit data. Microwaves have shorter wavelengths and are therefore generally used for short-distance communications. Radio waves have longer wavelengths and are therefore generally used for long-distance communications. Considering this, the waves used in both Wi-Fi and Bluetooth are technically microwaves. However, historically, the term 'radio waves' has been applied to the technology used in wireless data transmission.

14.9 Bandwidth and bit rate

One very important factor that affects the performance of a network is bandwidth. The bandwidth of a network is the measure of the frequencies available on the channels of communication in the network. Bandwidth is also used to describe the maximum amount of data that can be transferred across a network within a given time, which is usually one second. Therefore, the more bandwidth a connection has, the more data it can transfer at a single time. It is a common misconception that the bandwidth is a measure of the speed of a network. It is not.

The bit rate is a similar measure to bandwidth, in that it is a measure of how many bits of data are transferred in a given period of time. It is different from the bandwidth in that bandwidth is a term used to describe the performance ability of a network, whereas bit rate is used to describe the rate at which a particular file, for example, a video file, is transferred. The bit rate of a transfer will not exceed the bandwidth, because the bandwidth will be the maximum possible bit rate.

KEY WORDS

bandwidth: the range of frequencies available for a communication method which determines the transmission rate

bit rate: the rate at which bits can be transferred in data transmission

An example to demonstrate the two would be that a network could have a bandwidth of 100 Mbps but a video file that is transferred from one computer to another over that network may be transferred at a bit rate of 75 Mbps.

Bandwidth and bit rate are also important when streaming audio and video files. There are two different types of data streaming – real-time and on-demand streaming. In real-time data streaming, the data is streamed as soon as it is recorded by the camera (or any other recording device that may be used). In on-demand streaming, data is pre-recorded and streamed to the users device whenever they request the recording. When a file is streamed, it removes the need to download and store the whole file before it is viewed or listened to. Data is streamed as a series of bits to the receiving device. The receiving device will have a temporary storage area called a buffer. Data will be stored in the buffer, as it is downloaded, before it is needed as the video is viewed, or the song is played. Data is removed from the buffer to be played and simultaneously added to be ready to play when required. The bandwidth available will limit the quality of the sound or video file that can be streamed. If a user has a connection that has a bandwidth of 2 Mbps, it is highly unlikely they will be able to stream a 4K movie from an online streaming service. The data required to produce each frame in the video would be too much to be transmitted using the bandwidth available.

Question

2   What do you think would happen if a buffer were not used when streaming data?

14.10 Cloud computing

Cloud computing is a term that is used to refer to services that are hosted using the internet. These services could include the storage of data and software, and access to resources such as servers.

Cloud computing can be divided into three main categories, infrastructure as a service (IaaS), platform as a service (PaaS) and software as a service (SaaS):

Category	Description
IaaS	In this model of cloud computing the host provider hosts some of the network resources that are used by businesses, such as servers. Businesses can gain access to these resources using the internet.
PaaS	In this model of cloud computing the host provider hosts platform resources that can be used to build software applications. Users can gain access to these resources using the internet.
SaaS	In this model of cloud computing the host provider hosts software applications and makes them available to users using the internet.

Table 14.20: Cloud computing categories.

One of the most common uses of cloud computing by the individual is to store data. Many applications now offer the service of storing data linked to the application, and other personal data, on cloud resources. These are normally a collection of servers in a remote location.

There are several advantages and disadvantages of cloud computing:

Advantages	Disadvantages
Individuals and organisations do not need to purchase additional hardware to store data and software.	Individuals and organisations are reliant on a third party to keep their data secure and they have little control over the security measures that are put in place by the cloud provider.
Individuals and organisations do not need to host their own development platforms to develop applications software.	If the resources provided by the cloud provider fail, for example, a server fails, then the data or software stored on that server will become unavailable.
Organisations do not need to employ technical staff to maintain the hardware used to store data and software that is provided by the cloud provider.	Cloud computing resources can only be accessed using an internet connection, so if an internet connection cannot be found, the resources cannot be accessed.
Individuals and organisations do not need to worry about creating a backup of their data, because this is automatically carried out by the cloud provider.	
Individuals and organisations can access their data and software applications from anywhere in the world, as long as they have an internet connection.	
Individuals and organisations do not need to worry about updating software applications that are accessed using the cloud, because this will be carried out by the cloud provider.	

Advantages	Disadvantages
Organisations can quickly boost the performance of their network by employing more resources from the cloud. If an organisation is expecting more data traffic to their server, for example, they are having a sale of their products, accessed by their website, they could increase the capacity of the web server to allow it to handle the temporary increase in traffic. They could then reduce it again after the sale, to save costs.	

Table 14.21: Advantages and disadvantages of cloud computing.

Question

A company creates websites using style sheets.

3   Describe another scenario that would allow an organisation to take advantage of the ability to scale up resources using cloud computing.

PRACTICAL ACTIVITY 14.06

Use the internet to research a news story that outlines a security issue caused by cloud computing.

14.11 Satellite communication systems

Earlier in this chapter you learnt about cellular mobile communication networks. There is another type of mobile communication system that uses satellites.

A communications satellite is a machine that has been transported into space and set to orbit the earth. These satellites are used to transmit radio waves from one place on earth to another. The radio waves that are transmitted can carry most things radio waves on earth are used for, including telephone calls, internet data and television broadcasts.

Satellites are complex machinery. Their main components are a solar powered battery, a transponder and various antennas.

Any data that is intended to be sent using satellite communications will need to be converted to radio waves. The data is transmitted in the form of radio waves from a ground station on earth. This process is called the uplink. The radio waves travel through the layers of the atmosphere up to the intended satellite. This may be a chosen satellite, or the nearest in orbit to pick up the radio waves. The antennas on the satellite are the component that initially receive the radio waves. The transponder processes the data, which can often involve boosting the signal. The antenna then transmits the radio waves back to the destination ground station on earth. This process is called the downlink.

PRACTICAL ACTIVITY 14.07

Use the internet to research further information about what a ground station looks like and how they are used. See if you can find out where there are satellite ground stations in your country.

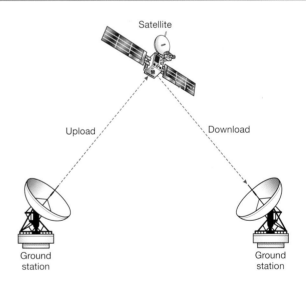

Figure 14.9: Uplink and downlink to a satellite.

Satellites are also used in navigation systems such as global positioning systems (GPS). A GPS uses satellites to work out a user's current location. One of the most well-known satellite navigation systems is the Navstar GPS. This system currently has 24 satellites in orbit. At any time on earth, a user will usually be in the line of sight for at least 10 of these satellites, however only three or four are actually needed to work out a user's location.

A process called **triangulation** is used to find the location of a user. The user will be in possession of a device, such as a mobile telephone, that receives radio signals. Each navigation satellite constantly beams radio waves that are sent toward earth. A user's device will receive these radio waves. A device must pick up radio waves from at least three satellites and the GPS will then be able to pinpoint their location.

KEY WORD

triangulation: the process of pinpointing the location of a device, using radio signals from a satellite

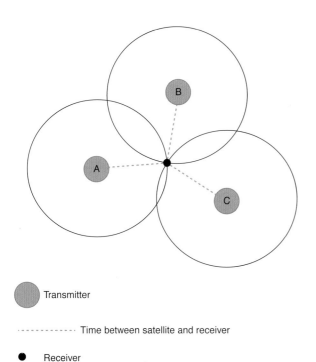

○ Transmitter

----------- Time between satellite and receiver

● Receiver

Figure 14.10: Triangulation by three GPS satellites.

If the user's device receives a signal from satellite A, this means they must be somewhere in the area currently covered by satellite A. If it also receives a signal from satellite B and satellite C, the user must be at the point where the area covered by all three of the satellites meets.

Many devices are equipped with GPS devices, including mobile telephones and cars. As well as giving the user the ability to find out their location, this technology can also be used by others for surveillance purposes. It is possible to use a GPS to find out where another person is by tracking their device. These devices often keep a log of all GPS activity, so it is possible for a person to gain access to that log and see exactly where the device (and therefore possibly the user) has been.

PRACTICAL ACTIVITY 14.08

Find out how GPS systems are being tested to create driverless vehicles.

14.12 Network security

Data is very precious. Some will argue that it has become more valuable to companies than resources such as oil. Unfortunately, for this reason, there are people that will create malicious systems that are designed to either steal data, so that it can be used for criminal activity, such as identity theft, or to damage data, and therefore cause damage to a company, often to their reputation. The use of networks, unfortunately, has made accessing data through malicious means a greater risk.

There are various risks that users should be aware of when using a network. Each of these risks is designed to damage or steal data.

The first risk is malware. A user will normally unknowingly download the malware onto their computer. The malware is often disguised in a file download or a link that the user is enticed into clicking. There are several types of malware, these include viruses, worms, spyware and ransomware. You can read more about these in Chapter 5.

An attack may come from a single third party and computer, or it could be distributed across many computers. This type of attack is called a botnet. Any user's computer could be made part of a botnet, often by the user downloading malware. Malware is downloaded onto the computer and will often stay dormant until the third party wants to use the computer in an attack. Each computer that is infected with this type of malware is called a bot. When the user wants to carry out an attack, they 'wake up' the malware in the bots and use them to form a botnet. A botnet can be used to carry out attacks such as a distributed denial of service (DDoS) attack. This is when the bots are used to send a huge number of requests to a web server all at once, causing the web server to struggle to deal with all the requests and eventually crash. This will prevent legitimate users accessing the websites stored on the web servers.

REFLECTION

What impact could it have on a business if people are not able to access their website?

Third parties may also want to hack computers to damage or steal data. Hackers will try to gain access to a system, normally by installing what is often known as a backdoor, in software. This is a mechanism, sometimes implemented using malware, or sometimes already present in a software download (this can be the case if the software is not legitimate), that allows a hacker to gain unauthorised access to a computer system, through the backdoor.

Third parties may also want to crack into computers to damage or steal data. Crackers will try a brute force approach to get into a computer by trying many different combinations of a password. They can also build software that will carry out this function for them. This allows them to gain unauthorised access to a computer system by using the user's log-in details.

Individuals and organisations can put a range of preventative methods in place to help protect their data.

The simplest form of protecting data is the use of physical methods. Organisations can put a barrier to entry at the opening of their office or building. They could also put a lock on a door to their office or a selected area in their office. Other physical methods that could be used are CCTV, security guard and alarm systems. CCTV will allow an organisation to see who is trying to gain unauthorised access. Security guards can stand guard and only allow authorised users to gain access to a place where the data is stored, for example, a server room. Places of this nature could also be secured using an alarm system, this will alert the organisation if unauthorised access is attempted.

PRACTICAL ACTIVITY 14.09

There are advantages and disadvantages to physical methods for securing data. Complete the table to outline what some of those advantages and disadvantages could be:

Physical method	Advantages	Disadvantages
Barrier		
Lock requiring a key or pin code		
Security guard		
CCTV		
Alarm system		

Data can also be protected using software-based methods.

An employee may be required to provide biometric data, such as their fingerprint, iris or facial features, to access data. A biometric device will scan their biometric data and check to see if it matches data stored in a database. If it does, the employee will be allowed to gain access. Biometric devices are useful because biological data is unique to the user and very difficult to fake. Biometric devices could also be used to secure individual devices in a similar way. Modern mobile telephones have biometric devices installed that require a user to provide, for example, their fingerprint, to gain access to the device.

The effects of malware can be prevented by using software, such as anti-malware, anti-virus and anti-spyware software. This type of software is designed to scan a computer system for malware. If it finds any, it quarantines the malware (put it in a designated safe area) and allows the user to delete it. Software of this nature can sometimes monitor the data that is downloaded in real-time. It can scan each download and, if it finds malware present, it can alert the user before the file is downloaded. The quicker this kind of software finds malware, the less damage the malware can carry out.

A firewall is another method that can be used to prevent unauthorised access or damage to data. A firewall can be hardware based or software based. A firewall examines incoming and outgoing traffic to a computer or a network. The firewall can be set to recognise malicious traffic by providing it with rules and criteria to check the traffic. If traffic is detected that does not meet the rules or criteria, then it can be rejected.

One way that an organisation can protect data is to only allow access to those that directly need that data. This is called access rights. The username that an employee is given in an organisation is often what indicates their access rights. The permission to access the data that the employee requires can be attached to their username, so they are not able to see any data that needs to remain confidential. This can prevent data being damaged.

One final method that an organisation and an individual can use to protect their data is encryption. Encryption will not stop the data from being stolen, but it will mean that if the data is stolen, it will be meaningless to the third party, unless they are able to get the key to decrypt it.

PRACTICAL ACTIVITY 14.10

There are advantages and disadvantages to software-based methods for securing data. Complete the table to outline what some of those advantages and disadvantages could be:

Software-based method	Advantages	Disadvantages
Biometrics		
Anti-malware		
Firewall		
Access rights		
Encryption		

The impact of security threats on individuals and organisations

Individuals and organisations need to carefully consider the impact of security threats. There are two main common reasons why perpetrators carry out security attacks – either to obtain personal data or as an act of sabotage or revenge.

Individuals need to be very cautious of any of their personal data being accessed and stolen. This could lead to criminal acts such as fraud and theft of their identity.

Organisations need to be very cautious of any of their stored data being accessed and stolen. They also need to be very cautious of their data being manipulated or destroyed. Data is a very precious asset to organisations, as it is used in the day to day functioning of the organisation. Without it, they are unlikely to be able to function at all. This could lead to a loss of profits, or if the data is stolen because the organisation's security is breached, this could lead to a negative reputation for the organisation, which may also lead to a loss of profits.

14.13 Disaster recovery management

In an organisation, a disaster is anything that may put the operations of the organisation at risk. This could be anything from a cyber-attack, power failure or a natural disaster. Disaster recovery is a planning mechanism that allows an organisation to plan for disaster and put in place measures that will minimise the risks. To be able to plan for protection against a disaster, the possible disaster first needs to be identified.

There are several stages that can be used to identify a risk that could cause a disaster, these include:

Stage	Description
Risk analysis	This is also known as a risk assessment. The organisation will first identify what they think could be a potential disaster. They will then consider what or who could be harmed as a result. They will finally think about how this could impact the organisation. Finally, they will develop methods to control the possibility and impact of the disaster.
	All parts of a company will be assessed, including its infrastructure, networks, hardware, software and people.
	The type of things that could cause disaster in an organisation may be a power cut, cyber-attack, fire, flood, denial of access to data, theft of data, corruption of data and hardware failure.
Perpetrator analysis	This process is often carried out as part of the risk analysis. The organisation will identify who they think could be a perpetrator that could cause a disaster to occur. A perpetrator is someone who carries out malicious or illegal acts.
Risk testing	In this stage of the process an organisation will rehearse the plans and strategies that have been developed during the risk analysis. This will allow employees in the organisation to understand exactly what they should do in the event of a disaster. An organisation can monitor what happens during the testing stage and can amend plans to take improved actions, or to correct the behaviour of employees, if they are not acting correctly. The type of plans and strategies that could be tested are: • restoration of data • replacement of hardware • reinstallation of software • emergency evacuation of offices • emergency protection methods for data.
Quantifying the risk	The process of quantifying a risk involves evaluating the risk and prevention methods for the risk in terms of cost and time. There are two key measurements that should be considered, maximum tolerable downtime (MTD) and recover time objective (RTO). • MTD is the maximum time that each part of the organisation could tolerate not having access to the essential parts of a network that they require. • RTO is the estimated maximum amount of time in which an organisation has in which to recover its network and resume operations.

Table 14.22: Stages of disaster recover management.

Earlier in the chapter you learned about methods that can be used to protect data and a network against a cyber-attack. An organisation will also need methods in place to prevent against other disasters that could occur:

• Power surge protection devices could be used to stop a surge in power damaging hardware.
• A back-up generator could be ready for use if an organisation suffers power failure.
• Back-ups of data could be stored in fire and flood proof cases so that data is not lost in a fire or flood. Back-ups could also be stored off site.

- Policies and procedures should be developed for staff to follow to prevent disaster such as fire and damage to equipment.

- Cloud computing could be used as a back-up for data and possible hardware resources.

In the event of a disaster occurring, data and resources will need to be restored. This can often mean the:

- the restoration of data from back-ups

- the re-installation of software

- replacement or repair of hardware.

All of these areas will be planned and assessed in a disaster recovery plan, which will consider how these will be carried out and what timescales should be expected

PRACTICAL ACTIVITY 14.11

Use the internet to research more specific information about what an organisation could include in a disaster recovery plan, for example, taking a detailed itinerary of equipment.

EXAM-STYLE QUESTIONS

1 Explain the function of the presentation layer in the OSI model.   [2]

2 Explain the function of the network layer in the TCP/IP model.   [2]

3 William wants to create a network in his home that will connect three computers, a printer, a mobile tablet device and a mobile telephone. He wants to minimise the costs in setting up his network.

   a Identify the network structure that would be suitable for William to use. Justify your choice.   [1]

   b Identify the components William will need to build the network and describe the role of each.   [4]

   c William wants to use the network to stream videos and music. Explain the importance of bandwidth and bit rate for this purpose.   [2]

   [Total 7]

4 Identify two protocols that are used in the transmission of emails. Describe the role of each protocol in the process.   [4]

5 Describe how the sound required to make a telephone call is sent from one mobile device to another, using a mobile network.   [4]

6 Emily stores data about her customers on a server in a server room in her office building. Emily wants to keep the data more secure, so she installs a biometric device required to gain access to the server room. She also installs a firewall.

   a Explain one advantage and one disadvantage of using a biometric device to secure access to the server room.   [2]

   b Describe how the firewall will help keep the data safe.   [4]

   [Total 6]

7 Discuss the impact of implementing a disaster recovery plan for an organisation.   [6]

SUMMARY CHECKLIST

- ☐ I can understand models that form the basis of a network, including the OSI model and the TCP/IP model.
- ☐ I can describe the structure of a data packet.
- ☐ I can describe a range of ways that data is transmitted, including circuit switching, packet switching and message switching.
- ☐ I can understand a range of network structures, including peer-to-peer, client-server, LAN, WAN, VPN, mobile and satellite.
- ☐ I can understand the role of a large range of network protocols and the responsibilities they have in the transmission of data.
- ☐ I can understand the role of a range of network components, including NIC/WNIC, hub, switch, repeater, WAP, bridge, router, cables and wireless technologies.
- ☐ I can understand the importance of bandwidth and bit rate when transmitting data.
- ☐ I can understand what is meant by cloud computing.
- ☐ I can understand the risks that could cause harm to a network and data and a range of methods that can be used to help prevent them.
- ☐ I can understand the process of disaster recovery management.

Project management

By the end of this chapter, you will be able to:

- describe the stages of a project
- describe the use of project management software for supporting projects
- discuss the strengths and weaknesses of project management software for supporting projects
- use and describe tools and techniques for project management.

Introduction

Project management is about applying a process to enable the completion of a project on time and within budget. It can be broken down into initiation, planning, execution and monitoring, and close stages. Project management software can be used to assist a project team throughout a project and tools such as Gantt charts, PERT and CPM can be used to aid project planning. Failure to complete projects on time, and within budget, can be embarrassing for organisations who have made promises on delivery and frustrating for the end user.

15.1 The stages of the project life cycle

Every project needs to be managed properly in order to ensure deadlines are met, **resources** are available and everybody knows what they are doing.

KEY WORD

resources: people, equipment, facilities or funding required to complete a project

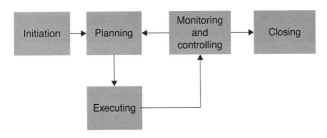

Figure 15.1: Project stages.

Project initiation

During the conception and **initiation** stage, the initial ideas for a project are identified and goals set. Key stakeholders are identified and decisions are made about whether or not it is appropriate to undertake a project by conducting a feasibility study. The feasibility study will determine whether the project is of benefit to an organisation based on resources, time and finance. Requirements for the project will be identified so that all stakeholders are aware of the expectations of the project. Objectives of the project, its scope, risks, approximate budget and approximate timescales will be defined and agreed with all stakeholders. An estimate of the resources that will be required will be made and a high-level schedule created which identifies proposed dates for completion of aspects of the project. A project brief or Project Initiation Document (PID) or initial statement of work (SoW) will be created. At the end of the project initiation stage, a phase review will be carried out to check that all aspects of initiation have been completed and that all stakeholders understand and agree the project brief.

KEY WORD

initiation: start of a project

Project planning

There is a common phrase, 'failing to prepare is preparing to fail'. This is true in all parts of life, but particularly with project planning. It is essential that the project is planned well so that all stakeholders know their responsibilities during all stages. A comprehensive budget will be formulated along with details of timescales for the progress of the project. Milestones will be set. These milestones show by which time certain aspects of the project must be complete. Tasks that have to be completed between each milestone will be identified and prioritised. A **Gantt chart** will be produced to show which tasks need to be completed and in which order. Resources, including personnel, will be allocated to tasks in a coordinated manner so that they are available at the right times. A very important part of planning is to ensure that appropriate amounts of time are allocated to each task and resource so that tasks can be completed on time, resources (especially personnel) are not over used and that personnel have work to do rather than not being used.

At the end of the project planning phase, a phase review will be carried out to check that the plan is achievable and that it meets the objectives of the project.

Project execution

Once all plans are in place and the start date arrives, the project can commence. It is critical that the plan is followed so that resources are used at the appropriate times. Any delays to a task can have a knock-on effect to successor tasks. The project manager will be expected to communicate roles and responsibilities to team members and set interim targets for each member to achieve within the timescales of the overall plan.

At the end of the project execution phase, an execution phase review will take place to learn lessons from what went wrong and to note examples of good practice. The review will cover questions such as:

- Was the project schedule maintained?
- Was the project within budget?
- Were all resources available when required?
- Has the project met the original requirements?

Project monitoring and control

Throughout the execution of the project, the project manager must monitor the progress and control what is happening. The project manager will be responsible for ensuring tasks are completed on time and rescheduling any tasks if there are delays. The project manager will need to monitor the performance of team members to ensure they are carrying out their agreed roles effectively. The project manager will need to monitor expenditure and compare it against the budget to ensure that overspends don't occur and keep a close eye on the scope of the project to make sure it doesn't extend beyond its agreed boundaries. Objectives will be regularly reviewed to ensure that the project is meeting its original objectives. There should be regular project review meetings where key stakeholders can discuss the progress of the project. At times, the project plan will need to be adjusted, so there is regular iteration between the execution, monitoring and control, and planning phases as shown in Figure 15.1.

Project close

When the project is ready to complete, a handover will take place from the project team to the client. Contracts will be terminated, which means some people may need to be deployed elsewhere or may need to look for alternative employment. Resources that have been assigned to the project will be released. A review of the project will take place between the client and the project management team, where requirements will be evaluated and successes will be celebrated. The client will be expected to sign off the project as completed, so that it is clear there is no further work to carry out and closure will have been achieved.

WORKED EXAMPLE 15.01

Before writing a textbook, authors are given a project brief that outlines the scope of what they are required to write about, the types of pedagogical items to include, the timescales for the delivery of manuscripts and payment information. This is all part of planning.

Prior to this, a publisher will have decided that they want to publish that particular textbook, and may seek approval from an exam board, which makes the publisher and the exam board the key stakeholders in this case. During planning, the publisher will have identified a project manager, an editor, a reviewer and authors, all of whom are required resources.

The execution stage includes the authors writing chapters for the textbook. This is monitored and controlled by the editor who stays in regular communication with the authors to check on their progress and to collect completed chapters. If timescales slip, then the project plan is revised as other execution stages such as reviewing, typesetting and proofreading are all dependent upon the manuscript being delivered.

The project comes to a close when the textbook is ready to be sent to the printers, once the authors, the publisher and exam board have approved the final proof.

Question

1   Explain why it is necessary to iterate between the planning, execution, and monitoring and control stages of project management.

15.2 Project management software

Planning

Most of the planning involved using project management software is concerned with scheduling tasks and allocating resources to those tasks. However, key milestones can be identified in advance. These are when crucial points in the project should be reached, so tasks should be scheduled to meet these milestones. Documents that are likely to be required can be allocated to milestones, such as success criteria and specifications. Templates can be used for setting up an initial project plan. These templates can be provided by the software or they could be templates that are created based upon an organisation's previously successful projects. Through the use of project templates, company standards can be set up for the way projects should be planned, so employees have a common, collaborative and recognisable structure.

Scheduling of tasks

Tasks are jobs that need to be completed as part of the project. Project management software will enable a project manager to create a Gantt chart to show an overview of the tasks that need completing on a timeline. Tasks will be assigned an estimated number of hours or days that they will take to complete, together with a deadline for completion. The project manager will be able to identify which tasks are dependent upon other tasks and so cannot start until those other tasks have been completed. Tasks can be delegated to other members of the team and put in a priority order to identify which should be completed first. Team members will be able to record how many hours have been spent on each task and identify when the task is complete. Milestones can be identified for crucial points of the project and these can be highlighted. A milestone is often a point at which a key part of the project has been completed or part of the project has been delivered (known as deliverables). The project manager will be able to see an overall calendar of all tasks that need to be completed, together with calendars for each team member that is responsible for those tasks.

Allocation of resources

Resources can be equipment, property or people that are required to complete a task. These resources will need to be defined within the project management software and their availability can be identified so the project manager knows when they can be used. Costs can be assigned to any resource, so the project manager can see how their use will affect the budget. Resources can then be assigned to tasks and a number of hours or days be assigned to the use of that resource. The software will help the project manager to avoid resource conflicts and also identify clearly situations where team members could experience overload. This is when a team member has too many tasks to complete during a period of time.

Costings

All resources will have costs allocated to them, so the project manager will be able to calculate the total cost of each task based on how many hours each resource is used for each task. The software can be used to keep a record of any expenses incurred by team members and account for these in the overall costs. Daily, weekly, monthly or custom analysis of expenditure and its comparison to the budget can be provided. The software can report on the total costs for each individual resource or set of resources. The costings information will be able to be exported to common formats such as spreadsheets for further manipulation and analysis.

Communication and collaborative working

Project management software can offer a large variety of communication tools which help team members to collaborate throughout the whole project:

- Calendars: each team member will have a calendar showing what they are doing at any time. These can be synchronised with third-party calendars, such as Google, iCal or Outlook, so that each member's availability is always up to date. This enables meetings to be scheduled with each team member. Documents can be attached to these meetings so that they are readily available to each participant.

- Instant messaging/video chat/video conferencing: these tools enable team members who are working remotely from each other to communicate in real time so that they can share ideas and discuss progress.

- Shared documents: all documents should be stored in a central repository so that they are available to the team members who require access to them. Documents can be assigned to tasks, resources or milestones so that they are available at the right time to the right people. Changes to the documents can be tracked so that each team member knows what modifications have been made and which is the latest version of the document. The software can email team members to inform them when changes to documents have been made or display an alert on their project dashboard, their home page for the project management software. This is a much more controlled manner of dealing with documents than email attachments and mixed revisions.

- Discussions/forums: these can be set up for tasks, documents or milestones so that discussions between team members can be held. This is particularly useful when all team members are not available at the same time. Team members will be able to see comments and suggestions that have been made by others and respond to them. Email notifications of new contributions to discussions can be sent or alerts can be displayed on project dashboards.

- Progress: the software can inform team members and the project manager of progress that is being made. Team members can update tasks to show how near to completion they are and this progress can be fed into the whole project plan. If changes are made to the project timeline, automated email notifications can be sent out to all affected team members.

> **KEY WORD**
>
> collaborate: work together

Decision making

All communications within the project management software can be logged and tracked so that if decisions have been made, then it is possible to clearly identify who made each decision and for what reasons. If problems or issues have been experienced, then these will be highlighted by the software and decisions can be made as to what adjustments need to be made, such as changing the timeline or allocating additional resources. These issues can also be monitored to check on progress of the resolution.

Graphs, charts and reports can be used to analyse the budget, scheduling and task progress. Comparisons can be made between the plan and what is actually happening during the execution of the project, and then decisions can be made to make changes if necessary. The software can show how much time was spent on each task compared to how much time was planned for that task, so that lessons can be learned for future tasks that are similar in nature.

The software will identify a **critical path** which will show all tasks that must complete on time if the project is to meet its deadline. This can then be monitored closely and delays can be anticipated in advance and resources diverted to critical tasks if necessary. The software will show an overview of the availability of resources and the time allocated to each and their respective costs, so that the project manager is able to reallocate them as necessary.

> **KEY WORDS**
>
> critical path: the tasks which must be completed on time for a project to complete on time

Weaknesses of project management software

The strengths of project management software have been detailed within the discussion of features above. However, there are also weaknesses of project management software that need to be considered. Good quality project management software is a large financial investment, especially if it needs to be used by several users. This initial investment can deter some organisations from using the software. Project management software is complex because it covers so many different aspects of project management. Project managers need extensive training to use the software effectively and team members also need training to use the components that are relevant to their tasks. The complexity of the software can also over complicate simple projects which could have been managed more effectively without the software.

Users can become too reliant on the software to remind them that tasks need to be completed. This can result in a task not being done until an alert pops up on someone's screen telling them they've missed a deadline. Online project management software will enable access for many users which is good for collaboration but it creates a risk that unauthorised users may access sensitive data that they shouldn't have access to. It's therefore important to ensure that any access control is set up properly.

Question

2   Explain how project management software can be used for allocating resources to tasks.

on time in order for the whole project to complete on time, and defines the minimum time in which the project can be completed. It is appropriate for projects where the time needed for each task is known, usually because they are common recurring tasks, for example construction tasks.

15.3 Tools and techniques for project management tasks

Critical path method (CPM)

The critical path method (**CPM**), also known as critical path analysis (CPA), finds a project's critical path. The critical path identifies which tasks must complete

> **KEY WORD**
>
> **CPM:** critical path method, also known as CPA (critical path analysis)
>
> **predecessor:** a task in a project that must be completed before another task can start

---

WORKED EXAMPLE 15.02

Figure 15.2 shows a network activity diagram for making a cup of tea.

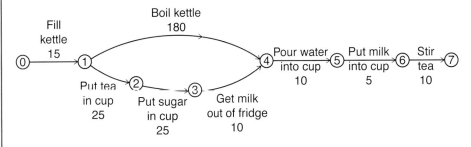

Figure 15.2: Network activity diagram for making a cup of tea.

The circles represent milestones in the project and are numbered for identification purposes. The tasks are represented by arrows. The numbers next to each task represent the number of seconds the task will take. For example, pouring water into the cup will take 10 seconds.

Some tasks can be completed in parallel to other tasks. For example, boiling the kettle can take place at the same time as putting tea in the cup, putting sugar in the cup and getting milk out of the fridge. Where there are parallel tasks, the longest timeline forms the critical path. In this case, 180 seconds to boil the kettle is longer than the 60 seconds it takes to do the three parallel tasks.

Sequential tasks cannot be carried out at the same time because they are dependent upon other tasks completing first. For example, boiling the kettle is dependent upon the kettle being filled with water and so cannot start until the kettle is filled with water. In this case, the kettle being filled with water is a **predecessor** to boiling the kettle.

The total length of the critical path is calculated by adding up all the sequential tasks plus the longest of each of the parallel sets of tasks. In this case that is 15 + 180 + 10 + 5 + 10 = 220 seconds, which is the shortest time it will take to complete the project. If any of the tasks on the critical path takes longer than planned, then the whole project will be delayed.

Some tasks aren't critical and have what is known as float time. The float time is the time an activity can be delayed without affecting the rest of the project.

In the example network activity diagram for making a cup of tea, getting the milk out of the fridge has a float time of 120 seconds because it can be delayed this long before it would catch up with milestone 4.

PRACTICAL ACTIVITY 15.01

Interpret the network activity diagram in Figure 15.3 for building an extension to a house.

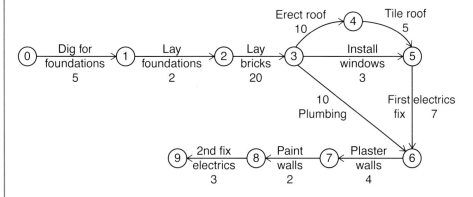

Figure 15.3: Network activity diagram for building an extension.

1   Identify the longest task.

2   How many milestones are there?

3   Which tasks are dependent upon the bricks being laid?

4   Which tasks can run parallel to installing the windows?

5   How many days is the critical path?

6   Which tasks form the critical path?

To create a network activity diagram you need to know the following information:

- the list of tasks
- how long each task will take
- which tasks are dependent upon predecessors.

This information can be shown in an activity dependence table.

WORKED EXAMPLE 15.03

Task	Days	Dependencies
A	3	
B	2	A
C	6	A
D	1	B
E	3	C
F	5	D
G	4	E, F
H	3	G
I	2	G
J	3	G

First, add any tasks to the diagram that have no predecessors.

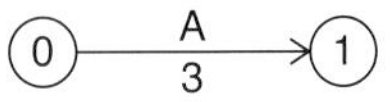

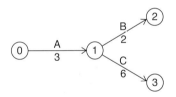

Figure 15.4: Network activity diagram part 1.

Then add on any tasks that are dependent on task A.

Figure 15.5: Network activity diagram part 2.

Continue task by task until there is a completed diagram.

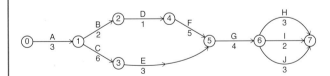

Figure 15.6: Network activity diagram part 3.

PRACTICAL ACTIVITY 15.02

Complete a network activity diagram for the following scenario:

Task	Days	Dependencies
A	3	
B	5	
C	4	
D	18	A
E	16	B
F	12	C
G	7	E, F
H	11	D, G
I	2	H

Network activity diagrams can be extended to include the earliest start time (ES) and earliest finish time (EF) of a task. The ES of the first task is 0 and the EF of the first task is the length of that task. The ES of all other tasks is the latest EF of its predecessors.

ES of task = latest EF of predecessors

The EF of any task is calculated as:

EF = ES + length of task

The float time can also be added to each task. The float time is calculated by subtracting the EF of a task from the ES of the next task:

Float time = EF of task – ES of next task

WORKED EXAMPLE 15.04

Figure 15.3 has been extended to Figure 15.7 below to show the ES in green, the EF in red and float time in blue.

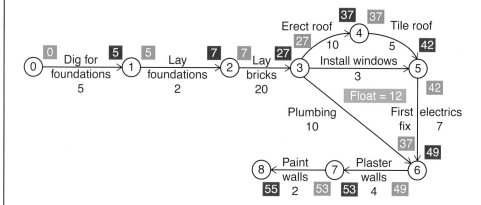

Figure 15.7: Extended network activity diagram.

The ES for dig for foundations is day 0 because it is the first task. The EF for dig for foundations is day 5 because the task will take 5 days. This means that the ES of the next task (lay foundations) is also day 5 because it can only start when the foundations have been dug.

EF for lay foundations = ES for lay foundations + length of lay foundations

EF for lay foundations = 5 + 2 = 7

When it comes to parallel tasks, the ES of a task is the latest EF of its predecessors. The EF for installing windows is day 30, but the EF for tiling the roof is day 42. As these are both predecessors for first fix electrics, the ES for first fix electrics must be day 42.

The ES for first fix electrics is day 42 but the EF for installing the windows is day 30 meaning there are 12 days of float time.

Note: when working in days, the EF and ES are considered to be the beginning of the day. For example, if the EF of task 2 is day 4 then task 2 should be finished by the beginning of day 4, or the end of day 3. This will then enable task 3 to start at the beginning of day 4.

PRACTICAL ACTIVITY 15.03

Extend the CPM from Practical Activity 15.02 to include the ES, EF and float time for each task.

Using a network activity diagram can help to allocate the right number of resources to a task. For example,

when a task needs to be completed earlier than planned, additional resources can be allocated to that task. This is known as 'crashing'. Those additional resources could come from tasks with high float times because it's not critical that those tasks finish at their planned earliest finish time. When there aren't any float tasks available or the necessary resources can't be found from float tasks, additional resources have to be found which incur additional costs. For example, in Figure 15.7, if the laying of bricks needs to be completed 5 days earlier then there are no float tasks available from which to use resources. However, if erecting the roof needed to be completed earlier than planned, then resources could be used from the plumbing task which has a float of 12 days.

Performance evaluation and review technique (PERT)

PERT is similar to CPM in that it is used to plan, schedule and manage projects and activities are based on predecessors. It is more suitable for research and development projects which are non-repetitive because estimates of time are used rather than definitive times.

Tasks or activities are represented by arrows and milestones are represented by nodes, usually a circle. PERT and network activity diagrams therefore look very similar.

The key difference with PERT is that the time for each task is estimated. To estimate the time, the following are used:

- most optimistic time
- most likely time
- most pessimistic time.

The most optimistic time is based on the assumption that everything will go right and there will be no problems. The most pessimistic time is based on the assumption that anything that can go wrong will go wrong.

The estimated time is then calculated as:

$$\text{estimated time} = \frac{4 \times \text{most likely time} + \text{optimistic time} + \text{pessimistic time}}{6}$$

Gantt charts

A Gantt chart is used to show the start and finish dates of each task, the predecessors for each task, the progress of each task and the current position within the project. Tasks are listed with their start and finish dates. A bar represents each task. Each bar can be shaded in to show the percentage of the task that has been completed. Arrows are used to show which tasks are dependent upon other tasks. A line or other indicator can be used to show the current position (time) within the project. It's also possible to identify the resources required, usually by listing the person responsible for each task.

To create a Gantt chart you need to know the following information:

- the list of tasks
- how long each task will take
- which tasks are dependent upon predecessors
- start date of the first task
- resources that are allocated to each task.

Note that some programs used to create Gantt chart (like Gantt Project) only work in days/months, so sometimes you might need to adapt this accordingly when the context is minutes/seconds or hours/minutes.

WORKED EXAMPLE 15.05

Figure 15.8 shows a Gantt chart for developing a book.

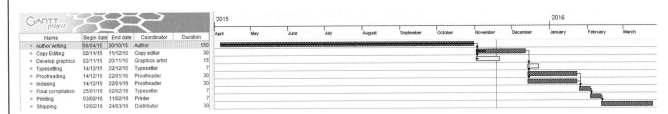

Figure 15.8: Gantt chart.

On the left-hand side you can see the task list together with beginning dates and times, coordinators and the duration. The yellow bars represent the time that each task takes. This makes it much easier to see the float time that is available. Dependencies are shown by the arrows from the end of a predecessor to the start of another task. The black lines represent how much of each task has currently been completed and the red line represents the current time. Therefore, assuming that the progress is correct, the project is running slightly behind schedule. The diagonal lines on the yellow bars represent the critical path.

PRACTICAL ACTIVITY 15.04

Interpret the Gantt chart in Figure 15.9 for building a house extension. The Gantt chart is saved as **15.01 House extension.gan** and was created using GanttProject, which can be used to open the files.

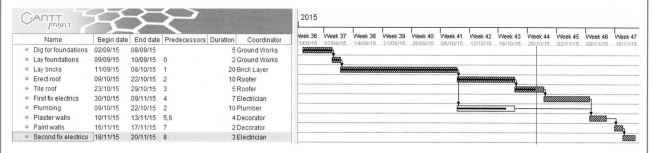

Figure 15.9: Gantt chart for house extension.

1   Which task has float time?

2   Which tasks are currently in progress (started but not finished)?

3   The plumbing appears to be behind schedule. Will this affect the whole project finish date? Why?

4   Which tasks are the predecessors for plastering the walls?

REFLECTION

Figure 15.10 is the resources chart for the house extension project. Have a look at when each resource will be being used. What do you notice about the weekends?

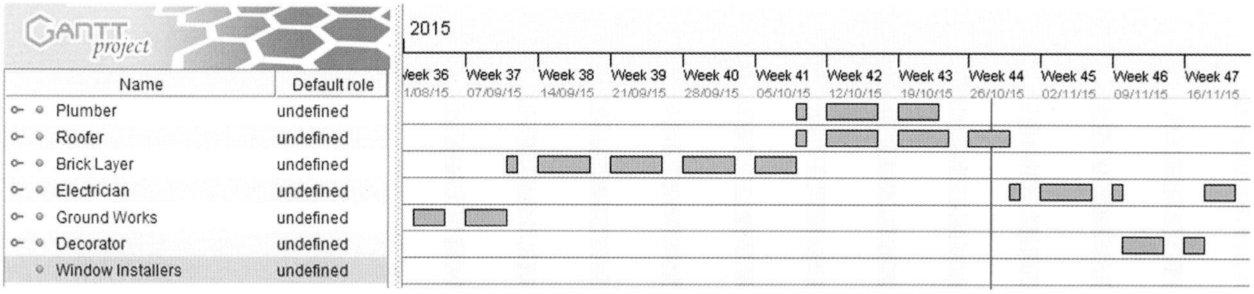

Figure 15.10: Resource chart for house extension.

WORKED EXAMPLE 15.06

Task A starts on 1 January 2020.

Task	Days	Dependencies	Resources
A	3		R1
B	2	A	R1
C	6	A	R2
D	1	B	R1
E	3	C	R2
F	5	D	R3
G	4	E, F	R3
H	3	G	R5
I	2	G	R2
J	3	G	R6

First, create a list of tasks, the duration and the resources required and identify the start and finish dates of the first task.

```
                                           JAN
                                       1 2 3 4 5 6 7

Task    Duration   Start    End    Resources
 A        3       1-1-20   3-1-20     R1      ▭
 B        2                           R1
 C        6                           R2
 D        1                           R1
 E        3                           R2
 F        5                           R3
 G        4                           R3
 H        3                           R5
 I        2                           R2
 J        3                           R6
```

Figure 15.11: Gantt chart part 1.

Then add on any tasks that are dependent on task A, to start the day after task A finishes.

```
                                           JAN
                                       1 2 3 4 5 6 7 8 9

Task    Duration   Start    End    Resources
 A        3       1-1-20   3-1-20     R1      ▭
 B        2       4-1-20   5-1-20     R1       ▭
 C        6       4-1-20   9-1-20     R2        ▭▭▭
 D        1                           R1
 E        3                           R2
 F        5                           R3
 G        4                           R3
 H        3                           R5
 I        2                           R2
 J        3                           R6
```

Figure 15.12: Gantt chart part 2.

Continue task by task until there is a completed Gantt chart.

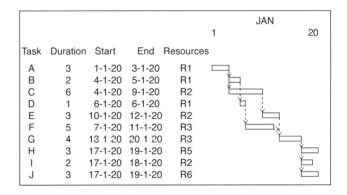

```
                                           JAN
                                      1                20

Task    Duration   Start     End    Resources
 A        3       1-1-20    3-1-20     R1
 B        2       4-1-20    5-1-20     R1
 C        6       4-1-20    9-1-20     R2
 D        1       6-1-20    6-1-20     R1
 E        3      10-1-20   12-1-20     R2
 F        5       7-1-20   11-1-20     R3
 G        4      13 1 20   20 1 20     R3
 H        3      17-1-20   19-1-20     R5
 I        2      17-1-20   18-1-20     R2
 J        3      17-1-20   19-1-20     R6
```

Figure 15.13: Gantt chart part 3.

PRACTICAL ACTIVITY 15.05

Complete a Gantt chart for the following scenario commencing on 1 April 2020.

Task	Days	Dependencies
A	3	
B	5	
C	4	
D	18	A
E	16	B
F	12	C
G	7	E, F
H	11	D, G
I	2	H

Work breakdown structure (WBS)

All of the methods discussed so far have broken the project down into manageable tasks. However, very large projects can become quite daunting if looking at hundreds of tasks all at once. To help manage those tasks, a hierarchical decomposition of the project can be created as a work breakdown structure (WBS). A WBS forms a hierarchical diagram with tasks allocated to sub-tasks or project phases.

In a software development project, the project might be broken down into the phases of a development life cycle as shown in Figure 15.14.

A team manager would then be responsible for each phase, so for example, an assistant project manager might be responsible for the testing phase of a software development project. Each phase would be broken down further to show the stages involved in each phase.

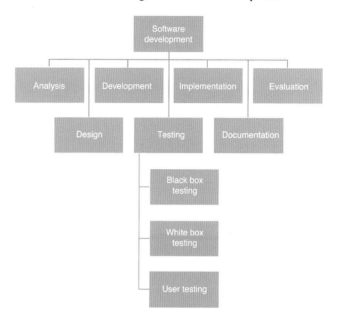

Figure 15.15: WBS for software development with testing expanded.

REFLECTION

Find some recent news stories that report about government projects that have not met their deadlines or budgets.

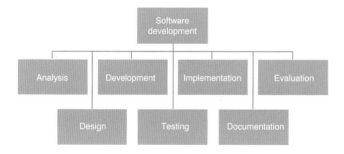

Figure 15.14: WBS for software development.

EXAM-STYLE QUESTIONS

A landscape gardening company has commissioned a software development company to develop a new piece of software that can be used by customers to view a model of what their new garden might look like. A project manager has been appointed to oversee the project.

At the end of the initiation stage of the project, a project brief will be created.

1 a   Identify four items that might be included in the project brief.   [4]

  b   Identify three other stages of project management that will be coordinated by the project manager.   [3]

[Total 7]

The project will involve a large team.

2   Describe four ways the project management software can help the project team to work collaboratively.   [4]

The project manager has the option of using critical path method (CPM) and a Gantt chart for planning the timescales of the project.

3 a   Compare CPA with a Gantt chart.   [2]

  b   Identify two features available in a Gantt chart that are not shown on CPA.   [2]

[Total 4]

The project manager has decided that PERT would be more appropriate than CPA for this project.

4   Explain why PERT is more appropriate than CPA for a software development project.   [3]

5   Explain how a work breakdown structure (WBS) can help a project team.   [3]

SUMMARY CHECKLIST

- [ ] I can describe the stages of project management including:
  - [ ] project initiation
  - [ ] project planning
  - [ ] project execution and monitoring
  - [ ] project close.
- [ ] I can describe the use of project management software for supporting projects.
- [ ] I can discuss the strengths and weaknesses of project management software for supporting projects.
- [ ] I can use and describe tools and techniques for project management tasks including:
  - [ ] Gantt charts
  - [ ] performance evaluation and review technique (PERT)
  - [ ] critical path method (CPM).

System life cycle

CONTINUED

- describe types of documentation and explain why each is needed
- describe the contents of documentation
- explain methods of evaluating a new system
- describe different types of maintenance and explain why each is needed
- explain how each type of maintenance is carried out
- explain different types of prototyping and explain why each is needed
- explain the advantages and disadvantages of each type of prototyping
- describe the stages and processes of different software development methodologies
- explain the advantages and disadvantages of different software development methodologies.

BEFORE YOU START

- Do you understand what a project is?
- Do you understand the structure of a database?
- Do you know what validation means?
- Are you able to draw a flowchart?

Introduction

A new system following the waterfall method of software development evolves through a system life cycle. Requirements are specified by the client and recorded by the analyst. The designer will then follow a requirements specification in order to produce a design specification which will show the client what the new system is likely to look like. When the user is happy with the design specification, the system will be developed based upon the design specification and the developed system will then be tested before being installed for the client. The client will be provided with user documentation. An evaluation will take place to review the system life cycle for the project. Any ongoing maintenance will be carried out by the maintenance team. Other methods for software development are also used including agile and Rapid Application Development (RAD).

16.1 Analysis

Analysis involves finding out how the current system works and what the requirements of the client are for the new system.

KEY WORD

analysis: finding out how the current system works and what the requirements of the client are for the new system

Methods of research

A variety of methods can be used to research current systems and the requirements of a new system.

Questionnaires

Questionnaires are used when information is required from a large number of users when it would be impractical to interview them all. A large number of users also means there is a large sample size for the results of the questionnaire to be quantified and compared. They are not suitable when there are only a small number of users involved because there is not a large enough sample size to gauge opinion and it would be quicker to conduct interviews than spend time preparing questionnaires. An exception to this would be if it is impossible to arrange an appointment time with a user or users, in which case questionnaires could be used as an alternative to interviews. The disadvantage of this is that it doesn't allow the analyst the opportunity to ask the user to elaborate on answers without contacting the user again.

Questions need to be asked in a way in which the required information can be elicited from users, but also so that the responses can be analysed collectively. This often means providing multiple choice responses so that each response can be counted. It's also important to ensure that the questionnaire does not take too long for users to complete as otherwise not many responses may be returned.

WORKED EXAMPLE 16.01

During the analysis for a new school reports system, the analyst wants to find out from pupils, teachers and parents what information should be included on the report. One question that could be asked would be:

Please rate from 1 to 5 the importance of the following information on the school report (1 is not important, 5 is very important):

- Attendance total half days
- Attendance percentage
- Number of negative behavioural events
- Number of positive praise events
- Academic grade for each subject
- Position/rank in class for each subject

- Percentage score for each end of year exam
- Average score for all exams
- Comment from subject teacher
- Targets from subject teacher
- Comment from house tutor
- Target grade.

This will allow the analyst to consider the importance attributed to each piece of information by the three different groups of people, which will contribute to deciding what is included on the reports and how prominent a position each piece of information will take.

An alternative way of asking this question would be:

Please list any information you would like to be included on the school report.

This would make it very difficult to quantify the responses and analyse the findings as each respondent would give very different answers. By providing the list, the analyst is able to give the respondents a starting point.

A mixture of multiple choice questions, opinion ratings and open questions should be used. This will provide a balance of quantitative analysis of closed questions and a qualitative analysis of open questions where users are able to suggest alternative ideas to those presented by the questionnaire. Questions should also be written in a way which does not threaten users and the way they currently do their work. Users should be given the opportunity to return their questionnaires anonymously because that means more honest answers are likely to be given.

Questionnaires should ideally be completed online. This means that the results are immediately stored and readily available for detailed analysis in the form of graphs and tables. Filters can be applied to the results and responses can be compared based on the answers given to another question. For example, a filter could be applied to compare the responses of all males who work part-time compared with males who work full-time.

Interviews

Interviews involve a direct conversation between the analyst and the client. Where there is a single end user or small group of end users then interviews are the perfect solution, because questions can be asked of the users and a conversation can take place which can expand upon answers that are given with follow-up questions searching for further detail. Even in large organisations, interviews can still be used with key stakeholders or representatives of user groups.

Questions to be asked during interviews should be planned and designed to elicit the required information from the client. The questions will vary depending on who is being interviewed. If management are being interviewed, then the questions will focus on the requirements of the organisation as a whole and the information that is required for decision making. If end users are being interviewed, then the questions need to be aimed at finding out what the users need to make their jobs more efficient. Interviews don't have to be with individual users. They can take place with groups of users or focus groups that represent user groups or customers.

The logistics of each interview also needs to be planned. It can sometimes be difficult to find a time when both the analyst and the client are available, especially if the client has a busy schedule. Honesty is important during interviews so that the analyst can get an accurate picture of how tasks are completed. This can sometimes be difficult to achieve because end users may not want to admit to taking shortcuts in their tasks or not carrying out tasks to the best of their ability. In these situations, anonymous questionnaires can get more honest responses. With interviews, the analyst has to be involved with every interview and this can result in a lot of time being used up early in the project.

Observation

Observation involves the analyst watching the processes that take place within an organisation to find out how everyday tasks are completed. This can involve sitting with users to understand the tasks they have to complete, with an opportunity to ask questions of the users to elicit further information that could be needed for a **requirements specification**. This can give a very good understanding of the current input data, processing methods and output information. Other options can include wandering around an office throughout the day to see how information is shared amongst users.

KEY WORDS

requirements specification: what a user needs a new system to do

One disadvantage of this method is that when users are being observed, they may do things differently from normal or they may be more efficient and so this does not give the analyst a true picture of what is happening. The analyst needs to be able to identify how long tasks genuinely take and any inefficiencies that could be improved upon. By observing users directly, the analyst can get first-hand experience of the inefficiencies and can plan to overcome these. Of course, some users may not like being watched

and this may cause them some stress, which means they don't perform as they would do normally. Although this method can take up a lot of time, it is the most insightful method of finding out how an organisation works.

Document analysis

Existing documents within an organisation can tell an analyst a lot about the information that is currently being used.

PRACTICAL ACTIVITY 16.01

Examine the receipt in Figure 16.1.

Figure 16.1: Receipt.

1   Identify the output information that is included on the receipt.

2   Identify any calculations that are likely to have taken place on the receipt.

3   Identify which information is likely to be the same for all receipts and which information is likely to be different for each receipt.

The analyst will need to see examples of any documents that show output information or give an indication of what data is being collected for input to a system. The analyst can sometimes also identify processes that take place by looking at documents. It's also possible to estimate the amount of data that is likely to be required if the volume of documents is known.

This method is not to be used on its own but must be used in conjunction with other analysis methods, because it is difficult to identify the processes just by looking at documents. Examination of the documents also only shows data that is currently output and doesn't give the analyst an opportunity to find out what additional data an organisation might need or what data the organisation does not need. This information can be found out by following up document analysis with interviews.

The content of specifications

There are three types of specification used within the life cycle. These can be summarised as shown in Table 16.1.

Requirements specification	Design specification	System specification
Created by the analyst.	Created by the designer.	Created by the designer.
Contract between developer and client.	Shows what the system will look like.	Identifies the software and hardware needed to run the system.
Identifies what the system must do.	Describes how the system should work.	Identifies the minimum hardware needed to run the system.
	Specifies the data structure to be used.	

Table 16.1: The different types of specification.

Requirements specification

A requirements specification is a contract between the developer and the client. It will specify exactly what the client needs the system to do so that the developer can produce a system that meets the client's needs. The analyst will usually write the requirements specification in consultation with the client who will approve it.

A requirements specification should include:

- the purpose of the system
- the main objectives of the system
- data that must be output from the system (for example, invoices, sales reports)
- data that needs to be input to the system to generate the outputs, including any screens or data collection forms
- validation and verification that is needed for input data

- processes that need to take place to convert inputs into outputs or to store data
- data that need to be stored
- functional requirements such as performance measures
- deadlines for each milestone within the project.

WORKED EXAMPLE 16.02

Here is an extract from a requirements specification for a new town council website. The extract shows specific data that is required on the home page in addition to that which will have been specified for all pages:

- Quick links
- Show list of links editable by content manager
- Initially to be:
  - How can I get involved? (go to Consultations)
  - How can I stand for council? (go to Elections arrangements)
  - When is the next steering group meeting? (go to Meetings)
  - When will I be able to vote for councillors? (go to Key dates)
  - What powers does the Town Council have?
  - How do I report a problem? (go to City Council sub-page)
  - When can I vote for councillors? (go to Elections 2016 arrangements)
- News list
  - Picture, news title, date (taken from list of news)
  - Button: view all news
  - To show latest four news articles
- What's on list
  - Picture, event title with hyperlink, date and time (taken from List of events, Key dates and Meetings)
  - Button: view all events
  - Button: view all key dates
  - To show next four events.

System specification

A **system specification** lists all the software and hardware that is needed for the new system. The software needs to be identified first as the hardware will depend upon what software is needed. Only software that is needed to run the system should be specified. There may be different software identified for different types of users and for servers.

Once the software is known, the minimum hardware required to run that software can be identified. In addition to this, the analyst needs to consider how much storage space is going to be required for the data being used by the system. The analyst will probably also recommend higher than minimum specifications so that the system functions at a reasonable speed. These specifications will include the processing power and the amount of memory required. External hardware components that are needed should also be specified and these should be based upon the requirements of the user.

Design specification

The **design specification** is produced by the designer and is an illustration of how the system will look, what the data structures will be and how the system will work. It is intended to give the user an idea of what the system will look like before it is developed so that the user's feedback can be incorporated into the final designs. The developer will then follow the designs.

> **KEY WORDS**
>
> **system specification:** the hardware and software needed to run the system
>
> **design specification:** illustration of how the system will look, what the data structures will be and how the system will work

Later in this chapter you will learn how to design:

- flowcharts
- data flow diagrams
- data collection forms
- screen layouts
- validation routines
- data dictionary.

In addition to this, a design specification will include:

- house style (logos, colours, fonts, styles, sizes)
- screen sizes
- connectivity diagram to show links between screens
- purpose of calculations.

Questions

1   Identify five stages in the system life cycle.
2   Explain why interviews are better than questionnaires for smaller groups of users.
3   State the purpose of the system specification.

16.2 Design

During the **design** stage, the overall structure of the system and details of the system components are designed without being developed. Diagrams can be used to describe how a current system works (during analysis) or they can also be used to demonstrate how a new system will work (during design).

> **KEY WORD**
>
> **design:** the stage in the life cycle when the design specification is produced

System processing

Data flow diagram

A data flow diagram (**DFD**) shows how data flows throughout a system. It is not about the order of processes, it is purely about the data flows. The elements shown in Table 16.2 are used within a DFD.

> **KEY WORD**
>
> **DFD:** data flow diagram which shows how data moves around a system

Element	Purpose	Symbol
Data flow	This is the data that is flowing throughout the system.	⟶
Process	This is an action that uses or manipulates data.	
Data store	This is a place where data is stored. This could be a hard disk, cloud storage or a paper file, for example.	
Data source or destination (inputs and outputs)	This is an external entity where the data originates or is destined.	⬭
Duplication data source or destination.	This is where we have more than one source where data originates or is destined, to avoid crossing data flow.	

Table 16.2: DFD elements.

DFDs can exist at many levels. At level 0, or context level, the diagram will show the whole system and the data flows between the whole system and any external entities, such as customers, suppliers, members, guests, etc.

WORKED EXAMPLE 16.03

A hotel accepts online bookings for its hotel rooms. Guests make a booking online and the booking is received by the hotel. When the customer arrives, they are given an electronic key which includes encrypted data that will unlock the door and allow purchases at the bar. At the end of the stay, the guest is presented with a bill which must be paid before leaving.

CONTINUED

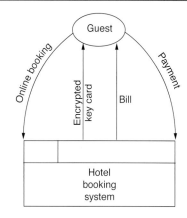

Figure 16.2: Level 0: DFD.

This DFD shows the system as the hotel booking system. It shows the guest as an external entity. It then shows the four items of data that flow between the guest and the booking system.

To create a level 0 DFD, you should identify the external entities and the data flows between the external entities and the system. It is important to remember that it is the data flow that is being represented and not physical objects. Each data flow will be in one direction only.

DFDs can also be considered to be one of the final stages of analysis as they can be used to record the data flows that are currently taking place within an existing system.

PRACTICAL ACTIVITY 16.02

Create a level 0 DFD for the following scenario:

A car hire company accepts bookings of cars by telephone. A credit card payment for the deposit is taken from the customer at the time of booking. When the customer arrives to collect the car, they have to provide details of their driving licence, which are stored by the car hire company. The car hire company will provide the customer with details of the insurance and breakdown services for the car. The customer must pay the remainder of the hire cost before taking the car. The customer will be presented with an invoice showing the payments made.

The next level is a level 1 DFD. This shows the flow of data within part of a system, or if the system is small within the whole system. If the DFD is showing just part of a system, then other parts of the system are considered to be external entities. Each flow of data must be linked to a process, because something has to happen to the data before it can be stored or passed onto an external entity.

WORKED EXAMPLE 16.04

Figure 16.3 is a level 1 DFD for the hotel booking system. Any other aspects of the hotel system are considered to be external entities.

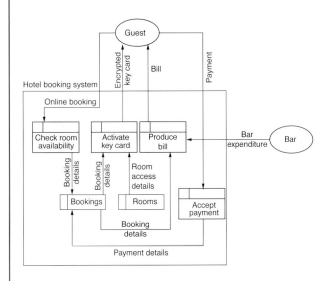

Figure 16.3: Level 1: DFD.

When the guest sends their online booking, the room availability is checked and the booking details are stored. When the guest arrives, their key card is activated by retrieving the room access details. When the guest is ready to leave, a bill is produced by retrieving the booking details and any bar expenditure from the bar system. When payment is made, the booking details are updated to confirm that payment has been made.

To create a level 1 DFD, first identify any external entities and any other parts of the system that will be classed as external entities. Identify the data flows to and from those external entities. Each data flow must have a process attached to it. A data flow cannot move directly from one external entity to another or from one data

store to another or between an external entity and a data store because a process is required to deal with the data. Ignore how the data will actually be processed and just focus on the data movements.

PRACTICAL ACTIVITY 16.03

Create a level 1 DFD for the car hire company introduced in Practical Activity 16.02. Assume the DFD will be for the whole system.

System flowchart

A **system flowchart** shows the flow of data and processes within a complete system. A system flowchart will show how various elements of an information system are related. System flowcharts were popular in the 1960s and 70s when punched card and magnetic tape were commonplace, but they are not as commonly used in modern systems analysis techniques. The elements shown in Table 16.3 are used within a flowchart.

KEY WORDS

system flowchart: an overview of how a system works in a diagrammatic format

Element	Purpose	Symbol
Manual input	Manual input into a computer system, for example using a keyboard.	
Arrow	Shows the direction of flow.	
Process	An activity within the system.	
Document	A single printed document.	

Element	Purpose	Symbol
Multi-document	Multiple printed documents.	
Magnetic disk	Storage on a magnetic disk, although in modern systems, other storage methods are likely.	
Magnetic tape	Data stored on a magnetic tape.	
Display	Output on a visual display.	

Table 16.3: Flow chart elements.

CONTINUED

Hotel bookings are input manually using a keyboard. While editing the booking, the data that has been input is displayed on the screen. Data for the guest who will be staying at the hotel is retrieved from the guests' file. When the data has been input, it is validated and the user is required to correct any errors. A process then saves the booking and prints a booking confirmation document which can be sent to the guest. Each morning, guest arrival sheets, which include information about each guest and the room they will be staying in, are printed. Also in the morning, a checkout list is printed which shows which rooms are due to be vacated that morning.

To create a system flowchart, identify the processes that take place within the system. Then identify the different files that will be used. Use arrows to connect process to data files with the arrow pointing towards the data file if data is being stored, or the arrow pointing towards the process if data is being retrieved. If user input is required, then add the manual input symbol at the appropriate place with the arrow pointing towards the process. Identify any documents that are produced by the system and link each one with a process with the arrow pointing from the process to the document.

WORKED EXAMPLE 16.05

Figure 16.4 is a flowchart for taking a hotel booking online.

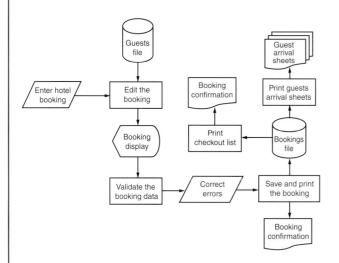

Figure 16.4: Online hotel booking flowchart.

PRACTICAL ACTIVITY 16.04

Create a system flowchart for the following scenario:

A pizza delivery company accepts orders for pizzas by phone. The customer is asked for their address and the system checks the address is in the delivery file. The customer is asked for their order and the telephone operator inputs the order into the system. The order is added to the orders file. Payment details are then taken from the customer which are saved to the payments file. A receipt is printed for the customer and an order sheet is printed for the cooks.

Data storage

Data dictionaries

A data dictionary should be created to describe how data will be stored in tables within a database. The fieldnames should be identified along with their data type, field size and format. Primary keys and foreign keys be identified, including the names of tables to which the foreign keys link to. Any input masks, validation rules or default values should be identified for each field along with an example of what typical data might look like.

WORKED EXAMPLE 16.06

This is an example of a data dictionary for a table about students.

Attribute	Data type	Length	Format	Validation Rule	Default Value	Sample Data	Primary Key	Foreign Key
Student ID	Integer	6	999999	Autonumber		459283	Yes	
Forename	Text	20	Xxxxx	Required		Mao		
Surname	Text	20	Xxxxx	Required		Zedong		
Other names	Text	50	Xxxxx	Required		Xi		
Tutor Group	Text	3	99X			12A		TUTOR GROUP – TgId
Date of Birth	Date	8	DD/MM/YYYY	<= 10 years before today		12/04/2007		
Date Joined	Date	8	DD/MM/YYYY	>= 10 years after date of birth		01/09/2018		
Date Left	Date	8	DD/MM/YYYY	> [Date Joined]				
Disability	Boolean	1		Required	False	True		

PRACTICAL ACTIVITY 16.05

Revise data types, field sizes, primary and foreign keys and validation from chapter 10. Complete the following data dictionary for a table of vehicles:

Attribute	Data type	Length	Format	Validation Rule	Default Value	Sample Data	Primary Key	Foreign Key
Vehicle Registration								
Make								
Model								
Engine size (cc)								
Transmission								
Number of doors								
Imported?								

An entity relationship diagram should be created to show the relationships between the tables that will be used. Refer to Chapter 10 for detailed information about entity relationships.

Files

Any files that will be used to import data should be designed, including the intended layout of data. Similarly, any files generated by the system should be designed, including the format in which the data will be exported. The type of files should be specified, for example, whether it is comma separated or tab delimited. The contents of each column should be specified including the expected data type, length and format of each column.

Input forms

Data collection forms

Data collection forms are documents that are used to collect data without the use of a computer. These could include membership application forms, questionnaires, job applications or reply slips. It is important to design the form in such a way that the required data can be collected.

When designing a data collection form, it is good practice to follow these principles:

- avoid colour as the document may not be printed in colour
- include instructions about how to complete the form
- give clear instructions about where the form should be returned
- identify which questions must be answered and which are optional
- provide enough space for each answer
- use tick boxes for multiple choice lists
- make it clear how many options are allowed to be chosen from a multiple choice list
- ensure all fonts are consistently used
- avoid cluttering the form with too much information or too many questions
- ensure the font style and size are legible

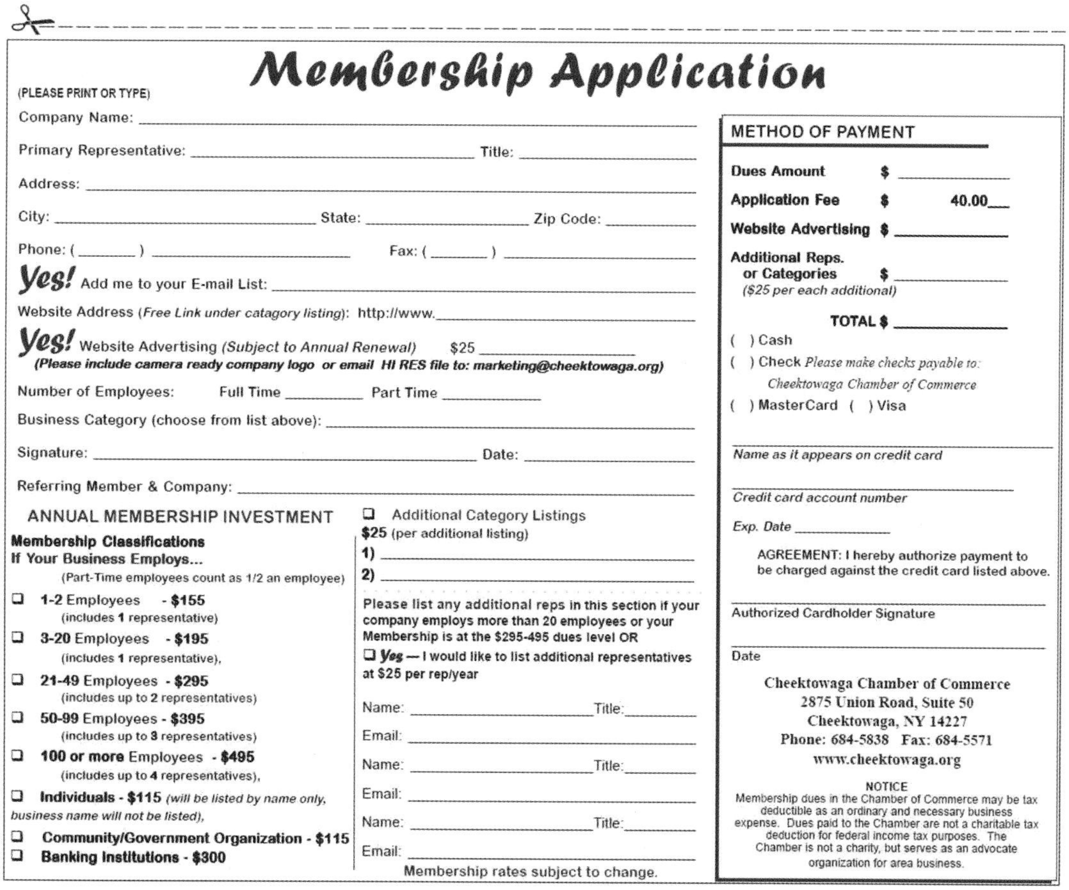

Membership Application

(PLEASE PRINT OR TYPE)

Company Name: ____

Primary Representative: ____ Title: ____

Address: ____

City: ____ State: ____ Zip Code: ____

Phone: (____) ____ Fax: (____) ____

Yes! Add me to your E-mail List: ____

Website Address (*Free Link under catagory listing*): http://www.____

Yes! Website Advertising (*Subject to Annual Renewal*) $25 ____

(Please include camera ready company logo or email HI RES file to: marketing@cheektowaga.org)

Number of Employees: Full Time ____ Part Time ____

Business Category (choose from list above): ____

Signature: ____ Date: ____

Referring Member & Company: ____

ANNUAL MEMBERSHIP INVESTMENT

Membership Classifications
If Your Business Employs...
(Part-Time employees count as 1/2 an employee)

- ❑ **1-2** Employees - **$155** (includes **1** representative)
- ❑ **3-20** Employees - **$195** (includes **1** representative),
- ❑ **21-49** Employees - **$295** (includes up to **2** representatives)
- ❑ **50-99** Employees - **$395** (includes up to **3** representatives)
- ❑ **100 or more** Employees - **$495** (includes up to **4** representatives),
- ❑ **Individuals - $115** (*will be listed by name only, business name will not be listed*),
- ❑ **Community/Government Organization - $115**
- ❑ **Banking Institutions - $300**

❑ Additional Category Listings
$25 (per additional listing)
1) ____
2) ____

Please list any additional reps in this section if your company employs more than 20 employees or your Membership is at the $295-495 dues level OR
❑ ***Yes*** **— I would like to list additional representatives at $25 per rep/year**

Name: ____ Title: ____
Email: ____
Name: ____ Title: ____
Email: ____
Name: ____ Title: ____
Email: ____

Membership rates subject to change.

METHOD OF PAYMENT

Dues Amount **$** ____
Application Fee **$** **40.00**
Website Advertising **$** ____
Additional Reps. or Categories **$** ____
(*$25 per each additional*)
TOTAL $ ____

( ) Cash
( ) Check *Please make checks payable to: Cheektowaga Chamber of Commerce*
( ) MasterCard ( ) Visa

Name as it appears on credit card

Credit card account number

Exp. Date ____

AGREEMENT: I hereby authorize payment to be charged against the credit card listed above.

Authorized Cardholder Signature

Date

Cheektowaga Chamber of Commerce
2875 Union Road, Suite 50
Cheektowaga, NY 14227
Phone: 684-5838 Fax: 684-5571
www.cheektowaga.org

NOTICE
Membership dues in the Chamber of Commerce may be tax deductible as an ordinary and necessary business expense. Dues paid to the Chamber are not a charitable tax deduction for federal income tax purposes. The Chamber is not a charity, but serves as an advocate organization for area business.

Figure 16.5: Example of a data collection form.

- if the respondent needs to complete a scale (e.g. 1–10), then explain what the scale represents (e.g. 1 = very dissatisfied, 5 = neither satisfied or dissatisfied, 10 = very satisfied).

PRACTICAL ACTIVITY 16.06

Explain how the application form in Figure 16.6 could be improved.

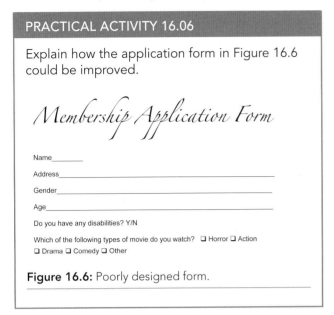

Figure 16.6: Poorly designed form.

Screen layouts

A screen can be used to ask the user for data to be input or to display information to the user or a mixture of both. For example, Figure 16.7 shows information about a property that is for sale. It also allows the user to change details about the property or add details about a new property.

Figure 16.7: Screen example.

When designing a screen it is good practice to follow these principles:

- use colour sparingly and appropriately; different colours could be used for questions and responses or for different types of data; colours that the

user expects should be used, for example green is usually seen as a positive colour and red as a negative colour

- ensure all fonts are used with consistency

- avoid cluttering the screen with too much information, but at the same time try to fit all information that needs to be viewed at the same time on a single screen

- ensure the font style and size are legible

- if the screen requires user input:

  - include instructions about how to complete the form

  - identify which questions must be answered and which are optional

  - provide enough space for each answer

  - use tick boxes for multiple choice lists that can have more than one response

  - use drop-down boxes (combo boxes) or option buttons (radio buttons) for multiple choice lists that can only have one response.

See Chapter 2 for detailed information about the types of form controls that can be used on input forms.

When designing a screen or collection form, it is only necessary to indicate where questions and responses will go, the types of response options and the styles to use. The layout of any information should also be indicated. The developer will then follow the design.

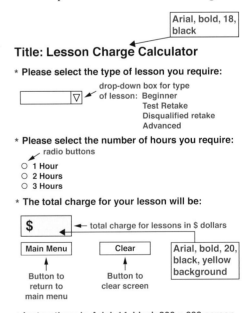

Figure 16.8: Example of a screen design.

Validation routines

> **PRACTICAL ACTIVITY 16.07**
>
> Revise validation routines from Chapter 1. Complete the following table.
>
> | Validation type | Description | Example |
> |---|---|---|
> | Presence | | |
> | Range | | |
> | Type | | |
> | Length | | |
> | Format | | |

Validation rules should be used wherever possible and be appropriate in order to reduce the number of possible input errors. They only need to be used for input data so any calculations or output data do not require validating. Drop-down boxes should always be used instead of lookup validation checks. For example, if a category needs to be selected, then a drop-down box should be used to select that category rather than requiring the user to type in the category.

When designing a validation rule, identify the input data that is to be validated, the type of validation rule to be used, the rule that will be used and the error message that should appear if the data input is invalid. Error messages should be positive and guide the user as to what to do to correct the error.

Input data	Validation type	Validation rule	Error message
Surname	Presence	Surname must be entered	Please enter a surname
Date of birth	Range	Date of birth must be at least 18 years earlier than today	Applicant must be at least 18 years old

Input data	Validation type	Validation rule	Error message
Application number	Type	Must be a whole number	The application number must contain only numbers
Telephone	Length	Must be between 3 and 15 digits	Telephone number must be between 3 and 15 digits
Product code	Format	XX999XX9	The product code must be in the format XX999XX9 where X is a letter from A to Z and 9 is a number from 0 to 9

Table 16.4: Examples of a design for validation.

Checking of data collected by forms

In addition to validation rules, any intended methods for verifying data input such as visual checking, double data entry or hash control should be specified. See Chapter 1 for detailed information about these verification methods.

Output reports

The design of output screen layouts follows the same principal as input forms except that there is no need for instructions or input fields.

Printed copy layouts

When designing a printed copy layout, as well as following the same principles for output reports, consideration needs to be made to the size of paper that will be used, the size of margins and the intended audience. Printed copies can often include tabular data.

WORKED EXAMPLE 16.07

This example shows a report for listing all the products available.

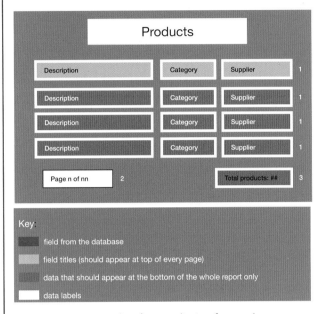

Figure 16.9: Example of report listing for products.

1 The description, category and supplier data will be repeated for each record in the PRODUCTS table.
2 n = page number, nn = total number of pages
3 ## = total number of products in PRODUCTS table

In addition to these points, the size of paper, size of margins, font styles and sizes, colours and any gridlines should also be specified.

PRACTICAL ACTIVITY 16.08

Design the layout of a report that will show a list of all the students in your class including their dates of birth and contact details.

Questions

4 Identify the purpose of a data flow diagram (DFD).
5 Identify one rule for data flows within a level 1 DFD.
6 Describe the difference between a tick box and an option button.

16.3 Development and testing

The **development** stage is often referred to as the implementation stage where the design is implemented. Due to the confusion between implementation of the design and implementation of the system, development is now a more commonly recognised and understood term.

KEY WORD

development: the stage in the system life cycle when the software is produced

Test data

When a system has been developed, it needs to be tested. In order to test the system, data has to be created that will be used for the purpose of testing. This is known as **test data**. The data used in this phase is a simulation of 'live data'. There will need to be enough test data generated to ensure that the system is able to cope under the pressures of large amounts of data in everyday use. There will also need to be specific types of data to test different scenarios within the software, including validation rules and queries.

KEY WORD

test data: data that will be used for testing a system

When testing the input of data that is to be validated, Table 16.5 shows the types of data that should be included as test data:

Type of test data	Description
Valid (also called normal data)	Data that will be accepted by the validation rule.
Invalid (also called abnormal or erroneous data)	Data that will not be accepted by the validation rule.

Type of test data	Description
Extreme (also called extreme data)	Data that will only be accepted by the validation rule because it is at the limit of acceptability.

Table 16.5: Types of test data.

WORKED EXAMPLE 16.08

To test the validation rule that gender must be 'M' or 'F', the following test data could be used.

Type of test data	Data
Valid (normal)	M, F
Invalid (abnormal or erroneous)	B

To test the validation rule that a date must be between 1/1/2017 and 31/12/2017, the following test data could be used.

Type of test data	Test data
Valid (normal)	12/5/2017
Invalid (abnormal or erroneous)	15/7/2012, 4/6/2019
Extreme	1/1/2017, 31/12/2017

PRACTICAL ACTIVITY 16.09

Select test data to test the input of numbers in the range 2500 to 5000.

Test data is also needed to test queries. Records will need to be created where there is data that meets the criteria of the query, does not meet the criteria of the query, only just meets the criteria of the query and only just fails to meet the criteria of the query. Where there is more than a single criterion, data should also be selected that only meets part of the criteria in case both parts have not been set up correctly.

WORKED EXAMPLE 16.09

The following data for records could be used to test the query for males over the age of 50 (including 50).

Record number	Gender	Age	Reason
1	M	65	Both criteria met
2	F	25	Both criteria not met
3	M	25	Gender part met, age part not met
4	F	65	Gender part not met, age part met
5	M	50	Age part only just met
6	M	49	Age part only just not met

The more criteria that are used and the more possibilities for extremes, then the more records that will be required to test the query fully.

PRACTICAL ACTIVITY 16.10

Data is stored about cars, including their make, model, registration number, transmission (automatic or manual), colour, distance travelled and year of registration. Select test data that could be used to test the query to find all automatic transmission cars that were registered before 2016.

The system will also be tested to see how it works under normal conditions and so a sample set of 'live data' will be used to test that the system functions correctly under normal conditions. 'Live data' is the actual data being used by the system once it has been implemented, and so a sample of 'live data' enables a simulation of a live system to take place. This type of testing with a sample of 'live data' will be carried out by the end-users in most circumstances. They will use the data as if they were doing their normal job, simulating different processes that they would carry out.

Alpha testing and beta testing

Alpha testing is carried out by the developers or a specialised team of testers before a system is delivered to the user. This usually takes place close to the end of the development stage when the application is nearly ready for the user. Alpha testing can take a long time because each time an error is found, testing has to be repeated when the error has been corrected and there may be knock-on effects to other parts of the system.

Beta testing is used when software is being made available to a large number of customers. Beta testers will be real customers who have been selected to test an early release of the application. Beta testing only takes place after alpha testing has been completed. Alpha testing is planned and structured using test data to follow all pathways through the software but beta testing involves customers using the software in a real world environment using real data. As bugs are found within a beta version, new beta versions will be released for further testing before a final version is released for sale.

> ### KEY WORDS
>
> **alpha testing:** initial testing of the software by a limited group of people
>
> **beta testing:** a sample of users test a pre-release version of the software

Black box testing and white box testing

Black box testing involves selecting input data and checking that the expected output data matches the actual output data, with no knowledge or understanding of what happens inside the black box. The black box could be the whole system or part of a system. **White box testing** involves the same process of input and output data but the internal structure and logic of the program are known to the tester.

> ### KEY WORDS
>
> **black box testing:** testing of inputs and outputs to a system or part of a system with no consideration for the workings of the system
>
> **white box testing:** testing the whole system in terms of structure and logic covering all paths through the system

White box testing usually takes place with small program modules and is carried out by the software developers who coded the programs. They will do this to ensure that each module works in the way it was intended, and because they know the inner workings of the module they can test pathways that a black box tester would not know about. The testing will be focused on whether detailed designs, such as validation rules, have been developed correctly.

Black box testing usually involves testing the whole system or user testing. It can be carried out by specialist testers or, in the case of user testing, by the intended users. No knowledge of programming or the way the system works is required. The testing will be focused on ensuring the requirements specification has been met.

White box testing needs access to a detailed specification, whereas black box testing does not require knowledge of how the system was developed. In black box testing, only a limited number of test scenarios are actually performed due to not knowing how each module works, but with white box testing, each module can be tested in-depth. Black box test plans are difficult to design because so many different input data options have to be considered along with pathways through the system, whereas with white box testing, test plans can be created for each calculation, navigation and input separately. With white box testing, the tester can identify the type of test data that will be required, particularly related to valid, invalid and extreme test data, but with black box testing, the tester may not know what the boundary values are expected to be. Due to needing to understand the code, skilled testers are required to carry out white box testing, whereas black box testing can be carried out by moderately skilled testers.

The importance of testing and having a test plan

Testing is necessary because no programmer or developer is perfect and errors are to be expected. These errors need to be found and rectified. It is important to ensure that the system is error free so that the users can use the system knowing that it will work reliably and behave as expected. Although it's almost impossible to ensure a system is completely free of errors, a **test plan** can help to minimise the number of errors by ensuring that all pathways through a system and types of data have been tested.

> ### KEY WORD
>
> **test plan:** a detailed and structured plan of how testing should be carried out

WORKED EXAMPLE 16.10

This extract, from a test plan, tests the input of data where the date must be between 1/1/17 and 31/12/17.

Number	Description	Type of test	Input data	Expected result	Pass/Fail
1a	Test the input of join date.	Valid	12/5/17	Accepted	Pass
1b		Extreme	1/1/17	Accepted	Pass
1c		Extreme	31/12/17	Accepted	Fail – error message
1d		Invalid	15/7/12	Error message: the join date must be in 2017.	Pass
1e		Invalid	4/6/19		Pass
1f		Extreme	31/12/16		Fail – accepted
1g		Extreme	1/1/18		Pass

The reason the test for 31/12/17 failed to be accepted may be because <31/12/17 was used in the validation rule rather than <=31/12/17. Similarly, the reason 31/12/16 failed to generate an error message may be because >= 31/12/16 was used in the validation rule rather than >31/12/16.

A test plan will identify all the tests that are needed for every input, every button, every link, every report, every screen and all other elements of a system. The test plan will include different types of test data, including valid, invalid and extreme, so that inputs are tested to their limits. Without this planning, important parts of testing would be missed out and errors could be left undiscovered. The plan will also cover all the user's requirements and ensure that they are tested.

A good test plan will provide a systematic outline of all features and functionality which will be continually updated to reflect any new risks as the software is developed. The test plan will ensure that all aspects of running a test are considered and prevent aspects being missed out. The test plan is also important so that testers know what the testing regime will involve and that there is a mechanism for ensuring each test is carried out as planned and signed off.

Test plans

A test plan will identify what is being tested, the type of test, the input data that should be used to test it, the expected result of the test and space to record the actual result. Each test will be numbered.

PRACTICAL ACTIVITY 16.11

Create a test plan to test the input of data for a character code between the letters D and P.

As well as inputs, it is important to test that all calculations work as expected. Each input for a calculation will need to be identified and an expected result determined. Table 16.6 shows an example of how testing of calculations might be planned and executed.

Number	Description	Type of test	Input data	Expected result	Pass/Fail
2	Discount formula works for 2 hours	Calculation	Charge per hour = $13 on quote worksheet	Test retake = $25 in 2 hours column	Pass
3	Function for lesson charge	Calculation	Lesson type = advanced Number of hours = 2 on quote worksheet	Total charge = $19	Fail = $1.90

Table 16.6: Examples of test plan for calculations.

Any links or buttons also need testing. Table 16.7 shows how a navigation button (main menu) and an action button (clear) would be tested.

Number	Description	Type of test	Input data	Expected result	Pass/fail
4	Main menu button	Button	Click on main menu button on quote worksheet	The main menu worksheet opens	Pass
5	Clear button works	Button	Lesson type = advanced, number of hours = 2 Click on the clear button on quote worksheet	Lesson type = (blank) Number of hours = (blank)	Fail – number of hours remained as 2

Table 16.7: Example of a test plan for buttons.

Questions

7 Describe the purpose of using extreme test data.
8 Describe two differences between alpha and beta testing.
9 Explain black box testing.
10 Explain the importance of having a test plan.

REFLECTION

What would be the implications of rocket launch system software not being fully tested?

16.4 Implementation

This section has the title 'Implementation', however, the term 'installation' can also be used. Implementation can have two meanings within the system life cycle and is sometimes understood to be the development stage where the design is implemented.

KEY WORD

implementation: the stage in the system life cycle when the software is installed for the user

There are four different methods of implementing (installing) a new system which can be remembered as the 4 Ps:

- parallel
- plunge (direct)
- phased
- pilot.

Parallel running

Parallel running is when a new system and an old system are run at the same time. On an agreed date, the new system will become live but the old system will continue to run. Data will need to be duplicated from the old system to the new system. New data will need to be input into both systems and output will be produced from both systems. This will continue until the organisation is confident that the new system is running satisfactorily.

Direct changeover

Direct changeover is when a date is chosen for the old system to stop running and the new system to start running. The systems do not run at the same time and there is a clear break from the old system to the new system. Data will need to be transferred from the old system to the new system before the new system can be used.

Phased implementation

With phased implementation, parts of the new system will be introduced one at a time. This often takes place when there is a large system with lots of functionality that can be easily separated into sections. The old system will run until a date that has been agreed, at which point part of the old system will be retired and part of the new system will start running. After a while, another part of the old system will be retired and another part of the new system will start running. This will continue until the complete new system is fully running.

Pilot implementation

Pilot implementation takes place when part of an organisation starts to use the new system while the rest of the organisation continues to use the old system. The new system is effectively being beta tested by the pilot group who may also be able to deliver training to the rest of the organisation when the system goes fully live.

Choosing an implementation method

The most suitable changeover method will always be dependent upon the individual circumstances surrounding a new system. Factors that will need to be taken into account will include:

- how critical the system is to the running of the organisation
- cost
- number of users in the organisation
- the size of the new system.

The advantages and disadvantages of each method is shown in Table 16.8.

Implementation method	Advantages	Disadvantages
Parallel	Less risky because if the new system fails the organisation can continue to run using the old system. The accuracy of the new system can be tested against the old system and any errors can be fixed.	Duplication of data input means additional staffing costs. There may need to be additional hardware installed at the same time as the old hardware is still being used, which will require physical space. Data may be input differently into the two systems, meaning that the data is not accurate in both.
Direct	This is cheap to implement because there is no duplication of work. The data being used will be consistent because it is only being used in one system at a time. There is no need for the new system to be compatible with the old system.	This is a risky method because any errors could lead to the system failing with no fallback. All the training will need to be done in advance of changeover and so if there are a lot of users this could result in some forgetting what they've learned by the time they start to use the new system.
Phased	If there are any errors, they will only affect the part of the system that has changed over rather than the whole system. End users can be trained how to use each phase of the new system and spend time using that phase before being trained in the next phase.	Delays can occur waiting for each phase to be running successfully before the next phase can start. Users will be using two different systems and they may get confused as to which system they should be using for which part of their work. This could lead to data being updated in the wrong system. Both the old and new system need to be compatible with each other in order for data to be used across both systems.

Implementation method	Advantages	Disadvantages
Pilot	If there are any errors, they will only affect the pilot group that are using the system. Any errors found by the pilot group can be fixed before the system is installed for all users. The pilot group can train other users on how to use the system because they will have experienced using it for real.	This is a slower method of changeover because the rest of the organisation has to wait until the pilot has been completed satisfactorily. Users in the pilot group might not be happy about using the new system while it may still have some errors in it and users not in the pilot group may be disgruntled that they have not been offered the opportunity to try the new software first. Both the old and new system need to be compatible with each other in order for data to be shared between the pilot group and the users still using the old system.

Table 16.8: Advantages and disadvantages of implementation methods.

Questions

11 Identify four methods of changeover.

12 Describe one situation when direct changeover would be more appropriate than parallel changeover.

13 Describe one situation when pilot changeover would be more appropriate than phased changeover.

REFLECTION

Find out what happened in 1992 when the London Ambulance Service Computer Aided Dispatch system failed. What lessons can be learned from this?

16.5 Documentation

Technical documentation

Technical documentation is an overview of the structure of the system, how it was put together and how it works. It will include a data dictionary to show how data has been structured within the system. Any programming code or macros will be annotated to explain their purpose and anything unusual, along with a list of variables including their datatypes and purpose. All validation rules will be listed with the criteria used for successful input and the error messages that they generate. The purpose of calculations within the system will be identified and an explanation given of how each calculation works. All buttons and links will be listed, including where they are located and what their function is. All files used by the system will be listed and their purpose identified. The technical documentation will also include flowcharts to show how different parts of the system work and other diagrams that may have been used during design and development such as entity relationship diagrams and screen connectivity diagrams.

KEY WORDS

technical documentation: an overview of the structure of the system, how it was put together and how it works

There will be an installation guide for the installation team and also in case the system has to be installed again in the future. All the results of testing will be recorded, including any known errors and bugs. Backup routines will be detailed to show where files are stored, how the routines were configured and how to restore from a backup. All security settings will be documented to show which groups have access to each part of the system and the permissions they have been granted. The software and hardware requirements will also be listed.

User documentation

User documentation is a user guide giving instructions to the user. It can be in electronic or printed format. A printed user guide should have a front cover that clearly identifies the name of the system and the whole guide should have a header or footer with page numbers. A contents page should be included with page numbers and an electronic version would include hyperlinks to those pages. An introduction to the purpose of the user guide should be included, but it only needs to be a few sentences. All the software and hardware requirements will be listed within the guide.

The main part of the user guide will be the instructions on how to use the system. This should include written instructions together with screenshots of the system or photographs of hardware. Arrows can be used to point to parts of screenshots or photographs. Bullets or numbering should be used to break instructions down into manageable tasks.

A glossary will show an alphabetical list of any technical terms that have been used within the user guide and a definition of each of those terms. There should be a troubleshooting section that includes a table of common problems (for example, error messages) together with a description of what might have caused the problem and possible solutions for overcoming the problem. An index will be included at the end of the user guide with page numbers for each popular term.

KEY WORDS

user documentation: a user guide giving instructions to the user on how to use the software

WORKED EXAMPLE 16.11

This is an example of a troubleshooting guide for a printer.

Problem	Cause	Solution
Orange light displayed on printer.	No paper in feeder tray.	Add paper to the feeder tray.
Red light displayed on printer.	Paper is jammed in the printer.	Open the paper feeder tray and check there is no paper stuck there. Open the back door and check there is no paper stuck there. Open the toner door, remove the toner and check there is no paper stuck there. If any paper is found, gently pull any paper that is stuck.
Error message on computer says 'Printer Offline'.	Printer is turned off. Printer is not connected to the computer.	Turn on printer. Ensure the USB cable is connected between the computer and the printer.

CONTINUED

Below is an example of a troubleshooting guide for an order processing system.

Problem	Cause	Solution
Microsoft Access [×] ⓘ Not enough items in stock OK **Figure 16.10:** Error message 1.	On the New order form you have specified a quantity larger than the amount currently in stock.	Enter a smaller quantity.
Microsoft Access [×] ⓘ Invoice cannot be paid if not dispatched OK **Figure 16.11:** Error message 2.	On the Order details form you have ticked the Paid box before the Invoice has been dispatched.	Check the invoice has been dispatched. If it has, then tick the Invoice dispatched box.

PRACTICAL ACTIVITY 16.12

Find a user manual for an electronic device or appliance at home. Identify the different sections that are used and compare them with those listed in Worked Example 16.10.

Why technical and user documentation is needed

Technical documentation is required so that anybody carrying out future maintenance on the system will be able to understand how the system was developed and how it is configured. It is unlikely that the person carrying out future maintenance is part of the original development team and so will not be familiar with the system without the technical documentation. Even if it is the same person or team carrying out the maintenance, they will need the documentation to remember the structure of the system.

User documentation is needed so that the user can learn how to use the new system or look up how certain features are supposed to work. The troubleshooting section will be important for the user to understand what has caused an error to occur and what they need to do in order to stop the error from occurring.

Questions

14 Give three sections you would expect to find in user documentation.

15 Describe the purpose of a glossary in user documentation.

16 Give a situation when technical documentation would be needed.

16.6 Evaluation

When a system has been developed and installed, the whole process will be evaluated. This is sometimes referred to as a review. The **evaluation** will consider how the project team and end users worked together so that lessons can be learned for future projects.

KEY WORD

evaluation: a formal review of a project

Users will be given questionnaires to find out what they think of the new system and how they feel it is improving their workflow (or not). Selected users will also be given specific tasks to complete that will be observed to see whether the new system is living up to its expectations. Some users will also be interviewed about their interaction with the new system.

The most important question to be asked will be whether the system meets the user requirements. Each requirement will be considered in turn to determine if it has been fulfilled. If it hasn't been fulfilled, then actions will be set to rectify the situation in the long run. The efficiency of the new system will also be discussed. Users will have been given an opportunity to feed back on how well the new system is working for them and if there are any problems. It is expected that the new system will work more efficiently than the old system. However, if there are problems that need addressing, then actions will be taken.

The requirements specification should have specified how easy the new system should be to use. This can be rather subjective and so it is difficult to measure. Again, feedback will have been gained from users as to how well they have adapted to the new system and how easy or not they find it to use now they are using it regularly. If there are issues regarding ease of use, then plans can be made to simplify any processes by adding additional features to the software if necessary.

There will also be an opportunity for users to make suggestions for future improvements or additions to the system.

Question

17 State three elements that might be evaluated after a system has been installed.

16.7 Maintenance

Maintenance takes place after a system has been delivered to a customer and it is being used. There are four reasons why maintenance might be required, which are outlined here.

> **KEY WORD**
>
> **maintenance:** changes made to a system after its implementation

Perfective maintenance

The idea of perfective maintenance is to be always looking to improve a system. There may not be anything wrong with the system, but there may be ideas to make the system perform better or to do additional tasks. Sometimes improvements might be possible because of new technology that has become available.

If a system remains in place for several years without any improvements, then it may become outdated and inefficient compared with other systems that are available. Users will also have new ideas and if they are likely to improve efficiency then they should be embraced.

For example, an online accounts application sends out automatic reminders to customers when payments haven't been made. These reminders are sent to a single customer contact. The system only allows for the contact details of one person to be stored. Many users of the accounts application have requested that the system be adapted to store details of multiple contacts for each customer and that contacts who should receive invoice payment reminders are identified within the software so that they go to the right person.

Adaptive maintenance

Systems need to adapt to changes. There could be changes to internal procedures within an organisation or changes over which the organisation has no control. For example, new government legislation could be introduced to which the system has to adapt. It's necessary to adapt to changes so that the system continues to work effectively and doesn't produce incorrect outputs. It's important that the system enables an organisation to comply with new laws. There is also a need to adapt to new technology such as a new operating system, new web browser and new hardware.

For example, the government introduced new requirements for organisations to provide pensions to all employees. The online accounts application needed to be updated to include a facility for checking that all employee payslips include pension payments unless they have opted out of the scheme. The accounting software was supposed to show a paper clip symbol to indicate that a receipt had been uploaded against a recorded expenditure. When a web browser was upgraded, this paper clip stopped being displayed. The software had to be adapted to work with the new web browser.

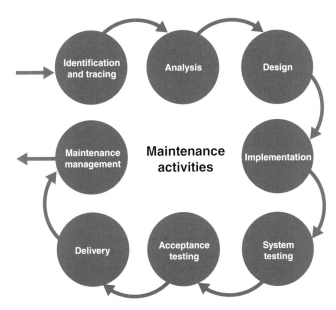

Preventative maintenance

Preventative maintenance is required to prevent problems arising within a system. This can apply to both hardware and software. Hardware should be regularly cleaned to stop dust from blocking any fans and regular scans of storage media should be carried out to ensure they are working properly. Heat should be monitored within systems for any abnormalities to prevent hardware failures. Data should be regularly checked for consistency and integrity. Performance of the system should be monitored to ensure that the processor, memory and storage are all working efficiently. By carrying out regular preventative maintenance, system downtime can be avoided.

Corrective maintenance

When errors or bugs are found within a system they need to be corrected. This will be the responsibility of the original developers, although it may be different people that carry out the maintenance. These errors need to be corrected so that the system can run efficiently and accurately and produce the results required by the organisation. Bugs that cause problems by making a system slow or by crashing a system can be very frustrating to users and reduce overall productivity.

For example, a graphics application would intermittently stop responding for several seconds. This was not supposed to happen and so corrective maintenance was required.

How maintenance is carried out

There are many ways in which maintenance to software can be carried out, but one widely used methodology similar to the software development life cycle (SDLC) is the maintenance process model. The maintenance process model includes the following stages:

Figure 16.12: Maintenance activities.

Maintenance needs to go through the same stages as software development because the software is being further developed. Testing is still very important because any changes made could affect existing parts of the system. The maintenance team can be formed using one of three different approaches:

- **separating development and maintenance**: the maintenance team will be different to the original development team.

- **combined approach**: the maintenance team will include both maintenance specialists and members of the original development team.

- **functional approach**: this is similar to the combined approach, but systems personnel are assigned to functional areas within an organisation where they are responsible for both development and maintenance within that functional area.

Maintenance starts with the identification and tracing stage. A modification request (or problem report) will be generated which could be a request by a user or it could be as a result of collating error logs from the system. The modification request must clearly describe the existing functionality of the system and the desired functionality of the system. The modification request will need to be classified as either perfective, adaptive, preventative or corrective maintenance.

During the analysis stage, a change impact analysis will take place. An impact analysis involves identifying all systems and software that will be affected by the change, the risks associated with the change, an estimate of the resources that will be required to implement the change and a cost-benefit analysis of the change. If the impact of the change is considered to be severe then an alternative solution may be sought. If the impact is manageable then the required modifications from the modification request will be analysed with the customer to form a requirements specification for the modification.

The design stage of the maintenance process model closely follows the design stage of the SDLC. There will also be a need to identify any new modules that are required, any modules that need to be replaced, any modules that need to be modified and any modules that need to be scrapped. Test plans will be created in preparation for the testing stage.

The implementation stage is very similar to the development stage of the SDLC but should not be confused with the implementation/installation stage of the SDLC. Implementation will involve following the design to implement the changes to modules. A technique known as software re-engineering will be used. Software re-engineering can involve:

- deciding whether the whole system needs re-engineering or just part of it

- performing reverse engineering to obtain specifications of the existing software

- restructuring the program (if required)

- restructuring the data (if required)

- forward engineering to get the re-engineered software through software engineering methods.

Reverse-engineering involves analysing and understanding the existing system to produce a system specification. This is required when original specifications are unavailable. The process involves examining the code in depth to generate a design. The design is then used to generate a system specification.

Program restructuring could involve re-writing the program in a different programming language or restructuring the way modules are used within a program. Program restructuring is often required to enable obsolete hardware to be decommissioned.

Throughout the implementation stage, modules that are introduced or modified should be tested, including their impact on other parts of the system. The impact on the rest of the system of scrapping any modules should also be tested.

During system testing, new and modified modules will be tested together as a group. This type of testing is known as integration testing because the testing is designed to expose faults in the interaction between integrated units. Following this, regression testing will take place. This is effectively re-running the original test plan for the original software to ensure that the software continues to perform as expected after the change. It is called regression testing because if a change causes a new fault, then that is a regression.

Acceptance testing involves the users testing the system following the change. Users will be able to confirm whether issues have been addressed by the change or if there are any adverse effects on the system following the change. Simple modifications to a system may not require this stage.

The delivery stage is similar to the implementation/installation stage of the SDLC where the existing software will be upgraded to include the modification that has been developed. This will include any additional training that is required by users and updates to the user documentation.

Maintenance management is an essential part of maintenance in terms of documenting changes. It involves ensuring that version control is in place and is fully documented. Version control identifies each update made to the software and will include technical documentation for that update. Without version control, software revisions become unmanageable and it is impossible to identify when changes were made and what impact those changes may have had on the software. This makes finding a bug in the system very difficult because there is no documentation to show the changes which may have caused that bug.

Question

18 Give a situation when corrective maintenance would be required.

REFLECTION

Discuss the types of software maintenance you have seen take place on mobile phones.

16.8 Prototyping

A **prototype** is a 'mock-up' of a software solution in a primitive form. It is used during the design stage to demonstrate how a system will look and work. It is usually focused on the user interface, rather than any data structures. It is used so that the client can get a feel for the new system before it is developed and can provide feedback that can then be acted upon. The client is also able to compare the prototype against the requirements specification. The client also has an opportunity to explain their requirements more clearly having seen the designer's interpretation.

> **KEY WORD**
>
> **prototype:** a 'mock-up' of a software solution in a primitive form

Types of prototyping

Incremental prototyping

This type of prototyping takes an iterative approach in that requirements are specified, an initial prototype is developed, the prototype is reviewed and then requirements are clarified and the prototype is improved based on feedback.

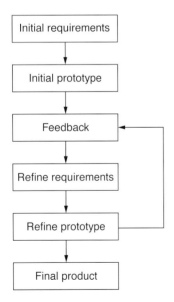

Figure 16.13: Iterative prototyping.

Each prototype will build upon the previous one and include more functionality until a final product is built. At each stage, only clearly understood requirements are developed. Each prototype can be functional and if required can be used by the client until the next iteration of the prototype is ready. This means that the end users may request enhanced or new features that they discover they require as the prototypes are being developed, features they wouldn't have envisaged at the initial requirements specification stage.

Evolutionary prototyping

Evolutionary prototyping follows a similar pattern to incremental prototyping in that it is iterative in nature. However, unlike incremental prototyping, there is no requirements specification at the start of the project, but instead there might be a goal or an aim. Both the analyst and developer begin the project by brainstorming ideas. The developer will start working on some of the best ideas so far while the analyst will discuss with the customer what the problem is and what is needed to solve the problem.

After a few days, the analyst and developer will compare notes. The developer will demonstrate how they have implemented ideas and the analyst will talk about what the customer has said. Following this discussion, the developer will continue with development focusing on the needs of the customer that are understood most clearly, while the analyst will get feedback from the customer and get more clarification on their needs. This process will continue as the product evolves from a goal to a usable piece of software. This evolutionary approach is often used by start-ups or where new ideas are being experimented with.

Throwaway/rapid prototyping

With throwaway prototyping, also known as rapid prototyping, the prototype will never become part of the final delivered software, but will be discarded. A loosely working model is created following a short investigation, with the aim being to get something tangible to the client as soon as possible for feedback as to how well the requirements are being met.

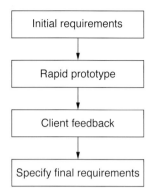

Figure 16.14: Throwaway prototyping.

This enables the requirements to be fine-tuned early in the process, which is more cost-effective than trying to make changes later when considerable work has been carried out. The main aspect to the prototype will be the user interface which the client will be able to test and experience. The interface will appear to work by being simulated.

The advantages and disadvantages of prototyping

The advantages and disadvantages of prototyping are shown in Table 16.9.

Advantages	Disadvantages
Problems can be identified early during the process and modifications made before it becomes very costly to make changes.	Requirements analysis can be rushed, meaning that prototypes don't reflect much of what the end users were expecting.
Requirements can be clarified and refined following feedback on the prototypes.	With rapid prototyping, the prototype can become rushed and, when trying to develop it into a working system, it may have significant design flaws or structural errors that carry through to the end solution.

Advantages	Disadvantages
The end users will be involved more in the process, giving them more ownership of the solution and providing valuable feedback.	When users see the prototype, they can often get lots of new ideas about features they would like to be included, which can lead to disappointment if these features can't be funded. This is known as 'feature creep'.
If the prototype is evolutionary, then users can get used to using parts of the system before having to use the whole system, which will reduce the need for bulk training. It's much cheaper to make changes earlier in the process than after real development has taken place.	When users see what looks like a working interface with a throwaway prototype, they don't realise how much more effort is required to make it into a working solution and may have false expectations as to the timescale. The iterative process of feedback can sometimes last too long if the user is regularly wanting changes to be made to the latest prototype.
By listening to feedback from end users, the developers will have a much better understanding of what the users are expecting and so a better quality solution will be provided.	The initial costs of developing a prototype are high compared with traditional designs.

Table 16.9: Advantages and disadvantages of prototyping.

Question

19 Compare and contrast evolutionary and throwaway prototyping.

16.9 Methods of software development

Types of development

Software development tends to fall into two main categories which are **incremental development** and **iterative development**. Both types of development can be followed mutually exclusively or in co-existence with each other.

> ### KEY WORDS
>
> **incremental development:** creating a system or adding new functionality in small parts
>
> **iterative development:** creating a system or adding new functionality in a repetitive cycle

Incremental development is about development in phases. Part of the software is developed fully, including improvements from feedback, before moving on to the next part of the software.

Iterative development is about planned rework throughout a project. It allows for feedback to be given by the customer and improvements to be made based on that feedback. It usually involves building a bit of every part of a solution before seeking feedback and then revisiting the whole solution to make improvements.

A typical analogy used to describe incremental and iterative development is that of an artist. A landscape artist following the incremental approach might start by painting a picture of a house and perfect that picture before moving on to painting something else. Then the artist may paint a tree and perfect that tree before moving on to the next object.

A landscape artist following the iterative approach would sketch an outline of the whole landscape. The artist might then start to add background colour to all parts of the landscape. The artist might then start to add details to all parts of the landscape. The artist will keep revisiting the picture and changing it until they are happy with the final picture.

Development methodologies
Waterfall method

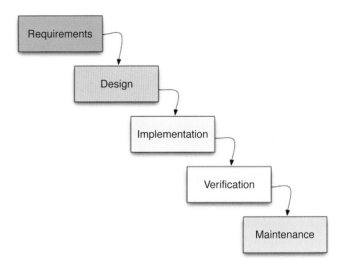

Figure 16.15: Waterfall method.

The waterfall method is an iterative development model. The waterfall method involves gathering all the user requirements at the beginning of the project. There will be considerable communication with the user at this stage in order to elicit the requirements of the potential solution. When the requirements are defined, the process runs 'downhill' like a waterfall.

During the design stage, the interface and the structure of the system will be designed. During implementation, often referred to as development, the system will be developed, which often involves programming. The purpose of the verification phase is to ensure that the project meets the customer's requirements. The system will then be used and during its use there may be problems that are discovered that need to be corrected or other changes that need to be made. This is known as maintenance.

As each stage starts, changes may need to be made to the previous stage as a result of user feedback or lessons that have been learned during that stage. This is what makes the model iterative.

The waterfall method relies upon the requirements being clearly defined, which is an unrealistic expectation, so it is fundamentally flawed. It was originally used in manufacturing and then adopted into computing, but with adaptions that included the need to revisit the requirements.

The system life cycle discussed in this chapter is based on the waterfall model and there are many variations in existence.

The advantages and disadvantages of the waterfall method are shown in Table 16.10.

Advantages	Disadvantages
Each stage is completed before moving onto the next stage making management of the project more structured and controllable.	The customer only sees the product at the end of the project.
It's a simple model to understand and use because each stage is distinctly separate from the other stages.	It's hard to measure progress within each stage because the milestones are just the beginning and end of each stage.
It works well for projects where the requirements are clearly understood and are unlikely to change.	It doesn't work well for complex projects where the requirements cover a large variety of aspects and aren't clearly understood by everyone involved.
The process followed and the resulting software are well documented, meaning new team members can get up to speed very quickly.	Projects can take longer to deliver than other methods because of the emphasis on planning and documentation.
The client and project team work to a set timescale and a set budget which removes a lot of uncertainty from projects.	Client involvement is limited to set times within the project which can lead to requirements not being met to the client's expectation.
The requirements are clearly set from the beginning of the project and are used to measure the project's success when it is completed.	The model doesn't accommodate changes to requirements.

Table 16.10: Advantages and disadvantages of the waterfall method.

Agile

The agile approach to software development is able to respond to a customer's changing requirements, even late in the development life cycle. It is expected that the customer's requirements will evolve as the project develops. The process can cope with change and harness that change for the benefit of the customer.

Following the agile approach, individuals and the interaction between people is valued more highly than design processes and tools. Similarly, it is more important that working software is developed than having comprehensive supporting documentation. Collaboration with the customer is expected to underpin the whole project with contract negotiations taking a less important role. While planning is necessary, flexibility is more important in the agile approach and so responding to change is essential. These are summarised in a manifesto for agile software development as valuing:

- individuals and interactions over processes and tools
- working software over comprehensive documentation
- customer collaboration over contract negotiation
- responding to change over following a plan.

Unlike the waterfall model which has separate phases throughout the system lifecycle, the agile approach uses iterations with each iteration including the planning, design, development and testing of part of the software. At the end of an iteration, a working solution for that part of the software is ready for demonstration. Several iterations are usually required before a product is ready to be released or updated.

As an iteration includes designers, developers and testers, they are expected to be located in the same place. This ensures a collaborative approach to each iteration. Each team will also include a customer representative, sometimes referred to as a product owner, who represents the client and must be available to developers throughout an iteration. Working closely together means that feedback is instantaneous and enables a flexible approach to be taken to the design and development. There will often be a daily 'scrum', which is a briefing session where each team member reports to the others on their work so far and their plan for their next stage of development.

One technique used in agile software development is pair programming where two programmers work at the same computer with one being the driver who writes the code and the other being the observer who reviews each line of code. The observer is expected to think about potential improvements that could be made and pre-empt potential problems that might take place.

Agile is both iterative and incremental. It's incremental because each iteration can be planned to be improved

upon in future iterations. It's important not to get the words iteration and iterative confused. Each iteration increments the existing functionality and each iteration is iterative in nature.

The advantages and disadvantages of agile software development are shown in Table 16.11.

Advantages	Disadvantages
The customer gets to see completed parts of software quickly which enables them to adapt their requirements for other parts of the software.	As requirements change, it's difficult to know how much a project is going to cost and how long it will take.
The customer, designers, developers and testers are constantly interacting with each other which reduces delay.	The project can easily go off track if requirements change too much.
If the business needs aren't fully known at the start of the project then they can evolve as the project progresses.	Experienced senior programmers are needed to be able to make quick decisions during each iteration.
There is unlimited access to the customer which means their needs are more likely to be met.	There will be minimal documentation produced which means new team members can take longer to get up to speed with the project and there can be a large learning curve when maintaining the software.
There is no complicated bureaucracy that delays decision making.	Projects may seem to never have an end in sight.
The customer doesn't have a fixed budget or timescale so customer needs can be met above timescales and budgets.	Not having a fixed budget or timescale creates a lot of uncertainty for the client and is not a popular move with senior members of an organisation.
Parts of the software can be deployed when they are ready so the customer sees the value of that software sooner.	The software, especially the user interface, can become disjointed because each iteration is worked on separately.
Bugs and problems can be fixed quickly because the designers, developers and testers for each iteration are working closely together.	

Table 16.11: Advantages and disadvantages of agile software development.

Rapid application development

Rapid application development (RAD) uses prototyping to develop a system in a very short time frame, usually less than six months. Instead of following a traditional requirements gathering approach, requirements are gathered through focus groups. Users are key players in the prototyping stage and provide feedback for refinements. This type of user involvement is known as joint application development (JAD) because the user is jointly involved with the developer in the development

of the system. Less time is spent on planning and design and more emphasis is put on the development phase.

> **KEY WORD**
>
> **rapid application development (RAD):** use of prototyping to develop a system in a very short time frame

Strict deadlines are allocated throughout the development of the system to ensure that the product is developed and finished on time by allocating time boxes to the development of each requirement. This requires understanding from the user that, if requirements are too complex, then they must be simplified or removed from the project. The RAD approach will also try to reuse any modules of software that already exist and are available, rather than always developing from scratch. Software application frameworks can be used to develop the solution whereby a complex graphical user interface can be created using drag and drop functionality. This enables users to be involved in the actual design of the interface as part of the JAD approach and they can see the interface taking shape in real time.

RAD is based on an incremental model in that each timebox will deliver specific functionality. However, it's not necessary to complete a timebox before moving onto another one as timeboxes can be developed in parallel.

The advantages and disadvantages of RAD are shown in Table 16.12.

Advantages	Disadvantages
The high level of user involvement means that the end solution is more likely to be suitable for the end users, who will also have ownership of the solution.	Requirements are not clearly specified from the outset and so the final solution may not meet the entire needs of the organisation.
Users are often not sure of what the requirements of a system should be from the outset and so the evolutionary approach of RAD enables the requirements to evolve.	Users are required throughout the whole process and they also have their normal day jobs to do. This can lead to work overload or the need for temporary staff.
As users are involved throughout the whole project, it is quickly recognised when a requirement is overambitious and therefore the requirement can be simplified or removed at an early stage.	The structure of the system may be compromised, leading to instability, as the focus is on the user interface and getting a system developed rapidly.
The strict deadlines ensure that the project will be completed on time and prevents 'feature creep'.	The strict deadlines mean that some parts of the project could be rushed and not completed to a high enough quality.
Prototyping of the interface with user involvement means less time is spent on design and more on development, leading to a shorter overall project.	Existing software modules will not have been designed for the exact requirements of the system and so may not provide sufficient functionality.
Software application frameworks mean that a user interface can be developed quickly and users can even be involved in configuring the layouts of screens and reports.	Software application frameworks don't produce particularly efficient code and so the end solution will not run as quickly as if it had been developed from scratch.
	Users who are not involved in the JAD approach may be disappointed that they didn't have a say in the process and the system may not meet their specific needs.

Table 16.12: Advantages and disadvantages of RAD.

Questions

20 Describe the differences between incremental and iterative methods of development.

21 Describe joint application development.

EXAM-STYLE QUESTIONS

Thornhill Estates runs several hotels. It would like a new software solution to manage room bookings, dinner reservations and purchases across all its hotels. It has asked a software developer to produce the software for them. The software developer will follow the system life cycle.

1 a State one purpose of analysis in the system life cycle. [1]

   b Suggest four reasons why questionnaires would be appropriate for researching how bookings are currently managed at the hotel. [4]

   c State three other methods that could be used to research the current booking system. [3]

[Total 8]

The analyst will interview a group of users to create a requirements specification.

2 State the purpose of a requirements specification. [1]

The designer will create a design specification based on the requirements specification.

3 a Identify three factors that should be considered when designing a screen layout. [3]

   b Using an example, show how a validation rule could be designed for the hotel booking system. [3]

   c Apart from keyboards, mice and monitors, describe three external hardware components that will be needed by the hotel system. [3]

[Total 9]

An evolutionary prototype approach will be used during the design and development of the software.

4 a Define the term 'prototype'. [1]

   b Justify the manager's choice of an evolutionary approach. [4]

[Total 5]

Once the system has been developed, it will need to be tested.

5 a Describe two differences between white box and black box testing. [4]

   b Explain one reason why beta testing might not be appropriate for the hotel system. [2]

   c Explain why invalid test data is used. [2]

[Total 8]

The system will be installed in a pilot approach and user documentation will be provided to the hotel staff.

6 a Justify the choice of the pilot approach of installation for the hotel system. [4]

   b Explain why the user documentation should include troubleshooting and glossary sections. [4]

   c Suggest four reasons why the hotel system may require maintenance in the future. [4]

[Total 12]

SUMMARY CHECKLIST

- ☐ I can describe the stages in the system life cycle.
- ☐ I can describe methods of research for a given situation.
- ☐ I can understand the content and purpose of specifications.
- ☐ I can construct diagrams to represent system processing and the flow of data through a system.
- ☐ I can design data storage, input forms and output reports.
- ☐ I can create a test plan and understand its purpose.
- ☐ I can select appropriate test data.
- ☐ I can describe the differences between alpha and beta testing.
- ☐ I can describe the differences between white box and black box testing.
- ☐ I can describe different methods of implementing a system.
- ☐ I can explain the advantages and disadvantages of each implementation method for a given situation.
- ☐ I can describe types of documentation and explain why each is needed.
- ☐ I can describe the contents of documentation.
- ☐ I can explain methods of evaluating a new system.
- ☐ I can describe different types of maintenance and explain why each is needed.
- ☐ I can explain how each type of maintenance is carried out.
- ☐ I can explain different types of prototyping and explain why each is needed.
- ☐ I can explain the advantages and disadvantages of each type of prototyping.
- ☐ I can describe the stages and processes of different software development methodologies.
- ☐ I can explain the advantages and disadvantages of different software development methodologies.

Chapter 17

Mail merge

LEARNING INTENTIONS

By the end of this chapter, you will be able to:

- use, create and edit source data using appropriate software

- create a master document structure

- link a master document to a source file

- specify rules selecting recipients and for managing document content

- set up manual completion, automatic completion and calculated fields

- use manual methods and software tools to ensure error-free accuracy

- perform mail merge.

- Do you know how to create documents using a word processor?

- Do you know how to create data sources using a database or spreadsheet?

Introduction

A **mail merge** is the automatic process of merging data, such as names and addresses, from a **source file** into a **master document**, such as a letter. You can save time writing the same letter to lots of different people when their data already exists in a data source.

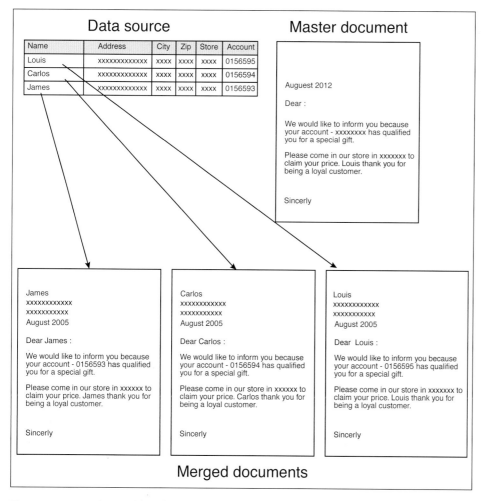

Figure 17.1: Mail merge documents.

17.1 Mail merge letters

Create a master document structure

A master document is the main letter, email, memo, fax or other document that you can send to all recipients from the data source.

WORKED EXAMPLE 17.01

17.01 Learner letter.docx is a master document. It is a letter written to learner drivers in a driving school. The words in italics are the data that needs to be inserted about each learner driver and will be obtained from the data source.

Pass 1ˢᵗ Driving School

Date will go here

Full name of recipient will go here
Full address of recipient will go here

Dear *forename*

We are conducting an annual check of our records. Could you please confirm that your telephone number is *telephone* and your mobile number is *mobile*.

We would be grateful if you could email us at info@pass1st.info with your email address.

Yours sincerely

Ben Dean
Senior Instructor

Figure 17.2: Master document.

Notice how a standard letter includes the letterhead of the organisation sending the letter, the date of the letter and the full name and address of the recipient of the letter. When you produce a letter on a computer, it should always have all the text (except the letterhead) aligned to the left.

PRACTICAL ACTIVITY 17.01

Create a master document that you will use to write to customers of the company IT Distribution Inc. You should create the letter in a standard letter format, including space for the recipient's name and address. Your letter should invite the customer to participate in a survey with the opportunity to win one of ten prizes each worth $250. Tell customers that the survey is available online and is available for two months from the date of the letter.

Create a source file

You need to create a source file that contains the data the computer will include in each mail-merged document. This source file usually consists of names and addresses and other information about the people you are writing to.

WORKED EXAMPLE 17.02

17.02 Driving School.mdb contains a table called Learner which includes the names, addresses, telephone numbers and mobile numbers of learner drivers in a driving school.

Source files can be in a variety of formats including:

- database table
- database query
- spreadsheet
- word-processed table
- variable length text file (for example, comma-separated values)
- fixed length text file
- email contacts.

PRACTICAL ACTIVITY 17.02

1   Examine the structure of the following data sources and identify which formats they are in:

a   17.03 Student.csv

b   17.04 Student.rtf

c   17.05 Student.txt

d   17.06 Student.xlsx

e   17.07 Student.mdb (examine the student table)

f   17.07 Student.mdb (examine the query)

2   Create a data source using a table in a word processor that will include the following **fields** (categories of information):

a   forename

b   surname

c   email address.

3   Create three records in the data source.

KEY WORD

field: a category of information from the data source

Link a master document to a source file

Your master document needs to know the source location of the data. You therefore need to link the master document to the data source.

WORKED EXAMPLE 17.03

17.01 Learner letter.docx has been linked to the Learner table in **17.02 Driving school.mdb**.

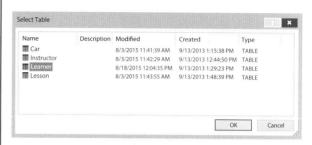

Figure 17.3: Database link.

The records from the data source are identified in the master document in the recipient list.

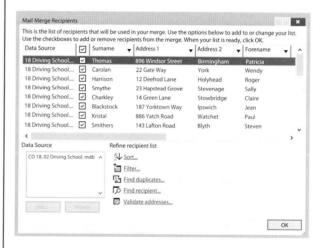

Figure 17.4: Recipients.

PRACTICAL ACTIVITY 17.03

1   Open the master document **17.08 New class.docx** and link it to each of the following data sources one at a time. Finish by linking it to the query from the database.

a   17.03 Student.csv

b   17.04 Student.rtf

c   17.05 Student.txt

d   17.06 Student.xlsx

CONTINUED

e 17.07 Student.mdb (link to the Student table)

f 17.07 Student.mdb (link to the query)

Open the letter that you wrote for IT Distribution Inc. Use it as a master document and link it to the table Customer in 17.09 Sales processing.mdb.

Set up fields

Having a link from the master document to the source file only tells the master document which file to use. The master document also needs to know which fields to put into the document and where to place them.

WORKED EXAMPLE 17.04

17.10 Learner letter with fields.docx includes the merge fields from the Learner table in 17.02 Driving school.mdb. The merge fields are highlighted in yellow and have been inserted in place of the placeholder names in Worked Example 17.01.

Pass 1st Driving School

14 June 2019

«Forename» «Surname»
«Address_1»
«Address_2»
«Post_Code»

Dear «Forename»

We are conducting an annual check of our records. Could you please confirm that your telephone number is «Telephone» and your mobile number is «Mobile».

We would be grateful if you could email us at info@pass1st.info with your email address.

Yours sincerely

Ben Dean
Senior Instructor

Figure 17.5: Merge fields.

When you eventually run the merge, the fields will be replaced with data from the Learner table.

PRACTICAL ACTIVITY 17.04

1 Use the master document 17.08 New class.docx that you linked to the query in the database 17.07 Student.mdb. Insert merge fields for forename, surname and class.

2 Open the letter that you wrote for IT Distribution Inc. and linked to 17.09 Sales processing.mdb. Insert merge fields in the appropriate places.

Perform mail merge using the master document and data sources

Now that you have entered the fields, the mail merge can be completed. You need to tell the software to carry out the merge process. It is usually possible to preview the results of the mail merge prior to printing or creating a new document with the merged letters. It is also possible to merge the letters to an email address for each recipient.

WORKED EXAMPLE 17.05

17.10 Learner letter with fields.docx can be previewed. The data from the first record of the data source 17.02 Driving school.mdb is highlighted in yellow.

Pass 1st Driving School

18 August 2015

Patricia Thomas
896 Windsor Street
Birmingham
B21 4BR

Dear Patricia

We are conducting an annual check of our records. Could you please confirm that your telephone number is 0555 555 555 and your mobile number is 0777 777 726.

We would be grateful if you could email us at info@pass1st.info with your email address.

Yours sincerely

Ben Dean
Senior Instructor

Figure 17.6: Merge preview.

1   Open **17.10 Learner letter with fields.docx** and merge to a new document. Notice how all the records have been included so that there is one letter for every learner.

2   As you have added merge fields, use the master document **17.08 New class.docx** to merge to a new document.

3   Open the letter that you wrote for IT Distribution Inc. Merge the letters to send as emails to the email address field in the Customer table.

Edit the source data

You can edit the source data by making changes to the source file. However, if a master document that is linked to the source file is open, then it is possible that the source file will be locked and you won't be able to edit it. You must remember to close the master document before making changes to the source file. Any changes made to the source file will be visible in the master document.

Some word processors allow the source data to be edited directly from within the word processor.

WORKED EXAMPLE 17.06

17.10 Learner letter with fields.docx has been used to edit the data source and change Patricia Thomas' surname to Donaldson.

Figure 17.7: Edit source data.

Be careful when you edit the data source because other users may be using it and so any changes you make would affect other users.

PRACTICAL ACTIVITY 17.06

1   Open **17.08 New class.docx** that you have already merged with **17.07 Student. mdb**. Edit the data source to change Chloe Carson's surname to 'Carlton'.

2   Open the letter that you wrote for IT Distribution Inc, and linked to **17.09 Sales processing.mdb**. Edit the data source to change Carmella Wishman's email address to 'carmella.w@wishman.com'.

Mail merge labels

You can use mail merge to create labels or similar documents such as business cards from a data source. You can set up the document as a table with each cell representing a label, business card or similar. Each cell will contain the merge fields from one record from the data source.

WORKED EXAMPLE 17.07

17.11 Instructor Labels.docx has been set up to use labels. It is set up to use the labels named L7263 which defines the measurements of the label.

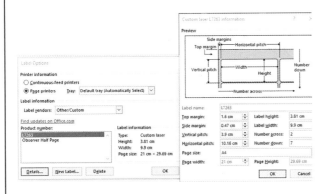
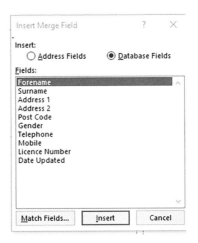

Figure 17.8: Setting up the labels.

The label layout has been merged with the Instructors table from **17.02 Driving School.mdb**. A table is created for each label and a <<Next Record>> field is added to each of the cells in the table except the first one. The <<Next Record>> field means that the next record from the data source will be displayed so that each cell contains data about a separate record from the data source.

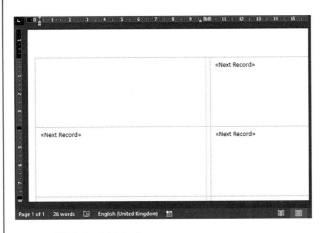

Figure 17.9: Initial label merge structure.

You can now add merge fields to the first label.

Figure 17.10: Adding merge fields to the labels.

You can update the rest of the labels to include the same merge fields as the first label. A preview of the labels shows the merged content.

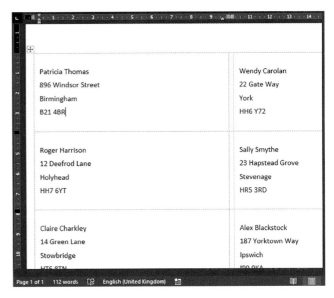

Figure 17.11: Preview of merged labels.

1   Create a new word-processing document and set it up to contain labels. Link the document to the data source **7.07 Student. mdb** using the query Qry Student Teacher.

2   Using merge fields, create a set of labels that shows each student's name, their class and their teacher.

3   Create a new word-processing document that is linked to the Sales Rep table from **17.09 Sales processing.mdb**. Use the mail-merge labels feature to create a business card for each sales representative. You can create business cards instead of labels by selecting a business card page layout from the label options.

17.2 Manipulating mail-merge documents

Create prompts

You can use master documents several times and on many different occasions. There may be some data that needs to be included within the master document that is not part of the data source but will change each time the mail merge is run. A **prompt** can be given to the user. This is a question that asks them what the data should be.

prompt: a question asked to the user which requires a response

17.12 Learner letter with fill-in prompt.docx asks the user to enter the name of the senior instructor who will sign the letter.

Figure 17.12: Fill-in.

The Fill-In prompt rule can be viewed as a merge field code.

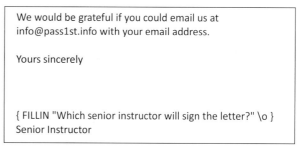

Figure 17.13: Fill-in code.

When you process the mail merge, the user is prompted for the name of the senior instructor.

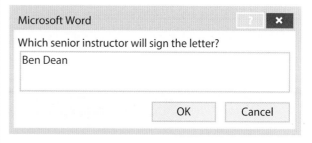

Figure 17.14: Prompt.

Note that Microsoft Word uses rules to control the way the mail merge works. Fill-In is one of these rules. It is most commonly used to ask for one item of data that will be the same for every letter. However, by deselecting 'Ask once', you could have a different response for every recipient.

PRACTICAL ACTIVITY 17.08

1   Open the master document **17.08 New class.docx** to which you have added merge fields. Add a Fill-In prompt for the name of the Head of Year.

2   Open the letter that you wrote for IT Distribution Inc. before you completed the mail merge process. Add a Fill-In prompt for the date when the survey will close.

There are occasions when the same data needs to be included more than once within a document. In these situations, an Ask prompt can be used instead of a Fill-In prompt. The Ask prompt stores the response in a bookmark which can be placed in more than one location in a document.

WORKED EXAMPLE 17.09

17.13 Learner letter with ask prompt.docx prompt asks the user to enter the date by which the information should be returned. You will notice that the difference from the Fill-In prompt is that the Ask prompt needs a bookmark to be defined. This has been defined as 'ActionBy'. You will also notice that the default text has been completed. This is necessary in order to be able to reference the bookmark.

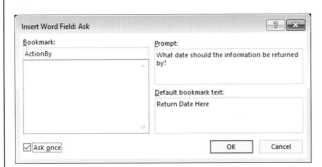

Figure 17.15: Ask.

You can view the Ask prompt rule as a merge field code, but its location is not important because the bookmark will be referenced in the required locations.

> Yours sincerely
>
> { FILLIN "Which senior instructor will sign the letter?" \o }
> Senior Instructor
> { ASK ActionBy "What date should the information be returned by?" \d "Return Date Here" \0 }

Figure 17.16: Ask code.

You now need to reference the bookmark in the document. You can do this by inserting a reference point.

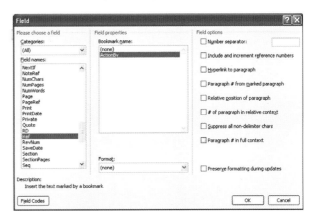

Figure 17.17: Reference point.

Here, you can see two reference points highlighted in yellow that have been inserted.

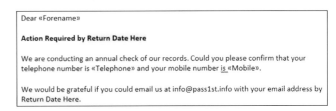

Dear «Forename»

Action Required by Return Date Here

We are conducting an annual check of our records. Could you please confirm that your telephone number is «Telephone» and your mobile number is «Mobile».

We would be grateful if you could email us at info@pass1st.info with your email address by Return Date Here.

Figure 17.18: Reference point text.

CONTINUED

You can also view these as merge field codes.

> Dear { MERGEFIELD Forename }
>
> **Action Required by { REF ActionBy * MERGEFORMAT }**
>
> We are conducting an annual check of our records. Could you please confirm that your telephone number is { MERGEFIELD Telephone } and your mobile number is { MERGEFIELD Mobile }.
>
> We would be grateful if you could email us at info@pass1st.info with your email address by { REF. ActionBy * MERGEFORMAT }.

Figure 17.19: Reference code.

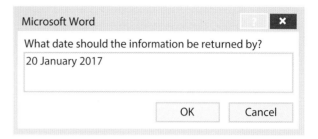

Figure 17.20: Prompt.

When you process the mail merge, you are prompted for the information return date.

If you look carefully at the field code for the Ask prompt you will notice that it includes the name of the bookmark. This can be useful in other ways because you can reference the data by other rules in the same way that data in fields can be referenced.

PRACTICAL ACTIVITY 17.09

Open the master document **17.08 New class.docx**. You will already have added merge fields to this. Instead of a Fill-In prompt, add an Ask prompt for the name of the Head of Year and assign a bookmark. Insert references to the bookmark at the end of the document where the Head of Year will sign and a new sentence that will inform the parents who the Head of Year will be.

Automatically select the required records

Data sources can often have thousands of records. The document that is being produced may not need to be merged with every record. It is therefore possible to set conditions to select which records will be included in the mail merge by using a **filter**.

KEY WORD

filter: selecting records from the source file based on conditions

WORKED EXAMPLE 17.10

17.14 Learner letter with filter.docx has filtered the records so that the letter will only be sent to male learners whose records haven't been updated since 1 January 2015.

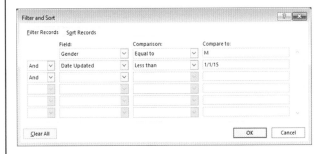

Figure 17.21: Filter.

The recipient list now only includes the filtered records, so the letter will only be sent to those recipients.

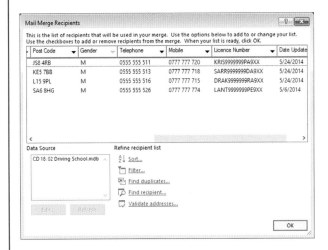

Figure 17.22: Filter records.

Sort the merged documents

The data source may not be sorted in the order in which the user wants to merge the documents.

WORKED EXAMPLE 17.11

17.15 Learner letter with sort.docx has sorted the records by surname and if any surnames are the same then by forename.

Figure 17.23: Selecting sort order.

PRACTICAL ACTIVITY 17.10

1   Open the master document **17.08 New class.docx** that you have added merge fields. Set the filter so that the letter is only sent to students in class 9F.

2   Change the filter so that the letter is sent to students in classes 9F or 9B.

3   Change the order of merged letters so they are sent to students in surname order. If any students have the same surname, then they should be sorted by forename.

4   Open the letter that you wrote for IT Distribution Inc. Set the filter so that the merged email is only sent to customers who have agreed to receive marketing and live in the state of California (CA).

5   Change the order of the merged email so they are sorted by postcode or ZIP code.

Rules for managing document content

Data sources are often fixed and cannot be changed. Therefore, any data manipulation may need to take place in the merge master document. The IF...THEN... ELSE rule can be used to insert text conditionally based on data within the data source.

WORKED EXAMPLE 17.12

17.16 Learner letter with condition.docx is to have a new sentence that asks users to confirm their gender has been stored correctly. You can see here how the IF statement was set up.

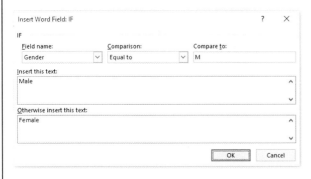

Figure 17.24: IF...THEN...ELSE..

This can be seen in field code view as shown here.

> Our records show that your gender is { IF { MERGEFIELD Gender] = "M" "Male" "Female" }.

Figure 17.25: IF...THEN...ELSE code.

This will work for situations where there are only two alternatives. However, when more than two alternatives are required, you will need to use a different method. One option is to use a series of IF...THEN...ELSE rules to cover each eventuality.

WORKED EXAMPLE 17.13

Some records may not have the gender recorded. In this situation, the letter should state 'your gender is not recorded in our records – please confirm your gender'. There are now three options: F, M or [blank] in **17.17 Learner letter with three conditions.docx.** ELSE cannot be used because it would apply the second outcome to both of options two and three. Here, three separate IF...THEN...ELSE rules have been used without defining the ELSE part.

> Our records show that your gender is { IF { MERGEFIELD Gender } = "M" "Male" }{ IF { MERGEFIELD Gender } = "F" "Female" }{ IF { MERGEFIELD Gender } = "" "not recorded in our records – please confirm your gender" }.

Figure 17.26: Separate IFs.

The other option you can use is a nested IF...THEN... ELSE rule. This involves using another IF...THEN...ELSE rule as the ELSE part of the original IF...THEN...ELSE rule. You can only manipulate this in field code view.

TIP

Note that the nested IF...THEN... ELSE rule do not work in Open/Libre office

WORKED EXAMPLE 17.14

17.18 Learner letter with nested conditions.docx has used a NESTED IF by entering the IF...THEN... ELSE rules within the ELSE parts of previous rules.

> Our records show that your gender is { IF { MERGEFIELD Gender } } = "M" "Male" }{ IF { MERGEFIELD Gender } = "F" "Female" }{ IF { MERGEFIELD Gender } = "" "not recorded in our records – please confirm your gender" }.

Figure 17.27: Nested IFs.

It achieves the same outcome as the previous example, but is a bit more complex. The speech marks need to be in exactly the right places, as do the curly brackets.

You can use AND or OR operators within the IF... THEN...ELSE rule. You can also include text from files as the outcome or pictures as the outcome. You may want to research how these can be achieved.

PRACTICAL ACTIVITY 17.11

1   Open the file **17.19 Vehicle Data Sheet. docx** which has been merged with the Car table from **17.02 Driving School.mdb.**

2   Change the field for the Transmission so that it automatically displays 'Manual' instead of 'M' and 'Automatic' instead of 'A'.

3   Open the letter that you wrote for IT Distribution Inc. Add a sentence that tells customers who live in California (CA) that they have a special discount. If they live in California then the sentence should read 'As you live in California, you are entitled to a special 10% discount until the end of this month.'

Rules for selecting recipients

One method of deciding which records will be included from the data source is to use a filter. Another method you can use is a rule, which is a merge field code that will control which records will be omitted. The rule is called SKIP IF and this will omit the record from the mail merge if the conditions are met.

WORKED EXAMPLE 17.15

17.20 Learner letter with selection codes.docx includes a SKIP IF rule that states that if the gender field is equal to "M" then the record should be skipped.

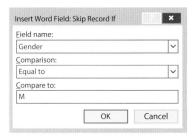

Figure 17.28: Skip If set up.

SKIP IF a rule is inserted into the document.

{ SKIPIF { MERGEFIELD Gender } = "M" }**Pass 1ˢᵗ Driving School**

Figure 17.29: Skip If code.

The rule should always be inserted at the beginning of the document. When using Microsoft Word, you will need to complete the merge to see which records have been skipped as they will still show when previewing the merge.

PRACTICAL ACTIVITY 17.12

1 Open the master document **17.08 New class.docx**.
    a Add a rule to skip records for class 9B.
    b Add a second rule to also skip records for class 9F.
2 Open the letter that you wrote for IT Distribution Inc. and remove any filters that you have applied.

CONTINUED

a Add a rule to skip records for customers who have chosen not to receive marketing (this is a Boolean field that can be TRUE or FALSE).
b Add additional rules to skip records for customers who are based in New York (NY), California (CA) or Texas (TX).

17.3 Arithmetic operators

There are occasions when the merged data needs to have a calculation performed on it. For example, a discount might be offered when writing or the tax might need to be calculated on a price. It may not be possible to perform this calculation within the data source itself and so a calculation can be performed on the merge field. When a calculation is performed, it is known as a **calculated field**.

KEY WORD

calculated field: an arithmetic calculation on a field from the data source

WORKED EXAMPLE 17.16

The file **17.21 Instructor letter with calculation. docx** has been merged with the Instructor table from **17.09 Sales processing.mdb**.

«Forename» «Surname»

Statement of Tax

Your hourly charge is £«Charge»

The amount of tax we collect from this is

Figure 17.30: Instructor letter.

The formula option has been selected and a formula added to multiply the charge by 0.2. The number format has been set to currency with two decimal places.

CONTINUED

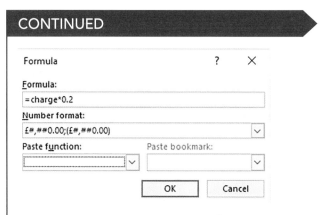

Figure 17.31: Setting up a calculated field.

This initially gives an error because 'charge' doesn't mean anything.

Figure 17.32: Bookmark error.

The field codes can be edited using Alt+F9 and the Charge merge field can be inserted in place of 'charge' within the calculation.

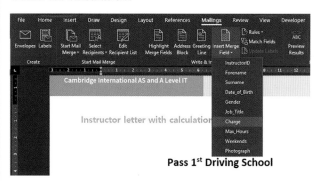

Figure 17.33: Including a merge field in a calculation.

The merge field is now included within the calculation.

Figure 17.34: Calculated field with merge field.

CONTINUED

The merge codes can be hidden (ALT+F9) to view the result of the calculation.

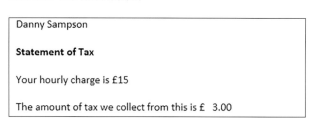

Figure 17.35: Preview of calculation.

PRACTICAL ACTIVITY 17.13

1   Open the file **17.19 Vehicle Data Sheet.docx** which has been merged with the Car table from **17.02 Driving School.mdb**.

2   Add a calculated field that states when the MOT (vehicle safety test) is due. The MOT is due three years after the vehicle was registered.

3   Open the file **17.21 Instructor letter with calculation.docx** which has been merged with **17.09 Sales processing.mdb**.

4   Add a sentence and a calculated field that tells the driving instructor their maximum number of hours available during weekdays (multiply the Max Hours by five).

5   Challenge: add a sentence and a calculated field that tells the driving instructor their maximum number of hours available during the week. This should include weekends for those who have opted to work weekends (if Weekends field set to TRUE).

Date and time fields

You can include the current date or time in a document. This doesn't have to be a merged document but can be any document. Each time you open the document or the field is refreshed, the current date or time will be displayed.

WORKED EXAMPLE 17.17

You can choose a variety of date and time formats. Ticking the Update automatically option will ensure the date or time is automatically updated.

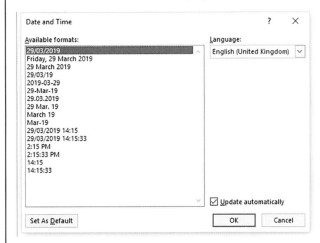

Figure 17.36: Inserting a date field.

PRACTICAL ACTIVITY 17.14

1 Open the file **17.19 Vehicle Data Sheet. docx** which has been merged with the Car table from **17.02 Driving School.mdb**.

2 Add a sentence that states the date and time the document was printed, for example 'This document was printed on <<date>> at <<time>>'. The date and time should automatically update.

3 Open the letter that you wrote for IT Distribution Inc. Add the current date to the beginning of the letter so that it updates automatically.

17.4 Document properties

Properties of the document can be included automatically including:

- filename

- author

- document title

- creation date

- number of pages.

PRACTICAL ACTIVITY 17.15

Open a word-processing file that you have created and that includes more than one page. Experiment by adding the document properties into your document.

Embedding data

You can embed data from another document. Embedding means that the data remains in the original source document but can be shown in a word-processed document. Any changes you make to the source document will be automatically updated in the word-processed document.

KEY WORD

embedding: importing data from a data source so that any changes to the data source are shown in the new document

Embedding tables

You can embed data in tabular format within a document. Any changes you make to the data in the data source will be updated in the document.

WORKED EXAMPLE 17.18

17.22 Attendance Report.docx is a report that has been written to summarise the attendance of students in a school. The attendance data has been embedded from the spreadsheet 17.23 School attendance.xlsx.

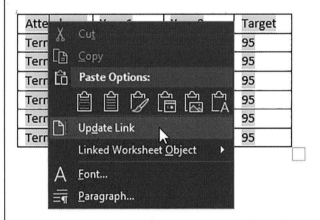

Figure 17.37: Paste and link.

Any changes you make to the selected data in 17.23 School attendance.xlsx will be updated automatically in 17.22 Attendance Report.docx the next time it is opened.

You can also update the data while the main document is open by clicking Update Link.

Figure 17.38: Updating embedded data.

Embedding charts

Similarly, you can embed data into a document from a graph or chart. Any changes to the original graph or chart will be updated automatically in the document.

WORKED EXAMPLE 17.19

17.22 Attendance Report.docx is a report that has been written to summarise the attendance of students in a school. The chart showing attendance data has been embedded from the spreadsheet 17.23 School attendance.xlsx. Here is the chart.

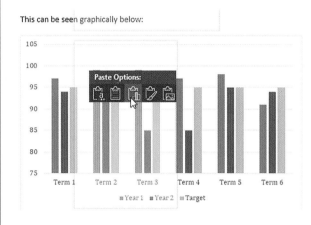

Figure 17.39: Embedding a chart from a spreadsheet.

Any changes you make to the chart in 17.23 School attendance.xlsx will be updated automatically in 17.22 Attendance Report.docx.

PRACTICAL ACTIVITY 17.16

1   Create a new word-processing document. Write a brief report summarising the results of the votes for head prefect at your school. The report should include embedded data from the table in 17.24 Graphs and charts.xlsx and an embedded pie chart from the same data source.

2   Save and close your report.

3   Open 17.24 Graphs and charts.xlsx and change the number of votes for Adrian Smith from 4 to 40.

4   Save and close the spreadsheet.

5   Reopen your report and check that the data and chart have updated automatically to show 40 votes for Adrian Smith.

17.5 Error-free accuracy and proofreading

You should carry out a number of checks before completing a mail merge.

- Run a spell check and grammar check on the master document.

- Visually check for any errors on the master document.

- Visually check for any errors on the preview or merged documents.

- Check that the correct records have been included in the filter.

Visual checking could include:

- reading the document from start to finish to see if there are any errors in grammar or spelling

- printing a copy of the document to read it instead of reading it on screen

- reading the document out loud so errors that may not be spotted visually are heard

- using a blank piece of paper to cover up the rest of the document so each line can be checked individually

- searching for common errors such as 'there' instead of 'their'.

Even if you run a spell check, it may not spot all the errors. These can include words that sound the same but are spelt differently, for example, stationery and stationary. The spell check will not be able to identify problems with layout, such as spaces that are missing or have been added by mistake. Errors in names are not spotted by a spell check and field codes will not be checked by the spell check. A visual check will also be required to see if all merge fields have been included.

WORKED EXAMPLE 17.20

17.25 Learner letter with errors.docx includes several errors.

Pass 1st Driving School

19 August 2015

«Forename»«Surname»
«Address_1»
«Address_2»
«Post_Code»

Dear «Forename»

We are conducting a anual check of our record. Could you please confirm that you're telephone number is «Telephone» and you're mobile number is «Mobile» .

We wood be greatful if you could email us at info@pass1st.info with your email address.

Yours sincerely

Ben Deane
Senior Instructor

Figure 17.40: Errors.

The grammar and spell checks have spotted some errors: 'a anual' should be 'an annual', 'wood' should be 'would' and 'greatful' should be 'grateful'.

The errors highlighted in yellow require visual checking as the grammar or spell checks have not identified them: 'record' should be 'records', 'you're' should be 'your' and 'Deane' should be 'Dean'.

The errors highlighted in blue also require visual checking but these may not be spotted until data is actually merged. Here, you can see what the data would look like when merged.

PaulKristal
886 Yatch Road
Watchet
JS8 4RB

Dear Paul

We are conducting a anual check of our record. Could you please confirm that you're telephone number is 0555 555 511 and you're mobile number is 0777 777 720 .

Figure 17.41: Merge errors.

There is no space between the forename and surname and there is an additional space after the mobile number.

The criteria for the filter are that letters should be sent to male learners whose records haven't been updated since 1 August 2015. This should mean letters going to 11 learners. However, only four letters will be produced.

Gender	Telephone	Mobile	Licence number	Date updated
M	0555 555 511	0777 777 720	KRIS9999999PA9XX	5/24/2014
M	0555 555 513	0777 777 718	SARR9999999DA9XX	5/24/2014
M	0555 555 516	0777 777 715	DRAK9999999RA9XX	5/24/2014
M	0555 555 526	0777 777 774	LANT9999999PE9XX	5/6/2014

Figure 17.42: Filter errors.

This has been spotted using a visual check. The error was due to the filter requiring an American layout of date which should be 8/1/15, rather than 1/8/15 that had been used. When corrected, the 11 learners are included.

Gender	Telephone	Mobile	Licence number	Date updated
M	0555 555 557	0777 777 724	HARI9999999RA9XX	6/8/2015
M	0555 555 511	0777 777 720	KRIS9999999PA9XX	5/24/2014
M	0555 555 512	0777 777 719	SMIT9999999SA9XX	6/8/2014
M	0555 555 513	0777 777 718	SARR9999999DA9XX	5/24/2014
M	0555 555 516	0777 777 715	DRAK9999999RA9XX	5/24/2014
M	0555 555 517	0777 777 714	BLAC9999999SA9XX	6/8/2014
M	0555 555 518	0777 777 713	DREW9999999JA9XX	6/8/2014
M	0555 555 519	0777 777 712	BROW9999999DA9XX	6/8/2014
M	0555 555 523	0777 777 777	PETE9999999PA9XX	6/8/2014
M	0555 555 525	0777 777 775	HARR9999999PA9XX	6/8/2014
M	0555 555 526	0777 777 774	LANT9999999PE9XX	5/6/2014

Figure 17.43: Filter correction.

PRACTICAL ACTIVITY 17.17

1   Open the master document **17.26 New class errors.docx**. Check the master document and merged letters for accuracy. The merged letters should be sent to students in classes 9F or 9B.

2   Change the filter so that the letter is sent to students in classes 9F or 9B.

REFLECTION

1   How long would it take you to write 100 personalised letters to customers without using mail merge?

2   What do you think are the advantages of using mail merge?

3   How could you apply what you have learnt about mail merge to your life? Are there any occasions for you when mail merge might be useful, for example in your social life?

4   When you created a mail merge document, did you make any errors? If so, what did you do to correct them?

REVIEW PRACTICAL ACTIVITY

1   Create a new word processing document and link it to the Product table in **17.09 Sales processing.mdb**

2   Create a product information sheet using mail merge fields from the Product table. The product information sheet should include the Product ID, Product Name, Quantity Per Unit, Unit Price, Units in Stock, Reorder Amount, Units on Order and Reorder Level.

3   Sort the data so that it will be merged in order of Product Name.

4   The product information sheets should only be printed for stock that has NOT been discontinued.

5   At the top of the product information sheet should be the date the sheet is printed. This should automatically be the current date.

6   At the bottom of the document should be the name of the person who printed the document. This should be populated using the word field FILL IN.

7   Use the word field SKIP IF to skip any products that are in Category ID 3.

8   If the Unit Price is above $60 then the phrase 'HIGH VALUE ITEM' should be displayed.

9   The Sale Price should be displayed. The Sale Price is 30% on top of the Unit Price.

10 The total value of stock for each product should be displayed.

11 Merge the product information sheets to a new document.

EXAM-STYLE QUESTIONS

1 Service to You is a company that carries out car servicing at the customer's home address. They store details in a database of the services they have carried out and when the next service is due. When a customer's car is due a service, Service to You use mail merge to write a letter to the customer to let them know.

    a Describe the term mail merge. [2]

    b Describe the steps involved in creating a set of mail merged letters. [6]

                            [Total 8]

2 Service to You sends out letters once a month.

  Explain how Service to You can use mail merge facilities to only send letters to customers whose cars are due a service in the next month. [4]

3 Amin has used a word processor to send mail merged invitations for his party to his friends. Describe how he could proofread his invitations. [4]

4 Sharene has written a report to her manager to show the sales figures for members of her team. She has embedded a graph in her report. Describe the term embedding. [2]

SUMMARY CHECKLIST

- [ ] I can use, create and edit source data using appropriate software.
- [ ] I can create a master document structure.
- [ ] I can link a master document to a source file.
- [ ] I can specify rules for:
  - [ ] selecting recipients
  - [ ] managing document content.
- [ ] I can set up fields for:
  - [ ] manual completion
  - [ ] automatic completion.
- [ ] I can use calculated fields.
- [ ] I can use manual methods and software tools to ensure error-free accuracy.
- [ ] I can perform mail merge.

> Chapter 18
Graphics creation

LEARNING INTENTIONS

By the end of this chapter, you will be able to:

- use common graphic skills
  - work with layers
  - use transform tools
  - use grouping or merging tools
  - use alignment and distribution tools
  - use layout tools
  - use colour picker tools
  - use crop tools
  - know and understand the properties of different colour systems
  - know and understand the need for different image resolutions
  - know, understand and select different bitmap and vector file formats
  - export an image in different file formats
  - change the opacity of all or part of an image.

- use vector images
  - create a vector image that meets the requirements of its intended application and audience
  - use vector drawing tools
  - use selection tools to select parts of a vector image
  - use fill tools to colour elements
  - use node and path editing
  - convert bitmap images into editable vector shapes.

- use bitmap images
  - use selection tools to select parts of a bitmap image
  - adjust colour levels
  - use tools/filters to alter parts of an image
  - resize an image/canvas

- know and understand the effects of different methods of compression on images.

- manipulate text
  - select font style
  - fit text to path or shapes
  - set text in a shape
  - convert text to curves.

BEFORE YOU START

- Do you know the differences between bitmap and vector images?
- Have you had some experience of creating images and changing images through software such as Microsoft Paint?

Introduction

In this chapter you will learn about image editing, including the difference between vector and bitmap images. The skills you need will be introduced using the photo-editing software Adobe Photoshop.

18.1 Type of images
Vector images

A **vector** image is created using shapes and coordinates. Mathematical formulas and calculations are used to draw the image and fill areas with colour. If you change the size of the image, the computer recalculates and redraws it. This means it does not go blurry (pixelate). The image itself is not saved. Only instructions on how to create the image are saved. For example, coordinates for a line and a calculation for drawing the line are stored, including the colour, width, and so on.

KEY WORD

vector: an image that uses geometric points and shapes; calculations are used to draw the image

Figure 18.1: A vector image.

Figure 18.2: An enlarged vector image.

Figure 18.3: A bitmap image.

Figure 18.4: A pixelated bitmap image.

Bitmap images

A bitmap image is made up of small squares called pixels. Each pixel can have one colour. If you change the size of the image, the pixels are enlarged or made smaller. By enlarging the pixels you pixelate an image and it goes blurry.

The use of vector and bitmap images

The most common form of a bitmap image is a photograph. When you take a photo, the camera records the colours as pixels and the quality of an image depends on the resolution. Other common bitmap images include ones that have been scanned, or produced using painting software. Resolution is the number of pixels per measurement, for example **dots per inch (DPI)**. The larger the DPI, the more pixels and therefore the more precise your image is.

Different images have different requirements for their resolution. If an image is going to be small and will not need enlarging then a smaller resolution will be acceptable. If you are going to enlarge an image to allow you to see more detail, then you need to have a higher resolution otherwise it might pixelate if it is a bitmap image.

The resolution also impacts the file size of the image – the higher the resolution, the larger the file size. This is important if you have limited storage space, or if you are uploading images to a website. The larger the file size is, the longer it will take to download the image.

Selecting a resolution depends on both the image requirements and the file size. For example: A bitmap photograph is taken that has a resolution of 1600×1200 pixels. Each pixel is 2 bytes in size, so the image will take up 3.84 megabytes.

One possible use: the image is going to be modified and then enlarged to print as a posted. This image will need a high resolution because it needs the detail and is going to be enlarged. The file size is not necessarily relevant here.

A second possible use: the photograph will be uploaded to a website for other people to view and then purchase. The full detail is not necessarily required here, it is more important that users can download it, and to save storage space on the server. Therefore the resolution could be lowered.

KEY WORDS
DPI/dots per inch: the resolution of an image

Vector graphics are created using a computer, often with specialist drawing software, but word processors usually provide some vector tools, such as drawing shapes and speech bubbles. They could be used, for example, to create a logo or an animation where characters can be drawn using a graphics tablet.

Figure 18.5: A graphics tablet.

Deciding between vector or bitmap graphics

If you scan a document (for example a photo), then you will create a bitmap image. As increasing the size of this image may result in **pixelation**, you must be careful to ensure the resolution is high enough. These pictures cannot be created as vector images, so if you want to use a photo of you and your friends, it will be a bitmap graphic.

KEY WORD
pixilation: when a bitmap image is enlarged, the pixels are enlarged and become visible causing the image to appear blurry

If you are creating a graphic using a computer, then you can choose between a bitmap and a vector image. If you produce a bitmap image, such as a photo, it may pixelate when enlarged. If you produce a vector graphic, it will not pixelate but will require a lot of work to look realistic.

Software exists that can turn bitmaps into vectors, and vectors into bitmaps. For example, if you scan a document, you can vectorise it. Most image manipulation software has this option.

The use and impact of image editing on society

This section explains some of the tools available to manipulate images. These tools can be used to edit images to both improve the image and make the image look worse. For example, in magazines, photos may be edited (airbrushed) to make people appear thinner or to remove blemishes, such as wrinkles and spots.

Figure 18.6: An example of airbrushing.

Another way image manipulation software may be used is to put people in scenarios (for example memes) that have never actually happened. For example, using a selection tool to copy a person from one image and place them in another. The image of the person can be edited, and the colours manipulated, so they appear to belong in the new scene.

Vector images can be used on their own or added to a bitmap image. For example in the meme shown in Figure 18.7, vector text has been added to the bitmap photo.

Figure 18.7: An example of a meme.

These are just two examples of how image manipulation can be used. Each have their positive and negative aspects. In the first example in Figure 18.6, the company using the image may increase sales by showing a perfect model. However, the image is not real and people may strive to achieve this impossible vision. This can contribute to mental-health problems. Memes can be used to draw attention to an advert or create humorous effects, but they can also be used negatively,

to make fun of people and situations and may be used without the consent of the person in the image.

Image editing can be used in politics both to promote a political agenda, for example enhancing images so they look more favourable, and to put people into situations where they have not actually been. Image editing may mean that false versions of real events can be presented in a positive way in order to mislead the audience intentionally.

Image editing can also be used in a negative way, to put opposing party members in unfortunate situations or to use memes to mock them, which can cause offence and influence people by creating images that are not real.

As well as being used for political purposes, image editing can also be used in the entertainment industry. Image editing is used to create posters, signs, CD and DVD covers, all of which are enhanced to increase their attractiveness and appeal. This can increase sales as the images are attractive, but it does not portray an image of real life.

Questions

1   Describe bitmap graphics.

2   Describe vector graphics.

3   State two advantages of vector graphics over bitmaps.

4   Explain the problems associated with image manipulation on society.

18.2 Common graphic skills

Layers

Layers contain parts of an image, or an effect, that can be built up on top of each other to create the final image. By using layers, you can move or edit elements of an image independently without affecting other elements of the image. Imagine that each layer is an individual piece of paper and you can move them above and below each other.

KEY WORD

layer: a 'surface' onto which an image or object is placed; each object is placed on a separate layer and they are stacked on top of each other (as though on different pieces of paper)

On the right-hand side of the screen is the layers menu.

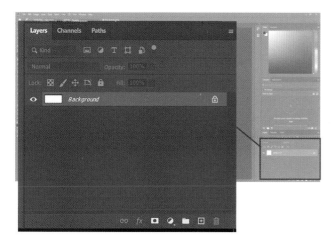

Figure 18.8: Layers menu.

To create a new layer, click the new layer symbol, then double click the layer name to change it.

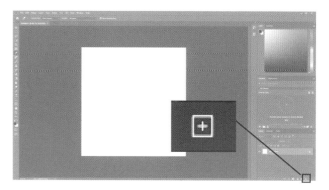

Figure 18.9: New layer symbol.

To delete a layer drag the layer, using the left mouse button, to the bin.

Figure 18.10: Bin symbol.

The layer that is on the top is in front. In this example the blue ellipse is in front of the rectangle, because the layer is higher up.

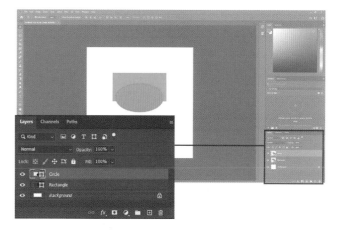

Figure 18.11: Ranking of layers.

To reverse these, and make the red rectangle come to the front, drag it above the circle layer.

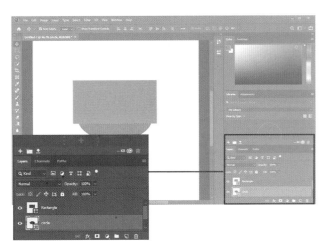

Figure 18.12: Ranking of layers (reversed).

To raise a layer, drag it one position up.

To lower a layer, drag it one position down.

To bring to front, drag the layer to the very top.

This allows you to order layers.

An alternative way is select the layer, then from the top menus select `Layer`, then `Arrange`. In this menu there are options to bring forward (raise), send backward (lower), bring to front, and send to back.

PRACTICAL ACTIVITY 18.02

1   Create two layers and draw an image in each layer. Move the layers to change the order.

2   Open a background image, for example, scenery such as a forest. Add new images such as additional trees, objects such as buildings and/or people in new layers. Position the layers so that the new objects are in front of the background.

3   Open **18.01 Background.jpg** in your image manipulation software. You may need to convert this to a different file type depending on the software you are using. Add a new layer to this image and use the drawing tools to add shapes, lines, and so on to the image. Use the drawing tools to draw a new tree or flower or other feature. Change the shapes, move them, delete them; the background layer should not change. Add further layers with additional shapes or objects.

Transform tools

Transform tools are used to change the size, rotation, distortion and skew of an item.

To transform an item, you first need to select its layer and then the part of the object you want to change. You can do this using any of the selection tools, for example, lasso, magic wand, rectangle select tool.

Scale/resize

Scale, or resize, lets you change the size of an object to make it larger or smaller.

Once you have selected the object, click `Edit` from the top menu, then `Transform` and `Scale`.

The squares will appear on the object and you can drag these to resize the object.

Move

This tool lets you move the shape you have selected. Click the `Move` tool from the toolbar, then drag the shape to where you want it.

Flip

This lets you create a mirror image of the shape, either horizontally or vertically.

From the top menu select `Edit`, then `Transform`. There are two options: `Flip Horizontal` and `Flip Vertical`. Click one of these to flip the object.

Shear/skew

Skew allows you to edit the edges of a shape while keeping it in proportion. For example, here the rectangle has had both of its edges skewed,

Figure 18.13: Skewed rectangle.

Skew is in the `Edit – Transform` menu. Once selected, move the squares on the object to skew the object.

Rotate

This lets you turn a shape. Click the `Edit` menu then `Transform` and select `Rotate`. Put your cursor near the corner of your object and you can free rotate it.

Grouping or merging

When creating an image, you may have multiple items (objects or shapes). These can all be moved individually, which can cause problems when you need them to stay together. You can group or merge items, which combines them into one item that can be moved and resized together.

To **group** two or more objects, click one object, hold down shift on the keyboard and select the other object; they will now become one. To ungroup the objects, click elsewhere on the screen and they will be separated.

Flatten will combine all of the separate layers in an image into one layer. To do this, right click one of the layers and choose `Flatten Image`.

KEY WORDS

group: join several images together

flatten: merge all layers into one single layer

PRACTICAL ACTIVITY 18.03

1   Using the image you manipulated in Practical Activity 18.02, select all the items you added in one layer (for example your drawing of a tree) and group or merge them. The item should now move as one, rather than as separate components.

2   Rotate one of the items you have added in a layer in Practical Activity 18.02, for example a tree. Move it to a new location.

3   Insert the bench from **18.02 Bench.jpg** into the background on **18.01 Background.jpg**. Resize the bench and move it into a suitable position.

Alignment and distribution tools

Align

This allows you to make two or more objects start at a set point, for example at the top, the left, the bottom or the right.

To **align** objects, first select them and then from the top menu choose `Layer`, `Align` and then one of the options.

KEY WORD

align: make objects start at the same position

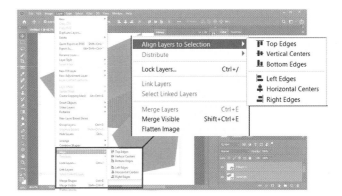

Figure 18.14: Align menu options.

Distribute

Distribute works on layers. It evenly spaces out the three (or more) layers selected, based on horizontal or vertical distances.

KEY WORD

distribute: make the space between objects the same

To use `Distribute`, highlight at least three layers. Select the `Layer` menu, then `Distribute` and choose which edge you want the distribute to use.

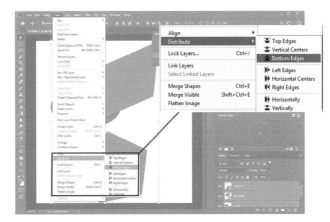

Figure 18.15: Distribute menu options.

Layout tools

Rulers

You can view a ruler on the horizontal and vertical axes of the screen. This lets you see how large an object is in inches.

To turn rulers on and off select the `View` menu and then click `Rulers`. The tick indicates that rulers are visible.

Figure 18.16: Ruler on/off options.

Rulers can be in cm, inches or pixels. To change the measurement, double click one of the rulers and then choose the units you want.

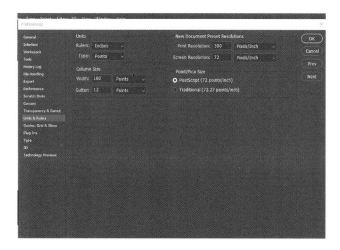

Figure 18.17: Ruler measurement unit options.

Grids

You can put a grid on the background of the image to help you align objects by using the lines to position them. The grid does not appear on any printout or exporting of the image, it is purely to help you create the image.

To turn the gridlines on or off, select the `View` menu, then `Show` and then `Grid`.

Figure 18.18: Grid options.

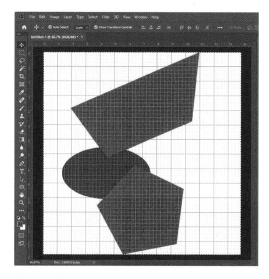

Figure 18.19: Image with grid options.

Guidelines

You can set a line at a specific point, for example at 3.5 inches in. These can then be used to align objects and make sure you are drawing images of the correct size.

WORKED EXAMPLE 18.01

Set a guideline

Create a new vertical guideline.

First click the View menu and then New Guide.

Then select Vertical from the new menu. Enter the position where you want the guideline to appear, in this case at 3.5 inches. Then click OK.

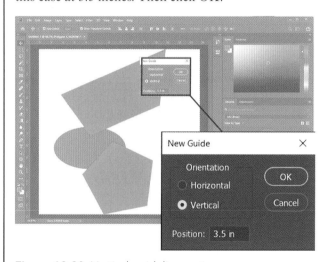

Figure 18.20: Vertical guideline option.

Snapping

Snap tries to help you by only allowing you to adjust, or draw, an object to meet gridlines. If you want more freedom to edit or draw the objects, you will need to turn snap off.

WORKED EXAMPLE 18.02

Set the shapes to snap to meet the gridlines.

First click View and then if Snap is not ticked, click it.

When you want more freedom, click on the Snap button again to untick it.

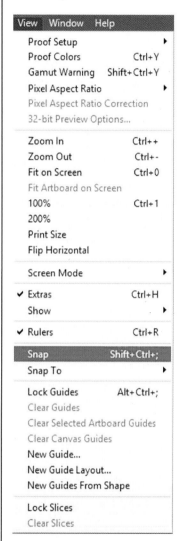

Figure 18.21: Snap options.

Crop tools

Cropping lets you select only part of an image to keep and removes everything else. To do this, select the crop tool from the menu and then drag the corners of the image in to show only the area you want to keep.

Crop the image so only a square from the centre of the image is produced.

First click on the `Crop` button on the left hand menu. Adjust the size of the box by clicking on the edges or corners.

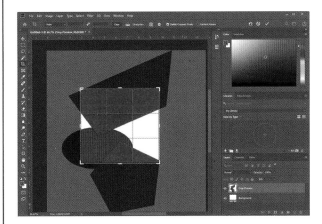

Figure 18.22: Cropping.

When you have a square in the centre of the screen, click `Enter` to complete the crop.

Using **18.01 Background.jpg**, crop the bottom layer of soil from the image and the top of the sky above the clouds. Make sure you have the correct layer selected before you begin, otherwise you will crop the wrong image.

Colour systems (RGB, HSL, CMYK, CMS)

A colour is developed by combining different colours in different quantities.

RGB

In school you have probably learnt about the primary additive colours, Red, Green and Blue. Every colour can be created from combining these colours in different quantities.

In Adobe Photoshop the amount of each colour is represented by a two-digit number, from 0 to F. This is called hexadecimal, the higher the number, the more of that colour is present. The letters are used to represent two-digit numbers, so A = 10, B = 11, C = 12, D = 13, E = 14 F = 15. So to have as much of one colour as you possibly can have, use FF. To have absolutely none of the colours, use 00.

Sometimes the numbers are replaced with whole numbers between 0 and 255. The most of a colour is 255, which is equivalent to FF. None of a colour is 0, equivalent to 00.

RGB colour codes are RRGGBB, which is the amount of red, then green, then blue. Look at this colour code: FF0000. This shows RR = FF (the highest), and no green or blue. So the colour is red. There are lots of colour mixers online to try.

KEY WORD

RGB: Red/Green/Blue colour system; all colours are a combination of quantities of red, green and blue

HSL

HSL stands for Hue–Saturation–Lightness.

KEY WORD

HSL: Hue/Saturation/Lightness colour system; all colours are a combination of the hue saturation and lightness selected

The Hue represents the base colour (red, yellow, green). The saturation is the % of that colour being used, with 100% being the highest. Lightness is a % from white to black.

For example, this is hue 100, with 50% saturation and 50% lightness.

Figure 18.23: Hue 100, with 50% saturation and 50% lightness.

Increase the saturation to 100%

Figure 18.24: Hue 100, with 100% saturation and 50% lightness.

Now increase the lightness to 95% (100% would make it white and invisible)

Figure 18.25: Hue 100, with 100% saturation and 95% lightness.

You can represent every colour using different values for hue, saturation and lightness.

Questions

5   What do the letters RGB stand for?
6   What colour will FF0000 create?
7   What colour will 00FF00 create?
8   What colour will 0000FF create
9   What colour will 000000 create?
10   What colour will FFFFFF create?

PRACTICAL ACTIVITY 18.05

Generating colours

Find a colour generator online and try experimenting with HSL.

Enter some numbers and try and guess what colour will appear.

Work as a pair and test each other, give your partner the numbers for a colour and ask them what colour they think it will produce.

CMYK

CMYK stands for Cyan–Magenta–Yellow–Black. These are the colours usually used by printers. Your printer will probably have a cartridge (or toner) for each of these four colours. By mixing these four colours you can create any colour.

KEY WORD

CMYK: Cyan/Magenta/Yellow/Black colour system; all colours are a combination of these four colours

Each colour is given a number as a percentage from 0 to 100, as to how much of the colour is included.

CMS

This is not a colour itself, but a CMS (Colour Matching System). This is a way that a piece of software can select a colour from an image and reproduce it. For example, if you have an image of a car and you want the shade of red used in the car, you can click the colour and find out what its RGB/CMYK values are and then use this later.

Adobe Photoshop has the magic wand tool that lets you click a colour and then use it elsewhere.

Colour picker tools

Colour options appear in a sidebar. Click the small colour square.

Figure 18.26: Colour options.

In the new menu you can manually select the colour based on the RGB and CMYK, and HSB (B for Brightness instead of Lightness).

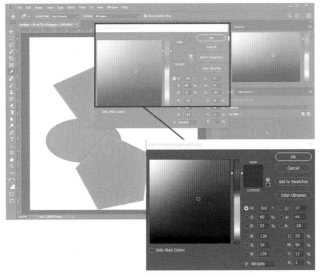

Figure 18.27: Colour options – manual selection.

You can also use the eyedrop tool to select a colour.

Click the tool from the menu, and then on the colour you want to select and it appears in the colour menu.

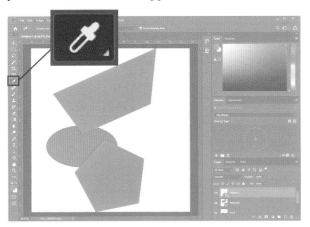

Figure 18.28: 'Eyedrop' colour selector.

Image resolutions

The image resolution is the amount of detail that is within an image: the number of pixels per inch. The more pixels you have, the more individual pieces of detail you can have. However, this has an impact on other areas. The more pixels you have, the more information you have to store, so the file size is larger.

The image has to be viewed in some way such as on a screen, or printed out. However, screens and printers have their own maximum resolutions so the resulting resolution is limited by the hardware being used to display or view it regardless of how much detail is in the image.

To change the resolution in Adobe Photoshop you need to change the size of the image. Click `Image` on the top menu bar and then `Image Size`.

You can then change the width and height of the image, and also the resolution. The larger the number, the more pixels there are per inch.

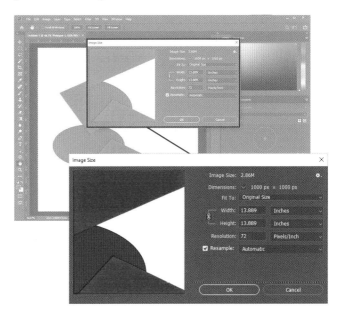

Figure 18.29: Width, height and resolution options.

File formats

There are a range of file types you can use to save your image. These can be selected by choosing an option when saving or exporting the image. Some of these are in the table 18.1:

File format	Image type	Description
.BMP	Bitmap	**Bitmap Image:** There are a range these formats, for example black and white, 256 colours, four-bit (16 colours), eight-bit (256 colours). The smaller the number of colours, the smaller the file size, but the quality also decreases.

File format	Image type	Description
.GIF	Bitmap	**Graphics Interchange Format:** This is a compressed format that will reduce the file size and is commonly used for online images. This format allows for transparency, as long as it was not created using an alpha option, and is also restricted to 256 colours.
.JPEG	Bitmap	**Joint Photographic Experts Group:** This is a common format that has a range of colour options to reduce file sizes. The image is compressed when saved and decompressed when opened. The level of compression can often be altered to gain a balance of compression versus quality. This type of image does not allow for transparency. Any areas that are transparent will be stored as white or black.
.PNG	Bitmap	**Portable Network Graphics:** This format uses lossless compression to reduce the file size. It has a range of colour options, and it keeps transparency in all images, which is not the case for all other options.
.TIFF	Bitmap	**Tagged Image File Format:** In this format, the number of colours can be adjusted to reduce the file size. This file type can save effects, such as the use of layers, if saving and reopening an image in the same software.
.SVG	Vector	**Scalable Vector Graphic:** It supports animations.
.PDF	Vector	**Portable Document Format:** This is a format used by Adobe products. It keeps documents as they were designed but in a common format.

Table 18.1: File formats.

There are two ways you can change the format. The first is to `Save As` and select a different file type.

The second is to `Export` the image. Click `File` then `Export As` to give you the options of PNG, JPG, and so on.

PRACTICAL ACTIVITY 18.06

Open an image you have already created. Save, or export, the image in each of the different file types. Compare the images and look at what the differences are.

Questions

11   Name three bitmap image formats.

12   Name one vector image format.

Opacity

Opacity means a lack of **transparency**, that is how solid and non-see-through the image is. Opacity is a percentage, which represents how transparent an image is. For example, 20 per cent opacity means that the image is 80 per cent transparent. This can be added as a mask to the entire image, or a small area of an image can be selected (using an appropriate selection tool) and then the opacity can be altered just in this area.

KEY WORDS

opacity: the lack of transparency of an image; at 0% opacity the image is fully transparent

transparency: being able to see through an object or surface

You can change the transparency (opacity) of a layer by selecting the layer in the layer menu, and then using the drop-down menu next to `Opacity` and the slider to adjust the value.

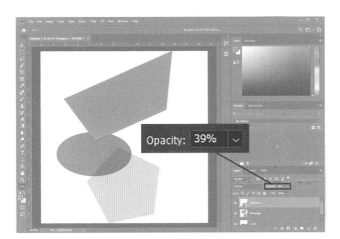

Figure 18.30: Opacity option.

WORKED EXAMPLE 18.04

Change the opacity of the magenta rectangle, so that the green rectangle can be seen through it.

First click on the layer for the magenta rectangle.

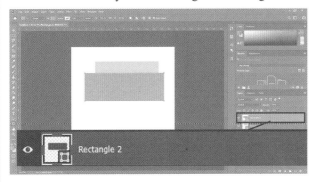

Figure 18.31: Layer option for magenta rectangle.

Click on the opacity button and drag the arrow to the left. Watch the magenta rectangle as you move it to get the transparency you need.

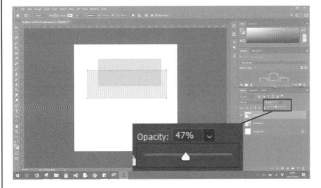

Figure 18.32: Transparency slider for layer.

18.3 Vector images

Vector drawing tools

Freehand drawing

There are a range of freehand drawing tools, all selected from the `Brush Tool` menu. Hold the left mouse button down on the menu to see the additional options.

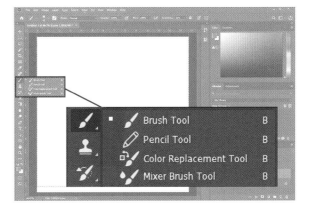

Figure 18.33: Freehand drawing tools.

Once you have selected your tool, and colour from the right-hand menu, draw your image on the **canvas**.

KEY WORD

canvas: the area in the software where you add and edit your images

Bezier curves

Bezier curves are named after the person who developed the now common way of drawing arcs in a computer.

KEY WORD

bezier curve: smooth curves made of paths that can be scaled indefinitely

A curve is created using the `Curvature Pen Tool` to draw a straight line first.

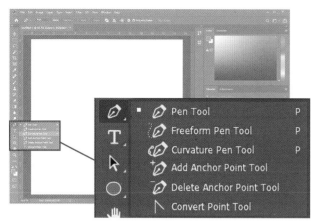

Figure 18.34: Pen tool menu.

Then select a midway point on the line and drag it outwards to create a curve.

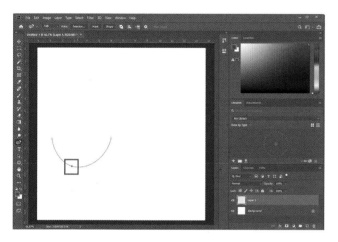

Figure 18.35: Curve 'mid' point.

Straight line

To draw in Adobe Photoshop hold the left mouse button down on the `Shapes Tool` and select `Line Tool`.

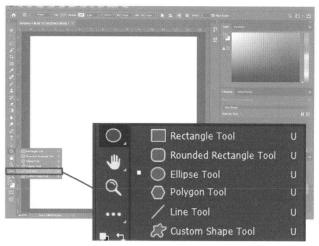

Figure 18.36: Line tool.

Shape tools

The `Shape` menu has inbuilt shapes to allow you to draw rectangles, ellipses (e.g. circles) and polygons.

Arcs, stars and other shapes such as arrows are all accessed from the `Custom Shape Tool` option. The drop-down menu gives other options such as arcs, stars and spirals.

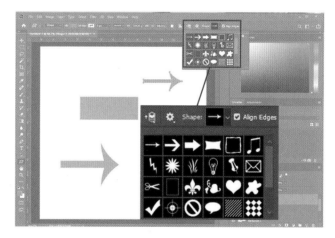

Figure 18.37: Custom shape tool.

Selection tools

A selection tool lets you access, edit and manipulate just one part of an image. You can choose which parts to change. There may be a range of different tools that you can access depending on your software. For example, the `Lasso Tool` lets you draw freehand around the area of an image you want to select. Hold the left mouse button down to select the area.

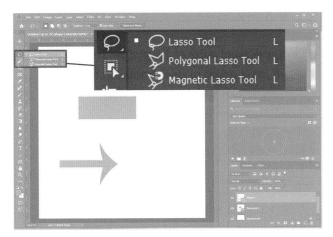

Figure 18.38: Lasso tool.

A `Rectangular Marquee Tool` provides you with a shape, such as a rectangle, that you can 'draw' over your image to select a rectangular area.

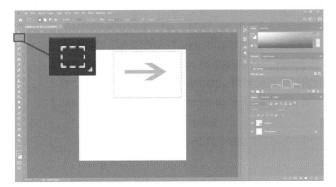

Figure 18.39: Selecting a rectangular area.

A `Magnetic Lasso Tool` will stick to an edge within an image, for example a line or a specific colour, which means you don't need to follow the line precisely.

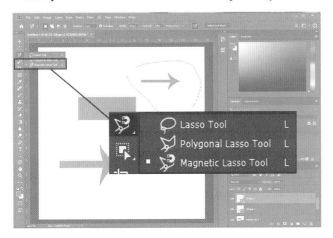

Figure 18.40: Magnetic lasso selection tool.

PRACTICAL ACTIVITY 18.07

Use a selection tool on **18.01 Background.jpg**. Select one of the trees. Create a new instance of this object (copy and paste it into a new layer), then use the `Transform` tools to adjust its position and size. Repeat this with the bench in **18.02 Bench.jpg**.

Fill tools

A `Fill Tool` lets you select a colour, then fill a selected area with that colour. For example, if you select red, then the `Fill Tool`, then click inside a rectangle, it will change the rectangle to red. Some software may require you to select the `Fill Tool`, then the colour.

To fill an image, select the `Fill Bucket Tool`, choose your colour and then click the image you want to change.

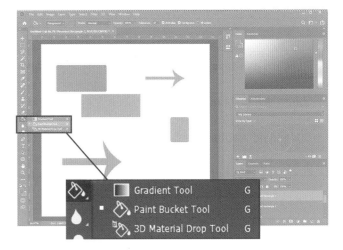

Figure 18.41: Fill tool options.

Fill gradient lets you select two colours and Adobe Photoshop will change the colour from one to the second. First you need to select the area that you want the gradient to be applied to, for example using the rectangle select tool.

Select the first colour, and then the second.

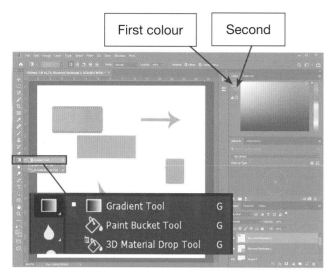

Figure 18.42: Colour gradient options.

There are a range of pre-set gradient fills that you can select from. Once you have chosen the `Gradient Fill Tool` these appear at the top of the screen.

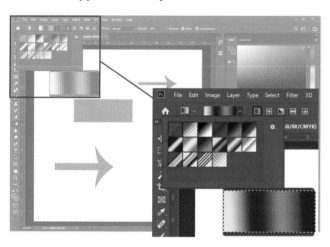

Figure 18.43: Pre-set gradient fills.

PRACTICAL ACTIVITY 18.08

Use a `Fill Tool` to change the colour of the sky, trees and mountains in **18.01 Background.jpg**. Make sure you have the correct layer selected first. Change the fill colour of the bench in **18.02 Bench.jpg** by use a fill pattern or gradient.

Node and path editing

Existing shapes

Shapes are made up of nodes (points that can be edited) and paths (between nodes). You can change these by right clicking an object and selecting `Warp`. This shows you the nodes and, by dragging these with the left mouse button, you can change the shape.

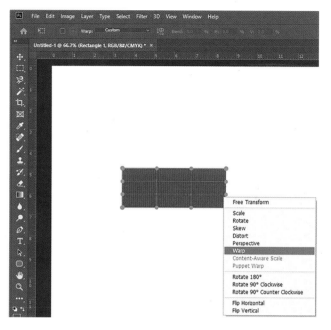

Figure 18.44: Warping option.

PRACTICAL ACTIVITY 18.09

Select the nodes on one of the mountains on **18.01 Background.jpg**. Manipulate the shape of the mountain. Make it higher and change the angles of each side. Repeat this with the copy of a tree you have made and change the shape of the trunk.

Pen tool

If you use the `Pen Tool` you can add new nodes and edit these to tailor your shape.

When you have drawn your line, or shape, with the pen, right click where you want a new node and select `Add Anchor Point`. This will give you,

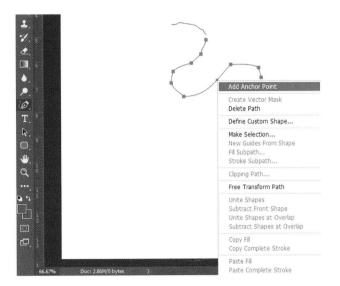

Figure 18.45: Adding an anchor point.

Choose the `Direct Selection Tool` to select one of the nodes and adjust it. This will give you a Bezier handle, which allows you to alter the curve by moving the squares to adjust the angles.

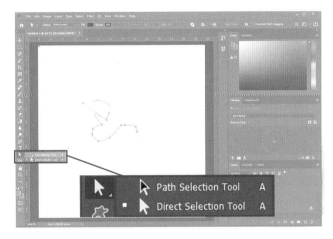

Figure 18.46: Direct selection tool.

Right clicking a node gives you the option to delete that node, which will simplify the shape (there are fewer points to edit).

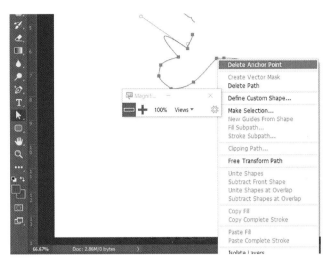

Figure 18.47: Menu option for deleting node.

You can align multiple paths by using the `Path Selection Tool` from the left-hand menu. Hold down `Shift` to select two or more paths, then choose the drop-down menu for `Align`. `Distribute` is also in this menu, so you can create the same distance between the paths.

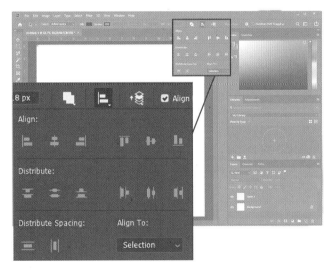

Figure 18.48: Alignment and distribution options.

Convert bitmap images into editable vector shapes

The images displayed in Adobe Photoshop will be bitmaps, but you can export these to **vector** shapes.

First highlight the area that you want to export, for example by using the `Magnetic Lasso Tool`.

Make sure the `Paths` menu is open (window from the top menu, then `Paths`).

From the `Paths` menu, choose `Make Work Path`.

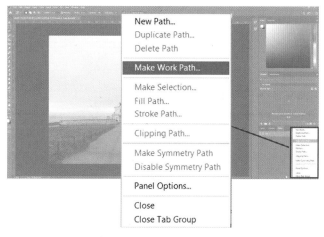

Figure 18.49: Make work path menu.

Set the tolerance: the lower the number, the more precise the shapes are.

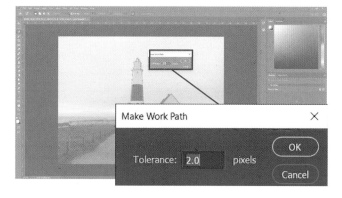

Figure 18.50: Setting tolerance.

Once you have the path, you need to export it as a vector. To do this, click `File`, `Export` and then `Paths to Illustrator`. This creates an illustrator vector file with your image.

Figure 18.51: Export menu.

Vector graphics are better for images that you need to create in different sizes, for example to enlarge for a poster, and make smaller for items such as business cards. This is because they do not pixelate when you change the size. However, not all images can be converted into exact vector graphics. For example, you can take some elements of a photo and convert it into a separate vector, but a whole photograph cannot be converted and retained with the same content.

> **TIP**
>
> You can trace bitmap images to convert them into vector images. An example of how to do this is shown in Chapter 19, Importing an image.

PRACTICAL ACTIVITY 18.10

1   J.B. Garden Landscaping need an image to put on their website. They would like a brown arrow pointing to the right, on top of a green rectangle. Create the image for J.B. Garden Landscaping.

CONTINUED

2 Haven's Creations would like you to create a logo of a series of clouds of different shades of grey overlapping each other. Create the image for Haven's Creations.

3 Robson's Refreshments would like you to create an image of a table with drinks bottles of different sizes on the top. Create the image for Robson's refreshments.

4 Bhavin's Buildings would like you to create a logo of a high-rise building. It should have at least 10 storeys and have the image of a cloud behind the top of the building. The building should be an appropriate colour to stand out against a pale blue background.

18.4 Bitmap images

Selection tools

The selection tools available with vector graphics can also be used with bitmaps, such as the Lasso Tool, but there are other tools as well.

Hold the left mouse button down to select the Magic Wand Tool. This allows you to select pixels based on their colour.

Figure 18.52: Quick selection tool.

Hold Shift as you left click the area you want to select. The tolerance lets you adjust which elements it selects. The tool works by selecting pixels that are of a similar colour (RGB colour for example) to the one you have clicked. The higher the tolerance, the wider range of

colours it will select. The lower the number, the more precise the colour needs to be.

For example, by selecting the red of the lighthouse there can be a high tolerance because there are no other colours similar around it. However, to select the top part of the lighthouse will need a very small number, because the white is very similar to the clouds and if the tolerance is too high then the clouds will be selected as well.

PRACTICAL ACTIVITY 18.11

1 Open **18.03 New York.jpg**. Add a new layer and add the image from **18.04 Helicopter.jpg**.

2 Move the helicopter to an appropriate position in the sky and rotate it so it fits into the skyline.

3 Open **18.03 New York.jpg** and **18.04 Helicopter.jpg**. Add further copies of the helicopter onto the New York image in the same layer. Select all of these layers (you may need to use the Shift or Ctrl button to select more than one), then group or merge the layers into one layer. You should now be able to move them together.

4 Use a selection tool (for example the Magnetic Lasso Tool) to highlight one of the buildings in **18.03 New York.jpg**. Copy this image and paste it into a new layer. Move the building so it looks as if it belongs in the city. Repeat this with other buildings to create your own version of New York.

5 Open **18.05 Frog.jpg**. Crop the image so only the face and eyes of the frog are visible.

Colour levels

An entire image, or just part of one, can be converted from colour into black and white, or duotone.

Greyscale can be selected by selecting the Image menu, then Mode and Grayscale.

> **TIP**
>
> Grayscale is the American spelling of greyscale.

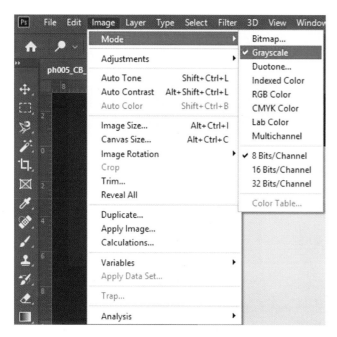

Figure 18.53: Selecting Greyscale mode.

This changes the whole image. If you only want one part to be in greyscale, then select the area you want using one of the selection tools. From the menus choose `Adjustments` and then `Desaturate`. Only the area you selected will become greyscale.

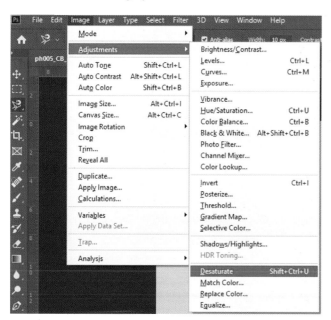

Figure 18.54: Selecting desaturate in adjustments menu.

This menu has other colour changes, such as `Hue/Saturation`, `Black & White`, and so on.

`Colour Balance` allows you to change the colour that you have selected. You can add, or remove, the different colours to, or from, the image to change the colour of the area you selected. Adobe Photoshop will keep the shades as they are because each pixel will be adjusted by the same amount, so if one was lighter to begin with, it will be lighter after the change.

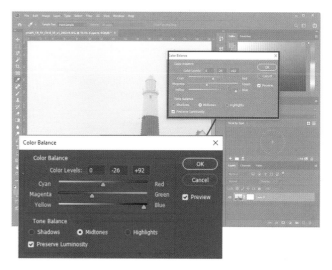

Figure 18.55: Colour balance sliders.

Within the colour balance there are options for `Shadows` and `Highlights`. These can be used to adjust images that may be too dark, or too bright. By adjusting the shadows or highlights you can make the image brighter, or darker.

`Brightness` allows you to increase the brightness of the image, or the part of the image selected. `Contrast` increases the difference between the different colours in the image. Both of these are selected from the `Image` menu, `Adjustments` and then `Brightness/Contrast`.

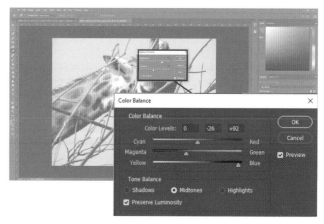

Figure 18.56: Brightness and contrast sliders.

PRACTICAL ACTIVITY 18.12

1 Open **18.06 Village.jpg**. Change the colour to black and white, duotone and a range of other colours. Compare turning an image to black and white then to duotone, rather than straight to duotone.

2 Take a photograph and open it in Adobe Photoshop. Change the image so only the main focus of the photograph is in colour; the rest should be in black and white.

Tools/filters

There are a range of tools and filters that can be used to edit images.

Clone creates an identical copy or part of an image. For example, if you have a tree that you would like to duplicate, by using this tool you can 'paint' a copy of the tree in a different place without having to trace the outline and copy it.

To use the clone stamp, select the `Clone Stamp` button.

Figure 18.57: Clone stamp button.

Hold `Alt` and click the area of the image that you want to copy. Move the cursor to where you want to paint the image, hold the left mouse button down and move it to draw the image.

The `Red Eye Tool` will automatically remove a red eye effect caused by a photo flash. Click the red eye tool and draw a box across (or click) the red pupil. You may need to do it more than once to get the whole area. The red eye tool uses the other colours from the eye to fill in the pupil.

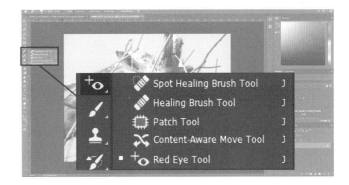

Figure 18.58: Red eye tool.

A filter can be used to add effects to an image or to change a small element of it. There are numerous filter tools you can use including the `Blur Tool`, the `Sharpen Tool`, and the `Smudge Tool`. These are can all be accessed from the left-hand toolbar.

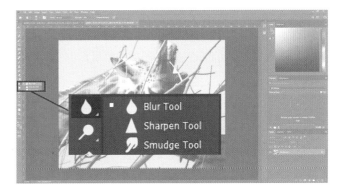

Figure 18.59: Blur, sharpen and smudge tools.

The `Blur Tool` reduces the focus on areas of the image. You can adjust the strength of the blur, and the size using the top toolbar. Drag the tool repeatedly over the area of the image you want to blur; the more times you go over the one area, the more blurred it will become.

Figure 18.60: Percentage of blur.

`Distort` and `Warp` both allow you to change the perspective of an image, or part of an image; for example if you have an image of a high-rise building and the perspective has curved the lines.

Figure 18.61: Warped images.

Both can be accessed from the `Edit-Transform` menu. Dragging in the boxes on the edges of the image can be used to distort or warp the image.

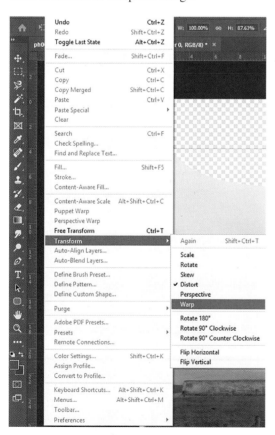

Figure 18.62: Selecting warp menu option.

The `Sharpen Tool` improves, or increases, the contrast between colours. For example, an edge between a light and dark area can be sharpened to make it more defined.

The `Smudge Tool` lets you change part of the image, for example expand it or stretch it out, almost as if you have dragged your finger through the drawing. Used subtly you can edit the size and shape of images.

PRACTICAL ACTIVITY 18.13

1   Select a photograph of yourself, or of your friends. (Make sure you have their permission before using an image of someone else.) Use the smudge, red eye remover and clone tools to edit the image and either make it better, or worse.

2   Create a 'spot the difference' puzzle. Take an image and create a copy of it. Make several subtle changes to this image and challenge someone to spot the differences between the two images.

3   Open **18.07 Fruit bowl.jpg**. Use the sharpen, distort and blur tools to alter the image. For example, you could make the fruit the focus by increasing the contrast and blurring other elements. You could also use other tools mentioned, for example the `Clone Tool`, to add more fruit to the image.

Resize an image/canvas

An image can be resized or scaled. Bitmap images may pixelate if they are increased too much in size. If part of an image needs to be resized, then you can use a selection tool to select the pixels you want to change and then use `Scale` to change the size, the same way as you would with a vector.

If the canvas needs to be enlarged, this can be done through the menu system by selecting `Image` and then `Canvas Size`.

Figure 18.63: Selecting canvas size menu.

You can then select the measurements (for example, pixels, cm or inches) and enter your new dimensions.

Figure 18.64: Canvas size measurement options.

The new background, outside the image, may appear as a checkerboard in grey and white. This means it is transparent. To change this, you will need to either fill the background with a colour, or colour gradient, or increase the size of the image to fill the new space.

18.5 Compression

Compression is a mechanism to reduce the file size on a file, in this case an image. You may need to compress an image because the file size is too large, for example to email to someone, or to store on your computer if you have limited space. On websites images may be compressed so that they do not take as long to download. There are two types of compression, lossless and lossy.

Lossless compression uses an algorithm to reduce the size of the image. When the image is decompressed, it is identical to the original. No data is lost. For example, you may put an image into a zip file format; when you unzip the image it will be identical. The effect of this is that the image you get is exactly the same image that you sent. It will not, however make the file as small as lossy compression will.

Lossy compression uses an algorithm to reduce the size of the image by removing some of the data. When the image is decompressed, it is not identical to the original. Data is lost. This means the image you get will not be identical to the original e.g. it may have fewer colours, or a lower resolution, but the file size will be smaller than lossless.

Lossy compression loses data, but it also compresses the image further (you can get a smaller file size). Two examples of lossy compression are changing the colour depth and changing the resolution.

Colour depth

The **colour depth** of an image is the number of different colours that can be represented. The higher the colour depth, the more colours you can use, but the larger the file size will become. This is because the colour depth is related to the bit depth.

The bit depth is the number of bits allocated to each pixel. If you have 1 bit per pixel, then there are two possibilities; 0 or 1. Each number is allocated a colour, e.g. 0 is red and 1 is blue. Therefore, 1 bit can only represent 1 colour.

Increase the bit depth to 1byte. 1 byte is 8 bits. In 1 byte there are 256 different unique numbers. If each unique number has a different colour, then 1 byte gives you 256 colours.

Increase it again to 2 byte (16 bits). Now there are 65536 different colours.

This all affects the file size. If your image has 100 pixels, then with 1 bit each pixel takes 1 bit of memory. $100 \times 1 = 100$ bits, or 12 bytes.

If each pixel has 1 byte, then 100×1 byte = 100 bytes.

KEY WORDS

lossless compression: a method of compression where the decompressed image is identical to the original

lossy compression: a method of compression where the decompressed image is not identical to the original

colour depth: the number of colours that can be represented in the image

---

To change the colour depth, select Image and then Mode. 8 bits means there are 8 bits per pixel; 16 means there are 16 bits per pixel, and therefore a greater range of colours.

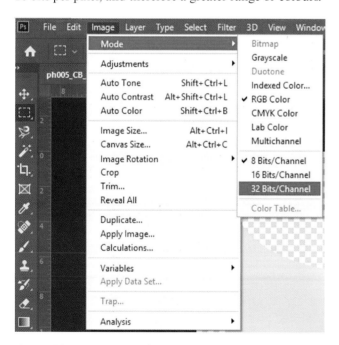

Figure 18.65: Image/Mode menu.

Changing the resolution by making it smaller will reduce the number of pixels per inch of the image. For example, for every square inch there might be 50 pixels instead of 100. This means there are half as many pixels, and therefore half as much data to store.

To change the resolution select Image and then Image Size, and change the number in the resolution box.

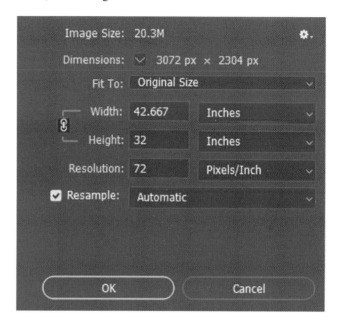

Figure 18.66: Inage size measurements.

18.6 Text

Add text to your image by selecting the Text Tool. You get the choice of horizontal or vertical. Click the tool and then where you want the text, then type the text.

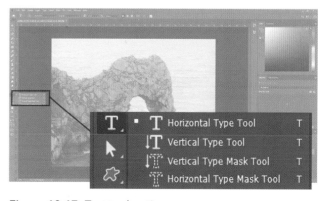

Figure 18.67: Text tool options.

Font style

By clicking your text, you then see font face and size options at the top of the screen.

Figure 18.68: Inserted text and text tool options.

Adobe Photoshop has a character window with additional options. Select `Window` and then `Character` if it is not already open.

Figure 18.69: Inserted text and character options.

Adding space between letters is called **kerning**. This can be changed by increasing or decreasing the number in the character space box.

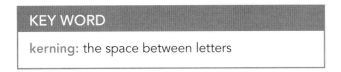

KEY WORD

kerning: the space between letters

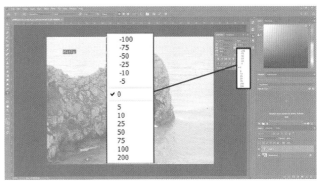

Figure 18.70: Inserted text and kerning options.

Changing the amount of space between lines is also available on this menu.

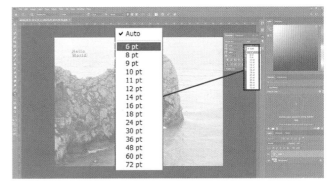

Figure 18.71: Inserted text and line spacing options.

Fit text to path or shape

When you have written your text, you can set it to match a shape. Choose the `Shape` option from the top menu and then choose the shape from the menu. Change the settings to adjust the size of the shape.

Set text in a shape

To add text within a shape, you first need to draw the shape (for example, using the custom shape tool). Click the `Text Tool` and then click inside the shape, and the text will be within the shape.

Figure 18.73: Inserting text in a shape.

Convert text to curves

You can convert text into an outline shape that you can then manually manipulate. To do this, select the text you want to convert, and then from the top menu choose `Type` and then `Convert To Shape`. You can now edit the text as though it was an ordinary shape.

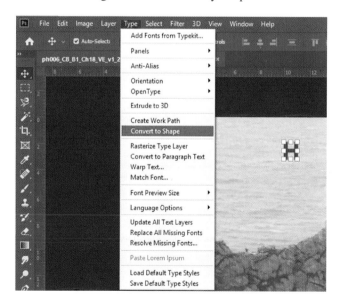

Figure 18.74: Converting text to shape option.

Create the following logo for Sunshine Holidays.

Figure 18.75: Finished logo.

Select the colour yellow from the palette and draw an ellipse.

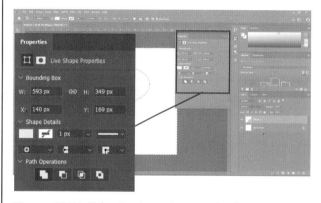

Figure 18.76: Selecting logo shape and colour.

Enter the text Sunshine Holidays in black, select the Arc shape and then change the Bend value until it is how you want it to appear.

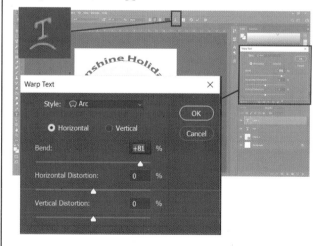

Figure 18.77: Inserting text with distortion sliders.

Adjust the shapes until they are in the correct position.

PRACTICAL ACTIVITY 18.14

Draw a curved line, similar to that in Figure 18.78, above the trees in **18.01 Background.jpg**. Give the image a title. Adjust the text size, colour and so on, so it fits in with the scene.

Figure 18.78: Curved line.

PRACTICAL ACTIVITY 18.15

1 J.B. Garden Landscaping need a bitmap image to be the faded background of their website. It should be made up of different plants including trees and flowers that have been combined from a range of images. Create the image and then fade it to 30 per cent opacity.

2 Haven's Creations sell cakes and would like an image of a single cake to add to their logo. Extract an image of a cake and position it in an appropriate place on their logo.

3 Robson's Refreshments have a new drink out named Robson's Berry Crush. They want a label that is 20 cm wide by 6 cm high for the drink. There must be images of a range of berries and the name of the drink in an appropriate place.

4 Bhavin's Buildings would like a border for the bottom of their website that has a range of buildings that appear as a skyline. Create the skyline border.

WORKED EXAMPLE 18.06

Plant Horizons is an online company that sells houseplants. They want the following logo to be created:

Figure 18.79: Finished logo.

First click on the arrow next to the Shape symbol. Select Nature from the options.

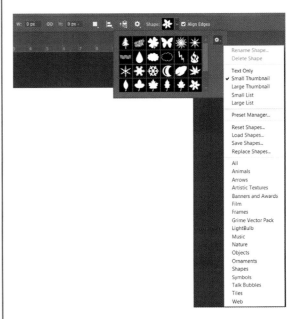

Figure 18.80: Selecting 'nature' shapes.

Select a shade of green from the palette.

Figure 18.81: Selecting green shade.

CONTINUED

Select the leaf and draw it on the screen.

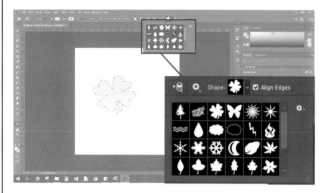

Figure 18.82: Selecting leaf shape.

Click on the text tool to add the company name. Choose your font style and size from the top menu. Choose the colour black, and centre-align the text.

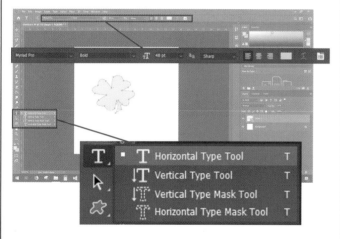

Figure 18.83: Selecting text options.

Type the company name; Plant Horizons.

WORKED EXAMPLE 18.07

Plant Horizons would like the following background image creating for their website.

Figure 18.84: Flower images.

Open the pink flower image and select the magnetic lasso tool.

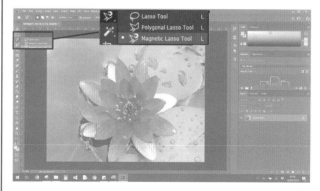

Figure 18.85: Image of pink flower.

Drag the tool around the image, click the left mouse button if it won't lock exactly where you want it to.

Figure 18.86: Flower selected with magnetic lasso tool.

CONTINUED

Copy the image and paste it into a new file that is 1000 pixels by 1000 pixels. Change the size of the image so it fits.

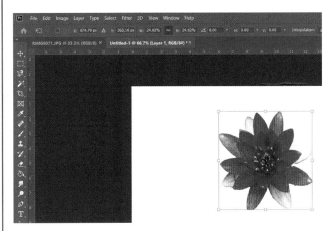

Figure 18.87: Selected flower image pasted into new file.

Open the image of the yellow flower and repeat the process. Change the opacity of both flowers to between 60 and 70 percent.

Figure 18.88: Yellow flower added.

Open the image of the orange flower and repeat the process.

Figure 18.89: Orange flower added.

Export the image as a gif.

Figure 18.91: Exporting image.

EXAM-STYLE QUESTIONS

1 Titania's Televisions needs a new logo.

The company has asked for there to be a rectangular television with a gradient fill from top to bottom and a small triangular stand similar to this image:

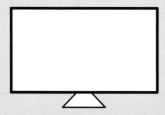

Figure 18.92: Blank television screen.

The outline should be in dark blue, and no more than 4pt thick.

The word Titania should be inside the television, in a sans-serif font, in an arc. The font colour should be green.

a Create Titania's logo and save it as a vector graphic. It should be no more than 250 by 250 pixels. **[13]**

b Explain why a vector graphic is more appropriate for a logo than a bitmap image. **[4]**

c Explain how lossy compression can reduce the file size of an image. **[6]**

[Total 23]

2 Kim's theme park needs an image for the homepage of her website.

a Draw a rollercoaster using a rectangle and distort the top. Add six evenly spaced circles for wheels, and a black line to act as a track and as a rectangle. Inside this rectangle should be the word Rollercoaster in a green sans-serif font, set across an arc to follow the rollercoaster shape. **[15]**

Figure 18.93: Rollercoaster logo.

b Suggest an appropriate file type to save the image. Justify your choice. **[3]**

c Explain the difference between the RGB and CMYK colour schemes. **[4]**

[Total 22]

SUMMARY CHECKLIST

☐ I can work with layers to raise, lower, bring to front and order layers.

☐ I can use transform tools to resize, skew, flip, rotate, move, scale and shear images.

☐ I can use grouping or merging tools to group, ungroup and flatten images.

☐ I can use alignment and distribution tools such as left, right, top and bottom alignment and vertical and horizontal distributions.

☐ I can use layout tools such as rulers, grids, guidelines, snapping.

☐ I can use colour picker tools.

☐ I can use crop tools.

☐ I can know and understand the properties of different colour systems (RGB, HSL, CMYK, CMS).

☐ I can know and understand the need for different image resolutions (impact of too high/low resolution on an image on screen/in print).

☐ I can know and understand how to select different bitmap and vector file formats (svg, bmp, jpg, png, gif, tif, pdf).

☐ I can know and understand how to change the opacity of all or part of an image.

☐ I can create a vector image using vector drawing tools such as:.

    ☐ freehand drawing, Bezier curves and straight lines

    ☐ shape tools: rectangles, ellipses, circles, arcs, stars, polygons and spirals.

☐ I can create a vector image using selection tools to select parts of a vector image.

☐ I can create a vector image using fill tools to colour elements (including gradient fills).

☐ I can create a vector image using node and path editing such as:

    ☐ adding and moving nodes

    ☐ deleting nodes to simplify paths

    ☐ using Bezier handles

    ☐ align and distribute nodes.

☐ I can convert bitmap images into editable vector shapes.

☐ I can know and understand the advantages and disadvantages of converting a bitmap image into an editable vector shape.

☐ I can create a bitmap image using selection tools to select parts of a bitmap image such as lasso, magic wand, colour select tools.

☐ I can adjust colour levels in a bitmap image such as brightness, contrast, colour balance, shadows, highlights, convert to greyscale.

☐ I can use tools/filters to alter parts of a bitmap image, such as distort, clone, blue, sharpen and red eye removal.

☐ I can resize an image/canvas.

☐ I can know and understand lossy and lossless compression.

☐ I can know how to change the colour depth and resolution of an image.

☐ I can know and understand the effects of different methods of compression on images.

☐ I can select font style (face, size, kerning, letter spacing and line spacing).

☐ I can fit text to path or shape (aligning text along a line or around a shape).

☐ I can set text in a shape.

☐ I can convert text to curves (convert fonts into editable vector shapes).

> # Chapter 19
> # Animation

Introduction

In this chapter you will learn about **animation** and how to use the animation software Adobe Animate. You will learn about different types of animations, and the components of an animation. There are tasks for you to try to explore the skills in the chapter, and to create your own animations.

KEY WORD

animation: a series of images that are played one after another to simulate movement

19.1 Types of animation

There are many forms of animation, and you have probably seen a lot of them without knowing there was any difference.

Cel (celluloid) **animation** was the first to be developed. This involves individually drawn frames (individual images), often drawn by hand. Each image is on a separate medium (for example a piece of paper), with the outlines drawn and then filled in with colour. By taking a photograph of each cel one at a time, when the images are viewed quickly it appears as animation. The original animations were made using cel animation, with thousands (if not millions) of individual frames.

Figure 19.1: Individual frames.

The basic principle of all animations is a series of individual images that are shown rapidly, one after the other.

Stop motion animation is where you use **objects** of other physical materials and take photographs of them in different positions. By making small changes to the positions of the objects, and taking a photograph each time, the images can then be viewed as an animation. Films and TV programs were often made using this technique.

KEY WORDS

cel animation: (also called cell animation) where individual images are drawn on separate pages then photographed, one frame at a time

stop motion animation: photographs are taken of objects; the objects are moved slightly each time and the photographs combined to create the animation

object: an image, or combination of images, that is manipulated as one item

Figure 19.2: Stop motion animation.

Time lapse is a form of photography, where a camera is set up and automatically takes a photograph at set-time intervals, for example, once a minute. The photographs are then shown in sequence to create an animation of what has happened. It is often used for events that take a long time, for example a plant growing.

Figure 19.3: Time-lapse photography.

A **flip book animation** is similar to a cel animation in that each frame is drawn individually, and usually by hand. In a flip book, the images are drawn in a book, each frame on a new page. The pages are then flipped by hand very quickly, so that the images appear to move.

Figure 19.4: Flip book animation.

CGI stands for Computer Generated Imagery. This refers to any images, whether still or moving, that are created using a computer. This could be **2D (two dimensional)** where the images are drawn on the x and y axis without any depth. They are usually cartoons which are created by a computer and not by hand.

CGI can also be **3D** (three dimensional). When most people say, or hear, CGI, they automatically think about 3D animations.

Figure 19.5: Computer-Generated Imagery (CGI).

Both 2D and 3D CGI can be animated.

Figure 19.6: 3D animation.

Figure 19.7: Frames showing a puffin landing.

Questions

1   Describe cel animations.
2   What is a time lapse animation?
3   How do you create a stop frame animation?
4   Name the animation that involves drawing an image in a book, and then changing the image.
5   What does CGI stand for?

Frame

Take a blank notepad and draw a shape in the bottom right-hand corner, then draw the same shape but in a slightly different position on the next page. Repeat this on a number of pages. You can then create a flip book animation (see Figure 19.4).

Each of these pages, or individual images, is called a **frame**. A computer animation is made up of a series of frames, which are played very quickly to give the illusion of movement. In reality, it is simply a sequence of individual images. Figure 19.7 shows a series of frames for a puffin landing.

> **KEY WORD**
>
> **frame:** one screen, or page, where an image is drawn; a series of these frames are played one after the other to create the animation

19.2 Stage

The area in animation software where you draw and create your animation is called the **stage**.

> **KEY WORD**
>
> **stage:** the area where the animation takes place; to be within the animation, the object must be on the stage

When you open Adobe Animate you will get a white rectangle. This is the stage. Whatever you want to appear in the animation must be in this stage.

The size of this stage is measured in pixels. You can change the size of the stage to meet your needs by increasing or decreasing the number of pixels in the width and height.

To change the stage size in Adobe Animate, click `Modify` and then `Document`.

You can then change the width and height in stage size. The drop-down menu lets you change from pixels to centimetres or inches, depending on which you want to use.

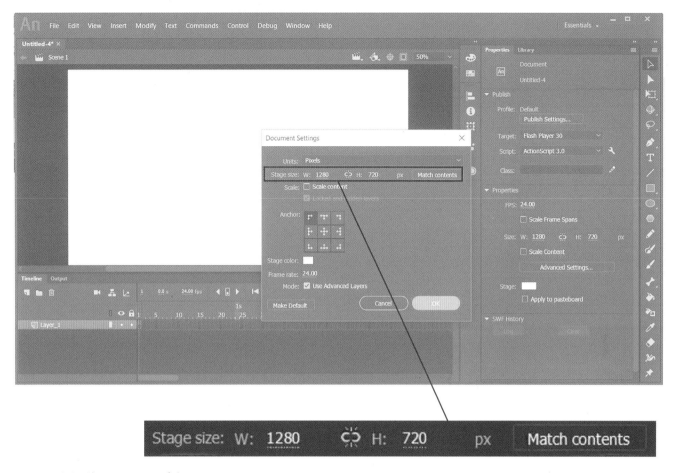

Figure 19.8: Changing size of the stage.

The stage has a set of *x*- and *y*-**coordinates** that you can use to position objects with more accuracy.

> **KEY WORD**
>
> **coordinates:** the position (*x* and *y*) of an object on the stage

The top-left corner has the coordinates (0, 0) and these then increase as you move down and across the image. In Figure 19.9, the ruler is visible at the top and left of the screen; this gives you the coordinates. This blue rectangle starts at *x*-position 0 (the left-hand edge) and its width is 313 (this is how far to the right the rectangle goes). Its *x* also starts at position *y* (the top edge) and its height goes down to 163.

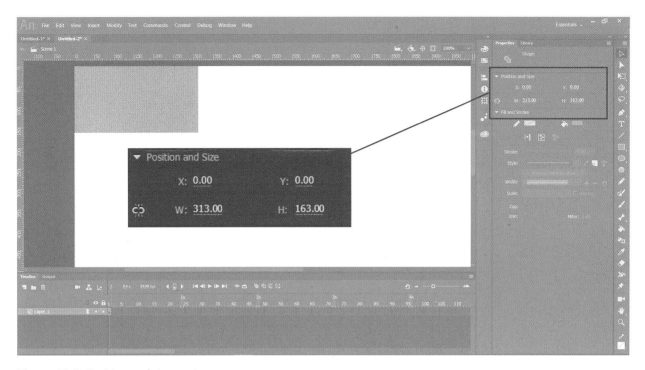

Figure 19.9: Position and size options.

When you select Modify and Document, you can also change the colour of the stage by clicking the Stage color box.

This will bring up a range of colours. Click the sphere in the top right to access even more colours, or you can type the colour code directly into the box.

The aspect ratio is the width and height of the stage. There are standard ratios depending on what you want to use the animation for. For example, if you are producing a film for widescreen televisions, you don't want the animation to be in a small square in the centre.

Common aspect ratios are shown in Table 19.1.

You need to consider where your animation is most likely to be viewed and when setting up your stage you must decide on the aspect ratio.

Adobe Animate helps you when you start a new document, by giving you some common options to choose from.

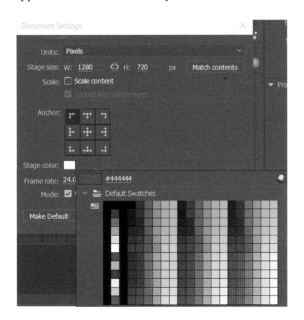

Figure 19.10: Colour options.

Ratio	Description
4:3	This is called standard. It is what old televisions used so is rarely used now. It is 4 units wide to 3 units high. It could be 2000 pixels wide by 1500 pixels high.
16:9	This is the ratio that is currently most widely used for TV. It is also commonly used in computer monitors and laptops, for consistency with television. It is 16 units wide to 9 units high.
2.35:1	This is widescreen and used for films. It is 2.35 units wide to 1 unit high.
16:10	Most modern mobile phones. It is 16 units wide to 10 units high.

Table 19.1: Common aspect ratios.

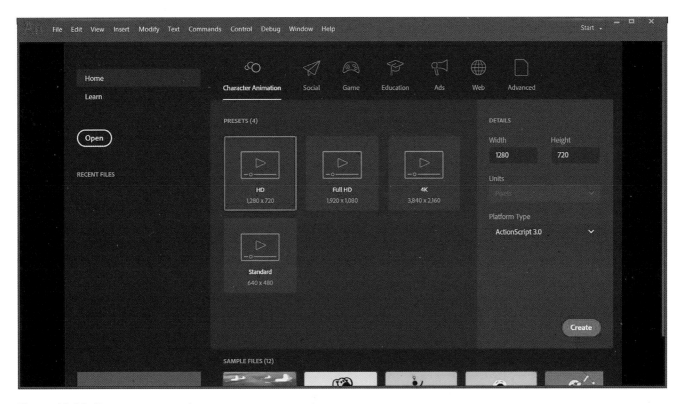

Figure 19.11: Common start options.

Use rulers, guides and grid settings

The stage has several features that can help you to lay out your animation.

Rulers can be turned on, and off. Click View from the top menu and then click Rulers.

The **grid** option displays a grid on the background of the stage. This can help you align objects to the same gridline. To turn the grid on or off, click View from the top menu, then Grid and then Show Grid.

There are options you can edit in the grid. By selecting Edit Grid, this brings up the menu. From here you can choose to display the grid over the objects instead of behind (the grid does not appear on the final animation).

There is the **snapping** option Snap to grid. This will make sure all objects align to one of the grid lines.

You can also change the space between the grid lines. Here this is 1 grid line every 10 pixels, but you can increase, or decrease it.

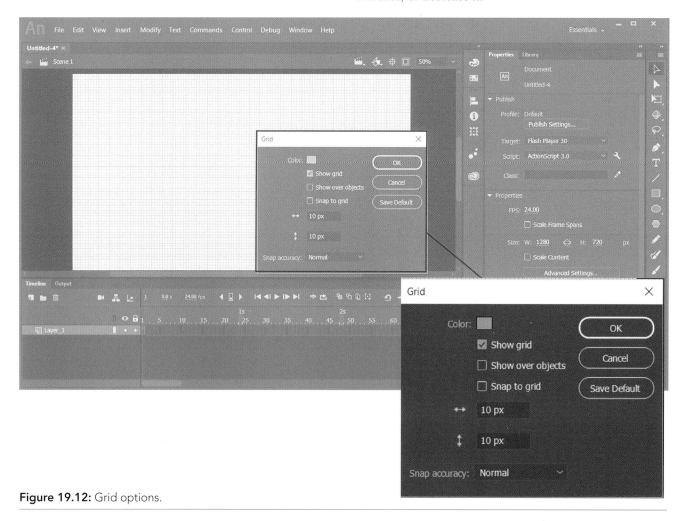

Figure 19.12: Grid options.

There are other snapping options, accessed from the `View` menu. These allow Adobe Animate to align objects automatically to:

- display lines from the object to let you line it up with other elements, using the option `Snap Align`

- other objects, using `Snap to Objects`

- specific pixels or lines of pixels, using `Snap to Pixels`.

You can add **guides** to your stage. Guides are lines that you can position to help you line up your objects. Turn on guides by selecting `View` from the top menu, then select `Guides` and then `Show Guides`.

The lines are then dragged down from the top of the screen as shown by the green arrows. The red lines are the guides that then appear. You can change the colour of these by choosing `Edit Guides` from the `Guides` menu.

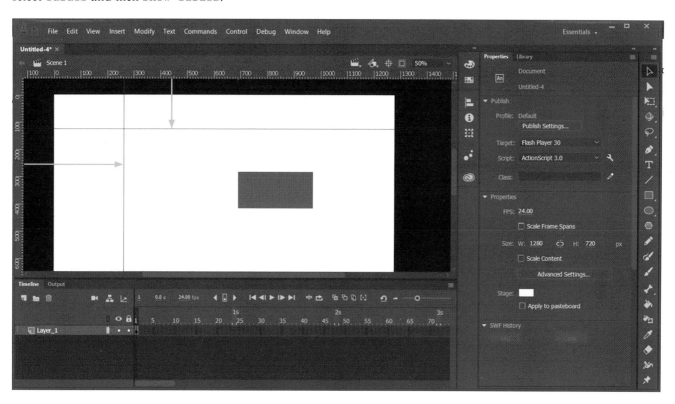

Figure 19.13: Positioning guides.

Questions

6   What is a frame in animation?

7   Describe what a ratio of 4:3 means and when is it used.

8   Name two other common ratios and when they are used.

9   Explain the purpose of rulers, grids and guides.

10 Explain the advantage(s) of using snapping.

19.3 Importing and creating Vector objects

Vector graphics are stored as points (or coordinates) and equations that are used to calculate the position, colour, and so on, of the image. There is much more about vector graphics in Chapter 18: Graphics Creation.

Drawing an image

The side toolbar has a range of shapes you can use to create vector graphics. Clicking one of these brings up its `Properties` menu, where you can select fill colours, line colours, size, style, and so on, before drawing the shape (or line) on screen. The black arrow lets you select items.

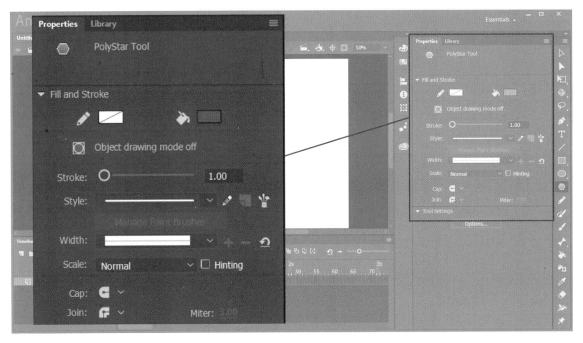

Figure 19.14: Properties options.

The `Line` and `Fill` options are accessed by clicking them independently.

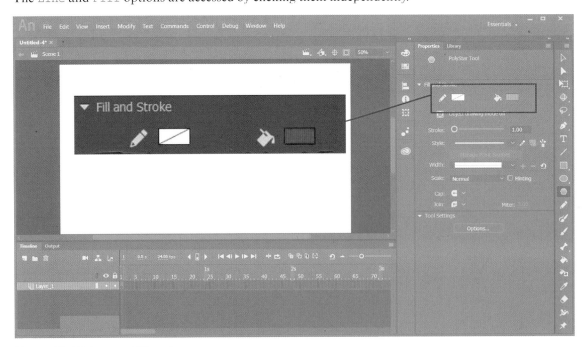

Figure 19.15: Line and fill options.

The menu to choose the colour from will then appear. Select the colour from the block.

> **TIP**
>
> Clicking on the sphere will show you a wider range of colours.

The lack of transparency of an object or a piece of text can be changed. In the software this may be referred to as the opacity or the alpha style. This is measured as a percentage. For example, 0% will have a fully transparent, invisible image. At 100%, the image is fully visible.

The visibility of an object can be set when it is created, and it can also be manipulated during an animation to make objects appear and disappear.

To change the opacity of an image, select its properties and go into its fill options. Here you can change the percentage of the opacity.

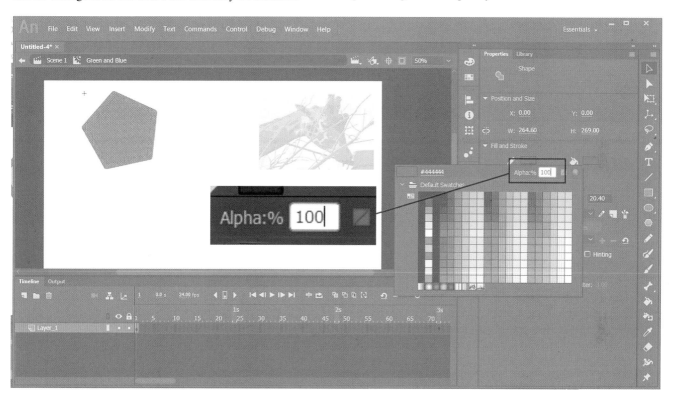

Figure 19.16: Opacity (Alpha %).

When you have selected a drawing tool, for example the paint brush tool, you have some additional properties to choose from.

The `Stroke` option is the size of the line you will draw. There are a range of styles that produce different patterns. There is only a line colour option, and no fill. This is because these tools only draw lines; they do not draw shapes to fill.

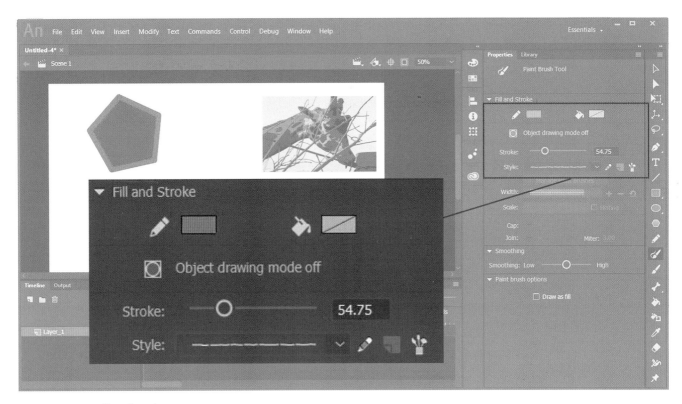

Figure 19.17: Fill and stroke options.

To change an image you can **transform** it. Use the selection tool to select the object you want to change (hold down `Shift` and click to select more than one element). Right click the item, select `Transform` and then `Free Transform`. This allows you to change the size of the object, rotate it, change its centre point (so you can rotate it from a different point). These can be accessed independently from the `Transform` menu.

You can manually adjust the size, rotation (orientation), skew, and so on, by selecting the `Transform` menu from the properties window and entering the rotation, or size transformation required.

Figure 19.18: Transforming options.

Questions

11 Describe vector graphics.

12 What is the difference between line and fill colours?

13 Which option do you select to rotate a shape or object?

Library and symbols

A **symbol** is one element that you have given a name. This allows you to perform motion and **morphing** inbetweening techniques on the symbols. If you select multiple items and convert them into one symbol, then they will become grouped together.

To convert a selection to a symbol, use the selection tool to right click the item. Then choose `Convert to Symbol`.

A new window will open. You need to give your new symbol a sensible name (something that describes it) because you might have hundreds of symbols and you need to be able to tell them apart.

The symbol now appears in the **library**. This is a record of all the symbols you have in your document. You can create a new instance of a symbol by dragging its name onto the stage. You could have 20 of the same symbol, and animate them separately. However, if you change the structure of one of the symbols, the rest will also change.

KEY WORDS

symbol: a component, for example, an image, of an animation that has a name and is put in the library; multiple copies of the object can be created

morphing: another term for shape tweening; one image changes into another image

library: a place that stores a list of images and objects/symbols in an animation

---

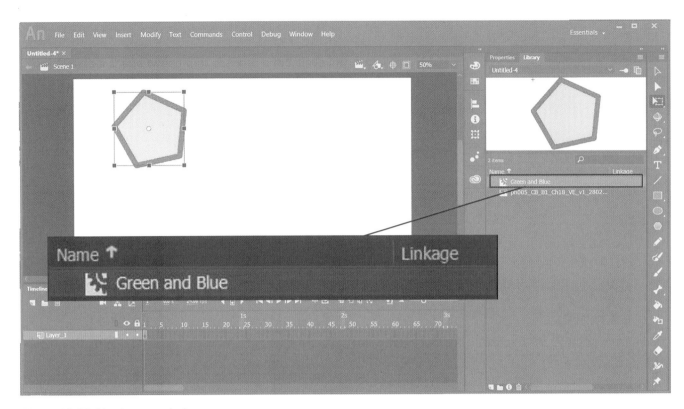

Figure 19.19: Naming a symbol.

Importing an image

You can import a pre-existing image into the library, or onto your stage (that is not as a symbol) for your animation, for example a photograph.

To import an image, click `File` from the top menu, then `Import` and either `Import to Stage` or `Import to Library`. Find your image and click `Open` to import it.

Bitmaps cannot be animated like vector graphics can be, because they are not made of coordinates and calculations that can be amended. A second problem with bitmap images is that when you enlarge them, they might pixelate. To try and prevent this you can try and convert the bitmap image into a vector graphic. This is called **tracing bitmaps**.

A disadvantage of exporting to a vector graphic is that you will lose some of the detail. If the image is a photograph then it might not appear exactly as the original. It will also not be able to be edited in the same way, for example using the bitmap image manipulation tools.

> **KEY WORD**
>
> **tracing bitmap:** a way of converting a bitmap image into a vector graphic

First put the bitmap image from the library onto the stage by dragging it.

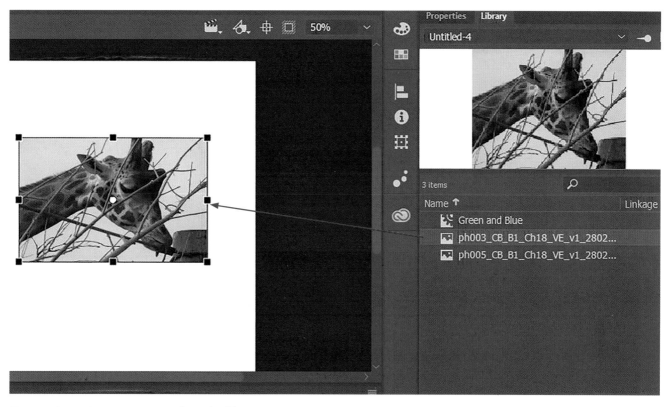

Figure 19.20: Getting an image from the library.

With the symbol selected, select `Modify` from the top menu, and then `Bitmap`, then `Trace Bitmap`.

The lower the colour threshold, the more accurate it will be. Adobe Animate will usually give you the most appropriate threshold automatically. Click `OK` and then your bitmap will be turned into a vector. You can select just some sections of the image and manipulate them independently.

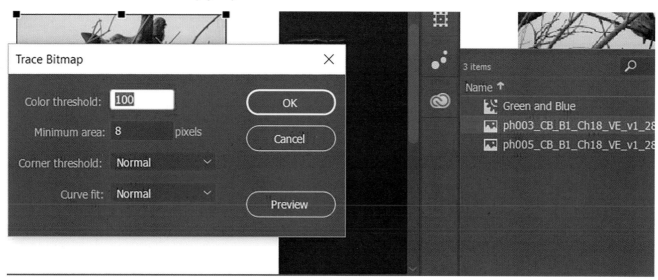

Figure 19.21: Bitmap manipulation options.

Text

Text can be added to the stage using the text tool which lets you edit the style, size and colour. Text is treated in the same way as objects, so you can use **layers**, **tweens**, change the opacity and manipulate text in the same way.

To add text, click the T on the toolbar, then on the screen where you want the text to appear.

KEY WORDS

layer: an object or image given its own timeline for independent manipulation

tween: (inbetweening) an animation where the start and end points are set; the computer generates the actual images to make the animation change

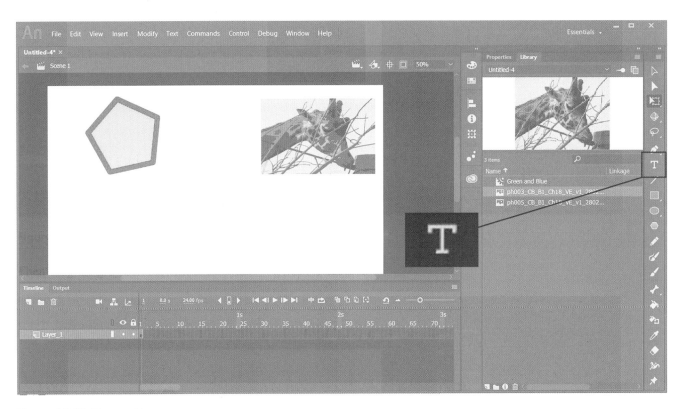

Figure 19.22: Text tool button.

Click Properties to change the font name, size, colour, and so on.

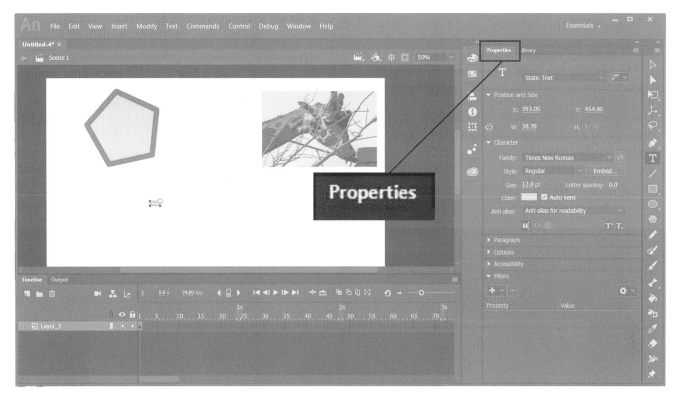

Figure 19.23: Text properties options.

Questions

14 Why do you have to change a shape to a symbol?

15 Why can't bitmap images be used in inbetweening?

19.4 Layers

An animation is made up of layers which each has its own set of frames that you animate independently. By using layers, you can independently manipulate different parts of an image, otherwise you would be manipulating the entire image, in the same way, every time.

Think about a stick person that you want to make walk. The elements that need to be separate would be:

- left arm
- right arm
- left leg
- right leg
- head
- body.

You might even need to split some of these down further, for example 'left arm' may need to be 'upper left arm', and 'lower left arm'. It all depends on how detailed your animation is going to be.

Each layer is shown on the left of the **timeline**. Each layer must have an appropriate and descriptive name, for example if it stores the left arm, then name it left arm.

> **KEY WORD**
>
> **timeline:** the place that controls the order the frames are run, the positioning of the layers, and so on

To create a new layer, click `Insert` and then `Timeline`, then `Layer`. To change its name, double click the layer name beside the timeline and enter your name. The name cannot have any spaces in it, so multiple words can be separated by a symbol, for example, `arm-Layer`.

You can even create folders for your layers. Complex animations may have hundreds of layers, so you can keep some of them together. Consider the stick person you are trying to make walk. You could make a folder called 'stick_person' and put all the layers for that person in the folder. Then they are all kept together, so you don't mix them up with other parts of the animation.

To create a folder, when you click `Insert`, then `Timeline`, select `Layer Folder`. Use your left mouse button to drag layers into the folder, and double click its name to rename it.

If two shapes are in the same layer, then they can delete each other. For example, in Figure 19.24, the two shapes are in the same layer.

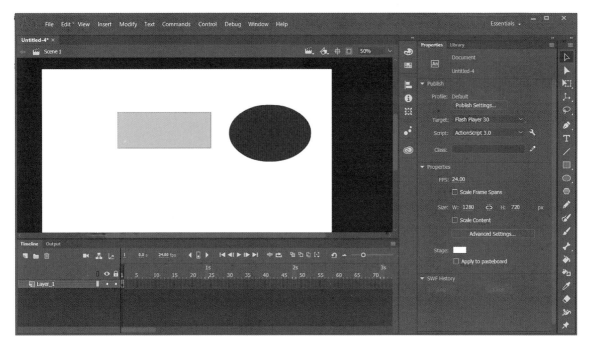

Figure 19.24: Shapes in the same layer.

If they are moved so the blue oval is over the green rectangle, the part of the rectangle covered is deleted.

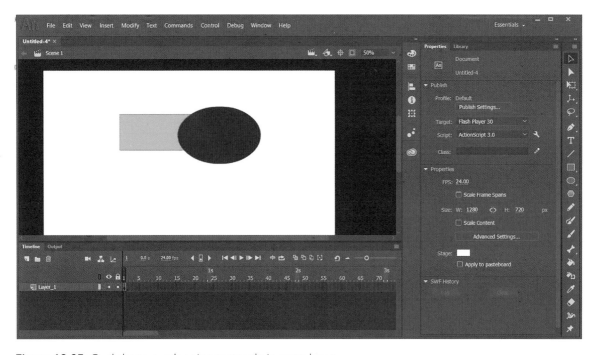

Figure 19.25: Oval shape overlapping rectangle in same layer.

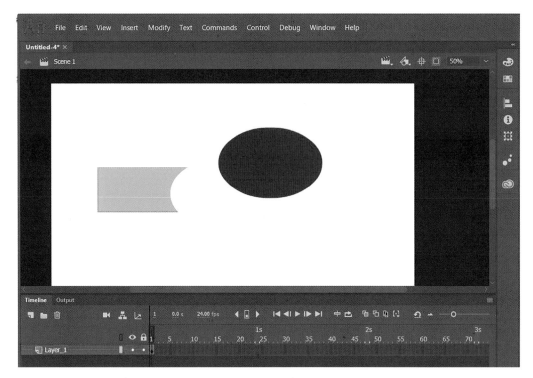

Figure 19.26: Part of rectangle in same layer deleted.

Layers also allow you to order objects. The item(s) in the highest layer in the timeline are in front of all the others.

In Figure 19.27, the layer 'blue_oval' is at the top, and on the stage it appears in front of the green rectangle.

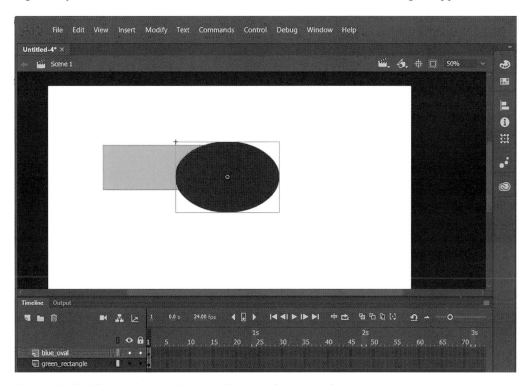

Figure 19.27: Blue oval in own layer overlapping the rectangle.

If the layers are swapped in the timeline then they will be reversed on the stage. The green rectangle is now in front.

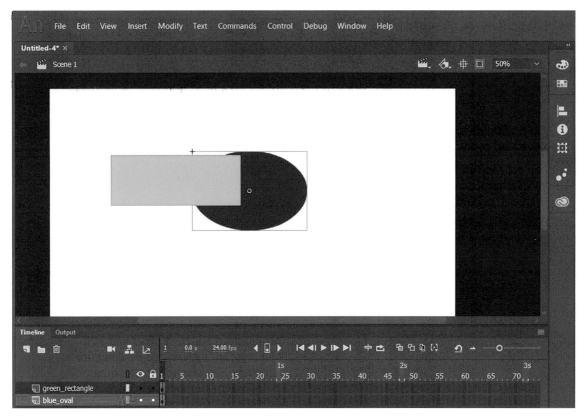

Figure 19.28: Order of layers swapped so that there is no deletion of part of the rectangle.

Timeline

A timeline is made up of frames, in chronological order from left to right. Each rectangle is one frame. In Adobe Animate every 5 is numbered.

A completely grey rectangle is a frame. A rectangle with a circle in is a keyframe (which you will learn about in the next section). When you create inbetween animations some of these frames could turn green or blue.

Figure 19.29: Timelines.

If there is no rectangle for a layer in a specific frame (for example frame 30), then the items in that frame do not exist when that frame runs. So, in Figure 19.30, 'blue_oval' does not have a frame beyond frame 10.

Whereas 'green_rectangle' has frames up to frame 15. This means on the current frame selected (frame 15 as shown by the red rectangle on the number 15), only the 'green_rectangle' is visible.

Figure 19.30: Green rectangle timeline.

Key frame

A **key frame** identifies a change in an image. These changes are represented by a • in the frame.

KEY WORDS

key frame: a location on a timeline which marks a frame that has a change in the animation, for example, a drawing has changed, or the start or end of a tween

Figure 19.31: Key frame dots.

For example, 'green_rectangle' is in one position in frame 1. It then changes in frame 2, and frame 3; it then does not change again. 'blue_oval' is created in frame 1; it does not change then until frame 10.

To add frames and keyframes, you need to right click the frame where you want to add a frame or keyframe, then choose `Insert Frame` (or `Insert Keyframe`) from the menu.

PRACTICAL ACTIVITY 19.02

1 Reopen the file **stickperson**. Create an animation with your stick person. Make them walk across the screen. Challenge yourself and make them perform other actions such as jumping, running and dancing. You could introduce a second person by copying your folder of layers and animating them separately.

2 Reopen the file **underwaterScene**. Add a fish to your underwater scene. Make the fish swim around the underwater scene using keyframes. Add bubbles coming from the fish that slowly rise to the surface.

3 Reopen the file **myName**. Create an animation, using frames and keyframes, to make your name appear letter by letter.

4 Create an animation to make a flower grow. Start with a seed and then make roots and a stem grow from the seed, before eventually it becomes a flower.

Timings and frame rate

A common misconception is that a frame represents a second, so that if there are ten frames, this takes ten seconds. This is not the case. The timing is measured in frames per second (fps), which can be changed, for example, 10 fps means that ten frames will be run each second. If you have 200 frames, the animation will last 20 seconds. The higher the fps rate, the quicker the frames change and the smoother the animation appears.

When designing an animation, you need to consider the fps, as this will affect the number of frames you need, and the extent to which you change the images in each frame. If you need an item to stay static for a set time, then it can be given frames (not key frames) where it exists but does not change. When it needs to change or move, a key frame is then added.

You can change the frame rate by entering a different number of frames above the timeline.

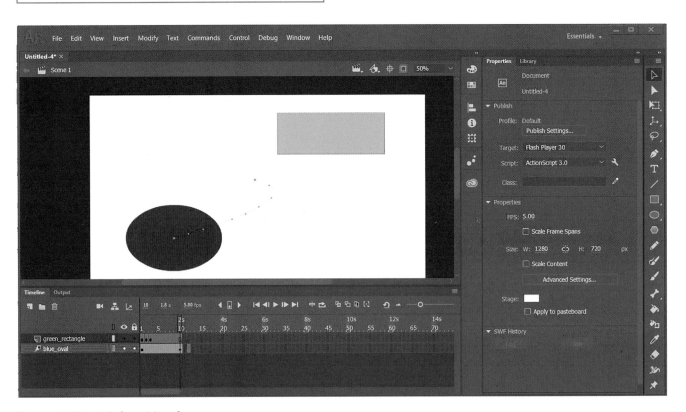

Figure 19.32: Path for adding frames.

Questions

16 What is a layer?

17 Why are layers used in animation?

18 What effect will increasing the frame rate have on an animation?

Inbetween animation

An animation created solely with frames and key frames can be quite robotic, unless you made very small changes in each keyframe, but this is time consuming. By inserting an inbetween animation (a tween), the computer will generate the animation for you (it fills in the spaces inbetween your frames). For example, if you want to move a drawing of a fish across the screen, you can set the start location (A), the end location (B) and then the computer will work out how to get the fish from A to B.

When applying a tween to a layer, it will affect every item in that layer. It is important to make sure that each individual item has its own layer.

There are two types of tween you can use, motion and shape (or morphing).

Motion tween

A motion tween only deals with the movement of an object, for example moving from one place to another, and rotation. If you use key frames, you have to position the object in each frame. Using a motion tween, the computer fills in the gaps in movement.

The item you tween needs to be set as a symbol before you start moving it.

To create a motion tween in Adobe Animate, create the first keyframe with the symbol where you want it to start, and frames up to the point where you want the tween to end.

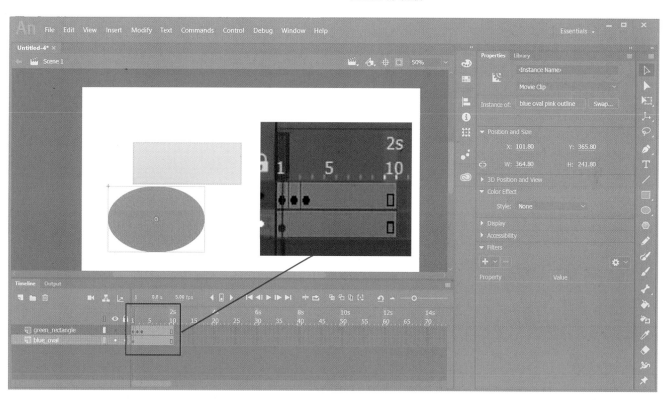

Figure 19.33: Starting a motion tween.

Then right click the frames you have added and select `Create Motion Tween`.

Insert a keyframe in the frame where you want the animation to end, and then with this frame selected, move the object to the position where you want it to be. You can also rotate it if required.

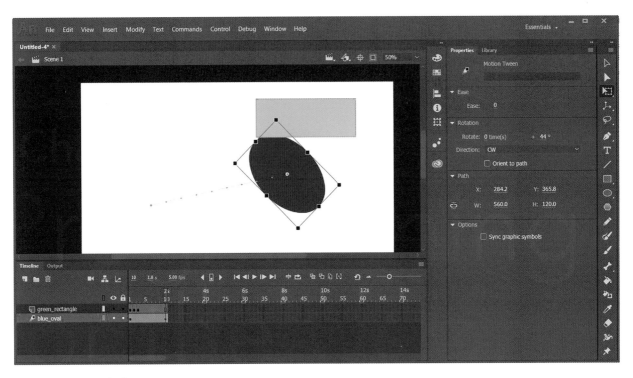

Figure 19.34: End of motion tween.

WORKED EXAMPLE 19.01

Create an animation where a red circle moves to each corner of the screen using inbetweening.

First rename the layer 'redcircle', choose the line colour red and fill colour red, then draw the circle.

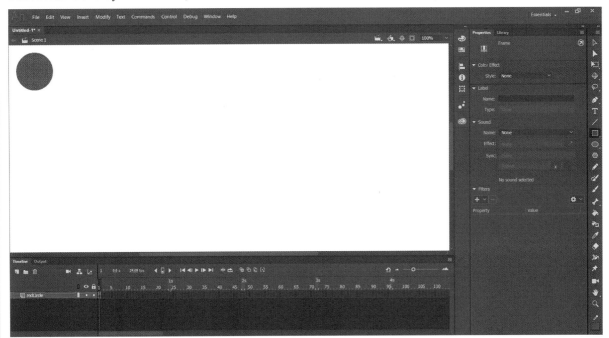

Figure 19.35: Rename the layer.

CONTINUED

Convert the red circle to a symbol with a sensible name.

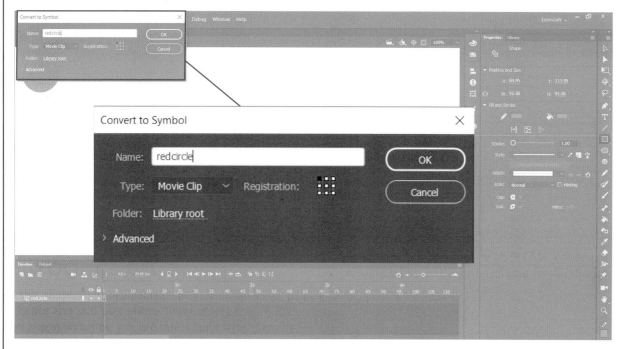

Figure 19.36: Convert the red circle to a symbol.

Add frames to frame 15, and then Create Motion Tween.

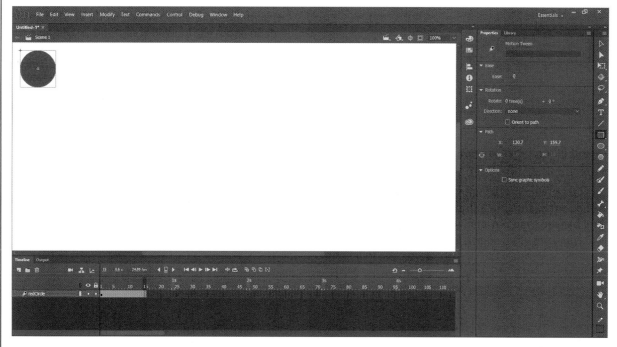

Figure 19.37: Add frames.

CONTINUED

Add a keyframe on frame 15, and move the circle to the top right corner of the screen.

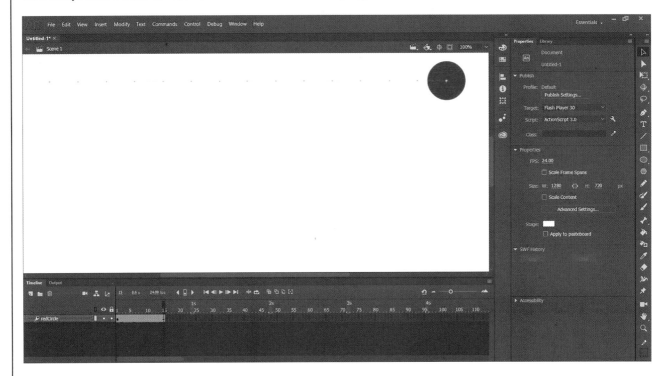

Figure 19.38: Add a key frame.

Repeat for all four corners.

PRACTICAL ACTIVITY 19.03

1   Create a ball and make it move around the screen.

2   Create a car animation where the car appears on screen and drives around a track that is drawn on the background using a motion tween. Save the file as **carAnimation**

3   Use a motion tween to create an animation of each letter of your name flying onto the screen one by one, eventually displaying your full name.

4   Add more fish to the file **underwaterScene** that you created earlier. Make each one move using a motion tween. Add a bubble for each fish and use a motion tween to make the bubbles float to the surface.

19.5 Paths

You can draw a path for a symbol to follow, and set a motion tween to follow this path.

To do this, first add the keyframe where you want the path to start, and another where you want it to end.

Right click and select `Create Classic Tween`. This will turn the frames blue and they will have an arrow in them.

Right click the layer and select `Add Classic Motion Guide`.

Use the drawing tools to draw the path, for example using a paint brush.

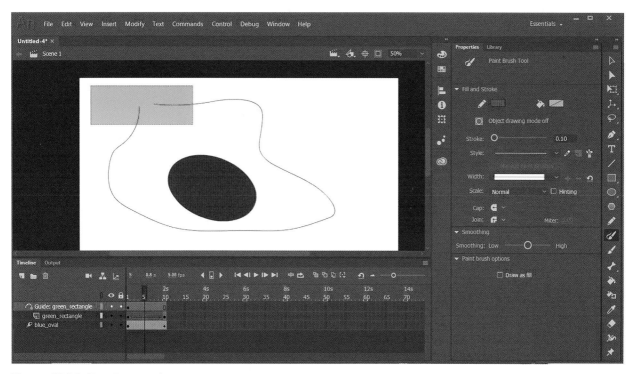

Figure 19.39: Drawing a path.

Select the first keyframe and drag the object so its centre (the circle that appears) locks onto the start of your path. Then select the last keyframe and drag the object so its centre locks onto the end of the path. That will create your motion path tween.

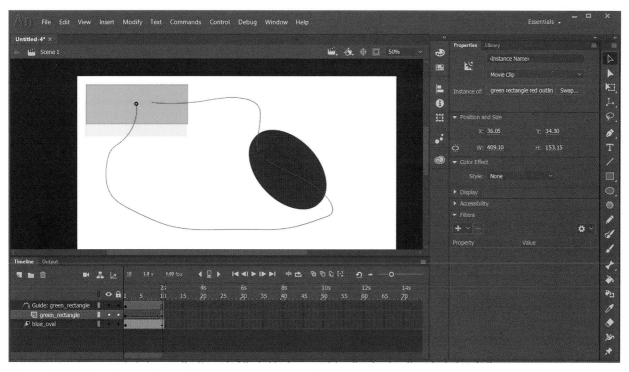

Figure 19.40: Creating motion path.

PRACTICAL ACTIVITY 19.04

1   Create a red ball. Draw a path for the red ball to follow and animate it so it follows the path.

2   Add a second ball with a new path, and animate it to follow that path.

3   Open the file **carAnimation** that you created earlier. Make the road include a number of bends. Draw a path to make the car move around the track.

4   Open the file **underwaterScene** that you created earlier. Add an octopus to your underwater scene. Draw a path for the octopus to follow and animate it.

Morphing (shape, size and colour)

Morphing allows a shape to be changed into a new shape, for example, a small, red square could be turned into a large, blue circle. The computer generates each step of the transformation for you.

A shape tween can also include movement. The shape will change while it moves.

In Adobe Animate, a shape tween cannot take place on a symbol (or object) such as a shape. This is because the symbol is in the library and it cannot be changed by a shape tween. To create the shape tween, draw your shape, image, line, and so on, and do not convert it to a symbol. However, it all still needs to be in the same layer so that other elements are not affected.

Add your image in the keyframe where you want your shape tween to start. Add frames to where you want it to finish, in the same way you would with a motion tween. This time, right click and select `Create Shape Tween`.

Right click in the frame where you want the tween to finish and then select `Insert Keyframe`.

With the new keyframe selected, either change the colour, shape or size of the image. Or, delete the contents of the frame, and draw a new image.

WORKED EXAMPLE 19.02

Create an animation where a black line turns into a blue circle, then a red rectangle, then back to a line.

First create a new file and add a layer with the name **shape**. Draw the line on the stage.

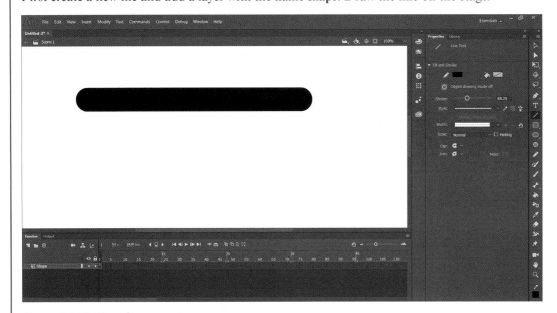

Figure 19.41: Line drawn on stage.

CONTINUED

Add frames, then right click and select Create Motion Tween. Right click on the last frame and create a keyframe. Delete the line in this keyframe and draw a blue **circle**.

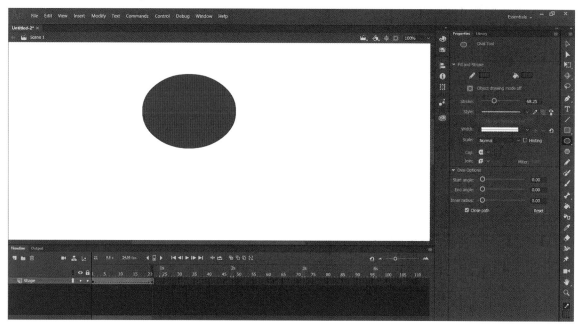

Figure 19.42: Blue circle in the last key frame.

Repeat the process this time drawing a red **rectangle**.

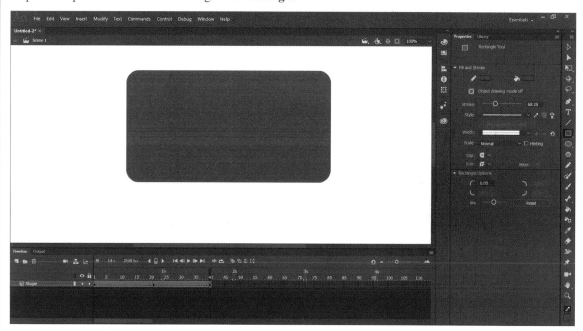

Figure 19.43: Red rectangle in the last key frame.

Repeat again but this time copy the line from frame 1 and paste it into your new keyframe.

PRACTICAL ACTIVITY 19.05

1   Create a shape tween that changes a red circle into a blue square.

2   Create a shape tween that changes a rain cloud into a sun.

3   Draw a scene that shows the changes during a year, for example a river and forest showing

  a   lush, green, sunny days

  b   leaves changing to red and orange and falling

  c   a frozen river with barren trees

  d   new growth emerging.

4   Open the file **underwaterScene**. Make the bubbles change shape, for example, get smaller as they move to the surface.

5   Open the file **myName**. Make each letter of your name morph into the next letter.

Property keyframes

Property keyframes allow you to even out the keyframes in a tween. For example, if you copy a tween the keyframes may not be evenly spaced and this will make the symbol move at different speeds. In Adobe Animate, turn on roving keyframes to stop this.

For example, in this tween the orange dots show the keyframe changes. They are not evenly spaced.

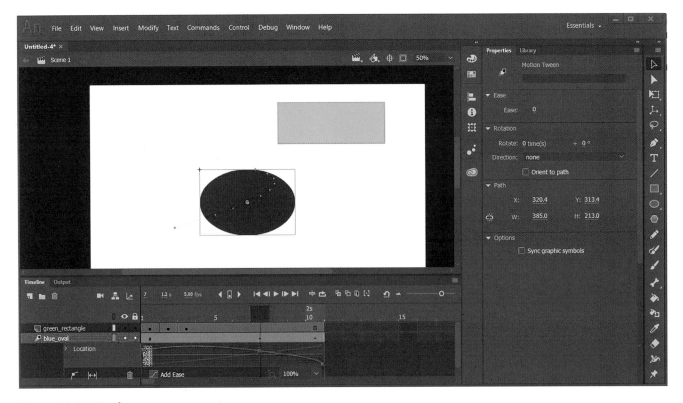

Figure 19.44: Key frames uneven spacing.

To change this, right click the tween in the timeline, select `Motion Path` and then `Switch keyframes to roving`. This will even out the spacings.

Viewing and controlling animations

To test-run the animation, click `Enter` on the keyboard, or click the play symbol above the timeline. There are other controls here too, such as stepping that lets you move the animation through one frame at a time.

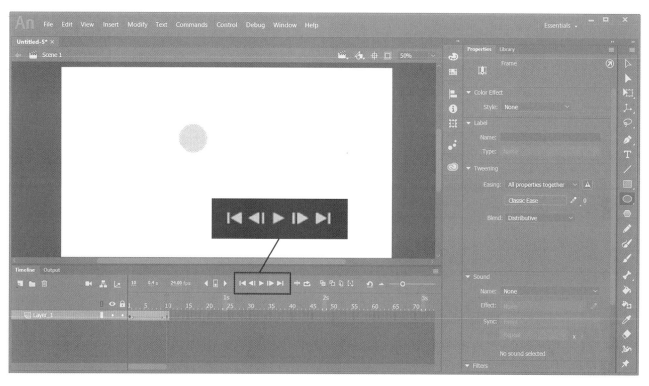

Figure 19.45: Animation play symbols.

To watch the video on loop, select the Loop option above the timeline.

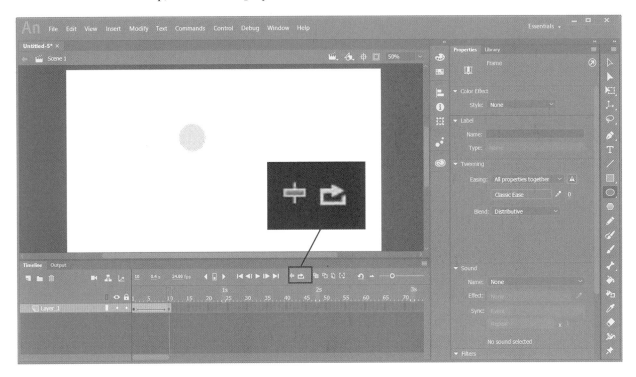

Figure 19.46: Animation loop option.

Then drag the grey box over the frames that you want to loop.

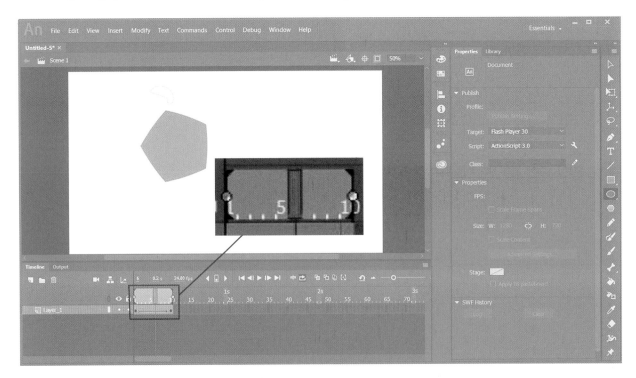

Figure 19.47: Selection of frames to be looped.

To stop the animation when it is playing, click the **play** button. This then becomes the pause symbol.

To view the animation looping continually in a separate window, hold down `Control` and click `Enter`.

19.6 Masks

A **mask** can make it so that only certain parts of an image are visible. In Adobe Animate, masks are added in their own layers.

Right click the layer you want to become a mask, and select `Mask`. The layer beneath automatically becomes a sub-layer of the mask.

Draw the shape that you want the mask to be in the first layer.

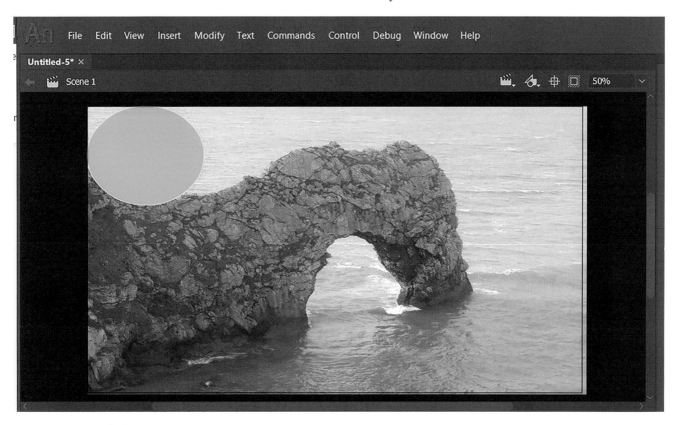

Figure 19.48: Mask shape.

Click the padlock to lock this layer. You will then be able to view the image through the masked area.

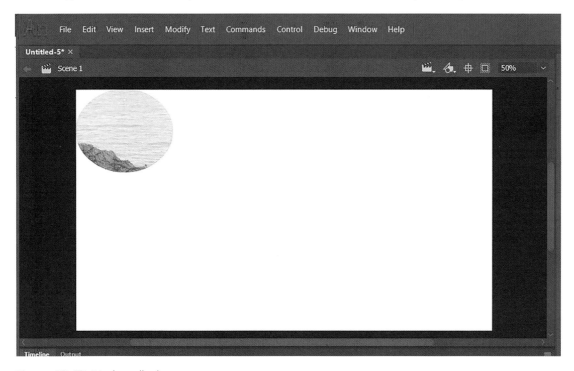

Figure 19.49: Mask padlock.

You can animate a mask as you would an ordinary symbol. Remove the padlock to unlock the layer, and then add a motion tween in the same way you would normally. Add the tween, add the keyframe, and move the symbol.

Figure 19.50: Adding motion tween to a mask.

1 Create an animated introduction to a TV show or film. Make sure you include images of the main characters and text introducing the title. Make use of opacity and tweens.

2 Extend your underwater scene to include a range of sea life. Animate the background and plants to create a continuous, repeating scene.

3 Create an animated cartoon that shows a day in the life of cartoon's central character. Use a range of techniques, including some key frame animation and tweens.

4 Choose your favourite TV show. Create a new show-intro to this show, using a range of animation techniques.

5 Create an animation about your school to advertise it to prospective students. Include a range of images from the school as well as your own vector graphics.

Questions

19 What is the difference between a frame and a keyframe?

20 What is the difference between a motion tween and a shape tween?

21 Explain why inbetweening produces smoother animations than frame-by-frame animations.

22 Describe the purpose of a mask and give an example of how it can be used.

Exporting

Once you have created your animation you will need to export it to a file format for use in other formats.

Click `File` from the top menu, then `Export`.

There are several export options to choose from.

Export option	Description
Image	This creates one image file for every frame in your animation.
Movie	You can create an .swf file, which is a Flash file commonly used in websites, although this is being phased out of use.
Video	You can create a video through Adobe Media Encoder, or convert to a .mov file.
Animated GIF	This will create an animated .gif file that you can integrate into a website.

Table 19.2: Animation export options.

Export your finished animations into an appropriate format. When you have developed your web development skill, use them to create a website to display your animations.

19.7 Animation variables

A variable is something that can change. In animation, this can have many different forms.

Variables can be items that you change as the animator. For example, the graphical elements that you have within the animation. Each one of these can be manipulated and changed during the animation. These are **primary variables** because they are the most important. They are the fundamental basis of the animation.

Animations have other elements, known as **secondary variables**. These might be sound or other components that are in the background. The rippling of water behind the objects is secondary, or the movement of clothing as a person walks, and the movement of trees in the wind. They are not the focal point of the animation but they are animated.

KEY WORDS

primary variable: the foremost parts of the animation, that is, the graphic components

secondary variable: the background elements of the animation, for example moving water/trees

Variables can also be used to control, or manipulate, parts of an animated object. In 3D animations, wire models are created on the computer of the objects being animated.

Figure 19.51: Wireframe.

Within these wire models an animation can create hinges called **avars**. By using these avars the position of that part of the animated object, or even the animated object itself, can be manipulated. For example, you could manipulate each part of a finger individually to make it move realistically.

EXAM-STYLE QUESTIONS

1 Saif owns a small independent comic shop named Saif's Comics.

   a Saif wants a short animation that will appear as a banner across the top of his website.

   Create an animation to meet the following requirements.

   - The aspect ratio must be 2.35:1.
   - The background must remain black throughout.
   - The name 'Saif's' should appear at the start of the animation, then each letter should fade out one at a time, taking 1 second for each one to fade.
   - The word 'Comics' should fade in as a whole word, taking 1 second to appear. It should stay on screen for 2 seconds, and then fade out one letter at a time (1 second for each fade).
   - The words should be in a large white font, taking up the full height of the animation.
   - The animation must be set to loop.
   - All animations must be smooth.
   - The animation must be exported in a suitable format for use on a website.   [13]

   b Describe the differences and similarities between cel animation, stop motion animation, and time-lapse animation.   [3]

                                                                        [Total 16]

2 Henry owns a property sales business named Henry's Homes.

   You have been provided with the following file: **Henry logo.jpg**

   a Create a short animation to advertise Henry's property sales business.

   The animation must meet the following requirements.

   - The aspect ratio must be 16:9.
   - The background should be pale blue.
   - The image 19.1 **Henry logo.jpg** should be on the left-hand side of the animation. It should start small and then increase in size, before decreasing again. This should repeat throughout the animation.
   - A white ball should come in from the left to the right, revealing the sentence 'We take pride in selling your property' for example,

   Figure 19.52: Revealing text.

CONTINUED

- When the ball disappears off the left-hand side of the animation, it should stay off for 1.5 seconds.
- When it returns, it should move from left to right. It should display the text 'No sale, no fee' (as a mask) as it passes over it before disappearing off to the right, for example,

Figure 19.53: Mask.

- The animation should be set to loop.
- All animations must be smooth.
- Animation should be exported in a suitable format for viewing on a computer.

[19]

b Describe what is meant by a **frame** and a **keyframe**. [2]

[Total 21]

3 Ying needs an animation for her independent film company: Films by Ying.

Figure 19.54: Films by Ying logo.

Create a short animation for the logo.

The animation must meet the following requirements.

- The screen ratio should be 16:10.
- The background should be white with the green outline already displayed.
- The letters should bounce in from the left. The Y should appear first, then the B, then the F.
- When all the letters are on screen they should remain for 2 seconds, and then fade out.
- The animation should loop.
- All animations should be smooth.
- The file should be exported as an animation gif.

[12]

SUMMARY CHECKLIST

- [ ] I can configure the stage/frame/canvas for an animation by:
  - [ ] setting colour, size, aspect ratio
  - [ ] using rulers, guides and grid settings
  - [ ] setting snapping options.
- [ ] I can import and create Vector objects including:
  - [ ] tracing bitmaps
  - [ ] adding text.
- [ ] I can control object properties including:
  - [ ] stroke and fill settings
  - [ ] size position and orientation
  - [ ] transparency.
- [ ] I can use inbetweening ('tweening') tools including:
  - [ ] show motion
  - [ ] show shape, size and colour changes.
- [ ] I can set paths for animation to follow.
- [ ] I can use layers.
- [ ] I can apply masks.
- [ ] I can control animations by:
  - [ ] adjusting frame rates
  - [ ] looping or stopping animations.
- [ ] I can know and understand the basic principles of animation including:
  - [ ] frames, key frames, property keyframes, timings, coordinates
  - [ ] inbetweening and the effect it creates
  - [ ] morphing and the effect it creates.
- [ ] I can know and understand different animation types and methods including:
  - [ ] cell animation, stop motion, time lapse, flip book, CGI, 2D, 3D.
- [ ] I can know and understand the use of animation variables when creating animations including:
  - [ ] primary, for example graphical elements
  - [ ] secondary, for example sound, components of animation
  - [ ] the use of animation variables to control the position of an animated object or parts of an animated object.

> Chapter 20
Programming for the web

LEARNING INTENTIONS

By the end of this chapter, you will be able to:

- use JavaScript to:
    - add interactivity to web pages
    - change HTML content
    - change HTML styles
    - show/Hide HTML elements
    - display data in different ways
- react to common HTML events
- provide user interaction
- use correct syntax to:
    - create statements
    - use JavaScript loops for iterative methods
    - create functions
    - use JavaScript timing events
    - add comments to annotate and explain code

- know and understand the structure and syntax of JavaScript code
- know and understand a range of object-based JavaScript programming techniques and terms
- describe and explain the terms and programming techniques listed here.

BEFORE YOU START

- Do you know how web pages are constructed using HTML code?
- Are you able to read and use HTML tags to create and edit web pages?
- Do you have experience of CSS (Cascading Style Sheet) and know how this is used to set the style, or presentation, of a website?

Introduction

In this chapter you will learn how to use JavaScript to enhance and add user interactivity to websites. When you access websites, you are interacting with them by clicking buttons, entering data and selecting from sets of options. This is often done using the scripting language JavaScript. JavaScript is written within the HTML code of a web page and the HTML code then calls this code. JavaScript can then be integrated with other languages such as PHP to allow your website to communicate with a database, but that is beyond the scope of this specification. JavaScript is useful to learn because you add additional content to your web pages to make them perform more actions and engage the user.

It is important that you understand how websites are developed, because this will allow you to edit and create your own websites, and give you more control over the content because you understand how it works and how the data can be manipulated. This can also be helpful when things go wrong, because when you understand what is happening in the scripts you have a better chance of finding the problem and fixing it.

20.1 Introduction to JavaScript

JavaScript uses keywords. These are words that you must use to tell the web page what to do.

JavaScript can be added to an HTML document. It is recognised by starting and ending the JavaScript code with a script tag. For example:

```
<script>
    Your JavaScript code would go here
</script>
```

This can be part of a web page. For example here is an alert box within an HTML web page:

```
<HTML>
    <BODY>
        This is my first web page
        <SCRIPT>
            alert("Hello World");
        </SCRIPT>
    </BODY>
</HTML>
```

As soon as this web page opens, a pop-up box will appear saying "Hello World".

The code does not need to be indented as it is in this example, but the indenting does make the code easier to read. You can see where you have opened and closed your tags so you don't accidentally miss any. alert is one of the keywords.

20.2 Outputting data

document.write

The code `document.write(theOutput)` will output the text inside the brackets to the web page. For example:

```
<script>
    document.write("Hello world");
</script>
```

This will display "Hello world" in the web page.

WORKED EXAMPLE 20.01

Create a web page that displays the title: My First JavaScript Web Page, at the top of the page.

First, put your basic HTML tags into the file you are using to create the website.

```
<HTML>
<BODY>

</BODY>
</HTML>
```

Inside the body tags, put your JavaScript tags.

```
<HTML>
<BODY>
    <SCRIPT>
    </SCRIPT>
</BODY>
</HTML>
```

Inside the JavaScript tags write your code to output My First JavaScript Web Page.

```
<HTML>
<BODY>
    <SCRIPT>
        document.write("My First JavaScript
Web Page");
    </SCRIPT>
</BODY>
</HTML>
```

CONTINUED

Notice that the text inside the brackets is in speech marks; this is because it is a **string** (Section 20.6 Variables and operators/**Data types**). If there aren't speech marks there, then the website tries to run the command `My`, then the command `First` and so on, which is meaningless.

Open your file in a web browser to see the result of the code.

KEY WORDS

string: a data type: data is stored as text which can be characters, numbers and symbols

data type: the type of data being stored, for example, a number, string (text)

.innerHTML

You can name elements within your HTML code. For example, you might want to name the first paragraph in your website paragraph:

```
<p ID = "paragraph1"></p>
```

In your script tag, you can instruct JavaScript to add the text to the document in the element with the ID `paragraph1`. For example:

```
<script>
    document.getElementById("paragraph1").
    innerHTML = "Hello World";
</script>
```

The first section is always the same:
`document.getElementById`

Within the brackets is the name of the element where you want the text to appear.

`.innerHTML` tells it that you want the text within that element. Then there is an equals sign, and the text you want to display.

WORKED EXAMPLE 20.02

Create a web page with two paragraphs and with different text in each paragraph.

The paragraphs are declared with the IDs `paragraph1` and `paragraph2`.

```
<HTML>
<BODY>
   <p id = "paragraph1"></p>
   <p id = "paragraph2"></p>
   <SCRIPT>
   </SCRIPT>
</BODY>
</HTML>
```

Add one line of code for each paragraph. The first will say: `"This is paragraph1"` and the second will say `"and this is my second"`.

```
<HTML>
<BODY>
   <p id = "paragraph1"></p>
   <p id = "paragraph2"></p>
   <SCRIPT>
      document.getElementById("paragraph1").innerHTML = "This is paragraph1";
      document.getElementById("paragraph2").innerHTML = " and this is my second";
   </SCRIPT>
</BODY>
</HTML>
```

Run it in your web browser and see what happens.

PRACTICAL ACTIVITY 20.01

Open file **20.01.html**.

Create two paragraphs on the webpage.

Use Javascript to write your first name to the first paragraph, and your last name to the second paragraph.

Figure 20.1: A pop-up box.

20.3 Pop-up boxes

Pop-up boxes can be used to display text or information. They do not write text to the web page; it appears in an extra box on top of the screen. For example, here is an Alert box,

There are three types of pop-up box: Alert, Confirm and Prompt.

alert

You have already seen an alert box; this displays text in a box over the top of a web page. It is usually used to alert the user of something. In this example, the text `"Hello World"` will be displayed in the alert box.

```
alert("Hello World");
```

You might sometimes see an alert with the word window in front of it; it is exactly the same result. For example:

```
window.alert("Hello World");
```

confirm

A confirm box has two options: `Ok` and `cancel`. For example, this confirm box will display `"Ok to proceed?"`

```
confirm ("Ok to proceed?");
```

The option chosen by the user is returned as a value that can then be used to decide what to do. In this example, the value returned is stored in the variable `answer` (see Chapter 4 Algorithms).

```
var answer = confirm ("Ok to proceed?");
```

prompt

A prompt box allows a user to enter some text and gives them the option of `Ok` and `cancel`.

```
prompt("What day is it?")
```

If `Ok` is selected, then the text input can be stored into a variable. In this example, it will be stored in the variable answer.

```
var answer = prompt("What day is it?")
```

PRACTICAL ACTIVITY 20.02

Open file **20.02.html**.

First, amend the code to output "Ready to continue?".

Then use a confirm box to store their response. Then output "Let's go".

---

console.log

Some web browsers allow you to view console mode. This is where you can make your webpage record events, write messages to, etc. that do not actually appear on the web page, but appear in a log. It is used for debugging.

For example, if you are writing a selection statement (IF statement), and you want to check if the JavaScript has gone into the statement, you can output a unique message to the log to confirm the script has run, for example output `"in IF statement"`. If that message does not appear, then you know where to start looking for the error.

To view console mode open your browser with the web page on, and click F12. There will then be a tab with console on it.

```
console.log("In the JavaScript")
```

Change the text in the speech marks to output a different message.

WORKED EXAMPLE 20.03

Create a web page that:

- firstly, displays an alert welcoming you to the website
- secondly, asks you to confirm that you want to proceed to the question
- thirdly, asks a question where you have to type an answer.

At each stage it should write a log to the console to say what it has done.

Start with the alert.

```
<HTML>
<BODY>
   <SCRIPT>
      alert("Welcome to the website")
   </SCRIPT>
</BODY>
</HTML>
```

CONTINUED

Add the confirmation using a confirm box.

```
<HTML>
<BODY>
    <SCRIPT>
        alert("Welcome to the website")
        var confirmed = confirm("Are you sure you want to proceed?")
    </SCRIPT>
</BODY>
</HTML>
```

This is storing the result in the variable confirmed. You are not going to do anything with this at this stage, but when you have learnt how to use selection, you can stop the next question being asked based on the response.

Add the question.

```
<HTML>
<BODY>
    <SCRIPT>
        alert("Welcome to the website")
var confirmed = confirm("Are you sure you want to proceed?")
var userAnswer = prompt("What is 10 + 10?")
    </SCRIPT>
</BODY>
</HTML>
```

After each of the actions write an appropriate message to the console log.

```
<HTML>
<BODY>
    <SCRIPT>
        alert("Welcome to the website")
        console.log("Alert")
var confirmed = confirm("Are you sure you want to proceed?")
console.log("Confirmation")
var userAnswer = prompt("What is 10 + 10?")
console.log("Question asked")
    </SCRIPT>
</BODY>
</HTML>
```

Open the website with the console log open and watch what happens.

PRACTICAL ACTIVITY 20.03

1   Create a web page that displays your name at the top of the page.

2   Create a web page that outputs a story as a series of alert boxes.

3   Add a console log to tasks 1 and 2 to confirm each box that has been successfully output.

4   Create a basic text web page using HTML. Edit the web page so that each element (for example, `paragraph`) has a name and display the text in JavaScript instead.

Questions

1   Which keyword(s) will output a box with a message?

2   Which keyword(s) will write data to the console?

3   Which keyword(s) will output a new box for a user to enter data?

4   What is the purpose of writing data to the console?

20.4 Changing images

You can set, or change, an image by using the `document.getElementById` command. Make sure the HTML code for your image (or image placeholder) has an ID. For example, here there is no image (`src` is `""` instead of a filename), and the element is named:

```
"firstImage":
    <img src="" id = "firstImage">
```

Instead of using `.innerHTML` there is `.src`. This is because you are not changing the HTML within the element, you are changing the filename of the image. In this case, the element will display the image with the name `"ss1.jpg"` that is saved in the same folder as the web page file.

```
document.getElementById("firstImage").src =
"ss1.jpg"
```

You can access and change other properties of images using the same `document.getElementById` command. Change the `.src` to the property you want to edit. For example, this code will set the height and width of an image:

```
document.getElementById("image1").height =
"500"

document.getElementById("image1").width =
"500"
```

WORKED EXAMPLE 20.04

Create a web page with the title `My Images`, and then two images underneath that are set using JavaScript.

First set up the structure of the website, the title and the placeholders for the two images with IDs.

```
<HTML>
<BODY>
<h1>Welcome to my website.</h2>
<img src = "" id = "image1">
<img src = "" id = "image2">
    <SCRIPT>

    </SCRIPT>
</BODY>
</HTML>
```

Then add the code to the JavaScript to set the images.

```
<HTML>
<BODY>
<h1>Welcome to my website.</h2>
<img src = "" id = "image1">
<img src = "" id = "image2">
  <SCRIPT>
     document.getElementById("image1").src = "IMG_1.jpg"
     document.getElementById("image2").src = "IMG_2.jpg"
  </SCRIPT>
</BODY>
</HTML>
```

PRACTICAL ACTIVITY 20.04

Open file **20.03.html** and edit it to create a webpage that displays four images of your favourite animal.

Use JavaScript to display four images of your favourite animal.

PRACTICAL ACTIVITY 20.05

1   Change the web page that displays your name at the top, to include an image of you (or something related to you).

2   Change your web page that outputs a story using alert boxes. Each time a new alert box appears, change the image that is on the web page so it matches the text in the alert box.

After the name of your element, put the command `.style` and then the name of the style you are trying to change, for example, `.color`, or `.fontSize`. After the equal sign is the value you want to assign to this style.

Look at the following examples:

1   This example sets the paragraph with the ID `"p1"` to have red font.
```
document.getElementById("p1").style.color = 'red';
```

2   This example changes the font to xx-large.
```
document.getElementById("p1").style.fontSize = "xx-large";
```

3   This example changes the background colour to blue.
```
document.getElementById("p1").style.backgroundColor = 'blue';
```

Table 20.1 has a list of some of the styles you can change, but there are many more that you can use.

20.5 Changing HTML style

In HTML you can change the colour and style of font, the background colour of a section of text, and so on. These are all different properties of the elements. You can change these in JavaScript by using the `document.getElementById` command.

Style	Options	Example
Font size	xx-small x-small small medium large x-large xx-large smaller (decreases by 1 unit) larger (increases by 1 unit)	`.style.fontSize = "xx-small"` `.style.fontSize = "smaller"`
Font style	italic oblique normal	`.style.fontStyle = "oblique"`
Font weight	normal lighter bold bolder 100 to 900	`.style.fontWeight = "bold"` `.style.fontWeight = "500"`
Font family	For example, Arial Courier New Verdana Times New Roman	`.style.fontFamily = "Arial"` `.style.fontFamily = "Courier New"`
Background colour	For example, Red Yellow #FF0052	`.style.backgroundColor = "red"`

Table 20.1: Styles.

WORKED EXAMPLE 20.05

Create a website that has two paragraphs of text.

Use JavaScript to make the first paragraph in:

- purple
- Arial font
- size small.

Make the second paragraph in:

- green
- Courier New font
- size x-large.

Start by creating the two paragraphs; these could be in HTML or in JavaScript.

```
<HTML>
<BODY>
  <p id = "p1">There was no possibility of taking a walk that day. We had been wandering, indeed, in the leafless shrubbery an hour in the morning; but since dinner (Mrs. Reed, when there was no company, dined early) the cold winter wind had brought with it clouds so sombre, and a rain so penetrating, that further out-door exercise was not out of the question.</p>
```

```
    <p id = "p2">I was glad of it: I never like long walks, especially on chilly afternoons:
dreadful to me was the coming home in the raw twilight, with nipped fingers and toes, and a
heart saddened by the chidings of Bessie, the nurse, and humbled by the consciousness of my
physical inferiority to Eliza, John, and Georgiana Reed.</p>

    <SCRIPT>

    </SCRIPT>
</BODY>
</HTML>
```

Set the font style for the first paragraph (p1).

```
<HTML>
<BODY>
    <p id = "p1">There was no possibility of taking a walk that day. We had been wandering,
indeed, in the leafless shrubbery an hour in the morning; but since dinner (Mrs. Reed,
when there was no company, dined early) the cold winter wind had brought with it clouds
so sombre, and a rain so penetrating, that further out-door exercise was not out of the
question.</p>
    <p id = "p2">I was glad of it: I never like long walks, especially on chilly afternoons:
dreadful to me was the coming home in the raw twilight, with nipped fingers and toes, and a
heart saddened by the chidings of Bessie, the nurse, and humbled by the consciousness of my
physical inferiority to Eliza, John, and Georgiana Reed.</p>
    <SCRIPT>
        document.getElementById("p1").style.color = 'purple';
        document.getElementById("p1").style.fontSize = "small";
        document.getElementById("p1").style.fontFamily = "Arial";
    </SCRIPT>
</BODY>
</HTML>
```

Set the font style for the second paragraph (p2).

```
<HTML>
<BODY>
    <p id = "p1">There was no possibility of taking a walk that day. We had been wandering,
indeed, in the leafless shrubbery an hour in the morning; but since dinner (Mrs. Reed,
when there was no company, dined early) the cold winter wind had brought with it clouds
so sombre, and a rain so penetrating, that further out-door exercise was not out of the
question.</p>
    <p id = "p2">I was glad of it: I never like long walks, especially on chilly afternoons:
dreadful to me was the coming home in the raw twilight, with nipped fingers and toes, and a
heart saddened by the chidings of Bessie, the nurse, and humbled by the consciousness of my
physical inferiority to Eliza, John, and Georgiana Reed.</p>
    <SCRIPT>
        document.getElementById("p1").style.color = 'purple';
        document.getElementById("p1").style.fontSize = "small";
        document.getElementById("p1").style.fontFamily = "Arial";
        document.getElementById("p2").style.color = 'green';
        document.getElementById("p2").style.fontSize = "x-large";
        document.getElementById("p2").style.fontFamily = "Courier New";
    </SCRIPT>
</BODY>
</HTML>
```

1 Change the web page that displays your name and an image of you. Write an introductory paragraph of text about yourself. Change the font style of both the title and the first paragraph using JavaScript. The title should be larger and centered in the page.

2 Work in pairs. You will be working together to create a web page that instructs a user on how to add JavaScript to a web page. Make sure you have a suitable title that is formatted appropriately using JavaScript. Whenever you use code in the text, this should be formatted to be Courier New. All other fonts should be Arial. Make sure you format the text using JavaScript. Take it in turns to add statements to format the text.

20.6 Variables and operators

A variable is a space in memory that is given a name (an identifier), where you can store data that can change while the program is running.

For example, you could create a space in memory called `name` and you could store the name `Luca` in there. You could later change it and store `Katerina`. You can check what is stored there by asking what is stored in `name`. The computer would tell you `Katerina`.

The identifier must be one word (that is, no spaces) and start with a letter. It must not be any word that is used by JavaScript (these are known as reserved words). For example, `var` is invalid because it is used by JavaScript.

Declaration

A variable **declaration** tells the program that you need a space in memory and what its identifier will be. An example variable declaration in JavaScript is:

KEY WORD

declaration: a statement giving the identifier of a variable or array

```
var name;
```

`var` tells JavaScript that you are creating a variable.

`name` is the name of this variable.

Assignment

Assignment means adding a value to that variable. For example:

```
name = "Luca";
```

The name of the variable comes first and `=` can be read as the word 'becomes'. This is the assignment operator. `Luca` is what is being stored. `Luca` is in speech marks (`" "`) because it is a string (see Table 20.2). For example:

```
age = 18;
```

This time the variable is called `age`, and `18` has been put into it.

You can change the value in the variable. For example:

```
name = "Katerina";
age = 21;
```

These values have overwritten the previous data.

Data types

The data stored in a variable will be of a set data type. Table 20.2 shows the main data types used in JavaScript.

Data type	Description	Example
Number	A numeric value	`age = 16` `score = 12.4`

String	Letters, characters and numbers. Any text string must start and end with either single or double quotation marks, for example '...' or "..."	`name = "Katerina"`
		`address = '24 Main Street'`
		`message = "Hello World"`

Boolean	True or False	`correct = true` `correct = false`

Data type	Description	Example
Array	A series of values of the same data type (see Section 20.13 'Arrays')	`numbers = [1,2,3]`
Object	A series of named values of the variable	`film = {title:"The House", genre:"Drama", length:96, releaseYear:2013}`

Table 20.2: Data types.

Data types are not declared when declaring a variable; it is assumed when a value is given to the variable. For example:

```
var name;
```

`name` could be of any data type. But if instead you put:

```
var name = "";
```

`name` is now a string.

For example, in:

```
var age;
```

`age` could be of any data type. But if instead you put:

```
var age = 0;
```

`age` is now a number.

Type conversions

You can convert one type of data into a second data type.

To convert data to a string, use the command `String()`. For example:

```
var stringNumber = String(999);

var stringBoolean = String(true);
```

To convert data to an integer, use the command `Number()` for example:

```
var numberString = Number("999");
```

Boolean data can be converted to numbers; true is converted to 1, and false to 0. For example:

```
var numberBoolean = Number(true);
```

Converting data to the correct form is important to make sure you get the data you expect. You will learn about addition in the next section ; the + symbol can be used to add together two numbers (for example 2 + 3 = 5), but it also joins together two strings (for example, "2"+"3" = "23").

> **WORKED EXAMPLE 20.06**
>
> Create a webpage that stores the first name, last name, and age of a person in variables. The script should then output all of this information in separate alerts.
>
> First create a variable for the first piece of data, first name.
>
> ```
> <HTML>
> <BODY>
>     <h1>This is all about me</h1>
>
>     <SCRIPT>
>         var firstName = "Katerina";
>     </SCRIPT>
> </BODY>
> </HTML>
> ```
>
> Create the next variable for last name, and then one for age.
>
> ```
> <HTML>
> <BODY>
>     <h1>This is all about me</h1>
>
>     <SCRIPT>
>         var firstName = "Katerina";
>         var lastName = "Singh";
>         var age = 28;
>     </SCRIPT>
> </BODY>
> </HTML>
> ```

CONTINUED

Output each of the variables, one at a time.

```
<HTML>
<BODY>
    <h1>This is all about me</h1>

    <SCRIPT>
        var firstName = "Katerina";
        var lastName = "Singh";
        var age = 28;
        alert(firstName);
        alert(lastName);
        alert(age);
    </SCRIPT>
</BODY>
</HTML>
```

PRACTICAL ACTIVITY 20.07

1   Create a web page that stores information about yourself in variables. Output this information into HTML elements to display the information about yourself.

2   Edit the story program you created before. Store each part of the story in individual variables. Output these variables instead of the text for the story.

3   Swap computers with a partner. Add a new part of the story in your partner's web page. Make sure you do not change anything that is already there.

20.7 Arithmetic operators

An **operator** is a symbol, or set of symbols, that perform an action. There are a number of these used in JavaScript. These are categorised as **arithmetic**, **comparison** and **logical**.

Table 20.3 shows the arithmetic operators.

Operator	Function	Example
+	Addition	x = 1 + 2; x is now 3
-	Subtraction	x = 5 - 1; x is now 4
*	Multiplication	x = 2 * 3; x is now 6
/	Division	x = 10 / 3; x is now 3.33
++	Increment (increase by 1)	x++;
--	Decrement (decrease by 1)	x--;
%	Modulus (return the remainder part of a division)	x = 11 % 5; x is now 1
floor()	Round down a calculation (remove the remainder)	x = floor(10/3);

Table 20.3: Arithmetic operators.

In an arithmetic calculation you can use numbers (**literals**) or variables.

KEY WORDS

operator: a symbol, or set of symbols, that perform an operation, for example, arithmetic operators

arithmetic operator: a symbol, or symbols, that perform a mathematical calculation; these often appear as algebraic operators that you will be used to using in mathematics

comparison operator: a symbol, or symbols, that compare the two sides of the operator and the result is either true or false

logical operator: symbols that represent the logical operations and, or, not

literal: the actual data being used (instead of a variable)

WORKED EXAMPLE 20.07

Create a web page that stores 9999 and 1000 in variables, and then calculates and outputs the result of:

- 9999 + 1000
- 9999 – 1000
- 9999 * 1000
- 9999 / 1000
- 9999 % 1000
- floor(9999 / 1000).

First, declare two variables and store 9999 and 1000 in each.

```
<HTML>
<BODY>
   <h1>Data Web page</h1>
   <SCRIPT>
      var firstNumber = 9999;
      var secondNumber = 1000;
   </SCRIPT>
</BODY>
</HTML>
```

Perform the first calculation, store the result in a new variable, then write this to the document.

```
<HTML>
<BODY>
   <h1>Data Web page</h1>

   <SCRIPT>
      var firstNumber = 9999;
      var secondNumber = 1000;
      var total = firstNumber +
      secondNumber;
      document.write(total);
   </SCRIPT>
</BODY>
</HTML>
```

Add each calculation in turn, and output each result. The same variable, `total`, has been used for each calculation because this saves memory (each new variable takes up a space in memory).

```
<HTML>
<BODY>
   <h1>Data Web page</h1>
   <SCRIPT>
      var firstNumber = 9999;
      var secondNumber = 1000;
      var total = firstNumber + secondNumber;
      document.write(total);
      document.write(" ");
      total = firstNumber - secondNumber;
      document.write(total);
      document.write(" ");
      total = firstNumber * secondNumber;
      document.write(total);
      document.write(" ");
      total = firstNumber / secondNumber;
      document.write(total);
      document.write(" ");
      total = firstNumber % secodnNumber;
      document.write(total);
      document.write(" ");
      total = floor(firstNumber /
      secondNumber);
      document.write(total);
      document.write(" ");
   </SCRIPT>
</BODY>
</HTML>
```

A second `document.write(" ")` command is put between each output, to put a space between each result.

Try the code with and without this statement and see what happens.

PRACTICAL ACTIVITY 20.08

1   Use prompt boxes to ask the user to enter two numbers (you will need one prompt for each number). Output the result of these two numbers added together.

2   Use prompt boxes to ask the user for their name. Output a message including their age, for example, "Hello Chin Hao".

3   Store 10 numbers in separate boxes. Add together all the numbers and output the result.

4   Use a prompt box to ask the user to enter a number. Subtract this number from 100 and output the result.

20.8 Functions

A function is a set of instructions that perform a specific task. It is independent code that only runs if it is called.

Functions are very useful for removing repeated code, especially when it may need to be repeated at different positions in the program. Instead of rewriting the code (which gives more opportunity for errors), just call the function.

Functions can be a) called (invoked) from within the JavaScript code, b) called when an event occurs such as clicking a button, and automatically run (self-invoked).

This section will include all these ways.

Every function has an identifier. In the following example the function is named `outputNums`.

```
function outputNums(){
    document.write(0);
    document.write(1);
}
```

The code inside this will not run unless the identifier is called. All the code that will run in the function needs to be inside the brackets { }.

To call the function, add the code:

```
outputNums();
```

WORKED EXAMPLE 20.08

Create a program that has a function to output "Hello World". Call the function several times from the main program.

First declare your function in the JavaScript and put the actions inside the { }.

```
<HTML>
<BODY>
    <h1>Welcome to my website</h1>
    <SCRIPT>
        function outputText(){
            document.write("Hello World");
        }
    </SCRIPT>
</BODY>
</HTML>
```

Then, call the function in the JavaScript code; this can go before or after the function.

```
<HTML>
<BODY>
    <h1>Welcome to my website</h1>
    <SCRIPT>
        outputText();
        function outputText(){
            document.write("Hello World");
        }
    </SCRIPT>
</BODY>
</HTML>
```

A function can take values from the program that calls it; these are called the parameters. It can also return a value back to the program that called it.

The following function, `addNums`, takes two numbers, `num1` and `num2`, adds these together and returns the result.

```
function addNums(num1, num2){
    return num1 + num2;
}
```

The `addNums` function can now be used within the code:

```
var result = addNums(2,3);
```

`num1` is given the value 2, `num2` is given the value 3. The function `addNums` adds these together (5) and returns the result. 5 is now stored in `result`.

Create a program that has a function to take two values as parameters and multiply them. The main program should then call the function, first with the numbers 2 and 3, secondly with the numbers 4 and 5, thirdly with the result of the first function call and the second function call. Then, display the result from the third function call.

First, create the function. It needs two parameters, and needs to return the result.

```
<HTML>
<BODY>
   <h1>Welcome to my website</h1>
   <SCRIPT>
      function multiplyNumbers(num1, num2){
         var result = num1 * num2;
         return result;
      }
   </SCRIPT>
</BODY>
</HTML>
```

In this function the result is saved in a variable before being returned, but it could just be returned directly.

The first call is with 2 and 3. The function returns a value, so this needs to be stored somewhere.

```
<HTML>
<BODY>
   <h1>Welcome to my website</h1>
   <SCRIPT>
      function multiplyNumbers(num1, num2){
         var result = num1 * num2;
         return result;
      }
      var value1 = multiplyNumbers(2,3);
   </SCRIPT>
</BODY>
</HTML>
```

Then, the second call with the numbers 4 and 5.

```
<HTML>
<BODY>
   <h1>Welcome to my website</h1>
   <SCRIPT>
      function multiplyNumbers(num1, num2){
         var result = num1 * num2;
         return result;
      }
      var value1 = multiplyNumbers(2,3);
      var value2 = multiplyNumbers(4,5);
   </SCRIPT>
</BODY>
</HTML>
```

Finally, call the function with the result of the two previous calls (value1 and value2) and output this result.

```
<HTML>
<BODY>
   <h1>Welcome to my website</h1>
   <SCRIPT>
      function multiplyNumbers(num1, num2){
         var result = num1 * num2;
         return result;
      }
      var value1 = multiplyNumbers(2,3);
      var value2 = multiplyNumbers(4,5);
      var value3 = multiplyNumbers(value1,
      value2);
      document.write(value3);
   </SCRIPT>
</BODY>
</HTML>
```

Open file **20.04.html** and amend it to store two numbers. Then, output the result of the numbers added together, subtracted, multiplied and divided.

When you create a function, you can create a variable inside it (local) or outside it (global). If the variable is local, then it only exists when that function is running. As soon as it ends and returns control, the variable disappears and is blank. This variable can only be accessed (for example output, changed) from within that function.

KEY WORDS

local variable: a variable declared within a function; it can only be accessed within the function

global variable: a variable declared outside a function; it can be accessed anywhere within the code

If the variable is global, then it exists as soon as the web page loads, and permanently exists. It can be accessed from anywhere in the JavaScript. However, this can waste memory, because it will always exist.

In this example, `number` is global. It is declared outside the function, but it can be accessed inside the function. Although the variable `newNumber` is local, it is inside the function and cannot be accessed outside of it.

```
<HTML>
<BODY>
    <h1>Welcome to my website</h1>
    <SCRIPT>
        var number = 0;
        function firstFunction(){
            alert(number);
            var newNumber = 10;
            alert(newNumber);
        }
    </SCRIPT>
</BODY>
</HTML>
```

PRACTICAL ACTIVITY 20.10

1   Create a function for each of the arithmetic operators. Use a prompt to ask the users to enter two numbers, then call the function for each of the operators and output each result.

2   Write a sentence to output to the screen with repeated words within it, for example, "when a word is repeated, the repeated word appears several times". Create a function for each word, and a separate function for the space between each word. Call the functions to output the sentence.

CONTINUED

3   Items in a shop are reduced by 10 per cent. Create a function to take a value as a parameter and return the reduced price. Create a function to ask the user to input the cost of an item using a prompt. Repeatedly call the function to output, and then the function to calculate the cost. Display the reduced price each time.

Questions

5   Define the term function.

6   What does the operator % do?

7   What is the difference between the operator ++ and --?

20.9 Form elements

You need to tell HTML that you are creating a form using the `<form></form>` tag. All the code to display buttons, drop-down boxes, and so on then comes within these tags.

An event can occur within the HTML code that can be acted upon by JavaScript, for example when a button is clicked. Within the HTML code for these **objects**, a JavaScript function can be called to perform an action.

KEY WORD

object: a series of named values all stored under one identifier

button

When the user clicks on an element, for example, an HTML button, it can be programmed to call a JavaScript function. For example, every time you click a button, the function `calculate()` is called and it performs a calculation and outputs a result.

This HTML code will create a button that says `"Click me"`:

```
<button onclick="outputMessage()">Click
me</button>
```

The code states that when the button is clicked (onclick), the JavaScript function `outputMessage()` will be called.

This function is then written in JavaScript:

```
function outputMessage(){
    document.write("Hello World");
}
```

Every time the button is clicked, the message `"Hello World"` will be displayed on the page.

WORKED EXAMPLE 20.10

Create a program that displays an image when a button is clicked.

First, create the button.

```
<HTML>
<BODY>
<button onclick = "showImage()">Click to
show image</button>
    <SCRIPT>
    </SCRIPT>
</BODY>
</HTML>
```

Then, create the function.

```
<HTML>
<BODY>
<button onclick = "showImage()">Click to
show image</button>
    <SCRIPT>
        function showImage(){
        }
    </SCRIPT>
</BODY>
</HTML>
```

Then, create the placeholder for the image.

```
<HTML>
<BODY>
<button onclick = "showImage()">Click to
show image</button>
<br>
<img src = "" id = "imageHolder">
    <SCRIPT>
        function showImage(){
        }
    </SCRIPT>
</BODY>
</HTML>
```

Lastly, put the code in the function to display the image and change any other of the properties, for example setting the height and width.

```
<HTML>
<BODY>
<button onclick = "showImage()">Click to
show image</button>
<br>
<img src = "" id = "imageHolder">
    <SCRIPT>
        function showImage(){
            document.getElementById
            ("imageHolder").src = "IMG_2.jpg"
            document.getElementById
            ("imageHolder").height = "500";
            document.getElementById
            ("imageHolder").width = "500";
        }
    </SCRIPT>
</BODY>
</HTML>
```

Text box

You can enter text into a text box, and you can then access this data and use it, for example, in a calculation.

This HTML code will create a text box with the identifier `enterColour`.

```
<input type="text" id="enterColour">
```

The data is accessed using `document.getElementByID().value` with the text box identifier in the brackets. For example, here the data in `enterColour` is stored in the variable `colourEntered`,

```
var colourEntered = document.
getElementById("enterColour").value;
```

An action is needed to tell JavaScript to get the data from the text box, for example clicking a button. This can then call a function where you get the data from `enterColour`.

You can write to a text box in a similar way. Put the command on the left of the assignment. This code will write `"Hello"` into the text box.

```
document.getElementById("enterColour").
value = "Hello";
```

All data accessed from text boxes is stored as a string, unless you tell it to convert it. For example, if number 22 was entered, this would be stored as "22". See Section 20.6 Variables and operators/Type conversions for how to convert it to a number.

WORKED EXAMPLE 20.11

Create a program that asks the user to enter two numbers, one in each separate text box. When the button is clicked, add these numbers together and output the result to both text boxes.

First, set up the form, with two text boxes and a button.

```
<HTML>
<BODY>
<input type = "text" id = "number1">
<input type = "text" id = "number2">
<button onclick = "addTogether()">Add</
button>
    <SCRIPT>
    </SCRIPT>
</BODY>
</HTML>
```

Declare a function. Within it, get the data from each text box and store each in their own variable.

```
<HTML>
<BODY>
<input type = "text" id = "number1">
<input type = "text" id = "number2">
<button onclick = "addTogether()">Add</
button>
    <SCRIPT>
        function addTogether(){
            var num1 = document.
            getElementById("number1").value;
            var num2 = document.
            getElementById("number2").value;
        }
    </SCRIPT>
</BODY>
</HTML>
```

CONTINUED

These values are currently strings.

Add the values together and store the result in a new variable. Then, write this variable to both text boxes.

```
<HTML>
<BODY>
<input type = "text" id = "number1">
<input type = "text" id = "number2">
<button onclick = "addTogether()">Add</
button>
    <SCRIPT>
      function addTogether(){
          var num1 = document.
          getElementById("number1").value;
          var num2 = document.
          getElementById("number2").value;
          var total = Number(num1) +
          Number(num2);

          document.getElementById("number1").
          value = total;
          document.getElementById("number2").
          value = total;
      }
    </SCRIPT>
</BODY>
</HTML>
```

PRACTICAL ACTIVITY 20.12

1 Create a program that asks the user to enter their name into a text box. Output their name in an alert box.

2 Change your calculator program, so there are two text boxes for the user to enter a number into each. When a button (for example +) is clicked, perform the calculation and output it.

Drop-down box

A drop-down box gives the user options to choose from.

This HTML code will create a drop-down box called `colours`. It will create three options: purple, orange and blue. Each `<option>` will be a new choice in the drop-down box:

```
<select id = "colours">
    <option>purple</option>
    <option>orange</option>
    <option>blue</option>
</select>
```

The item selected is accessed using:
```
document.getElementById("colours").
options[document.getElementById("colours").
selectedIndex].text;
```

This is a long piece of code, but there is a way to shorten it. `document.getElementById("colours")` appears twice in the same line. Instead of writing it twice, you can store this in a variable, for example:

```
var coloursID = document.
getElementById("colours");
```

Then use this variable instead, giving the code:

```
coloursID.options[coloursID.selectedIndex].
text;
```

This will need to go within a function that is called, for example, from a button. This function will access the chosen option and output it in an alert.

```
function displayChoice(){
    var coloursID =
    document.getElementById("colours");

    alert(coloursID.options[coloursID.
    selectedIndex].text);
}
```

Radio button

You can give the user a range of options that they can see, but can only select one of. This is done with a radio button.

This HTML code will create a radio button for Purple, Orange and Blue:

```
<form>

<input type="radio" name="colours"
value="purple">Purple<br>

<input type="radio" name="colours" value
="orange">Orange<br>

<input type="radio" name="colours" value
="blue">Blue<br>

</form>
```

The radio buttons must be within a form so they are grouped together, otherwise you may be able to select several.

In the JavaScript, you need to check which one has been selected using a `for` loop and an `if` statement (you will learn more about these in Section 20.12 Selection and Section 20.14 Loops). This function needs to check each of the radio buttons you have created, in turn, to find out which one has been checked.

```
function checkColours(){
    var colour = document.forms[0];
    for(i=0; i<3; i++){
        if(colour[i].checked){
            document.write(colour[i].value);
        }
    }
}
```

- The first line in the function stores the first form elements in the variable `colour` (this just saves having to write it all out every time).

- The `for` loop goes through each element; 0, then 1, then 2.

- Each time, it checks if that radio button has been selected.

- The next line only runs if the `if` is true, then it outputs the content of the choice (the colour chosen).

WORKED EXAMPLE 20.12

Create a program where a user can choose a colour from a drop-down box, and an animal from a radio button. The program should then combine these and output the name of the new animal when a button is clicked.

First, create the drop-down box with the colour options.

```
<HTML>
<BODY>
<select id = "colour">
    <option>red</option>
    <option>yellow</option>
    <option>purple</option>
    <option>orange</option>
    <option>green</option>
</select>
    <SCRIPT>
    </SCRIPT>
</BODY>
</HTML>
```

CONTINUED

Then, create the radio buttons.

```
<HTML>
<BODY>
<select id = "colour">
   <option>red</option>
   <option>yellow</option>
   <option>purple</option>
   <option>orange</option>
   <option>green</option>
</select>
<form id = "animals">
   <input type = "radio" name = "animals" value = "elephant">Elephant <br>
   <input type = "radio" name = "animals" value = "tortoise">Tortoise <br>
   <input type = "radio" name = "animals" value = "dolphin">Dolphin <br>
   <input type = "radio" name = "animals" value = "kangaroo">Kangaroo <br>
</form>
   <SCRIPT>
   </SCRIPT>
</BODY>
</HTML>
```

Create the button.

```
<HTML>
<BODY>
<select id = "colour">
   <option>red</option>
   <option>yellow</option>
   <option>purple</option>
   <option>orange</option>
   <option>green</option>
</select>
<form id = "animals">
   <input type = "radio" name = "animals" value = "elephant">Elephant <br>
   <input type = "radio" name = "animals" value = "tortoise">Tortoise <br>
   <input type = "radio" name = "animals" value = "dolphin">Dolphin <br>
   <input type = "radio" name = "animals" value = "kangaroo">Kangaroo <br>
</form>
<button onclick = "createAnimal()">Create the animal</button>
   <SCRIPT>
   </SCRIPT>
</BODY>
</HTML>
```

CONTINUED

Create the JavaScript function and access the data in the drop-down box and store it in a variable.

```
<HTML>
<BODY>
<select id = "colour">
   <option>red</option>
   <option>yellow</option>
   <option>purple</option>
   <option>orange</option>
   <option>green</option>
</select>
<form id = "animals">
   <input type = "radio" name = "animals" value = "elephant">Elephant <br>
   <input type = "radio" name = "animals" value = "tortoise">Tortoise <br>
   <input type = "radio" name = "animals" value = "dolphin">Dolphin <br>
   <input type = "radio" name = "animals" value = "kangaroo">Kangaroo <br>
</form>
<button onclick = "createAnimal()">Create the animal</button>
   <SCRIPT>
      function createAnimal(){
         var dropDownName = document.getElementById("colour");
         var colourChosen = dropDownName.options[dropDownName.selectedIndex].text;
      }
   </SCRIPT>
</BODY>
</HTML>
```

Add JavaScript code to check the radio buttons and get the value of the one selected.

```
<HTML>
<BODY>
<select id = "colour">
   <option>red</option>
   <option>yellow</option>
   <option>purple</option>
   <option>orange</option>
   <option>green</option>
</select>
<form id = "animals">
   <input type = "radio" name = "animals" value = "elephant">Elephant <br>
   <input type = "radio" name = "animals" value = "tortoise">Tortoise <br>
   <input type = "radio" name = "animals" value = "dolphin">Dolphin <br>
   <input type = "radio" name = "animals" value = "kangaroo">Kangaroo <br>
</form>
```

```
<button onclick = "createAnimal()">Create the animal</button>
   <SCRIPT>
      function createAnimal(){
         var dropDownName = document.getElementById("colour");
         var colourChosen = dropDownName.options[dropDownName.selectedIndex].text;
         for(i=0; i<4; i++){
            if(animalRadio[i].checked){
               var animalChosen = animalRadio[i].value;
            }
         }
      }
   </SCRIPT>
</BODY>
</HTML>
```

Output the two selected values.

```
<HTML>
<BODY>
<select id = "colour">
   <option>red</option>
   <option>yellow</option>
   <option>purple</option>
   <option>orange</option>
   <option>green</option>
</select>
<form id = "animals">
   <input type = "radio" name = "animals" value = "elephant">Elephant <br>
   <input type = "radio" name = "animals" value = "tortoise">Tortoise <br>
   <input type = "radio" name = "animals" value = "dolphin">Dolphin <br>
   <input type = "radio" name = "animals" value = "kangaroo">Kangaroo <br>
</form>
<button onclick = "createAnimal()">Create the animal</button>
   <SCRIPT>
      function createAnimal(){
         var dropDownName = document.getElementById("colour");
         var colourChosen = dropDownName.options[dropDownName.selectedIndex].text;
         for(i=0; i<4; i++){
            if(animalRadio[i].checked){
               var animalChosen = animalRadio[i].value;
            }
         }
      }
      alert(colourChosen + " " + animalChosen;
   </SCRIPT>
</BODY>
</HTML>
```

PRACTICAL ACTIVITY 20.13

Open file **20.05.html**.

Complete the program to give the user five fruit to select, and five colours to select.

When the button is pressed, output these two words combined e.g. 'orange banana'.

PRACTICAL ACTIVITY 20.14

1   Create a form that lets the user choose from a series of options in a drop-down box. Change the text displayed in the web page to the option they have selected.

2   Repeat Task 1, using a radio button instead of a drop-down box.

3   Create a form that lets the user create their own sentence using a series of drop-down boxes and radio buttons. Users should be able to select the first word of the sentence from one object, then the second from the next, and so on. When the user clicks a button, output the sentence using an alert.

20.10 Detecting events

You have already used `onClick()` in the section on buttons. There are other events that you can detect in JavaScript, such as the following:

onload

When onload is attached to an element, it will run when the element is called or loaded. In this example, when the web page (the body tag) loads, the function will run.

```
<HTML>
<BODY onload="outputText()">
  <SCRIPT>
    function outputText(){
      alert("Hello World")
    }
  </SCRIPT>
</BODY>
</HTML>
```

onchange

This can be attached to an element that the user can change, for example a drop-down box. In this example, when the user changes their option in the drop-down box, the function will be called.

```
<HTML>
<BODY>
<select id = "colours" onchange="outputText()">
  <option>purple</option>
  <option>orange</option>
  <option>blue</option>
</select>
  <SCRIPT>
    function outputText(){
      alert("Hello World")
    }
  </SCRIPT>
</BODY>
</HTML>
```

onmouseover

This will run when the user moves the cursor over an element, for example an image. In this example, when the user puts their cursor over the image, the image will change.

```
<HTML>
<BODY>
<img src="IMG _ 1.jpg" id =
"imageHolder" width=500 height=500
onmouseover="changeImage()">
  <SCRIPT>
    function changeImage(){
      document.
      getElementById("imageHolder").src =
      "IMG _ 2.jpg"
    }
  </SCRIPT>
</BODY>
</HTML>
```

onmouseout

This will run when the user moves the cursor off an element, for example, an image. In this example, when the user moves the cursor away from the image, a different function is called.

```
<HTML>
<BODY>
<img src="IMG _ 1.jpg" id = "imageHolder"
onmouseover="changeImage1()"
onmouseout="changeImage2()" width=500
height=500 >
    <SCRIPT>
        function changeImage1(){
            document.getElementById
            ("imageHolder").src = "IMG _ 2.jpg"
        }
        function changeImage2(){
            document.
            getElementById("imageHolder").src =
            "IMG _ 1.jpg"
        }
    </SCRIPT>
</BODY>
</HTML>
```

onkeydown

When attached to an element where the user can enter data, for example, a text box, it will run when the user clicks a key on the keyboard (types a letter). In this example, every time the user types a letter a message will output.

```
<HTML>
<BODY>
    <input type="text"
    onkeydown="outputLetter()">
    <SCRIPT>
        function outputLetter(){
        alert("Letter clicked")
    }
    </SCRIPT>
</BODY>
</HTML>
```

20.11 Showing and hiding HTML elements

HTML elements (for example paragraphs) can be made visible (so they appear and are on screen), and invisible (so they disappear and cannot be seen).

The `.visibility` option can be set to `"visible"` or `"hidden"`. For example, this code will set the element `"text1"` to be invisible:

```
document.getElementById("text1").style.
visibility = "hidden";
```

A second way of doing this is by using the `style.display` option of `"none"` (hidden) or `"inline"` (visible). To make the text box invisible, use the code,

```
document.getElementById("text1").style.
display = "none";
```

WORKED EXAMPLE 20.13

Make an image disappear when the cursor moves over it, and make it reappear when the mouse moves off it.

First set up the web page with the starting image.

```
<HTML>
<BODY>
    <img src = "IMG_1.jpg" id = "theImage">
    <SCRIPT>
    </SCRIPT>
</BODY>
</HTML>
```

CONTINUED

Create one function to make the image appear, and another to make it disappear.

```
<HTML>
<BODY>
   <img src = "IMG_1.jpg" id = "theImage">
   <SCRIPT>
      function imageDisappear(){
         document.getElementById("theImage").style.visibility = "hidden";
      }
      function imageAppear(){
         document.getElementById("theImage").style.visibility = "visible";
      }
   </SCRIPT>
</BODY>
</HTML>
```

Now, set onmouseover and onmouseout for the image.

```
<HTML>
<BODY>
   <img src = "IMG_1.jpg" id = "theImage" onmouseover = "imageDisappear()"
onmouseout="imageAppear()" width = 500 height = 500>
   <SCRIPT>
      function imageDisappear(){
         document.getElementById("theImage").style.visibility = "hidden";
      }
      function imageAppear(){
         document.getElementById("theImage").style.visibility = "visible";
      }
   </SCRIPT>
</BODY>
</HTML>
```

PRACTICAL ACTIVITY 20.15

1   Create a web page where the user can choose to view an image by clicking a button.

2   Create a web page with several images and a button. Each time the user puts their mouse over an image, it disappears and they get a point (stored as a global variable). When the user clicks the button it tells them their score.

20.12 Selection

A conditional statement lets you specify which, if any, statements are to be run. This is done through a **condition**, and whether that condition is true or false.

KEY WORD

condition: a statement that can be evaluated as true or false, for example 5 > 6 (this is false because 5 is not greater than 6)

Comparison operators

Table 20.4 shows the different comparison operators.

Operator	Function	Example
>	Greater than	5 > 6; This is false.
<	Less than	5 < 6; This is true.
>=	Greater than or equal to	5 >= 6; This is false.
<=	Less than or equal to	5 <= 5; This is true.
==	Equal to	5 == 6; This is false.
===	Equal to and of the same data type	5 === "5"; This is false because the first is a number and the second is a string.
!=	Not equal to	5 != 6; This is true.
!===	Not equal to or not of the same data type	5 !=== "5"; This is true, because they are not the same data type.

Table 20.4: Comparison operators.

if

if checks a condition. If it is true, the first block of code is run,

```
if (myVariable < 6) {
    message = "Yes it is!";
}
```

The code assigning "Yes it is" to the variable message is only carried out if the data in the variable myVariable is less than 6.

if is always the first in a selection statement. It can be on its own, or it can be combined with else and elseif statements.

else

An else statement gives you an option to run code if the condition within the if is false:

```
if (myVariable < 6) {
    message = "Yes it is!";
}else{
    message = "No it isn't!";
}
```

If the data in the variable myVariable is less than 6, then "Yes it is!" will be assigned to message. If it is not less than 6 (so it is 7 or more) then "No it isn't!" will be assigned to message instead.

else if

else if allows you to have multiple conditions that you set to different outcomes. It still starts with an if, but you can then have as many else if conditions as you need. You can also have an else, but this would need to go at the very end.

```
if (myVariable < 6) {
    message = "Yes it is!";
}else if (myVariable == 6){
    message = "They're the same";
}else{
    message = "It's smaller";
}
```

In this example, if the value in myVariable is less than 6 then "Yes it is!" is assigned to message.

If it is not less than 6, it is compared to see if it is equal to 6. If it is, then "They're the same" is assigned to message.

If it is not less than 6, and not equal to 6, then "It's smaller" is assigned to message.

WORKED EXAMPLE 20.14

Create a program that displays a different image depending on which option was chosen from a drop-down box.

First, create the web page with a drop-down box, image placeholder and button.

```
<HTML>
<BODY>

Which image would you like to see?
<select id = "choice">
   <option>Image 1</option>
   <option>Image 2</option>
</select>

<button onclick = "displayImage()">Display</button>
<img src = "" id = "imagePlaceHolder width = 500 height = 500>

   <SCRIPT>

   </SCRIPT>
</BODY>
</HTML>
```

Write the function to get the value from the drop-down box, and then check what the value is using an `if` statement.

```
<HTML>
<BODY>
Which image would you like to see?
<select id = "choice">
   <option>Image 1</option>
   <option>Image 2</option>
</select>
<button onclick = "displayImage()">Display</button>
<img src = "" id = "imagePlaceHolder width = 500 height = 500>
   <SCRIPT>
      function displayImage(){
         var dropDownName = document.getElementById("choice");
         var imageChosen = dropDownName.options[dropDownName.selectedIndex].text;
         if(imageChosen == "Image 1"){
               document.getElementById("imagePlaceHolder").src = "IMG_1.jpg";
         }else{
            document.getElementById("imagePlaceHolder").src = "IMG_2.jpg";
         }
      }
   </SCRIPT>
</BODY>
</HTML>
```

Logical operators

A comparison can include more than one statement by including a logical operator.

There are three logical operations: AND, OR and NOT. These operators can also be used in loops that you learn about later in this chapter.

The three logical operators are shown in Table 20.5.

Operator	Function	Explanation	Example

&&	AND	Is true if the condition before and after are both true. If one is false, then it is false.	`(5 < 6) && (7 < 10)`
			 Both are true, so the result is true.
			
			 `(5 > 6) && (7 < 10)`
			 The first statement is false, so the result is false.

||	OR	Is true if one or both of the conditions are true. If both are false, it is false.	`(5 < 6) ||`
			 `(7 < 10)`
			 Both are true, so the result is true.
			
			 `(5 > 6) ||`
			 `(7 < 10)`
			 The second is true, so the result is true.

!	NOT	Replaces a true with false, or a false with true.	`!(5 < 6)` This is false because 5<6 is true, but the ! will change this to false.

Table 20.5: Logical operators.

WORKED EXAMPLE 20.15

Create a program that asks the user to enter two numbers and output a message depending on the numbers.

- If either number < 10, output "Too small"
- If either number > 100, output "Too large"
- If both numbers < 50 and >= 10, output "below"
- If both numbers are >= 50 and < 100, output "above"
- Otherwise, output "mixed"

Set up the form with two text boxes and a button.

```
<HTML>
<BODY>
   <input type = "text" id = "num1">
   <input type = "text" id = "num2">
   <button onclick = "calculate()">Calculate</button>
</BODY>
</HTML>
```

CONTINUED

Create the function to get the numbers when the button is clicked.

```html
<HTML>
<BODY>
    <input type = "text" id = "num1">
    <input type = "text" id = "num2">
    <button onclick = "calculate()">Calculate</button>
    <SCRIPT>
        function calculate(){
            var number1 = document.getElementById("num1").value;
            var number2 = document.getElementById("num2").value;
        }
    </SCRIPT>
</BODY>
</HTML>
```

Write the if statement to check each of the conditions in turn.

```html
<HTML>
<BODY>
    <input type = "text" id = "num1">
    <input type = "text" id = "num2">
    <button onclick = "calculate()">Calculate</button>
    <SCRIPT>
        function calculate(){
            var number1 = document.getElementById("num1").value;
            var number2 = document.getElementById("num2").value;
            if(number1 < 10 || number2 < 10){
                alert("Too small");
            }else if(number1 > 100 || number2 > 100){
                alert("Too large");
            }else if(number1 < 50 && number2 < 50){
                alert("Below");
            }else if(number1 >= 50 && number 2 >= 50){
                alert("Above");
            }else{
                alert("Mixed");
            }
        }
    </SCRIPT>
</BODY>
</HTML>
```

In the worked example, the later `elseifs` did not need to check that the number was also above 10, or less than 100. This is because the `if` statements run in order, so if the first condition is true then none of the other comparisons will take place, and the program will jump to the last `}`.

Questions

8   What is the result of 10 < 2?

9   What is the result of 10 === 100?

10   What is the result of "ten" !=== "eleven"?

11   What is the result of "a" == "a"?

12   What is the result of 10 > 2 && 10 > 10?

13   What is the result of "house" == "house" ||
10 >= 12?

14   What is the result of !(55 < 66)?

switch

Combining multiple `ifs` can get difficult to manage. A switch statement is more efficient because it does not perform all of the conditions every time. It can take a variable (or expression) and then check its value against a series of options. These options can be values, as in the following example, or variables.

```
number = 5;

switch(number) {

case 4;

    message = "It's 4";

    break;

case 5;

    message = "It's 5";

    break;

case 6;

    message = "It's 6";

    break;

default;

    message = "It was none of these";

}
```

This statement will take the value stored in the variable number and compare it to the first case statement; in this code, case 4. If it is equal to it, it will write

"It's 4" into the variable message, then run the break statement which forces it to break out of the switch statement (that is, it will not then compare the value with the next case).

The default catches a value that is not caught by any of the previous case statements.

Ternary operator

The ternary operator is a special type of selection statement. It has a single comparison, and can then assign a variable a value dependent on whether this comparison is true or false.

```
var valueToUpdate = (inputData < 10) ?
"Below":"Above";
```

This statement says: If the value in `inputData` is less than 10, store `"Below"` in the variable `valueToUpdate`, otherwise store `"Above"` in the `valueToUpdate`.

PRACTICAL ACTIVITY 20.16

1   Create a web page that has a person's age stored in a variable. Using an `If` statement, output a different message, depending on their age. For example, if they are between 13 and 19: "You are a teenager".

2   Extend your story program. This time ask the user to enter data, for example an answer to a puzzle and, if they get it correct, or give a specific answer, then give them the next part of the story.

3   Create a web page with one button. Each time the button is clicked, a different image is displayed (up to five images). You will need a global variable to keep track of how many times the button has been clicked.

4   When the web page loads, ask the user to confirm that they want to see the image using a confirm box. If the user clicks OK, make the image visible, otherwise make it invisible.

5   Create a web page to allow a user to enter their mark in a test. Convert this to a grade (for example A is 80%) and output it.

CONTINUED

6 Create a game where the user has to guess what number the game has stored. Each time they guess, the web page will tell them if they need to guess higher, or lower, or got it correct. If they get it correct, tell them how many guesses it took. You will need a global variable to track the number of guesses.

7 Create a function that takes four numbers as parameters. Find and output the largest of these numbers.

8 Extend Task 7 to find the smallest of the numbers as well.

PRACTICAL ACTIVITY 20.17

Open file **20.06.html**.

Complete the program to input 2 numbers, and then output the largest.

20.13 Arrays

An **array** is a data structure that allows you to store multiple values under one name. It is often represented as a table, with each value given a number with which to access it (known as the array index). For example:

```
var colours = ["orange", "purple", "green",
"yellow", "grey"];
```

KEY WORD

array: a data structure that can store multiple items under one identifier; the items are of the same type

This code declares an array, called `colours`, with five elements. These are shown as a table in Table 20.6.

Index	0	1	2	3	4
Value	orange	purple	green	yellow	grey

Table 20.6: An array.

Data can be extracted from this array. For example, this code would store purple in `myFavColour`:

```
var myFavcolour = colours[1];
```

Data can be replaced in this array. For example, this code will replace `yellow` with `pink`:

```
colours[3] = "pink";
```

Data can be added to this array. For example, this code will make a new index, 5, and put `blue` in it:

```
colours.push("blue");
```

The length of the array can be found. For example, this code will return 5:

```
var arrayLength = colours.length;
```

WORKED EXAMPLE 20.16

Store five words in an array. Create a web page that asks the user to enter a number between 1 and 5

Display the word in that index.

First, set up the web page, declare an array and store the data in it.

```
<HTML>
<BODY>
Enter a number between 1 and 5.
<input type="text" id="wordToOutput">
<button onclick="outputWord()">Press me</button>
   <SCRIPT>
      var words = ["One", "Two", "Three", "Four", "Five"];
   </SCRIPT>
</BODY>
</HTML>
```

CONTINUED

Get the value input. Check its value and subtract 1 to get the index (if they enter 1, this will output index 0).

```
<HTML>
<BODY>
Enter a number between 1 and 5.
<input type="text" id="wordToOutput">
<button onclick="outputWord()">Press me</button>
    <SCRIPT>
        var words = ["One", "Two", "Three", "Four", "Five"];
        function outputWord(){
            var inputNumber = document.getElementById("wordToOutput").value;
            inputNumber = inputNumber - 1;
            alert(words[inputNumber]);
        }
    </SCRIPT>
</BODY>
</HTML>
```

Only the numbers 1 to 5 can be entered, so the input can be checked and an error output if it is not valid.

```
<HTML>
<BODY>
Enter a number between 1 and 5.
<input type="text" id="wordToOutput">
<button onclick="outputWord()">Press me</button>
    <SCRIPT>
        var words = ["One", "Two", "Three", "Four", "Five"];
        function outputWord(){
            var inputNumber = document.getElementById("wordToOutput").value;
            inputNumber = inputNumber - 1;
            if(inputNumber >= 1 && inputNumber < 5){
                alert(words[inputNumber]);
            } else {
                alert("Invalid number, it must be between 1 and 5");
            }
        }
    </SCRIPT>
</BODY>
</HTML>
```

1 Create an array that stores the names of ten different films. Output each of these films, in turn, on a web page. Each film should be on a new line.

2 Store a list of image names in an array. Ask the user to choose an item from a drop-down menu. Depending on their choice, output one of the images (for example the first option in the drop-down box should output the image in index 0).

3 Create a web page with a text box and a button. Each time the user enters a number in the text box, and clicks the button, put the number into the next array index (you will need to keep track of the number of elements in the array using a global variable). Output the largest number and smallest number of those in the arrays.

20.14 Loops

A loop is a construct that repeats the code inside it a set number of times based on a condition. Another name for it is iteration.

It can be used when you want to perform the same action multiple times. For example, you may want to output a number ten times. Instead of writing the same line of code ten times, you can put it in a loop, which reduces the amount of code.

You may not know how many times some code needs to be run. For example, you want to multiply a number by itself until it is greater than 1000. You will not know, at the start, how many times this code needs to be run.

There are two types of loop: count controlled, and condition controlled.

A count controlled, for example a `for` loop, repeats a set number of times. A condition controlled, for example `while` and `do/while`, repeat when a condition is true.

for

In a `for` loop, you need to know the number of times the loop is to run. The following code adds the value of the total to itself ten times:

```
for (count = 0; count < 10; count++){
    total = total + total;
}
```

`count` is a variable that is declared for the loop. It usually counts the number of times a loop is run, although it can be used in other ways. This statement can be excluded if, for example, you want to use a variable that already exists.

The second element, `count < 10`, is the condition. As long as this is true, the loop will run. This code can be excluded, but then the `for` loop will run continually unless you include a break statement. This is a line of code that tells the program to stop the construct it is currently in (that is, the loop) and go to the next line of code after the loop.

The third element is what happens each time the program gets to the end of the loop, and goes back to the beginning. In this case, the variable `count` increments (increases by one). This statement can be excluded if, for example, you want to change the variable elsewhere within the loop.

This `for` loop will output the first 12 square numbers:

```
for (count = 1; count <= 12; count++){
    alert(count * count);
}
```

for/in

If you have an object that you need to loop through each element, for example to output them all, you can use a `for/in` loop:

```
var film = {title:"The House",
            genre:"Drama", length:96,
            releaseYear:2013};

var count;

for (count in film){
    document.write(film[count]);
}
```

This code will output each of the elements within the object film.

while

A `while` loop runs the code while a condition is true:

```
var count = 0;
while(count <= 12){
    document.write(count * count);
    count++;
}
```

This loop will display the first 12 square numbers. A counter (count) is declared before the loop. The value of this is checked in the condition to see if it is less than or equal to 12. If it is, it enters the loop, otherwise it skips it and jumps to the code below the closing. Within the loop, this counter is incremented.

A `while` loop does not need to use a counter. For example,

```
var check = true;
while(check = true){
    document.write("It's true");
}
```

At the moment this loop will run infinitely. While the variable check is true, it will continue to run. This is a common programming error. The variable would need to change within the loop so that at some stage it is no longer true.

A break statement can be inserted into a loop to stop it running. For example, a loop could run forever, but a selection (`if`) statement within it could catch a condition that calls break. This will then break out of the loop.

do/while

In this loop the condition is checked at the end of the loop, which means the loop will always run at least once:

```
var count = 0;
do{
    document.write(count * count);
    count++;
}
while(count <= 12);
```

In this example, `0*0` will always be output, then the value of `count` is checked and it decides if the loop will run again.

WORKED EXAMPLE 20.17

Create a program that asks the user to enter their username and password. All valid usernames and passwords are stored in a 2D array (username in one index, password in the other). Output whether the user has got it correct, or not.

First, set up the web page to let the user enter a username and password, and click a button.

```
<HTML>
<BODY>
Username <input type = "text" id = "txtUsername">
Password <input type = "password" id = "txtPassword">
<button onclick = "checkUsername()">Enter</button>
    <SCRIPT>
    </SCRIPT>
</BODY>
</HTML>
```

CONTINUED

The input box is set to type *password*, this means that *s will appear instead of the password when text is typed into the box.

Set up a global array with the valid usernames and passwords.

```
<HTML>
<BODY>
Username <input type = "text" id = "txtUsername">
Password <input type = "password" id = "txtPassword">
<button onclick = "checkUsername()">Enter</button>
   <SCRIPT>
      var logins = [["test1","pass123"],["test2","password"]];
      function checkUsername(){
      }
   </SCRIPT>
</BODY>
</HTML>
```

Store the username and password entered.

Loop through all the array elements and check the first index in each to compare the usernames.

```
<HTML>
<BODY>
Username <input type = "text" id = "txtUsername">
Password <input type = "password" id = "txtPassword">
<button onclick = "checkUsername()">Enter</button>
   <SCRIPT>
      var logins = [["test1","pass123"],["test2","password"]];
      function checkUsername(){
         var username = document.getElementById("txtUsername").value;
         var password = document.getElementById("txtPassword").value;
         for(count in logins){
            if(logins[count][0] === username && logins[count][1] == password){
               alert("Welcome");
            }
         }
      }
   </SCRIPT>
</BODY>
</HTML>
```

CONTINUED

Set a flag to track if they are let in. If they are not, output the username or password are incorrect.

```
<HTML>
<BODY>
Username <input type = "text" id = "txtUsername">
Password <input type = "password" id = "txtPassword">
<button onclick = "checkUsername()">Enter</button>
    <SCRIPT>
        var logins = [["test1","pass123"],["test2","password"]];
        function checkUsername(){
            var username = document.getElementById("txtUsername").value;
            var password = document.getElementById("txtPassword").value;
            for(count in logins){
                if(logins[count][0] === username && logins[count][1] == password){
                    alert("Welcome");
                }
            }
            if (flag == false){
                alert("Sorry that's incorrect");
            }
        }
    </SCRIPT>
</BODY>
</HTML>
```

PRACTICAL ACTIVITY 20.19

1   Create a web page that has a series of colours stored in an array. Use a loop to go through each element in the array and output it on a new line on the web page.

2   Create a web page that stores a number in a variable. Use a loop to output the 12-times-table for this number.

3   Create a web page that stores a number in a variable. Output that number of asterisks (*) on a web page

4   Create a web page that asks the user a question, such as what is the user's favourite colour. It then searches through an array to output a sentence related to purple.

20.15 Timing events

JavaScript has an inbuilt timer that lets you delay performing a task within a function, or perform an action at a set interval.

setTimeout

This allows you to set a delay before something happens, for example before an output appears. The call follows the structure:

```
setTimeout(function(){

    Event to delay;

}, timeToDelay);
```

The time to delay is in milliseconds: 3 seconds = 3000, 4 seconds = 4000.

In this example, the prompt box appears after a two-second delay:

```
setTimeout(function(){

    prompt("Do you want to continue?");

    }, 2000);
```

WORKED EXAMPLE 20.18

Create a web page that makes a line of text appear, then an image, then another line of text, then another image, with a two-second delay between each.

First, set up the web page; there needs to be space for two images, and two pieces of text.

```
<HTML>
<BODY>
    <p id="firstText"></p>
    <img src="" id="firstImage" width = 300 height = 300>
    <p id="secondText"></p>
    <img src="" id="secondImage" width = 300 height = 300>
</BODY>
</HTML>
```

Write the function with each element on a separate delay timer. Call the timer when the website first loads (the body onload).

```
<HTML>
<BODY>
    <p id="firstText"></p>
    <img src="" id="firstImage" width = 300 height = 300>
    <p id="secondText"></p>
    <img src="" id="secondImage" width = 300 height = 300>
    <SCRIPT>
        function displaySequence(){
            setTimeout(function(){
                document.getElementById("firstText").innerHTML = "This is the first image"";
            }, 2000);
            setTimeout(function(){
                document.getElementById("firstText").src = IMG_1.jpg";
            }, 4000);
            setTimeout(function(){
                document.getElementById("secondText").innerHTML = "This is the second image";
            }, 6000);
            setTimeout(function(){
                document.getElementById("secondText").src = "IMG_2.jpg";
            }, 8000);
        }
    </SCRIPT>
</BODY>
</HTML>
```

setInterval

This allows you to make something happen repeatedly. For example, every two seconds you can output the same alert box.

The call follows the structure:

```
setInterval(function(){
   Event to repeat;
}, timeBetweenRepeats);
```

In this example the alert appears every second

```
setInterval(function(){
   alert("Hello");
},1000);
```

In both `setTimeout` and `setInterval`, you can include more than one line. For example, this code declares a global variable, `counter`, and both outputs its value then increments its value every second:

```
var counter = 0
function delayOutput(){
   setInterval(function(){
      alert(counter);
      counter++;
   },1000);
}
```

You can only have one delay running at a time, because JavaScript is not designed to keep multiple threads running; each interval will be one thread that is counting.

WORKED EXAMPLE 20.19

Create a web page that outputs the next element in an array of colours every two seconds.

First, set up the global array of colours, and a `counter` to keep track of how many have been output.

```
<HTML>
<BODY onload="sequence()">

   <SCRIPT>
      var colours=["grey", "purple", "red",
      "green", "yellow", "orange"];
      var counter = 0;
   </SCRIPT>
</BODY>
</HTML>
```

Create the function to output the `counter` element of the array and increment `counter`.

```
<HTML>
<BODY onload="sequence()">

   <SCRIPT>
      var colours=["grey", "purple", "red",
      "green", "yellow", "orange"];
      var counter = 0;
      function sequence(){
         setInterval(function(){
            alert(colours[counter]);
            counter++;
         }, 2000);
      }
   </SCRIPT>
</BODY>
</HTML>
```

This could give an array out of bounds error because `counter` keeps incrementing, and if it gets to 6; there is no sixth element. So this needs catching and setting back to 0 using selection.

```
<HTML>
<BODY onload="sequence()">

   <SCRIPT>
      var colours=["grey", "purple", "red",
      "green", "yellow", "orange"];
      var counter = 0;
      function sequence(){
         setInterval(function(){
            alert(colours[counter]);
            counter++;
            if(counter > 5){
               counter = 0;
            }
         }, 2000);
      }
   </SCRIPT>
</BODY>
</HTML>
```

PRACTICAL ACTIVITY 20.20

1   Edit your story from previous tasks so that timers are used to delay different parts of the story. For example, instead of displaying all of the text for one phase at a time, display one sentence, then the next, and so on

2   Create a web page that displays an image every few seconds, and if the user clicks on the image then they get a point and the image is hidden. When they have gained 10 points, output a message telling them that they have won.

3   Create a program that tells a joke with an alert, after a set time the answer appears.

4   Create an array of JavaScript terms and definitions. Every five seconds display another term and its matching definition.

5   Edit Task 4 to become a test; the term appears first, and then after a short time the definition appears.

20.16 String manipulation

A string manipulator allows you to perform actions on a string and extract information from it. When counting letters in a string, the first letter is letter 0, the second letter is letter 1, and so on. Spaces and all symbols all count as letters.

Table 20.7 shows the most common string manipulation methods you may need.

Operator	Description	Example

`substring (startLetter, endLetter);`	Return the letters from the position of *startLetter* to *endLetter*	`word = "Hello World";`
		
		`subword = word.substring(7,11);`
		
		`subword` will now hold `"World"`
		
		The variable, word, is used together with the operator, that is `word.substring`

`substr(start, noOf);`	Starting at the *start* letter, return the *noOf* (number of) letters	`word = "Hello World";`
		
		`subword = word.substr(2,4);`
		
		`subword` will now hold `"llo"`

`replace("string", "string");`	Finds the first string and replaces it with the second string	`word = "Hello World";`
		
		`newW = word.`
		
		`replace("World","Friends");`
		
		`newW` will now hold `"Hello Friends"`

`length`	Returns the length of a string	`wordL = "Hello".length;` `wordL` will store `5`.

`concat("string1", "string2")`	Concatenate will join string1 and string2 together.
	
	You can have more than two strings
		`word1 = "Hello"';`
		
		`space = " "';`
		
		`word2 = "World"';`
		
		`final = word1.concat(word1, space, word2)';`
		
		`final` will now store `"Hello World"`

Operator	Description	Example

`String1 + String2`	+ works in the same way as concat on a string and joins two strings together	`word1 = "Hello";`
		`space = " ";`
		`word2 = "World";`
		`final = word1 + space + word2;`
		`final` will now store `"Hello World"`

`toUpperCase()`	Converts the string to uppercase	`word = "Hello";`
		`final = word.toUpperCase();`
		`final` will now store `"HELLO"`

`toLowerCase()`	Converts the string to lowercase	`word = "Hello";`
		`final = word.toLowerCase();`
		`final` will now store `"hello"`

`charAt(number)`	Returns the character in the string at location number	`word = "Hello";`
		`letter = word.charAt(4);`
		`letter` will now store `"o"`

Table 20.7: String manipulation.

WORKED EXAMPLE 20.20

Create a web page that generates a username for a user. The username uses the last three characters of their last name, the first four characters from their first name, and the year from their date of birth. Output their username to the user.

First, set up the web page with space for all three pieces of data to be entered, and a button.

```
<HTML>
<BODY>
First name <input type = "text" id = "txtFirstName"><br>
Last name <input type = "text" id = "txtLastName"><br>
Year of birth <input type = "text" id = "txtYear"><br>
<button onclick = "createUsername()">Create username</button>
    <SCRIPT>
    </SCRIPT>
</BODY>
</HTML>
```

CONTINUED

Get the data from the text boxes when the button is clicked.

```
<HTML>
<BODY>
First name <input type = "text" id = "txtFirstName"><br>
Last name <input type = "text" id = "txtLastName"><br>
Year of birth <input type = "text" id = "txtYear"><br>
<button onclick = "createUsername()">Create username</button>
    <SCRIPT>
        function createUsername(){
            var firstName = document.getElementById("txtFirstName").value;
            var lastName = document.getElementById("txtLastName").value;
            var yearBirth = document.getElementById("txtYear").value;
        }
    </SCRIPT>
</BODY>
</HTML>
```

Get the characters you want from the variables.

```
<HTML>
<BODY>
First name <input type = "text" id = "txtFirstName"><br>
Last name <input type = "text" id = "txtLastName"><br>
Year of birth <input type = "text" id = "txtYear"><br>
<button onclick = "createUsername()">Create username</button>
    <SCRIPT>
        function createUsername(){
            var firstName = document.getElementById("txtFirstName").value;
            var lastName = document.getElementById("txtLastName").value;
            var yearBirth = document.getElementById("txtYear").value;
            firstName = firstName.substring(0,3);
            var lengthLN = lastName.length;
            lastName = lastName.substring(lengthLN-3, lengthLN);
        }
    </SCRIPT>
</BODY>
</HTML>
```

CONTINUED

Concatenate the data and output it.

```html
<HTML>
<BODY>
First name <input type = "text" id = "txtFirstName"><br>
Last name <input type = "text" id = "txtLastName"><br>
Year of birth <input type = "text" id = "txtYear"><br>
<button onclick = "createUsername()">Create username</button>
  <SCRIPT>
     function createUsername(){
        var firstName = document.getElementById("txtFirstName").value;
        var lastName = document.getElementById("txtLastName").value;
        var yearBirth = document.getElementById("txtYear").value;
        firstName = firstName.substring(0,3);
        var lengthLN = lastName.length;
        lastName = lastName.substring(lengthLN-3, lengthLN);
        username = lastName + firstName + yearBirth;
        alert(username);
     }
  </SCRIPT>
</BODY>
</HTML>
```

PRACTICAL ACTIVITY 20.21

Open file **20.07.html**

Amend the program to take two words as input, and then output alternate letters from each word until there are no letters left in one word.

For example, 'horse house' would output 'hhoorussee', and 'red yellow' would output r'yeedl'

PRACTICAL ACTIVITY 20.22

1   Create a program that stores the first name, second name and age of a person. Output these in a sentence, for example Roberto Mantovani you are 20 years old.

2   Create a program that stores the first name and second name of a person in variables. Combine and output the first two letters of their first name with the first two letters of their second name.

CONTINUED

3   Create a form that takes a person's first name, second name and favourite number. Create a username for them in a function, using the first letter of their first name, their second name and their favourite number. Output their username in a sentence.

20.17 Comments

A comment is text that you add to your code, which the interpreter (the software that runs your program) does not run. Comments can be used to make notes about how your code works so other developers can understand what you have done.

To add a comment, write //, then anything after that will be a comment. For example:

```javascript
var count = 0; //number to act as
    // counter in loop
while(count <= 12){ //loop 0 to 12
    //displaying square numbers
    document.write(count * count);
    //output square numbers
    count++; //increment counter
}
```

You can make a comment go over several lines without having to put `//` in front of each line. Start the comment with `/*` and end it with `*/`. For example:

```
/* This program will generate the username

It takes 3 characters from the last name

And 2 characters from the firstname */
```

PRACTICAL ACTIVITY 20.23

Open your story program and add comments to explain the main elements of the code.

20.18 Iterative methods

An iterative method is a function (or task) that is repeated, for example applied to each element in an array.

every

This iterative method will check every element in an array against a condition. It will return true if every item meets the condition, or false if at least one element does not meet it.

The following code creates a function called `isTen` with `item` as a parameter.

```
function isTen(item){
    return (item == 10);
};
```

An array, `numbers`, is declared. The function `isTen` is applied to the array using the every method:

```
var numbers = [10, 20, 30, 40, 50, 60];
var everyCheck = numbers.every(isTen);
```

This code:

- declares an array called numbers
- calls an every method and sends the array elements using the code `function(item, index, array)`
- the condition is `item == 10`
- the result of this is returned and stored in the variable `everyCheck`.

It will return `false`, because not all elements in numbers are equal to 10.

some

The `some` method checks if at least one item meets the condition:

```
function equalTen(item){
    return (item == 10);
};
var numbers = [10, 20, 30, 40, 50, 60];
var someCheck = numbers.some(equalTen);
```

This time, the method will return true, because at least one of the elements is equal to 10.

filter

The `filter` method will return an array with all the elements that meet the criteria:

```
function lessThirtyFive(item, index,
array){
    return (item <= 35);
};
var numbers = [10, 20, 30, 40, 50, 60];
var filterArray = numbers.
filter(lessThirtyFive);
```

This time, the method will return [10, 20, 30] because these are all the elements that are less than, or equal to, 35.

forEach

`forEach` runs a task, or command, on every element within the array. It does not return any value:

```
function addOne(item, index, array){
    item = item + 1;
    document.write(item);
}
var numbers = [10, 20, 30, 40, 50, 60];
numbers.forEach(addOne);
```

This time, the method will take each item, add 1 to it, then output the new value. The actual value stored in the array is not changed.

map

map runs a task, or command, on every element within the array and returns the new, edited array:

```
function mapOne(item, index, array){

   item = item + 1;

}

var numbers = [10, 20, 30, 40, 50, 60];

var mapArray = numbers.map(mapOne);
```

This time, the method will take each item and add 1 to it. It will return the following edited values that are now stored in mapArray: 11, 21, 31, 41, 51, 61.

WORKED EXAMPLE 20.21

Create a web page that checks if every number stored in an array is greater than 0.

First, set up a button to run the code. Set up an array with numbers.

```
<HTML>
<BODY>
<button onclick = "checkValues()">Create
username</button>
   <SCRIPT>
      var numbers = [-1, 0, 2, 5, -6, -8,
      1.5, 6];
      function isGreaterThan0(){
      }
   </SCRIPT>
</BODY>
</HTML>
```

In the function, add the three parameters and the condition.

```
<HTML>
<BODY>
<button onclick = "checkValues()">Create
username</button>
   <SCRIPT>
      var numbers = [-1, 0, 2, 5, -6, -8,
      1.5, 6];
      function isGreaterThan0(item, index,
      array){
         return(item > 0);
      }
   </SCRIPT>
</BODY>
</HTML>
```

Call the function from the array.

```
<HTML>
<BODY>
<button onclick = "checkValues()">Create
username</button>
   <SCRIPT>
      var numbers = [-1, 0, 2, 5, -6, -8,
      1.5, 6];
      function isGreaterThan0(item, index,
      array){
         return(item > 0);
      }
      function checkValues(){
         var result = numbers.
         every(isGreaterThan0);
         alert(Result);
      }
   </SCRIPT>
</BODY>
</HTML>
```

PRACTICAL ACTIVITY 20.24

1   Create an array with a series of numbers.

   a   Create a function that will multiply each number in the array by two and output the result, but do not store the result.

   b   Create a function that will multiply each number in an array by ten, store the results and output them.

   c   Create a function that will check if *any* of the numbers are greater than 20.

   d   Create a function that will check if *all* the numbers are greater than 20.

   e   Create a function that will return an array with all elements in that are greater than or equal to ten.

20.19 Trap errors

Errors can occur in a variety of places in a program and for a variety of reasons. For example, a user may have input invalid data, a calculation may not be possible or on the wrong data type, or the programmer may have made an error themselves. These errors might stop the web page working.

To trap these errors, `try` and `catch` code is used. Within the `try` block are the statements that are attempting to run. You can throw a specific error message to be output after each statement. The `catch` block states what to do with the error message if generated:

```
var x = 21;
try{
    if(x>20) throw "over 20";
    if(x<=10) throw "less than 11";
}
catch(e){
    message.innerHTML= e;
}
```

This code checks if the value of x is greater than 20.

If it is, it sets the error (e) to be `"over 20"`.

If it isn't, it compares it to `<= 10`.

If it is, it sets the error (e) to `"less than 11"`.

The `catch` takes this error, if it is generated, and then displays it.

This code can be used to validate data on entry. Using `ifs` in this way will ensure all conditions are met, whereas a `case` statement may not catch all possible errors.

PRACTICAL ACTIVITY 20.25

1   Create a web page that asks the user to guess a stored number that is between 1 and 100. Throw appropriate errors if numbers outside of this range are entered.

2   Create a web page that asks the user to enter registration information for a website. Throw an error if any inappropriate or invalid data is entered, for example an inappropriate date of birth.

3   Ask a partner to feedback on your web pages. Discuss what other features you could add to enhance the pages. Add any of the comments that you feel would be appropriate.

20.20 Using external scripts

You can write your JavaScript code in a separate document and then import it into your HTML document.

Create a separate document and write your JavaScript code inside it. Save the file with a sensible name and the extension .js

Inside this document write the JavaScript code that would usually go within the script tags, for example:

```
var value1 = 5;
var value2 = 10;
document.write(value1 * value2);
```

You then call this code within your HTML document. The name of the file goes within the script tag, in this example the JavaScript file `javascriptparagraph.js` is being imported into this webpage:

```html
<html>

    <script src="javascriptparagraph.js">
    x</script>

</html>
```

PRACTICAL ACTIVITY 20.26

Take one of the webpages you created as part of this unit. Remove the JavaScript code and put it into a separate document. Remember to give the file the extension .js

Import this external JavaScript file into your HTML program.

REFLECTION

1   How did you solve errors that you encountered while writing web pages?

2   What approach did you take to solving a task? Did you plan the web page first, or start programming straight away? Why did you choose this approach?

3   Did you find any extra code that was outside of the requirements? How did you learn how to use this code? Did you learn better through independent experimentation?

EXAM-STYLE QUESTIONS

1   Kim runs a theme park. She wants a web page to allow a customer to submit a question. The web page must:
    • include space for the customer to enter their first name, last name, query, and email address
    • check that none of these data items have been left blank
    • check that the email address includes an @ symbol
    • give the user a confirmation that their request has been submitted (if there is no error).
    Suitable error messages must be used if any of the requirements are not met.
    Add comments to explain each JavaScript construct used.
    a   Create the web page and error messages.   [11]
    b   Explain why comments are added to the code of a website.   [3]
    c   Explain the importance of trapping errors and giving appropriate error messages in a web page.   [4]
    d   Kim would like an image adding to the web page. When the user moves their cursor over the Image 1

Figure 20.2: Image 1.

Figure 20.3: Image 2.

CONTINUED

it should change to the second Image 2 from the provided files, 20.08 Image1.jpg and 20.09 Image2.jpg.

Edit the web page for Kim. [3]

[Total 21]

2 Terry owns a restaurant. People can put in a request for a reservation using an online form.

The form needs to allow a user to:

- select a day from Tuesday, Wednesday, Friday, Saturday or Sunday
- select a time (bookings are made every half an hour from 17:00 to 20:30)
- enter the number of people; there is a minimum of 1, and a maximum of 10
- select whether they would like the set menu, or not
- enter their name and a contact telephone number.

   a Create the web page. Make sure all fields have been validated so only acceptable data can be entered, and cannot be left blank. There should be suitable error messages if any data is not valid. The data should only be successfully submitted if it is all valid. [12]

   b Comment on your code from part (a) to explain the key constructs used. [2]

   c Explain how you used selection in your answer to part (a). [3]

[Total 17]

3 Two loops are `while` and `do while`.

Explain the difference between how these two types of loop run. [2]

4 Describe what an array is in programming. [3]

SUMMARY CHECKLIST

- [ ] I can add interactivity to web pages.
- [ ] I can change HTML content and styles.
- [ ] I can show/hide HTML elements.
- [ ] I can display data in different ways.
- [ ] I can react to common HTML events.
- [ ] I can provide user interaction.
- [ ] I can create statements.
- [ ] I can create loops for iterative methods.
- [ ] I can create functions.
- [ ] I can use timing events.
- [ ] I can add comments to annotate and explain code.
- [ ] I can describe the structure and syntax of JavaScript code.
- [ ] I can describe a range of object-based JavaScript programming and terms.

> Answers

1 – Data processing and information

1   For example, #000000 (there must be no explanation, just the data).

2   For example, context is added to #000000 because we are told it is a colour code. Meaning is added by telling us it is the colour code for black.

3   For example, measure it himself.

4   For example, accept measurements given by the customer.

5   For example, he can rely on the measurements he has taken himself to be accurate.

6   Accuracy, relevance, age, level of detail, completeness.

7   The user guide could be written for an old operating system that has since been updated on the phone.

8   WELL DONE

9   To ensure data that is input matches the source data.

10 Presence, range, type, length, format, check digit, lookup.

11 Data can match the rules but still be incorrect (for example, date of birth of 29/1/13 matches the rule of a data type but it may be that the date should have been 29/1/03).

Data can be checked against the source, but the source maybe incorrect (for example, the name 'Siohan' is written on the original source and is visually checked to have been entered as 'Siohan' but the actual spelling should have been 'Siobhan').

12 •   When a customer makes a payment, they will phone the telephone company and an operator will record the payment using a graphical user interface as an interactive process.

•   At the end of each month, the telephone company will produce the telephone bills overnight by reading data about phone calls and payments from the transaction files and updating the master file as a batch process.

13 •   A video-conference requires participants to be able to see and hear each other at the time that communication takes place.

•   If the conference is not in real-time, then the participants will be waiting to hear what other participants have said – and this may be several seconds or minutes after it has happened.

•   Real-time is required so that the participants can communicate at the same time with each other rather than having to wait long periods of time before being able to respond.

Exam-style questions

1   Data that has context/meaning [1], for example, EW1 5RG is a postcode [1].

2   a   Any four from the following [4]:

Credit card information is sensitive [1] because it could be used for fraud [1].

HTTPS is an encrypted method of passing information over the web [1] which will mean the credit card information will be scrambled [1] and unusable by anybody without a key [1].

b   The sender encrypts the message using an encryption key [1]. The same key is used to decrypt the message by the recipient [1].

c   Any two from the following [2]:

The sender uses the public key of the recipient to encrypt the message [1]. The message is sent in an encrypted format [1]. The recipient uses their private key to decrypt the message [1]. The sender and recipient need to exchange digital certificates [1].

d For example, the user could be asked to enter their password twice [1] or the user could type their password and then visually check it [1].

3 **a** To ensure that data matches a given set of rules [1].

b For example, presence check [1] to ensure news story [1] is present [1].

Or, for example, format check [1] to ensure email address [1] contains @ symbol [1].

4 All of the following [4]:
- An online processing system processes data in transactions
- … whereas a real-time processing system process data as soon as it is input.
- Online processing systems are often used in booking systems, where all the data for the transaction can be collected and then processed
- … whereas real-time processing systems are used when the immediacy of the data is vital, such as air traffic control systems.

5 Any two from the following [2]:
- A collection of fields about a main element of a data system.
- Stores all of the more permanent data about the customer / employee.
- A transaction file is normally used to update a master file.

6 Any three from the following (2 marks for each) [6]:
- Stores information about minimum stock levels that should be maintained for each product – these will depend upon how quickly stock is used and how long it takes to order new stock.
- Stores information about up-to-date current stock levels of each product.
- Stores information about re-order amounts for each product – how many of each product should be ordered when the minimum stock level has been reached – these will depend

upon how quickly stock is used and any discounts that are applied for bulk purchasing.
- Stores information about planned deliveries of replacement stock.
- Stores information about the cost of purchasing each product and, for the retail industry, the prices to be charged for each product.
- Stores information about dates that each batch of stock was supplied so that the oldest stock can be used first.
- Stores information about suppliers that can be used to supply each type of product.
- Stores information about location of each product in stock so that it can be found when needed.

7 Any four from the following [4]:
- System stores current stock level, minimum stock level and re-order amount.
- As each stock item is sold or used, the current stock level is reduced by one.
- When the current stock level reaches the minimum stock level, a new order for stock is placed.
- The amount ordered for the stock will be the re-order amount.
- When the stock delivery arrives, the number of items received is added to the current stock level.

2 – Hardware and software

1 Any two from the following [2]:
- serving multiple terminals
- serve ATMs
- host business databases
- host web sites

- transaction processing
- batch processing
- statistical analysis.

2 Any two from the following [2]:
  - quantum mechanics calculations
  - weather forecasting
  - climate research.

3 Reliability, availability and serviceability.

4 Data centres / mainframes / supercomputers generate a lot of heat so natural cold air can be circulated, which is cheaper than artificial cooling.

5 MFLOPS measure floating point instructions per second and supercomputers use floating point instructions for scientific calculations.

6 Allocating memory to software; sending data and instructions to output devices; responding to input devices such as when a key is pressed; opening and closing files on storage devices; giving each running task a fair share of processor time; sending error messages or status messages to applications or users; dealing with user logons and security.

7 To translate source code into object code ready for execution.

8 When testing a program, an interpreter can translate just the code that is being tested which saves translation time; source code can be translated into object code for more than one operating system.

9 For example, antivirus; backup; data compression; disk defragmentation; format; file-copying; deleting.

10 To stop viruses or malware from being executed and causing damage to files and programs

11 Software that already exists and is readily available to be purchased.

12 For example, the client has to wait a long time for it to be developed; it is expensive because the client has to cover the whole development cost; the software won't have been used by other customers before so bugs are likely to be found when the software is used; the only support available will be from the company that developed the software.

13 The device may not have much memory to carry out complex operations.

14 Any two from the following [2]:
  - they are difficult to learn
  - users have to remember the commands
  - typing errors can be easily made.

15 Windows, Icons, Menus, Pointers.

16 Examples are:

No hands are required [1], which makes them useful when cooking / driving a car [1].

The user does not need to have access to a physical device [1], which means commands can be given from anywhere in a room [1].

Exam-style questions

1 a 1 MIPS [1] or FLOPS / MFLOPS [1].

  b Reliability: Disruption to a mainframe computer could be extremely expensive when lots of users are affected [1] so it's important that hardware is self-checking and can recover automatically [1] / so it's important that software has been tested extensively to avoid failure [1].

    Availability: Mainframe computers can be used by thousands of users at a time [1] so it's important that the system is available at all times [1].

    Serviceability: Mainframe computers can be serving users or batch processing tasks 24 hours a day [1] so any downtime for upgrades or replacement hardware needs to be minimal [1].

2 The device driver includes instructions for the printer [1] so the operating system can communicate with the printer [1].

3 a Any from the following [4]:

    Data is stored in track sectors [1] which are segments of a track [1] on a magnetic platter [1]. The read/write head moves to the correct track [1] and magnetises/demagnetizes sectors [1]. Data is stored in clusters of adjacent track sectors [1] (where possible).

  b Over time data has been deleted from the disk [1] leaving only small clusters of space [1] meaning that new large files have to be written across multiple clusters [1], which will be in different locations on the disk [1].

4 Any six from the following [6]:

Custom written software will meet all of the requirements for waste management [1] because it is written especially for the council [1]. Custom software can be designed especially to be compatible with existing systems [1] such as the web interface used by residents [1]. Custom written software will be very expensive [1] compared with off-the-shelf software [1]. The council will have to wait a few months [1] for the system to be developed for them [1]. There may be very good alternative off-the-shelf solutions [1], which would be able to be used instantly [1] at a much lower cost [1] and with a lot of support available [1]. In conclusion, the council should investigate existing off-the-shelf solutions before committing to the cost and development time of a custom-written solution [1].

5 a Any three from the following (3 marks each point) [9]:

- Labels [1] text that can't be edited by user [1], for example, an instruction to the user [1].

- Text boxes [1] for the input of text [1], for example, input of a postcode where waste collection has been missed [1].

- Tick boxes [1], which can be selected or not selected [1], for example, selecting which waste collections have been missed [1].

- Option buttons / radio buttons [1] where only one option can be selected from a group [1], for example, selecting whether it is just one property or the whole street that has been missed [1].

- Drop down box / combo box / list box [1] where user can select an item from a list [1], for example, selecting an address for a postcode [1].

- Buttons [1] that user can click on to confirm an action [1], for example, to move to the next question about the missed collection [1].

- Spinner [1] which can be used to select a number by increasing/decreasing value [1], for example, number of people who live in a household [1].

b Any two from the following [2]:

- Command Line Interface / CLI [1]

- dialogue / voice-controlled interface [1]

- gesture (based) interface [1]

- menu interface [1].

6 Any two from the following (2 marks each point) [4]:

- Compiler translates source code all at once [1]; interpreter translates one line at a time [1].

- Compiled code will only work on target operating system [1]; interpreter can translate code for current operating system [1].

- Compiled code is ready to be executed immediately [1]; interpreter has to generate code a line at a time which delays execution time [1].

- Compiling code can take a while to complete [1]; interpreting parts of code can be done immediately for on-the-fly testing [1].

3 – Monitoring and control

1 Students may notice things like:
- the temperature of the room
- any sounds in the room
- any sounds outside the room
- how light it is in the room
- whether anyone is moving in the room.

2 Infrared sensors can collect data about the infrared radiation given off by lifeforms.

Electromagnetic field sensors collect data about electromagnetic fields that are often given off by man-made electronics.

Touch sensors can collect data about force/pressure or about electrical fields. A resistive touch sensor collects data about the pressure that is placed upon it. A capacitive touch sensor collects data about changes in an electrical field.

A proximity sensor collects data about how close a nearby object is. This can be done through emitting an electromagnetic field, or infrared light and measuring the change in return.

3 **a** A sensor could provide incorrect readings if it has not been calibrated correctly or the sensor hardware may be faulty.

b A control system will be reliant on the accuracy of the readings from the sensor. If the sensor is measuring a dangerous situation, then human lives could be at risk if the control system does not take the correct safety action.

4 A pH sensor could be used to measure the level of pollution in the river. The pH sensor could be placed in the water and continually send data back to a microprocessor. The microprocessor can check the data against a storage range of values. The stored range of values represent the correct pH level for the river. If the data from the sensor falls outside this range, an alert can be raised to tell staff at the factory that there may be pollution coming from the factory into the river. The factory can then investigate this.

The data from the sensor could also just be continually collected and stored on a computer, so that an employee at the factory can manually analyse the data to see if there is any change in the pH that might indicate that pollution from the factory is present in the river.

5 **a** Possible flow chart could be:

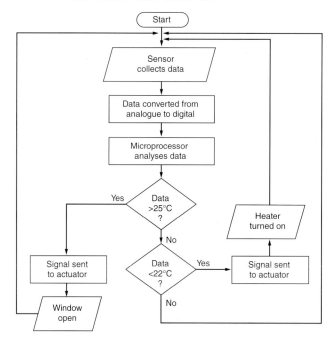

b • Closing the window when too cold.

   • Turning off the heater when too hot.

6 Possible algorithm could be:

• Infrared sensor continually sends data to microprocessor.

• Data is converted from analogue to digital so that it can be processed.

• Microprocessor compares data received from sensor to stored values.

• If the data is outside the accepted range, the microprocessor sends a signal to sound an alarm. It will also send signals to actuators to trigger metal bars to drop to block each door and window.

7 Possible flowchart could be:

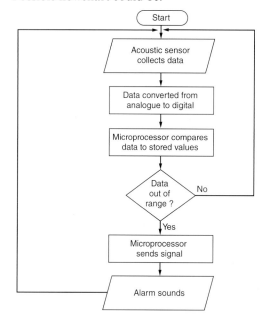

8 Possible algorithm could be:

• Pressure sensor continually sends data to microprocessor.

• Data is converted from analogue to digital so that it can be processed.

• Microprocessor compares data received from sensor to stored values.

• If the data is < 5kg, the microprocessor sends a signal to sound an alarm. It will also send signals to actuators to trigger metal bars to drop to block each door and window.

Exam-style questions

1   It is an input device that collects data from the surrounding physical environment. [1]

2   It is an integrated circuit that is used in monitoring and control systems. [1]

3   It is a type of motor that is used to move and operate another mechanism or systems.. [1]

4   Any three from the following [3]:

•   Take two different readings with the sensor

•   Compare the readings to a device measured at the ideal standard.

•   Calculate the range for the sensor readings by subtracting the low reading from the high reading.

•   Calculate the range for the ideal readings by subtracting the low reading from the high reading.

•   Use a formula to calculate the correct value for each reading.

5   Any two from the following [2]:

•   It means a human doesn't need to carry out the task of analysing the data.

•   Automatic action can be triggered as a result of the analysis by the microprocessor.

•   A microprocessor is likely to be more accurate than a human when analysing data.

6   All of the following [4]:

•   A monitoring system takes in data readings and simply records them for human analysis

•   … or can output a simple alert so that manual action can be taken.

•   A control system requires no human interaction.

•   A control system takes in data readings that are analysed and an automated action is taken.

7   Any five from the following [5]:

•   The touch sensor continually sends data to the microprocessor.

•   The microprocessor converts the data from analogue to digital.

•   The microprocessor compares the data to stored values.

•   If the cooling liquid level is too low, the microprocessor sends a signal to an actuator to open a value and allow more cooling liquid to enter.

•   If the cooling liquid level is too high, the microprocessor sends a signal to an actuator to open a value and allow cooling liquid to drain out.

•   The process will be continually repeated until the system is switched off.

8   All of the following [6]:

•   Input for sensor.

•   Process for converting data to digital.

•   Process for comparing data.

•   Decision for comparing data to 12 microns.

•   Process to send signal to turn screen off if greater than 12 microns.

•   Screen turns on/stays on if less than 12 microns.

Possible flowchart:

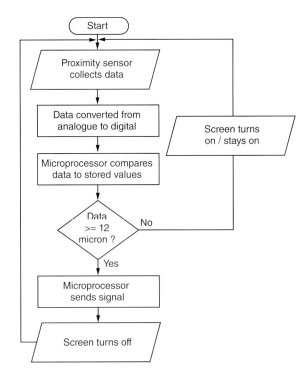

4 – Algorithms and flowcharts

1   A series of steps that perform a task or solve a problem.

2   A series of steps, flowchart, pseudocode.

3   A rectangle with rounded corners .

4   The text 'Enter a number' is output.

    The user inputs a number, it is stored in the variable number.

    The words 'Your number is' and the contents of the variable number are output.

5   An operation that changes something.

6   Power of

7   x = 3 * 7

8   The user inputs two numbers, the first is stored in the variable num1, the second in num2.

    The number in num1 and num2 are added together and stored in the variable total.

    The value of num1 is output, with a + symbol, then the value in num2, then an = sign and then the value in total.

    The value in total then becomes the value in num1 minus the value in num2.

    The value of num1 is output, with a − symbol, then the value in num2, then an = sign, and then the value in total.

9   2

10 Code is run dependent on a condition.

11 Yes

12 No

13 No

14 Code is repeated a set number of times or until a conditions is met or unmet.

15 Code is repeated a set number of times.

16 When you know the number of times iteration must take place.

17 Starting value, end value, amount value changes in each loop.

18 When you don't know how many times a loop should run, or the loop runs until a condition is met or unmet.

19 0

20 A section of code, that has its own name, that is separate from the main program and can be called from anywhere in the code.

21 To create reusable components.

    To avoid repeated code.

22 A value that is sent to a subroutine.

23 A construct within another construct, e.g. selection inside iteration.

24 Change decision box from 'Is counter = 10?' to 'Is counter = 20?'

25
```
largest = -9999
    FOR counter = 0 to 50
            INPUT number
            If number > largest THEN
                    largest = number
            ENDIF
    NEXT counter
    answer = largest * largest
    OUTPUT answer
```

Exam-style questions

1   Series of instructions; Flowchart; Pseudocode [2].

2   Process; Input/Output; Start/Stop [3].

3   20 [1].

4   Change process box 'answer = count * 5' to 'answer = count * 9' [1].

5   Change continue = False to continue = True [1].

6   a   generate1 [1]

    b   Two [1]

    c   symbol; number; value1; value2; outputS; count [2]

    d   ***** [1].

7   1 mark per bullet [6].
    • Start and stop symbol.
    • Looping from 0 to 100 (or equivalent)
    • … using correct selection statements.
    • A mechanism for working out if it's odd (mod or incrementing by 2).
    • Outputting the numbers.
    • Correct data flows with no lost connectors.

8   1 mark per bullet [9].
    • Taking two numbers as input.
    • Taking a symbol as input.

- Checking if the symbol is +
- ... and all other symbols.
- Use of a subroutine for one calculation
- ... that has the two numbers as parameters
- ... and performs the correct calculation
- ... and outputs the result.
- All other subroutines work correctly.

5 – eSecurity

1
- A VPN can improve security as it encrypts data that is sent across the network.

- A VPN can allow data to be sent anonymously, so if data is intercepted, the intruder may not be able to find the identity of the sender.

2 It is a type of malicious software. When it is unknowingly installed on a user's computer, it can allow a hacker to have remote access and control of a computer system.

3 The Confiker worm targeted windows operating system. It infected millions of systems. Its purpose was unclear as the authors never used much of its potential. It created the ability for the authors to install and run software on computers from a remote location. It could also be used to remotely control those computers and use them in some type of botnet attack. One popular method that the worm used to spread was through the use of memory sticks.

This caused many businesses to ban the use of memory sticks for transporting data and anti-virus and anti-malware software to be repeatedly run on computers on a network until the worm was no longer detected. It can still, however, be detected on many computers today.

4 Many companies were making use of spyware to monitor the actions of users online. This data was being analysed and collated and results could be sold to target users in what was felt to be unethical ways, e.g. targeting specific people with certain kinds of voting marketing to try and influence their choices further.

The GDPR is a regulation that now exists to make sure that data is not collected and sold in this way without a user's consent. The law requires users to be transparently informed about what data is collected about their online habits and how that

data will be used. It also gives them the right to decline the collection of their data.

5 Mobile phones are often infected with spyware as it is buried into the download of apps. This is why it is important to make sure that only trustworthy apps are downloaded.

Spyware can be used to track data such as contacts, images, call logs, messages, browsing habits and it can make audio recordings of calls.

6 One example of its use is to hide a rootkit on a CD/DVD that is downloaded onto the user's computer when the CD/DVD is inserted. The rootkit could be used to limit the user's ability to copy the CD/DVD. This can stop user's creating pirated copies of the CD/DVD.

7 a Search engines use bots as web crawlers to build an index of all the webpages available on the world wide web.

b User's computers are infected with malware that turns the computer into a bot. The name given to a computer in this state is a zombie bot. When a perpetrator wants to launch an attack on a web server, to bring it down, it wakes up all the zombie bots, by accessing them from a remote location, and causes each bot to send numerous requests to the webserver. All the bots together create a bot net.

8 The practice of POLP is based on the principle that a user should only be given access to the data and resources that they required for legitimate reasons. This is created by making sure that every user or process in a system should have the least authority possible to perform the job.

Exam-style questions

1 Any three from the following [3]:
- Set strong passwords.
- Encrypt personal data.
- Use a firewall to monitor traffic.
- Regularly scan computer with detection and prevention software.
- Only visit and use trusted sources.
- Do not open any email attachments from unknown and untrusted sources.
- Check the URL of any link.

- Be cautious about any personal data shared.
- Set all privacy settings to the most secure setting.
- Report and block suspicious activity.

2 Phishing involves clicking a link in an email that takes a user to the fake website, whereas pharming downloads malicious code onto a user's computer that redirects them to the fake website [1].

3 All of the following [2]:

- They can both involve a user receiving a fake email.
- They are both designed to collect a user's personal data.

4 Any four of the following [4]:

- virus
- adware
- trojan
- rootkit
- worm
- malicious bots
- spyware
- ransomware.

5 All of the following [5]:

- Firewall monitors incoming and outgoing traffic from a computer system.
- User can set rules and criteria for the data, which could include detecting known viruses.
- User can close certain ports on firewall that are often used by hackers to infiltrate a firewall.
- Firewall compares traffic to rules and criteria set.
- Firewall can decline traffic if it does not meet the rules and criteria set.

6 Any five of the following [5]:

- A user could click a link / open an attachment / download software that could trigger the download of spyware onto the user computer.
- The spyware could be software, such as a key logger.
- The spyware will record all the keypresses the user makes.
- The recorded keypresses are sent to a third party.
- The third party analyses the data looking for patters and trends.

- If a patter is identified, this could be data that is used as a password.

7 a A rootkit is a computer program that enables a person to gain administrator access to a victim's computer [1].

b Any one of the following (2 marks per bullet) [2]:

- Set a strong password for the computer.
- Only download data from trusted sources.
- Don't insert a USB that you find into your computer.

c All of the following [2]:

- Steal a user's personal data.
- Use the user's computer as part of a larger cyber security attack.

8 a It encrypts the data [2].

b Any two from the following [2]:

- Store data in the cloud.
- Keep an up-to-date backup of data, away from the computer system.
- Only open and use software from trusted sources.

6 – The digital divide

1 a If a person does not have high-speed internet, they may not be able to use all the resources available on learning platforms, such as streaming videos and taking part in video-conferences.

b This could increase the digital divide between those living in a city and those living in rural locations. It is likely that those living in a rural location will not be able to get as high speeds for their internet connection as those in a city.

2 a They may not be able to use facilities such as video conferencing (e.g. facetime and skype) on their mobile telephone, so they cannot enjoy the increased communication method that seeing the other person face to face can bring.

b They may not be able to access their social media and the instant messaging facilities that are often built into social media platforms.

c   The lack ability to communicate using these services may make them feel isolated and they may feel like they are left of out of online social situations.

3   They may have better access to high education.

They may have better access to job opportunities and promotion prospects.

4   Possible responses could be:

Task	Pre-technology	Post-technology
Sending a list of places you want to visit, to a friend.	Writing them a letter and sending it by post.	Sending them a text message.
Arranging to meet a friend for lunch.	Calling them on a landline telephone.	Calling them on a mobile telephone.
Buying a cinema ticket.	Going to the ticket office at the cinema.	Using a mobile application to buy the ticket and downloading the ticket to the mobile phone.
Researching recipes for your favourite food.	Going to the library to look at recipe books.	Using a search engine to research the recipes.
Finding out how much money is left in your bank account.	Going to the cashier desk at the bank.	Using online banking facilities.

5   People could use the online circumstances to improve their education, or learn new skills, and this could lead to better job opportunities.

6   High-speed internet for education purposes could mean that movies and television shows could be streamed in high definition, improving the viewing experience for the audience.

Exam-style questions

1   The term refers to the technology divide between countries, demographic groups and economic areas [1].

2   Any two from the following [2]:
- people living in cities vs people living in rural areas.
- people educated in using technology vs people uneducated in using technology.
- older people vs younger people.
- areas that are more industrially developed vs areas that are less industrially developed.
- different socio-economic groups.

3   All of the following [4]:
- The infrastructure in place to allow the use of effective technology can differ greatly depending on a person's geographical location.
- Those in rural locations may have less infrastructure that those in cities.
- Those in third world countries may have less infrastructure that those in third world countries.
- If the infrastructure is not available, a person may not be able to use the technology available

4   All of the following [4]:
- Lots of resources are available on online learning platforms.
- People can use these resources to enhance their own learning.
- This can lead to improved opportunities for people, including better job opportunities.
- If people cannot access these learning resources, they may find that they are behind others in their education and cannot access the same opportunities.

5   Any four from the following [4]:
- The use of satellite technology
- … this can provide access to the internet to those in remote locations and where the infrastructure is not in place.

- Government promotes the business and products that could be on offer

- … in hope that other countries will invest in their infrastructure to allow them to utilise the necessary technology.

- Company initiatives that encourage the recycling and donation of technology

- … these can then be given to those in circumstances that may mean they cannot afford to but the technology.

- The use of classes to teach the use of the technology

- … this can be especially useful for older people who may not feel confident in using technology.

7 – Expert systems

1. A user may become frustrated as they are not able to input the data and get the result that they are looking for.

   The user may not understand the data that is being presented to them.

2. The knowledge could not be updated, and the data stored could be incorrect or outdated. This means that the results produces by the expert system may be incorrect or outdated.

3. Any scenario in which a decision or diagnosis can be provided based on factual data.

4. Any scenario in which a decision or diagnosis would need to be given based on an emotional response.

5. Advantages could be:

   - Person may not need to visit the doctor.

   - Person may be able to go straight to a pharmacy and get correct medication.

   - Person may be able to get an understanding of whether the medical condition could be serious, and how quickly they need to visit the doctor.

   Disadvantages could be:

   - Person may not go to the doctors with a serious condition.

- Person may get an incorrect diagnosis and get incorrect medication as a result.

6. Questions could include:

   - How old are you?

   - Do you smoke?

   - How much alcohol do you drink in a week?

   - How much exercise do you do in a week?

   - Have you had any previous illnesses?

   - Have you ever had surgery?

7. Questions could include:

   - How many legs does it have?

   - Does it have a tail?

   - Does it have fur?

   - How tall is it?

   - What colour is it?

   - What kind of noise does it make?

Exam-style questions

1. Knowledge base [1].

2. Inference engine [1].

3. All of the following [2]:

   - The role of an expert system is to attempt to reproduce the decision-making process of a human being.

   - The role of an expert system is to try and replicate the judgement of a human that has an expert knowledge in a certain field.

4. Any three from the following [3]:

   - Forward chaining is based on data driven reasoning.

   - It is dependent on the data that it is provided with.

   - It is better for solving open-ended problems.

   - The system takes data input by the user, then moves from rule to rule to provide a possible outcome.

5 A goal driven problem [1].

6 Any two from the following (2 marks per bullet) [4]:

- An expert system could be used to self-diagnose medical conditions

  … a user can input medical symptoms and gain an understanding of what medical conditions this could be.

- An expert system could be used to diagnose a fault on a car

  … a car can be attached to an expert system that will analyse data from the car and find the fault.

- An expert system can be used to act as an opponent in a game

  … the game could use the data input by the user to make decisions about the game play of the opponent.

- An expert system can be used as a tool in financial planning

  … the user can input their financial details and the system can help with processes such as managing their debt.

- An expert system can be used as a tool in providing insurance

  … the user can input their personal data and the system can tell them what insurance products are available to them.

- An expert system can be used to find out the identification of a plant or an animal

  … the user can input data about the features and characteristics of the item and the system can provide information about what it thinks it is.

- An expert system can be used to help plan out delivery schedules

  … the deliveries a driver needs to make can be input into the system and the system can plan the best route for making the deliveries..

8 – Spreadsheets

1 The named range can be referenced directly by name instead of by cell references; it can be used as an absolute reference when replicating a lookup function.

2 A formula is a simple calculation using basic arithmetic of +, -, x, ÷ whereas a function is a predefined complex calculation that can be called by name and includes a series of formulas that the user is unaware of.

3 When formulas and functions are replicated, absolute cell references remain the same whereas relative cell references change in relation to the row or column.

4 A tax rate could be stored in a single cell. A set of prices would be stored in a column. When calculating the tax to be applied to the first price in the column, the price would be a relative reference (for example, B3) and the tax would be an absolute reference (for example, $F$1). These two references would be multiplied together and then replicated down the spreadsheet. B3 would change to B4, B5, etc. as it is replicated to each row below but $F$1 would remain the same.

5 **a** Any three from the following:

- Length check: to check the product code is six characters long.

- Format check: to check the product code is three letters, two numbers, one letter.

- Lookup check: to check the product code exists in a list of product codes.

- Presence check: to check the product code has been input.

b Any two from the following:

- Type check: to check the value is an integer.

- Range check: to check the value is more than zero.

- Presence check: to check a quantity has been input (if not used for **a**).

6

Test data input value	Type of test data	Expected result	Reason for choosing data
Customer = Null	*Abnormal/Invalid/ Erroneous*	*Error: 'You must input a customer'*	*It will check to see if a customer has not been input*
Customer = 'Any Customer Name'	*Normal/Valid*	*Value accepted*	*It will check to see if a customer can be input*
Product Code = XYZ12AB	*Normal/Valid*	*Value accepted*	*It will check to see if a valid product code can be input*
Product Code = XY21C (any code that is not 6 digits)	*Abnormal/Invalid/ Erroneous*	Error: 'You must input a product code with 6 characters'.	*It will check if a product code is not 6 characters*
Quantity = 'a'	*Abnormal/Invalid/ Erroneous*	*Error: 'Quantity must be an integer'*	*It will check to see if the quantity is not an integer*
Quantity = 1	Extreme	Value accepted	It's the smallest allowable quantity.
Quantity = 3 (any number 3 or more)	*Normal/Valid*	Value accepted	*It will check to see that an integer above 0 will be accepted*

7 Line, because it shows how data has changed over a period of time.

8 Pie, because it is showing each piece of data in proportion to the rest of the data.

Exam-style questions

1 a Horizontal set of cells [1], for example, for one car [1].

  b i Arithmetic calculation [1] any example using plus, minus, divide, multiply, exponent [1].

   ii E2*4.55 [1].

   iii Any two of the following [2]:

   Complex calculation [1]; reserved word in spreadsheet [1]; ready-made formula [1].

   iv Lookup or vlookup or hlookup or index [1].

2 a Any two of the following [2]:

   Select column D [1] apply a filter [1] of fuel type = petrol [1].

  b Any two of the following [2]:

   Apply conditional formatting [1] to fuel type column [1] where diesel, petrol and lpg are each set to a different colour [1].

3 Any four from the following [4]:

Relative referencing used for cost per gallon [1] so when the formula is replicated [1] it refers to the cost per litre on the next row down [1]. Absolute referencing used for the fuel type table [1] within the lookup function for cost per litre [1] so that when replicated down the lookup function keeps referencing the fuel type table [1].

4 a Any three of the following [3]:

   Variables can be used to change the distances travelled [1], what-if questions can be asked such as 'what will be the cost if the car travels 300 miles?' [1], formulas and functions can be used to calculate the total cost [1]; graphs and charts can be used to compare the costs of each car [1]; formulas and functions will automatically recalculate so results can be seen instantly [1]; conditional formatting can be used to show cars that cost a specific amount [1]; goal-seek can be used to find out the optimum speed to travel at [1].

b   Any one of the following [1]:

the model will only be as good as the rules [1]; the speed the car is travelling out will need to be taken into account [1]; unforeseen circumstances such as traffic jams will affect the costs [1].

9 – Modelling

1   The ability to change variables within the software; asking what-if questions to see what the result of changing variables might be; formulas and functions to carry out the mathematical calculations that form the basis of the model; automatic recalculation of formulas and functions; rules that define how the model behaves; layers of abstraction so that different parts of the model can be viewed and analysed separately.

2   Variables can be used to change the rental costs; formulas and functions can be used to calculate the total cost of each of the premises; graphs can be used to show the distances from important locations for each of the premises; goal-seek can be used to find out what the rental cost would need to be to match the current costs; conditional formatting could be used to show the cheapest and most expensive options.

3   Fuel costs can be saved by not having to fly real aircraft; wear and tear of aircraft does not take place during training, which saves on maintenance costs; instructors do not need to be present for all training sessions; unforeseen or dangerous circumstances can be invoked to test the pilot's reaction without experiencing the real danger.

4   The learner driver does not get to experience the real reaction of a car; the simulator is only as good as the model it is based upon, meaning that the simulator will not react exactly the same as a car would.

Exam-style questions

1   a   Any three of the following [3]:

- Variables can be used to change the distances travelled [1].

- What-if questions can be asked such as 'what will be the cost if the car travels 300 miles?' [1].

- Formulas and functions can be used to calculate the total cost [1].

- Graphs and charts can be used to compare the costs of each car [1].

- Formulas and functions will automatically recalculate so results can be seen instantly [1].

- Conditional formatting can be used to show cars that cost a specific amount [1].

- Goal-seek can be used to find out the optimum speed to travel at [1].

b   Any one of the following [1]:

- The model will only be as good as the rules [1].

- The speed the car is travelling at will need to be taken into account [1].

- Unforeseen circumstances such as traffic jams will affect the costs [1].

2   a   Any four of the following [4]:

Dangers such as hazards, other cars, pedestrians, etc. can be avoided [1] because the simulator can model these instead of using the real road [1]. Learners do not always need to have an instructor present [1] because the simulator does not pose any danger [1]. Learners can experience circumstances they may not normally encounter [1] such as a child running into the road [1] because these can be modelled [1]. The learner can practice complex manoeuvers without holding up other road users [1] because the simulator can model the presence of other traffic [1].

b   Any two of the following (2 marks for each point) [4]:

- There are too many variables to be modelled [1] and so the simulator won't always match a real car [1].

- There is no consequence for making a mistake in a simulator [1], which may lead to drivers becoming over confident when using a real car and making mistakes which cause damage or an injury [1].

- Not all driving situations can be replicated [1], meaning that the simulator won't give a full experience of driving a car [1].

- Simulators can cause nausea [1] that wouldn't happen in a real car [1].
- The driving school would need to invest in the purchase [1], which could be extremely expensive for a small school [1].

3 Any four from the following (2 marks for each) [8]:

- Nuclear science is very dangerous so experimenting with simulations is much safer.
- Variables such as coolant temperature can be changed to see the effect on nuclear reactions.
- What-if questions can be asked to see what the effect of changes to variables would be.
- Goal-seek could be used to see what variables need to change to achieve a desired reaction.
- The simulation could be sped up rather than waiting several days or years to see a real world outcome.
- Nuclear simulations require a lot of computing power due to the large number of reactions taking place.
- Not all possible inputs can be simulated meaning the results of the simulation would not reflect exactly what might happen in the real world.

10 – Databases and file concepts

1 A field that is a unique identifier for each record.

2 Simple query uses one criterion, whereas a complex query can use multiple criteria.

3 To allow the user to decide the parameter value of the query, such as choosing the class for which to display student records.

4 Decide the file format; decide whether to use fixed length or variable length fields; decide whether to include field names; decide where to save the file.

5 Referential integrity is a form of lookup validation that ensures data exists in a related table. It is important because it prevents data from being entered that is not valid and that does not have any related data, so it ensures data is linked.

For example, an order must have a customer. If a customer that does not exist is entered, then this can create mismatched orders which can be lost because they are not linked to the customer.

6 Non-atomic data; no repeating groups of data; unique primary key.

7 No attributes can be dependent on a non-key attribute.

8 Duplicate data is removed from a database, which reduces the database size and removes the potential for errors and inconsistencies; the database will perform better because searches can be carried out on indexed fields; maintenance tasks such as rebuilding indexes can be completed more quickly because there is no longer any redundant data; the database is more flexible because it is easy to add new fields to tables without affecting other columns and new tables can be added without affecting existing tables.

9 Any three data dictionary components listed with related description, for example, field size is the maximum length of data for a field.

10
- text
- date/time
- date/time
- text
- integer
- text
- Boolean/logical

11 Starts with zeros and numbers can't start with zero; may contain spaces, which requires a text data type which allows spaces; may contain hyphens or brackets, which can't be stored as a number data.

12 Different software applications store files in different ways and so generic file types are needed to transfer data between software applications.

13 Read through the index until the required data is found in the key column; identify the corresponding storage address; go directly to the storage address; read sequentially until the record is found.

14 Sequential access requires the data to be stored in order, which is a problem when new records need to be added and old records are deleted, whereas direct access does not require a sequential order and so new records can be added using a hashing algorithm and found again using the same hashing algorithm.

15 Collates data from databases and other sources; interconnects data from different sources; analyses data to provide the data that is required by management; produces summary reports and charts for managers that will help with decision making.

Exam-style questions

1 a All of the following [3]:

charity [1]; donor [1]; donation [1].

b Both of the following [2]:

One charity has many donations [1]; one donor makes many donations [1].

c Both of the following [2]:

Each donation will need to be for a charity that already exists and from a customer that already exists [1]. This will prevent donations from unknown donors or to unknown charities and therefore ensure the money gets to where it needs to go [1].

2 a Both of the following [2]:

Apartment ID [1]; Customer ID [1].

b i alphanumeric or text or string [1].

ii Boolean [1].

iii integer [1].

c All of the following [4]:

Query would include all three tables [1]; dynamic parameter would be used for the Apartment ID or Apartment Name [1]; dynamic parameters would be used to compare the start date and end date [1]; the names of the customers would be included as fields in the query [1].

d Both of the following [2]:

Complex queries have two or more criteria [1]; there are three criteria for Apartment ID, start date and end date [1].

e Any three of the following (2 marks for each point) [6]:

- field names [1] to identify each field [1].
- validation rules [1] to restrict data entry for each field [1].
- relationships [1] between each table [1].

- primary keys [1] which are unique to each table [1].
- data types [1] to define the type of data that is stored in each field, for example, alphanumeric [1].

3 All of the following [4]:

- STUDENT (Student ID, Forename, Surname, Address 1, Address 2, Address 3, ZIP, Telephone, Tutor Group) [1].
- TUTOR (Tutor Group, Forename, Surname) [1].
- LOAN (Book ID, Student ID, Return Date) [1].
- BOOK (Book ID, Title) [1].

4 Both of the following [2]:

Proprietary formats are used by manufacturers of software applications for their applications only [1] whereas open-source file formats can be used by any application that supports them [1].

11 – Sound and video editing

1 3840 × 2160 pixels (or 4096 × 2160 in the movie industry).

2 Black bars are sometimes added to make a video the correct aspect ratio for the screen. If the video is a different aspect ratio to the screen, the black bars will fill the empty parts of the screen.

3 Formats could include:

- MP4
- MOV
- AVI
- FLV.

4 Compression methods are:

- MP4 – lossy
- MOV – lossy
- AVI – can be both
- FLV – lossy.

5 a 10.58 MB

b It increases to 21.17 MB, so it doubles in size.

Exam-style questions

1   The proportion of a screen or video width to its height [1].

2   One from the following [1]:

- The video clip may be too long.

- To remove part of the video clip.

3   Both of the following [2]:

- They can be used to provide further information about the image or video shown.

- They can be used to provide further information about where a user can learn more about the context of the image or video.

4   Both of the following [2]:

- It makes the video file smaller, so it is quicker to download / stream.

- It makes the video file smaller to it takes less storage space.

5   It will not reduce the file size as much as lossy, so it will take up more storage space [1].

6   Both of the following [2]:

- The sample rate is the number of times sound is sampled in a second.

- If the sample rate is increased, it will increase the overall size of the file.

12 – IT in society

1   The business could mine data about what kind of qualifications and what kind of people are employed by its competitors.

The business could use data mining to find out what characteristics of an employee are a good match for their company.

Exam-style questions

1   All of the following [3]:

- A cryptocurrency is a type of digital currency.

- A cryptocurrency is decentralised.

- A cryptocurrency uses encryption algorithms and cryptographic techniques as a security method.

2   Four from the following (two per advantage and disadvantage) [4]:

Advantages

- Don't need to carry physical money.

- User can stop transactions if digital method is lost/stolen.

- All transactions are encrypted.

- Can speed up payment.

- Don't need to exchange physical currency in foreign countries.

Disadvantages

- Always the risk that a transaction can be hacked.

- Some people may lose track of their spending as they don't hand over actual money.

- Some people are anxious about using digital payment methods, especially contactless ones.

3   Four from [4]:

- A chatroom is an online service that allows multiple users to send each other instant messages

- … whereas a forum allows users to post questions and thoughts for other users to respond to.

- A chatroom is designed to be a live conversation

- … whereas a forum is designed to allow user to return to the forum at any time to see what other users have posed as a response.

- A chatroom is not normally monitored by a moderator

- … whereas a forum will often have a moderator checking the posts meet the rules.

4   Eight from [8]:

- Stage 1 is the business understanding stage

- … it is where the objectives are set and the criteria for success are established.

- Stage 2 is the data understanding stage

- … this involves the initial collection of data from the various sources available.

- Stage 3 is the data preparation stage

- … this is where the data is taken through a whole process of selection, cleansing, construction and formatting.

- Stage 4 is the data modelling stage

- … during this stage various test scenarios are generated to model the data.

- Stage 5 is the evaluation stage

- … this is when the results generated by the models are evaluated.

- Stage 6 is the deployment stage

- … this is when a report is created to present the findings of the data mining to stakeholders.

5   Four from [4]:

- It can be used by businesses to aid planning

- … informing any actions that are taken on a daily basis.

- It can be used by governments to aid national security

- … by analysing intelligence gathered to highlight current activity in a country.

- It can be used in surveillance

- … surveillance data can be analysed to predict issues such as criminal activity.

6   Six from (max four for advantages) [6]:

Advantages

- A large selection of courses are available

- … so a user can enhance their learning in anything that they are interested it.

- Can provide an employee with a competitive advantage

- … as it demonstrates their motivation to learn and improve in their own time.

- They are free of cost

- … so all users who can access them will be able to learn.

- The number of people on a course is often unlimited

- … so people do not have to wait for a place to become available.

- User can learn at their own rate

- … this means that users are more able to fit the learning around the own schedule.

Disadvantages

- There are a huge selection of courses available

- … this may overwhelm a learner if they do not know which one to choose.

- There are often a large number of people on a course

- … so the tutor/educator may not have a lot of dedicated time to help each person on the course.

- … it may also be difficult for a tutor/education to keep track of the progress of each person on the course.

- Some learners may struggle to complete the tasks

- … and may choose to only complete those ones that they know will be assessed.

7   Six from [6]:

- This would mean that banks create their own version of a digital currency.

- This may mean that physical currency disappears altogether.

- This could save money for the government as they do not need to think about the cost of creating the physical currency.

- This could save the bank money as they do not need to have huge security system in places, like vaults, in which physical currency is stored.

- This could cost the banks money as they will need to have very strong security systems for their digital currency.

- The speed of the exchange of money from bank to bank could be improved.

- Criminal activity such as money laundering may decrease.

- Some people do not like the idea of the invasion of privacy that will exist by tracking each digital currency transaction.

8 All of the following [6]:

- Banks heavily rely on IT to keep all the records about their customers. If they had to store paper versions of this data, it would take up huge amounts of physical storage space.

- IT can be used in the form of ATMs to access physical currency that we have stored in our bank account. This means that a user no longer needs to go into a bank branch to queue to get money out of their account.

- IT can be used for online banking, allowing a user to access many financial and banking facilities online, without the need to go into a bank branch.

- IT can be used for online banking, allowing users to access many banking and financial services 24/7.

- IT can be used for online banking, allowing users to see all the transactions instantly, without needing to wait for a paper statement to be delivered.

- People can use comparison websites to compare the offers of banks and financial services. This means they can easily find the best and right deal for their circumstances.

13 – New and emerging technologies

1 Possible uses could be:

- It could be used to limit access to certain areas.
- It could be used to provide doctors with information about patients.
- It could be used to provide patients with information about the hospital.

2 It could use lossless compression methods to compress the data.

3 Advantage could be:

If the surgeon can see a very detailed image of the patient, this can improve the accuracy of their surgery.

Disadvantage could be:

It would require a high-speed internet connection and if this is not available there may be a lot of lag on the stream, or it may not be able to stream at all.

4 The user will be required to have a high-speed internet connection. The technology will need to have a large amount of RAM so that it can process and handle the amount of data streaming to the device. The computers used to edit the video files will need to have powerful graphics cards to be able to render the amount of data required to create the video file.

Exam-style questions

1 Two from (max one per advantage/disadvantage) [2]:

Advantages can include:

- Allow greater access to important health statistics.
- Users can sync their devices and challenge each other to improve motivation for exercise.
- User can get alerts without the need to check their mobile phone.

Disadvantages can include:

- People can become obsessed with their health statistics, developing an unhealthy relationship and damaging thoughts.
- There can be compatibility issues between devices.
- The accuracy of some health trackers can be dubious.
- Some people are concerned about the security of their data that is gathered by the device.

2 Three from [3]:

- 3D printing could be used to create prosthetic limbs.
- 3D printing could be used to create blood vessels.
- 3D printing could be used to engineer tissue.
- 3D printing could be used to create medical tools.

3 All of the following [4]:

- It will allow the surgeon to have a very detailed image of the patient
- … this can increase the accuracy of the surgery.
- It can allow the level of detailed required to carry out remote surgery

... this means that specialist surgeons do not need to make tiring journey around the world to perform surgery.

4 Two from (2 marks each) [4]:

- They often require more power consumption
- ... therefore, more carbon emissions may be released to create the level of power required.
- They often encourage users to replace previous versions of devices
- ... resulting in technology being thrown away into landfill, that can leach dangerous metals into soil if not disposed of correctly.

5 All of the following [3]:

- NFC has allowed electronic payments to become contactless.
- The user no longer needs to put a PIN into a device for small transactions
- ... they can just touch their device or card to the NFC base device.

6 Eight from [8]:

- AI can replace the need for employees to do tedious tasks in manufacturing
- ... so an employee does not need to become bored and unmotivated by completing a repetitive task.
- AI can replace the need for employees to do dangerous tasks in manufacturing
- ... so an employee's life does not need to be put in danger to complete dangerous tasks.
- AI can allow manufacturing to be carried out for longer periods of time
- ... as it does not need to rest like a employee.
- AI can allow tasks to be carried out to a higher standard
- ... as it is capable of a greater level of accuracy than an employee.
- ... it can also have faster reaction time than an employee.
- AI can be used to replace employees in manufacturing
- ... which can be very concerning to humans as they may lose their job.

7 Six from [6]:

Advantages:

- The organisation will be able to store very large amounts of data in a much smaller space
- ... this can save costs such as warehouse space and hardware costs to store the data.
- The organisation will be able to make their data storage much more portable
- ... this can help move data to archive much more easily
- ... it can also mean that very large amounts of data can be transported to other locations around the world without the need for an internet connection, which could compromise its security.
- The organisation will be able to transfer data at a much faster speed than other storage methods
- ... as millions of bits of data can be stored in a very short space of time.

Disadvantages:

- The organisation may find that the data storage is not compatible with their previous methods of data storage
- ... therefore, they may find that they cannot read and write data from one storage to another, if required
- ... therefore, they may find it costly to replace all the technologies involved.

14 – Communications technology

1 Example could include:

- It could be used in a remote control.
- It could be used in a game controller.

2 The stream would keep stalling all the time as it would be waiting for the data to download.

3 Example could include:

- Seasonal products, so more resources can be available when the seasonal product is at its height of business.

- When they have a new product available, so may have a sudden influx of traffic.

Exam-style questions

1 All of the following [2]:

- The function of the presentation layer is to prepare data ready for use in the application layer

- Preparation could involve translating, encrypting and compressing the data

2 Any two from the following [2]:

- It breaks data down into packets

- It transmits the data from network to network

- It uses two main protocols, the IP and the ICMP

3 a One for network, two for justification [1]:

- He should set up a LAN network.

- He will need limited network hardware.

- Any other network functionality would be redundant.

b Any four from the following [4]:

- Transmission media

- … this will create a wired connection if needed between any of the devices.

- Wireless access point

- … this will create a wireless connection between the devices.

- … this will allow all devices to be connected using a single component.

- Router

- … he will need this to connect his network to the internet if he wants this functionality.

c All of the following [2]:

- The bandwidth and the bit rate will limit the download time for the data.

- If the bandwidth and the bit rate are not high enough, the data will not stream in a timely enough fashion for it to play smoothly.

4 Four from the following (one for protocol name, one for description) [4]:

- SMTP.

- Used to send emails from a computer to a mail server, and between mail servers.

- POP.

- Used to retrieve emails from a mail server.

- IMAP.

- Used to retrieve emails from a mail server.

5 All of the following [4]:

- The network is broken down in cells.

- The data is sent from the mobile telephone to the radio base station in the current cell that the mobile telephone is created.

- The data is routed through each cell until it reaches the cell of the receiving mobile telephone.

- The data is then sent from the base station to the mobile telephone.

6 a Both of the following [2]:

- Data required for biometric device is unique to each person and therefore very difficult to replicate.

- Biometric devices can be expensive to purchase and implement.

b All of the following [4]:

- The firewall will monitor data coming into and out of the network.

- The user can set rules and criteria for the traffic.

- The firewall compares the traffic to the rules and criteria

- … and will reject any traffic that does not meet them.

7 Six from the following [6]:

- By implementing a disaster recovery plan and organisation has a plan in place for recovering data in the event of a disaster.

- The process of the plan will force the organisation to assess what poses a risk to their data and resources

- … they can then begin to think about what measures they can put in place to minimise the risks.

- As part of the process they will carry out run throughs of what will be done in the event of different disasters

- … this can mean that employees are familiar with what they need to do should a disaster occur.

- The process of planning for disaster recovery can be time consuming and expensive

- … however, the cost of not having a plan in place could be far greater, if the organisation loses all of its data.

15 – Project management

1 During monitoring and control of the execution, resources may become unavailable, timescales may not be met and the budget may be exceeded. If this happens, plans will need to be revised to allocate different resources, adjust timescales and adjust expenditure.

2 Resources will have been defined within the software including their availability and costs. The project manager can then select available resources and allocate them to tasks where they are required. Allocation of already assigned resources at specified times will be prevented by the software. The project manager will be able to assign an amount of time to each resource for each task. The project manager will be able to see the costs involved for each resource and how much each task will cost.

Exam-style questions

1 a Any four of the following [4]:

Objectives [1]; scope [1]; risks [1]; budget [1]; approximate timescales [1]; stakeholders [1]; resources [1].

b Any three of the following [3]:

Planning [1]; execution [1]; monitoring/control [1]; close [1].

2 Any four of the following [4]:

Calendars can show what each team member is doing [1]; instant messaging / video chat / video-conference can enable remote workers to share ideas and discuss progress [1]; documents can be shared in one place [1] with tracked changes so any modifications can be monitored [1]; discussions / forums can be setup so team members can discuss specific tasks / documents / milestones [1]; current progress can be updated by team members so the project manager can see how the project is progressing [1].

3 a Any two of the following [2]:

Both charts can show the critical path [1]; both charts show the length of time each task takes [1]; both charts show predecessors/dependencies [1].

b Any two of the following [2]:

Resource allocation [1]; start/finish dates [1]; task progress [1].

4 Software development projects have tasks with unknown timescales [1] and PERT is designed to deal with uncertainties [1] by calculating estimated times for each activity [1].

5 Any three of the following [3]:

The WBS will break the project down into sub projects [1] which can be managed separately by assistant project managers [1]. Each team member only needs to be concerned with their phase of the project [1] and can ignore other phases [1]. The project manager can organise activities into phases or sub-tasks so they are more manageable [1].

16 – System life cycle

1 Feasibility; analysis; design; implementation/development/coding/programming; testing; installation/implementation; maintenance; documentation; evaluation.

2 The analyst can expand upon questions that have been asked during the interview to gain further information from the user; questionnaires take time to create and so it is unnecessary when a small group of users can all be interviewed.

3 To identify the hardware and software required to operate the developed system.

4 To show the data flows within a system.

5 Each data flow must have a process attached to it. A data flow cannot move directly from one external entity to another or from one data store to another or between an external entity and a data store.

6 A tick box allows more than one response where as an option button only allows one response.

7 To test that a validation rule accepts data that is within the acceptable range.

8 Alpha testing is carried out by the development team whereas beta testing is carried out by users; alpha testing is planned and structured whereas beta testing is ordinary everyday use; alpha testing uses test data whereas beta testing uses real data.

9 Tester will use input data to test part of a system or a whole system and check the expected results against actual results without knowing or understanding the code inside the black box.

10 A test plan will identify all the tests that are needed for every input, every button, every link, every report, every screen and all other elements of a system. The test plan will include different types of test data including valid, invalid and extreme so that inputs are tested to their limits. Without this planning, important parts of testing would be missed out and errors could be left untested. The plan will also cover all the user's requirements and ensure that they are tested.

11 Parallel; direct; phased; pilot.

12 If it would be too costly or take too long to input data into both systems, then direct would be more appropriate.

13 If there are a lot of users then pilot changeover will enable training to take place in stages rather than all at once; If the new system is not very big and doesn't have features that can be separated then pilot could be used instead of trying to phase something that can't be broken into parts.

14 Cover, contents, introduction, hardware/software requirements, instructions, glossary, troubleshooting, index.

15 To give definitions of any technical terms used in the user documentation.

16 When a system requires maintenance.

17 Working relationship; efficiency of system; bugs or errors in the system; ease of use of the system; possible improvements to the system.

18 If a bug or error is found within a system.

19 Evolutionary prototyping develops each prototype further whereas throw-away prototyping involves disposing of the prototype. Evolutionary prototyping involves refining user requirements after each evolution of the prototype and throw-away prototyping also involves refining requirements after the prototype is developed. Both methods involve producing a basic version of what the user interface will look like. Both methods involve getting feedback from the user early during the project.

20 With incremental development, a part of the software is fully developed before moving on to the next part of the software whereas with iterative development, the phase of a system (e.g. design) is completed before feedback is sought and improvements made.

21 JAD involves both users and developers working together to develop a working prototype with the user being able to refine the design and layout as the development progresses. Software application frameworks will be used to develop the prototype and end-solution.

Exam-style questions

1 a Any one from the following [1]:

To find out how the current system works [1]; to find out the requirements of the client [1].

b All of the following [4]:

There will be lots of staff in several hotels [1] so there won't be time to interview them all but questionnaires can get information from all staff [1]; the data will need analysing [1] and so the questions can be written in a way that will gather responses in a structured manner [1].

c All of the following [3]:

Interviews [1]; observation [1]; document analysis [1].

2 To identify what the client needs the new system to do [1].

3 a Any three from the following [3]:

Use of colour [1]; consistent use of fonts [1]; avoiding clutter [1]; legibility of fonts [1]; instructions to the user [1]; optional vs compulsory questions [1]; sufficient space for answers [1]; tick boxes or drop down boxes or option buttons for multiple choice lists [1].

b   Any three from the following [3]:

Example could identify the input data [1], type of validation [1], rule [1] and error message [1]. For example, Number of nights, Type check, Must be numeric, Please enter a numeric value.

c   Any three from the following [3]:

Printer to print invoices for the customer [1]; barcode scanner to read barcodes on customer booking printout or mobile phone display [1]; magnetic stripe / smart card reader/writer to initiate room keys [1]; touch screen for the point of sale terminal in the bar and restaurant [1].

4   a   A 'mock-up' of a software solution; partially completed product used for evaluation/ feedback [1].

b   All of the following [4]:

Evolutionary prototyping develops each prototype further whereas throw-away prototyping involves disposing of the prototype so the prototype can grow rather than having to start again [1]. Evolutionary prototyping involves refining user requirements after each evolution of the prototype which will enable the landscape gardening company to better understand their own requirements as the prototype develops [1]. The landscape gardening company can canvass opinion from customers on what the user interface will look like [1]. The project team can get feedback from the landscape gardening company early during the project [1].

5   a   All of the following [4]:

White box testing requires understanding of the module or system being tested [1] whereas black box testing only requires input data and output data to be used [1]; white box testing is usually carried out by the developer [1] whereas black box testing is usually carried out by the user or specialist testers [1].

b   Both of the following [2]:

Beta testing requires a very large user base [1] and usually applies to off-the-shelf software whereas the hotel system will need to be used consistently by all staff within all the hotels [1].

c   All of the following [3]:

It's needed to check that the system can cope with invalid data [1] and reject it appropriately [1] without system errors occurring [1].

6   a   Any four from the following [4]:

There are lots of hotels [1] so one hotel could pilot the system and identify any problems [1], which could be rectified before the system is implemented in other hotels [1]. Only a small group of staff need to be trained in how to use the system initially at the one hotel [1]. The hotel that pilots the system could be used to train staff from the other hotels how to use the new system [1].

b   Troubleshooting will show common errors and how to solve them [1] so if the staff come across one of these errors they can find out what to do [1]. Glossary will include definitions of technical terms used in the documentation [1] so if staff don't understand a term in the documentation they can look it up [1].

c   Errors may need correcting [1]; the system may need to be adapted due to organisational or external changes [1]; to prevent problems from occurring [1]; to improve on the software [1].

17 – Mail merge

Exam-style questions

1   a   Both of the following [2]:

Mail merge is the automatic addition of data from a source file [1] such as names and addresses into a master document such as a letter [1].

b   Any six from the following [6]:

Create the master document [1]; link the master document to the data source[1]; insert merge field codes[1]; spell check the master document[1]; visually inspect the master document to check for accuracy[1]; set up any filters that are required[1]; preview the mail merge[1]; check the preview for accuracy including the correct records and layout[1]; run the mail merge to produce the letters [1].

2   All of the following [4]:

Filter will be required [1] that compares the date of service [1] from the source file [1] with the date specified by the user [1].

3   Any four from the following [4]:

- Read the text carefully to find/correct typographical errors/mistakes in grammar/ style/spelling [1].

- Printing a copy to read on paper rather than reading on screen [1].

- Read the invitation out loud to himself [1] so he hears problems he may not read [1].

- Use a blank sheet of paper to cover up the lines below the one he is reading [1].

- Use the search function to find mistakes he is likely to make [1], or example 'its', 'there'.

- Compare the spelling of names with a list of names spelt correctly [1], for example, a class list [1].

- Run the mail merge and check for errors on the merged documents [1].

- Check the data for the merged fields is displayed correctly [1].

- If he has used a filter, check the correct records have been included [1] by comparing the merged invitations with his filtered list [1].

4   Any two from the following [2]:

Embedding is inserting data from a source document into the current document [1] {then either of the following} so that any changes to the source document are updated in the current document [1], for example, any changes to the source data for the graph will automatically update the graph in the report [1].

18 – Graphics creation

1   Image made of small squares called pixels

Each pixel can have one colour

2   Image stored as coordinates and calculations.

3   They do not pixelate when enlarged

The file size is usually smaller

4   Images are edited before being presented to the public.

People think the images are real and aspire to meet their unrealistic standards.

5   Red, Green, Blue

6   Red

7   Green

8   Blue

9   Black

10   White

11   Any three from: BMP, GIF, JPEG, PNG, TIFF

12   Any one from: SVG, PDF

Exam-style questions

1   a   1 mark per bullet [13]:

- Rectangle created.

- Triangle created and positioned central to rectangle.

- Outline of both objects is dark blue

- … … less than 4 pt thick.

- Gradient fill used for television.

- Text says Titania

- … inside the television

- ..in green

- … sans-serif font

- … in an arc.

- Font is a suitable size for the television.

- Image saved as vector

- … no more than 250 by 250 pixels.

b   1 mark per bullet [4]:

- Vector is made of points and calculations

- … when it is resized the proportions are kept

- … it does not pixelate

- … unlike a bitmap.

c   1 mark per bullet [6]:

- Lossy compression removes some data.

- … the decompressed image is not the same as the original.

- Reduce the number of colours
- … fewer colours means less data to store per pixel.
- Reduce the resolution
- … means fewer pixels to store therefore less data.

2 a 1 mark per bullet [15]:
- Rectangle created
- … warped/distorted on the top edge only
- … appropriate level of distortion to match image.
- Six circles added
- … in black
- … all identical
- … and evenly spaced.
- Black rectangle drawn
- … outline only.
- Word rollercoaster added
- … in green
- … in sans-serif font
- … set to an arc
- … inside the rollercoaster rectangle
- … an appropriate size.

b For example [3]:
- .jpg
- Compresses the image to reduce the file size.
- There is no transparency.

c 1 mark per bullet [4]:
- RGB colours are made up of red green and blue
- … values between 0 and 255/FF for each colour.
- CMYK are made of cyan, magenta, yellow and black
- … values are a percentage between 0 and 100.

19 – Animation

1 Each frame was drawn individually by hand.

Each frame was a different medium/sheet.

Photographs of the frames are taken.

The photographs are run through very quickly.

2 Photographs are taken of an object.

Every set number of seconds.

The photographs are run one after the other.

3 Position an object/series of objects.

Take a photograph.

Move the objects minutely and take another photograph.

The photographs are run one after the other.

4 Flip-book animation.

5 Computer-generated imagery.

6 An individual image.

7 The stage is 4 units wide to 3 units high.

Old televisions.

8 16:9 – modern televisions, monitors and laptops.

2.35:1 – widescreen and films.

16:10 – modern mobile phones.

9 Help you layout objects.

Help you align objects.

10 Objects will be automatically aligned.

Saves time in attempting to align them.

Increases precision.

11 Images are stored as coordinates and calculations.

Images can be resized without pixelating.

12 Line changes the line around the edge of an image.

Fill changes the colours inside the image (inside the lines).

13 Orientation

14 To allow you to perform motion tweening and morphing on it.

15 Because they are not stored as coordinates so their coordinates cannot be changed.

16 A self- contained image / set of images that have their own independent animations.

17 To allow different images / parts of images to be animated independently, that is, without affecting the other images.

18 Increase the speed.

19 A frame keeps the same content, a key frame is used when something needs to be changed, or added or removed.

20 Motion can only move an object. Shape can move it, change its shape, size and/or colour.

21 It calculates all the spaces between the two key frames and fills in the gaps so that it is not jumping from one position to the next, but is smoothly moving.

22 Only the elements inside/outside the mask can be seen, for example, a shape moves across the screen and you can only see the image inside that screen.

Exam-style questions

1   a   1 mark per bullet [13]:
- Aspect ratio is 235:1.
- Black background throughout.
- Starts with Saif's name clearly visible.
- Letters fade
- … 1 at a time
- … taking 1 second for each to fade.
- Comics appears when Saif's name åhas disappeared
- … taking 1 second to fade in
- … stays on screen for 2 seconds
- … fades out one letter at a time with 1 second for each fade.
- Font is white and appropriate size (takes up full height of animation).
- Animation loops.
- Animation is exported in a suitable format for a website.

    b   1 mark per bullet [3]:
- All have individual images as frames.
- Cel uses hand-drawn images whereas stop-motion animation and time-lapse animation are photographs of real-life objects/items.
- Stop-motion animation and cel animation both require a person to manipulate each

frame (by moving items or drawing items) whereas time-lapse animation is automatic.

2   a   1 mark per bullet [19]:
- Animation is 16:9 ratio.
- Background is pale blue.
- Logo is on left-hand side of the animation.
- Logo starts small
- ..increases gradually to full size
- … then decreases small again
- … repeatedly throughout animation.
- Ball appears from right-hand side and moves to the left
- … and out of sight
- … displays text as it rolls
- … leaving correct text behind it.
- Ball is off screen for 1.5 seconds
- … then returns and moves from left to right
- … as a mask
- … displays text as it moves over it
- … and only as it moves over it.
- Animation is set to loop.
- Animations are smooth.
- Export to a suitable format.

    b   Frame: one single image of an animation [1].

    Key frame: a frame where a change happens for that object/symbol [1].

3   1 mark per bullet [12]:
- Screen ratio is 16:10.
- Background is white.
- Green outline matches that on logo.
- … and is displayed throughout.
- Letters bounce in from left.
- … in correct order.
- All letters stay on screen for 2 seconds
- … then they all fade out
- … together.

- Animation loops.
- Animations are smooth.
- File is exported as a .gif.

20 – Programming for the web

1 alert

2 console.log

3 prompt

4 To view what is running/happening in the webpage.

For debugging purposes.

5 A self-contained piece of code that can be called from another part of the program, it runs and then returns control back to the code that called it.

6 Modulus, the remainder after division.

7 ++ increments/adds 1 to a value, -- decrements/ subtracts 1 from a value.

8 False

9 False

10 True

11 True

12 False

13 True

14 False

Exam-style questions

1 a 1 mark per bullet [11]:
- Suitable input for first name
- … with suitable error if blank.
- Suitable input for last name
- … with suitable error if blank.
- Suitable input for query
- … with suitable error if blank.
- Suitable input for email address
- ..with suitable error if blank
- … detecting if there is an @

- … and suitable error message if here is not.
- Confirmation given if no errors

b 1 mark per bullet [3]:
- To explain how the code works.
- So other developers know how your code works
- … so they can change it/improve it.

c 1 mark per bullet (up to 4) [4] :
- To stop the web page crashing.
- So the web page outputs a message
- … instead of doing nothing.
- Otherwise the user will not know what they have done wrong.
- Otherwise the user will not know what to do to correct the error.

d 1 mark per bullet (up to 3) [3]:
- Web page still contains and works as required in part (b).
- Image1 appears in web page when loads
- … changes to Image 2
- … when the user moves their cursor over it.

2 a 1 mark per bullet [12]:
- Field to select day
- … limited to only valid options.
- Field to select time
- … limited to only valid options.
- Field to select number of people
- … limited to only valid options.
- Option to select set menu.
- Fields to enter name and telephone number.
- Appropriate error messages for invalid data on one field
- … and on all other fields where appropriate.
- Confirmation of submission given
- … only if all valid.

b 1 mark per bullet [2]:

- At least one appropriate comment

- ... and all constructs commented.

c 1 mark per bullet (up to 3) [3]:

- Description of checking data entered

- ... against criteria.

- Outputting error messages if invalid.

- If no error messages then submission allowed.

3 1 mark per bullet [2]:

- While may never run the code inside it; Do while will always run the code once.

- While checks condition at start of loop; Do while checks condition at end of loop.

4 1 mark per bullet [3]:

- Stores multiple pieces of data

- ... under one identifier

- ... all of the same data type.

> Glossary

Absolute cell reference: a cell reference that does not change when it is copied into other cells, usually by placing a $ sign before the cell reference

Actuator: a type of motor that is used to move and operate another mechanism or device

Algorithm: a set of instructions or steps to be followed to achieve a certain outcome

Align: make objects start at the same position

Alignment: positioning text so that it is in line, for example on the left, right or centre

Alpha testing: initial testing of the software by a limited group of people

Analysis: finding out how the current system works and what the requirements of the client are for the new system

Animation: a series of images that are played one after another to simulate movement

Anti-malware: software that is used to identify malware on a computer and remove it

Anti-virus: software that is used to identify a virus on a computer and remove it

Arithmetic operator: a symbol, or symbols, that perform a mathematical calculation; these often appear as algebraic operators that you will be used to using in mathematics

Array: a data structure that can store multiple items under one identifier; the items are of the same type

Artificial intelligence: a computer system designed to simulate human intelligence

Aspect ratio: the proportion of a screen or video width to its height

Assignment: giving a variable a value

Attribute: a category of information within an entity

Automation: the ability to operate automatically

Avar: a hinge on a wire-model object that lets you manipulate its position

Backward chaining: breaking a goal down into sub-goals that allow the system to work backward from the goal

Bandwidth: the range of frequencies available for a communication method which determines the transmission rate

Batch processing: sets of data are processed all at one time without user interaction

Beta testing: a sample of users test a pre-release version of the software

Bezier curve: smooth curves made of paths that can be scaled indefinitely

Biometric: unique physical characteristic of a person that can be used by a computer for identification purposes

Bitmap: an image made up of small squares, called pixels; each individual pixel can only be one colour

Bit rate: the rate at which bits can be transferred in data transmission

Black box testing: testing of inputs and outputs to a system or part of a system with no consideration for the workings of the system

Boolean: a data type, either true or false

Bridge: a network component that connects segregated parts of a LAN

Broadband: a method of data transmission that is capable of transmitting a high level of traffic

Calculated field: an arithmetic calculation on a field from the data source

Calibration: the process of testing and modifying a device to make sure that it is taking the correct readings

Canvas: the area in the software where you add and edit your images

Cel animation: (also called cell animation) where individual images are drawn on separate pages then photographed, one frame at a time

Cell: a single unit/rectangle of a spreadsheet formed at the intersection of a column and a row where data can be positioned; its reference (name/address) is based on its column and row

CGI: an abbreviation of computer generated imagery; any image (still or moving) that is created using a computer

Client: a computer in a network that is not a central point of control

Clip: short piece of a video or audio file

CMYK: Cyan/Magenta/Yellow/Black colour system; all colours are a combination of these four colours

Collaborate: work together

Colour depth: the number of colours that can be represented in the image

Comparison: comparing two items of data resulting in True or False

Comparison operator: a symbol, or symbols, that compare the two sides of the operator and the result is either true or false

Compiler: translates high-level programming language into an executable file in machine code

Compound key: two or more fields that form the primary key. Each field that comprises the compound key are themselves keys from another table

Compression: reducing the file size of a file, for example, an image

Concatenate: to join two strings together

Condition-controlled loop: a loop that runs based on a condition, not the number of times it will run

Condition: a statement that can be evaluated as true or false, for example 5 > 6 (this is false because 5 is not greater than 6)

Construct: a control structure, such as a loop or a conditional statement

Control system: a system that manages or regulates a process by physically changing aspects of the system depending on collected data

Coordinates: the position (x and y) of an object on the stage

Count-controlled loop: a loop where you know the number of times it will run

CPM: critical path method, also sometimes known as CPA (critical path analysis)

Critical path: the tasks which must be completed on time for a project to complete on time

Custom-written software: software that is written especially to meet the requirements of a client

Data: raw numbers, letters, symbols, sounds or images without meaning

Database: a structured method of storing data

Database management system: software used to manage a database

Data dictionary: metadata (information) about the database

Data driven: a system dependent on the data that it is provided with

Data mining: the process of collecting large sets of data and analysing them to identify patterns and trends

Data type: the type of data being stored, for example, a number, string (text)

Decision: a comparison is used to decide if code is run, or not

Declaration: a statement giving the identifier of a variable or array

Demographic: a particular section of a population

Design: the stage in the life cycle when the design specification is produced

Design specification: illustration of how the system will look, what the data structures will be and how the system will work

Development: the stage in the system life cycle when the software is produced

Device: a hardware component of a computer system consisting of electronic components

DFD: data flow diagram which shows how data moves around a system

Direct data source: data that is collected for the purpose for which it will be used

Distribute: make the space between objects the same

DPI/dots per inch: the resolution of an image

Economic: considering a country in terms of their production and consumption of goods and services

Electronic currency: a payment method that occurs in a digital form

Embedding: importing data from a data source so that any changes to the data source are shown in the new document

Emerging technologies: a technology that is still in development to allow it to reach its full potential

Encryption: scrambling data so it cannot be understood without a decryption key so that it is unreadable if intercepted

Entity: a set of data about one thing (person, place, object or event)

Entity relationship diagram: a diagram that represents the relationships between entities

Evaluation: a formal review of a project

Execution: the development stage of a project

Explanation system: a component of an expert system that provides an explanation of how an outcome was achieved

Export: to prepare data for use in another application

Field (databases): a common word for attribute

Field (mail merge): a category of information from the data source

Filter (mail merge): selecting records from the source file based on conditions

Firewall: a security measure that can be implemented to monitor traffic into and out of a computer and prevent external users gaining unauthorised access to a computer system

Flat file: a database stored in a single table

Flatten: merge all layers into one single layer

Flip book animation: each page of a book that has a different image drawn on; when flicked through they create an animation

FLOPS: floating point operations per second – used to measure the performance of supercomputers

Flowchart: a set of symbols put together with commands that are followed to solve a problem

Foreign key: a field in a table that refers to the primary key in another table

FOR loop: a count-controlled loop

Formula: a mathematical calculation using +, −, × or ÷

Forward chaining: a system that moves forward from rule to rule until it reaches a possible outcome

Frame (sound and video): a single image in a video file

Frame (animation): one screen, or page, where an image is drawn; a series of these frames are played one after the other to create the animation

Function (Algorithms): a separate piece of code that has an identifier and performs a task; it can be called from elsewhere in the code and returns a value

Function (Spreadsheets): a ready-made formula representing a complex calculation

Gantt chart: a chart used for planning a project

Gateway: a network component that joins different LANs together

Geotag: an electronic tag that assigns a geographical location

Global variable: a variable declared outside a function; it can be accessed anywhere within the code

Goal driven: a system that is dependent on a finding a desired goal

Goal seek: looking to see what a variable needs to change to for a goal in terms of output to be achieved

Grid: a tool that displays a grid on the background of the screen to help with alignment

Group: join several images together

Guides: lines that you can drag on the stage to help you position objects

Heuristic: the ability to use a value to determine which is the best pathway to select

Hologram: a 3D image that is created using laser beams and mirrors

HSL: Hue/Saturation/Lightness colour system; all colours are a combination of the hue saturation and lightness selected

HTTPS: Hypertext Transfer Protocol Secure

Hub: a network component that joins computers together and forwards data packets to all connected devices

Identifier: the name given to a variable, subroutine or function

Implementation: the stage in the system life cycle when the software is installed for the user

Import: to bring in data from another application

Increment: add 1 to something

Incremental development: creating a system or adding new functionality in small parts

Index: a list of keys or keywords which identify a unique record and can be used to search and sort records more quickly

Indirect data source: data that was collected for a different purpose (secondary source)

Information: data with context and meaning

Infrastructure: the facilities that are needed for the

operation of a society, such as roads, buildings and utilities

Initiation: start of a project

Input: putting data into an algorithm

Integer division: where only the whole number is given from a division

Interpreter: translates and executes a high-level programming language a line at a time

IP address (Internet Protocol address): a unique address given to a device, normally by a router

Iteration: a loop to repeat a section of code for a fixed number of times or until a required outcome is achieved

Iterative development: creating a system or adding new functionality in a repetitive cycle

Key frame: a location on a timeline which marks a frame that has a change in the animation, for example, a drawing has changed, or the start or end of a tween

Kerning: the space between letters

Knowledge base: a component of an expert system that stores the knowledge provided by experts

Knowledge base editor: a component of an expert system that is used to amend or update the knowledge base

Layer (Graphics): a 'surface' onto which an image or object is placed; each object is placed on a separate layer and they are stacked on top of each other (as though on different pieces of paper)

Layer (Animation): an object or image given its own timeline for independent manipulation

Library: a place that stores a list of images and objects/symbols in an animation

Literal: the actual data being used (instead of a variable)

Local area network (LAN): a relatively small network that is located within a single building or site

Local variable: a variable declared within a function; it can only be accessed within the function

Loop: code that is repeated

Logical operator: symbols that represent the logical operations and, or, not

Lossless compression: a method of compression where the decompressed image is identical to the original

Lossy compression: a method of compression where the decompressed image is not identical to the original

MAC address (Media Access Control address): a unique address given to a device by the manufacturer

Macro: a set of instructions that can be completed all at once

Mail merge: the automatic addition of data, such as names and addresses, from a source file into a master document, such as a letter

Mainframe computer: powerful computer serving several terminals

Maintenance: changes made to a system after its implementation

Malware: software that is malicious

Mask: a layer that involves shapes, or other components, that restrict what can be seen of the other layers

Master document: the main document that will be used for all records

Master file: a table in a database containing information about one set of things, e.g. employees

Microprocessor: an integrated circuit that is used in monitoring and control systems

Model: a representation of a process

Modulus division: when the remainder is given from a division

Monitoring system: a system that observes and often records the activities in a process

Mono: a sound clip that has a single track

Morphing: another term for shape tweening; one image changes into another image

Nested loops: one construct that is inside another construct

Network: two or more computers or devices connected together so they can communicate and share data and resources

Network interface card: a network component required to attach a computer to a network

Normal form: the extent to which a database has been normalised

Normalisation: process of structuring data in a database

Object (Animation): an image, or combination of images, that is manipulated as one item

Object (Programming): a series of named values all stored under one identifier

Off-the-shelf software: general purpose software available to a large market

Online processing: also known as interactive processing, data is input by the user and feedback given in the form of outputs

Opacity : the lack of transparency of an image; at 0% opacity the image is fully transparent

Operating system: software that manages the hardware within a computer system

Operator: a symbol, or set of symbols, that perform an operation, for example, arithmetic operators

Orientation: the direction of text, for example horizontal or vertical

Output: displaying data from an algorithm to the user

Packet: a unit of data in data transmission

Parameter (Algorithms): a piece of data that is sent to a subroutine

Parameter (Databases): data used within the criteria for a query

Peer: a computer of equal importance in a peer-to-peer network

PERT: performance evaluation and review technique

Pixel: a small square of one colour; these are combined to create a bitmap image

Pixilation: when a bitmap image is enlarged, the pixels are enlarged and become visible causing the image to appear blurry

Predecessor: a task in a project that must be completed before another task can start

Primary key: a field that contains the unique identifier for a record

Primary variable: the foremost parts of the animation, that is, the graphic components

Procedure: a type of subroutine that does not return a value to the main program

Process: an action performed to some data to make a change

Prompt: a question asked to the user which requires a response

Protocol: a set of rules or standards that ensure data is transferred between devices correctly

Prototype: a 'mock-up' of a software solution in a primitive form

Pseudocode: a syntax-less language that is used to convey an algorithm

Query: a request for data from a table or combination of tables

rapid application development (RAD): use of prototyping to develop a system in a very short time frame

Range: a selection of cells

Real-time processing: data is processed as soon as it has been input and outputs are generated immediately

Record: a common word for entity

Referential integrity: data in the foreign key of the table on the many side of a relationship must exist in the primary key of the table on the one side of a relationship

Relationship: the way in which two entities in two different tables are connected

Relative cell reference: a cell reference that changes when it is copied into other cells

Repeater: a network component that is used to boost a signal in data transmission

REPEAT UNTIL loop: a condition-controlled loop that runs until the condition is true

Requirements specification: what a user needs a new system to do

Resolution: the number of pixels per 'measurement' an image or a single frame in a video contains (for example, dots per inch)

Resources: people, equipment, facilities or funding required to complete a project

Reverberation: the number of echoes of the sound and the way that they decay – reverberation can be natural (caused by the room in which the sound is played) or introduced by editing software

RGB: Red/Green/Blue colour system; all colours are a combination of quantities of red, green and blue

Router: a network component that uses a computer's IP address to send data packets to a destination outside the current network

Ruler: a tool that lets you see the position of items on the screen, and helps you draw them to the correct size

Rules base: a part of the knowledge base that contains all the rules to be analysed by the expert system

Sample rate: the number of times sound is sampled in a second

Sample resolution: the number of bits that are used to represent each sound sample

Secondary variable: the background elements of the animation, for example moving water/trees

Selection: use of a conditional statement to decide a course of action or which section of code to run

Sensor: an input device that collects data from the surrounding physical environment

Server: a computer in a network that is a point of control

Simulation: using a model to predict real-life behaviour

Snapping: a feature that will predict where you want objects placing, by aligning them to other objects, images or gridlines

Social networking: the use of websites and apps that allows users to communicate and interact

Software: programs which give instructions to the computer

Source file: the file containing the data that will be merged into the master document

Splice: join together two or more sound or video clips

Spreadsheet: software that can organise, analyse and manipulate data organised in a grid of rows and columns

SSL: Secure Socket Layer

Stage: the area where the animation takes place; to be within the animation, the object must be on the stage

Stereo: a sound clip that has multiple tracks

Stop motion animation: photographs are taken of objects; the objects are moved slightly each time and the photographs combined to create the animation

String: a data type: data stored as text which can be characters, numbers and symbols

Subroutine: a set of instructions that have an identifier and that are independent from the code. It is called from another part of the program and returns control when it was finished

Supercomputer: large computer with parallel processing to complete highly complex tasks quickly

Switch: a network component that uses a computer's MAC address to send data packets to a destination within a network

Symbol: a component, for example, an image, of an animation that has a name and is put in the library; multiple copies of the object can be created

System flowchart: an overview of how a system works in a diagrammatic format

System software: software needed to operate a computer system

System specification: the hardware and software needed to run the system

Table: a collection of related data, organised in rows and columns (for example, about people, places, objects or events)

Technical documentation: an overview of the structure of the system, how it was put together and how it works

Test data: data that will be used for testing a system

Test plan: a detailed and structured plan of how testing should be carried out

Time lapse: a camera automatically takes a photograph every set period (for example, once a minute) and these are combined to create a film

Timeline: the place that controls the order the frames are run, the positioning of the layers, and so on

TLS: Transport Layer Security

Tracing bitmap: a way of converting a bitmap image into a vector graphic

Track: a specific recording, for example, of one instrument or voice – the tracks can then be edited separately and combined to play concurrently

Transaction file: data that is used to update a master file

Transform: changing the dimensions, rotation, colour fill, opacity, etc. of an object over a certain number of frames between two key frames

Transition: the method with which one video clip merges into a second clip

Transparency: being able to see through an object or surface

Triangulation: the process of pinpointing the location of a device, using radio signals from satellites

Tween: (Inbe*tween*ing) an animation where the start and end points are set; the computer generates the actual images to make the animation change

2D: two dimensional: only on the x and y axis, for example a traditional cartoon

3D: three dimensional: has an x, y and z axis

User documentation: a user guide giving instructions to the user on how to use the software

User interface: communication between the user and the computer system

Utility software: software that performs some sort of maintenance on the computer system

Validation: the process of checking data matches acceptable rules

Variable: a space in the memory of a computer that has an identifier, where you can store data; this data can be changed

Vector: an image that uses geometric points and shapes; calculations are used to draw the image

Verification: ensuring data entered into the system matches the original source

Virtual Private Network: an encrypted connection that can be used to send data more securely across a network

Wide area network: (WAN) a relatively large network that is normally two or more LANs that are linked

What-if analysis: experimenting with changing variables to see what would happen to the output if those variables changed

WHILE loop: a condition-controlled loop that runs while the condition is true

White box testing: testing the whole system in terms of structure and logic covering all paths through the system

Wireless access point: a network component that receives and transmits radio signals to allow wireless (Wi-Fi) connection to a network

> Index

network security 323–5
network simulators 178
networked learning 278
networks 303
    components 314–17
    fundamental models 303–4
    structures 307–13
news, IT use in 282–3
NFC (near field communication) 286–7
NICs (network interface cards) 314
night vision 299–300
node editing 413–14
non-volatile memory 21
normal form 225–9
    first (1NF) 225–7
    second (2NF) 227–8
    third (3NF) 228–9
normalisation
    database 225–9
    sound clip 259–60
nuclear science research 185
numeric data 231–2, 478

object code 33, 235
objects 430, 436–7, 479, 484
    ordering 447–8
observation 346
off-the-shelf software 37–8
onchange 492
one-to-many relationships 192, 193, 194, 237
one-to-one relationships 191–2, 193–4
onkeydown 493
online banking 9, 281–2
online courses 277, 278–9
online processing 21–3
online shopping 282
online tutorials 278
onload 492
onmouseout 493
onmouseover 492
opacity 409–10, 426, 439
open-source file formats 235
open source software 38
operating systems 31–2
operators 478–82
    arithmetic 388–90, 480–2
    assignment 478
    Boolean (logical) 113, 154, 208, 214, 480, 497–9

comparison 480, 495–6
    ternary 499
optical data storage 297–8
orientation 128
OSI (open systems interconnection) 303–5
output 56–9, 470–1
output devices 31
output reports 355–6
overdubbing 257

PaaS (platform as a service) 321
packet switching 306–7
packets 304
padlocks 9, 462
page formatting 121–2
panning 248, 249
parallel running 360, 361
parameters 73, 214
    dynamic 214–15
    static 214
parity check 16
path editing 413–14
paths 454–61
PDF (portable document format) 409
peer-to-peer networks 307–9
peers 307
pen tool 413–14
perfective maintenance 365
personal data 88–92
PERT (performance evaluation and review technique) 338
pharming 91–2
phased implementation 360, 361
phishing 89–90
photographs 398
physical layer 304
pie charts 168
pilot implementation 361, 362
pilot training 184
PIN (personal identification number) 22, 81, 91, 266
pivot charts 159–60
pivot tables 156–9, 160
pixelation 397, 398, 399–400, 442
pixels 398, 437
planning, project 330–1, 332
plant identification 117
platter 35
play symbols 459, 461
PNG (portable network graphics) 409

Pokémon Go 291
politics 400
    IT use in 283
POP (post office protocol) 305, 314
pop-up boxes 471–4
population growth models 179
predecessors 334, 336, 338, 339
preparatory analysis 326
presence check 11
presentation layer 304
pressure sensors 48
preventative maintenance 366
primary keys 189, 191–4, 196–7, 201, 225, 227–8
primary variables 463
print servers 309
printed copy layouts 355–6
printing, 3D 298–9
privacy issues 271, 284
private key 8, 10, 313
procedures 72
processes 56, 59–61
progress, project 333
project management 330–41
    software 332–4
    stages of life cycle 330–2
    tools and techniques 334–41
prompt box 472
prompts 383–5
proofreading 392–3
property keyframes 458–9
proprietary file formats 235
proprietary software 38
prosthetic limbs 293
prosthetics, bespoke 298–9
protocols 286
prototyping 368–9, 373
proxy servers 309
pseudocode 54, 56
public key 8–9

QR codes 287
queries 199–200, 206–15
    complex 208–10, 213
    cross-tab 212–13, 214
    data export from 224
    nested 210–11, 213
    simple 206–8, 213
    summary 212–13, 214
    to find duplicate records 211–12
questionnaires 344–5, 346, 365
queue management 180

> Acknowledgements

The authors and publishers acknowledge the following sources of copyright material and are grateful for the permissions granted. While every effort has been made, it has not always been possible to identify the sources of all the material used, or to trace all copyright holders. If any omissions are brought to our notice, we will be happy to include the appropriate acknowledgements on reprinting.

Thanks to the following for permission to reproduce images:

Cover image: adventtr/Getty Images

Inside: Chapter 1 opener Agsandrew/Shutterstock; fig 1.01 MBI/Alamy Stock Photo; fig 1.02 gilaxia/GI; fig 1.03 Anatolii Babii/Alamy Stock Photofig 1.18 Monty Rakusen/GI; fig 1.20 Image Source/GI; Chapter 2 opener Sergey Nivens/Shutterstock; fig 2.01 MediaNews Group/GI; fig 2.02 Sean Gallup/GI; fig 2.08 Encyclopaedia Britannica/GI; Chapter 3 opener Lucapierro/GI; Fig 3.01 Andriy Onufriyenko/GI; Fig 3.05 Jonathan Kitchen/GI; Fig 3.06 Dennis Galante/GI; Fig 3.07 Petegar/GI; Fig 3.08 4FR/GI; Fig 3.09 Andrew Brookes/GI; Fig 3.10 Westend61/GI; Fig 3.11 Std/GI; Fig 3.13 Kosamtu/GI; Chapter 4 opener Yagi Studio/GI; Chapter 5 opener Wk1003mike/Shutterstock; fig 5.01 sorbetto/GI; fig 5.03 Westend61/GI; fig 5.04 Jasper James/GI; fig 5.05 Peter Dazeley/GI; fig 5.06 Jon Feingersh/GI; fig 5.07 Artpartner images/GI; fig 5.08 Jeffrey Coolidge/GI; fig 5.09 Troy Aossey/GI; fig 5.10 Vladwel/GI; fig 5.11 Seksan Mongkhonkhamsao/GI; fig 5.12 Wutthichai Luemuang/GI; fig 5.13 AFP Contributor/GI; Chapter 6 opener Aeriform; fig 6.01 Imaginima/GI; fig 6.02 Marques Madayag/GI; fig 6.03 Luis Alvarez/GI; fig 6.04 Construction Photography/Avalon/GI; fig 6.05 Filadendron/GI; fig 6.06 AAMIR QURESHI/GI; fig 6.07 Eternity in an Instant/GI; fig 6.08 Klaus Vedfelt/GI; fig 6.09 Vitranc/GI; Chapter 7 opener KrulUA/GI; fig 7.01 JGI/Jamie Grill/GI; fig 7.02 Busakorn Pongparnit/GI; fig 7.03 Compassionate Eye Foundation/Mark Langridge/GI; fig 7.06 WebMD symptom checker screenshort used by permission of WedMD; fig 7.07 Matsou/GI; fig 7.08 STAN HONDA/GI; fig 7.09 Audtakorn Sutarmjam/GI; fig 7.10 Alistair Berg/GI; fig 7.11 Jonathan Minster/GI; fig 7.12 Mabus13/GI; Chapter 8 opner Gregor Schuster/GI; fig 8.58 Image Professionals GmbH/Alamy Stock Photo; Chapter 9 opener Viaframe/GI; Chapter 10 opener Jorge Rey/GI; Chapter 11 opener Don Farrall/GI; fig 11.01 Patrick Daxenbichler/GI; fig 11.02 Tetra Images/GI; fig 11.16 BrianAJackson/GI; Chapter 12 opener Violetkaipa/GI; fig 12.01 Yuoak/GI; fig 12.02 EyeEm/GI; fig 12.03 Jonathan Evans/GI; fig 12.04 FrankRamspott/GI; fig 12.05 MediaProduction/GI; fig 12.06 Jason Butcher/GI; fig 12.07 Maskot/GI; fig 12.08 Moment/GI; fig 12.09 Hoch Zwei/GI; fig 12.10 Klaus Vedfelt/GI; fig 12.11 Monty Rakusen/GI; fig 12.12 John Lamb/GI; fig 12.13 Stephen Brashear/GI; Chapter 13 opener Martin Barraud/GI; fig 13.01 DAVID MCNEW/GI; fig 13.02 Jasmin Merdan/GI; fig 13.04 THOMAS SAMSON/GI; fig 13.05 Patra Kongsirimongkolchai/GI; fig 13.06 Busakorn Pongparnit/GI; fig 13.07 Flashpop/GI; fig 13.08 SolStock/GI; fig 13.09 MrPliskin/GI; fig 13.11 Yuichiro Chino/GI; fig 13.12 Charles O'Rear/GI; fig 13.13 Westend61/GI; fig 13.15 Dean Mouhtaropoulos/GI; fig 13.16 Vgajic/GI; fig 13.17 Peter Macdiarmid/GI; fig 13.18 Guido Mieth/GI; Chapter 14 opener Mina De La O/GI; fig 14.02 luxxtek/GI; fig 14.03 Jelena83/GI; fig 14.04 Vtls/Shutterstock; fig 14.05 Yangyang/GI; fig 14.07 Bortonia/GI; fig 14.08 Tomasz Zajda/GI; Chapter 15 opener Hero Images/GI; Chapter 16 opener MimaCZ/GI; Chapter 17 opener Yagi Studio/GI; Chapter 18 opener Artishokcs/GI; fig 18.01 & 18.02 Lilu330/Shutterstock; fig 18.03 & 18.04 Yadid Levy/Alamy Stock Photo; fig 18.05 Wavebreak Media ltd/Alamy Stock Photo; fig 18.06 kris Mercer/Alamy Stock Photo; fig 18.07 petoei/Shutterstock; fig 18.61 1Photodiva/GI; Chapter 19 opener Jauhari1/GI; fig 19.01 Hakule/GI; fig 19.02 Photofusion/GI; fig 19.03 N-Photo Magazine/GI; fig 19.04 Rakop Tanyakam/GI; fig 19.05 VasjaKoman/GI; fig 19.06 Pagadesign/GI; fig 19.07 Mike Turtle/GI; fig 19.51 Duncan1890/GI; Chapter 20 opener BEST-BACKGROUNDS\Shutterstock; fig 20.02 Thomas Barwick/GI; fig 20.03 Thomas Barwick/GI

Video source files: SimonSkafar/GI, maradek//GI, Eternity In An Instant/GI, Photolibrary Pty Limited/GI

Keys: GI: Getty Images